Mas

Modern British History

Palgrave Master Series

Accounting
Accounting Skills
Advanced English Language
Advanced English Literature
Advanced Pure Mathematics
Arabic
Basic Management
Biology
British Politics
Business Communication
Business Environment
C Programming
C++ Programming
Chemistry
COBOL Programming
Communication
Computing
Counselling Skills
Customer Relations
Database Design
Delphi Programming
Desktop Publishing
Economic and Social History
Economics
Electrical Engineering
Electronic and Electrical Calculations
Electronics
English Grammar
English Language
English Literature
Fashion Buying and Merchandising
  Management
Fashion Styling
French

Geography
German
Global Information Systems
Human Resource Management
Information Technology
Internet
Italian
Java
Management Skills
Mathematics
Microsoft Office
Microsoft Windows, Novell
  NetWare and UNIX
Modern British History
Modern European History
Modern United States History
Modern World History
Networks
Organisational Behaviour
Pascal and Delphi Programming
Philosophy
Physics
Practical Criticism
Psychology
Shakespeare
Social Welfare
Sociology
Spanish
Strategic Management
Statistics
Systems Analysis and Design
Theology
Visual Basic
World Religions

www.palgravemasterseries.com

Palgrave Master Series
Series Standing Order ISBN 0–333–69343–4
(outside North America only)

You can receive future titles in this series as they are published by placing a standing order.
Please contact your bookseller or, in case of difficulty, write to us at the address below with
your name and address, the title of the series and the ISBN quoted above.

Customer Services Department, Macmillan Distribution Ltd
Houndmills, Basingstoke, Hampshire RG21 6XS, England

Mastering

Modern British History

Third Edition

Norman Lowe

palgrave

First edition 1984
Reprinted 4 times
Second edition 1989
Reprinted 8 times
Third edition 1998

Published by
PALGRAVE
Houndmills, Basingstoke, Hampshire RG21 6XS and
175 Fifth Avenue, New York, N. Y. 10010
Companies and representatives throughout the world

PALGRAVE is the new global academic imprint of
St. Martin's Press LLC Scholarly and Reference Division and
Palgrave Publishers Ltd (formerly Macmillan Press Ltd).

ISBN 0–333–72106–3

This book is printed on paper suitable for recycling and
made from fully managed and sustained forest sources.

A catalogue record for this book is available
from the British Library.

10   9   8   7   6   5   4
07   06   05   04   03   02   01

Printed in China

Contents

List of maps

List of tables

List of illustrations

List of figures

Preface to the third edition

The third edition of this book brings the story of British history up to the general election of 1997 and the end of the Thatcherite era and the eighteen-year period of Conservative domination. This edition is specifically designed to help Advanced Level students and undergraduates; all the chapters contain new material, taking into account the latest research and the most recent interpretations, and there are new chapters and sections. The questions are all 'A' level style, and some are taken from 'A' level papers. I hope that the general reader will find the book informative and enjoyable, and will find the source material stimulating and enlightening.

I am grateful once again to my old friend Glyn Jones of Bede College, Billingham, who read the new material and made many helpful suggestions, and to Suzannah Tipple at the publishers for her help, encouragement and advice. I must thank my wife, Jane, and my daughters, Sara and Victoria, who between them read the entire typescript, spotting mistakes and polishing up my English style.

NORMAN Lowe

Note about money values and sources

Before the change of currency in 1971, British money consisted of pounds (£), shillings (s) and pence (d); 12 pence (12d) were equal to one shilling (1s, sometimes written 1/-); 20s were equal to £1. In terms of the new decimal coinage, 1s = 5p, 50s = £2.50, and so on.

It would have been impossible in a book of this size to give the source for every single statistic. I have taken statistics of general election results, population, and trade union membership, unless otherwise stated, from Chris Cook and John Stevenson, *The Longman Handbook of Modern British History 1714–1987* (Longman, 1988). Useful for financial statistics was B. R. Mitchell, *British Historical Statistics* (Cambridge, 1988) which provided me with the figures of income tax rates in Section 8.2). The sources of the statistical tables are given in the text.

Full details of relevant books and articles by historians mentioned in the text are given in the Further Reading List.

Acknowledgements

The author and publishers would like to thank the following photograph sources: Associated Press p. 398; Hulton Getty pp. 8, 75, 261, 475, 513; National Portrait Gallery p. 110; Popperfoto pp. 51, 83, 180, 196, 213, 233, 238, 361, 407, 415, 534; Topham pp. 16, 35, 135, 158, 241, 301, 359, 439, 451, 453, 537, 571.

The author and publishers would like to thank the following for permission to use copyright material: Addison Wesley Longman Ltd for Tables 15.2 and 25.1 taken from C. Cook and J. Stevenson, *The Longman Handbook of Modern British History 1714–1987* (1988) Longman, pp. 194, 217; The Associated Examining Board and Northern Examinations and Assessment Board for questions from past examination papers; Guardian News Service Ltd and the Office for Official Publications of the European Communities (for Eurostat data) for Figure 32.1 taken from *The Guardian*, 17.7.97, p. 12; Hodder & Stoughton Ltd for Tables 21.1 and 21.2 taken from R. Wolfson, *Years of Change* (1978) Edward Arnold, pp. 137, 138; Macmillan Press Ltd for Tables 32.1 and 33.1 taken from D. Childs, *Britain Since 1939: Progress and Decline* (1995) pp. 248, 253; John Murray (Publishers) Ltd for Figure 30.1 taken from J. Watson, *Success in World History Since 1945* (1989) pp. 150; Oxford University Press for Table 15.3 taken from A. J. P. Taylor, *The Struggle for Mastery in Europe 1848–1918* (1971) pp. xxix–xxx; Penguin Books Ltd for Tables 25.2 and 25.3 taken from J. Stevenson, *British Society 1914–45* (1984) pp. 270, 271. Copyright © John Stevenson, 1984; International Thomson Publishing Services for Tables 15.1, 15.2, 15.4 and 15.5 taken from P. Mathias, *The First Industrial Nation* (1969) Methuen, pp. 481–7, 468, 486, 472–5.

Every effort has been made to trace all the copyright holders, but if any have been inadvertently overlooked the publishers will be pleased to make the necessary arrangements at the first opportunity.

⬡ 1 Introduction

1.1 Prologue: Waterloo

In the late evening of Sunday, 18 June 1815, as the smoke and rain-clouds cleared to reveal the setting sun, the Battle of Waterloo drew to an end. Napoleon's Imperial Guard and the whole French army were in retreat. As they streamed away from the battlefield leaving behind a mass of artillery and baggage, they were harassed by British and Prussian cavalry. Meanwhile the two allied generals, Wellington and Blucher, met briefly and congratulated each other on their victory. In the chaos, Napoleon himself was held up for over an hour only four miles from the battlefield, at the village of Genappe. There was utter confusion as several thousand men struggled and fought to cross the only bridge over the River Dyle. With only minutes to spare before the Prussian cavalry caught up, Napoleon at last forced a path through, and galloped away towards Charleroi and Laon.

He reached Paris on 21 June, and realizing the hopelessness of the situation, he abdicated four days later. He was exiled to the tiny island of St Helena in the South Atlantic; the long series of wars which had lasted almost continuously since 1792 (Britain became involved in 1793) was over. Wellington was horrified by the carnage at Waterloo: the British had lost a quarter of their army – over 15 000 dead and wounded – including nearly all his personal staff. He shrank from ever having to use force again. Wellington was to play a prominent part in public life for over 30 years after Waterloo; when he was Prime Minister (1828–30), it was this reluctance to resort to force which in 1829 was to lead him to agree to Catholic emancipation rather than risk a civil war in Ireland (see Section 2.7(b)).

1.2 Themes of change after 1815

Britain in 1815 was a victorious nation, apparently at the height of her power and prestige. But there was to be no tranquillity after the turmoil of the previous 22 years; the period following the Battle of Waterloo turned out to be crammed with important changes and developments. Some of them, like the Industrial and Agricultural Revolutions, were already under way before the outbreak of war with France in 1793; others, like falling prices and industrial slumps, came in the aftermath of the wars. These changes brought with them innumerable problems – poverty, discontent and violence. The ruling classes, badly shocked at the fate of the aristocracy during the French Revolution, were nervous in case a similar outbreak occurred in Britain.

(a) *Industrially and commercially, Britain led the world for much of the nineteenth century*

In 1815 Britain was still in the throes of what is known as *the Industrial Revolution*, which lasted from the 1740s until the 1850s. Historians still disagree about exactly when this revolution started and finished; in fact, one can argue that it has never really come to an end and is still happening today. Some historians do not like to use the word 'revolution' because they think it implies too sudden a change and they feel that in reality the process was too gradual to be called a revolution. Nevertheless 'Industrial Revolution' is still a convenient phrase to describe the introduction of the many new inventions and techniques which transformed the Midlands, the North, and parts of Scotland from being mainly rural areas where the majority of people worked in agriculture, and where such industry as existed was carried on in homes or in small factories, into a mainly industrial society of large power-driven mills and factories concentrated in sprawling industrial towns.

The cotton textile and metal industries were the centrepiece of the revolution. The main inventions included Hargreaves's spinning jenny (1764), Arkwright's water frame for spinning, first used in his big mill at Cromford in Derbyshire (1771), Crompton's spinning mule (1779), Watt's rotary steam-engine (1781) and Cartwright's power loom (1785). In 1785 a steam-engine was first used to power a cotton spinning mill, and by 1800 at least 500 of them were in operation. The need for armaments during the war acted as a stimulus to the metal industries and resulted in the widespread adoption of coke-fired blast furnaces for producing iron. At the same time there was an expansion in the coalmining industry.

However, the main expansion of industry took place after 1815. For example, power-loom weaving had not caught on by 1815, even though Cartwright's loom had been available for 30 years. Yet by 1835, after it had been improved by Horrocks, there were 85 000 of them in use in England and 17 500 in Scotland; whereas imported cotton for weaving amounted to a modest 82 million pounds in 1815, it had soared to 1000 million pounds in 1860. Coal production rose sharply from about 15 million tons in 1815 to 44 million tons in 1846. Together with the industrial expansion went a marked population increase from about 18 million in 1811 to over 27 million in 1851. The increase was most noticeable in the industrial towns and cities, so that by 1851 about 80 per cent of the labouring population worked in some form of manufacturing industry. Another development of crucial importance was the introduction and spread of the railway; the greatest era of railway building was between 1830 and 1860.

During the last quarter of the nineteenth century, Britain began to lose her economic lead, and by the outbreak of the First World War in 1914, Germany and the USA had taken over Britain's position as the world's greatest manufacturing power.

(b) *Agriculture had also seen the appearance of new techniques and changes, usually referred to as the Agricultural or Agrarian Revolution*

Early in the eighteenth century, new crops were being introduced – turnips, clover and sainfoin – which provided winter fodder for cattle. Thomas Coke of Holkham in Norfolk demonstrated how yield could be greatly increased by using marl to enrich light soils, by using bones as fertilizer, and by improving land drainage. Robert Bakewell of Dishley in Leicestershire concentrated on careful and scientific breeding of animals, and showed that by allowing only the best specimens to breed, it was possible to produce far superior cattle and sheep. Another important aspect of the agricultural revolution was *the spread of enclosures*, An enclosure was the fencing- or hedging-in of a large area of medieval strip and furrow land, along with the common pasture land, to form large fields. Enclosures were essential if progress was to be made, because it was impossible to introduce the new scientific farming methods on the open field strips, which survived from medieval times in the counties of eastern and southern England.

Although these improvements had been creeping in throughout the eighteenth century, making possible a marked increase in agricultural production, they were by no means in general use over the whole country. As in industry, the agricultural changes only reached their peak in the years after 1815.

On the debit side, enclosures had the unfortunate effect of depriving many of the smallest farmers of their land. For a variety of reasons, British agriculture went through a serious depression in the 20 years after Waterloo. This was followed by a period of prosperity lasting until about 1875, but then a further period of depression set in. Consequently, another important theme running through the century, even when the industry as a whole seemed prosperous, was *poverty among agricultural labourers*, especially in the South and East of England.

(c) *Governments began to intervene more in an attempt to solve the new problems caused by industrial and agricultural changes, and by the population growth*

There were problems of overcrowded towns, excessively long hours of work, child labour, dangerous conditions in mines and factories, and dire poverty among many working-class people. Another important theme in the nineteenth century was therefore *the emergence of working-class movements like the Chartists and the Trades Unions*, which hoped, in their different ways, to improve social and working conditions. The state introduced new regulations dealing with health matters and conditions at work, but ignored some other problem areas. For example, it did very little to help the poor, except provide workhouses for them to live in when they could no longer manage at home.

Towards the end of the nineteenth century there was a great argument going on about whether or not the state – the government – should be expected to do anything to help poor people. *Should the state introduce old age pensions, health insurance, unemployment insurance and social security?* The traditional Victorian view was known as *laissez-faire*: the belief that the government should interfere as little as possible with people's lives and activities; they should be left alone in freedom to organize their own lives. The poor should be encouraged to help themselves and not expect to be helped out by the state. This is known as *individualism* or *self-help*.

The opposing view, which was gradually becoming more widespread after about 1870, was known as *collectivism*. This is the belief that the state has a duty to look after the welfare of its people and to do its best to improve things for the poor. Gradually politicians of all parties (though not all politicians) came to accept that it *was* the state's job to provide social services. One of the great themes of the twentieth century was therefore *the development of the Welfare State*. This means a state in which the government tries to provide the best possible services for everybody, in health care, education, housing, pensions and unemployment benefit. Other ideas which became associated with the Welfare State were the belief that the government should do its best to make sure that everybody had a job, and that probably the best way of achieving this was for the government to plan and organize the economic life of the country; in other words, there should be *a managed economy*. This, in theory, would help to reduce unemployment and keep costs under control.

The first steps towards a Welfare State were taken by the Liberal governments of 1905–15. Later governments continued to build on these foundations and the Labour governments of 1945–51 can be said to have more or less completed the Welfare State.

They also went some way towards introducing a managed economy by *nationalizing important industries* such as coal, gas, electricity, steel and transport; this means that these industries were taken into state ownership, instead of being privately owned.

During the period of Conservative government from 1979 until 1997, there were worries about the escalating costs of the Welfare State and the burden which it placed on the economy. The Conservatives believed that the nationalized industries were not as efficient as they ought to have been, and consequently almost all of them were *privatized*, that is, sold off into private ownership. The individualism versus collectivism debate was reopened. Many Conservatives believed strongly in self-help, and since the economy was not as successful as it might have been during the 1980s, the future of the Welfare State seemed in some doubt.

(d) *Many changes and developments took place in politics – the way the country was governed*

In 1815 Britain was a union of England, Wales, Scotland and Ireland. The country was governed by a monarch (King George III in 1815) and a parliament of two houses (the House of Commons and the House of Lords) which sat at Westminster. England and Scotland had shared the same monarch since 1603, but it was only in 1707 that the Scots had reluctantly agreed to give up their own parliament in Edinburgh and send MPs to Westminster instead. Wales had been conquered by Edward I of England in 1283 and the country was united with England by an Act of Parliament in 1536. The Welsh had never had a parliament of their own, and their MPs always sat at Westminster.

English kings had claimed control of Ireland since Henry II of England first went over to Ireland in 1172, but it was only in the sixteenth century that it was conquered by the English. After that, the English government encouraged English and Scottish Protestants to settle in Ireland in what were known as 'plantations'. This happened especially in Ulster, and the idea was to 'civilize' the Catholic Irish. The Irish had their own parliament until 1800, but Roman Catholics, who formed almost 90 per cent of the population, had only been allowed to vote since 1793; even then, Catholics were not allowed to become MPs. In 1800 the Irish agreed to give up their parliament in Dublin in return for the promise of *full Catholic emancipation*; this was the granting of full political and civil rights, so that Catholics could become MPs at Westminster. However, for a number of reasons the British government failed to keep its promise about emancipation. Irish Catholics, poverty-stricken and frustrated, were highly indignant at this betrayal, and throughout the nineteenth century *the country was usually in some sort of turmoil*. This was a constant problem for successive British governments, which tried *different methods of pacifying Ireland*.

The Irish campaigned first for Catholic emancipation (achieved in 1829) and then for the repeal (cancellation) of the 1800 Act of Union so that they could have *Home Rule* – their own parliament in Dublin from which they could control their own internal affairs. This long and bitter struggle dragged on throughout the nineteenth century; it ended temporarily in 1922 with *the setting up of the Irish Free State* (known as the Irish Republic or Eire since 1937). However, this did not include the six counties of Ulster (Northern Ireland), which remained part of the United Kingdom, and many Irish patriots would never rest until Ulster was united with the Republic.

Britain's parliament, which contained, in the House of Commons, elected representatives of the people, played an important part in governing the country. In comparison with other European rulers, the powers of the British monarch were somewhat restricted; for this reason the British system is sometimes described as *a limited monarchy*. On the other hand, Russia, for example, was ruled by the Tsar (Emperor), who was *an autocratic or absolute monarch*. This means that he had complete power, there was no parliament to restrict him, and theoretically he could do exactly as he wished. The British system was therefore the envy of *liberals* all over Europe. Nineteenth-century European liberals (not to be confused with the British Liberal party) were people who wanted to limit the power of autocratic monarchs and replace autocracy with a system in which the middle classes had some say in the government.

Although the British parliament had a great deal of power, *in 1815 the system was not democratic*. Democracy is a system of government through which a country is ruled by elected representatives of the people. However, the House of Lords was not elected – members (peers) inherited their seats. The House of Commons *was* elected, but the franchise (the right to vote) was restricted to men, and only the wealthiest ones at that. Both parliament and local government were controlled by wealthy aristocratic landowners who dominated the two main political parties – Whigs and Tories. It was one of the ironies of the early nineteenth century that Britain, the world's greatest industrial power, should be governed by a group of wealthy agriculturalists who, on the whole, knew little about industry.

There was constant pressure for this state of affairs to be remedied. The most striking aspect of the campaign was *the struggle for parliamentary reform*: the extension of the vote to all adult males, and a fairer distribution of seats and constituencies. It was thought in many circles that to get a parliament which was genuinely representative of all the people was the best way of bringing about an improvement in the miserable conditions of the working classes. Progress towards achieving these aims was made in the Parliamentary Reform Acts of 1832, 1867 and 1884; but in 1900 Britain was still not a democratic country: only 27 per cent of the adult population (aged 21 and over) were allowed to vote. All women and 40 per cent of men were excluded from voting, and nothing had been done to make the House of Lords more democratic.

The next stages in the reform of parliament in the early twentieth century were the campaigns to limit the powers of the House of Lords and to get votes for women. The reform of the House of Lords was achieved by the Parliament Acts of 1911 and 1949, though members were still not elected. After a long and bitter struggle by the suffragettes, the vote was given to women (aged 30 and over) by the Representation of the People Act (1918), and the process was completed by the Equal Franchise Act of 1929 which gave women the vote at 21.

Important changes took place in the party system. In 1815 there were two main political parties – Whigs and Tories. In the mid nineteenth century *the Whigs developed into the Liberal party*, which, under the leadership of W. E. Gladstone, appealed to the growing urban middle classes, to skilled workers and to religious nonconformists. *The Tories developed into the Conservative party*; originally it was a party of rich English landowners and supporters of the Church of England, but under the leadership of Peel and Disraeli it began to attract more widespread support. It was the most successful party at staying in power: since 1874 (when Disraeli won a general election), the Conservatives have been in power themselves, or as leading members of coalitions, for roughly two-thirds of the time.

During the struggle for Irish Home Rule *the Irish Nationalists became an important third party*, but they almost faded out after the Irish Free State was set up in 1922. *The Labour party was formed in 1900*, and by 1924 it had replaced the Liberal party as the main challenger to the Conservatives. The rapid decline of the Liberals and the rise of Labour were two of the most fascinating political developments of the early twentieth century, which historians are still trying to explain. Other important developments were the formation of the Welsh Nationalist party (Plaid Cymru) in 1925 and the Scottish Nationalist party in 1928.

(e) *In foreign affairs Britain's prestige abroad stood high in 1815*

This was mainly thanks to the crucial role Britain had played in the defeat of France and to her developing industrial strength. Her attitude to Europe and the rest of the world was complex: traditionally the British were reluctant to get mixed up with European affairs; they had only become involved in the wars against France for reasons of self-defence. After 1815, their instinct was the same, and towards the end of the nineteenth century this policy became known as one of *splendid isolation*. They managed to avoid major foreign entanglements – apart from the Crimean War (1854–6) and the Boer War (1899–1902) – until the outbreak of the First World War in 1914. In practice, however, Britain was never genuinely isolated for long:

- Britain found herself drawn into European affairs because of disagreements with autocratic governments, especially those of Austria and Russia, *which were determined to destroy liberalism and nationalism*. Nationalism is the desire of peoples to rid themselves of foreign rulers and have governments of their own nationality. For example, Greeks wanted to break away from Turkey, Poles from Russia and Italians from Austria. Nationalism could also be the desire to unite all people of the same nationality into one powerful state; this was important in Italy and Germany which were both divided up into a number of separate states. Britain tended to sympathize with both liberalism and nationalism, especially where it suited her interests.
- Britain was also drawn into Europe, whether she liked it or not, by trading interests, since Europe was her most important market for exports until the end of the nineteenth century. British governments *gradually abolished tariffs (import and export duties) and other trade restrictions* so that British manufacturers could enjoy *free trade*. The British were always on the alert in case another power threatened to dominate Europe. British governments always talked about *preserving the balance of power*, by which they seem to have meant taking measures to make sure that no single country controlled the rest, in the way that Napoleon and the French did in the years before 1815. If that happened, British profits and political influence would suffer. In practice, the five great powers of Europe – Britain, Austria, Prussia (Germany from 1870), France and Russia – more or less balanced each other.
- Britain became involved in the pursuit of *imperialism – building up an empire*. The idea was that it would be good for Britain to take over territory abroad which would be valuable for trade. The British already controlled some overseas territory including India, Canada, the Cape of Good Hope and Hong Kong; in the last quarter of the nineteenth century they joined other European powers in taking over large sections of Africa. This operation took place mainly between 1880 and 1912 and became known as *the 'Scramble for Africa'*. During the 1890s the phrase *Pax Britannica* became popular, though the ideas behind it had been in circulation long before that; it was the idea that the British Empire was comparable with the Roman Empire, that Britain, all-powerful because of her naval supremacy and her economic prosperity, would bring the benefits of peace and civilization to the foreign peoples under her rule. At its largest, Britain's empire covered something like one-fifth of the world's land area and contained about a quarter of the world's population. After the Second World War ended in 1945, Britain's empire gradually became independent and her world role changed.
- After Germany was united in 1870 the situation in Europe began to change with the development of a system of alliances: France and Russia (known as the Dual Alliance) balanced Germany, Austria and Italy (the Triple Alliance). At first Britain stayed outside the system, sticking resolutely to *splendid isolation*. But the Boer War (1899–1902) showed how dangerous it was to have no allies; so Britain moved away from isolation, signed agreements with Japan (1902) and France (1904), and became involved in the First World War (1914–18). Some historians have suggested that Britain

could have had more influence in Europe and could therefore have done more to prevent the outbreak of war, if she had not spent so much time and energy building up her empire.

●   Britain continued to show her mixed feelings about Europe and foreign entanglements after the Second World War. She refused to sign the Treaty of Rome (1957) setting up the European Economic Community (EEC), but later changed her mind and eventually joined the community in 1973. When the community began to move towards more political unity, calling itself the European Union (from 1992), Britain feared that she would lose her sovereignty (control over her own internal affairs), and resisted moves towards a European super-state.

Summary of major themes and developments after 1815

● Britain's industrial supremacy, followed by gradual decline after 1914.
● Agriculture: cycle of depression > prosperity > depression up to 1914; poverty among agriculural labourers.
● Growth of population and towns and associated social problems.
● Working class movements – Chartists, trades unions, the Labour party.
● Social reform – factories, mines, education, public health.
● The role of the state in society; the individualism v. collectivism debate; development of the Welfare State.
● Problems in Ireland – the struggle for Home Rule.
● The struggle for reform of parliament – votes for everybody, constituency changes and changes to the House of Lords.
● Changes in the political parties – decline of the Liberals and rise of Labour.
● Imperialism – the rise and fall of the British Empire.
● Britain and foreign affairs – splendid isolation, the *Pax Britannica*, First and Second World Wars.
● Britain and Europe after 1945 – The European Economic Community and the European Union.

You can follow these themes through the book by using the detailed index at the end.

2 Britain under the Tories 1815–30

Summary of events

In 1815 *King George III* was still on the throne. Now aged 77, he had been King since 1760. Since 1811 he had been insane, and there seemed no possibility of a cure, although he had recovered from two earlier attacks of madness in 1788 and 1802. His eldest son, George, acted as Regent, and the period from 1811 until 1820, when the unfortunate George III died, is known as *the Regency*. In 1820 the Prince Regent became *George IV* and reigned until 1830. He was extremely unpopular and had a bad reputation because of his extravagance, immorality, laziness and selfishness.

Politically, *the Tories were in power*. They had been in government more or less since 1783, though the Prime Minister, the 45-year-old *Lord Liverpool* (Robert Banks Jenkinson), had been premier only since 1812. His predecessor, *Spencer Perceval* (Prime Minister 1809–12), had been shot dead as he entered the lobby of the House of Commons, by a bankrupt financier. Liverpool was mild-mannered and modest, and his greatest strength was his ability to manage and reconcile the ministers in his cabinet,

Illus. 2.1   Robert Banks Jenkinson, Lord Liverpool, Prime Minister 1812–27

who had a disturbing tendency to squabble among themselves. Another strength of the government was *Lord Castlereagh*, a first-rate Foreign Secretary and leader of the Tories in the Commons. Outwardly cold and imperturbable, he was nevertheless deeply sensitive, and was eventually driven to suicide in 1822. The main opposition group to the Tories was known as the Whigs. The modern labels – Conservative and Liberal – were not yet in use.

Liverpool's government was unfortunate in having to deal with probably the most complex set of problems ever faced by a British government up to that date: economic and social distress, the demand for Catholic Emancipation in Ireland, and widespread disturbances which suggested that Britain might be on the verge of a revolution like the one which had broken out in France in 1789. Strong measures were taken to maintain law and order, but very little was done to relieve the distress. However, in 1822, Liverpool brought new blood into the government in the form of some politicians with more progressive ideas – *George Canning, Robert Peel and William Huskisson*. As a result of this, a number of much needed reforms and improvements were introduced, which caused this phase of the government to be described as '*Liberal' Toryism* ('liberal' meaning 'open-minded and favourable to reform').

Early in 1827 Lord Liverpool suffered a stroke, and without his conciliatory skills, the Tories began to fall apart. In April 1827 *George Canning* became Prime Minister, but he died in August. His successor, *Frederick John Robinson, Lord Goderich*, had the greatest difficulty in persuading enough people to serve in his cabinet, and soon resigned in despair. George IV turned next to *the Duke of Wellington*, who, in January 1828, succeeded in forming a government whose most memorable act was the granting of Catholic Emancipation. The Wellington government lasted until November 1830 when *Lord Grey* became Prime Minister of a Whig government.

2.1 What were the British political parties in 1815 and what did they stand for?

The main groups were Whigs, Tories and Radicals, though it is important to realize that they were not rigidly organized with manifestos and special policies as they are today. Leading figures had their own groups of supporters; sometimes relations between these groups were not good: among the Tories, the rival Castlereagh and Canning groups were notoriously hostile to each other. Parties therefore consisted of loosely linked factions; there was very little idea of party discipline and MPs often voted as they saw fit. For most of the time there seemed little to distinguish Whigs from Tories, since wealthy landowners formed the backbone of both groups.

(a) *Whigs*

The names 'Whig' and 'Tory' originated during the reign of Charles II (1660–85) at the time when there was some controversy about whether or not Charles's brother, James, should be allowed to succeed to the throne on Charles's death. The Whigs were the people who wanted to exclude him on the grounds that he was a Roman Catholic, whereas the Tories were those who were not prepared to exclude him. Both words – Whig and Tory – were terms of abuse flung by each side at the other. 'Whig' was short for 'whiggamor', a nickname for western Scots who came to Leith for corn; 'tory' was Irish for 'robber' or 'brigand'. By 1815 the origins of the groupings had largely been forgotten. The Whigs had no particular programme or policy and were not even united. Broadly speaking they stood for:

- a reduction in crown patronage (the monarch's power to appoint people to certain important positions and offices);
- sympathy towards Nonconformists (Methodists and other groups who had broken away from the Church of England);
- care for the interests of merchants and bankers;
- a vague sympathy towards the idea of some reform of the voting system, although they were unable to agree on a scheme.

Leading Whigs – all wealthy landowners – were Lord Grey, Lord Grenville, Lord Althorp, William Lamb (later Lord Melbourne) and Lord John Russell. Perhaps the most gifted of all was Henry Brougham, a brilliant lawyer, who was rather set apart from the rest by his comparatively modest background.

(b) *Tories*

On the whole, Tories stood for the preservation of the *status quo*:

- They wanted to maintain the powers of the monarch and the Anglican Church (the Church of England); they were much less tolerant of Nonconformists than the Whigs were.
- They had been badly frightened by the French Revolution and consequently they believed in the strict maintenance of law and order.
- Unlike some of the Whigs, most Tories opposed any reform of parliament, though the more progressive were in favour of some cautious humanitarian reform.

Leading Tories of the more rigid type were Henry Addington (Lord Sidmouth), Lord Castlereagh, Lord Eldon and the Duke of Wellington. The 'reforming' Tories included George Canning, Robert Peel, William Huskisson and F. J. Robinson (Lord Goderich). The Tories, like the Whigs, were often deeply divided; in 1809 Castlereagh and Canning had disagreed so violently over the conduct of the war that Castlereagh had challenged his colleague to a duel with pistols. This actually took place at 6 o'clock one morning on Putney Heath, and ended with Castlereagh slightly wounding Canning in the thigh. The duel caused something of a sensation, and both men had to retire from the cabinet for a time. After 1812 the Tories were more united, which says much for Liverpool's skill as a manager and conciliator.

(c) *Radicals*

They had been greatly encouraged by the French Revolution (which began in 1789) and by its slogan 'liberty, equality and fraternity'. They only had a handful of MPs in 1815, the most influential being Sir Francis Burdett and Joseph Hume; but outside parliament, Radical leaders such as Major John Cartwright, Henry 'Orator' Hunt, Francis Place (whose tailor's shop in Charing Cross Road became a famous Radical meeting-place), and William Cobbett (the journalist and publicist of the movement), were busy organizing mass meetings, marches and petitions. The word 'radical' (from the Latin 'radix' – a root) meant someone who wanted fundamental reforms which got to the root of problems. Early-nineteenth-century Radicals were not an organized party, but they had one aim in common: they wanted a thorough reform of the political system and an improvement in the conditions of the working class, though they did not always agree about how these were to be achieved. They were greatly influenced by the ideas of *Jeremy Bentham* (1748–1832), which were known as *Utilitarianism*. A lawyer like his father, Bentham claimed that the function of governments was to promote 'the greatest happiness of the greatest number of people'; this could be achieved in two ways:

1   The government and administration of the country must be made as efficient as possible; anything which was not efficient or useful – whether it was the education system, the penal system, the prison system or the voting system – must be modernized.

2   The government should interfere as little as possible with the lives and activities of individual people, since this was the best way of achieving the greatest happiness. Such a policy was known as *laissez-faire* (meaning literally 'leave alone') – allowing people to act as they wanted, without government restrictions. Thus one of the Radicals' pet theories was *free trade*: the belief that import and export duties should be abolished because they interfered with the natural flow of trade.

There was something of a contradiction in these Radical ideas – in fact, more government interference than ever before might be necessary in order to achieve efficiency in, for example, the education system. But this did not prevent Radicalism, with its clubs and debating societies, from swelling into the great protest movement of the early nineteenth century, supported by the working classes, by middle-class humanitarians (people who wanted society organized in a humane fashion) and by some industrialists.

2.2 Why was there so much discontent and distress among ordinary people after 1815?

The trouble was caused by a combination of many different developments which, for the sake of simplicity, can be divided into three groups:

(a) *The industrial and agricultural revolutions caused widespread poverty in both town and country*

1   *Enclosures* (see Section 1.2(b)) probably caused hardship in some areas. The movement towards enclosure had been taking place piecemeal since the fifteenth century, but it had gathered pace after 1760, and there was a late surge during the war years as farmers took advantage of the high demand for wheat. There has been disagreement among economic historians about how serious and widespread the effects were. It used to be argued that enclosures ruined the yeomen (farmers of medium-sized holdings) and small peasant farmers, who were evicted from their land because they could not afford the expenses involved. Some recent historians claim that the hardship has been exaggerated. Whether they are right or not, the fact is that much of the country – Kent, Essex, Sussex and the West Country – had been enclosed long before 1815; in some areas – Lancashire, Cheshire, Northumberland and Durham – the open-field system had never existed.

There must therefore have been other reasons for the poverty in these areas in the years immediately following 1815. One obvious explanation is that *the rapid population growth made many farm labourers redundant*. Nevertheless, it is likely that in areas where enclosures did take place during the war years, large numbers of smallholders lost their two or three acres, together with their right to use the common pasture for their animals, and so were reduced to landless labourers. One historian, E.P. Thompson, suggested that this was a deliberate policy by wealthy farmers in order to swell the reserves of cheap labour who could be called in for haymaking, harvesting, roadmaking, fencing and draining.

2   *The Speenhamland System* aggravated rural poverty. The pool of cheap labour kept farm labourers' wages so low that in 1795 the magistrates at Speenhamland in

Berkshire decided to supplement wages from the poor rates, either by food or money, depending on the price of bread and the size of a labourer's family. This system spread rapidly, though it was never common in the North of England. Although the magistrates acted through humanitarian motives (as well as the need to calm unrest and perhaps prevent revolution), the system had two unfortunate effects: farmers reduced wages still further, or refused to employ men for a full week, knowing that however inadequate their earnings were, they would be topped up by the magistrates. In addition, the money had to come out of the poor rate (a special rate charged by the parish for the maintenance of the poor); this meant that the rest of the ratepayers were having to subsidize the wealthy farmers, a highly unpopular state of affairs, particularly as poor rates on average doubled between 1795 and 1812.

3 *The new machines in agriculture, factories and mines* often reduced the demand for labour and caused hardship in certain trades. The best-known example is the hand-loom weavers of Lancashire, Yorkshire and Cheshire, who were gradually being forced out of business by the power-loom. They were already past their heyday in 1800, because their earlier prosperity had attracted too many extra weavers, thus enabling employers to force down wages. But as the power-loom was adopted more widely after 1815, their plight became much worse. One set of statistics puts the average weekly wage for hand-loom weavers at 21s in 1802, 14s in 1809, 8s 9d in 1817, 7s 3d in 1828 and 6s in 1832. And there was worse still to come; according to William Cobbett after a visit to Halifax in 1832: 'It is truly lamentable to behold so many thousands of men who formerly earned 20 to 30 shillings per week, now compelled to live on 5s, 4s, or even less' (see note about money on p. xviii).

4 *In the industrial towns there were unpleasant working and living conditions.* It is difficult to generalize about this, and in fact historians have disagreed about how objectionable working conditions actually were. However, there is no doubt that in many mills men had to work long hours (a 16-hour day was common); children from the age of five could be expected to work a 14-hour day; and there was resentment at the way wages were paid in some trades – there was the 'truck' system by which workers received part of their wages in goods or in vouchers, which could only be spent at the 'truck' shop kept by the mill- or mine-owner. What was also distressing for industrial workers was the loss of freedom, together with the regimentation of factory life, plus the fact that wages probably failed to keep pace with rising prices.

Nor can there be any doubt that the growth of industrial towns was too rapid for proper planning and housing. For example, Liverpool mushroomed from only 82 000 in 1801 to 202 000 in 1831, Manchester/Salford grew from 95 000 to 238 000 over the same period, and Glasgow from 77 000 to 193 000. Much of the extra population came in from the surrounding countryside, but in Lancashire there was a great influx of Irish immigrants. Cheap, jerry-built housing was thrown up close to the factories, water supplies and sanitation were primitive, and overcrowding was dangerously unhealthy. In Manchester in 1820 at least 20 000 people, including many Irish immigrants, were living in cellars. This excess of cheap labour was one of the reasons why industrial wages stayed so low.

(b) *The after-effects of the wars aggravated these problems*

1 *The end of the war brought a sharp fall in corn prices*, causing bankruptcies among poorer farmers. The price reached a peak in 1812 at an average per quarter of 126s 6d; it fell dramatically to 65s 7d in 1815, and by January 1816 it was down to 55s 6d. The fall was caused by the fact that farmers, having taken more land under

cultivation to meet demand during the war, were now over-producing. Imported foreign corn was available again, and in addition, the harvests of 1813 and 1814 were outstandingly good. Many small owner-occupiers, already in debt because of the costs of enclosure, high war-time taxes and the increase in the poor-rate, could not stand the reduction in profits, and went out of business. Wealthier farmers reduced wages and laid off some of their labourers, adding to the unemployment pool.

2   *There was a sudden industrial slump causing widespread unemployment.* The reasons for this were several: now that the war was over, the government stopped buying armaments and uniforms, which meant the loss of orders worth about £50 million. European manufacturers, worried by British competition, brought pressure to bear on their governments to introduce tariffs (import duties), making British goods more expensive in Europe, and thus protecting the developing European industries. After a short boom (a period of increasing exports) in 1815, British exports fell away again and had dropped 30 per cent by 1818. Roughly half the blast furnaces in the country had to close down, and there was a corresponding reduction in the demand for coal. On top of this, there were over 200 000 demobilized soldiers and sailors flooding the labour market, making a grand total of perhaps half a million unemployed by the end of 1816.

(c) *Some of the government's actions made the situation even worse*

1   *The Combination Laws (1799–1800)* made combinations (trade unions) illegal, and though the laws were not effective, they aroused resentment.

2   *The Corn Laws of 1815* forbade the import of foreign wheat until the price of home-grown wheat had risen to 80s a quarter; this was considered to be a sufficiently profitable level to enable landowners and farmers to keep all their labourers in work. This increased the price of wheat which rose to 76s 2d a quarter in 1816 and to 96s 11d in 1817, sending the price of a four-pound loaf up from 10d to 1s 2d. Although this pleased farmers, it was disastrous for unemployed workers, and it brought a shower of accusations that the Tory landowners were looking after themselves at the expense of the poor.

3   *Income tax was abolished in 1816.* It had been introduced originally in 1797 to raise extra cash for the war effort. William Pitt, then the Prime Minister, had pledged to remove it as soon as the war was over. Liverpool, under pressure from wealthy industrialists, merchants, bankers and landowners who wanted rid of income tax, kept Pitt's pledge. However, the income tax was bringing in about £15 million a year, which the government could ill afford to lose, especially as the interest they had to pay on the National Debt (money borrowed by the government to finance the war and for other purposes) amounted to over £31 million a year. To make up for the loss, Liverpool's government increased the taxes on a wide range of goods, including tea, sugar, tobacco, beer, paper, soap and candles. While the rich were relieved of income tax, the poor, who had not paid income tax since it only applied to people earning over £60 a year, now found themselves burdened with at least some of the extra taxes on popular goods. The government's unpopularity reached a new peak.

4   The government showed very little sympathy or understanding when people protested, and replied with a policy of repression which embittered people further (see Section 2.4).

2.3 How was the discontent expressed?

Some people expressed their views peacefully in pamphlets, speeches and petitions; but there were also marches and demonstrations, many of which ended violently. The government was convinced that there was a widespread and centrally organized conspiracy, but in fact this was probably not the case.

(a) *The Radicals kept up a constant stream of criticism of the government and the way society was organized*

In 1816 Cobbett began a 2d weekly edition of his pamphlet *Political Register* (known as Twopenny Trash) which was soon selling 44 000 a week. His themes were the crushing burden of taxation on ordinary people and the need to bring about a reform of parliament: 'We must have that first, or we shall have nothing good. . . . Any man can draw up a petition and any man can carry it up to London.' He advocated universal male suffrage (the vote for all men) and a general election every year, thereby keeping parliament firmly in touch with the wishes of the people. This would enable a start to be made on vital social reforms. On the whole the Radicals favoured peaceful protest, realizing that violence would discredit their cause, though Henry Hunt tended to get involved in agitation.

(b) *The Luddite Riots (1811–17)*

These had already started before the end of the wars. They involved workers in three trades – the croppers (woollen cloth dressers and finishers) of the West Riding of Yorkshire, the cotton weavers of Lancashire and the framework-knitters of the Midlands, particularly Nottingham. All these workers were suffering economic hardships for a variety of reasons, including the use of new labour-saving machinery. They began to relieve their feelings by smashing machinery and setting fire to factories. Beginning in Nottinghamshire, the movement took its name from Ned Ludd, a youth who was reputed to have smashed up some machinery in a fit of temper. During 1811 almost 1000 frames valued at over £6000 were destroyed, and the government retaliated by making frame-breaking punishable by death.

The outbreaks soon spread to Yorkshire and Lancashire; mills were attacked in Leeds, Manchester, Stockport and many other centres. At Rawfolds in the Spen Valley, a mill-owner used troops to fight off the Luddites, killing two of the attackers; at Middleton, near Manchester, a power-loom mill was attacked by a crowd of several thousands, but they were driven back by musket-fire; after ten people had been killed, the crowd retaliated by burning down the mill-owner's house (April 1812). The government took a strong line, using troops to break up demonstrations and hanging 17 Luddites at York (January 1813). The main phase of Luddism was over by this time, though sporadic outbursts occurred until 1817. The Marxist historian, E. P. Thompson, believed that Luddism was more than just an economic and industrial protest movement, and that it had political aims as well. He saw it as an important step forward in the political consciousness of the working classes and he thought the Luddites were part of a great underground revolutionary movement. Many other historians go along with Thompson on the question of political aims (mainly the reform of parliament), but are not convinced by his evidence of a widespread revolutionary network. (For a fuller discussion of this debate see John A. Hargreaves, 'Luddism', in *Modern History Review*, September 1995.)

(c) *The Spa Fields Meetings in London (1816) led to disturbances*

There were three separate meetings (15 November, 2 and 9 December), the second of which ended in a riot. The main speaker was 'Orator' Hunt, who urged the need for a reform of parliament, universal suffrage, voting in secret (by ballot) and annual elections. However, the organizers of the meeting were more extreme than the Radical Hunt; they included Arthur Thistlewood and Thomas Preston who wanted the eventual overthrow of the monarchy. They believed the army was on the verge of mutiny and hoped to excite the crowd into attacking prisons, the Bank of England and the Tower of London. Even before Hunt began to speak, a section of the crowd had rampaged through the streets and ransacked a gunsmith's shop. It was only dispersed by troops after several hours' rioting.

(d) *The March of the Blanketeers (1817) set off from Manchester to present petitions to the Prince Regent in London*

Manchester, full of unemployed weavers, was the centre of an impressive reform movement, and the march was well organized. About 600 men, mostly poor weavers, walked in groups of ten with blankets on their backs, each group carrying a petition (ten was the maximum number allowed by law to present a petition) asking the Prince Regent to help their unfortunate industry. About 200 were arrested at Stockport and most of the remainder were chased away by cavalry at Macclesfield. One man was allowed through to present the petition, but nothing came of this pathetic incident except that 13 of the leaders were sent to prison.

(e) *The Derbyshire Rising (1817) was one of a number of similar incidents which took place in Yorkshire and the Midlands*

Encouraged by a government spy known as Oliver (W. J. Richards), about 300 poor stocking-makers and quarrymen from the Derbyshire villages of Pentridge and Ripley, led by Jeremiah Brandreth, set off to seize Nottingham Castle, 14 miles away. Brandreth had assured his followers that the whole country was about to rise with them, and that a provisional government would be set up which would send relief to the workers. A detachment of cavalry already alerted by Oliver was waiting at Nottingham, and the rising ended ignominiously as the men ran off. Three of the leaders, including Brandreth, were executed.

(f) *The Peterloo Massacre in Manchester (1819) was the most famous incident of the period*

After a quiet year in 1818 thanks to an improvement in trade and the previous year's good harvest, 1819 brought a slump in exports and a return to unemployment. This led to new Radical demands for reform and a plan to hold a meeting of Radical leaders from all over the country in London. The Manchester Radicals organized an open-air meeting in St Peter's Fields, to be addressed by Henry Hunt, who was to be Manchester's representative at the London meeting. About 60 000 men, women and children turned up, and although many carried Radical banners, they were not armed and there was no disorder. The magistrates allowed the meeting to begin and had troops standing by in case there was trouble.

While Hunt was speaking, the magistrates apparently lost their nerve, decided the meeting was illegal, and ordered the yeomanry (local volunteer troops) to arrest him. Unfortunately they had difficulty forcing a way through the solidly packed crowd, and regular troops were sent to help. They charged in with drawn swords, the crowd pan-

Illus. 2.2   The Peterloo Massacre of August 1819

icked and stampeded, and 11 people were killed and 400 injured; 161 of the injured had sabre wounds. Hunt was arrested but soon released on bail.

There were protests from all over the country at the magistrates' handling of the situation and the incident soon became known as the 'Peterloo Massacre' – an ironic comparison with the army's activities at Waterloo. However, the government, afraid that the country was on the verge of revolution, congratulated the magistrates on their prompt action and used the incident to justify passing *the Six Acts* – a further tightening up of restrictions on Radical activities (see Section 2.4(b)4) – which, among other things, banned any further large meetings.

(g) *The Cato Street Conspiracy (1820) was the final and most extreme act in this series of protests*

The leaders, who included Arthur Thistlewood and Thomas Ings, a butcher, were apparently moved to desperation by the latest government restrictions. They conceived a half-baked plan to murder the entire cabinet at a dinner, parade the heads of the ministers on pikes, capture the Tower, Bank and Mansion House (the residence of the Lord Mayor of London) and proclaim a republic. However, government spies knew all about it and the conspirators were arrested at a house in Cato Street (off the Edgware Road). Five leaders, including Thistlewood, were executed and five others transported. The incident was not particularly important except that it seemed to justify the Six Acts. Apart from an abortive attempt to start a general strike in Glasgow, the agitation died down towards the end of 1820 as the economic situation improved.

2.4 What steps did Liverpool's government take to combat the unrest in the period before 1820?

(a) *The government's attitude to the problem*

The government's main concern seems to have been to stem the violence and keep order rather than to remove the causes of grievance. It was because of this that they came in for so much criticism at the time from the Radicals and later from liberal historians. In fact it is easy to understand the reaction of the Tories: they had been elected by the wealthy landlords; they had seen the horrors of the French Revolution which had started with similar protests in 1789 (Lord Liverpool had actually witnessed the storming of the Bastille); and their landowning supporters had a great deal to lose if a similar revolution broke out in Britain. It is important to remember that there was no police force at the time, and only a limited number of troops; consequently the government had to rely for law and order on local magistrates who had little experience of handling such situations, who had no idea of crowd control, and who were liable to panic, as they did at Peterloo. The widespread nature of the disturbances after 1815 convinced the Tories that unless firm action was taken, the whole country would erupt into revolution. They were probably mistaken: there is very little evidence of any co-ordinated conspiracy to overthrow the government; the Radicals were not in favour of violence, and extremists like Thistlewood were only a small minority. Nevertheless the Tories, ignoring the fact that some of their policies (Corn Laws and abolition of income tax) were making matters worse, embarked on *a policy of repression* (keeping people under control, restricting liberties, quelling riots and stamping out violence), directed by Lord Sidmouth, the Home Secretary.

(b) *Repressive policies*

1 *The government used spies and informers* who usually pretended that they had been sent by Radical groups in London to help organize agitation in the provinces. Having contacted local reformers, they reported full details back to Lord Sidmouth; sometimes they acted as *agents provocateurs* – they encouraged reformers with violent tendencies to come out into the open and take action. The most notorious of these informers, W. J. Richards (known as Oliver), while not actually planning such activities as Brandreth's Derbyshire Rising, seemed to have encouraged them enthusiastically. This exaggerated the threat to law and order but enabled the government to arrest possible revolutionary leaders, and it appeared to justify the rest of their repressive programme. According to E. P. Thompson, 'the government wanted blood – not a holocaust, but enough to make an example'.

2 *The Game Law of 1816* made poaching and even the possession of a net for catching rabbits punishable by transportation to Australia for 7 years. This was designed to stamp out the sudden increase in poaching which took place after the introduction of the Corn Laws, but it was not as effective as the government hoped because juries were reluctant to convict when the penalty was so severe for such a minor offence.

3 *The Habeas Corpus Act was suspended in 1817.* This Act (meaning literally – you must have the body) had been passed originally in 1679 and gave the right to demand a written order for a prisoner to appear in court so that he could be charged with an offence; this was to protect people from being kept in prison for long periods without being charged. If the Habeas Corpus Act was suspended, a person who had committed no offence could be arrested and held for an indefinite period without charges and without trial to prevent him from committing an

offence he might have in mind. It was the Spa Fields affair which prompted the government into the 1817 suspension. The government also banned *seditious meetings* (meetings which might have discussed or caused disobedience or violence against the government) and sent letters to magistrates urging them to be firm with agitators. Together these government actions were nicknamed the '*Gagging Acts*'. They allowed the arrest of scores of Radical leaders, though not Cobbett who had left smartly for the USA.

4   *The Six Acts (1819) were the government's reply to Peterloo*; these were the most drastic measure taken so far:

- Magistrates could search houses, without warrants, for unauthorized firearms; there were severe penalties if any were found.
- Drilling and military training by private individuals were forbidden.
- Political meetings to present petitions must involve only people from the parish in which the meeting was taking place; this was to prevent huge gatherings like those at Spa Fields and St Peter's Fields.
- Magistrates could search houses, without warrants, for seditious literature.
- Magistrates could try people charged with political offences immediately without waiting for the local assizes where they would have been tried by judge and jury. This was because juries were sometimes reluctant to convict when it was obvious that evidence came from informers.
- The stamp duty on pamphlets and periodicals was increased, making them more expensive; most of them now cost at least 6d, and the government hoped this would reduce the circulation of Cobbett's *Political Register* and other radical publications.

Hundreds of prosecutions followed and during 1820 the agitation and violence gradually died away.

(c) *Minor reforms*

The government introduced a few improvements:

- *The Factory Act of 1819* (the work of Sir Robert Peel senior) forbade the employment of children under 9 in the mills, and limited the working hours of 9–16-year-olds to 12 hours a day. Unfortunately this was largely ineffective: it applied only to cotton mills, and magistrates were expected to enforce the regulations, a task quite beyond them; what was needed was a large body of professional inspectors.
- Another ineffective reform was *the Truck Act of 1820* which attempted to control abuses in the system of paying wages in ways other than in money.

In conclusion it has to be said that the gradual disappearance of agitation during 1820 was not caused solely by the government's repression and certainly not by their reforms. It had much more to do with the recovery in exports which helped to reduce unemployment; there was also a series of good harvests which brought down the price of bread. As Cobbett remarked, 'I defy you to agitate a fellow with a full stomach'.

2.5 Who were the 'liberal' Tories and why did Lord Liverpool bring them into the government in 1822–3?

(a) *The new men*

They included George Canning who became Foreign Minister and Leader of the House of Commons, replacing Castlereagh who had just committed suicide. Sir Robert Peel (junior), aged only 33, became Home Secretary, replacing Sidmouth who had retired. W. J. Robinson (aged 40) became Chancellor of the Exchequer in 1823, and William Huskisson (aged 50) became President of the Board of Trade in the same year. As well as being open to new ideas, they came from more middle-class backgrounds than the majority of landowning Tories. Canning's father was a barrister and his mother an actress, a profession not then considered respectable; it was a handicap that Canning took a long time to live down. Peel's father was a wealthy Lancashire cotton manufacturer.

(b) *They were brought into the government for a number of reasons:*

● Castlereagh's suicide made a major cabinet reshuffle necessary. Canning was the obvious candidate to take over as Foreign Secretary; this meant that some members of Canning's group of supporters, such as Huskisson and Robinson, would be brought in too.
● They were all in their different ways more progressive than the men they replaced, and were prepared to introduce some reforms. By drafting them into the government, Liverpool hoped to improve social and economic conditions sufficiently to win the support of moderate reformers all over the country, as well as the support of the manufacturers. By removing some of the causes of distress, he hoped to reduce the demand for a reform of parliament, which he and his colleagues certainly did not favour.
● 1822 was a suitable time to begin reforms since law and order had been restored and it would therefore not look as though the government was being swayed by violence.
● Moderate reform would be a blow at the Whigs who were split between the aristocratic members, who were not keen on reform, and the left wing of the party, who were sympathetic towards the Radicals.
● The Tories had been seriously embarrassed by what was known as *the Queen's Affair* (1821). On the death of George III in 1820, the Prince Regent became George IV. Already secretly married to the Roman Catholic Mrs Fitzherbert, he had, in 1795, married Princess Caroline of Brunswick. Since he and Caroline had lived apart for many years, George was determined that she should not be crowned Queen, and he persuaded Liverpool to introduce a Bill of Divorce into parliament on the grounds of Caroline's adultery. The King was himself highly unpopular because of his extravagance and his mistresses; the general public, the Radicals and most of the Whigs rallied to Caroline's support, though she was certainly no saint. Public opinion seemed so solid in its support of Caroline that the government dropped divorce proceedings. In London huge mobs celebrated, and cabinet ministers had their windows smashed. George still tried to ignore her, and the London public was treated to the spectacle of the Queen, cheered on by huge crowds, trying to force her way into Westminster Abbey to take part in the Coronation Service. She had to abandon the attempt, and fortunately for George, she died a month later. As well as bringing the popularity of

the monarchy to its lowest point ever, the Affair had also shown how out of touch the government was with public opinion. This may well have reinforced Liverpool in his decision to bring in some new blood.

2.6 What reforms did the 'liberal' Tories introduce between 1822 and 1830 to deserve this title?

Huskisson and Robinson, both able administrators and financiers, were quick to grasp the importance of overseas trade, and were prepared to remove antiquated restrictions which were hampering Britain as a trading nation. Peel was ready to listen to proposals for reforming prisons and the system of maintaining law and order; he was even persuaded to support Catholic Emancipation, though he had begun by being resolutely against it. Canning favoured Catholic Emancipation and supported his colleagues in their social and economic policies. They were all influenced by the ideas of Jeremy Bentham (see Section 2.1(c)), that governments should aim for greater efficiency. Two important points to remember, however, which have sometimes caused confusion, are:

1   Very few of the Tories were in favour of making parliament more democratic; only after the death of Canning (1827), who was against change, did the 'liberal' Tories begin to consider a modest reform of parliament; therefore they were not fully 'liberal' (the word could mean 'in favour of democratic reform' as well as 'wanting a general removal of abuses').
2   The change of policy was not as sudden as some historians have made out. The beginnings of reform had already taken place before 1822. The Factory Act (1819) and the Truck Act (1820) have already been mentioned (see previous section); in addition, there had been the partial abolition of the pillory (1816) and the abolition of the whipping of women (1820); a Commons Committee of Enquiry had been set up in 1819 to study the weaknesses of the legal system; the Board of Trade had already admitted the need for commercial reform before Huskisson arrived. Even Canning's foreign policy, which seemed to favour liberalism overseas (see Section 3.3(a)), had its beginnings under his predecessor, Castlereagh.

However, what had been a mere trickle of reform became a flood after 1822.

(a) *Huskisson and the move towards Free Trade*

The problem was that British merchants were hampered by numerous *tariffs* (import duties) and other restrictions. Some of these had been imposed originally to protect British industry from foreign competition by making foreign goods more expensive than similar goods produced in Britain. Others had been imposed to raise money during the wars with France. There were, for example, heavy duties on imported raw materials which were now needed on a much larger scale than ever before, because of the expansion of British industry. In 1820 the merchants of London, Manchester and Glasgow had petitioned the government for *free trade* (the abolition of all duties), since they were convinced that British industry could beat all foreign competitors and no longer needed protection. They also argued that if Britain continued with tariffs, foreign countries would do the same in order to protect their industries from British goods. Huskisson was a follower of *Adam Smith* (1723–90), a Scottish philosopher and political economist, who in his book *The Wealth of Nations* (1776) had condemned monopolies and too much state control, and had argued in favour of free trade, competition and private enterprise as the most successful ways of encouraging a nation's economy to develop.

- Huskisson reduced import duties by varying amounts on a wide range of raw materials and other goods: cotton, wool, silk, linen, tea, coffee, cocoa, wine, rum, spirits, books, glassware, china, porcelain, manufactured textiles, iron, copper, zinc, tin and many others. For example, the duty on imported raw silk was slashed from 5s 7$^1/_2$d per pound to 4d per pound. The duty on imported manufactured goods not specifically mentioned in the list was reduced from 50 to 20 per cent.
- He removed restrictions on the trade of Britain's colonies: they could now trade directly with foreign countries for the first time, instead of all such trade having to pass via Britain first. Many goods imported from the colonies now paid lower duties than similar goods from foreign countries (such as wheat and timber from Canada; wool from Australia paid no duty at all). This was known as *imperial preference* and was designed to encourage trade with the British Empire.
- He modified an obsolete set of restrictions known as the Navigation Laws (introduced in the seventeenth century) which said that goods being imported into Britain and her colonies had to be carried in British ships or in ships of the country where the goods originated. This had been designed to prevent the Dutch from capturing the world's carrying trade, but by the 1820s it was quite unnecessary, and other countries were beginning to retaliate with similar policies; this meant that British ships were being excluded from European ports or were being forced to pay high duties. Huskisson's *Reciprocity of Duties Act (1823)* enabled the government to sign agreements with foreign governments, allowing completely free entry of each other's ships. During the next six years, 15 of these agreements were signed, with, among other countries, Prussia, Sweden, Denmark, Brazil and Colombia.
- He modified the 1815 Corn Law by introducing a sliding scale of import duties (1828): if British wheat was selling at over 73s a quarter, there would be no duty on imported foreign wheat; as the price fell, the duty increased.

In the long term Huskisson's work bore fruit: cheaper raw materials enabled manufacturers to produce goods at lower prices, so that British exports and shipping increased steadily as her industries became more competitive; smuggling began to disappear, since the reduction in duty made it unnecessary. In the short term there were a few problems: the government lost the revenue (income) which it had collected from the higher import duties, and in December 1825 there began a sudden slump in exports caused mainly by over-production. Unemployment increased again, and in Lancashire there were more outbreaks of machine-breaking. Some people blamed Huskisson, though this was absurd, because many of his reforms only applied from the beginning of 1826. In fact, he had taken Britain through the first crucially important steps towards Free Trade. Sadly his career was cut short in 1830 when he was knocked down and killed by a locomotive at the opening of the Liverpool and Manchester Railway.

(b) *Repeal of the Combination Laws (1824)*

Since 1800 the Combination Laws had made trade unions illegal. A campaign to get these laws repealed (cancelled) was mounted by Francis Place, the famous Radical tailor of Charing Cross, whose shop was a favourite meeting-place for London Radicals. He was supported in parliament by the Radical MPs Joseph Hume and Sir Francis Burdett, and by many other Benthamites. *Their arguments were*:

- the laws were inefficient – trade unions did, in fact, exist, but called themselves friendly societies; these were organizations which workers paid into in order to get sickness and unemployment benefit.

- workers were dissatisfied simply because unions were illegal; once they had full rights, workers would co-operate with employers for the greater prosperity of both, and unions would no longer be necessary.

In 1824 Hume succeeded in having a parliamentary committee of inquiry set up to study the situation. So well did Hume and Place train the workers who gave evidence that Huskisson was persuaded to take the extremely liberal step of repealing the Combination Laws. However, the results horrified both Radicals and industrialists. Hundreds of trade unions came out into the open and hundreds of new ones were formed. In 1825 there was a wave of strikes as workers demanded wage increases – their share of the general prosperity. Under pressure from industrialists, the government was preparing to reintroduce the Combination Laws, but Place and Hume managed to salvage something for the unions: *the Amending Act (1825)* permitted trade unions to exist for the purpose of negotiating about wages and hours of work, but they were not allowed to 'molest' or 'obstruct'. Although this made it difficult to conduct strikes, it was at least an important step forward in trade union organization.

(c) *Peel and law and order*

Part of Peel's talent was that he was willing to listen to and be persuaded by reasonable arguments. He studied carefully the recommendations of humanitarian reformers such as Sir Samuel Romilly, Sir James Mackintosh, John Howard and Elizabeth Fry. Bentham himself had criticized the inefficiencies of a legal system which had grown up piecemeal over 600 years. *The penal code* (the list of punishments for various crimes) was far too severe: over 200 offences, including minor ones like stealing a loaf of bread, damaging Westminster Bridge and impersonating a Chelsea pensioner, were punishable by death. Another 400 were punishable by hard labour in the convict settlements of Australia. In a notorious case in 1813 a boy had been hanged for stealing a sheep. In practice the system broke down because juries often refused to convict if it meant execution for a trivial offence, and many criminals went unpunished.

Conditions in prisons were atrocious: they were overcrowded, filthy, insanitary and disease-ridden; child offenders were put together with hardened criminals; jailers were often brutal, and there was a ludicrous system whereby they were unpaid, and had to make a living from fees paid to them by prisoners. Peel introduced a series of reforms which, between 1823 and 1830, radically changed the whole system of law and order:

1 *Penal code reform*: the death penalty was abolished for over 180 crimes, and in the remainder (except for murder and treason) it was left for the judge to decide whether the death penalty should be imposed. Punishments for other offences were made less severe. The barbaric practice of burying suicides at crossroads with a stake through the heart was abolished. In addition, the jury system was drastically reorganized, and the government stopped using spies to report on possible trouble-makers. These were splendid liberal and humanitarian reforms, but there was still some way to go: people could still be sent to jail for debt and transported to Australia, while public hangings continued until 1868. Peel was unable to do much about the procedure of the law courts which remained slow and cumbersome.

2 *The Jails Act (1823)* removed some of the worst abuses from the prison system: magistrates were to inspect prisons at least three times a quarter; jailers were to be paid instead of having to extort cash from prisoners; women prisoners were to be looked after by women jailers; all prisoners were to have some elementary education and receive visits from doctors and chaplains. However, the act applied

only to the large prisons in London and 17 other cities – smaller prisons and debtors' prisons remained as before.

3   *The Metropolitan Police Act (1829)* introduced the London police force. The Bow Street Runners and the army of elderly night-watchmen were not very efficient at keeping the peace; Peel was convinced that the law would be more effective if there was some organization to track down and deter criminals. The Act provided for 1000 paid constables, soon to be increased to 3000, under the control of a commissioner with headquarters at Scotland Yard. The scheme was to be financed by a special rate. The new police wore top-hats and blue coats with belts, but were armed only with truncheons to avoid the charge that they were a military force. Soon nicknamed Bobbies or Peelers after their founder, they reduced the crime rate spectacularly; as criminals moved out of the capital, provincial city authorities and then country areas began to copy the London force. *It was a controversial reform*: many people felt that the police were just another form of repression, and they resented the police rate. Even a parliamentary committee set up to consider the problem had announced in 1822: 'It is difficult to reconcile an effective system of police with that perfect freedom of action and exemption from interference which are the great privileges and blessings of society in this country.' However, respect for the police increased as crime and violence were reduced over the whole country.

(d) *Religious reforms*

Peel and Wellington (then Prime Minister) piloted two important and liberal religious reforms through parliament:

1   *The Repeal of the Test and Corporation Acts (1828)*. These antiquated laws dating back to the seventeenth century said that only Anglicans (members of the Church of England, the official state Church) could hold important positions in the state and on town corporations. Non-Anglicans included Dissenters or Nonconformists (such as Methodists, Unitarians, Presbyterians and Baptists) and Roman Catholics. For years the Acts had been ignored as far as Nonconformists were concerned, and their repeal was simply a recognition of what happened in practice. But the repeal was only partial: *the restrictions still applied to Roman Catholics.*

2   *The Catholic Emancipation Act (1829)* was passed amid tremendous controversy which ruined Peel's popularity with the Tories and finally caused the party to disintegrate (see next section). Roman Catholics could now sit in parliament and hold all important offices except Lord Chancellor of England or Ireland, and Lord Lieutenant of Ireland.

(e) *For Canning's 'liberal' foreign policies see Chapter 3*

2.7 Why did the Tory party disintegrate in 1830?

Between 1827 and 1830 a series of events and problems occurred which split the Tory party and allowed the Whigs to form a government.

(a) *The resignation of Lord Liverpool*

Liverpool resigned at the age of only 57 in March 1827 after suffering a paralytic stroke. This removed the only man among the leading Tories who had the gift of holding together the various factions in the party. The old squabbles re-emerged: George Canning became Prime Minister, but Peel, Wellington and five other ministers resigned because they disapproved of his foreign policy and his sympathy for Catholic Emancipation. Canning even had to bring some Whigs into his cabinet to make up the numbers, which shows how loose party organization was at that time. After Canning's death in August, Goderich failed to form a cabinet, and in desperation, George IV asked Wellington to form a government. He succeeded but soon fell out with Huskisson and the other 'liberal' Tories who resigned after a disagreement over parliamentary reform. Though Peel remained in the government, Wellington had lost the support of the 'liberal' Tories (now referred to as Canningites), the left wing of the party.

(b) *The crisis in Ireland culminating in Catholic Emancipation split the party further*

1 *The problem in Ireland* arose from the fact that although almost 90 per cent of the people were Roman Catholics, most landowners and all important government officials were Protestants. Catholics had the vote, but were not allowed to sit in parliament. This was a source of great bitterness, especially as the Irish had only agreed to the Act of Union (1800), giving up their own parliament, on condition that Catholics were allowed full political and civil rights, i.e. Catholic Emancipation. The British government had failed to keep its promise because George III refused to agree to emancipation, on the grounds that he would be violating his Coronation Oath in which he had sworn to uphold the Protestant religion. Since George IV held the same view, no progress could be made.

2 *The campaign for emancipation was led by Daniel O'Connell*, an Irish Catholic landowner and barrister, and an exciting speaker. After emancipation had been achieved, he hoped to get the Union dissolved and the Irish parliament restored to run internal affairs, though he was quite happy for the link with England to remain as far as foreign policy was concerned. His methods were non-violent: in 1823 he founded *the Catholic Association* to which Catholics, including poor tenant farmers, paid a penny a month (the Catholic rent). It soon became powerful, with a weekly income of £1000 and the full support of Roman Catholic priests. At elections the Association backed Protestant candidates who were pledged to vote for emancipation at Westminster, and anti-Catholic candidates were defeated in two by-elections. The repeal of the Test and Corporation Acts made O'Connell even more determined.

3 *The crisis point was reached with the County Clare election of 1828.* Vesey Fitzgerald, the MP for County Clare, was standing for re-election (he had just been promoted to President of the Board of Trade, and a newly-appointed minister had to resign his seat and submit himself for re-election). Though Fitzgerald was a Protestant landlord, he was in favour of emancipation and had been a popular MP. O'Connell decided to stand against him to show how strongly Catholics felt about the issue, though as a Catholic he would not be able to take his seat even if he won. The franchise (right to vote) was restricted: the minimum qualification was the ownership of land worth £2 a year (these voters were known as 40 shilling freeholders). However, there were enough Catholic tenant farmers with the vote to swing the election for O'Connell who won a triumphant victory. Ireland was seething with excitement at the prospect of scores of Catholics winning seats at the next general election. There seemed every possibility of violence and even civil

war if O'Connell and other future Catholic MPs were debarred from Westminster. The Catholic MPs might well set up their own parliament in Dublin, and that could lead to the breakup of the Union.

4   *Faced with this prospect, Wellington and Peel decided to give way.* Both had been bitter opponents of emancipation for years, on the grounds that it would lead to the breaking of the Union between England and Ireland (which it eventually did); but both were convinced that only concessions would prevent civil war. Wellington himself said: 'I have probably passed a longer period of my life engaged in war than most men and I must say this: if I could avoid by any sacrifice whatever even one month of civil war, I would sacrifice my life in order to do it.' Wellington persuaded the rest of the cabinet to support them, and Peel introduced the Bill for Catholic Emancipation into the Commons. Wellington bullied the Lords into passing it, and George IV accepted it after several stormy scenes (April 1829). Catholics could now sit in both houses of parliament and hold all important offices of state in Britain except monarch, regent, Lord Chancellor of England or Ireland, and Lord Lieutenant of Ireland. As a parting shot, the government forced O'Connell to fight the County Clare election again and raised the property qualification for voting to £10, so that the 40 shilling freeholders no longer had the vote; this did not prevent O'Connell from winning again.

The results of emancipation were important: Peel and Wellington could claim to have averted civil war in Ireland, but the treatment of O'Connell and the 40 shilling free-holders lost the government most of the goodwill that emancipation should have won for them from the Irish Catholics. The Protestant Tories, especially the Irish landlords, never forgave Peel and Wellington for their 'betrayal'. Peel resigned, and a bitter joke circulated that he had changed his name from Peel to Repeal. Wellington was so incensed at one of his critics, Lord Winchelsea, that he challenged him to a duel, which took place in Battersea Park (neither man was wounded). Having earlier lost his left wing over parliamentary reform, Wellington had now lost the support of right-wing Tories (known as the Ultras) over Catholic Emancipation. Emancipation was a great encouragement to supporters of parliamentary reform; it showed that the constitution could be changed peacefully, and by weakening the Tories it opened the way for the Whigs, who had plans for reform, to come to power the following year.

(c) *In 1830 there were new outbreaks of violence all over England*

The causes of the outbreaks were complex: bread prices were high following the poor harvest of 1829; there was a sudden slump in exports which brought unemployment to the Midlands and North; revolutions in France and Belgium helped to fuel the unrest. All over the South of England labourers burnt ricks and smashed the threshing-machines which were throwing them out of work. Strong measures were needed, but Wellington's government seemed too weak for decisive action.

(d) *The demand for reform of parliament revived*

After a lull during the period of calm and prosperity since 1821, interest in parliamentary reform revived again, for a variety of reasons (see Section 4.3). Many of the Whigs now supported the demand because they thought it was the best way to prevent revolution. It was Wellington's refusal to consider even the mildest reform measure that brought about his downfall. At the general election in the autumn of 1830 (caused by the death of George IV and the accession of his brother William IV), candidates who favoured reform did well; when parliament met in November, there was pressure for reform from Whigs and from 'liberal' Tories. Though he had compromised over emancipation, Wellington remained unmoved by the arguments for reform. In spite of the fact that the election system was hopelessly out of date, he announced that he thought it was the best that could be devised. Soon afterwards he was outvoted by a combination of Whigs and Tories and immediately resigned. The Whig leader, Lord Grey, became Prime Minister of a joint Whig, Radical and Canningite government.

2.8 Verdict on the Tories

No simple straightforward verdict is possible. Students at 'A' level and beyond who look more deeply at these Tory governments soon realize that historians disagree about several aspects of their policies. Here there is space to refer only briefly to some of the areas of dispute as an introduction to further study. There is a fuller discussion of some of these points in the article by Graham Goodlad, 'Liberal and High Tories in the Age of Liverpool' in *Modern History Review*, November 1995. The traditional view still accepted by writers such as Derek Beales is that the Tories were reactionary (against progress, wanting to put the clock back to an earlier situation) until 1822, when they suddenly became 'liberal' reformers. More recently several new points have been suggested:

● There was no sudden change in 1822; the first signs of change were already there, and the process was simply speeded up after 1822 (see Section 2.6). J. E. Cookson suggests that the government was not reactionary before 1822: they were extremely cautious and thorough and 'were held back by their desire to present reforms which would have the widest possible acceptance'.
● A clear distinction needs to be made between the Tories' political policies and their economic policies; though they may not have been progressive as far as political matters were concerned (the majority were against parliamentary reform as late as 1827), they were prepared to make concessions on economic matters.
● The motives of the Tories have provoked argument: the traditional view is that they followed policies (Corn Laws, abolition of income tax) favouring their own class – wealthy landowners – for purely selfish reaons. However, Boyd Hilton believes that they acted through disinterested motives: they wanted to secure food supplies and full employment and therefore supported agriculture because it seemed the most promising area of expansion. Later they realized their mistake, that industry was the major growth area, and consequently, in the 1820s, they began to favour industrialists.
● There is disagreement about the personal achievement of Lord Liverpool. Disraeli described him as 'the arch-mediocrity'. Others see him as the arch-reactionary responsible for repression and opposition to parliamentary reform. On the other hand, he allowed important reforms to be introduced between 1822 and 1827 and showed enormous skill in holding a difficult cabinet together for 15 years. 'If Liverpool was an arch-mediocrity,' writes historian N. H. Brasher in his defence, 'then it is a pity that Britain has had so few of the breed since.'

Questions

1 **Peterloo: 16 August 1819**
   Study Sources A to G and then answer the questions which follow.

A letter from five Lancashire magistrates to Lord Sidmouth (the Home Secretary), 1 July 1819

We cannot have a doubt that some alarming insurrection is being thought about. We applaud the behaviour of many of the labouring classes, which has been peaceful until now, but we do not count on this continuing. Urged on by the speeches of a few desperate rabble rousers, we anticipate, at no distant period, a general rising, and possessing no power to prevent the meetings which are held weekly, we as magistrates are at a loss how to stem the influence of *the dangerous and seditious doctrines* which are continually spread around.

Source: quoted in R. Walmsley, *Peterloo: the Case Reopened*, Manchester University Press, 1969.

Source B

A letter from the Home Office to the Manchester magistrates, August 1819

Careful thought convinces him [Sidmouth] the more strongly, the inadvisability of attempting forcibly to prevent the meeting on Monday. Every discouragement and obstacle should be thrown in its way. He has no doubt that if anything illegal is done or said, it may be the subject of prosecution. But even if they should offer sedition ... it will be the wisest course to abstain from any endeavour to disperse the mob unless they should proceed to acts of felony or riot.

Source: quoted in P. Revill, *The Age of Lord Liverpool*, Blackie, 1979.

Source C

Report in The Times, *whose correspondent, John Tyas, was arrested along with Hunt, although he was well known as a strong critic of Hunt*

One banner read 'Taxation and no Representation is unjust'; on another banner 'Equal Representation or Death; on a third 'Annual Parliaments, Universal Suffrage, and Vote by Ballot'.

A posse of 300 or 400 constables marched into the field about 12 o'clock. Not the slightest insult was offered to them. The cavalry drew their swords and brandished them fiercely in the air: upon which they rode into the mob which gave way before them. Not a brickbat was thrown at them – not a pistol was fired during this period: all was quiet and orderly. They wheeled round the waggons until they came in front of them.

As soon as Hunt and Johnson had jumped from the waggon (to surrender) a cry was made by the cavalry, 'Have at their flags'. They immediately dashed not only at the flags which were in the waggon, but those which were posted among the crowd, cutting indiscriminately to the right and left in order to get at them. This set the people running in all directions, and it was not until this act had been committed that any brickbats were hurled at the military. From that moment the Manchester Yeomanry Cavalry lost all command of temper ...

Of the crowd a large portion consisted of women. About 8 or 10 persons were killed, and besides those whom their own friends carried off, above 50 wounded were taken to the hospitals; but the gross number is not supposed to have fallen short of 80 or 100 grievously wounded.

Was that meeting at Manchester an unlawful assembly? We believe not. Was the subject proposed for discussion (reform of the House of Commons) an unlawful object? Assuredly not. Was anything done at this meeting before the cavalry rode in upon it, contrary to the law or in breach of the peace? No such circumstances are recorded in any of the statements which have yet reached our hands.

Source: *The Times*, 19 August 1819.

Source D

A cartoon (dated September 1819) by George Cruikshank, showing the Peterloo Massacre

MANCHESTER HEROES

Figure 2.1

The head in the top left corner, representing the Prince Regent, is saying: 'Cut them down, don't be afraid, they are not armed, courage my boys ... and he that kills most shall be made a Knight errant and your exploits shall live for ever in a song.' The cavalryman is saying 'Cut them down, cut them down.' The child is saying 'Oh pray Sir don't kill mummy, she only came to see Mr Hunt.' The bystanders are shouting 'Shame, murder'.

Source: British Museum.

Source E

A letter in The Courier *written by an eyewitness*

The meeting was then addressed by the several orators, showing much menacing attitude, and the shouts seemed to rend the very air and shake the foundation of the ground. The constables were tauntingly insulted wherever they were observed to stand; sticks and hats always waving on every acclamation.

About half past one the magistrates deemed it expedient to read the Riot Act, and instantly after, the platform was surrounded in a masterly manner. The manoeuvre would have taken place without bloodshed had not the mob assailed the civil and military authorities with every resistance in their power, and particularly with missiles. Consequently the cavalry charged in their own defence; not without first being witness to a pistol shot from the multitude, against one of the gentlemen in our Yeomanry, who now lies in imminent danger.

Note: As the law stood in 1819, if a crowd did not disperse within an hour of the reading out of the Riot Act, then they were liable to be arrested.

Source: quoted in P. Sauvain, *British Economic and Social History 1700–1870*, Stanley Thornes, 1987.

Source F

A private letter from Lord Liverpool to George Canning, 23 September 1819

When I say that the actions of the magistrates at Manchester were justifiable, you will understand that I do not by any means believe that the course they pursued on that occasion was in all its parts prudent. A great deal might be said in their favour even on this head. But whatever judgement might be formed in this respect, being satisfied that they were substantially right, there remained no alternative but to support them.

Source: quoted in A. Aspinall and E. A. Smith (eds), *English Historical Documents, vol. ll, 1783–1832*, Eyre & Spottiswoode, 1959.

Source G

The view of a Marxist historian, E. P. Thompson, in his book The Making of the English Working Class, *first published in 1963*

My opinion is (a) that the Manchester authorities certainly intended to employ force, (b) that Sidmouth knew – and approved of – their intention to arrest Hunt in the midst of the assembly, and to disperse the crowd, but that he was unprepared for the violence with which this was carried out. . . . It really was a massacre. Hunt had exerted himself in the week before the event to ensure obedience to his request for 'quietness and order'. The presence of so many women and children was overwhelming testimony to the peaceful character of the meeting.

Source: E. P. Thompson, *The Making of the English Working Class*, Penguin edition, 1980.

(a) Using the evidence of these sources and your own knowledge, explain what was meant at the time by the phrase in Source A – '*dangerous and seditious doctrines*'. (6 marks)

(b) What message is the cartoonist in Source D trying to put across? (4 marks)

(c) (i) Compare the interpretations of the events in Manchester given in Sources C, D and E. (6 marks)

    (ii) What reasons can you suggest for the differences? (4 marks)

(d) Using the evidence of the sources and your own knowledge, explain how far you agree with the two opinions (a) and (b) given by E. P. Thompson in Source G. (10 marks)

(Total 30 marks)

2 To what extent was the discontent and distress of the period 1815–20 caused by the after-effects of the wars with France?

3 'After 1822 the policies of the Tory governments underwent fundamental changes.' How accurate is this view of the activities of the Tory governments in the period 1815–30?

③ Foreign affairs 1815–30

Summary of events

The period was dominated by two outstanding Foreign Secretaries, *Robert Stewart, Lord Castlereagh* (from 1812 until his death in 1822) and *George Canning* (1822–7). After Canning's death, the key influence on foreign policy was Wellington, who became Prime Minister in 1828.

The most pressing problem at the end of the Napoleonic Wars was how to deal with the defeated France, and at the same time how to redraw the map of a Europe whose frontiers and governments had been drastically reorganized by Napoleon. The Bourbon monarchy was restored in the person of Louis XVIII, and other details were dealt with by *the First and Second Treaties of Paris* (May 1814 and November 1815). In the intervening period, Napoleon escaped from exile on the island of Elba and had to be crushed once and for all at Waterloo. The wider problems of Europe were settled at *the Congress of Vienna* (1814–15), though the arrangements, like those of most peace treaties, were controversial and were to cause problems later.

1815 saw the formation of *the Holy Alliance*, the brainchild of Tsar Alexander I of Russia; its members pledged themselves to rule their countries according to Christian principles. More important was *the Quadruple Alliance* of Britain, Austria, Prussia and Russia, a continuation of the 1815 alliance which had defeated Napoleon; this became *the Quintuple Alliance* in 1818 when France was allowed to join. Its aims, broadly speaking, were to maintain the Vienna Settlement and preserve peace by holding Congresses to solve any awkward problems which arose. After the initial Congress at *Aix-la-Chapelle* (1818) it gradually became apparent that Britain was not in agreement with the other members of the alliance about how to deal with the revolutions which had broken out in Naples, Spain and Portugal, where liberals (see Section 1.2(d)) were trying to force autocratic monarchs to allow democratic constitutions. Following the Congresses of *Troppau* (1820) and *Laibach* (1821), troops were sent in to suppress the revolutions in Spain and Naples, in spite of strong objections from Castlereagh who disapproved of interfering in the internal affairs of other states.

There were other revolutions as well, this time caused by nationalism (see Section 1.2(e)): the Spanish colonies in South America were trying to assert their independence, while the Greeks were struggling to break away from Turkish rule. These problems were considered at the Congress of *Verona* (1822). Unlike the outbreaks in Naples and Spain, these revolutions were successful, partly because of British support. In the case of the Greek revolt, Russia and France agreed with Britain; the Austrians and Prussians were so incensed at Canning's attitude that no further Congresses met, and the Congress System (sometimes known as the Concert of Europe) was at an end. The general feeling in Britain was that this was no bad thing since the Austrian and Prussian idea of preserving peace and the Vienna Settlement seemed to be to keep as many autocratic governments in power as possible.

Key events in British foreign affairs 1812–30

	1812	Castlereagh becomes Foreign Secretary
May	1814	First Treaty of Paris
Oct	1814–	
June	1815	Congress of Vienna
June	1815	Battle of Waterloo – Napoleon finally defeated and exiled to St Helena
Nov	1815	Second Treaty of Paris
Nov	1815	Quadruple Alliance of Britain, Austria, Russia and Prussia signed – Congress System begins
	1818	Congress of Aix-la-Chapelle. France joins the Alliance which becomes the Quintuple Alliance
	1820	Revolutions break out in Spain, Portugal, Naples and Piedmont
	1820	Congress of Troppau meets – Castlereagh refuses to attend because he knows other members want to crush revolutions
	1821	Congress of Laibach – Castlereagh again refuses to attend – Congress decides to send Austrian troops to crush revolutions in Naples and Piedmont
August	1822	Castlereagh commits suicide
Sept	1822	Canning becomes Foreign Secretary
	1822	Congress of Verona authorizes French army to crush revolution in Spain
July	1823	Canning sends British naval squadron and later 5000 troops to help Portuguese revolutionaries who are eventually successful
	1825	Britain recognizes Mexico, Colombia and Argentina (former Spanish colonies) as independent republics
July	1827	Canning signs Treaty of London: Britain, France and Russia promise to help Greeks win independence from Turkey
August	1827	Canning dies
Oct	1827	Battle of Navarino – British and French fleet destroys Turkish/Egyptian fleet – leads to recognition of Greek independence (1830).

3.1 What were the aims of the statesmen who met at Vienna in 1814–15 and to what extent were their aims fulfilled in the Vienna Settlement?

The leading personalities at Vienna were Prince Metternich (Austrian Chancellor), the Tsar Alexander I of Russia, Count Hardenburg (Prussian Minister) and Lord Castlereagh.

(a) *Their aims were:*

- To make sure that the French, who were held responsible for the wars, paid for their misdeeds.
- To further their own interests and make sure that the victorious powers gained some compensation for their pains.
- To prevent any further French aggression which might threaten the peace and security of Europe. This could be done by strengthening the states bordering on France and by making sure that the four leading powers remained on good terms with each other in order *to maintain a balance of power* (no single state would be powerful enough to dominate the rest). Rulers who had been expelled by Napoleon should be restored, as far as possible, as the best guarantee of peace and stability (this was known as the principle of *legitimacy*).

There were disagreements about details: each had different ideas about what constituted a balance of power. Castlereagh was worried in case the settlement was too hard on the French so that it made them bitter and likely to go to war again to regain their losses; he argued that 'it is not our business to collect trophies, but to try, if we can, to

Map 3.1   Europe in 1815

bring the world back to peaceful habits'. There were jealousies lest one country gained more than another: Prussia wanted Alsace-Lorraine (from France) and the Kingdom of Saxony, and Alexander wanted the whole of Poland; in each case the other states were suspicious and refused to allow it. Austria wanted to make sure that Russia did not take over from France as the most powerful nation on the continent of Europe.

Throughout the entire negotiations Talleyrand, the French representative, was extremely active in protecting French interests and salvaging what he could from the disaster.

(b) *How successful were they?*

1 The treatment of France was finalized by the Second Treaty of Paris (November 1815); though harsher than the First Treaty, it was still reasonably lenient. France was to be reduced to her 1790 frontiers, which meant losing some territory to Belgium and some to Piedmont (see Map 3.1). She had to pay an indemnity (a fine) and have an army of occupation until the fine was paid; in addition, she lost many of her overseas colonies. The terms might have been much more stringent if Talleyrand had not exploited the mutual suspicions of the other powers so shrewdly: for example, France was allowed to keep Alsace-Lorraine in spite of Prussia's determination to get it, because the other states thought this would make Prussia too powerful. The statesmen were successful in their aim: France was penalized yet not embittered enough to want a war of revenge (note the contrast with the treatment of the defeated Germany at Versailles in 1919 – see Section 22.6).

2 The victorious powers all gained territory mainly at the expense of countries which had been unlucky enough to end the war on the losing side. Britain gained Ceylon (Sri Lanka), Mauritius, Trinidad, Tobago, St Lucia, Malta, Heligoland, the Cape of Good Hope, and a protectorate over the Ionian Islands. After some complicated bargaining, Prussia received about two-fifths of Saxony, the Rhineland, Western Pomerania, Danzig and Posen; Russia received Finland (from Sweden) and part of Poland; Austria was given Lombardy and Venetia in North Italy and a stretch of Adriatic coast. As compensation for losing Finland, Sweden was given Norway, taken from Denmark; this move was pressed by Britain so that the entrance to the Baltic would not be controlled by a single power.

3 Two of France's smaller neighbours were strengthened: the Austrian Netherlands (Belgium) were combined with Holland to make a strong barrier state to the north-east. Piedmont (also known as Sardinia) in North Italy on France's eastern frontier, regained most of Savoy and Nice (taken by France in 1796) and was given the port of Genoa. The Bourbon family was restored to the Kingdom of Naples in the person of Ferdinand I, though they had a bad reputation for misgovernment. The Pope was restored to the Papal States. Also in Italy, the Duchies of Parma, Modena and Tuscany were given to Austrian princes. Austria, in fact, had a firm grip on northern Italy; this was thought necessary to deter a possible French invasion of Italy. In general, therefore, the statesmen's aims seemed to have been fulfilled: a balance of power had been achieved and the Quadruple Alliance of Britain, Austria, Prussia and Russia seemed likely to preserve good relations.

There was, in fact, no major conflict in Europe until the Crimean War (1854–6), though of course there are many other reasons besides the Vienna Settlement for this long period of comparative peace.

On the other hand *there were criticisms of the settlement*. The main one was that it ignored the principle of nationalism: Belgians were placed under Dutch rule, Italians under Austrians; Finns, Norwegians and Poles were placed under foreign governments merely to suit the wishes of the great powers. German nationalists were disappointed: they wanted Germany united into one powerful state, whereas the settlement reduced the old Germany of over 360 small states to 38 (known as the German Confederation); this was an improvement, but not at all what the nationalists had hoped for. By restoring autocratic rulers such as the Pope and Ferdinand I of Naples, the Congress also ignored the newly developing principle of liberalism. Although there was no major war for many years, there were a number of disturbances which resulted directly from the settlement – the Belgian struggle for independence; revolutions in Naples, Piedmont and the Papal States, and the Italian fight to throw off Austrian control. The great powers were concerned in case these disturbances escalated into a major war as the French revolution had. In conclusion, it has to be said in defence of the settlement that in 1815 nationalism was still a very new principle, produced mainly by the French Revolution. It was hardly to be expected that the statesmen of Europe would allow themselves to be influenced by such a new and, to them, suspect ideal.

3.2 What were the aims and achievements of Lord Castlereagh in foreign affairs after the Congress of Vienna (1815)?

Robert Stewart, Viscount Castlereagh, was an Irish Protestant aristocrat brought up in County Down. At the end of the Congress of Vienna he had enormous prestige among the statesmen of Europe and already had considerable achievements to his credit. He had played an important part in building up and maintaining the alliance which had finally brought down Napoleon. At Vienna he had successfully played the role of con-

Illus. 3.1 Robert Stewart, Viscount Castlereagh, Foreign Secretary 1812–22

ciliator, persuading Prussia to tone down her demands, so that France gained a lenient peace. He had prevented both Prussia and Russia from gaining too much, and had consequently preserved the balance of power. He must take much of the credit for Britain's territorial gains after the defeat of Napoleon; these confirmed British naval supremacy, providing valuable bases, sources of raw materials and markets – the basis for her future imperial and commercial expansion.

(a) *Castlereagh's aims after the Congress of Vienna*

His main concern was to preserve peace, and he hoped that this could be achieved by continuing the co-operation between the great powers started at Vienna, thereby maintaining the balance of power. He wanted regular meetings of the powers to solve problems and quell disturbances by a *Concert of Europe* (states acting in concerted agreement together) instead of by confrontation. However, he did not believe it was right for the great powers to intervene in the internal affairs of other states, and did not want Britain to become involved in any such action. Thus in 1818 when Alexander I proposed that they should sign a written guarantee to preserve all frontiers and monarchs in Europe, Castlereagh refused. His attitude was summed up perfectly by a statement he issued in December 1815: 'It is the province of Great Britain to encourage peace by exercising a conciliatory influence between the Powers, rather than put herself at the head of any combination of Courts to keep others in check.... It is not my wish to encourage on the part of this country, an unnecessary interference in the ordinary affairs of the Continent.' As to specific details, he was keen to get the army of occupation removed from France and France accepted as an equal again by the other powers; this would boost Louis XVIII's popularity and help stabilize the country. Castlereagh felt it was wrong to penalize the Bourbon government too heavily for the behaviour of Napoleon.

(b) *Castlereagh's achievements*

It seemed as though his policies were beginning well; however, after 1818 his actual achievements were limited.

1   With the help of Metternich, Castlereagh was responsible for *the Quadruple Alliance* (November 1815) of Britain, Austria, Russia and Prussia. They agreed to maintain the peace settlement and to hold regular Congresses to discuss any threats to peace and stability. The frontiers of France were guaranteed and the powers would intervene in France to prevent any attempt to restore the Bonapartes. This was an important achievement, because regular conferences in peacetime were a new idea in diplomacy.

2   *The Congress System got under way with the Congress of Aix-la-Chapelle (1818)*. It met to consider what to do about France which had paid off the 700 million franc indemnity and was settling down under Louis XVIII. It was decided that the army of occupation should be withdrawn and that France should take part in future Congresses, transforming the Quadruple into the Quintuple Alliance. Relatively minor problems dicussed and agreed upon were the rights of Jews in Europe, Swedish payments to Denmark for the acquisition of Norway, and the treatment of Napoleon on St Helena. A discordant note was sounded when the Tsar Alexander I, carried away by his Holy Alliance (which had been signed by all European rulers except George III, who was insane, by the Pope and by the Sultan of Turkey), proposed that the powers should guarantee all frontiers and all monarchs; this would have meant intervening to suppress all revolutions, including those

provoked by bad government. Castlereagh was able to carry the Austrians and Prussians with him in rejecting this proposal. Again Castlereagh seemed to have scored a considerable success: France had been accepted again on equal terms, he had launched his new method of European diplomacy and had avoided a split in the Alliance. Unfortunately for Castlereagh the fragile harmony of the Alliance could last only so long as there were no revolutions and no divergent interests among the powers.

3 *1820 was a year of revolutions inspired by liberalism*, in protest against autocratic government. In January, troops were gathering at Cadiz before sailing to attempt the recapture of Spain's New World colonies (Mexico, Argentina, Chile, Peru and Colombia) which had declared themselves independent during the wars. Instead the troops turned on the government and forced King Ferdinand VII to grant a democratic constitution. Similar revolutions in Portugal, Naples and Piedmont also achieved democratic constitutions. Metternich and Alexander, alarmed at the prospect of disturbances spreading from Italy into their own territories, summoned ...

4 *The Congress of Troppau (1820)*. Castlereagh, knowing that they intended to use the Alliance to quell the revolutions and destroy the new constitutions, refused to attend, merely sending his half-brother, Lord Stewart, as an 'observer'. Castlereagh expressed his attitude in a famous State Paper (May 1820); it was not that he approved of liberal revolutions – in fact he sympathized with Metternich's fears; but he was unwilling to involve Britain in general commitments on the continent. It was not morally right for the great powers to force their wishes on smaller countries: 'the Alliance ... was never intended as a Union for the government of the world ... such a scheme is utterly impractical and objectionable'. In addition he knew that the Opposition in parliament would be furious if Britain supported intervention, and he was extremely suspicious of Russian motives, since Alexander was itching to send an army through Europe to crush the Spanish revolution. Unimpressed by Castlereagh's objections, the other representatives issued *the Troppau Protocol* (a first draft of terms to be agreed), which asserted their right to intervene in any country where a revolution seemed in danger of infecting other countries. Castlereagh rejected the Protocol and there was clearly a serious split in the Alliance. The Congress adjourned in disarray.

5 *The Congress of Laibach (1821)* was a continuation of the previous one. Castlereagh again sent his half-brother to show his disapproval. He did concede, however, that the Austrians should intervene in Naples, provided it was not done in the name of the Alliance. As a result, Austrian troops quelled the revolts in Naples; they went on to deal with the revolt in Piedmont as well, a step Castlereagh did not approve. No action was taken against Spain and Portugal at this stage. Just before the Congress ended, the European situation was further complicated by the outbreak of the Greek revolt against Turkish rule. Relations between Britain and the rest remained tense, and it was obvious that Castlereagh's idea of international co-operation was being misused by Britain's allies, though he could not quite bring himself to break away from the Alliance completely. A further Congress was planned for Verona in 1822 to consider the Spanish and Greek problems, but before it met, Castlereagh had committed suicide (August 1822).

His mind had given way under the strain of what historian R. J. White calls 'his courageous attempt to be with Europe but not of it, a diplomatic tight-rope act which must have been a nightmare for the chief performer'. He also had the difficult job of leading the unpopular Tory government in the Commons (as an Irish peer, Lord Castlereagh was not entitled to a seat in the House of Lords, and therefore sat in the House of Commons, whereas the Prime Minister, Lord Liverpool, an English peer, was able to sit in the House of Lords). In addition, though he appeared cool and arrogant, Castlereagh was a shy and sensitive man who was deeply hurt and disturbed by his unpopularity and by the abuse he had to suffer. He already unpopular with the liberals and radicals in 1815 for allowing the restoration of so many autocratic monarchs. Later he was blamed for the government's repressive policy (see Section 2.4). Not being a good speaker, he failed to explain his foreign policy clearly; consequently, the opposition in parliament and the general public thought he was committed to supporting autocracy, which seemed to be borne out by his approval of Austrian intervention in Naples. During the summer of 1821 he was convinced that sinister characters were trying to ruin his reputation by accusing him of homosexuality. He became so unbalanced that although his friends removed his pistols and razors, he succeeded in cutting his throat with a penknife. So great was his unpopularity that crowds hissed and jeered as his coffin was carried into Westminster Abbey.

Though his career was tragically cut short at the early age of 53, Castlereagh's achievements after Vienna deserve to be remembered: he must take the credit for the introduction of the Congress System; this was a new departure in international co-operation and personal contact between the statesmen of Europe, a policy which he pursued with commonsense and restraint.

3.3 What were the aims and achievements of Canning in foreign affairs (1822–7) and how did his policies differ from those of Castlereagh?

(a) *Canning's aims*

Canning was not radically different from Castlereagh in his attitude, though there were differences of method and style.

- Canning was not an enthusiastic supporter of liberalism and revolution abroad, but he did believe that whenever there was bad government, change must come.
- Like Castlereagh, Canning did not approve of great powers interfering all over the world as they saw fit – if a change was necessary, as for example in Greece, the process should be supervised by whichever of the powers was most closely concerned and not simply squashed by the whole Alliance.
- Whereas Castlereagh had merely protested against the Metternich policy of intervention, Canning intended to be more decisive and actually help the revolutionaries in Greece and Portugal. Even here, though, the difference was not completely clearcut, since just before his death, Castlereagh had been contemplating sending a fleet to help the Portuguese liberals.
- Where he differed most from Castlereagh was that his overriding concern was to protect British interests rather than to preserve the Alliance. As Canning's biographer, Wendy Hinde, puts it, 'his policy was based on a careful, even opportunist calculation of what would best preserve peace and promote England's prestige and prosperity'. Not being a founder-member of the Alliance, he had no special affection for it, and did not know the European rulers and politicians personally; if it suited Britain's interests, he was quite prepared to withdraw from the Alliance. 'For *Europe*, I shall be desirous now and then to read *England*', he wrote soon after becoming Foreign Secretary.
- Whereas Castlereagh's policies were misunderstood, Canning took the trouble to

explain to the public what he was trying to achieve; this gained him public support and popularity, though other politicians often disapproved and thought him flashy – one critic remarked that Canning's trips round the country 'speechifying and discussing the intentions of the Gov't were ridiculous ... quite a new system among us ... which excites great indignation'.

● Canning's specific aims were to prevent the French from interfering in Spain, preserve the new Portuguese constitution, maintain the independence of the Spanish colonies with which Britain had developed valuable trade, and help the Greeks, while at the same time making sure that the Russians did not gain too much advantage from the situation.

(b) *Canning's achievements*

1 Canning failed in his first specific aim – to keep the French out of Spain. At *the Congress of Verona (1822)* it soon became clear that Britain's representative, Wellington, was isolated, since all the other powers were determined to destroy Spain's new liberal constitution. British protests were ignored and a French army was authorized to invade Spain; by April 1823 the Spanish liberals had been defeated and Ferdinand's full powers restored. It was a diplomatic failure for Britain, and public opinion was outraged at the presence of French troops in Spain again, only ten years after they had been driven out by Wellington. However, Canning's anti-French speeches won him popularity at home, which increased as some important successes followed.

2 He was successful in upholding the liberal constitution in Portugal. Canning's fear was that unless Britain took decisive action, the French and Spanish, carried away by their crusade against liberalism, might invade Portugal and might even be tempted to regain the lost Spanish colonies in the New World. Following an appeal for help by the Portuguese Foreign Minister, a British naval squadron was sent to Lisbon (July 1823), and later, when it looked as though a Spanish army was about to enter Portugal, Canning despatched 5000 British troops to defend the Portuguese liberals. This was immensely popular with the public at home: it was felt that Canning had restored Britain's prestige after the Spanish failure, and had defied Metternich and the other reactionaries in the Alliance.

3 Together with the USA, Britain was instrumental in preserving the independence of Spain's former colonies. The situation reached crisis point in the autumn of 1823 when Ferdinand VII of Spain proposed another Congress to consider action; it was obvious that Spain and France, and probably the other powers as well, were in favour of a joint expedition to recapture the lost colonies. Canning was determined this should not happen, for several reasons: he felt that the people of South America and Mexico should have the right to remain free from such a reactionary tyrant as Ferdinand VII; he feared that the French might keep some of the Spanish colonies for themselves; probably most important of all, Britain stood to lose the valuable export trade which had developed with the new states, as the Spanish refused to guarantee Britain's right to trade with the colonies if they were recovered. By now Canning was convinced that the Congress System was a waste of time: 'We protested at Laibach and Verona and our protests were treated as waste paper.' Consequently he rejected the idea of a further Congress and warned Polignac, the French ambassador, that Britain would use her fleet in the Atlantic to prevent any expedition reaching South America.

Support for the British stand came from the USA which had already recognized the colonies' independence. In December 1823 President Monroe told Congress (the US parliament) that if any European power interfered in any part of America, whether it be North, Central or South, the USA would oppose it by force. This American policy became known as *the Monroe Doctrine*. The President's motive was to make Central and South America into a US sphere of influence and to warn off the Russians in case they had designs on the rest of America via Alaska, which belonged to Russia. The Monroe Doctrine was actually anti-British as well as anti-the rest of Europe; moreover Canning was disappointed that the USA had recognized the colonies as republics – he would have preferred monarchies. However, the Americans were well aware that their navy alone would be ineffectual and that only with the help of British sea-power could they enforce the Monroe Doctrine. In 1825 Canning recognized Mexico, Colombia and Argentina as independent republics and signed trade agreements with them. Metternich and the others, faced with the double threat from Britain and the USA, abandoned all hope of recovering the colonies.

Canning was triumphant: the Alliance had been thwarted and the British defeat over Spain avenged; 'I called a New World into existence to redress the balance of the Old', he remarked. Prospects for British trade were good and Britain had shown that she could take effective action independently of the European powers. The Congress System was almost, but not quite, finished.

4 *Canning became involved in helping the Greeks in their fight against the Turks*, but he died (1827) before he could see it through. Though the Greeks eventually won full independence (1830), the circumstances were not particularly to Britain's advantage.

The origins of the situation lay in what was known as the Eastern Question: the Turkish Empire (also known as the Ottoman Empire) had once stretched far into south-eastern Europe as well as across Northern Africa. In 1683 the Turks had unsuccessfully besieged Vienna, and since that failure, they had gradually been in retreat. The Turkish government usually neglected and misgoverned its outlying provinces; by 1815 it had lost its authority over North Africa and much of the Balkans, though nominally these areas were still part of the Ottoman Empire. It was because of the obvious Turkish weakness that the Greek nationalists were stirred to try and assert their independence.

In essence, the Eastern Question was the Russian attempt to take advantage of the weakening Turkish Empire, and the attempts of other powers, especially Britain, to prevent this happening (see Section 9.2(c), Chapter 10 and Section 14.4 for later recurrences of the Eastern Question).

Canning's motives for intervention in the Greek revolt were:

- The Greeks were not having a great deal of success since the Sultan of Turkey had received help from Mehemet Ali, the ruler of Egypt. Ali's son Ibrahim had arrived in Greece with a large army, and by 1825 he was well on the way to crushing the rebellion. There was much sympathy in Britain for the Greek cause, and many volunteers, including Lord Byron, had gone out to fight for them. The Greeks themselves sent a deputation to Britain begging for help. All this put Canning under pressure to send active assistance to the Greeks.
- By the early part of 1826, it was clear that the Russians were about to intervene on the Greek side. Alexander I had been keen to help, but Metternich had dissuaded him on the grounds that revolutions, even against the Turks, must not be encouraged. However, Alexander died in December 1825, and the new Tsar Nicholas I was ready for immediate intervention. Russian policy since 1815 had been to suppress revolutions, but this one was different: Nicholas was horrified at the slaughter of Greek Christians by Egyptian and Turkish Muslims; above all though, Greek success would further

weaken Turkey. Canning therefore decided that Britain must act too in order to make sure *firstly* that Turkey would not be weakened too much so that she could still serve as a buffer against Russian expansion in the Balkans, and *secondly* that Russia should not gain too much advantage, such as for example, possession of Constantinople.

- Canning may have intervened in order to break up the Congress System, knowing that Anglo-Russian co-operation would infuriate Metternich.

Consequently Canning, now Prime Minister, negotiated *the Treaty of London (July 1827)* by which Britain, Russia and France agreed to bring about Greek self-government, by force if necessary; a joint naval expedition set out for Greece. The Austrians and Prussians objected strenuously at this support of revolution and the Turks refused to negotiate. In August Canning died (aged 57) from inflammation of the liver and lungs, probably brought on by overwork. Meanwhile the combined 27-ship fleet was blockading the Turkish-Egyptian fleet of 81 ships in *Navarino Bay*. Though they were under orders to avoid hostilities, the British Admiral Codrington decided to force the issue by sailing into the bay. The Turks opened fire and a full-scale battle developed lasting four hours. It was a disaster for the Turks and their allies; 61 ships and about 4000 men were lost (October 1827). This battle was of great importance: Ibrahim was cut off from supplies and reinforcements; French troops landed and organized the evacuation of his troops. There was now no prospect of the Turks recapturing Greece whose independence was recognized in 1830, although her frontiers were not decided until 1832.

After Canning's death Wellington reversed his policy and withdrew Britain from the treaty alliance, because he did not approve of aiding and abetting revolutionaries. The government apologized to the Turks and removed Codrington from his command. With no Canning to keep a watchful eye on them, the Russians declared war on the Turks and forced them to sign *the Treaty of Adrianople (1829)* which gave the area round the Danube delta to Russia.

In the end, *Canning's work in the Near East had mixed success*. He had helped to achieve a completely independent Greece, which in 1832 was recognized as a Kingdom, with Otto of Bavaria as the the first King. However, his wider aim of limiting Russian gains by co-operation with her had been ruined by Wellington, who had failed to grasp Canning's intentions. Russia had substantially increased her influence in the Balkans, and Turkey had suffered military defeat.

5   One result of the Greek revolt which, from Canning's point of view, can be seen as an achievement, was that it marked the end of the Quintuple Alliance and the Congress System as an instrument for crushing revolutions: for the first time Russia was acting *with* Britain and France in opposition to Austria, and there could be no further pretence that Europe was united. Canning had been prepared to break up the Congress System for a variety of reasons: to avoid binding commitments on the continent, to help liberals and nationalists (though this motive must not be exaggerated), but primarily to further Britain's trading and other interests. Metternich had been thwarted; no wonder he was delighted at Canning's death and thanked God for delivering Europe from 'this malevolent meteor'.

Questions

1 Castlereagh and foreign affairs
Read the Sources A to E and then answer the questions which follow.

Extracts from the diary of Charles Greville, who was clerk to the Privy Council (1821–59) and a close personal friend of Wellington

As a speaker he [Castlereagh] was monotonous and never eloquent ... but he was always heard with attention ... I believe he was considered one of the best managers of the House of Commons who ever sat in it ... and he was possessed of good taste, good humour and agreeable manners. With these qualities, it may be asked why he was not a better Minister.

    I believe he was seduced by his vanity, that his head was turned by emperors, kings and congresses and that he was resolved that the country which he represented should play as conspicuous a part as any other in the political dramas which were acted on the Continent. The result of his policy is this ... that we have associated ourselves with members of the Holy Alliance, and gone along with the acts of ambition and despotism in such a manner as to have drawn upon us the hatred of the nations of the Continent.

Source: quoted in P. W. Wilson (ed.), *The Greville Diary*, Doubleday & Co., 1927.

Source B

Extracts from the diary of Mrs Arbuthnot, the wife of a Tory politician

Castlereagh managed the foreign affairs of the country with a judgement and ability that will hand down his name with honour to posterity, when those of his pathetic critics will be buried in oblivion.... When he had to make a statement or an opening speech, he was generally flat and dull and scarcely commanded the attention of the House ... but his management was so good, and he was himself so gentlemanlike and so high minded, that he was one of the most popular leaders the Government ever had.

Source: quoted in F. Bamford and the Duke of Wellington (eds), *Mrs Arbuthnot's Journal, vol. 1*, Macmillan, 1950.

Source C

Comments from a modern historian, Asa Briggs

There was a vigorous debate in Parliament when the Whigs strongly criticised Castlereagh's surrender to European 'reaction', not knowing that Castlereagh in private was referring to the Holy Alliance (September 1815) between the absolute monarchs of Russia, Prussia and Austria as 'a piece of sublime mysticism and nonsense'.... In fact, during these years Castlereagh managed to steer clear of the Holy Alliance and refused to identify Britain too closely with the policies of the European powers.... Before he committed suicide in 1822 Britain had begun to part company with the other great powers on the question of intervention to maintain autocratic government in Spain, Portugal and Sicily.

Source: Asa Briggs, *The Age of Improvement*, Longman, 1959.

Extracts from Castlereagh's confidential State Paper, 5 May 1820

The principle of one state interfering by force in the internal affairs of another, in order to enforce obedience to the governing authority, is always a question of the greatest moral as well as political delicacy. . . . It is important to observe that to generalise such a principle and to think of reducing it to a system, or to impose it as an obligation, is a scheme utterly impracticable and objectionable. . . . This principle is perfectly clear and intelligible in the case of Spain. We may all agree that nothing can be more lamentable, or of more dangerous example, than the recent revolt of the Spanish army . . . but it does not follow that we have therefore equal means of acting upon this opinion . . .

Besides, the people of this country would probably not recognise that our safety could be so far threatened by any state of things in Spain as to warrant their government in sending an army to that country to meddle in its internal affairs. We cannot conceal from ourselves how generally the acts of the King of Spain since his restoration have made his government unpopular, and how impossible it would be to reconcile the people of England to the use of force in order to replace power in his hands.

Source: quoted in A. Aspinall and F. A. Smith (eds), *English Historical Documents vol XI*, Eyre & Spottiswoode, 1959.

__ Source E _____

Another modern historian, Jasper Ridley, writes about events in Spain, 1820–22

In 1820, the Spanish army gathering at Cadiz to embark for South America to recapture the Spanish colonies, mutinied and overthrew *the absolutist monarch* Ferdinand VII. They reintroduced *the liberal constitution* of 1812. . . . Metternich, Tsar Alexander II, the King of Prussia and Louis XVIII united to suppress liberalism and Louis XVIII asked permission of the powers to invade Spain and restore Ferdinand. At the Congress of Verona in 1822 only Britain opposed the proposal and worked for a compromise. The government tried to persuade the Spanish liberals to restore some of Ferdinand's powers, hoping this would prevent a French invasion. The liberals indignantly rejected the British proposals. The French army therefore crossed the frontier and overran Spain without much difficulty. The liberal leaders surrendered to Ferdinand on promise of their lives, but he broke his word and had them all shot. He now established an even more brutal police state than that which had existed before 1820. . . . The Opposition attacked the government's policy and accused Castlereagh of allowing France to 'conquer' Spain.

Source: Jasper Ridley, *Lord Palmerston*, Constable, 1970.

(a) Using the sources and your own knowledge, explain what was meant at the time by the two phrases in Source E:
  (i) absolutist monarch;
  (ii) liberal constitution. (4 marks)
(b) Comment on the similarities and differences in the two assessments of Castlereagh put forward in Sources A and B. (6 marks)
(c) What are the strengths and weaknesses of diaries (like the ones quoted in Sources A and B) as sources of information for historians? (4 marks)

(d) How useful is Source D as evidence of the true motives behind Castlereagh's foreign policy? (6 marks)

(e) Using the sources and your own knowledge, explain to what extent you would agree with the statement at the beginning of Source B, that 'Castlereagh managed the foreign affairs of the country with a judgement and ability that will hand down his name with honour to posterity'. (10 marks)

(Total 30 marks)

2 Compare and explain the foreign policies of Castlereagh and Canning.

3 To what extent can British foreign policy be described as 'liberal' in the period 1815–30?

Parliament and the Great Reform Act of 1832

Summary of events

In 1830 the agitation for a reform of parliament and the system of elections burst out afresh after a lull from 1821, during a period of good trade and comparative prosperity. The demand for reform dated back into the middle of the previous century.William Pitt (premier from 1783 until 1801 and again from 1804 until his death in 1806) tried to introduce some modest changes in 1785; he proposed redistributing some of the worst 'rotten' boroughs, but the idea was dropped largely because of opposition from George III. This new agitation seemed more widespread than before; this was shown by the general election held in the autumn of 1830, when candidates who favoured reform did well. Wellington, the Tory Prime Minister, said that he saw no need to change the system, but the Whig government which came to power in November, decided to introduce a Reform Bill which would remedy some of the worst faults of the system. The Whigs came up against many problems as they tried to steer their Reform Bill through parliament. It was defeated once in the Commons and twice in the Lords, but it eventually became law as the 1832 Reform Act or the Great Reform Act. After all the excitement, the reformers found that the terms of the Act were something of an anti-climax; several more Reform Acts were needed before Britain could be regarded as a genuinely democratic country.

4.1 How are laws made?

It might be helpful at this point to outline briefly the stages through which any proposed government measure has to pass before it becomes law.

● The proposed changes are known as *a Bill*; this is read out in the House of Commons (*first reading*) and then printed, after which it gets a *second reading*.
● Next the proposals are debated by the MPs and a vote is taken. If a majority of the MPs is in favour of the Bill, it passes to the next stage . . .
● *The committee stage*. Here each clause is carefully considered by an all-party committee of between 16 and 50 MPs who have special knowledge about the subject of the Bill. If necessary they can suggest amendments (changes) to the Bill before sending it back to the Commons. Here it goes through . . .
● *The report stage*. MPs consider the suggested amendments and may also propose further changes. When the Bill has been sorted out into its final form . . .

- *A third reading* takes place, followed by a short debate and another vote. These votes are known as *divisions*, because MPs register their votes by moving out into the lobbies of the House of Commons and dividing into two groups: those who approve of the Bill file back through one lobby; those against, through another.
- A Bill which has passed all three readings in the Commons is sent to the House of Lords where it goes through all the same stages again. A controversial Bill may well be defeated in the Lords; this happened twice to the Whig Reform Bill. This is one of the main functions of the House of Lords – to act as a check and to make the government think again about Bills or parts of Bills which might be considered to be ill-advised.
- If a Bill is approved by the House of Lords, it is sent to the sovereign (the King or Queen) to be signed. This is known as receiving *the Royal Assent*. Once the monarch has signed it, the Bill becomes *an Act of Parliament* and is ready to be put into operation as a new law. Nowadays the sovereign always gives the Royal Assent to Bills which have passed both Houses of Parliament. The last sovereign to refuse to do so was Queen Anne in 1707, but since then the monarch has gradually withdrawn from the business of party politics. The sovereign is said to be 'above politics', and she has to act 'on the advice' of her Prime Minister; in other words, she has to go along with the wishes of the Prime Minister and cabinet. However, both George III and George IV could still have some influence on government policy; if the government knew the King disapproved of a certain policy, it would delay introducing a Bill or hold it up in parliament so that it never reached the King; this happened with Catholic Emancipation and with Pitt's earlier attempt at parliamentary reform.

4.2 What was wrong with the system before the Great Reform Act?

Very few changes had been made since the eighteenth century, so the system was completely out of date and took no account of the recent alterations and shifts in population caused by the Industrial Revolution. Though Britain was rapidly becoming an industrialized nation, parliament, and therefore the running of the country, were still dominated by landowners.

(a) *Constituencies were not organized to give fair and equal representation to all parts of the country*

There were two types of constituency: *counties* and *boroughs*. There were 122 county MPs, 432 borough MPs, 100 from Ireland and two each from the universities of Oxford and Cambridge.

The absurdities of the system were many:

- English and Irish counties were each represented by two MPs irrespective of size and population. Yorkshire, for example, had 17 000 electors while Rutland only had 609.
- Scottish and Welsh counties only had one MP each, and both Scotland (45 seats) and Wales (24 seats) were under-represented compared with England's 489 seats.
- Most English borough constituencies had two MPs whereas those in Scotland, Wales and Ireland were allowed only one. Again the electorate (the group of people allowed to vote) varied widely: Westminster, Preston, Bristol, Leicester and Liverpool had over 5000 voters, while at the other end of the scale Old Sarum (Wiltshire) had seven, and Gatton (Surrey) had six. These tiny constituencies were known as *rotten*

boroughs, because they had fallen into decay. Old Sarum was no more than a mound of earth, Gatton had dwindled to six houses, and Dunwich (Suffolk), which had once been a thriving community, had gradually fallen into the sea as the coast eroded away. Altogether there were 56 boroughs with fewer than 40 voters each, yet each of them was represented in the House of Commons by two MPs.

●   Expanding industrial cities such as Birmingham, Manchester, Leeds and Sheffield had no MPs because they had not been boroughs in the late seventeenth century, when the last major redistribution of seats had taken place. Consequently the Midlands and North of England were greatly under-represented compared with the South: in 1831 Lancashire with a population of 1.3 million had only 14 MPs, while Cornwall with 300 000 people had 42 MPs.

(b) *The franchise (right to vote) was restricted and inconsistent*

Women were not allowed to vote at all. *In county constituencies* the franchise was fairly straightforward: since 1430, men who owned freehold (land or property) worth 40 shillings had had the vote. The fact that the value of money had declined meant that the county electorate was often larger than that in the boroughs. Sometimes the holders of certain church offices were considered to be freeholders – the bellringer at Westminster Abbey was allowed to vote in Middlesex.

Borough constituencies varied widely and there were five different categories:

1   *Freeman boroughs* (Liverpool and Coventry) were the most common: here the vote went to all who had received the freedom of the city, usually by inheritance, by marrying the daughter or widow of a freeman, or by purchase.
2   *Burgage boroughs*: the vote went to owners of certain pieces of land or property; these usually had small electorates, e.g. Clitheroe (Lancashire) with fewer than 50 voters.
3   *Scot and lot boroughs*: the vote for all male householders who paid local rates; these varied in size from Westminster (over 5000 voters) to Gatton (six).
4   *Potwalloper boroughs*: the vote for all males who owned a house and fireplace to boil a pot on; some of these were large – Preston had over 5000 voters, Bedford and Northampton both had over 1000.
5   *Corporation boroughs*: the vote went only to members of the corporation; here the electorates were small: out of 29 such boroughs in England, 26 (including Andover, Bath, Portsmouth, Scarborough and Truro) had fewer than 50 voters.

What they all had in common was that the system of choosing their two MPs was not at all democratic. In the whole of England, only seven boroughs out of a total of 202 had more than 5000 voters, while 56 had fewer than 50 voters each.. In the whole of Britain, which had a population of around 24 million (1831 census), there were fewer than 500 000 voters.

(c) *The way in which elections were carried out encouraged bribery and corruption*

●   There was no secret ballot and votes were cast openly, so that the candidates knew how each elector had voted. Electors often had little freedom, particularly if the candidate happened to be their landlord. There were many cases of tenants being evicted because they had dared to vote against the local squire.
●   In constituencies with large electorates, candidates resorted to outright bribery in the way of cash payments, jobs, government posts, contracts, and sometimes free beer. An election in Liverpool in 1830 cost the two candidates over £100 000 between them.

The voting lasted the usual 15 days and the state of the contest was known from day to day. They were paying £15 a vote at the beginning, but on the last day, with the candidates neck and neck, each vote was costing £150.
- In the very small borough constituencies, dealings were not quite so blatantly sordid. Usually there was no contest: the local landowner would nominate his MP and the handful of voters would approve, probably encouraged by a few gifts. Boroughs of this type were known as *pocket boroughs* (or nomination boroughs) and were a valuable asset to their owners, who could sell the nomination to the highest bidder.

4.3 Why did the demand for reform revive in 1829–30?

There had always been a small group of Whig MPs in favour of moderate parliamentary reform. The Whig leader, Lord Grey, had come out in support of reform as far back as 1793; other prominent supporters included his son-in-law, Lord Durham (known as 'Radical Jack'), Lord Brougham and Lord John Russell. By 1829 there were further pressures:

(a) *The ever-increasing class of prosperous businessmen and manufacturers*

Though many of them were MPs, *they resented the domination of parliament by landowners*. It seemed as though the latter protected their own interests with measures such as the Corn Laws, whereas the unfortunate manufacturers still had to pay duties on their imported raw materials; they felt that they were paying more than their fair share of taxes. Generally referred to as *the middle class*, they wanted the system changing, not to one of complete democracy in which all adults had the vote, but just enough to give themselves a fair representation in the Commons.

(b) *The passing of Catholic Emancipation in 1829* (see Section 2.7(b))

This provided an added stimulus because it split and weakened the Tory party which was the chief enemy of reform. Some of the right-wing Tories (Ultras) were so furious with Wellington that they came out in favour of reform just to spite him. They hoped to reduce the number of pocket boroughs, many of whose MPs had been used by Wellington to get Emancipation through.

(c) *There was a sudden slump in the economy*

This hit both agriculture and industry. The effects were seen most dramatically in the Midlands and South of England where farm labourers' riots broke out in protest against irregular employment and low wages. In some areas disturbances were sparked off by the introduction of threshing-machines which reduced the number of labourers needed. In other areas, workers were protesting against having to pay tithes; this was a tax amounting to one-tenth of annual income, payable either in cash or produce, to the local vicar for the upkeep of the church. Beginning at Orpington (Kent) in June 1830, the outbreaks spread rapidly and involved the burning of hayricks and barns, smashing of threshing-machines and attacks on parsons. There was a spate of threatening letters signed 'Swing' or 'Captain Swing' (apparently a reference to the swinging stick of the flail used in hand threshing). The new Whig government acted decisively to curb these *'Swing Riots'*; Lord Melbourne, the Home Secretary, set up special courts which tried nearly 2000 offenders. Nineteen were hanged, over 600 sent to gaol, and nearly 500 transported to Australia. By the summer of 1831 order had been restored, but the outbreaks had been alarming enough to convince many Whigs that moderate reform of parliament was the best way to avoid revolution.

(d) *Strikes in the North of England*

Here *John Doherty* had founded a trade union for cotton spinners, and strikes broke out in the Manchester area in protest at wage reductions. In October 1830 there was a coal strike at Oldham and miners began to join Doherty's union. The signs were ominous: a visitor at the opening of the Liverpool–Manchester Railway (September) noted: 'Tricolour flags (the French revolutionary standard) were displayed at some parts of the line. The spirit of the district was detestable.'

(e) *Jeremy Bentham continued to advocate a reform of parliament*

Bentham and his supporters (known as 'Philosophic Radicals') (see Section 2.1(c)) had been pressing their case for many years. In 1817 Bentham had published a pamphlet calling for annual general elections, secret ballots, and the vote for all males at 21. At first these demands were far too extreme for most people, but now some of them began to be taken up in unexpected quarters. *Thomas Attwood*, a Birmingham banker from a Tory background, founded *the Birmingham Political Union* (January 1830). 'The general distress which now affects the country,' he wrote, 'can only be permanently remedied by an effectual Reform in the Commons.' The Union aimed to unite the middle and working classes; similar unions quickly appeared in London and other cities and later they organized themselves into a nationwide movement known as *the National Political Union*. It won the support of workers because it seemed the only peaceful way to achieve social reform.

(f) *Revolutions in Europe had an important influence on Britain*

Particularly important was the revolution in France which overthrew King Charles X and put Louis Philippe on the throne (July 1830). This probably encouraged the reformers and may have frightened many of the ruling classes (though not Wellington) into giving way.

(g) *The death of George IV helped the reformers*

The reformers were fortunate that George, who was against any changes in parliament, died in June 1830. His successor, William IV, was by no means enthusiastic, but was prepared to go along with some changes. It was the practice to hold a general election on the accession of a new monarch. This took place in July–August 1830, and it was no surprise that reform candidates did well. When the Tory Prime Minister, Wellington, continued to stick to his view that the existing system was perfect, he was outvoted by a combination of Whigs and progressive Tories, and a Whig government was able to come to power.

4.4 Why was there so much opposition to reform?

It might appear that the case for reform was so strong that no sane-minded person could possibly oppose it. However, the system had plenty of vigorous supporters whose arguments and motives were:

● It had worked perfectly well in the past and therefore there was no need to change it.

● Rotten boroughs were useful because they allowed both parties to introduce their promising up-and-coming young men into the Commons; they were also essential to provide seats for unpopular ministers.

● All the people who benefited in any way from the system were reluctant to have it changed. For example, corporation members and freemen opposed an extension of the franchise because the more electors there were, the less they could expect to pick up in bribes.

● If the small boroughs were abolished, the resulting loss of the franchise would be an interference with the property rights of those people concerned; it would be like taking away someone's house or land, and once such practices were allowed, no property would be safe.

● The majority of Tories, though certainly not all of them, wanted to uphold the system because the nomination boroughs (pocket and some rotten boroughs) provided the basic core of their MPs (well over 200, whereas the Whigs had only about 70).

● Even small changes in the system must be restricted because they would encourage demands for more, and appetites would not be satisfied until full democracy had been introduced. This would upset the constitution and make the House of Commons more powerful than the Lords. This was why Peel was against reform: 'I was unwilling to open a door which I saw no prospect of being able to close.'

● Landowners were afraid that their interests would not be well served by a House of Commons dominated by the middle classes, particularly as some of the reformers were also advocating repeal of the Corn Laws.

4.5 The passing of the Bill

Although the Whigs were well aware of the strength of Tory feelings, it is unlikely that they foresaw how bitterly they would fight the Reform Bill. Instead of taking a few weeks to pass, as they expected, it took 15 months, and there were riots, marches, and a general election before it became law. The stages were:

● Lord John Russell introduced the Bill (March 1831), which proposed, among other things, to abolish over a hundred rotten and pocket boroughs and to give their MPs to the industrial North and Midlands. It would also allow more people to vote. It was quite a mild measure, to change things just enough to bring the new business and manufacturing classes into the system. As Professor Norman McCord puts it, the Bill was designed 'to recruit to the political nation, groups who could be seen as useful, . . . to admit the responsible, respectable, trustworthy few and to exclude the dangerous many. . . . What the Whigs intended was the enfranchisement of the possessors of property and information . . . those who could make an informed use of the vote.'

The Bill was greeted with jeers and howls of derision from the Tories, and though it passed its second reading in the Commons by a majority of one, the Tories were able to defeat it in the committee stage.

Illus. 4.1   Charles, 2nd Earl Grey, the Whig Prime Minister
responsible for the 1832 Reform Act

- The Prime Minister, Lord Grey, persuaded William IV to dissolve parliament, and a general election followed (April). Naturally the Tories held on in their rotten and pocket boroughs, but in the counties, where the electorate was larger, the Whigs made sweeping gains and came back with a majority of 136.
- Russell introduced a slightly different version of the Bill which passed the Commons with a comfortable majority of 109 (September). However, after a debate lasting five nights it was defeated in the Lords by a majority of 41, of whom 21 were bishops. There was an immediate outburst of public anger against the Lords, and *the Morning Chronicle* appeared with black borders as a sign of mourning for the Bill. There were riots in Derby and Nottingham, where the castle was destroyed (it was the property of the unpopular Duke of Newcastle who had expelled tenants for voting against his candidates). In Bristol rioters burned down the bishop's palace and other public buildings, and it took three troops of cavalry to restore order; at least 12 people were killed and around 400 seriously injured. Things were more orderly in

Birmingham, but about 100 000 people attended Attwood's protest meeting; the Political Unions organized similar meetings all over the country. Several peers and bishops known to have voted against the Bill, and even some who had not, were attacked by mobs, and the Duke of Wellington had his windows smashed (he retaliated by putting up iron shutters).

● A third version of the Bill passed the Commons (March 1832) and two readings in the Lords, but in the committee stage the Tories passed an amendment which would have weakened the Bill (May). Grey asked the King to create 50 new Whig peers, enough to give them a majority; when William refused, Grey resigned.

● With excitement in the country at a new climax, William invited Wellington to form a government. The Duke was prepared to do his duty and help the King: for six days he tried to form a cabinet, intending to introduce a much watered-down version of the Bill. But most Tories regarded this as another Wellington betrayal, and when Peel refused to support him, the Duke had to admit failure.

● Grey returned to office amid growing agitation. Attwood was urging non-payment of taxes and one MP wrote in his diary, 'the whole country is in a state little short of insurrection'. Now thoroughly alarmed, William agreed to create as many new peers as were necessary.

● Seeing no way out, the Tory peers stayed away in large numbers, and there was no need for the King to create any new peers. Consequently on 4 June 1832 the Bill passed its third reading in the Lords by 106 to 22, and on 7 June it received the Royal Assent.

There is disagreement among historians about how close Britain was to revolution during the Reform Bill crisis. The traditional view, which is also held by more recent writers such as E. P. Thompson, is that without the Reform Act there would almost certainly have been widespread revolution. According to Thompson, 'Britain was within an ace of revolution', and he went on to argue that only the compromises and concessions provided by the Act averted full-scale revolt. On the other hand some writers, including the American historian J. Hamburger, believe that the violent incidents were not as serious as historians have thought. Hamburger thinks that the danger was deliberately exaggerated by James Mill and other Radicals in order to frighten parliament into passing the Bill. One of the main pieces of evidence to support his theory is that during the riots in Bristol, the better-off working class became so disgusted with the behaviour of the rioters (mostly unemployed labourers) that they ignored them and went home; if Britain had been genuinely on the verge of revolution, these riots should have acted as the starting-pistol.

4.6 What were the terms of the Act and how far did they put right the faults of the system?

(a) *The terms of the Act changed both the representation and the franchise*

1 Boroughs with a population of less than 2000 (56 in all) lost both MPs.
2 Boroughs with a population of between 2000 and 4000 (31 in all) lost one MP.
3 This made 143 seats available for redistribution: 65 were given to the counties (e.g. Yorkshire received an extra two, giving it six in all); 65 were given to boroughs which had never had an MP (these included Leeds, Birmingham, Manchester, Sheffield, Bolton, Oldham and Bradford); eight were given to Scotland and five to Ireland. The total number of MPs in the Commons remained the same (658).

4   In borough constituencies the vote was given to the owners or occupiers of property rated at £10 a year or more.
5   In county constituencies the vote was given to owners of copyhold land valued at £10 a year (copyholders were tenants whose families had held a particular piece of land for generations; the proof of their right to occupy the land was a copy of the original manorial court-roll entry which first allowed their ancestors to hold the land). The vote was also given to holders of land on long leases worth £10 a year, holders of land on short leases worth £50 a year and to tenant farmers who paid £50 a year rent (40 shilling freeholders kept the vote).
6   Eligible voters had to register, i.e. have their names put on the electoral roll, for a fee of one shilling (5p).

(b) *A few of the worst faults were remedied but many still remained*

● Rotten boroughs disappeared but the constituencies still varied enormously in size of electorate: there were 35 boroughs with less than 30 voters while Westminster now had 11 600 and Liverpool 11 300. Although the industrial towns were given MPs, the South was still over-represented: 370 MPs came from south of a line from the Wash to the Severn, whereas the area north of the line (excluding Scotland), which had a larger population, returned only 120. Scotland, Ireland and Wales continued to be under-represented compared with England.

● The electorate of Britain increased from about 478 000 to 813 000 (though estimates of the figures vary) out of a total population of 24 million. This was a long way from being democratic: large sections of the population – agricultural labourers and the vast majority of industrial workers – still had no vote. Certain boroughs which already had something approaching a democratic franchise had a smaller electorate than before; at Preston, everyone who spent the night before the election in the town had been allowed to vote, but under the new system, all the workers were excluded, and the Radical Henry Hunt lost his seat as a result. The continuing unfairness of the new system was shown in another way: over Britain as a whole, one in seven adult males now enjoyed the vote; however, while this worked out at one in five in England, it was only one in eight in Scotland, and even worse, one in twenty in Ireland.

● The Act did not introduce voting by secret ballot: consequently bribery, corruption and 'influencing' of the voters continued unabated. John Hobhouse (a Radical) paid out a total of £6000 to encourage the electors of Nottingham to support him in the elections of 1834 and 1837. At Ipswich between £20 and £30 was being paid quite openly for one vote during the election of 1841 (see *Pickwick Papers* for Charles Dickens's hilarious description of a corrupt election, after 1832, in the imaginary borough of Eatanswill).

● The Act did not change the length of parliaments: this remained at seven years (introduced in 1716), and it stayed at that until 1911 when it was reduced to five years.

● There was no dramatic change in the membership of the House of Commons. Some businessmen and industrialists came in, but the wealthy landowners still predominated. Many of the pocket boroughs had survived and there were at least 50 boroughs in England and Wales where some member of the local gentry could nominate the MP. In the counties the position of the landowners was strengthened by the fact that the tenant farmers who now had the vote felt obliged to support their candidates. Thus, as M. G. Brock remarks: 'Much the same men continued to run much the same system.' Since the position of the House of Lords remained unchanged, the Tory fears of being edged out of control were not justified, at least for the time being.

(c) *Other results of the Great Reform Act*

- Politically aware members of the working classes were bitterly disappointed because they had not been given the vote; they began to look towards Trades Unionism and Chartism (see Chapters 6 and 19).
- The new registration of voters led the parties to form committees in the constituencies to keep the rolls up to date and to make sure of maximum support. In spite of some initial corruption (such as trying to remove known opponents from the list while keeping dead supporters on it), these committees were eventually to develop into the local party organizations, and so the party system was strengthened.
- The disappearance of so many rotten boroughs reduced the crown's influence in politics. The real importance of the Act turned out to be not the changes which it introduced, but the fact that it was the first breach in the system. Much to the disappointment of Grey and the Whigs who hoped it would be enough to satisfy appetites, it led to demands for further reform of parliament. These in turn led to a series of peaceful political changes in which parliament reformed itself, in 1867, 1884, 1911, 1918 and 1928. The Act also encouraged those who were advocating other types of reform – in factories, mines, poor law and local government.

Questions

1 **The campaign for parliamentary reform**
   Read Sources A to G and then answer the questions which follow.

Source A

A speech by Lord John Russell in the House of Commons when he introduced his first Reform Bill, 1 March 1831

What then would be the surprise of a stranger from afar if he were taken by his guide, whom he had asked to conduct him to one of the places of election, to a green mound, and told that this green mound sent two members to parliament. Or if he were shown a green park with many signs of flourishing vegetable life but none of human habitation, and told that this green park sent two members to parliament. But his surprise would increase to astonishment if he were carried into the North of England, where he would see large flourishing towns full of trade and activity, and were told that these places had no representatives in the assembly which was said to represent the people. Thus the confidence which the people used to have in the construction and constitution of the House of Commons is gone for ever. The whole people call loudly for reform.

Source: *Hansard*; quoted in L. Evans and P. J. Pledger, *Contemporary Sources and Opinions in Modern British History, vol. I*, Warne, 1967.

Source B

Extracts from The Extraordinary Black Book, *written to draw attention to the faults of the system; published 1831*

The great fount of evil is the *rotten boroughs*, from which has flowered national calamities, ruinous wars, lavish expenditure and enormous debt. They are the obstacle to every social improvement – civil, commercial, legal and ecclesiastical. By means of them the nobility have been able to double their private incomes and to fill every lucrative office in the army, navy and public administration with their friends and dependants. . . . Because of the boroughs, all our institutions are oppressive and aristocratic. . . . The aristocratic spirit pervades everything . . . all is privilege.

At Nottingham, one gentleman confessed to having paid out in the election of 1826, above £3000 in bribery in a single day. . . . At Hull, one of the sitting members dared not appear before his constituents because he had not paid 'the polling money' for the last election.

Source: quoted in D. Holman (ed.), *Portraits and Documents: Earlier 19th Century*, Hutchinson, 1985.

Source C

A speech by the Duke of Wellington in the House of Lords, 2 November 1830

He was fully convinced that the country possessed at the present moment a legislature which answered all the good purposes of legislation, and this to a greater degree than any legislature had ever answered in any country whatever. He would go further and say that the legislature and the system of representation possessed the full and entire confidence of the country . . . the representation of the people at present contained a large body of the property of the country and the landed interests which had a predominant place. Under these circumstances he was not prepared to bring forward any measure [of reform].

Source: as for Source A.

Source D

English boroughs and their electors in 1830

Number of electors	Number of boroughs
Over 5000	7
1001–5000	36
601–1000	22
301–600	24
101–300	36
51–100	21
50 or fewer	56

Source: M. Brock, *The Great Reform Act*, Hutchinson, 1973.

Source E

Analysis of the House of Commons elected in 1830; total number of MPs – 658

Relations of peers	256
Placemen and pensioners	217
Officers in the army	89
Officers in the navy	24
Lawyers	54
East Indian Interests	62
West Indian Interests	35
Bankers	35
Agricultural interests	356
Miscellaneous	51

Source: *The Extraordinary Black Book*, 1831 (see Source B).

Report of a meeting held on Hunslet Moor (near Leeds), 20 September 1819

It was resolved that a reform in the Constitution of the Commons House is an absolute necessity, the present corrupt system having nearly produced *a disruption of society*. Therefore in order to put an end to these great and national evils, we deem it vital that the present System of Electing Members to Parliament should be abolished and the Elective Franchise be extended to all persons who are called on to contribute, either by taxes or labour, to the support of the State, and that Elections be taken by the ballot annually.

Source: quoted in D. G. Wright, *Democracy and Reform 1815–85*, Longman, 1970.

Source G

Speech by Sir Robert Peel in the House of Commons, 21 September 1831

This Bill [the Reform Bill] does not violate the forms of the constitution – I admit it, but I assert that, while it respects those forms, it destroys the balance of opposing powers; it is a sudden and violent transfer of an authority which has until now been shared by all orders in the state, exclusively to one.

Source: *Hansard*; quoted in D. G. Wright (see Source F).

   (a) Using your own knowledge and the information in the sources, explain what the writer meant by the following phrases:
      (i)   rotten boroughs (Source B);
      (ii) a disruption of society (Source F).   (4 marks)
   (b) In what ways does the evidence in Sources D, E and F support the criticisms of the existing parliamentary system made in Sources A and B?   (10 marks)
   (c) Compare the view of the old parliamentary system put forward in Source C with the one put forward in Sources A and B. How do you explain these differences?   (8 marks)
   (d) Using your own knowledge and the evidence of the sources, explain:
      (i)   Sir Robert Peel's reaction to the Reform Bill (Source G);   (4 marks)
      (ii) how far you think the Reform Act of 1832 would have satisfied the people at the meeting on Hunslet Moor (Source F).   (4 marks)
                                          (Total 30 marks)

2   '[After the 1832 Reform Act] much the same men continued to run much the same system' (M. G. Brock). Why then is the Act seen as such an important landmark in British political history?

Whig reforms and failures 1833–41

Summary of events

Following the Great Reform Act, a general election was held in which the Whigs won a large majority (December 1832). They remained in office, except for two short breaks, until the Tory victory in the general election of 1841. Grey remained Prime Minister until 1834 when, at the age of 70, he resigned. This was partly because he felt that his main ambition – to introduce a moderate reform of parliament – had been achieved, and partly because there was a split in the cabinet about how to deal with the continuing unrest in Ireland. The 55-year-old *William Lamb, Lord Melbourne*, took over the premiership. However, he had difficulty forming a cabinet, and in discussions with the King, William IV, he offered to resign. William, who had had enough of the Whig reforms by this time, accepted the offer, and in effect dismissed the government. He invited Peel to form a ministry, even though the Tories lacked a majority in the Commons. A general election had to be held (January 1835), and although the Tories gained many seats, Peel was well short of a majority. Nevertheless he was Prime Minister from December 1834 until April 1835 (known as 'Peel's 100 days'), but he was repeatedly defeated and forced to resign. William had no choice but to recall Melbourne and the government which he had sacked; this demonstrated that the traditional practice of the Commons supporting whatever Prime Minister the King wanted no longer applied. It was one of the by-products of the Great Reform Act and it meant that the monarch would from then on play less and less part in politics.

William IV died in 1837 and was succeeded by *Queen Victoria* who reigned until her death in 1901. She was the daughter of William's deceased younger brother, Edward, Duke of Kent. The usual general election took place after the death of the monarch, though this was the last time the custom was followed. The Whig majority was greatly reduced, and in May 1839 Melbourne resigned after his government had secured a majority of only five votes in an important division. This dismayed Victoria who had found Melbourne most helpful and sympathetic when she had taken over the throne at the tender and inexperienced age of 18, and who looked on the Whigs as her friends. It was assumed that Peel would form a government, but an odd incident occurred, which became known as *the Bedchamber Crisis*. Peel, cautious about taking office again without a majority, asked Victoria to remove some of the leading ladies of the Queen's household who were related to the former Whig ministers, and replace them with Tory ladies. Victoria refused, whereupon Peel abandoned the idea of forming a government, and Melbourne returned yet again, for a further two years as Prime Minister. In 1840 Victoria married her cousin, *Prince Albert of Saxe-Coburg*, and became less dependent on Melbourne.

Though Melbourne himself was not interested in change, *the Whigs were responsible for some important reforms*, particularly in the early part of the ministry before they began to run out of steam. There was the abolition of slavery, attempts to improve factory conditions, grants for education, and reform of the Poor Law and of town government. At the same time the Whig Foreign Secretary, *Lord Palmerston*, conducted a successful and popular overseas policy (see Chapter 9). On the other hand *there were problems which the Whigs seemed incapable of understanding*: unrest among the unemployed, the Chartist movement, trade depressions and a failure to balance their budgets, which all help to explain the Whig defeat in 1841.

5.1 The Whig attitude to reform

Most of the members of the Whig government, wealthy aristocrats, seemed to think that the Great Reform Act was the one gesture towards reform that they were required to make; left to themselves they would have been quite content to meander along without taking any further positive action. Melbourne himself, though amiable and cultured, was against nearly all the reforms being discussed. 'I am for holding the ground already taken', he remarked, 'but not for occupying new ground rashly.' He claimed that passing new laws was only an incidental duty of governments and believed that there were no really serious problems to be solved. Two of the most progressive Whigs, Lords Brougham and Durham, were dropped from the cabinet in 1835.

However, it is easy for historians, and students, with the benefit of hindsight, to be too critical of these nineteenth-century politicians for what might be seen as a lack of vision. It is important to remember that at the time:

●   There was no tradition of wide government intervention in the life of the nation.
●   Most people disapproved when governments *did* try to extend their powers and suspected that their motives were just for party political or personal gain.
●   Governments did not have the administrative machinery and resources to operate an interventionist policy.
●   Policies of this sort would cost money, and there was a widespread feeling against increasing taxation. Even the Radicals, who wanted efficient government, also demanded 'cheap government'.

In spite of all this, the Whig government came under considerable pressure from several directions to keep up the flow of reforming measures:

(a) *The Benthamite Radicals*

The ideas of Jeremy Bentham (see Section 2.1(c)) had enormous influence. Ever since the publication of his first pamphlet in 1776 Bentham had persevered with his doctrine of *Utilitarianism*: the acid test of all laws and institutions should be – are they efficient and useful? If not, they must be changed or scrapped. He must take some of the credit for the Great Reform Act; once that had been achieved, why should governments not continue to give way to pressure and concede reform in other areas of inefficiency? Although Bentham himself died in 1832 just before the Reform Bill passed, his followers kept up the pressure, publishing reports and recommendations, and generally harassing the Whigs. The most important were *Edwin Chadwick* who produced reports on the poor law, public health (see Section 12.4(c)) and the police, and *Joseph Parkes* who investigated the defects of town government. On the other hand, many Radicals were not enthusiastic about factory reform, since they were themselves factory-owners and did not approve of government interference.

(b) *The Humanitarian movement*

This was composed of people from many different spheres of life, who all had one aim in common – to improve the living and working conditions of the working classes. They were supported by *the Evangelical Movement* of the Church of England, a group which felt that the Church was not showing enough concern for the plight of ordinary people, and was consequently losing support to the Methodists. Evangelicals believed in a life of prayer and service to others, and they saw it as their Christian duty to maintain Christian principles in public life. Many Humanitarians were Tories: for example William Wilberforce, leader of the anti-slavery movement; Michael Sadler and Lord Ashley (later Lord Shaftesbury), the factory reform campaigners, were Tory MPs as well as Evangelicals.

(c) *Progressive factory-owners such as Robert Owen and John Fielden*

These two men in particular demonstrated that better conditions and shorter working hours increased rather than reduced output. They tried to influence other industrialists as well as governments to follow their example (see Section 12.3(b and g)).

5.2 The first round of reforms: slavery, factories and education (1833)

(a) *The abolition of slavery in the British Empire (1833)*

1   The problem was that although the slave trade had been prohibited in 1807 by the British government, after a long campaign led by the humanitarian Tory MP *William Wilberforce*, slavery itself was allowed to continue. This encouraged the smuggling of slaves who continued to be shipped across the Atlantic in appalling conditions, traders cramming as many slaves as possible into their ships. There were 670 000 slaves in the West Indies alone. In 1821 Wilberforce brought out a pamphlet explaining the arguments in favour of abolition, and in 1823 *T. F. Buxton*, a Tory MP, founded *the Anti-Slavery Society*. In 1833 the Whig Colonial Secretary, Lord Stanley, introduced an Emancipation Bill.

2   *There was a good deal of opposition to the Bill*, especially from the owners of sugar plantations in the West Indies and from merchants involved in the sugar trade: abolition would mean loss of property (a good slave might be worth around £50); there would be a labour shortage which would push up production costs, to the advantage of competitors in the USA who would still have their slaves; and there was the fear of unrest and disturbances if former slaves ran riot after gaining their freedom. Many MPs had money in sugar production and trade: W. E. Gladstone's father was a sugar merchant in Liverpool, and he gave his son, newly elected to parliament in 1833, strict instructions to vote against the Bill.

3   *The terms of the Act*, which passed with a large majority, were:

- All slaves were to be set free within a year, and were then to serve apprenticeships of up to seven years to their former owners; this was to ease the transition from a slave economy to a wage-earner system.
- The government paid £20 million compensation to the slave-owners.

4   *The Act was successful* in the sense that it did away with a system that was morally wrong, although it caused some economic problems. Planters complained that the compensation was insufficient, and many went out of business. In Jamaica and Guiana, freed slaves preferred to settle in villages of their own instead of working on the plantations; this led to labour shortages and high wages and helped to cause a general depression in the West Indies. In Cape Colony (South Africa) many Boers, convinced that farming would be unprofitable without slaves, decided to leave, and they embarked on the Great Trek (see Section 14.3(d)). Nowhere was anything done to enable the slaves to make good use of their freedom; instead, black people remained illiterate and exploited.

(b) *Althorp's Factory Act (1833)*

This was the first effective attempt at factory regulation (for full details see Section 12.3(d)).

(c) *The first government grant for education*

1   Having stipulated in Althorp's Factory Act that children ought to receive at least two hours schooling a day, the government felt it ought to try and make this possible. There were no state schools, and the only education for the masses was provided by two rival religious bodies or voluntary societies, one Anglican, one Nonconformist. In 1833 the government gave its first annual grant of £20 000 to be divided between the two societies. This was increased to £30 000 in 1839, and the Privy Council was to keep an eye on how the money was spent (in fact most of it went on building new schools).

2   The grants established an important principle: that the state should accept some responsibility for educating the poor. On the other hand, the amounts of cash involved were pitifully small and the system remained totally inadequate. Bentham's proposal that the government should set up its own system separate from the voluntary societies was ignored; consequently religious rivalry continued to be an unfortunate feature of the haphazard system.

5.3 Reform of the Poor Law: the Poor Law Amendment Act (1834)

(a) *What was wrong with the existing provision for the poor?*

●   The system dated back to the late sixteenth century: each parish was expected to look after its own poor, and it became the traditional practice for paupers (people who were so poor that they were unable to support themselves) to be sent back to the parish of their birth. The cash to provide relief for the poor came from a special rate paid by the inhabitants of the parish. The 1601 Poor Law Act had classified paupers into three groups:

1   those who couldn't find work (able-bodied poor)
2   those who were too ill, too young or too old to work (impotent poor)
3   those who refused to work (idle poor).

In practice the system varied widely throughout the 15 000 parishes: in some parishes relief payments were made to the poor at home; during the eighteenth century it became more common for relief to be given to all types of poor only inside the parish workhouse. From the late eighteenth century onwards, however, the system was unable to cope with the vastly increasing numbers of poor people during periods of unemployment and low wages.

● *The Speenhamland System* adopted in the South after 1795 was a well-meaning attempt to deal with the problem, but it made the situation worse (see Section 2.2(a)2). Depending on the size of a labourer's family and the price of bread, relief payments were made out of the parish poor rates to supplement low wages. However, this type of *outdoor relief*, as it was known (to distinguish it from *indoor relief* given in the workhouse), encouraged employers to lower wages still further. In addition it introduced a new principle: poor relief was originally intended for people who, for whatever reason, were out of work; now it was having to cope with people who were in jobs. This placed a tremendous burden on the parish, much to the disgust of the people who had to pay the ever-increasing rates. In 1795 the total money spent by the 15 000 parishes on poor relief was £2 million; in 1830 it was not far short of £8 million.

● *The Swing Riots of 1830–1* (see Section 4.3(c)) highlighted the complete breakdown of the system and frightened the government into taking some action.

(b) *A Commission was appointed to investigate the working of poor relief*

Appointed in February 1832, its main objective was to find ways of saving money on the poor rates rather than to ease the plight of the poor, which the Humanitarians wanted. The most influential member of the Commission was *Edwin Chadwick*, a Manchester lawyer and a fanatical Benthamite. He was determined that the system should be made uniform and efficient so that it gave value for money. The Commission's Report (February 1834) condemned outdoor relief: 'every penny bestowed ... is a bounty to indolence and vice.' It also disapproved of the slack way in which many workhouses were run: able-bodied poor were being kept at the parish's expense 'in sluggish sensual indolence'. The Commission's recommendations became the 1834 Act, which, according to Chadwick himself, was like 'a cold bath – unpleasant in contemplation but invigorating in its effects'. On the other hand some historians have suggested that the old system was not as bad as the reformers claimed, and that the Benthamites exaggerated the evidence to make it look more wasteful and over-generous than it really was.

(c) *Terms of the Act*

● Outdoor relief would no longer be provided for the able-bodied poor, though in some cases help would continue to be given to the sick and aged at home.

● For the able-bodied poor, and also for the impotent poor who could not be helped at home, relief would be provided in workhouses.

● In order to make larger and more efficient units, parishes were to be grouped into Unions. It was intended that each Union would contain separate workhouses for the able-bodied, impotent and idle poor.

● Conditions in workhouses were to be made as unattractive as possible, so that the poor would make every effort to find work and only come to the workhouse as a last resort. Existence in the workhouse had to be more miserable than the life of the poorest labourer outside. This would encourage 'self-help' and prevent the poor from looking on the workhouse as a haven of refuge; it was known as the *'less eligibility'* principle.

● Each Union was to have paid officials to operate the system; they were to be appointed by the unpaid Board of Commissioners and their secretary, Edwin Chadwick.

(d) *How successful was the new system?*

It was a success in the narrow sense that it helped to reduce the poor rates. Between 1830 and 1834 the average annual expenditure on poor relief had been around £7 million; between 1835 and 1839 it averaged only £4.5 million. Thus the Benthamites saw it as an ideal reform, and it was popular with the majority of ratepayers. However, in every other respect the Act aroused the most bitter criticism, both from the working classes who suffered hardship from it, and from the Humanitarians who thought it cruel and cold-blooded. Most newspapers were severely critical, and there was a flood of pamphlets and petitions, as well as hostile demonstrations and attacks on workhouses and Guardians. *The main criticisms were*:

- The new system ignored the causes of poverty and unemployment and assumed that to be poor was always the fault of the pauper – lack of initiative, laziness or drunkenness – and that people would be able to find jobs if they tried hard enough. Unfortunately this theory made no allowances for the regular trade recessions and slumps which caused unemployment.
- The stoppage of outdoor relief for able-bodied poor caused great hardship in the South. Thousands of labourers in full-time work were not receiving a living wage, and wives and children had to take whatever work they could get in the fields to avoid starvation. The situation would have been much worse had it not been for a series of good harvests, which kept bread prices low, and for railway building which provided extra jobs.
- In the industrial North it proved impossible to stop giving outdoor relief. Unfortunately for all concerned, there was a trade recession in 1837–8 just when the Commissioners began applying the Act in those areas. Outdoor relief was essential as unemployment pay if workers were not to starve in their thousands, and there were far too many to be accommodated in the workhouses. In Huddersfield a mob organized by Richard Oastler, a local Tory Evangelical, gate-crashed the first meeting of the new Board of Guardians and chased them off; it was a further two years before they were able to begin operating. At Bradford the Guardians had to be protected by cavalry, while at Todmorden on the Lancashire–Yorkshire boundary, John Fielden, a mill-owner, led a campaign to boycott the election of Guardians. Police constables were attacked and troops had to be quartered in the town to keep order. Not until 1897 was a workhouse built in Todmorden. At Colne in Lancashire nobody could be found to act as Guardians.
- Although by 1838 over 13 400 of the 15 000 parishes had been grouped into 573 Unions, in the majority of them it proved too expensive to provide separate workhouses. Each parish within the Union was still responsible for meeting the cost of its own poor, which meant that the poorest parishes faced the largest expenses. It was not until 1865 that the system was changed so that parishes within the Union shared the cost more equally. This meant that in the years immediately after 1834, all types of poor, including children, were herded together with criminals, prostitutes and lunatics. As Charles Dickens showed in *Oliver Twist*, conditions were poor. Some historians have suggested that opponents of the new poor law deliberately exaggerated the worst features of workhouse life, and that conditions were in reality fairly tolerable. But it seems certain that during the first 15 years at least, workhouse life was harsh. Husbands and wives were separated (this was relaxed in 1842), children were separated from parents, meals had to be eaten in silence and diets were sparse; the jobs provided in the

workhouses – stone-breaking, bone-grinding and picking old rope to pieces – were either back-breaking or painful on the fingers. There was a famous scandal in the Andover workhouse in 1845 when inmates working on bone-crushing were so hungry that they were found to be eating rotting marrow and fat from the bones. No wonder workhouses became known among the workers as Bastilles (after the notorious fortress-prison in Paris).

Thus the new Poor Law did not end poverty, and consequently thousands of workers were driven to support Chartism (see Chapter 6). Although conditions in workhouses improved after 1865, there was still a great stigma attached to people who were forced into them, and the poor always viewed workhouses with fear and suspicion.

5.4 The reform of town government: the Municipal Corporations Act (1835)

(a) *Why was reform needed?*

The governing and running of towns was confused and inefficient. There were about 250 boroughs, each with its own corporation (mayor, councillors and aldermen) which ran the town's affairs. There were wide variations in how the corporations were chosen and how they functioned, but the disturbing feature was that in 186 of them, only the members of the corporation itself were allowed to vote; they normally re-elected themselves or brought relatives or friends on to the council. These small cliques (known as closed corporations) fixed the local bye-laws and taxes, and it was impossible for the mass of ratepayers to get rid of unpopular councils by voting them out. Most of the corporations used their privileges for personal or party advantage, and ignored matters such as water supply, drainage and street cleansing which they were supposed to look after. Even more ludicrous was the fact that the newly expanded industrial towns had not been recognized as boroughs and had no corporation at all. Here living conditions in overcrowded slums were a threat to public health; in 1831–2 there was a cholera epidemic which began in Sunderland and spread across the country, causing thousands of deaths (see Section 12.4(c)). It was inevitable that once the Whigs had accepted the principle of parliamentary reform, local government reform would soon follow.

Following the same procedure as with the Poor Law, the Whigs appointed a Royal Commission to investigate the problem (July 1833). The Commission secretary, *Joseph Parkes*, a Radical lawyer, was determined to act quickly: 285 towns were investigated, most of which were found to be unsatisfactory. Consequently, with the help of Parkes, a Bill was drawn up and introduced into the Commons by Lord John Russell (June 1835). It became law in September 1835.

(b) *Terms of the Act*

- The closed corporations were abolished; borough councils were to be elected by all the male ratepayers who had lived in the town for three years.
- Councillors were elected for three years, one third to be elected annually.
- Councillors would choose the mayor (to hold office for one year) and a group of aldermen (for six years).
- Each borough was to have a paid town clerk and treasurer, and accounts were to be properly audited.
- It was compulsory for councils to form a police force; councils were allowed, if they

so desired, to take over social improvements such as proper drainage and street cleansing.
- Towns and cities which had no councils could apply to become boroughs.

There was plenty of opposition to the Bill. It went through the Commons smoothly enough but received a rough ride in the Lords. Since most of the closed corporations were controlled by Tories, the Tory peers claimed that the Bill was an attack on personal privileges and property, in the same category as the abolition of rotten boroughs, and that it was a further step in the destruction of the constitution. However, although some amendments were made to the Bill, Peel and Wellington restrained the Tory peers from throwing it out altogether.

(c) *How successful was the new Act?*

There was a marked improvement over the previous haphazard and disorganized system, and the Act established the principle of elected town councils. At the same time *it had several failings*:

- By making it optional instead of compulsory for the new councils to make social improvements, the Act missed an opportunity to do something positive about the awful conditions in most towns. By 1848 only 29 boroughs had taken any action. One reason for the poor response was that ratepayers were often only interested in keeping the rates down.
- Many towns failed to apply to become boroughs because the procedure was complicated and expensive. In 1848 there were still 62 large towns without a council.
- Although the new system was more democratic than before, it was mainly of benefit to the middle classes; very few working men were wealthy enough to be ratepayers.

However, although progress was slow, the Act did at least set up the machinery which would enable future social and health reforms to be carried out effectively in the towns.

5.5 Other Whig reforms

The Whig governments also introduced a number of less spectacular but none the less important changes:

(a) *The compulsory registration of births, marriages and deaths (1836)*

This typically Benthamite measure was extremely important: without it, it would have been impossible to apply the Factory Acts which sought to protect children and young people; they could now rely on their birth certificates to prove their age.

(b) *Religious reforms (1836)*

The government was responsible for two measures which did something to reduce Nonconformist resentment against the powers and privileges of the Church of England:

- *The Marriage Act* recognized marriages in Nonconformist chapels and Roman Catholic churches as legal, provided that a civil registrar was there.
- *The Tithe Commutation Act* replaced the tithe (a tax of one-tenth of annual

produce to be paid to the church) with a cash rent. Though this was a move in the right direction, non-Anglicans felt it should have been abolished altogether. The Act was popular with the Irish Catholic tenant farmers who tended to come off better with a fixed money rent, and it helped to keep Ireland fairly peaceful until 1841.

(c) *Limited Liability Companies were permitted (1836)*

These were companies in which the shareholders did not have to pay the full losses if the company went bankrupt. This encouraged investment and proved to be an enormous boost to the spread of railways. The government sanctioned 1500 miles of new railway in 1836–7 and the first main line was opened between London and Birmingham.

(d) *The Penny Post*

The brainchild of Rowland Hill, the Penny Post was introduced in 1840. He managed to convince the Whigs that the existing letter post, in which charges were made according to the weight of the letter or parcel and the distance it travelled, was actually losing the Post Office money; time was wasted while the postman waited at every house for payment. Hill's suggestion was adopted: the fee was to be paid in advance by means of an adhesive stamp; the charge was one penny for a half ounce letter. The Post Office objected, but Hill was proved right: business soared and so eventually did profits (though the scheme lost heavily for the first few years). The new system was swift and efficient.

5.6 Why did the Whigs lose the 1841 election?

The Whigs had a number of failures and showed a fatal lack of understanding in certain areas, all of which contributed to their defeat:

(a) *They showed no real understanding of the causes of unemployment*

This was the case in both industry and agriculture, and the Whigs tended to fall back on repression. The first instance of this occurred with the Swing Riots (1830–1), and there were several more. When working people began to join Robert Owen's Grand National Consolidated Trades Union (founded in 1833) in their thousands, the government decided to make an example of six farm labourers from the village of Tolpuddle in Dorset who had started their own union. They were sentenced to seven years' transportation for having sworn an illegal oath (1834). The GNCTU soon collapsed in the face of determined government opposition (for full details see Section 19.2).

(b) *Important Whig reforms slowed to a mere trickle after 1836*

This was partly because of Melbourne's unprogressive attitude and partly because their Commons majority was dwindling all the time. But the unpopular fact remained that the Whigs did nothing to improve either the appalling working conditions in mines or the unhealthy social conditions in towns. Hardly anything was done to continue Huskisson's commercial reforms, yet there was still a long way to go before Free Trade was achieved. As a result, trade seemed to be stagnating.

(c) *Further working-class hostility was aroused*

The government, already unpopular because of the harshness of the new Poor Law, rejected the first Chartist petition in 1839 (see Chapter 6). By the middle of 1841 Britain was moving into a severe depression; Manchester cotton mills were soon to be at a standstill, and in Birmingham almost 100 000 people were being given poor relief. Just before the election Feargus O'Connor, one of the Chartist leaders, instructed all Chartists who had a vote to support the Tories as a protest against the Whig Poor Law.

(d) *The Whigs failed to produce an attractive programme*

The Tories, on the other hand, were now united under the leadership of Peel and they had a promising new programme which had appeared in 1834 as the Tamworth Manifesto (see Section 7.1(b)). Peel's reputation had grown during his ten years in opposition, and it was known that he had plans for encouraging trade and industry and therefore employment. The Tories (now known as Conservatives) seemed more likely to be able to deal successfully with the country's emergency than the tired and jaded Whigs.

It was no surprise when the Conservatives won the general election of June 1841, emerging with a comfortable majority of over 70.

Questions

1 Poor Law reform
Study Sources A to G and then answer the questions which follow:

Source A

A letter to a newspaper by George Nicholls, Overseer of the Poor at Southwell (Nottinghamshire), 1822

Instead of giving way to the impulse of our feelings, by giving relief when something like distress approaches us, the overseers must resolutely refuse all parochial aid, except relief to the aged, infirm and impotent.

The poor house ought to be so conducted as that the labouring part of the community might not see it as being better furnished, better provided, more comfortable than their homes. They should not, in winter, see all its chimneys cheerfully smoking, when their own homes are cold ... nor all comforts filling the abode of the pauper, when their own habitations presented scenes of want and wretchedness. The dread of a poor house has decreased in about the same ratio as pauperism had increased, owing to the humane and well-meant endeavour to improve these receptacles, which are now so generally converted into abodes of comfort and even of apparent elegance. I wish to see the poor house looked to with dread by our labouring classes and the reproach for being an inmate of it extended downwards from father to son. Let the poor see and feel that their parish, although it will not allow them to perish from absolute want, is yet the hardest taskmaster and the most harsh and unkind friend they can apply to.

Source: quoted in N. Longmate, *The Workhouse*, Maurice Temple Smith, 1969.

A report by by Sir Francis Head (one of the investigators appointed by the 1832 Royal Commission) after a tour of workhouses in Kent in 1832

The River Workhouse, on the old Dover Road, is a splendid mansion. The dignity and elegance of its architecture, its broad double staircase, its spacious halls, the lofty bedrooms and its large windows form a 'delightful retreat', splendidly contrasted with the mean little rate-paying hovels at its feet ...

In the smaller workhouses, minute classification has been found impossible. All that can be done is to put the males of all ages into one room and all the females into another. In either case the old are teased by the children who are growled at until they become cowed into silence.... In one workhouse I saw a room full of sturdy labourers sitting round a stove with their faces scorched and half-roasted. As we passed them they never rose from their seats and had generally an over-fed, a mutinous and an insubordinate appearance.

Source: as for Source A.

Some of the recommendations of the Royal Commission on the Poor Laws, 1834

The first and most essential of all conditions is that his situation on the whole shall not be made as eligible as the situation of the independent labourer of the lowest class. Throughout the evidence it is shown that in proportion as the pauper class is elevated above the condition of independent labourers, the condition of the independent class is depressed; their industry is impaired, their employment becomes unsteady and its recompense in wages is diminished. Such persons therefore are under the strongest inducement to quit the less eligible class of labourers and enter the more eligible class of paupers. The converse is the effect when the pauper class is placed in its proper position, below the condition of the independent labourer.

The chief measures which are recommended are:

First, that except as to medical attendance, all relief whatever to able-bodied persons or to their families, otherwise than in well-regulated workhouses, shall be declared unlawful and shall cease.... All who receive relief from the parish should work for the parish exclusively, as hard and for less wages than independent labourers work for individual employers.

Source: quoted in L. Evans and P. J. Pledger, *Contemporary Sources and Opinions in Modern British History, vol. 1*, Warne, 1967.

Report of a meeting of Poor Law Guardians at Stow (Suffolk) in 1837

The Board have now been acting in the execution of the Poor Law Amendment Act more than twelve months and think themselves justified in pronouncing it sound in principle, producing practical results exceeding their expectations and requiring but little alteration in detail. The expenditure of the several parishes within this Union has been reduced in the aggregate 44.75 per cent without diminishing the comforts of the aged and infirm. The Board attribute this reduction mainly to their having offered admission to the House instead of giving money out of doors to those whose idleness formerly made them continuous applicants for Relief.

That symptoms of returning industry are clearly visible amongst this class throughout the Union.

That in particular this Board is convinced that the present arrangements for medical relief are such as to ensure attention to the wants of the Poor.

Source: quoted in R. Watson, *Edwin Chadwick, Poor Law and Public Health*, Longman, 1969.

Source E

Comments on the New Poor Law by Nassau Senior, made in 1842; he was chairman of the Royal Commission on the Poor Laws 1832–4

A more general estimate of the improvement may be made by comparing the total amount of the poor rates in 1834 with the amount in 1840. The amount for 1834 was £7 511 218, that for 1840 was £5 110 683 – the difference being nearly one third.

We attach, however, comparatively little importance to the financial results of the Poor Law Amendment Act. We are grateful to the Commissioners not for having saved £2 400 000 a year, but for having stopped the progress of the plague and improved the morals of the people. The general result may be stated to be that the labourer, finding himself no longer entitled to a fixed income, whatever his idleness or misconduct, becomes stimulated to activity and honesty by the double motive of hope and fear.

Source: as for Source C.

Source F

Extracts from The Condition of the Working Classes, *by Friedrich Engels, published in 1844. Engels was a German socialist writer and philosopher who lived mostly in England after 1842*

Since the rich have all the power, the working classes must submit to have the law actually declare them as not required. This has been done by the New Poor Law. The regulation of these workhouses, or as the people call them, Poor Law Bastilles, is such as to frighten away everyone who has the slightest prospect of life without this form of public charity. The workhouse has been made the most repulsive residence which the ingenuity of a follower of Malthus can invent. In the workhouse at Greenwich in the summer of 1843, a boy of five years old was punished by being shut in the dead room, where he had to sleep upon the lids of the coffins. At Bacton (Suffolk) in January 1844, patients who were often restless at night or who tried to get up, were tied fast with cords passed under the bedstead, to save the nurse the trouble of sitting up at night.

Source: as for Sources C and E

(a) How useful and how reliable are Sources A, B and C as evidence about the poor law system before the 1834 reforms? (10 marks)

(b) (i) In what ways does Source F either support or contradict the claims made in Sources D and E? (4 marks)

(ii) What reasons can you think of to explain why the writers of Sources D and E were so pleased with the 1834 Act whereas the writer of Source F disapproves so strongly? (4 marks)

(c) Using the evidence of the sources and your own knowledge, explain how far you think the Poor Law Amendment Act of 1834 was successful. (8 marks)

(d) What difficulties face the historian in trying to write an objective account of the New Poor Law? (4 marks)

(Total 30 marks)

2 Why did the Whig reforms arouse so much opposition before they were introduced, and so much criticism afterwards?

3 Explain why the Whigs, after introducing an apparently impressive programme of reforms between 1832 and 1836, lost the general election of 1841 to the Conservatives.

6 Chartism

Summary of events

Chartism was a movement which boiled up in the mid-1830s out of working-class discontent and disillusionment with the reforms of the Whig governments. It was the first working-class political organization, and so, in a sense, it was the forerunner of the Labour party. With branches all over Britain, including Ireland, it aimed to change the parliamentary system so that the working classes would be in control. The Chartists drew up their political demands in a six-point list known as *the People's Charter*. Three times, in 1839, 1842 and 1848, the Charter was presented to parliament in the form of a gigantic petition containing millions of signatures; three times it was overwhelmingly rejected by the Commons. After each rejection there were outbreaks of violence organized by the more extreme Chartist leaders, but on each occasion the government took swift action to restore order.

After the failure of the third petition in 1848 the movement gradually died out; it seemed at the time to have been a rather pathetic failure. However, it did have some important effects, and in time, though not until long after the Chartists themselves were all dead, five of its six political aims were actually achieved.

6.1 Why did the Chartist movement come into existence?

The movement was caused quite simply by an overwhelming feeling of misery among the working classes, together with the conviction that they were not getting a fair deal at the hands of the wealthy and governing classes. There was a whole range of grievances, some of which, such as the ill-effects of the industrial revolution, had been building up and worsening over many years, while others had arisen more recently in the 1830s.

(a) *Poor conditions in factories, workshops and mines*

The Whig Factory Act of 1833 had brought in a 12-hour limit on the working day for young people of 18 and under, but it only applied to textile factories, and even this was not effective in many cases. Lord Shaftesbury continued the campaign to get a 10-hour day introduced for women and young people. There was no limit on the working hours of men. Serious injury and death were common in many factories where dangerous machinery was not properly fenced off; the 1840 committee of enquiry mentioned one case of a girl who had been caught by the hair and scalped from the nose to the back of the head. Conditions in mines were even more horrifying (see Section 12.1).

(b) *Poor living conditions*

Industrial towns were generally overcrowded and unhealthy, with no proper sanitation and sewage disposal. Edwin Chadwick's *Report on the Sanitary Condition of the Labouring Population* which appeared in 1842 revealed some appalling details: one-fifth of the inhabitants of Liverpool were living in one-room cellars; in Leeds the streets were a foot deep in accumulated rubbish; in London workers had to drink untreated water from the Thames. No wonder there were constant epidemics of cholera, typhoid, tuberculosis and diphtheria; roughly one-third of all children died before they reached the age of five. In the decade 1831–40 the death rate over the country as a whole was 23 per thousand, which was bad enough; in industrial Lancashire it was 37 per thousand.

(c) *Disillusionment with the 1832 Reform Act*

It soon became clear that the high hopes of the workers that real democracy was about to arrive had not been realized. The working classes were not given the vote, and in some boroughs such as Preston and Westminster, working men actually lost the vote as a result of the Act. Pocket boroughs, 'influence' and bribery still survived and would continue to do so as long as there was no secret ballot (see Section 4.6(b)). Even the Municipal Reform Act (1835) brought no benefit to working men: again it was only the middle classes who received the vote

(d) *The collapse of trade unionism*

In the late 1820s a number of trade unions were formed, and Robert Owen attempted to unite them into his Grand National Consolidated Trades Union (formed 1833); but the movement was dogged by all kinds of problems, including government hostility (see Section 19.2(c)). After the affair of the Tolpuddle Martyrs (1834) and the arrest and trial of the Glasgow cotton spinners' leaders (1837), the unions collapsed and many of their members joined the Chartists.

(e) *Anger at the 1834 Poor Law*

This was particularly strong in the North where the Commissioners first attempted to apply the new system in 1837 (see Section 5.3(d)).

(f) *Trade depression, unemployment and hunger*

The immediate cause of the Chartist outbreaks was always the same. J. R. Stephens, a north-country Methodist preacher, summed it up well when he declared that the movement 'is a knife-and-fork question, a bread-and-cheese question'. Some categories of workers – the handloom weavers of Lancashire, Wales and Scotland and the Leicester stocking weavers – had all been suffering falling wages and unemployment for years; they were the most consistent supporters of Chartism. But in 1837 a general trade depression set in, which affected workers in most industries, and which only began to ease off in 1842. By the summer of 1837 there were 50 000 out of work or on short time in Manchester. In 1839 a Lancashire handloom weaver could expect to earn at best five shillings (25 pence) a week, while a Leicester stocking knitter was managing only four shillings and sixpence. General Napier, who was in charge of the troops sent to keep order in the Midlands and North, noted that 'everywhere people are starving in the manufacturing districts ... and the guardians of the poor are guardians of their own pockets'.

All these grievances could be, and were, blamed on the 'rotten Whigs', as a Leicester Chartist described them in 1840. They were held directly responsible for the Reform Act, the New Poor Law and the treatment of the Tolpuddle Martyrs, and indirectly for bad conditions, depression and unemployment, which they had done next to nothing to improve.

6.2 How did the movement begin and what sort of people joined it?

(a) *The early days – the London Working Men's Association*

It is difficult to pinpoint exactly when and where the movement began because there were so many protest groups and societies in different parts of the country which didn't necessarily call themselves Chartists to begin with. However, it is usual to take the founding of *the London Working Men's Association* in 1836 as the starting point. It was formed by a number of skilled craftsmen, including *William Lovett*, a cabinet-maker, and *Francis Place*, the veteran Radical tailor. In 1837, at a meeting between the LWMA and some Radical MPs, the Charter from which the movement took its name was drawn up. Almost immediately other protest groups began to affiliate until by 1838 there were over 100 branches all over the country. In 1840 the National Charter Association (NCA) was formed, and the movement became well organized, with annual subscriptions and local branch meetings. By 1842 the NCA could boast 400 branches and 50 000 members.

(b) *The rank-and-file membership was overwhelmingly working class*

There was a great deal of middle-class support in the early stages, with the involvement of men like Thomas Attwood, Robert Owen and Joseph Sturge, a Birmingham corn-miller; but they tended to abandon the movement in the early 1840s as the more violent elements came into prominence. The most reliable and consistent membership came from the craftsmen who were being forced out of business by new machines (northern handloom weavers and Black Country nail-makers); and from workers in areas of declining industry (Wales, Wiltshire and the south-west where the old textile industries were in dire straits). Staffordshire potters were consistent supporters, and so were the framework knitters of the East Midlands. In other industrial areas, for example the coalfields of Yorkshire, South Wales and the north-east, workers became involved with Chartism in times of slump and unemployment but drifted away when trade recovered. In agricultural areas membership was even less consistent: in Suffolk, for example, though there were Chartist groups in Ipswich and Saxmundham, it was difficult to sustain the involvement of agricultural labourers because of their relatively isolated situation in the countryside.

6.3 What were the Chartists' aims and how did they hope to achieve them?

(a) *Aims*

Basically the Chartists wanted a drastic change in the parliamentary and political system so that the working classes would be in control. As Bronterre O'Brien, one of the Chartist leaders, put it in 1833, 'they aspire to be at the top instead of the bottom of society – or rather that there should be no bottom or top at all'. Only when this happened, or so they believed, would anything positive be done to achieve what was arguably their primary aim – to improve the general plight of working people. *The Charter contained their six specific political demands*:

1   Universal male suffrage (a vote for all men at the age of 21).
2   Voting by secret ballot.
3   Equal electoral districts (constituencies) so that each MP would represent roughly the same number of voters.
4   No property qualification for parliamentary candidates, to enable working men to stand for parliament.
5   Payment of MPs, so that working men who had no other income except from their trades, would be provided for when they left their jobs to enter parliament.
6   Annual elections. In the words of a Chartist voter, this would be 'the most effectual check to bribery and intimidation ... though a constituency may be bought once in seven years, no purse can buy a constituency in each ensuing twelvemonth'.

All the branches agreed on the six points, but at different times and in different places, Chartist groups put forward further aims, some of them economic and social in character. Most of them wanted the abolition of taxes on newspapers. *The London Democratic Association* (a rival group to the LWMA) mentioned 'the repeal of the infamous New Poor Law, an eight hour day for all workers in factories and workshops, and the abolition of child labour'. They were convinced that education for the working classes was vitally important, and supported the promotion of 'public instruction and the diffusion of sound political knowledge'. Their programme was summed up as the destruction of inequality and 'the establishment of general happiness'. The Birmingham group wanted the abolition of the Corn Laws.

(b) *Methods*

From the outset there were serious differences of opinion about how these aims were to be achieved. Like so much else to do with the Chartists, this is difficult to generalize about because many of the leaders changed their minds as the campaign developed. For the sake of simplicity, though, they can be divided into the 'moral force' and the 'physical force' Chartists.

●   *Lovett, Place and the LWMA* (together with Attwood, the Birmingham banker) were probably the most consistent leaders. They were moderate and peaceful, hoping to achieve their aims by discussion and persuasion, by means of orderly meetings and pamphlets. They accepted that this could only happen gradually, but it would be 'without commotion or violence' and without breaking the law.
●   *Feargus O'Connor* was impatient with the moderates. An Irish Protestant who had become MP for Cork in 1832, he wanted quick results. After founding the London Democratic Association (1837), he took over the Leeds Radical newspaper, the

Northern Star, which he soon turned into the main Chartist propaganda weapon, with a weekly sale of 50 000 copies. A brilliant agitator and fiery speaker, he swayed the masses into supporting the idea of a general strike and also seemed to favour an armed revolution. However, he was not himself prepared to risk force, and backed out on more than one occasion. Not surprisingly, he fell out with every other important Chartist leader at one time or another, but somehow retained his popularity with the rank and file.

- *Bronterre O'Brien*, an Irish lawyer, and *Julian Harnay*, who helped organize the groups in Sheffield and Newcastle, were two of the real militants, both quite prepared to use force. Harnay, who went around in a red cap and fancied himself as the British version of Marat (a French revolutionary leader murdered in 1793), wanted a full-scale revolution on the French model. However, even they cooled down after *John Frost*, another militant, had been sentenced to transportation for life after leading an uprising in Newport (Monmouthshire) in 1839.

6.4 The three phases of the Chartist movement

(a) *Phase One: 1838–9*

- During 1838 there was a series of huge open-air meetings addressed by Chartist leaders: 100 000 gathered on Glasgow Green to hear O'Connor, at least 30 000 at Manchester and a similar number at Leeds. When O'Connor tried to address a meeting in Newcastle, the crowd was dispersed by cavalry.
- In February 1839 a National Chartist Convention met in London to organize a petition and its presentation to parliament. It was here that the first serious differences of opinion occurred as the leaders argued about how best to proceed. Some of the extremists wanted to proclaim a general strike immediately, while Lovett and Attwood hoped to keep within the law. Attwood and the Birmingham contingent walked out in disgust at the extremists, though for the time being the moderates just about kept control. In May the Convention moved to Birmingham where there was more support for Chartism, and the petition was completed after some vast meetings in the Bull Ring, at which Lovett, O'Brien and Harnay appeared.
- The first Chartist petition containing one and a quarter million signatures was brought to the Commons in a decorated cart. It was introduced by Attwood who asked that parliament should grant the six points. The Home Secretary, Lord John Russell, led the attack on the petition and it was overwhelmingly rejected by 235 votes to 46 (July 1839).
- This rejection suggested that nothing could be achieved by moderation, and the physical force supporters seized the initiative, attempting to organize a general strike or 'sacred month' as the Chartists called it. There were protest meetings, riots, fights and strikes, with many leaders calling for an armed uprising. The Whig government, which had reacted cautiously when Lovett and the moral force leaders were in the ascendant, now decided to act. The army was increased by 5000 and new police forces set up in Birmingham, Manchester, Bolton and other industrial centres. General Napier, who was in charge of forces in the North, sympathized with the working classes and blamed the situation on 'Tory injustice and Whig imbecility'. He tried to avoid confrontation and showed local Chartist leaders how suicidal any attempt at revolution would be, given the strength of his artillery and cavalry. This, together with the arrest of many of the leaders, probably prevented any serious outbreak in the Midlands and North.

Illus. 6.1 The Chartists attempt to seize Newport, 1839

● The most serious violence took place in Wales, where conditions in the mining valleys were probably the worst in Britain. This was *the Newport Rising* (November 1839) organized by John Frost, a local draper and former mayor of Newport. Frost led 5000 miners in an attack on the town, apparently aiming to release a Chartist leader from gaol. However, the authorities knew well in advance and positioned troops in the Westgate Hotel. As the Chartists approached they were met by volleys of musket fire; at least 20 were killed and the rising soon ended in confusion. Frost and two other leaders were sentenced to death, but this was changed to transportation.

Although there were occasional incidents and a number of large open-air meetings, there was a lull in Chartist activity during 1840–1, partly because all the main leaders, even the peaceful ones like Lovett, were in gaol, and also because there was a temporary revival in trade.

(b) *Phase Two: 1842*

● As the most influential leaders finished their sentences and emerged from gaol, the Chartists gathered themselves together for another effort. Members were to pay a penny a week each to build up a strike fund.

● Another National Convention met and a second petition was drawn up containing three and a quarter million signatures. Reputed to be six miles long, it was carried to parliament in a huge procession of over 100 000 people, with brass bands playing. It was introduced in the Commons by Thomas Duncombe, supported by John Fielden, and although Peel and the Conservatives were now in power, it suffered a similar fate to that of the first petition – it was rejected by 287 votes to 49 (May 1842).

● Again violence followed the rejection, though this was probably caused as much by wage reductions which took place in all industrial areas from Scotland down to the Midlands, as the depression reached its worst. At Wolverhampton strikers besieged the workhouse and had to be dispersed by dragoon guards. In the Lancashire 'Plug Riots', strikers hammered the plugs out of factory boilers, forcing them to close down. By

August, work in the industrial North was at a standstill: there was serious rioting in towns such as Preston, Rochdale, Stockport, Bury and Bolton, while in Manchester several policemen were killed and thousands of strikers looted food shops. The situation seemed close to a general strike and perhaps even a revolution.

● O'Connor, who had so often advocated violence, was horrified by this turn of events, and condemned the strike in the *Northern Star*. Peel's government took prompt action and rushed troops to trouble spots, using the new railways. Within a week order had been restored and hundreds of Chartist leaders thrown into gaol; strikers had no choice but to return to work. Again there was a lull in Chartism, and membership declined rapidly as trade revived in 1843.

(c) *Phase Three: 1847–8 – the Chartists' last fling*

● In the mid–1840s, O'Connor, still the most exciting and influential of the Chartist leaders, put all his energies into his *Land Plan*. The idea was to buy country estates where thousands of Chartists from industrial towns could settle, each family with its own smallholding (small area of land). As well as making the settlers independent, this would also ease the unemployment situation in manufacturing areas. O'Connor founded the Chartist Co-operative Land Society in 1847. Chartists bought shares in the company for £1. 6s each, and eventually four Chartist colonies were started: O'Connorville near Watford, Lowbands and Snig's End near Gloucester and Charterville near Witney (Oxfordshire). Each family had a two-, three-, or four-acre plot and a cottage, and paid an annual rent of £1. 5s an acre.

● Early in 1847 another trade depression set in and unemployment soared. By May there were 24 000 out of work in Manchester and 84 000 on short time. This new wave of distress brought the Chartists back to politics again and in July O'Connor was elected MP for Nottingham. Encouraged by the news of a successful revolution in Paris (February 1848), they set about producing their third petition. It was completed early in April 1848 at another National Convention in London; this time it contained five points (secret ballot was the one omitted), and it was reported to have been signed by almost six million people.

● There was to be an open-air rally on Kennington Common on 10 April (see Source B in question 1 at the end of the chapter) followed by a mass procession to Westminster to present the petition. Some of the speakers at the Convention urged revolution and it was decided that if this third petition was rejected, the Chartists would call a National Assembly to force parliament to accept the Charter. It was said that O'Connor had even drawn up a new constitution with himself as president of a British republic.

● In fact both O'Connor and O'Brien played down the physical force approach in their speeches, but Russell's Whig government took no chances. The march on parliament was banned and O'Connor was told that only 10 people would be allowed through to present the petition. The Duke of Wellington stationed troops at key points in the capital and signed up 150 000 special constables. The Kennington Common rally went ahead but far fewer people turned up than had been expected and heavy rain dampened the Chartists' enthusiasm. No attempt was made to storm parliament, since it would have been difficult to force a way across the bridges over the Thames; the event ended lamely with O'Connor and a handful of supporters delivering the petition to the Commons in three cabs.

● When it was examined closely the petition was found to contain less than two million signatures, some of which – Queen Victoria, Wellington, Mr Punch, Sir Robert Peel, Flatnose and No Cheese – made it look ridiculous. Again the Commons rejected it by a huge majority.

- At the same time O'Connor's Land Scheme found itself in serious difficulties: much of the land was poor, the settlers had no experience of farming, the smallholdings were not large enough to support whole families, and O'Connor himself, though certainly not dishonest, made a hopeless muddle of the finances. In August 1851 the National Land Company was wound up in complete failure.
- Although there were some violent incidents in the Midlands and North following the rejection of the third petition, Chartism never again achieved the same impact. O'Connor could still draw a crowd of 20 000 in Leicester in 1850, but in general there was a slow fade-out of the movement after 1848. By 1852 the circulation of the *Northern Star* was down to only 1200 from its 1839 peak of around 50 000. O'Connor became insane and had to be confined in an asylum at Chiswick; he died in 1855.

6.5 Why were the Chartists unsuccessful in the 1840s and what was the significance of the movement?

(a) *Reasons for their lack of success*

From the beginning the Chartists' demands were too advanced for the time, and they had no chance of having their six political demands accepted at that particular point; there was no way that a parliament still dominated by aristocratic landowners was going to hand over power to the working and lower middle classes, which is what acceptance of the petition would have amounted to. In addition:

- There were serious divisions and disagreements among the leaders about whether to use moral persuasion or physical force. Lovett was hopeful that the industrial society would eventually lead to prosperity for all, but O'Connor hated the new machinery and wanted a society of small landholders; his Land Scheme was condemned as impractical by the other leaders. O'Connor outshone all the rest and made much more impact nationally, but unfortunately he was reckless and unstable, seeming to preach violence one minute and drawing back the next.
- There were many local differences which made unity difficult and central organization weak.
- The Chartists never won sufficient middle-class support; many potential backers who sympathized with the six points were frightened off by the Chartists' violence and by their attacks on wealth and property, and they preferred to put their energies and cash into the more respectable Anti-Corn Law League (see Section 7.5). In 1841 when Lovett seemed to be bridging the gap between the classes by attracting the support of Joseph Sturge, a weathy corn-miller, O'Connor attacked Lovett, accusing him of trying to 'domesticate the charter', and this New Move, as it was called, broke down. Many middle-class people preferred a limited extension of the franchise to include just themselves, and they were not willing to share political power with the workers.
- The Chartists' aims were too complicated: as well as the six points, there were numerous other social and economic aims which meant that they were trying to achieve too much all at once, which tended to confuse people. This was in marked contrast to the Anti-Corn Law League which knew exactly what it wanted (the abolition of the Corn Laws) and hammered away at that single aim until it was achieved. The Chartists might have done better to have concentrated on getting MPs elected so that they would have had a more effective voice in the Commons (as the League did).
- The authorities kept one step ahead of the Chartists and always knew of their plans; for instance, police spies had informed them about the Newport Rising in 1839.

Both Whig governments (in 1839 and 1848) and Peel's Conservatives (in 1842) took prompt action, arresting leaders, moving troops swiftly by train to areas of disturbances, and using the new electric telegraph.

● The reforms of Peel's government between 1841 and 1846 (see Sections 7.2 and 7.3) led to some improvement in trade and conditions. Britain was moving into a period of great economic prosperity which was reflected to some extent in rising wages and increased food consumption: the average price of a four pound loaf which had cost eleven and a half pence in 1847 was under seven pence in 1850. As living standards improved, support for the Chartists and their complicated programme melted away and workers preferred to join trades unions or the co-operative movement.

(b) *Significance of Chartism*

It would be wrong to dismiss Chartism as insignificant simply because it failed to achieve its political aims in the 1840s.

● It was a remarkable achievement for a working-class movement at that time to develop such a high degree of communication, organization and control on such a large scale. Mass meetings like the one on Glasgow Green in 1838 did not happen by accident, and must have taken considerable preparation and planning, especially as most of them passed off peacefully and without violence. Professor Clive Behagg points out that the movement developed 'a sense of community . . . and a Chartist culture: a network of schools, discussion groups, libraries, churches and other meeting places where politics could be debated and views exchanged'.
● Chartism's most important achievement was that it focused public attention on the appalling hardships of working people. It was no coincidence that Peel and the Conservatives (1841–6) immediately took steps (Mines Act, Factory Act, Commission on Public Health in Towns leading to the 1848 Public Health Act) to try and remove the grievances which had given rise to Chartism in the first place.

6.6 When was the Chartists' political programme achieved?

Bit by bit over the next 80 years, five of the six points were achieved. First to come was the abolition of the property qualification for MPs in 1858, followed by the introduction of the secret ballot in elections (1872). Manhood suffrage was achieved in stages by the Reform Acts of 1867 and 1884 and by the Representation of the People Act of 1918, which went further than the Chartists had intended by giving the vote to women aged 30 and over; in 1928 women were given the vote at 21. These acts also redistributed seats so that constituencies became approximately equal (though even today there are some variations: Northern Ireland constituencies contain many more voters than the average constituency in the rest of Britain). Payment of MPs was introduced in 1911. The only one of the points not achieved is annual elections; however, the 1911 Parliament Act did reduce the length of parliaments so that there has to be a general election every five years instead of every seven.

Questions

1 **The Chartist campaigns**
   Study Sources A to F and then answer the questions which follow.

Extracts from the Chartist petition drawn up in 1838

We, your petitioners, dwell in a land whose merchants are noted for their enterprise, whose manufacturers are very skilful and whose workmen are proverbial for their industry.... Yet we find ourselves overwhelmed with public and private suffering. We are bowed down under a load of taxes, and our workmen are starving. Capital brings no profit, labour no reward; the workhouse is full and the factory deserted. We have looked on every side to find out the causes of distress, and we can discover none in nature or in Providence.

It was the fond expectation of the people that a remedy for most of their grievances would be found in the Reform Act of 1832.... They have been bitterly deceived.... *The Reform Act has transferred power from one domineering faction to another*, and left the people as helpless as before ...

We perform the duties, therefore *we must have the privileges of free men*. Therefore we demand universal suffrage. To be exempt from the corruption of the wealthy and the violence of the powerful, the suffrage must be secret. We demand annual parliaments and ... for every representative chosen, a fair payment for the time which he is called upon to devote to the public service.

Source: quoted in R. G. Gammage, *History of the Chartist Movement*, Browne & Browne, 1854.

Source B

The Chartist poster advertising the 1848 meeting on Kennington Common

CHARTIST
DEMONSTRATION!!
"PEACE and ORDER" is our MOTTO!

TO THE WORKING MEN OF LONDON.

Fellow Men,—The Press having misrepresented and vilified us and our intentions, the Demonstration Committee therefore consider it to be their duty to state that the grievances of us (the Working Classes) are deep and our demands just. We and our families are pining in misery, want, and starvation! We demand a fair day's wages for a fair day's work! We are the slaves of capital—we demand protection to our labour. We are political serfs—we demand to be free. We therefore invite all well disposed to join in our peaceful procession on

MONDAY NEXT, April 10,

As it is for the good of all that we seek to remove the evils under which we groan.

The following are the places of Meeting of THE CHARTISTS, THE TRADES, THE IRISH CONFEDERATE & REPEAL BODIES:

East Division on Stepney Green at 8 o'clock; City and Finsbury Division on Clerkenwell Green at 9 o'clock; West Division in Russell Square at 9 o'clock; and the South Division in Peckham Fields at 9 o'clock, and proceed from thence to Kennington Common.

Signed on behalf of the Committee, JOHN ARNOTT, *Sec.*

Figure 6.1

Extracts from the objects of the London Working Men's Association, 1839

2. To seek by every legal means to place all classes of society in possession of their equal political and social rights.
7. To publish our views and sentiments in such a form as shall best serve to create a moral yet energetic public opinion; so as eventually to lead to a gradual improvement in the condition of the working class, without violence or commotion.

Source: quoted in D. Holman (ed.), *Portraits and Documents: Earlier Nineteenth Century 1783–1867*, Hutchinson, 1965.

Source D

From a speech by William Taylor, a Lancashire Chartist leader, in 1839

We are to be free, though we wade through streams of blood. . . . Do we read in ancient or modern history of any nation in bondage becoming free without the use of physical force?

Source: quoted in Christopher Thorne, *Chartism*, Macmillan, 1966.

Source E

From a newspaper article in The Bolton Chronicle, *Saturday 17 August 1839*

SERIOUS AND ALARMING RIOTS IN BOLTON
On Sunday last the Chartists marched to church . . . and a great fear was expressed by inhabitants of the town that violence would be attempted; therefore about 15 000 special constables were sworn in. It is not for us, as reporters, to express our opinion regarding the origin of such Chartist meetings . . . whether incited by the mayor or his friends, it is not for us to consider.
   TUESDAY – at five o'clock [a.m.] the Chartists again assembled, numbering about 300. The police officers at first made no attempt to disperse the mob when it first collected, but later arrested the leaders. Then showers of stones were thrown in all directions and the commotion arrived at a tremendous pitch. The mayor and the magistrates consulted and the riot act was read. The military was instantly called out and their prompt arrival discouraged the multitude.

Source: *The Bolton Chronicle*, 17 August 1839.

Source F

Comments from Sir Charles Napier, the general sent to deal with the Chartists in the North of England in 1839

[1839] June 29th. I hate the poor law, but it is not a cause of the mischief in itself, it is only a train to fire the mine: the evils produced by the manufacturing system and the debt are attributed by the people to the new poor law . . . a population starving one week, earning forty shillings the next . . .
   August 17th. Bolton is the only place where shot has been fired, but only three there, and those from the eagerness of the magistrates.
   August 19th. Everywhere a sudden calm has succeeded the storm; it is unnatural,

for the causes of discontent still exist. The fact is that the Chartist leaders' calculations are quite at fault; *they have found the difficulty of uniting their people in simultaneous efforts*. The mayor and corporation of Bolton are said to be Chartists and the constables everywhere are, more or less, and all avow that the people are oppressed. Men are restless and discontented with poverty; they have all its sufferings and have not the principal pleasures.

Source: quoted in R. Brown and C. Daniels (eds), *Nineteenth Century Britain*, Macmillan, 1980.

(a) Using your own knowledge and the evidence of the sources, explain what the writer meant at the time by the following sentences in Source A:
  (i) The Reform Act has transferred power from one domineering faction to another. (2 marks)
  (ii) We must have the privileges of free men. (2 marks)
(b) (i) Compare the evidence in the sources about the different aims and the different methods of the Chartists. (8 marks)
  (ii) Explain why there seems to be some disagreement among these sources. (4 marks)
(c) What questions would historians ask in order to assess the reliability of newspaper articles (as in Source E) and eyewitness accounts (as in Source F)? (6 marks)
(d) Sir Charles Napier writes in Source F that the Chartist leaders 'have found the difficulty of uniting their people in simultaneous efforts'. Using the sources and your own knowledge, explain how far you would agree that this was the main reason for the Chartists' failure in the 1830s and 1840s. (8 marks)

(Total 30 marks)

2 Explain which you think were more important to the Chartists – their political aims or their economic and social aims.

7 | Sir Robert Peel, the Conservatives and the Corn Laws 1830–46

Summary of events

At the end of 1830 the Tory party had disintegrated in the wake of Catholic Emancipation (see Section 2.7(b)) and was also deeply divided about what attitude to adopt towards reform of parliament. Reaching rock bottom in 1833, the party gradually began to revive under the leadership of Sir Robert Peel. When Melbourne's Whig government began to falter, Peel and his party – now known as Conservatives – held office for a short time (December 1834 to April 1835), but lacking a majority, they soon had to resign. Peel's reputation grew steadily and in August 1841 the Conservatives won a large electoral majority. Peel was Prime Minister from 1841 until 1846.

He had to face some alarming problems: an economic slump, appalling working and living conditions in industrial areas, agitation and violence from the Chartists, and pressure from the Anti-Corn Law League. Abroad, there were strained relations with the USA and France (see Section 9.3). However, Peel showed the same determination as he had earlier when he was Home Secretary (1822–30). Often facing opposition from many of his own party, he pushed through *important economic reforms* (reintroduction of income tax, further steps towards free trade, and the Bank Charter Act) and *social reforms* (Mines Act, Factory Act and an enquiry into health conditions in towns).

These were considerable achievements, and all seemed to be going well, when Peel was brought down by *the repeal of the Corn Laws*. Influenced by the Anti-Corn Law League's campaign and by a disastrous famine in Ireland, Peel decided that the Corn Laws must go. Many of the Tory landowners, amounting to about two-thirds of the party, were bitterly opposed to the repeal, convinced that it would damage British agriculture and reduce their profits by letting in too much cheap foreign corn. Whig support enabled Peel to get the repeal act through parliament, but the rebel section of his party soon forced him to resign and the Conservatives split into two groups. After doing so much to rebuild his party during the 1830s, it seemed as though Peel had now destroyed it again.

7.1 Peel and the revival of the Tory/Conservative party

(a) *Peel's early career*

Peel was the son of a wealthy Lancashire cotton manufacturer (also called Robert) who

Illus. 7.1   Sir Robert Peel: founder of the modern Conservative Party?

had bought a large estate at Tamworth (Staffordshire) which he represented as a Tory MP from 1790. The elder Peel had great political ambitions for his son; he sent him to Harrow and Oxford and secured him a seat in parliament in 1809 when he was only 21. The young Peel soon made a good impression with his speeches and in 1812 Lord Liverpool appointed him Chief Secretary for Ireland, a position he held until 1818. This was a difficult period in Ireland with the Irish Catholics violently opposing the Act of Union. Peel acquitted himself well, managing to contain the violence by setting up the Irish Constabulary, the first effective police force Ireland had ever had. With his reputation as an able and honest administrator standing high, Peel became Home Secretary in 1822, and was responsible for the penal code reform and the introduction of the Metropolitan Police (see Section 2.6(c)). Following the downfall of the Tory government in November 1830, the Whigs were in power for most of the next ten years; it was during this time that Peel devoted himself to building up the new Conservative party.

(b) *What was Peel's contribution to the development of the Conservative party?*

- Peel gave the party a new image, both in his speeches in parliament, and outside parliament in a document known as *the Tamworth Manifesto*. This was issued in December 1834 as an election address to the people of Tamworth which he represented in parliament after his father's death in 1830. In it he explained that although he had at first opposed parliamentary reform, he now accepted the 1832 Reform Act as 'a final and irrevocable settlement of a great constitutional question'. He and his party were in favour of 'a careful review of institutions ... undertaken in a friendly temper, combining, with the firm maintenance of established rights, the correction of proved abuses, and the redress of real grievances'; in other words, he was prepared to introduce moderate reform wherever there was a genuine need for it, while at the same time preserving all that was good about the British system. In a later speech Peel referred to these aims as 'conservative principles'. The Tamworth Manifesto was important because it formalized the party's new programme; it showed that the Conservatives, as they were now called, stood for a safe programme of cautious reform midway between the old Tories, who were against all change, and the Radicals, whose ideas about reform were alarming to moderates.
- He gained wider support for his party from moderate people of all classes, particularly from middle-class manufacturers and businessmen who felt neglected by the Whigs. The attractiveness of the Tamworth Manifesto and the party's new image were partly responsible for Peel's success, plus the fact that he came from a middle-class background himself.
- Under Peel, local Conservative associations and clubs were set up all over the country, so that the party was far more highly developed at local level than the Whigs. According to Professor Norman Gash, however, Peel did not take the initiative here: 'he had notoriously little interest in the humdrum details of party management'; F. R. Bonham, the Tory election manager, was responsible for this improvement.

As a result, the gap between Conservatives and Whigs gradually closed in the elections of 1835 and 1837 until in June 1841 Peel led his party to a triumphant victory, winning a majority of 76. Reasons for the Conservative success are fully explained in Section 5.6. In less than ten years Peel had revived and given new direction to a party which had seemed defunct. Some historians, like Norman Gash, think he deserves to be remembered as the founder of the modern Conservative party; others feel that Disraeli has a better claim to this distinction, since Peel, having revived the party, almost killed it off again with his repeal of the Corn Laws (see Section 7.6).

7.2 What did Peel do to help the British economy?

The country was facing serious economic problems when Peel became Prime Minister in 1841. Exports had fallen sharply, bringing an industrial slump; industry seemed to be stagnating, and there had been a series of poor harvests since 1837, which kept bread prices high. As well as causing hardship and misery for the workers, the slump was accompanied by a financial crisis in which many small banks collapsed. The Whigs had left a deficit (the amount spent over and above income) of over two million pounds. Peel aimed to encourage trade and to do something to ease the problems of the workers. He acted positively:

(a) *He took important steps towards free trade*

Although Huskisson had removed many tariffs (import and export duties) in the 1820s (see Section 2.6(a)), the Whigs had taken no further action; there were still about 1200 commodities subject to tariffs. Peel, influenced by a group of northern industrialists calling themselves *the Manchester School* (they included John Bright and Richard Cobden), came to believe that tariffs were stifling British industry. Their argument was that import duties made raw materials (such as cotton, wool and iron ore) more expensive, thereby keeping production costs too high. Foreign countries resented British tariffs and were less willing to trade than they would otherwise have been. Tariffs, including the duty on imported corn, made imported food more expensive and caused difficulty for the poor. Removal of tariffs would bring down the cost of British goods abroad, increase exports, stimulate industry and provide more jobs. In addition, the cost of living would be cheaper, to the benefit of the working classes. In Peel's own words: 'We must make this country a cheap country for living, and thus induce people to remain and settle here. Enable them to consume more by having more to spend.' In his *budgets of 1842 and 1845* he boldly swept away a large proportion of the remaining duties, so that after 1845:

- duties on over 600 articles had been removed completely;
- duties on about 500 others had been greatly reduced.

To take a few examples, this meant that there were no longer any export duties at all, and there was no import duty on raw cotton, livestock, meat and potatoes. Cheese imported from British colonies paid a duty of only 1s 6d per hundredweight instead of 10s 6d. There was even a slight reduction in the import duty on corn, though not enough to satisfy the Anti-Corn Law League.

These measures worked exactly as Peel had hoped: they helped to bring about a trade revival, exports increased, unemployment fell rapidly, and food was cheaper (though bread was still more expensive than it need have been, thanks to the Corn Laws). Britain began to move out of the 'hungry forties' and into a Golden Age of Victorian prosperity which lasted until around 1873 (see Section 15.1).

(b) *Income tax was reintroduced*

This was at the rate of seven pence in the £ on incomes over £150 a year (1843). This controversial tax had been abolished by the Tories in 1816 (see Section 2.2(c)), but Peel brought it back as a temporary measure for three years to make up for the losses in revenue (annual income) which the government would suffer with the abolition of so many duties. It turned out to be so profitable that Peel persuaded parliament to renew it for a further three years; since then no government has been able to afford to abandon it.

Between them, the trade revival and the income tax were strikingly successful: Peel had soon turned the Whig deficit of two million pounds into a healthy surplus.

(c) *The Bank Charter Act (1844)*

This was an important financial measure made necessary because many banks were unreliable. The problem was that all banks, no matter how small, could issue banknotes, with no limit on the amount. When demand for currency was high among businessmen (for example to finance railway building), there was a tendency for banks to issue too much paper money which they lent out for investment in new companies. If any companies got into difficulties (as many railway companies did), investors often lost their money and could not repay the bank. Some banks, having over-issued notes, lacked sufficient gold reserves to see them through, and always during a slump, some small banks would collapse. This gave the impression that the currency was unsound, and Peel realized that trade could only expand if the currency was stable. The 1844 Act aimed to bring about 'by gradual means the establishment of a safe system of currency'.

- No new banks were allowed to issue notes.
- Existing banks were restricted to their average issue during the three months preceding the passing of the Act; if any existing banks amalgamated, they lost the right to issue notes.
- The Bank of England could issue notes worth up to £14 million, but any paper money issued beyond that had to be covered by gold reserves in the Bank's vaults.

The Act was generally successful: it had the effect of gradually phasing out the note-issuing function of ordinary banks, so that the Bank of England came to control the amount of currency in circulation; there was less danger of over-issuing notes. English currency became extremely stable and London was regarded as the world's leading monetary centre.

(d) The Companies Act (1844)

This Act dealt with another finance and business problem: the fact that there were no controls on the formation of companies. Anybody could start a company simply by publishing an advertisement, and could then begin receiving money from foolish investors. During the 1830s many such dubious companies went bankrupt, or dishonest directors absconded with the capital; either way the investors suffered. The Act aimed to prevent 'reckless speculation' (investing money when there is a risk that it might be lost): all companies now had to be officially registered and were to issue prospectuses and regular accounts. The Act had some success but its weakness was that it did not apply to companies which had to get special approval from parliament; these included railway companies, where some of the worst racketeers operated.

7.3 What did Peel do about Britain's social problems?

Peel was well aware of the disgraceful conditions in some factories, mines and industrial towns. On the other hand he knew that not all manufacturers were blameworthy: his own father had been a humane and enlightened employer. His instinct told him that the best way of dealing with problems was not to pass laws, but to wait until his economic policies bore fruit; then all the workers would have jobs, and would be able 'to consume more by having more to spend'; hardships would gradually disappear. Another reason for not taking direct action was that he might lose the support of middle-class businessmen if he tried to regulate working hours and conditions. However, when unemployment reached a new peak in 1842, and troops had to be despatched to deal with Chartist violence (see Section 6.4(b)), a new urgency came into the situation. Peel was also under constant pressure from Shaftesbury and the Ten Hour Movement (which wanted a ten-hour working day for women and children). Eventually *the Mines Act (1842)* and *a Factory Act (1844)* did something to improve conditions (for full details see Section 12.3(e–f)). Most of the credit for these Acts belongs to Shaftesbury rather than to Peel; in fact, Peel himself was responsible for defeating Shaftesbury's proposal of a ten-hour maximum working day, and both Acts had serious weaknesses.

Again under pressure, this time from Edwin Chadwick, the government appointed a Royal Commission to enquire into the 'state of Large Towns and Populous Districts', which produced alarming findings in 1844 and 1845. Peel, now hampered by the Corn Law crisis, took no further action, and it was left to Russell's government to introduce the first Public Health Act in 1848. Social reform was therefore not Peel's most successful area.

7.4 Peel, O'Connell and Ireland

(a) *Ireland after the 1800 Act of Union*

Following the passing of this much-hated Act which took away the Irish parliament (see Section 1.2(d)), nearly every British government in the nineteenth century had to deal with problems of one sort or another in Ireland. We have already seen (Section 2.7(b)) how the Tory party split over Catholic Emancipation in 1829. The Irish were not satisfied with emancipation, partly because success had been soured when, at the same time, the Tories took the vote away from the 40 shilling freeholders.

When the Whigs were in power (1830–41), Daniel O'Connell, the Irish leader who now sat at Westminster as MP for County Clare, did not press his next great ambition – *the repeal of the Act of Union*. For most of the time he co-operated with the Whigs, hoping to win some concessions, such as the abolition of tithes, which were highly unpopular with the Catholic peasants. However, there were some outbreaks of violence, and it was disagreement about how to deal with these that caused Grey to resign as Whig Prime Minister in 1834. O'Connell did secure a few concessions, including the Tithe Act (see Section 5.5(b)) and the inclusion of Irishmen in the Irish police force, but overall he was disappointed.

(b) *Ireland during Peel's ministry*

Irish affairs had come to the forefront again by 1843, and in 1846 they were instrumental in bringing Peel down and splitting the Conservative party.

1   O'Connell's comparative lack of success after 1829 meant that he was beginning to
     lose his hold over the Irish; younger and more violent men – Smith O'Brien,
     Gavan Duffy and John Mitchel, calling themselves '*Young Ireland*' – were
     impatient with O'Connell's moderation. The ageing leader, now 65, decided to
     stage a last attempt to force the British to repeal the Act of Union, by agitation
     and the threat of civil war, a policy which had worked with Peel and Wellington in
     the case of Catholic Emancipation. Supported by the Catholic priests, O'Connell
     began to address large meetings, stirring up intense excitement; he told a crowd of
     over 100 000 at Tara (the seat of medieval Irish kings) that within a year the Act of
     Union would be smashed and the Irish would have a parliament of their own. The
     climax of the campaign was to be a vast open-air meeting at Clontarf (October
     1843).
2   Peel was determined not to be frightened into giving way again; he believed,
     rightly, that this time Ireland was not on the verge of civil war as it had been in
     1829. He announced that the Union would never be cancelled and that rebellion
     would be crushed. Troops were sent to Ireland and the Clontarf meeting banned.

3   This placed O'Connell in a difficult situation: if he allowed the meeting to go ahead, it would be treated as rebellion, while if he cancelled it, 'Young Ireland' could accuse him of surrendering to the British. In the event, he was not prepared to risk violence; he called the meeting off, and it was clear that Peel had outmanoeuvred him in the war of nerves.

4   O'Connell was arrested, tried for conspiracy (remarks in his earlier speeches were said to be seditious), found guilty, sentenced to one year in gaol and fined £2000. The House of Lords reversed the verdict and O'Connell was released, but there was no disguising his defeat. His influence gradually faded as 'Young Ireland' assumed the leadership; he died in 1847.

5   Peel combined his firm line with some mild concessions. He was convinced that Ireland would never be calm and stable until the government won the support of the educated Catholic community, and he had been making concessions to them since 1843. He appointed *the Devon Commission* to investigate problems of land-holding in Ireland; this reported in 1845 but there was no time to act before the government fell. He tried to please the Catholics by increasing the annual government grant to Maynooth College (which trained Catholic priests) from £9000 to £26 000. However, this aroused hostility among his Protestant supporters, many of whom voted against it; in fact the grant was only approved by the Commons because the Whigs voted for it. These were courageous moves by Peel, but they left the Conservatives deeply divided, and this prevented him from tackling the country's basic problem – poverty. Unfortunately worse was soon to come both for Peel and the Irish ...

6   By July 1845 it was clear that the Irish potato crop had been ruined by blight; the country was on the verge of famine, bringing new urgency to the Corn Law repeal problem.

7.5 The struggle for the repeal of the Corn Laws 1838–46

Along with Chartism, the campaign to repeal the Corn Laws was the other great protest movement of the nineteenth century. The two movements provide a striking contrast: Chartism a failure, the Anti-Corn Law League a triumphant success in 1846.

(a) *Formation of the Anti-Corn Law League*

●   Ever since the introduction of the Corn Laws (1815) banning the import of foreign corn until the price of home-grown corn reached 80 shillings a quarter (see Section 2.2(c)), critics had argued that they should be repealed, because they kept bread prices far too high. Huskisson's sliding scale of import duties (1828) did nothing to alter their general argument that the Corn Laws were in operation simply to guarantee farmers high profits by keeping out as much foreign corn as possible.

●   Between 1830 and 1835 harvests were good and wheat prices fairly low; in 1835 for example, wheat averaged 39s 4d a quarter and a four-pound loaf cost 7d compared with 96s 11d a quarter and 14$\frac{1}{2}$d a loaf in 1817. After 1835 there was a run of poor harvests, corn was more scarce and prices rose. In 1839 wheat averaged 70s 8d a quarter and a loaf 10d – not as disastrous for the poor as in 1817, but bad enough, bearing in mind the serious industrial depression which began in 1837. Tenpence a loaf was the average – at times in 1839 it was as high as 13$\frac{1}{2}$d (1s 1$\frac{1}{2}$d); this was when unemployment was rising and a Lancashire hand-loom weaver was earning no more than 5s a week; a family of two adults and three children would need at the very minimum five loaves a week.

● Agitation for repeal was strong in Manchester, the main distress centre. Here the Anti-Corn Law Association was started in 1838, followed by similar groups in other cities. In March 1839 they merged into the Anti-Corn Law League with its headquarters in Manchester. It was inspired mainly by manufacturers and businessmen; the leaders were *Richard Cobden*, a southerner who ran a calico factory in Manchester, and the Quaker, *John Bright*, a Rochdale cotton manufacturer.

(b) *Arguments for and against abolishing the Corn Laws*

The case for abolition involved a lot more than just cheaper bread, though that was an important consideration:

1 Removal of the Corn Laws was part of the general move towards free trade already started by Huskisson. Like all other duties, they were seen by Benthamites as an unnatural restraint on trade; they kept imports of foreign corn to a minimum and forced bread prices up simply to ensure good profits for landowners. According to Cobden and Bright, this was un-Christian. Abolition would bring cheaper bread, to the benefit of the poor. For this reason the League attracted a good deal of working-class support, so that it became a powerful alliance of middle classes and workers.

2 Once bread prices fell, real wages would increase (workers would be able to buy more with their wages even though the actual money paid to them was the same), enabling workers to buy not only more bread, but more of other goods as well. This would provide a much-needed stimulus to British industry.

3 The importing of foreign corn would encourage British farmers to become more competitive so that they would have no need of protective tariffs.

4 Buying corn from abroad would encourage foreign countries to import more British manufactured goods. As trade between nations expanded all round, it would improve international relations and contribute towards world peace. This argument appealed especially to the pacifist Bright and gave the campaign the flavour of a moral crusade.

The case for retaining the Corn Laws was put strongly by the landowners and by their ally, *The Times* newspaper.

1 Removal of the Corn Laws would allow an influx of cheap foreign wheat which would ruin British farmers and cause mass unemployment among farm labourers, who would migrate to the towns, adding to the existing problems of overcrowding and leaving the countryside depopulated.

2 Britain would become too dependent on foreign corn which might be cut off in wartime.

3 The whole campaign was a selfish middle-class capitalist plot: manufacturers only wanted cheaper bread so that they could reduce wages. This argument had some success among industrial workers and helps to explain why the Chartists were hostile to the League.

(c) *Methods and activities of the League*

Their simple and logical case was put, over and over again, by Cobden, Bright and other leaders; there was no violence and they almost always kept within the law:

- They used masses of paper propaganda: they published a fortnightly and later a weekly newspaper called *The Anti-Bread Tax Circular* and bombarded the public with millions of leaflets and pamphlets hammering home their arguments and ridiculing their opponents. They made excellent use of the new Penny Post (introduced 1840) and made sure that every elector received at least one batch of League literature.
- They held mass meetings both in the open air and indoors. In Manchester the Free Trade Hall was built to hold 8000 people (1843); in the same year a League headquarters was set up in London which organized no fewer than 136 meetings in that year alone. The country was divided into 12 areas each with a paid agent whose job was to arrange meetings and speakers. Cobden and Bright emerged as expert orators, though in the early days many League speakers had a rough reception from Chartists in industrial towns and from farmers in country areas. At a meeting in Manchester the audience hurled chairs at the speakers on the stage, while at Saxmundham (Suffolk) a speaker was thrown down a flight of stairs and had to be rescued by police.
- Much time and effort were expended in fund-raising – the wealthy middle class often needed persuasion to put their names on the donation lists and there were bazaars and tea-parties to organize. In 1843, over £50 000 was raised; in 1844, £100 000; a bazaar in Covent Garden Theatre (May 1845) raised £25 000.
- Cobden won the support of Daniel O'Connell, who provided an enormous boost by ensuring that Irish workers co-operated with the League, rather than with the Chartists. At meetings in the north, Irish labourers often acted as bodyguards against Chartist rowdies.
- Like the Chartists, the Leaguers presented a number of monster petitions to parliament, but as soon as it became obvious that these were useless, they concentrated on getting as many MPs as possible elected to parliament. Their first attempt was encouraging: at a bye-election in Walsall (January 1841) they put up J. B. Smith who stood as an *Abolitionist*. After a violent campaign, Smith was only narrowly defeated by the Tory candidate (363 votes to 336). The League used its funds to enable members who had no vote to buy 40 shilling freehold property (these could usually be bought for between £30 and £60) which carried the right to vote; in the general election of 1841 eight Abolitionists were elected, including Cobden himself for Stockport. Bright won a bye-election at Durham in 1843, and by 1845 there were 12 Abolitionist MPs. Now the League could bring constant pressure to bear on the government; as Cobden himself remarked, 'you speak with a loud voice when you are talking on the floor of the House, and if you have anything to say that hits hard . . . it reaches all over the kingdom'.

(d) *Stages in the repeal*

1 In the first two years the League made little progress: there was violent opposition from Chartists and farmers, and Russell, the Home Secretary, refused to receive deputations and petitions.

2 After the 1841 election the Abolitionist MPs began to make some impact, so much so that Peel slightly reduced the corn import duties laid down in Huskisson's 1828 sliding scale. He hoped that this would be sufficient to silence the more moderate League supporters, and in fact there was something of a lull in the campaign until 1845.

3 At some time between 1842 and the beginning of 1845 (*before* the Irish famine) Peel himself made up his mind that the Corn Laws were not serving any useful purpose and that British farmers ought to be perfectly capable of maintaining their profits without them, provided they modernized their methods. An up-to-date farming system would make a perfect partnership with expanding industry. No doubt the League's arguments were partly responsible for Peel's change of mind:

after Cobden had delivered a particularly effective attack on the Corn Laws in the Commons (March 1845), Peel screwed up his notes and whispered to the MP sitting next to him, 'You must answer this, for I cannot.' Peel's problem was that the Conservative party was pledged to keep the Corn Laws, and if he moved too quickly, he would infuriate the landowners and split the party, again. He hoped gradually to prepare the party for repeal and then allow the country to decide at the next general election, due in 1848.

4   In the summer of 1845 the Irish potato crop was ruined by blight. In a country where the basic diet consisted entirely of potatoes, this was disastrous. With the poor facing starvation, Peel arranged for £160 000 worth of maize to be imported from the USA to be sold at 1d a pound to the Irish. But this was soon used up; in hundreds of villages in the west of Ireland there was no food of any sort, and thousands were dying of starvation. At the same time the English and Scottish potato crop failed and the corn harvest was a poor one; however, corn grown in Ireland was being exported to England. In November 1845 Peel told his cabinet that the Corn Laws must go immediately; this was the only way to get cheap food into Ireland. Whether he really believed this or whether he was using the Irish famine as an emergency excuse to force repeal through, is not certain. (In fact repeal made little difference to the tragic situation in Ireland.) Either way, a majority of the cabinet opposed the idea, and Peel resigned (December 1845).

5   After Russell failed to form a Whig government, Queen Victoria recalled Peel who had by now won over most of his cabinet, but not his party. A Repeal Bill (which would phase out the Corn Laws over the next three years) was introduced into the Commons. There was a fierce debate lasting five months, during which about two-thirds of the Conservative MPs revolted against Peel. The Protectionists were led by Benjamin Disraeli and Lord George Bentinck. They made bitter personal attacks on Peel, claiming that the situation in Ireland was not serious enough to warrant such a Bill, and accusing Peel of breaking his promises and betraying his party again, as he had over Catholic Emancipation. Some said Disraeli's real motive for the attacks was revenge for Peel's refusal to include him in the government in 1841.

6   The Repeal Bill passed the Commons (May 1846), but only with Whig support: the rebel Conservatives (231 of them) all voted against Peel; only 112 Conservatives voted with him. Thanks to Wellington's support, the Bill passed the Lords without too much trouble and became law in June. But Disraeli and the Protectionists were determined on revenge. To help restore order in Ireland Peel had introduced a Coercion Bill into the Commons; on the same night as the Corn Law Repeal Bill passed the Lords, Disraeli and some of the rebel Conservatives combined with the Whigs and the Irish MPs to defeat the Coercion Bill. Peel resigned and never held office again.

(e) *What were the effects of the Corn Law repeal?*

Oddly, after all the controversy and excitement, the results of the repeal were an anti-climax:

● There was no dramatic fall in wheat prices for the simple reason that whenever the British harvest was poor, so was the European one; there was no vast inflow of European wheat, and supplies from North America were not yet available in large enough quantities. However, economists believe that repeal did at least keep British wheat prices steady at a time when world prices generally were rising.

● British farmers did not suffer immediate ruin; they soon developed better methods

– use of fertilizers, more mechanization, drainage pipes, stronger strains of wheat – which all helped to increase yield per acre. As town populations increased steadily, the demand for food grew and farmers were ensured reasonable profits. It was not until the 1870s that British farming began to suffer competition from massive imports from America (see Section 15.4).

● Repeal did not seem to help the Irish significantly; the 1846 potato crop failed as badly as the one in 1845, and 1847 saw only a slight improvement, so that the famine continued until 1848 when there was a good harvest. Since there were no large stocks of life-saving European corn available and Irish-grown corn continued to be exported to England throughout the famine, the condition of the Irish poor was pitiful. To add to their miseries a cholera epidemic broke out in December 1846. It is estimated that at least a million people died from starvation and disease and a further million emigrated to Canada and the USA (for the next phase in Irish history see Section 8.1(a)).

● Repeal probably encouraged other countries to reduce duties on goods from Britain, although there were many other reasons for this reduction; there was much more behind the British trade expansion than the abolition of the Corn Laws.

● It destroyed Peel and split the party; after this, the Conservatives were out of office (except for two short and ineffective periods in 1852 and 1858) until 1866. However, landowners were still the dominant group in parliament, whereas the middle classes, the largest section of voters, were still in a minority. Cobden had hoped that the Anti-Corn Law League would develop into a new middle-class political party capable of seriously challenging the landowning class. As time passed, he suffered disappointment: once the single aim uniting all the various sections of the middle class had been achieved, the alliance fell apart; the middle classes were far too diverse and varied in character and interests to be represented by one political party.

Of course, in June 1846 none of these results could be foreseen; as far as the League members were concerned, all else was forgotten as they celebrated their triumph.

(f) Why was the Anti-Corn Law League successful?

● The League concentrated on the one aim which was simple to understand (unlike the Chartists who tried to achieve too much all at once), and their arguments were reasonable and logical.

● It was a middle-class inspired movement which provided it with sufficient funds to form a national organization and mount an effective propaganda campaign (the Chartists – violent and threatening revolution – failed to win significant middle-class support).

● They had outstanding and united leaders (especially Cobden and Bright) who were successful in winning 12 seats to put their case effectively in parliament. It was this continued pressure, plus the strength of their case, which convinced Peel that the Corn Laws must eventually go, though not necessarily immediately (the Chartist leaders were less able, could not agree on what tactics to follow, and failed to make an impact in parliament).

● The Irish famine helped bring matters to a head, causing Peel, or perhaps giving him the excuse, to abandon the Corn Laws earlier than he would otherwise have done.

7.6 Was Peel a great statesman?

Taking the *Oxford Dictionary* definition of a statesman as 'a person taking a prominent part in the management of state affairs', there can be no disputing that Peel was a statesman. But there have been widely varying views about how 'great' he was. W. Bagehot, writing in 1856, thought that although Peel was a great administrator, he was not a great statesman because he was not capable of creative thought; he merely borrowed other people's ideas. Bagehot made the point, well worth thinking about, that Peel had begun by opposing most of the measures which were later considered his greatest achievements (such as Catholic Emancipation and the repeal of the Corn Laws); he was good at repealing things but not so impressive when it came to thinking of something new. G. Kitson Clark, writing his biography of Peel in 1936, believed that in spite of all his successes, there was 'a lack of vision in Peel'.

On the other hand, Peel's was a career full of striking achievements, first as Irish Secretary (1812–18), then as Home Secretary (1822–30) and finally as Prime Minister. Norman Gash sums up his premiership clearly and simply: 'Financial stability had been achieved, trade revived, Chartism virtually extinguished, O'Connell's repeal movement checked, the great institutions of state safeguarded, and good relations with France and the USA restored. . . . More than any other one man he was the architect of the early Victorian age.'

Yet how could he be a great statesman if he betrayed his Conservative party and left it in ruins? The answer is simple: Peel believed that the national interest was more important than party. When the Conservatives refused to go along with him over the Corn Laws, Peel was disgusted with them and disillusioned with party politics. Soon after the split he wrote: 'Thank God I am relieved for ever from the trammels of such a party.'

Some more recent writers have not been as glowing as Norman Gash in their assessment of Peel; it has been suggested that:

- his role as founder of the modern Conservative party has been exaggerated;
- Wellington deserves as much credit for the development of the party as Peel;
- his political judgement was often seriously at fault during his premiership;
- he failed to understand the way the party political system was changing after 1832.

(For a discussion of these points see R. Foster, 'Peel and his Party', in *Modern History Review*, September 1993.)

Peel died in 1850 at the age of 62, from injuries sustained when he was thrown from his horse. Although many who knew him in politics thought him dull and cold (O'Connell said that when he smiled it was like the gleam of the silver plate on a coffin lid), the general public certainly felt that the country had lost its most brilliant politician. Among the many tributes which poured forth was this excruciating but no doubt sincere verse:

> Talk of Canning and Pitt for their talents and wit,
> And all who upheld that high station,
> Oh! there has ne'er been such a noble Premier
> As Sir Robert before in the nation,
> In every way he carried the sway,
> For the good of his country, God rest him.

Questions

1 Peel, Disraeli and the Abolition of the Corn Laws, 1846
Study the Sources A to G and then answer the questions which follow.

A speech by Richard Cobden, 1839

We propose to keep people well informed as to the progress of our campaign by means of the penny post, by one letter a week. . . . We intend to visit every borough in the kingdom, and we shall invite the electors to meet us. We shall urge them to have a *Free-trade candidate* to supplant every *monopolist* who still retains a seat for a borough . . .

The single and undisputed object of the League is to put down commercial monopoly. . . . The Corn-law is the great tree of monopoly, under whose evil shadow every other restriction exists. Cut it down by the roots and it will destroy the others in its fall. The sole object of the League is to put an end once and for ever to the principle of maintaining taxes for the benefit of a particular class.

Free Trade! What is it? Why, the breaking down of barriers that separate nations . . . those barriers behind which nestle feelings of pride, revenge, hatred and jealousy, which every now and then burst their bounds, and deluge whole countries with blood . . . those feelings which assert that without conquest we can have no trade. . . . I see in the Free Trade principle that which will draw men together, thrusting aside the antagonism of race, creed and language, and uniting us in the bonds of eternal peace.

Source: J. Bright and J. E. T. Rogers (eds), *Speeches by Richard Cobden*, Macmillan, 1880.

A speech by Sir Robert Peel in the House of Commons during the debate on the Corn Law Repeal Bill, February 1846

This night you will select the motto which is to indicate the commercial policy of England. Shall it be 'advance' or 'recede'? Which is to be the fitter motto for this great Empire? Survey our position, consider the advantage which God and nature have given us. . . . Iron and coal, the sinews of manufacture, give us advantages over every other rival in the great competition of industry. Our capital far exceeds that which they can command. Our national character, the free institutions under which we live, an unshackled press . . . all combine to place us at the head of these nations which profit by the free interchange of their products. And is this the country to shrink from competition?

Choose your motto. 'Advance' or 'Recede'. Vote for 'Advance' and it will encourage in every state the friends of a liberal commercial policy. Sardinia has taken the lead. Naples is relaxing her protective duties and favouring British produce. Can you doubt that the United States will soon relax her hostile Tariff? Act thus and you will have done whatever human wisdom can do for the promotion of commercial prosperity. . . . Of course there is no guarantee that prosperity will continue without interruption – it seems to be unavoidable that the time of depression shall follow the season of excitement and success . . . may God grant that by your decision tonight you will have the consolation of knowing that such calamities have not been caused by laws of man restricting, in the hour of scarcity, the supply of food.

Source: quoted in L. Evans and P. J. Pledger, *Contemporary Sources and Opinions in Modern British History, vol. 1*, Warne, 1967.

From 'Peel and his Party', by Ruscombe Foster, in Modern History Review, *September 1993*

Peel's conversion to Catholic Emancipation is generally accepted to have been based on the conviction that civil war in Ireland was the unacceptable alternative, not on the merits of Emancipation itself.... For Wellington therefore, the corn law crisis was a case of *deja vu*, for Peel seemed again to be capitulating in face of the spectre of civil unrest in Ireland which loomed as a result of the potato famine. 'Rotten potatoes have done it all', he fumed. 'They have put Peel in his damned fright.' This famous outburst is usually dismissed as an old man's irascibility. Perhaps it should be taken more seriously. After all, it was accepted that repeal could not immediately alleviate the plight of the Irish peasant.... It looks more plausible that Peel was galvanised into action (using the Irish situation as a pretext) through fear that if he did not act, the Anti-Corn Law League would use the disaster to increase social unrest on the free trade issue in England.... A fear of mob disorder, therefore, may have played a bigger part in Peel's decision-making than he would readily admit.

Extracts from speeches by Benjamin Disraeli in the House of Commons during the debate on the Corn Law Repeal Bill, February–May 1846

When we complain of the right hon. gentleman [Peel] not treating his party fairly, we speak of the great body of the community whose views they represent.... I say that it is the first duty of a minister to maintain a balance between the two great branches of national industry ... and we should give a preponderance to the agricultural branch; this is not in order to pamper the luxury of the owners of land, but it is because our present system is the only security for self-government; the only barrier against that centralising system which has taken root in other countries. My constituents are not landlords; they are not aristocrats; they are not great capitalists; they are the children of industry and toil; but they believe that their social and political interests are involved in a system by which their rights and liberties have been guaranteed; and I agree with them. I have the same old-fashioned notions ...

When I examine the career of this minister [Peel] I find that for between 30 and 40 years, he has traded on the ideas and intelligence of others. He is a burglar of others' intellect ... there is no other statesman who has committed petty larceny on so great a scale.

Source: quoted in R. Grinter, *Disraeli and Conservatism*, Arnold, 1968.

From Politics and the People 1835–1850 *by K. H. Randell, published in 1972*

At the end of February, 231 Conservatives voted against the second reading of the Corn Bill, while only 112 voted for it. But what surprised Peel more was the vigour of his opponents, which transformed what he imagined would be a short if bloody battle into a five months campaign. It was not until the 28 June that the bill passed its third reading in the Lords, and by that time Peel had been the recipient of more malicious criticism than he could ever have thought possible. The attacks were led by Benjamin Disraeli, who could hardly believe that fate had made so vulnerable the man who had refused to admit his suitability for office in 1841, and who had since done nothing to make good his mistake.

Source F

From Disraeli and Conservatism *by R. Grinter, published in 1968*

Peel's repeal of the Corn Laws in 1846 was the decisive compromise with industry by the party of agriculture. Disraeli condemned this whole policy; the argument that he merely seized an opportunity for personal advance is very attractive, as he quickly made free trade part of Conservative policy, and found his party excluded from office for a generation by distrust of his tactics. But there was also a genuine and lasting dislike of all that the Whig/Liberal group stood for and the repeal would advance – the doctrine of the equality of man and the methods of private enterprise that drove industry forward.

Source G

From an article in a journal, the Fortnightly Review, *1878*

The growing distrust felt towards the Prime Minister, Sir Robert Peel, as he pursued his liberalising course in economic policy, made a Protectionist Party possible, and to its formation Mr. Disraeli devoted himself. . . . But it was not within his moral right to call disgraceful conduct which he had earlier praised. Sir Robert Peel was the convert, the honest convert, of public opinion. The proper contrast is between the statesman who does something about delayed convictions at the right time, and the trading politician who resists measures which he knows to be just and necessary, in order to humour a particular group of people or to justify personal spite or ambition.

Source: quoted in R. Grinter, *Disraeli and Conservatism*, Arnold, 1968.

(a) Using your own knowledge and the evidence of the sources, explain what the writer meant at the time by the following phrases in Source A:
   (i) Free-trade candidate;
   (ii) Monopolist. (4 marks)
(b) How useful is Source A as evidence of the Anti-Corn Law League's aims and methods? (6 marks)
(c) (i) How do Sources B, C and G differ in the evidence they provide about Peel's motives for repealing the Corn Laws? (4 marks)
   (ii) What reasons can you suggest for these differences? (4 marks)
(d) Compare and explain the evidence in Sources D, E, F and G for Disraeli's motives in attacking Peel. (8 marks)
(e) How reliable are speeches in parliament (like Sources B and D) as evidence for the historian? (4 marks)
(Total 30 marks)

2 'Peel's place as the founder of modern Conservatism is unchallengeable. . . . The age of revolt was giving way to the age of stability; and of that age, Peel had been the chief architect' (Norman Gash). How far would you agree with this assessment of Peel's achievement?

8 Domestic affairs 1846–67: Russell, Gladstone, Disraeli and the Reform Act of 1867

Summary of events

Although this was a time of general economic prosperity, *the political scene was confused and unstable* following the Conservative split over the Corn Law repeal. Those Conservatives (112 of them), including W. E. Gladstone and Lord Aberdeen, who had voted with Peel for the abolition of the Corn Laws, were known as *Peelites*. Those who had wanted to keep the Corn Laws (*Protectionists*) were led officially by Lord Derby, though it was Disraeli who supplied the brains and led the Conservative party in the Commons. The two groups would have nothing to do with each other and the Peelites usually voted with the Whigs. This enabled Lord John Russell, the Whig leader, to form a government with Peelite support, even though the Whigs lacked an overall majority.

The Whigs improved their position in the 1847 general election, winning 325 seats to the Tory Protectionists' 243. However, the Peelites with 89 seats* held the balance, and the Whigs could not afford to ignore their wishes if they wanted to remain in power. In the 1852 election the Peelites dwindled to 45 (Peel himself had died in 1850), but they still held the balance, and actually formed a coalition government with the Whigs; the Peelite leader, Lord Aberdeen, was Prime Minister (1852–5). In the election of 1857 the Peelites were down to 29, and after that they gradually faded out as most of them joined the Whigs (or Liberals, as they were now called). But the Conservatives had still not recovered fully from the split, and were only in government for three short spells during this period. The list of governments (see box) illustrates the instability.

Domestic politics were for the most part uneventful during these years, with certain exceptions, notably the final fling of Chartism in 1848 (see Section 6.4(c)), and some useful social reforms introduced by Russell's government of 1846–52. Gladstone, who was Chancellor of the Exchequer for much of the time between 1852 and 1866, continued the move towards Free Trade, his policies reaching a climax with a series of remarkable budgets (1860–4). The most striking feature on the domestic scene was not in politics – it was the great surge of industrial and agricultural prosperity sometimes referred to as the Golden Age of Victorian Britain (see Section 15.1).

In the middle of the period much of the public's attention was occupied with events abroad – *the Crimean War of 1854–6* (see Chapter 10) and *the Indian Mutiny of*

---

* The problem with the Peelites is that they were never an organized party, so it is difficult to be sure who were Peelites and who weren't at any given time. You will probably find different estimates of the numbers of Peelite MPs in different books. The figures used here are from R. Blake, *The Conservative Party from Peel to Thatcher* (Fontana, 1985), p. 46.

1857 (see Chapter 11). Public interest in foreign affairs was maintained during Palmerston's second spell as Prime Minister, from 1859 to 1865.

During the 1860s the question which came again to the forefront was the need for a further reform of parliament. After long wrangling reminiscent of the struggle to get the 1832 Reform Act through, Derby's Conservative government was responsible for *the Reform Act of 1867*, another major step towards a democratic system of parliamentary government. Much to the disgust of the Conservatives, the newly enlarged electorate responded at the general election of 1868 by voting in a Liberal government with a majority of over 100.

8.1 How successful were the domestic policies of Russell's government of 1846–52?

Broadly speaking the government had its main successes up to 1850, but after that it ran into trouble and achieved little of any significance.

(a) *Continuing problems in Ireland*

Ireland was again the most pressing problem, with famine, cholera, dysentery and fever continuing until 1852. Clearly massive amounts of relief were necessary, and although Russell's government did something to help, it was nowhere near enough. During the first half of 1847 a network of soup kitchens was set up providing free soup for about three million people. However, at the same time, stricter rules made it more difficult for the poor to get financial payments, and the government reduced its financial contribution, announcing that from August 1847 the Poor Law must deal with the problem; in other words the Irish taxpayers must foot the bill for famine relief themselves. This meant that the Irish Poor Law, which had been intended to cope with perhaps 100 000 paupers, was having to deal with about a million and a half people during the winter of 1847–8. Potato blight was still a problem in some areas as late as 1850; the deaths continued, though the majority were caused not by starvation, but by famine-related diseases. The terrible suffering and loss of life (which was confined to Ireland) demonstrated to the Irish people that Ireland was not being treated as an equal with the rest of Britain, and it only served to fuel Irish hatred of the English (see Section 13.3(a) for the next phase in Irish history).

(b) *The Chartist outburst of 1848*

Although this turned out to be the final fling of Chartism, it could well have got out of hand. However, the government acted positively and the situation was decisively dealt with (see Section 6.4(c)).

(c) *Social reforms*

These included *two Factory Acts, Fielden's in 1847 and Grey's in 1850*; both were concerned with limiting the working day for women (see Section 12.3). Another important reform was *the Public Health Act of 1848* (see Section 12.5(a)). This was a pioneering piece of legislation which allowed Local Boards of Health to be set up to improve sanitation and water supply, but the fact that it was not compulsory robbed it of much of its effectiveness. The government grant for education was increased in 1847 (see Section 12.7(a)).

(d) *The government loses its way*

After 1850 the government aroused opposition and lost support over several issues:

● The 1851 budget was highly unpopular among manufacturers and businessmen who had hoped to see income tax (standing at 7d in the £) abolished.
● Russell appeared to be against parliamentary reform when he opposed a private member's bill which would have made the voting qualification the same in both counties and boroughs. The Radicals, already disappointed over the budget, were so annoyed with Russell that they voted for the motion which was passed against Russell's wishes. At this point the Prime Minister resigned (February 1851), but the Conservatives, lacking a majority, failed to form a government, so Russell came back for another year. This was long enough to see through the Great Exhibition (see Section 15.1(a)).

But the government grew steadily weaker and was finally brought down by Palmerston in retaliation for his dismissal by Russell a few weeks earlier (see Section 9.4(e)).

8.2 What contribution did Gladstone make to the development of the British economy while he was Chancellor of the Exchequer?

William Ewart Gladstone, the son of a wealthy Liverpool merchant, was educated at Eton and Christ Church, Oxford, and first entered parliament as a Tory in 1832. For a time he was President of the Board of Trade in Peel's 1841–6 government, helping to formulate Peel's great tariff reforms. When the Conservatives split over the repeal of the Corn Laws, Gladstone remained a Peelite, which kept him out of office until 1852, when he became Chancellor of the Exchequer in the Whig–Peelite coalition (until 1855). The Conservatives tried to entice him back, but he was now moving firmly towards the Liberals, and when Palmerston invited him to take up his old post,

Gladstone accepted. He was Liberal Chancellor of the Exchequer from 1859 until 1865, and became Liberal leader in the House of Commons on Palmerston's death.

(a) *Gladstone had strong views about economic policy*

• While serving with Peel, he had been converted to the idea of Free Trade. The more manufacturers and businessmen could be freed from having to pay tariffs, the more cheaply they could produce their goods. These would be all the more competitive on the world market and British exports would increase.

• Full employment and low food prices would enable the working class to enjoy a share of the general prosperity.

• Gladstone believed it was important to keep both government expenditure and taxation to a minimum: 'All excess in public expenditure ... is not only a pecuniary waste, but above all, a great moral evil.' He hoped to abolish the income tax and generally make government finance more efficient.

• The result of all this would be to create the right environment for people to prosper, to live economically and to build up their savings; in other words, people should help themselves, rather than expect the government to spend vast amounts of cash on welfare schemes.

(b) *Gladstone's aims put into practice*

1   *The attack on tariffs* began immediately in the 1853 budget: he abolished nearly all remaining duties on partially manufactured goods and on food, including fruit and dairy produce, and halved nearly all remaining duties on fully manufactured goods; these changes affected over 250 separate articles. The 1860 budget continued this trend, import duties being abolished on a further 375 articles; this left only another 48 articles still being taxed. Even this was whittled down further when Gladstone reduced the duty on sugar (1864) and later halved the duty on tea (from 1s to 6d a pound).

2   *Income tax reduction* proved more difficult to achieve; Gladstone hoped to phase it out gradually, ending it altogether in 1859. He was reluctant to abolish it at a stroke in his 1853 budget because he needed the revenue it brought in to make up for that lost from the tariffs he was abolishing. His plans were thwarted by the outbreak of the Crimean War in 1854 which forced him to raise income tax to 10d in the £ on incomes from £100 to £150 a year and 1s 2d on incomes over £150. After the war he realized it was far too valuable a tax to disappear completely, but he reduced it again to 6d in 1865 and to 4d in 1866 and 1867.

3   *The Cobden Treaty (1860) with France* sprang from a mixture of political and economic motives. The details were worked out by Richard Cobden negotiating with Napoleon III's government in Paris. Cobden was convinced that Free Trade between the great nations would remove many of the causes of international friction. Since the British were eternally suspicious of Napoleon III's intentions, Gladstone was prepared to give Cobden a free hand in the hope of reducing tension. The agreement was that France reduced import duties on British coal and manufactured goods and in return Britain reduced duties on French wines and brandy, all of which fitted in well with Gladstone's tariff policy.

4   Gladstone brought in a clever new practice in the way laws dealing with financial matters were passed. Instead of introducing a number of separate bills, he combined them all into one large bill for the 1861 budget. This brought greater speed and efficiency into the passing of financial legislation. However, his real

motive was to manoeuvre the House of Lords into approving the abolition of the duty on paper; in 1860 they had voted out the bill abolishing the duty, in case it encouraged the growth of a cheap left-wing press. The Lords could hardly throw out the entire budget just to save the paper duty; so Gladstone had his way and the combined budget has remained until the present day.

5   *The Post Office Savings Bank (1861) was opened*, and after only a year it had attracted 180 000 investors who deposited between them almost two million pounds. This was a most important achievement not only because it encouraged ordinary people to save, but also because it provided the government with a new supply of cash which it could draw on if necessary.

(c) *Gladstone's policies had far-reaching effects*

1   Free Trade provided a great stimulus to the British economy. The 1860 Cobden Treaty alone produced a three-fold increase in trade with France by 1880. In general between 1850 and 1870, British exports increased fourfold, while the outstanding success story was provided by coal exports which increased in value fivefold during the same 20-year period. Of course all this was not due solely to Gladstone's tariff policies: there were other causes, such as the improvement in communications (railways and steamships); but Gladstone certainly created the right atmosphere for the great Victorian boom to develop (see Section 15.1).

2   The working classes were probably better fed, since wages rose rather more than food prices. There was, for example, a marked increase in the consumption of commodities such as tea and sugar. On the other hand, Gladstone's economy drive meant that much needed social reform in the fields of public health, sanitation, housing and education could not take place.

3   Gladstone's reputation among fellow politicians and with the general public was much enhanced by his achievements. It was no surprise when he became leader of the Liberals in 1868, and his popularity partly explains the Liberal victory in the general election held later that year.

8.3 Why did the demand for parliamentary reform revive in the early 1860s?

After the passing of the 1832 Reform Act, most people, including Lord John Russell, who had introduced the bill, believed that this was the end of the matter. But gradually the situation changed and several influences, both internal and external, combined to bring about a widespread feeling that further reform was necessary.

(a) *There had been important population changes since 1832*

The total population of Britain increased from 24 million in 1831 to 29 million in 1861; by 1865 the adult male population of England and Wales had risen to over five million, and yet of those, only a fraction over a million had the vote. The vast majority of the working class was still voteless. People had continued to move into the ever-expanding industrial areas, but there had been no corresponding changes in constituencies and no new ones created. Clearly some extension of the vote and some redistribution of seats was necessary.

(b) *Pressure from Radicals both inside and outside parliament*

The Radicals, with John Bright as their acknowledged leader, kept up constant pressure for reform. Bright was convinced that democracy, as it operated in the USA, Canada and Australia, should be tried in Britain. During the winter of 1858–9 he launched himself upon a series of great speeches which brought reform more publicity than it had enjoyed for a decade; it was time, he argued, that ordinary people were given a share in controlling their own fortunes; 'palaces, baronial castles, great halls, stately mansions, do not make a nation. The nation in every country dwells in the cottage', he told a Birmingham audience in October 1858.

(c) *The Trade Union movement campaigned for reform*

During the 1850s, associations of skilled workers, known as Model Unions, began to spread (see Section 19.3). These new craft unions were more moderate than earlier unions, and their leaders, men like Robert Applegarth of the Sheffield carpenters, and bricklayer George Howell, demonstrated that they were responsible people, concerned to improve standards for the workers and to reform parliament by legal means, not by revolution. They were in contact with Radical MPs, and succeeded in impressing a large section of the Liberal party, and many of the Conservatives as well, with their sense of responsibility. As early as 1861 working men in Leeds were organizing reform conferences, and in March 1864, *the Reform Union*, an alliance of middle and working class reformers, was set up at a meeting in the Manchester Free Trade Hall.

(d) *The American Civil War (1861–5) was an important external stimulus*

For most Radicals this was a simple case of freedom (the North) struggling to assert itself against tyranny and slavery (the South), and the war provided splendid publicity for the idea of equal rights and opportunities within a nation. The war had another effect: the northern blockade of southern ports cut off cotton supplies to the industrial towns of Lancashire, bringing serious unemployment and hardship during late 1861 and right through 1862. Yet by the end of 1862, as the cotton workers realized that the North stood for the abolition of slavery, they swung their support firmly behind the North, whose warships were the direct cause of their distress. This reaction impressed many politicians as a sign of working-class political maturity.

(e) *Gladstone was converted to the idea of reform*

A combination of Radical and trades union pressure was responsible for Gladstone's conversion. He first revealed his change of mind publicly in the Commons in 1864 when he said: 'Every man who is not incapacitated by some consideration of personal unfitness or political danger, is morally entitled to come within the pale of the constitution.' This angered his Prime Minister, Palmerston, who was still against reform and who retorted, 'I entirely deny that every sane man has a moral right to a vote.' Gladstone's approval of the Lancashire cotton workers' political maturity led him to declare that it was 'a shame and a scandal that bodies of men such as these should be excluded from the parliamentary franchise'. The death of the anti-reform Palmerston in 1865 removed the most serious obstacle to reform within the Liberal party.

(f) *The visit of Giuseppe Garibaldi to London (April 1864)*

This gave added publicity to the idea of liberal reform. In 1860 he had played a vital and heroic part in the unification of Italy, and he was still popular with the British public as a liberal and a democrat. A group of his admirers eventually became *the Reform League* (February 1865) which had extensive trade union support.

(g) *The Conservatives accepted that pressure would eventually bring about further reform*

Disraeli, the Conservative leader in the Commons, was even prepared to introduce limited reform of parliament himself, provided it didn't go too far. His reasoning seems to have been that if further reform really was inevitable, as Bright kept telling everybody, then the Conservatives ought to jump in and take the credit for it. In fact the Tories did bring in a very mild reform bill (March 1859), but it was thrown out; most of the Liberals voted against it because it did nothing to extend the vote in the boroughs and would have brought very few workers into the system.

8.4 What were the stages by which reform was achieved?

(a) *The Liberal Reform Bill fails*

Russell and Gladstone introduced a moderate reform bill in March 1866, which proposed to give the vote in the boroughs to householders paying £7 a year rent (instead of £10) and in the counties to tenants paying £14 a year rent (instead of £50). This was expected to bring an extra 400 000 voters onto the lists. No mention was made of redistributing seats. There was lively opposition in the Commons from:

- *The Conservatives*, who thought the Bill went too far. *Lord Cranborne (later Lord Salisbury)* compared the state to a joint-stock company, arguing that 'the wildest dreamer never suggested that all the shareholders should hold a single vote without reference to the number of shares they might hold'. Even Disraeli thought the Bill would bring into parliament 'a horde of selfish and obscure mediocrities, incapable of anything but mischief'.
- *A section of the Liberals led by Robert Lowe*, who claimed that the working classes were ignorant of politics, would be incapable of deciding who to vote for and would be open to bribery. They were full of 'venality, ignorance, drunkenness and the facility for being intimidated'. Bright nicknamed Lowe and his supporters *the Adullamites* (after the Bible story about the discontented Israelites who left Saul and went to join David in the cave of Adullam – see 1 Samuel 22, verses 1–2).

The opposition introduced an amendment to reduce the number of new voters, and when the Commons passed the amendment, Russell (now aged 74) resigned. It was a sad end to Russell's career in politics, since he had hoped to bow out with parliamentary reform as his crowning achievement.

(b) *Pressure for reform mounts*

The incoming Conservative government hoped to move slowly and introduce some mild reform in 1868. However, public interest was now thoroughly aroused, and *pres-*

sure built up for immediate action. Bright embarked on another speaking tour to campaign for reform; there was a short, sharp economic crisis which developed in 1866, several companies went bankrupt and there was widespread unemployment. Bread was expensive following the poor harvest of 1865 and there was a sudden cholera epidemic which killed 8000 people in London alone. In July a demonstration was planned to take place in Hyde Park. When the government closed the park to the meeting, there were some disturbances, during which 1400 yards of railings were demolished. It was the combination of all these circumstances which convinced the Conservatives that reform could not wait. Derby and Disrael decided to make a bid for popularity which would prolong their stay in office and 'dish the Liberals'.

(c) *Disraeli's 'leap in the dark'*

Both Disraeli and Derby were prepared to introduce a much more drastic bill than Gladstone's if it would bring the Tories a long period in power. Their problem was that Cranborne and his supporters in the cabinet threatened to resign if the bill went too far; so in February 1867 a measure was introduced which was so mild that it caused an uproar in the Commons when it was read out. It was obvious that the Liberals would not vote for it, and rather than be forced to resign, Disraeli decided to risk upsetting Cranborne by introducing a more radical measure. Cranborne and two other cabinet members resigned, but Disraeli pushed ahead with his bill. As it passed its various stages in the Commons, the Liberals proposed several amendments, all of which were accepted; this made the final bill even more extreme. This Conservative bill became law in August 1867, and is usually known as *The Second Reform Act.*

8.5 What were the terms and effects of the 1867 Reform Act?

(a) *Terms*

1 *In the boroughs* the vote was given to all householders (both owner-occupiers and tenants) who paid rates, provided they had lived in their house for at least one year. Lodgers paying £10 a year rent also received the vote.
2 *In the counties* the vote was given to all ratepayers paying £12 a year in rates, and to copyholders and leaseholders holding land valued at £5 a year.
3 Boroughs with a population of under 10 000 lost one MP. This released 45 seats for redistribution; 25 of them were given to the counties, 15 to boroughs which had not had an MP up till now, one was given to the University of London, and a third member was given to Liverpool, Manchester, Leeds and Birmingham.
4 The franchise in Scotland was brought into line with the English pattern, and seven seats were transferred from England to Scotland.
5 In Irish boroughs the vote was given to £4 ratepayers.

(b) *Effects of the 1867 Act*

Apart from the obvious one of increasing the size of the electorate, the effects of the Act were something of an unknown quantity at the time. Even Derby admitted that they were 'making a great experiment and taking a leap in the dark', while the historian Thomas Carlyle said it was 'like shooting Niagara'.

1   The size of the electorate was almost doubled from about 1.36 million to 2.46 million.
2   Most of the new voters were industrial workers living in the towns, so for the first time there was something approaching democracy in the boroughs.

However, there were some other results which showed that the leap in the dark fell a long way short of full democracy:

3   In the counties the voting qualification was high enough to keep agricultural labourers (the majority of the rural population) and people such as miners living in rural pit villages without the vote. This was completely illogical discrimination, but it was designed to preserve the power of wealthy farmers and landowners. If democracy had to be conceded in the boroughs, the wealthy were determined to salvage at least something for themselves in the countryside.
4   Voting was still held in public; the lack of secrecy meant that working-class borough voters were bound to be swayed by their employers and landlords (the 1872 Ballot Act solved this problem – see Section 13.2(f)).
5   The distribution of seats still left a lot to be desired. Many small towns with only just over 10 000 inhabitants – such as Tiverton – still had two MPs like Glasgow, which had over half a million. The South and East were still over-represented compared with the industrial Midlands and North; Wiltshire and Dorset between them were represented by 25 MPs for a population of 450 000, yet the West Riding of Yorkshire with over two million had only 22 MPs.

As time went on, other results became apparent which had not been foreseen in 1867:

6   The increased borough electorates meant that there were too many voters to bribe; politicians began to realize that they must explain and justify their policies, and gradually the whole nature of politics changed as the election campaign in the constituencies became the accepted procedure. The Liberals were the first to appreciate this, with Gladstone leading the way in the 1868 general election.
7   The creation of the large three-member constituencies like Birmingham and Manchester led to another development: the rule was that each elector could only vote for two candidates; this meant for example, that one of the three Birmingham Liberal candidates might not poll enough votes to be elected, while the other two received far more than was necessary. It was, in fact, the Birmingham Liberals who first realized that this wastage of votes could be avoided by having a local organization to make sure that there was an equal distribution of Liberal votes between the three candidates so that all three were elected. The Conservatives soon followed suit, and before long, party organizations developed both at national and constituency level to whip up support at election times and to nurse the voters between elections.

In spite of his triumph, Disraeli (who became Prime Minister on Derby's retirement) still lacked a Commons majority, and hoped that the 1868 election would bring its reward. To his intense disappointment the Liberals won with a majority of 112. *Reasons for the Liberal victory were*:

● Gladstone and Bright conducted a vigorous election campaign, speaking all over the country, whereas Disraeli merely sent a printed election address to his own constituents, and missed a splendid opportunity of winning over the new borough voters with a programme of much-needed social reform.
● Gladstone won middle- and working-class Nonconformist support by announcing that the Liberals would disestablish the Anglican Church in Ireland (the Anglican Church would no longer be the official state church in Ireland).

Questions

1 The passing of the 1867 Parliamentary Reform Act

Study Sources A to F and then answer the questions which follow.

Source A

A speech by John Bright, 1866

We now come to the Rochdale District Co-operative Corn Mill Society, which does a large business. It has a capital of £60,000 and turns over £164,000 per annum. It has also a committee, but neither the president, nor treasurer, nor secretary, nor any one of this committee has a borough vote. Now what is taking place in Rochdale societies is occurring in greater or less degree in all the societies, of which there are five or six hundred throughout the country. . . . You have one million electors now, and there are eight million of grown men in the United Kingdom; can you say that only one million shall have votes and all the rest are to remain excluded? Is the thing possible?

Source: quoted in D. G. Wright, *Democracy and Reform 1815–1885*, Longman, 1970.

Source B

A speech by W. E. Gladstone in the House of Commons, April 1866

An enormous benefit has been effected by the freedom of the press, when for the humble sum of a penny, or even less, newspapers are circulated by the million, carrying home to all classes of our fellow countrymen, accounts of public affairs, enabling them to feel a new interest in those affairs. . . . And the working community has responded fully to all calls made upon it to improve itself. Take for example the Working Men's Free Libraries throughout the country. . . . Then again, Sir, we called upon them to be thrifty, and we started for them the Post Office savings banks; and what has been the result? There are now 650,000 depositors in those savings banks. Parliament has been striving to make the working class progressively fitter and fitter for the franchise; and can anything be more unwise, not to say more senseless, than to persevere from year to year in this plan, and then blindly refuse to recognise its logical upshot – namely, the increased fitness of the working class for political power.

Source: quoted in L. Evans and P. J. Pledger, *Contemporary Sources and Opinions in Modern British History, vol. 1*, Warne, 1967.

Source C

Extracts from speeches by Robert Lowe, a Liberal MP, in the House of Commons, May 1867

The right hon. gentleman opposite [Disraeli] has adopted a course which is infinitely creditable to his dexterity as a tactician. He well knew that had he proposed the measure as it is now before us, and shown it to his party at first, they would have started back from it in horror. . . . The right hon. gentleman has treated them as we treat a shy horse . . . take him gently up, walk him round the object, and then, when the process has been repeated often enough, we hope we shall get the creature to pass it quietly . . . clearly he was determined from the beginning that household suffrage was the principle he intended to introduce . . .

You are about to take away the management of affairs from the upper and middle classes, and you are about to place it in the hands of people of whose politics you know nothing, for the best of all possible reasons – because they do not know what their politics are themselves. But they will not always be without politics; and what will they be? Their politics must take one form – Socialism . . .

The first stage will be an increase of corruption, intimidation and disorder, of all the evils that happen usually in elections. The second will be that the working men of England, finding themselves in a full majority, will awake to a full sense of their power. They will say 'We can do better for ourselves; we have our trade unions; we have our leaders all ready.'

Now, I ask the House again, with the example of America before us, is it wise to push forward in this direction? We see in America, where the people have undisputed power, that they do not send honest, hardworking men to represent them in Congress, but dealers in office, bankrupts, men who have lost their character and been driven from every respectable way of life, and who take up politics as a last resource.

Source: as for Source A, and also quoted in R. Grinter, *Disraeli and Conservatism*, Arnold, 1968.

Source D

Conservative historian Robert Blake writes that there are three main theories to explain why Disraeli and the Conservatives, after rejecting a mild Liberal reform measure, themselves introduced a much more far-reaching Bill only a year later

ONE – the Liberal theory: that the Bill in its final form was forced on Disraeli by Gladstone, as the price paid by unscrupulous Tories for remaining in office. The true facts were recognised by the newly enfranchised town householders who showed their gratitude to Gladstone by returning the Liberals with an increased majority in the first election after the new Act.
TWO – the Tory democracy theory: that the Reform Act was not forced on a reluctant Disraeli, but fulfilled an aim which he had held for many years – to further some kind of alliance between the aristocracy and the urban working class . . . The social reforms of 1875 and 1876 lend further colour to the view that the Conservatives were appealing to the working man. Far from yielding to pressure in 1867, Disraeli was educating his party.
THREE – the Labour theory: that the politicians were subject to the pressure of mass working class agitation expressed through the activities of the Reform League. According to this theory, the really crucial event was the demonstration by the League in Hyde Park in May 1867, in defiance of the government's ban. This, it is alleged, is the direct cause of Disraeli's adding another 400,000 voters to the borough electorate.

Source: R. Blake, *The Conservative Party from Peel to Thatcher*, Fontana, 1985.

Source E

A speech by Disraeli in the House of Commons during the Reform Bill debate, July 1867

I think that the danger would be less, that the feeling of the larger numbers would be more national, than by giving the vote just to a sort of class set aside, looking with suspicion on their superiors, and with disdain on those beneath them. I think you would have a better chance of touching the popular heart, of evoking the national sentiment, by bringing in the great body of those men who occupy houses and fulfil the duties of citizenship by the payment of rates.

Source: as for Source A.

Source F

From a biography of Gladstone, written by John Morley, a Liberal politician

It was at Mr Gladstone's demand that lodgers were given the vote, and that the distribution of seats was extended into an operation of enormously larger scale.

Source: J. Morley, *The Life of William Ewart Gladstone, vol. 1*, Macmillan, 1903

- **(a)** What methods do Bright and Gladstone use in Sources A and B to put over their case for more parliamentary reform? (6 marks)
- **(b)** How successfully do you think Lowe (in Source C) puts the case against more parliamentary reform? (6 marks)
- **(c)** Using the evidence of the Sources and your own knowledge, explain why you think Lowe's views on parliamentary reform were so different from those of Bright and Gladstone, although all three were members of the Liberal party. (5 marks)
- **(d)** Judging by the evidence of the Sources and your own knowledge, which of the three theories mentioned by Blake (Source D) about the passing of the 1867 Reform Act do you think seems most plausible? (13 marks)

(Total 30 marks)

2 Read the following extract from a speech about electoral reform made by Gladstone in the House of Commons in 1866, and then answer the questions which follow.

> I believe the composition of the House might be greatly improved and that the increased representation of the working classes would supply us more largely with the ... members we want, who would look not to the interests of classes, but to the public interest.

- **(a)** Why was parliamentary reform such a controversial issue in 1866–7? (8 marks)
- **(b)** Examine the implications of the Second Reform Act of 1867 for both governments and political parties in the period to 1880. [NEAB] (12 marks)

Lord Palmerston and Foreign Affairs 1830–65

Summary of events

John Henry Temple, Viscount Palmerston, was a leading figure in British politics for much of the nineteenth century. He had a remarkable career lasting from 1807 until 1865, when he died at the age of almost 81; for the whole of that period he was a member of the House of Commons. This might seem surprising since English peers normally sit in the House of Lords; but in fact, though Palmerston was born in London, the peerage had been given to the family for their estates in Ireland. Irish peers were not entitled to sit in the House of Lords, and this meant that Palmerston, like Castlereagh, was eligible to become an MP in the Commons.

Palmerston began as a Tory MP in 1807 and was made Secretary at War in 1809 (aged only 25), a position he held until 1828. He had a reputation as an efficient administrator but was perhaps better known for his numerous love affairs. He was in sympathy with Huskisson and the 'enlightened' Tories; when Huskisson disagreed with Wellington, Palmerston also resigned and soon joined the Whigs. When the Whigs came to power in 1830, Grey appointed him Foreign Secretary. His career after that is shown in the box below.

Palmerston's career from 1830 to 1865

1830–41	Foreign Secretary in Whig governments of Grey and Melbourne
1846–51	Foreign Secretary in Lord John Russell's Whig government
1852–5	Home Secretary in Lord Aberdeen's Whig/Peelite coalition
1855–8	Liberal Prime Minister
1859–65	Liberal Prime Minister

During his first two periods at the Foreign Office, Palmerston became immensely popular with the general public because he was prepared to stand up to foreign countries, giving the impression that the British were far superior to all other peoples. In his relations with other politicians and ambassadors he could sometimes be arrogant and abrasive; he upset Queen Victoria, who felt he should have consulted her more. In 1851 the Prime Minister, Russell, insisted that he resign because he had acted rashly without

Illus. 9.1   Lord Palmerston

informing either the Queen or the rest of the cabinet. In 1852 Lord Aberdeen made Palmerston Home Secretary, a position which would give him less chance of offending foreigners. However, for much of the time he could be approachable, good-humoured and witty, and had a gift for dealing with ordinary people, with whom he remained hugely popular to the end, even though he consistently opposed the extension of the vote to the working classes.

While he was away from the Foreign Office, the Crimean War (1854–6) broke out; without Palmerston to look after foreign affairs, the government ran the war badly (see Section 10.2). Many people felt that only Palmerston had the necessary flair to bring the war to a successful conclusion and eventually the Queen, against her will, appointed him Prime Minister. This seemed to bring new energy to the conduct of the war, which soon ended with what appeared to be advantageous terms for Britain. From 1859 to 1865 Russell was Foreign Secretary, and though he was not a man to be ignored, Palmerston usually had his own way. With the earlier rift between them now healed, the two men made a good partnership and successes in foreign affairs continued. After 1862 Palmerston encountered setbacks and suffered a decisive diplomatic defeat at the hands of the Prussian Minister-President, Bismarck. The long run of successes was over, and the two veterans, Russell over 70 and Palmerston nearing 80, seemed out of step with the times.

9.1 What were the principles behind Palmerston's conduct of foreign affairs?

1 He was determined to defend British interests wherever they seemed threatened and to uphold Britain's prestige abroad. Whether it was a question of protecting British trade with China, maintaining the British position in India (against Russian ambitions), opposing the spread of French influence in Spain, or looking after the interests of British citizens abroad (like Don Pacifico), Palmerston was prepared to take whatever action he thought necessary.

2 Like Canning, he wanted the public to be aware of those interests, and he developed a remarkable skill in using the press to publicize the issues and enlist support from all classes in society.

3 He was in favour of the spread of liberalism (the introduction of constitutional governments like the one in Britain). He believed that following the 1832 Reform Act, the British system was ideal and that similar systems should replace the autocratic monarchies of Europe, even if this had to be achieved by revolution. Thus he welcomed the revolutions in France (1830) and Greece (1843 and 1862). There were limits to his liberalism, however; after 1832 he was strongly against any further extension of the vote in Britain, and he remained so until his death in 1865 (see Section 8.3(e)).

4 He supported nationalism, sometimes actively, especially if British interests were being advanced, as in the Belgian revolt against Holland (1830–9) and Italian unification (1859–60).

5 He hoped to maintain world peace and wanted Britain to be 'the champion of justice and right'. Ideally this should be achieved by diplomatic means rather than by interfering militarily in the internal affairs of other states.

6 He wanted to preserve the balance of power, which, put at its simplest, meant making sure that no one country became strong enough to dominate the rest of Europe.

In practice none of these principles was binding, except the first: this was of paramount importance. Palmerston was a great improviser, using events and circumstances to maintain Britain's status as a great power. Although he approved of nationalism, he sent no help to the Poles or the Danes (1863 and 1864); he wanted liberalism to spread, yet he continually supported Turkey against Russia, and there could hardly have been a less liberal state than Turkey; the important consideration was that this policy protected British interests against Russia. 'We have no eternal allies and we have no perpetual enemies', he said in parliament. 'Our interests are eternal, and those interests it is our duty to follow.'

9.2 Palmerston as Foreign Secretary 1830–41: how successful was he?

Palmerston took over at the Foreign Office at a difficult time; he was faced almost immediately with three tricky problems: the Belgian revolt against Holland, revolutions in Spain and Portugal, and the outbreak of war between Egypt and Turkey. All three involved, in some way or other, *British relations with France.*

(a) *The Belgian revolt*

1   Although in 1815 it had seemed a good idea to unite Belgium with Holland (see Section 3.1(b)3), the arrangement had not been a success. The Belgians felt that their interests were being ignored by the Dutch-dominated government. Revolution broke out in Brussels (August 1830); by October Dutch troops had been chased out and Belgium declared an independent state. This could not be ignored by the other powers since it was a breach of the 1815 Vienna Settlement which they had all promised to uphold. The situation provided a searching test for Palmerston: if he used it well, he could turn it to advantage for Britain – an independent and friendly Belgium would be good for British trade and naval interests. The new constitutional French king, Louis Philippe, who had himself just been brought to power by the revolution of June 1830, favoured the Belgians and could be expected to support them. But though both Britain and France seemed to be working for the same end – Belgian independence – the danger for Britain was that the new Belgium might turn out to be very much under French influence, and the French were still viewed as the traditional British enemy. A further complication was that the autocratic governments of Austria, Russia and Prussia wanted to suppress the Belgians in order to discourage would-be revolutionaries in their own territories.

2   *Palmerston's aims were*: to co-operate with Louis Philippe so that together they would be strong enough to warn off Austria, Russia and Prussia, thus preventing a European war and ensuring Belgian independence. At the same time he wanted to make sure that if French troops entered Belgium in response to Belgian requests for help, they would leave smartly as soon as the Dutch were defeated. Palmerston suspected that once French troops were entrenched in Belgium, Louis Philippe might be tempted to annex the country, and he was determined to resist any such move.

3   *Palmerston took the lead* as chairman of an international conference which met in London in November 1830. Working closely with the French representative, Talleyrand, who wanted to maintain good relations with Britain, Palmerston prevailed upon both sides to accept a ceasefire. Belgian independence was recognized in principle, even, surprisingly, by Austria, Russia and Prussia, probably because their attention was occupied by other revolutions in Poland and Italy. The Dutch king William also accepted the decision, though reluctantly (January 1831).

    This was by no means the end of the crisis; two questions remained to be settled: to choose a king for the new state, and to fix its frontiers. A new alarm occurred for Britain when the Belgians invited Louis Philippe's second son to become their king. Palmerston, seeing this as almost a union between France and Belgium, threatened war if the French accepted, and began fleet movements; Louis Philippe, who was cautious and sensitive to Britain's feelings, declined the invitation and the throne was given to the pro-British Leopold of Saxe-Coburg.

    The frontier question caused further problems: Leopold demanded that Luxemburg should be included in Belgium, and when the London conference seemed likely to support him, the Dutch king, who was also Grand Duke of Luxemburg, broke the ceasefire and sent troops to occupy Belgium (August 1831). French troops moved in and within ten days had driven the Dutch out. Thus the situation which Palmerston had dreaded had now come about: French troops, established deep in Belgium, were reluctant to withdraw. Again Palmerston took a firm line: 'One thing is certain', he warned, 'the French must go out of Belgium or we have a general war, and war in a given number of days.' Again Louis Philippe gave way, though French public opinion was outraged at this second climb-down. The dispute dragged on until in 1839 the Dutch at last recognized Belgian independence and neutrality, which all the great powers agreed to guarantee in *the Treaty of London*.

4   *Palmerston had been strikingly successful*: thanks to his efforts, a new constitutional state friendly to Britain had been created in an area vitally close to the British coast. The French had been kept out of Belgium; though relations with France were strained for a time, the two governments worked well together during the later stages of the dispute, especially after Leopold married Louis Philippe's daughter. All this had been achieved without a European war. It gained Palmerston the reputation of being a champion of nationalism, but of course his primary aim had been to do what was best for Britain. Even Talleyrand was impressed: 'Palmerston', he wrote, 'is certainly one of the most able, if not the most able, man of business whom I have met in my career.'

(b) *Portugal and Spain*

1   *The problems*: by a strange coincidence the rightful rulers of both Portugal and Spain were child queens – Maria of Portugal and Isabella of Spain. The supporters of both favoured constitutional (liberal) government, and both were opposed by uncles (Miguel in Portugal and Carlos in Spain) who favoured autocratic government and aimed to destroy the liberal constitutions.

   In Portugal Maria had been kept in power by British troops sent by Canning (see Section 3.3(b) 2), but when Wellington withdrew them, Miguel seized the throne. Early in 1832 Maria's party rose in revolt against Miguel; they captured Oporto, and civil war developed.

   Meanwhile *in Spain*, Isabella's mother, acting as Regent for the three-year-old queen, was in the process of setting up a constitutional government, when Carlos raised an army against her. As a first step he crossed into Portugal to help Miguel. The situation was similar to the one in Belgium: France strongly supported both constitutional parties, while Russia, Austria and Prussia were itching to interfere in order to maintain autocracy.

2   *Palmerston's aims were clear*: he intended to support the queens, working in close conjunction with the French (who were proposing joint action). As in the case of Belgium, he was determined to prevent the French from gaining more than their fair share of influence; there were important British naval and commercial interests to be safeguarded in the Mediterranean, and Gibraltar, at the southern tip of Spain, was a British colony. Finally he hoped that joint Anglo-French action would deter Russia, Austria and Prussia from intervening.

3   Palmerston was responsible for sending both direct and indirect help; a British fleet cruised menacingly off the Portuguese coast while British finance equipped a naval expedition commanded by British officers. In 1833 this force defeated Miguel and drove him out of Portugal. The following year Palmerston masterminded a treaty between Britain, France, Spain and Portugal in which they promised joint action against the uncles. This *Quadruple Alliance* began promisingly: Miguel was prevented from returning to Portugal and Carlos was captured and brought to Britain as a prisoner.

4   *British policy seemed to be successful* in the short term, 'a capital hit and all my own doing', boasted Palmerston.

   In Portugal, success was lasting; Miguel never returned, constitutional government of a sort survived, and Portugal became a firm ally of Britain.

   In Spain, however, success was only shortlived; Carlos soon escaped, made his way back to Spain and resumed the struggle for the throne. The civil war (known as the Carlist Wars) lasted until the defeat of Carlos in 1839, and by then Britain's relations with Isabella's government were somewhat strained because of a row over Spain's non-payment of debts to Britain. The Quadruple Alliance broke up in 1836 when the French withdrew, apparently annoyed at Britain's good relations with Spain and Portugal. Added to the disagreement over the Near East (see below) it meant that Anglo-French relations were anything but good. But at least French influence in the Iberian peninsula had been kept to a minimum and the alliance lasted long enough to keep Austria, Russia and Prussia out.

(c) *Mehemet Ali, Turkey and the Eastern Question 1831–41*

1   In 1831 a crisis occurred stemming from the Greek revolt against Turkey (see Section 3.3(b) 4) which was to end successfully for the Greeks in 1833. Mehemet Ali, nominally the Turkish governor of Egypt (though he was practically independent), had been promised a reward for helping the Sultan Mahmud against the Greeks, but had received nothing. He demanded Syria, but when Mahmud refused, Mehemet's son, Ibrahim Pasha, moved his troops into Syria. The Turks tried to drive them out but were soundly defeated at Konieh (December 1832). Ibrahim advanced towards Constantinople, the Turkish capital, whereupon Mahmud issued a general appeal for help. Since most of the powers were occupied with Belgium, the Tsar Nicholas I of Russia eagerly seized this opportunity for intervention in Turkey. A Russian fleet entered the Bosphorus, while Russian troops moved towards Constantinople, both ostensibly to defend the capital against Ibrahim (see Map 10.1 on p. 131).

2   Palmerston was dismayed at the Russian presence in Turkey; he suspected them of wanting to annex the European part of Turkey including Constantinople, so that they could control the Dardanelles, the exit from the Black Sea. Russian warships would be able to sail through the Straits at will, posing a serious threat to Britain's interests in the eastern Mediterranean and possibly even to India. His aim therefore was to end the conflict between Mahmud and Mehemet as quickly as possible, and so remove the Russians' excuse for intervention.

3   *Palmerston sent a British fleet* into the eastern Mediterranean, and Britain, France and Austria, all worried about Russian expansion, threatened and cajoled the Sultan into giving Syria to Mehemet. Ibrahim withdrew his troops from Turkey so that the Russians had no excuse for staying. However, the Tsar Nicholas, who was in a strong position, could not resist demanding a high price for his help. He forced Mahmud to sign *the Treaty of Unkiar Skelessi* (July 1833) by which Russia and Turkey agreed to give each other military help whenever necessary; Turkey would allow Russian warships free passage through the Dardanelles, and would close them to ships of every other country in wartime.

4   *This was a setback for Palmerston* and a diplomatic triumph for the Russians who would now be extremely powerful in the eastern Mediterranean; Turkey was reduced almost to a protectorate of Russia, dependent for survival on Russian military support. Palmerston fumed and fretted and was determined to destroy the Treaty of Unkiar Skelessi. However, Nicholas ignored all protests, and for six years no opportunity offered itself.

5   *Palmerston's chance came in 1839* when the Sultan, who had never intended to let Mehemet keep Syria, suddenly launched an invasion. Once again Ibrahim was called into action and yet again the Sultan's armies were decisively defeated. The earlier situation seemed about to repeat itself as Ibrahim moved towards Constantinople. The French complicated the situation by aiding and advising

Mehemet on military matters; they were hoping to build up their influence in Egypt to add to their recent capture of Algiers (1830) at the western end of the Mediterranean. The future seemed bleak for Turkey when Mahmud died (July 1839) to be succeeded by a 16-year-old boy.

6   *Palmerston this time was prepared*: he aimed to preserve Turkey as a reasonably strong state capable of standing up to Russian ambitions. Help for Turkey must be provided jointly by several European powers, not just by Russia alone. Another motive for wanting to bolster up Turkey, as Jasper Ridley (one of Palmerston's biographers) points out, was because Palmerston was afraid that 'the collapse of Turkey would lead to a scramble for the pieces which would trigger off a major European war'. He was also determined to frustrate the French, and he knew he could count on Russian support in that. Above all though, Palmerston hoped to use the situation in order to destroy the Treaty of Unkiar Skelessi. The first step towards all this was to curb Mehemet Ali, who, according to Palmerston, was 'an ignorant barbarian, a former waiter at a coffee shop', but who impressed some western ambassadors as courteous, witty and charming.

7   *Palmerston made most of the running*: in July 1840 he engineered an agreement in London between Britain, Russia, Austria and Prussia; France was not even consulted. The four powers offered Mehemet Ali terms: he could remain as hereditary ruler of Egypt and keep the southern half of Syria, provided he immediately made peace with Turkey. Though it was not an unreasonable offer, Mehemet rejected it, expecting French military help if the powers moved against him. A major European war seemed likely, and Franco-British relations, which had recently been harmonious over the settlement of Belgium, reached rock bottom. However, Palmerston was convinced that although the French premier, Adolphe Thiers, was in an aggressive mood, the cautious Louis Philippe would never risk taking on four other powers. He instructed the British ambassador in Paris to inform Thiers that 'if France begins a war, she will to a certainty lose her ships, colonies and commerce.. and that Mehemet Ali will just be chucked into the Nile'.

8   *Allied action against Mehemet Ali now went ahead*: a British and Austrian force captured his ports of Acre and Beirut, while a British fleet bombarded Alexandria (in Egypt). Louis Philippe knew that it would be madness for France to get involved, and Thiers was forced to resign. Mehemet had to accept harsher terms from the powers (this time including France). He was allowed to remain ruler of Egypt but had to return Syria to the Sultan. A further agreement known as *the Straits Convention* was signed in July 1841. By this, all the powers, including Russia, agreed that the entrance to the Black Sea should be closed to the warships of *all* nations while Turkey herself was at peace. This cancelled Russia's special advantage by the Treaty of Unkiar Skelessi; Nicholas made this concession in the hope of gaining British friendship.

9   This complex problem turned out to be probably *Palmerston's greatest triumph*: he had bolstered up Turkey so that there were no disagreements among the powers over who should take what; Russian expansion had been controlled and the routes to India safeguarded; French ambitions in the eastern Mediterranean had been thwarted – and all without a war. Palmerston's actions showed clearly that his major concern was to protect British interests even if it meant abandoning co-operation with constitutional France and working with the autocratic governments of Russia and Austria which he had opposed over Belgium, Spain and Portugal.

(d) China and the Opium War

1 *Early in 1839 a dispute arose between Britain and China* about the British import of opium from India into the Chinese port of Canton. British merchants had built up the opium trade into a highly profitable operation. The Chinese government claimed that opium smoking was ruining the health of the population, and banned the trade. They seized opium worth over a million pounds belonging to British merchants at Canton, and poured it into the sea. Tension increased when the British refused to hand over to the Chinese some British sailors who had killed a Chinaman in a drunken brawl. The reason given was that the Chinese used torture to extract confessions and therefore the British refused to accept the jurisdiction of Chinese courts.

2 *Palmerston demanded compensation for the opium* and guarantees that British merchants would be free from interference. The Chinese rejected both requests and Palmerston despatched a naval and military expedition to Canton. His aim was partly to defend British honour and win compensation, but more important, to force the Chinese to open up their vast market of 350 million people to more British trade (until now the British had only been allowed to trade at Canton). The fighting which followed is known as *the Opium War*.

3 The British fleet bombarded and captured Canton and had no difficulty in forcing the poorly led and equipped Chinese to sign an agreement based on Palmerston's demands. *The Treaty of Nanking* (signed in August 1842 by Peel's Conservative government after the Whig defeat) allowed the British to trade at five treaty ports (Canton, Shanghai, Amoy, Foochow and Ningpo), exempted British merchants from Chinese law, granted six million pounds compensation and leased the island of Hong Kong to Britain (until 1997). Other European powers were granted similar privileges.

4 *The Opium War seemed to be a success*, and a whole new and vast market seemed to be assured for British exports. However, there was to be more trouble later as the Chinese tried to reduce their concessions. In addition Palmerston was severely criticized in the Commons on the grounds that it was morally wrong to force Britain's will on a weak and defenceless country.

The Whig government fell in August 1841 and Palmerston was away from the Foreign Office for over five years. His policies had been triumphantly successful, especially during his last two years in office. Even the Conservative Disraeli wrote about his 'brilliant performances'; and according to Jasper Ridley (one of Palmerston's biographers), 'by 1841 the Palmerston legend was already firmly established'.

9.3 Conservative interlude 1841–6

The Conservative Prime Minister, Peel, allowed his Foreign Secretary, Lord Aberdeen, a fairly free hand. Aberdeen was much less aggressive and bombastic than Palmerston, and favoured a policy of calmness and conciliation whenever possible. He did not like the idea of Britain interfering in the internal affairs of other countries and withdrew the troops Palmerston had sent to Portugal. He settled peacefully a potentially dangerous dispute with the USA over its frontiers with Canada in Maine and Oregon. Much of Aberdeen's time and energy was spent trying to improve relations with France, which Palmerston had left in some disarray. He found he could work amicably with the new French minister, Francois Guizot, with whom he reached compromise agreements on policing the Atlantic (in a joint attempt to stamp out the slave trade) and on the establishment of a French protectorate over the Pacific island of Tahiti.

More troublesome was the affair of *the Spanish Marriages*. Louis Philippe was anxious for one of his sons to marry the young Queen Isabella of Spain. The British objected to this, suspicious that some kind of union might take place between France and Spain; this, plus the French occupation of Algiers, made the British nervous about the safety of Gibraltar. They suggested that Isabella (aged 11 in 1841) should marry a Saxe-Coburg prince (who would be friendly to Britain) or one of her own Spanish cousins (which would at least keep the French out). Early in 1846 an understanding was reached that Isabella should marry one of her cousins and Louis Philippe's son should marry Isabella's younger sister, but only after Isabella had had children, so that there would be little chance of the two crowns becoming united. However, nothing was put in writing, and it was at this stage in the negotiations that Peel's government fell because of the Corn Law crisis, and Palmerston returned to the Foreign Office (June 1846).

9.4 Palmerston at the Foreign Ministry again 1846–51

Palmerston was less successful at winning specific advantages for Britain during his second turn in office, and he was outmanoeuvred by Louis Philippe over the Spanish Marriages. However, incidents such as the Don Pacifico Affair and the visit of General Haynau, though empty triumphs in themselves, greatly added to Palmerston's popularity with the public.

(a) *The Spanish Marriages 1846*

● Palmerston had been thoroughly impatient with Aberdeen's delicate handling of this problem and was determined to settle it quickly. The French, deeply distrustful of him and expecting him to press the claim of the Saxe-Coburg prince (a cousin of Prince Albert), saw a chance to get revenge on Palmerston for the Mehemet Ali affair. Following French bribery of the Spanish Queen Mother, two weddings took place: Isabella married her cousin, the elderly Duke of Cadiz, who was rumoured to be sexually impotent, while her sister Luisa married the Duke of Montpensier, Louis Philippe's younger son.

● *This was a diplomatic defeat for Palmerston*: if Isabella had no children and Luisa became queen, Spanish and French interests would be closely united. Even Queen Victoria for once found herself in agreement with Palmerston and wrote to Louis Philippe accusing him of breaking the previous agreement. In the end though, the marriages did Louis Philippe no good: the recent co-operation between France and Britain was brought to an abrupt end, which gave great comfort to Russia and Austria. Isabella had children (though probably not her husband's), so that Montpensier was excluded from the Spanish throne, and in 1848 Louis Philippe himself was overthrown by a revolution.

(b) *1848: the year of revolutions*

1 During this momentous year (the year of the third Chartist petition), revolutions took place in many European countries, inspired by a mixture of liberalism and nationalism; for example:

- Louis Philippe was replaced by a republican government
- the Italians of Lombardy and Venetia tried to throw off Austrian rule
- the people of Hungary and Bohemia fought for more national freedom from Austria
- in Vienna, Chancellor Metternich was forced to flee.

2   *Palmerston's attitude showed his policy in all its contradictions.* He had some sympathy with all the revolutionary movements, particularly the Italians: 'I cannot regret the expulsion of the Austrians from Italy', he wrote; 'her rule was hateful to the Italians.' With his reputation as a friend of liberals and nationalists, he might have been expected to do all in his power to help the revolutionaries. *But British interests came first*: though he liked the idea of an independent united state of Italy, he wanted the tottering Austrian empire to survive as a check to Russian expansion. He was also worried in case the new French republic sent military help to the Italians, which could give the French too much influence in northern Italy.

3   Britain therefore took no direct action, though as usual there was plenty of verbal activity from Palmerston. He tried to persuade the Austrians to grant independence to Lombardy and Venetia before the French intervened; nothing came of it, and the French dithered so long about whether to send help, that the Austrians regained control of Italy. Eventually all the revolutions in Austria, Germany and Italy were brought under control, and all Palmerston could do was protest against the atrocities committed by the Austrians against the Hungarian rebels. He supported the Turks when they refused to hand over to the Austrians the Hungarian nationalist leader, Louis Kossuth, who had escaped to Constantinople; after British warships were despatched to the Bosphorus, the Austrians and Russians took no action.

4   A general war had been avoided and the balance of power preserved; but although Palmerston's support for Kossuth was popular with the British public, there can be no disguising the fact that Britain had made very little impact on the main course of events in 1848.

(c) *The Haynau incident (1850)*

In September 1850 the Austrian General Haynau came to Britain on an official visit. He was one of the generals responsible for putting down the revolutions in Italy and Hungary, where he had ordered numerous hangings and the flogging of women. While he was visiting Barclay and Perkins' Brewery in Southwark, some of the workmen, realizing who he was, set upon him and chased him through the streets. He took refuge in a public house and had to be rescued by police. Victoria demanded that an apology should be sent to the Austrians; Palmerston sent an official apology, but added that Haynau had been asking for trouble in coming to Britain in view of his unpopularity, and that he regarded Haynau as 'a great moral criminal' because of the atrocities he had committed. Palmerston showed the Queen a copy of the apology, but only after it had been sent. Victoria was furious with him, particularly since he had recently promised not to send any despatches before she had first read and approved them. It was obvious that if Palmerston continued to act without consulting the Queen, there would soon be a major showdown.

(d) *The Don Pacifico affair (1850)*

1   There was a long-standing dispute between King Otto of Greece, and Britain, France and Russia, arising from the refusal of the Greeks to pay even the interest

on the massive loans granted by these governments to help the newly independent Greece establish itself in 1832. The dispute came to a head when Don Pacifico, a Portuguese Jewish merchant and money-lender who lived in Athens, had his house burned down by an anti-Semitic mob. Don Pacifico had been born in Gibraltar and could therefore claim to be a British citizen; when the Greek government rejected his demand for £27 000 compensation, he wrote directly to Palmerston asking for British support.

2   Palmerston threatened force, but for a long time the Greeks ignored him. Early in 1850 a British fleet was in the eastern Mediterranean (protecting Kossuth); Palmerston decided to use it to frighten the Greeks into paying compensation. For a month British warships blockaded the Piraeus (the Port of Athens) and other main ports, seizing all Greek merchant ships. After a good deal of haggling, it was agreed that some compensation would be paid, though not the original sum demanded, which was far too high (Don Pacifico was actually paid £6550).

3   This was something of a success for Palmerston; British prestige abroad had been maintained, but his high-handedness and belligerence caused a first-rate political row. The French and Russians, who had agreed, along with Britain, to protect the new state of Greece, protested strongly that they ought to have been consulted. Queen Victoria, Prince Albert, the Conservatives and even some of his own cabinet thought Palmerston had gone too far. When it looked as though his opponents might force him to resign, he rose magnificently to the occasion with a brilliant speech lasting four and a half hours, delivered to a crowded House of Commons. He defended his entire foreign policy since 1830 and ended: 'as the Roman in days of old held himself free from indignity when he could say *Civis Romanus sum* (I am a Roman citizen), so also a British subject, in whatever land he may be, shall feel confident that the watchful eye and the strong arm of England will protect him against injustice and wrong'. The speech won Palmerston a comfortable vote of confidence (June 1850); but the blaze of popularity which followed, tended to obscure the fact that Britain had gained nothing from the affair except to annoy France, Austria and Russia, who claimed that Palmerston was nothing more than a bully, especially when dealing with weaker states.

The Don Pacifico Affair was one of several incidents which brought relations between Palmerston and Victoria and Albert to breaking point, and culminated in Palmerston's resignation.

(e) *The affair of Louis Napoleon and the downfall of Palmerston (1851)*

1   The breaking point between Queen and Foreign Minister came in 1851, and ironically it was concerned with affairs in France. Louis Napoleon Bonaparte, the nephew of Napoleon I, had been elected President of the French Republic in 1848 following the overthrow of Louis Philippe. On 2 December 1851, in a cleverly organized *coup d'état*, he had himself proclaimed President for the next ten years, and became virtually a dictator.

2   Palmerston approved of this, believing that a strong government would prevent France from falling under socialist control. Queen Victoria would have preferred to see Louis Philippe restored; both she and Russell (the Prime Minister) felt that Britain should remain strictly neutral and make no comment. However, Palmerston acted carelessly: without consulting the Queen or the cabinet, he told the French ambassador that he congratulated Louis Napoleon on his success.

3   This was the chance the Queen had been waiting for and she demanded that Palmerston should be sacked immediately. Russell, knowing that this time

Palmerston could expect very little support for his action (the British public was still suspicious of all Bonapartes and feared the worst a year later when Louis Napoleon had himself declared Emperor Napoleon III), asked for and received his resignation.

4   By resigning, Palmerston avoided a confrontation with Victoria and Albert, but left unsettled the question of who really controlled British foreign policy: was it the Foreign Secretary or was it the monarch, who by tradition usually had the last word in foreign affairs? Though he was furious at having to leave the Foreign Office, Palmerston agreed to go in order to avoid a public dispute with the Queen which might have damaged the monarchy. However, he blamed Russell for not standing by him; early in 1852 he and his supporters took great delight in voting with the Conservatives to bring down Russell's government. This brought in Lord Derby's short-lived Conservative government (February–December 1852), followed by Lord Aberdeen's coalition (a government made up of people from different political parties) which got Britain involved in the Crimean War (1854–6).

9.5 The final phase: Palmerston as Prime Minister 1855–65

Palmerston became Liberal Prime Minister in February 1855 after Aberdeen's coalition had failed to bring the war to a speedy conclusion. Except for one short period, Derby's second Conservative government (February 1858–June 1859), Palmerston remained Prime Minister until his death in October 1865. For the first year he was fully occupied with the Crimean War (see Chapter 10). After this came a second war with China, problems of Britain's attitude towards Italian and German unification, and a dispute with the USA which came close to involving Britain in the American Civil War (1861–5).

(a) *The second war with China 1857–60*

1   The Chinese had been reluctant to keep to the terms of the 1842 Treaty of Nanking and tried to keep out as many foreign merchants as possible; the authorities at the treaty ports regularly victimized Chinese merchants who traded with the British. To protect these friendly merchants, the British started granting British registration to Chinese vessels trading at Hong Kong, hoping that the Chinese would not dare interfere with ships flying the British flag. In 1856 the Chinese authorities in Canton seized a small ship called the *Arrow* which belonged to a Chinese pirate and had been robbing merchant ships off Canton. The *Arrow* had been registered as a British ship and was flying the British flag; consequently the British consul in Canton demanded the release of the crew and an apology for insulting the British flag. The Chinese released the crew but refused an apology, whereupon British warships from Hong Kong bombarded Canton, causing considerable damage.

2   Palmerston was placed in an awkward situation: since the *Arrow* was a pirate ship (and its British registration had expired) the Chinese had a good case; the British governor of Hong Kong who ordered the bombardment should have consulted Palmerston first. However, Palmerston felt obliged to support the British officials once they had taken their stand. *He had a double motive*: there was the need to

uphold British prestige and avenge the insult to the flag; more important, he was determined to force the Chinese to accept full-scale trade with Britain, whether they wanted it or not.

3   After winning a general election (in which the Liberal majority was increased) fought on the Chinese issue (March 1857), Palmerston felt justified in sending a strong expedition to press British claims. The French supported the British and together they captured Canton (1858) and Peking (1860), after which the Chinese agreed to all demands. Several more ports, including Tientsin, were opened to trade with western powers: foreign diplomatic representatives were to be allowed at Peking; the opium trade, instead of being banned, was to be regulated by the Chinese authorities.

4   *Palmerston had triumphed again* and his popularity rose to new heights; British merchants were delighted at the prospects of a trade expansion with the Far East; even foreign powers, for once, were happy with Palmerston, since they too hoped to take advantage of the opening-up of China. Again, however, as with the Opium War and the Don Pacifico Affair, Palmerston's actions can be questioned from a moral point of view. The 1856 bombardment of Canton was a breach of international law; the war itself was another example of Palmerston bullying a much weaker country.

(b) *Palmerston and Italian unification 1859–60*

1   Early in 1859 Italy was still divided into a number of separate states. Lombardy and Venetia in the north belonged to the Austrians; three small states, Parma, Modena and Tuscany, were ruled by Austrian dukes; the three largest states were independent: Piedmont (including the island of Sardinia) was ruled by King Victor Emmanuel and his Prime Minister, Count Cavour; the Papal States (including Rome) belonged to the Pope; the Kingdom of Naples (including the island of Sicily) was ruled by Francis II.

2   Italian nationalists wanted to free the northern states from Austrian domination, and Cavour hoped to bring about a united Italy under Piedmontese leadership, with a democratic constitution similar to Britain's. In 1859 the Piedmontese, with considerable military help from Napoleon III, attacked the Austrians, defeated them twice (at Magenta and Solferino) and captured Lombardy. The French pulled out of the operation before Venetia had been captured, but Parma, Modena and Tuscany announced their intention of uniting with Piedmont. The Austrians immediately rushed more troops into Venetia with the clear intention of preventing the union.

3   *At this point Palmerston acted*: he announced that Britain would not allow armed intervention by the Austrians; 'the people of the Duchies have as good a right to change their rulers as the people of England, France, Belgium and Sweden', he claimed. The Austrians decided against intervention and the Duchies remained with Piedmont.

4   The next step towards Italian unification began in 1860 when the nationalist leader Giuseppe Garibaldi led an armed force by sea from Genoa (in Piedmont) and captured Sicily from the unpopular king of Naples. Again the British were able to help: British warships protected Garibaldi's invasion force as it went ashore in Sicily. Later they were in the vicinity as Garibaldi's expedition crossed the Straits of Messina from Sicily to the mainland. Napoleon III had threatened to stop him but dared not make a move against the British fleet. Consequently Garibaldi captured mainland Naples which soon united with Piedmont to form the Kingdom of Italy; all these changes were recognized as legal by the British government.

5   *As usual Palmerston's motives were mixed*: both he and Russell, as well as British
    public opinion as a whole (apart from Victoria and Albert), were sympathetic
    towards Italian nationalism and unification. They disapproved of Austria's
    repressive rule in northern Italy and of the atrocious government in Naples which
    Gladstone had described after a visit there in 1851 as 'the negation of God'. But as
    usual there was more to it than that: if there was to be a new state of Italy,
    Palmerston wanted to make sure it would be grateful and friendly to Britain. This
    would be to Britain's advantage in the Mediterranean and a valuable
    counterbalance to French hostility in that area. Friendship might also lead to a
    lowering of Italian tariffs against British goods, which would be of great benefit to
    British merchants.

6   Palmerston's Italian policy turned out to be his last great success in foreign affairs.
    He and Russell won the reputation as friends of the new Italy, whose unification
    had been made possible because Britain had restrained other powers from
    intervening. British sea-power had enabled her to make this contribution.

(c) *Britain and the American Civil War 1861–5*

1   In 1861 war broke out between the North and South of the USA, partly over the
    question of slavery (which existed mostly in the South) and partly over whether
    states had the right to leave the Union (which the South was trying to do). Public
    opinion in Britain was divided in sympathy: middle and working classes, who were
    very much against slavery, tended to sympathize with the North, especially after
    President Lincoln promised to abolish slavery throughout the USA (1863).
    However, in political circles there was much support for the South (the
    Confederates) on the grounds that all peoples should have the right to decide who
    they wished to be ruled by.

2   With sympathies so divided, Palmerston and Russell announced that Britain would
    remain strictly neutral. However, both North and South hoped to attract British
    help. Two incidents occurred, both involving ships – the *Trent* and the *Alabama* –
    which caused tension between Britain and the North.

3   *The Trent Incident* took place in November 1861 when two Confederate agents,
    Mason and Slidell, were on their way to Europe on board the *Trent*, a British ship,
    to try and whip up support for the South. A Northern cruiser stopped the *Trent*,
    and the agents were seized and taken to Boston. This was a breach of international
    law and an insult to the British flag, which must be avenged. Palmerston wrote a
    very strongly worded protest demanding an apology and the release of Mason and
    Slidell; extra troops were dispatched to Canada, and feelings ran high on both
    sides. Fortunately Prince Albert persuaded Palmerston to tone down some of his
    more insulting phrases, and Lincoln was sensible enough to give way. The agents
    eventually arrived in Britain, but had no success with their mission. Prince Albert
    probably deserves much of the credit for keeping Britain out of the war. It was to
    be his last contribution to politics; he died from typhoid in December 1861 at the
    early age of 42.

4   *The Alabama Incident (1862)* could have been avoided if Palmerston or Russell
    had acted promptly. The South, attempting to build up a navy, had ordered a
    number of warships from British yards. The first one sailed from Liverpool in
    March 1862 disguised as a merchant ship, but eventually became the cruiser
    Florida which proceeded to attack Northern merchant ships. A second ship
    destined to become the *Alabama* was being built at Birkenhead; Lincoln's
    government protested that this was a breach of the 1819 Foreign Enlistment Act

which forbade the building and equipping in Britain of military vessels meant for either side in a war in which Britain was neutral. Although the Northern protest was reasonable, Russell delayed so long before ordering the vessel to be detained, that she slipped out of the Mersey, and for the next two years inflicted severe damage on Northern merchant shipping. The North blamed the British government and claimed compensation; Russell denied all responsibility and refused to pay compensation or to allow the matter to go to arbitration. However, he later had three further ships detained, so avoiding any more friction with the North. (Later still, after the North had won the war, Gladstone accepted arbitration – see Section 13.4(b).)

5   Meanwhile the Northern blockade of Confederate ports was preventing exports of raw cotton from reaching the Lancashire textile industry. During 1862 *the cotton famine reached its worst*, throwing over half a million people out of work in Britain's most important export industry. The situation only eased in the spring of 1863, as alternative supplies of cotton began to arrive from Egypt.

In the spring of 1863 the 'two dreadful old men', as Queen Victoria called Palmerston and Russell, were still handling foreign affairs with some success. They had made a contribution to Italian unification, and though they had bungled the *Alabama* incident, they had at least kept Britain out of the American Civil War. But in the last two years of his government, Palmerston suffered two failures – over the Polish revolution and the affair of Schleswig-Holstein. Palmerston's inept handling of these two situations was described by Lord Derby, a leading Conservative, as a policy of 'meddle and muddle'.

(d) *Palmerston and Poland 1863*

●   Poland was in an unfortunate situation; it had once been an independent state, but between 1772 and 1795 it had been divided up between Russia, Austria and Prussia who all seized large areas for themselves. Like the Italians, the Poles looked forward to the day when they could escape from foreign rule and have a united Poland; but there was little chance of this happening, since the Poles, unlike the Italians, had three lots of foreigners to expel.

●   In 1863 the Poles in Russia broke out in revolution, and Russian troops were moved in to crush the rising. Bismarck (the Minister-President of Prussia) gave diplomatic support to the Russians, in case the outbreak should spread to the Polish areas of Prussia.

●   Palmerston and Napoleon III protested to the Tsar about his brutal treatment of the rebels, and hinted at some action to support the Poles. However, when Napoleon III proposed a European congress, Palmerston rejected the idea because he suspected Napoleon's motives. No help of any sort arrived and the Poles were quelled with great cruelty.

●   *This was Palmerston's first obvious failure in foreign affairs* and was a striking contrast to his role in helping the Italian nationalists. In Italy, the presence of the British fleet was enough to warn off the Austrians; the Russians were already in Poland, and only a major military effort by Britain and France could have driven them out. Palmerston and Russell knew from the beginning that such action was out of the question and should not have made threats which they could not carry out. Their actions only encouraged the Poles to resist longer than was sensible and left them feeling distinctly let down. Britain had been clearly outmanoeuvred by the Tsar, and Napoleon III, who should have been treated as an ally, was mortally offended. All in all, British prestige took a severe knock.

(e) *Palmerston, Bismarck and Schleswig-Holstein 1863–4*

1   In 1863 a long-standing dispute came to a head over whether the Duchies of Schleswig-Holstein should belong to Denmark or remain independent (see Map 3.1 on p. 33). By *the Treaty of London (1852)* the great powers had decided that the Duchies should remain as independent units, but the new king of Denmark, Christian IX, who also happened to be Duke of Schleswig-Holstein, was under pressure from Danish public opinion to incorporate the Duchies into Denmark. A majority of the people of Holstein were German-speaking, and German nationalists were strongly opposed to any move which would take Germans into Denmark. In November 1863 Christian announced the incorporation of Schleswig, though this was a breach of the 1852 treaty. Bismarck, who had ambitions of extending Prussian control over the whole of North Germany, saw this as an opportunity to take Schleswig-Holstein for Prussia. He threatened military action unless the Danes dropped their claims; he insisted that the 1852 agreement should be kept, but naturally made no mention of his own designs on the Duchies.

2   *Palmerston decided that Britain must support Denmark.* Again there was the usual mixture of motives: British public opinion was strongly pro-Danish; the Prince of Wales had recently married Princess Alexandra of Denmark, which led the Danes to expect British help. Palmerston was also rightly suspicious of Bismarck: 'what is at the bottom of the German design is the dream of a German Fleet and the wish to get Kiel as a German seaport'. A strong Denmark would increase British influence in Northern Europe.

3   Palmerston therefore told parliament that if any state attacked Denmark, 'those who made the attempt would find that it would not be Denmark alone with which they would have to contend'. This was intended to frighten Bismarck off and encourage the Danes.

4   Bismarck, who had Austrian support, guessed that Palmerston was bluffing and that Britain would need French help, which they were unlikely to get after Palmerston's abrupt rejection of Napoleon III's proposal for a European congress. In February 1864 a joint Prussian and Austrian force invaded the Duchies; but when the Danes appealed urgently for British help, the cabinet decided not to risk involvement in a major war against both Prussia and Austria.

5   The Danes had no alternative but to surrender (July 1864). Bismarck dropped the pretence that the Prussian action had been taken to uphold the 1852 treaty, and the two Duchies were handed over to Prussia and Austria.

6   *Palmerston had failed again*: he had seriously underestimated the astuteness of Bismarck and the growing threat of the Prussian army; this led him to make threats which Britain could not carry out with sea-power alone. At the same time he refused to consider joint military action with the French in case Napoleon seized the Rhineland. From the beginning he had been supporting a state which was in the wrong; if Britain had insisted on a Danish withdrawal from the Duchies, there would have been no treaty violation, and Bismarck would have had no excuse for the invasion. British encouragement of the Danes had played right into Bismarck's hands.

Palmerston died in October 1865 after catching a chill. On the whole he had been remarkably successful; only in the last couple of years did he seem to be getting out of touch with important developments. He failed to see that Bismarck and not Napoleon III was likely to be the main threat to the balance of power, and continued acting as though Britain was still the dominant power in Europe, as she had been immediately after 1815. But circumstances were changing: in less than six years after Palmerstons's death, the Prussians had defeated both the Austrians and the French, Napoleon III was a refugee in England, and Bismarck had united Germany. In all these highly important events British influence was nil. The balance of power had shifted decisively, and not in Britain's favour.

Questions

1 Palmerston and the reactions to his foreign policies
Study Sources A to G and then answer the questions which follow.

Source A

Extracts from speeches in the House of Commons by Lord Palmerston, 1848–9

The principle on which I have thought the foreign affairs of this country ought to be conducted is, the principle of maintaining peace and friendly understanding with all nations, as long as it was possible to do so consistently with a due regard for the interest, the honour, and the dignity of this country. *My endeavours have been to preserve peace. All the governments of which I have had the honour to be a member, have succeeded in accomplishing that object* . . .

We have a deep interest in the preservation of peace because we are desirous to carry on with advantage those peaceful relations of trade that we know must be injured by the interruption of our friendly relations with other countries. On the other hand it is essential for the protection of that commerce to which we attach so much importance, that it should be well understood by every nation on the face of the earth that we do not intend to submit to wrong, and that the maintenance of peace on our part is subject to the indispensable condition that all countries shall respect our honour and our dignity, and shall not inflict any injury upon our interests. . . . At the same time I am quite ready to admit that interference ought not to be carried on to the extent of endangering our relations with other countries

Source: quoted in D. Holman (ed.), *Earlier Nineteenth Century 1783–1867*, Hutchinson, 1965; and F. E. Huggett, *What They've Said about Nineteenth Century Statesmen*, Oxford, 1972.

Source B

A letter by Lord Shaftesbury, the Tory humanitarian social reformer, written in 1876

The institution of a true and vigorous foreign policy suited to the honour and position of the Kingdom of England was one of Lord Palmerston's guiding principles. . . . Vigorous assertion of this principle in the face of very hostile and sensitive powers, was often misinterpreted as a readiness for war, nay even as recklessness. . . . From war, I believe, he shrank with horror; but he was strongly of the opinion that the best way to avoid it was to speak out boldly, and ever be prepared to meet the emergency. Both in private and in public life he was of a very gentle and forgiving spirit. There might be, but very rarely, but now and then little bursts of irritation, but they soon passed away. Of public resentments he had no memory at all. In all my experience I have not seen any man so kind to all alike, so delicate, tender and considerate . . .

Source: quoted in Jasper Ridley, *Lord Palmerston*, Constable, 1970.

Article in The Times, *on the death of Palmerston, 19 October 1865*

One of the most popular statesmen, one of the kindliest gentlemen, and one of the truest Englishmen that ever filled the office of Premier, is today lost to the country. The news of Lord Palmerston's death will be received in every home throughout these islands, from the palace to the cottage, with a feeling like that of personal bereavement. The secret of his popularity was his boundless sympathy with all classes of his countrymen. Nor was his kindness and friendliness merely superficial ...

Others may advise Her Majesty with equal wisdom and sway the House of Commons with equal or greater eloquence; but his place in the hearts of the people will not be filled so easily. His name will long be connected in the minds of Englishmen with an era of unbroken peace and unparalleled prosperity.

Source: *The Times*, 19 October 1865.

The opinion of Talleyrand, a French statesman who was ambassador to Britain from 1830 to 1834

Lord Palmerston is certainly one of the ablest statesmen I have ever met with in all my official career. He possesses indefatigable energy, and iron constitution, inexhaustible mental resources and great facility of speech in Parliament. ... There is one point in his character, however, which to my mind, entirely outweighs all these advantages, and would prevent his being considered in the light of a real statesman – he allows his passions to influence him in public affairs, to the extent of sometimes sacrificing the greatest interests to his personal feelings; nearly every political question resolves itself with him into a personal one; and whilst seeming to defend the interests of his country, it is nearly always those of his hatred or revenge that he is serving. He is very skilful in hiding this secret motive, under what I might call patriotic appearances.

Source: quoted in F. E. Huggett, *What They've Said about Nineteenth Century Statesmen*, Oxford, 1972.

A private and confidential letter from Prince Albert to Lord John Russell, the Prime Minister, written in 1850

The Queen has two distinct complaints to bring against Lord Palmerston. ... First, his policy has generally had the effect that England is universally detested, mistrusted and treated with insult even by the smallest powers. There is not a sovereign or a government who do not consider Lord Palmerston as a personal enemy; there is not a people who is not convinced that their internal disagreements and sufferings are stirred up by England, in order to keep them weak and unable in consequence to compete with the English manufacturers. Since 1846 England has not had a single success [in foreign affairs] ...

Secondly, as a minister the sovereign has a right to demand from him that she should be made thoroughly acquainted with the whole object and tendency of the policy to which her consent is required, and, having given that consent, that the policy is not altered from the original line, that important steps are not concealed from her and her name used without her sanction. In all these respects Lord Palmerston has failed towards her. . . . Besides which he has let it appear in public as if the sovereign's negligence in attending to papers sent to her caused delays and complications.

Source: quoted in D. Holman (ed.), *Earlier Nineteenth Century 1783–1867*, Hutchinson, 1965.

Source: quoted in D. Holman (ed.), *Earlier Nineteenth Century 1783–1867*, Hutchinson, 1965.

Source F

A private note written by Palmerston to Sir George Bonham, the Governor of Hong Kong, 29 September 1850

The Time is fast coming when we shall be obliged to strike another Blow in China. These half-civilised governments such as those of China, Portugal, Spanish America, all require a dressing every eight or ten years to keep them in order. Their minds are too shallow to receive an impression that will last longer than some such period, and a warning is of little use. They care little for words and they must not only see the Stick but actually feel it on their shoulders before they yield to that only argument which to them brings conviction.

Source: quoted in W. C. Costin, *Great Britain and China, 1833–1860*, Oxford, 1937.

Source G

Some information from a modern historian about Palmerston's relations with China

Following the Opium War with China (1839) in which Britain forced the Chinese to open to her, five ports, relations between the two remained strained. In 1856 the British at Hong Kong became involved in a dispute with the Chinese at Canton over a vessel built and owned by Chinese merchants and wrongly flying the British flag as a screen for acts of piracy. The British demanded an apology from the Governor of Canton for his seizure of the pirates aboard the *Arrow*, and when this was refused, the British bombarded the city. A state of war with China resulted . . .

Lord Derby brought forward a motion in the House of Lords strongly condemning the government's Chinese policy. . . . When the debate ended in the defeat of the government by 16 votes, Palmerston ordered Parliament to be dissolved. In the following general election Palmerston and the Liberals were returned triumphantly to power with a majority of 70. He had opened his address to his electors at Tiverton by a volley of violent phrases: the Chinese governor of Canton was 'an insolent barbarian who had violated the British flag, and planned the destruction of British subjects by murder, assassination and poison'. This address clearly suited the electors of the day and the victor flatly refused to change his policy by one iota. The disgraceful war against the Chinese continued.

Source: R. W. Seton-Watson, *Britain in Europe 1789–1914*, Cambridge, 1955.

(a) In 1848 Lord Palmerston said '*My endeavours have been to preserve peace. All the governments of which I have had the honour to be a member, have succeeded in accomplishing that object*' (Source A). To what extent do the Sources and the information in Chapter 9 support the truth of Palmerston's statement?   (7 marks)

(b) (i)   In what ways could Palmerston's note (Source F) be taken as a contradiction of what he says in Source A?   (5 marks)

    (ii) What explanations can you offer for any apparent contradictions?

                      (4 marks)

(c) Compare and contrast Sources B, C, D and E in their interpretations of Palmerston's career.   (12 marks)

(d) What are the advantages and disadvantages of Sources A to F for the historian trying to make a balanced assessment of Palmerston's career?   (12 marks)

                      (Total 40 marks)

2   Consider the view that 'Palmerston's influence on British foreign policy served British interests less effectively in the period 1846–65 than in the period 1830–41'.

                      [AEB]

The Crimean War 1854–56

Summary of events

The Crimean War involved Britain, France, Turkey (also known as the Ottoman Empire) and Piedmont all fighting Russia. It was caused partly by *the Eastern Question* and partly by *the ambitions of Napoleon III of France which brought him into conflict with the Tsar Nicholas I of Russia.*

A joint allied force arrived in the Crimea (September 1854) with the object of capturing Sevastopol, the great Russian naval base. The allies, badly organized and ill-equipped, made heavy weather of the campaign, though they managed to win the three major battles that were fought: *the crossing of the River Alma* (September 1854), *Balaclava* (October), which included the notorious Charge of the Light Brigade, and *Inkerman* (November). Sevastopol eventually fell (September 1855) and the new Russian Tsar, Alexander II, faced with pressing financial and social problems, was prepared to end hostilities. After long negotiations *the Treaty of Paris* was signed in March 1856. At the time both Britain and France were highly satisified with the peace terms, but as it turned out, the war had not solved the Eastern Question permanently; 20 years later it was to flare up again (see Section 14.4).

Apart from its military and political importance, the Crimean War was remarkable for two other reasons. For the first time, a newspaper correspondent, William Howard Russell of *The Times*, sent back detailed reports so that the British public was better informed than ever before about what was happening on the spot. Partly because of Russell's vivid descriptions of the disgraceful conditions, *Florence Nightingale* and her team of nurses went out to try to bring some order to the chaos in the base hospitals where the wounded were looked after.

Recently, historian Andrew Lambert put forward a new interpretation of the Crimean War in a book published in 1990 (*The Crimean War: British Grand Strategy Against Russia, 1853–56*, Manchester University Press). He points out that the term 'Crimean War' is misleading; it wasn't actually used at the time and only came to be applied in the 1890s. He argues that the campaign in the Crimea was only one part of a much wider struggle against Russia which involved other campaigns in Asia Minor, the White Sea, the Baltic and the Pacific. Events in the Crimea attracted most attention among contemporaries, and so historians have tended to focus on that campaign and ignore the other areas of fighting.

10.1 What caused the war?

There have been differing opinions over the years about exactly why the war broke out. Some historians believe that Nicholas I of Russia deliberately provoked a war with Turkey so that he could destroy the Ottoman Empire and seize a large slice of the Balkans for Russia. Others believe that none of the countries involved really wanted a war and that they all drifted into it because of a series of misunderstandings. The second view, held by such historians as A. J. P. Taylor and M. S. Anderson, is the more widely accepted one today. Several issues and rivalries were at stake:

(a) *The basic hostility was between Russia and Turkey over the Eastern Question*

Section 3.3(b) 4) explained how the Turkish Empire, weak and badly governed, was in decline. Regarded by other states as 'the Sick Man of Europe', it was expected to fall apart in the near future. The Russians wanted to profit from this situation as much as possible; they were handicapped militarily and commercially by the fact that most of their ports were ice-bound for many months of the year, while ships sailing to and from the ice-free Black Sea ports, could, in wartime, be prevented by the Turks from passing through the Bosphorus and the Dardanelles, the two narrow straits which form the outlet from the Black Sea (see Map 10.1). If the Russians could gain influence in the Balkans down as far as Constantinople, it would enable them to control the Straits. In 1833 the Treaty of Unkiar Skelessi had given the Russians much of what they wanted, but their advantage had been cancelled out by the Straits Convention of 1841 (see Section 9.2(c)).

By 1852 the Turks had had no success in reorganizing or strengthening their Empire, and experienced observers were convinced that it would collapse shortly. The British ambassador at Constantinople, Stratford Canning, an admirer of the Turks, resigned in 1852, believing that 'the Turkish Empire is evidently hastening to its dissolution'. There was also the question of religion: the Russians, who were Greek Orthodox Christians, saw themselves as the protectors of the Christian inhabitants of Turkey (in the Balkans and Armenia) against the cruelties of the Muslim Turks.

(b) *The Russians seem to have been torn between two possibilities:*

● To divide the outlying provinces of Turkey up between themselves (taking parts of the Balkans) and Britain (taking Egypt and Crete). Nicholas had suggested this during a visit to Britain in 1844. However, the drawback was that other powers, Austria and France, might also want a share.
● To try and preserve the Turkish Empire in its weak state in the hope that they, the Russians, would be able to exercise close control over the government at Constantinople; this would reduce the influence of other states to a minimum.

Russian indecision explains why there has been disagreement about their real intentions; A. J. P. Taylor believed that by 1852 the Russians had decided on the second policy. Either way there was bound to be friction between Russia and Turkey.

(c) *Napoleon III of France starts the crisis which leads on to war*

Having recently become Emperor, Napoleon needed a success in foreign affairs and was eager to win the support of French Roman Catholics. In the mid eighteenth cen-

Map 10.1   The Eastern Question and the Crimean War

tury, the Sultan had granted French Roman Catholic monks the right to look after *the Holy Places* in Palestine. These included the Church of the Nativity and the Grotto of the Holy Manger in Bethlehem, and two churches in Jerusalem, all of which were held sacred by Christians. The republican government which came to power in France in 1793 was hostile to Catholics and withdrew its support from the monks. Gradually Greek Orthodox monks had taken over control of the Holy Places, and it was this situation which gave Napoleon his chance to interfere. He demanded that the Sultan should grant the privilege of guarding the Holy Places solely to the French monks. After the French ambassador had sailed through the Dardanelles in a 90-gun warship on his way back to Constaninople, the Sultan gave way to the French demands (1852).

(d) *Tsar Nicholas fears growing French influence in Turkey*

Nicholas was now afraid that the French might soon rival Russian influence in Turkey.

He sent Prince Menschikoff to Constantinople to demand that the rights of the Greek Orthodox monks should be maintained, and in addition, that the Tsar should be recognized as the protector of all Christians living in the Turkish Empire. If this were allowed it would give the Russians a permanent excuse to interfere in Turkish affairs. The Sultan restored the privileges to the Orthodox monks, but rejected Menschikoff's further demands (May 1853), although the Russians were threatening to invade the Turkish provinces of Moldavia and Wallachia.

(e) *The British distrust Russia's intentions*

The British government suspected, probably wrongly, that the Russians were plotting the destruction of the Turkish Empire, and they hated the idea that Russian warships might be able to come and go through the Dardanelles as they pleased. It was widely believed that Russian influence in Afghanistan was the first step in an attempt to oust the British from control of India. After Russian troops had helped the Austrians to suppress the 1848 Hungarian revolution, British public opinion became violently anti-Russian. However, Lord Aberdeen's coalition government was divided about what line to take:

● Palmerston (who was Home Secretary) and Russell wanted to stand up to the Russians; Russell was convinced that 'the question must be decided by war, and if we do not stop the Russians on the Danube we shall have to stop them on the Indus' (a river in northern India close to the frontier with Afghanistan). Andrew Lambert suggests that Palmerston thought Russia (along with the USA) was likely to become a serious rival to Britain in the league table of the world's most powerful nations, and he saw the situation as a chance to defeat Russia and weaken her so much that her challenge to British interests would be delayed for many years.

● Aberdeen was more cautious: he disliked the idea of supporting the Turks, who often persecuted Christians, against the Christian Russians. He believed the problems could be solved by negotiations; his attitude probably gave Nicholas the impression that Britain would not support Turkey if he were to step up Russian pressure. However, Aberdeen, influenced by Palmerston and Russell, and by British public opinion and the press, agreed to send a naval force to Besika Bay just outside the Dardanelles (June 1853). It was soon joined by a French force.

(f) *Events escalate towards war*

1　Nicholas was not impressed by this British and French action and thought it was all bluff. Having threatened Turkey, he now felt the threats must be carried out. Confident of support from Austria and Prussia, he sent troops to occupy Moldavia and Wallachia (July 1853), though they made no further moves towards Constantinople. Palmerston blamed Aberdeen for the Russian occupations, believing that if the British and French fleets had sailed into the Black Sea as he had proposed, instead of remaining outside the Dardanelles, the Russians would not have dared to violate Turkish territory.

2　Palmerston wanted the British fleet to move into the Black Sea and arrest Russian warships which could be held hostage until Russian forces withdrew from Moldavia and Wallachia. Aberdeen rejected this idea and the British cabinet was so divided that no decisive action was taken either to warn the Russians off or to promise support to the Turks.

3　The Austrians, also suspicious of Russian intentions around the Danube, organized a conference in Vienna to find a solution. Attended by Prussians, French and British, the conference produced proposals known as *the Vienna Note*. It was suggested that the Sultan should make a few concessions to the Tsar, and should consult both Russians and French about his policy towards the Christians. Nicholas, now realizing that help from Austria and Prussia was unlikely, accepted the proposals, but the Turks rejected them, thinking that Nicholas was weakening.

4   Nicholas met Francis Joseph, the Austrian Emperor, and Frederick William IV of Prussia, in a final attempt to win support, but the most they could agree was to remain neutral if war broke out. However, the British and French, who knew of the meetings but not what had been decided, thought that the three monarchs had hatched a new plot to divide the Turkish Empire up between the three of them. Consequently on 8 October 1853, the British government ordered the fleet to Constantinople, where it was joined by French warships.

5   The Sultan, feeling certain of British and French support, had already declared war on Russia on 4 October, though Stratford Canning (now Lord Stratford de Redcliffe and back as British ambassador to Turkey) persuaded the Turks to take no action for the time being.

6   When the British and French fleets approached Constantinople, the Turks could restrain themselves no longer; on 23 October their troops crossed the Danube and attacked the Russians in Wallachia. The Russians replied by attacking and sinking part of the Turkish fleet near Sinope on the Black Sea (30 November). Though this was a justifiable action since war had been declared, British public opinion regarded it as a 'massacre', and pressure intensified on the government to declare war on Russia.

7   The British government still dithered about what to do next and it was Napoloeon who took the lead by sending the French fleet into the Black Sea. This forced Aberdeen to order the British fleet to follow (January 1854). Still there was no declaration of war: the allies were there to protect Turkish shipping.

8   Britain and France made one last effort to avoid all-out war: in February they sent Nicholas an ultimatum demanding the withdrawal of Russian troops from Moldavia and Wallachia. When this was ignored, the two western allies declared war on Russia (March).

M. S. Anderson sums up the causes clearly: the war 'was thus the outcome of a series of misjudgements, misunderstandings and blunders, of stupidity, pride and obstinacy rather than of ill will'. A. J. P. Taylor makes the point that all the participants got themselves into situations from which they could not retreat without their prestige being seriously damaged, and that the war was caused by fear and suspicion of each other rather than by conscious aggression towards each other. The British government must take its share of the responsibility for not taking a tougher attitude towards the Russians much earlier, which might have dissuaded Nicholas from sending his troops into Turkey; once committed to the occupation of Moldavia and Wallachia, the Russians could hardly withdraw without seeming to climb down. Governments are usually blamed for involving countries in war, but on this occasion, Aberdeen did all he could to keep Britain out of it; it was the pressure of public opinion expressed through influential newspapers like *The Times* that pushed the British government into action.

10.2 Events in the war

(a) *The Russians withdraw*

The British military expedition commanded by the 66-year-old Lord Raglan, a veteran of the Peninsular War, arrived at Gallipoli and Scutari together with the French, in May 1854. Their objective was to protect Constantinople and to help the Turks drive the Russians from the occupied provinces. As the allied forces moved towards Varna, the Russians unexpectedly withdrew from Moldavia and Wallachia (August). This was not simply through fear of the approaching allied forces but also because:

● They were finding it difficult to maintain their position against Turkish attacks.
● The Austrians, afraid that their interests would be threatened by Russian control of the Danube, threatened to declare war on the Russians unless they withdrew.

The Russian withdrawal took the wind out of the allies' sails, since their objective had been achieved without a shot being fired. As Taylor put it: 'they were thus faced with the problem – how to check an aggressive power when it is not being aggressive?' The governments decided that having progressed so far, a blow of some sort should be struck at the Russians. It was decided that the expedition should sail across the Black Sea from Varna to the Crimean peninsula to capture the naval base of Sevastopol. This, it was hoped, would destroy Russian power in the Black Sea, and make life easier for Turkish shipping.

(b) *British and French successes*

The 60 000 strong allied force (30 000 French, 26 000 British and 4000 Turks) landed at Eupatoria to the north of Sevastopol, and in spite of numerous problems, it had some successes:

1 Faced by a Russian army of about 40 000, *the allies managed to force their way across the River Alma* (20 September) and advanced towards Sevastopol. Instead of attacking the city immediately, they marched round it and set up a base at Balaclava, to the south, which was thought to be a good harbour. This would enable supplies to be brought in so that the allies could lay siege to Sevastopol.
2 *The Battle of Balaclava* (25 October) was fought when the Russians launched a surprise attack in an attempt to push the invaders into the sea. The British held off the attack, and the troops distinguished themselves with great bravery, particularly the cavalry. The 'thin red line' of the Heavy Brigade delayed the Russian advance until reinforcements arrived; more famous was 'the Charge of the Light Brigade', led by Lord Cardigan. This was a courageous but mistaken attack on some Russian heavy artillery which achieved nothing and was extremely costly – 113 men were killed and 134 wounded out of 673.
3 A second Russian attack under cover of fog was driven off at *Inkerman* (5 November). Again the British and French troops acquitted themselves impressively; though they lost 775 men killed, they inflicted four times that number of deaths on the Russians and took many prisoners.

However, it was almost a year before the allied objective was achieved and Sevastopol fell (September 1855). In the meantime the troops had to endure the most appalling conditions during the severe winter of 1854–5.

(c) *Weaknesses in the British military system*

By the end of 1854 it was clear that *many mistakes had been made and that there were serious shortcomings in the British military system*, some of which were revealed by William Howard Russell, *The Times* war correspondent:

Illus. 10.1 British troops landing in the Crimea to take part in the siege of Sevastopol

- There were disagreements between the British and French commanders, the most serious of which was over what to do immediately after the crossing of the Alma. Raglan wanted to advance and make a swift attack on the north side of Sevastopol, but his French counterpart, St Arnaud, refused on the grounds that they lacked sufficient troops for a frontal attack. While the armies were marching round to the south of the city, the Russian engineer Totleben seized his chance to strengthen its fortifications. Whereas an immediate attack would have had an excellent chance of success, the delay probably added months to the campaign. Balaclava was a bad choice for a base – its harbour was too small and it was served by primitive roads which Raglan did nothing to improve, so that they became almost impassable in the winter.
- The officer class was less efficient that it might have been because of the practice of selling commissions; wealth rather than ability was what counted. A prime example of incompetence was the Charge of the Light Brigade; although the cavalry performed brilliantly, they charged up the wrong valley, thanks to a badly worded order from Raglan and a less than intelligent response from Lords Cardigan and Lucan. Military organization matched the poor leadership. There had been hardly any modernization or improvement in the army since the Battle of Waterloo 40 years earlier. The troops were poorly equipped, poorly trained and badly paid. In its desire to save money, the government refused Raglan's request for a special corps to handle food and other supplies and transport; thus the army was constantly short of food, clothing and ammunition. In the winter blizzards of 1854–5, the troops were still wearing the summer uniforms they had arrived in; they were completely unprepared for a winter campaign.
- Medical arrangements were grim: the wounded and sick had to endure a nightmare journey across the Black Sea to the base hospitals at Scutari. The hospitals were badly

organized and had no properly trained nursing staff. There was a chronic shortage of beds, dressings, bandages, soap, food and drugs. Many patients had to be left lying on the bare floor, and sanitation was non-existent. More people died from dysentery and cholera than from wounds sustained in battle.

(d) *Palmerston takes over*

Public opinion became increasingly critical of the government for its incompetent handling of the war. In February 1855 Aberdeen resigned and Palmerston became Prime Minister for the first time. The public expected great things from the new leader, and the situation began to improve as soon as he took office. However, this was not all Palmerston's doing. Florence Nightingale and her team of trained nurses had already begun to reorganize the Scutari hospitals, reducing the death-rate and improving morale. Reinforcements and adequate supplies were arriving and a decent road had been built from the harbour at Balaclava to the trenches around Sevastopol. *Palmerston's contribution was to*:

● send out a 'sanitary commission' which greatly improved conditions both at Scutari and in the Crimea;
● set up a special transport department which largely solved the problem of supply;
● sack some of the more inefficient administrators in the Crimea – what he called 'that knot of Incapables who have been the direct cause of the disability and deaths of thousands of our brave men'.

(e) *The fall of Sevastopol and the end of the war*

Gradually, as the allies brought in reinforcements, solved the supply problems, and even constructed a light railway from Balaclava harbour to the trenches, the siege tightened around Sevastopol. Even so, several assaults during the summer of 1855 failed, and it was not until September that Sevastopol was captured. Some sections of the British public, including Queen Victoria, wanted the allies to follow up their victory by forcing the Russians out of the Crimea altogether. However, both sides had had enough: although the allies were now occupying Sevastopol, the Russians had installed heavy artillery on the northern outskirts of the city; this meant that the allies never felt very secure, and any further advance was out of the question. Nicholas I had died from pleurisy after catching a chill while reviewing his troops (March), and the new Tsar, Alexander II, was anxious for peace so that he could concentrate on Russia's many internal problems. In January 1856 the Austrians threatened to declare war on Russia unless he agreed to peace negotiations. Historian Andrew Lambert believes that what finally convinced Alexander that it was time to start talking was a British threat to attack Kronstadt, the Russian Baltic naval base situated on an island just off St Petersburg (the Russian capital). In August 1855 a British fleet had destroyed the Russian dockyard at Sweaborg (near the modern city of Helsinki) on the Baltic Sea. Very little was made of this at the time because all attention was concentrated on the fate of Sevastopol. The British were planning to follow up this success by a similar but much larger attack using a huge fleet known as the 'Great Armament'. It was to consist of some 350 gunboats, mortar vessels and rocket firing boats and a force of Royal Marines which were to bombard and capture Kronstadt. This was timed for April 1856, and if successful, it would leave St Petersburg itself open to a direct British attack. Totleben was already at work fortifying Kronstadt, but it seems likely that Alexander decided to negotiate rather than risk the loss of his vital Baltic naval base.

10.3 The Treaty of Paris (1856) and the results of the war

(a) *The Paris Peace Conference*

Peace talks opened in Paris in February 1856, much to the delight of Napoleon III, whose prestige reached a high point. *The terms of the treaty (signed in March) were*:

- Moldavia and Wallachia were to have self-government for internal affairs, though they still had to acknowledge Turkish suzerainty (the right of general supervision). The powers agreed to guarantee this new semi-independence and Russia had to give up its claim to protect the provinces.
- Russia had to hand over the southern part of Bessarabia to Moldavia, which meant that the Russian frontier no longer reached up to the River Danube. In addition, the Danube was to be a free waterway for all nations.
- The Straits Convention of 1841 (see Section 9.2(c) 8) was repeated: the Black Sea was neutralized – no warships were allowed on it but it was open to merchant shipping of all nations. The treaty added that the Russians must not build any military or naval strongholds along the Black Sea coast.
- Russia had to abandon its claim to protect the Christians in Turkey, and the independence of the Turkish Empire was guaranteed. In return the Sultan promised to treat his Christians fairly and to modernize and strengthen his state.

(b) *How far were Britain's war aims achieved?*

The general idea had been to check Russian expansion in the Balkans, to keep the Russian navy out of the Mediterranean and to bolster up the Turkish Empire to act as a buffer against Russia. To some extent all three aims were achieved:

1. Russian influence in the Balkans was checked when Moldavia and Wallachia were given semi-independence. When the provinces united to form the new state of Romania (1858), it acted as a real barrier against any further Russian attempt to annex parts of the Balkans.
2. Russia was not allowed to have a fleet on the Black Sea and so could not threaten British sea-power in the Mediterranean. However, this clause of the treaty was difficult to enforce without keeping a Franco-British fleet permanently cruising around the Black Sea to make sure the Russians behaved themselves. In 1870 during the Franco-Prussian War, the Russians announced that they no longer recognized the ban and that they would build a Black Sea Fleet and fortify the coastline. The neutralization of the Black Sea therefore lasted only just over 14 years.
3. The Turkish Empire had been protected and saved from collapse, but in fact the Sultan kept neither of his promises and Turkey remained as weak as before.

Ever since the war there has been debate about whether the results justified the cost in money and lives – Britain alone lost over 22 000 killed. Cobden and Bright thought it was a waste of time, since the threat from Russia was a 'phantom'. More recently historians have taken a different view: Asa Briggs (in *The Age of Improvement*, Longman, 1959) believes that the war 'dealt a very real blow to Russian influence in Europe as a whole. In the aftermath of the 1848 revolutions, Russian power had reached its peak; it was never to be so strong again until the twentieth century.' Andrew Lambert points out that *this check to Russian influence in central Europe left a power vacuum; this enabled Bismarck to create the united Germany which was to prove a much greater threat to Britain than anything ever presented by Russia.* For the time being though, British seapower was at its peak: no other state could begin to rival the Royal Navy in sheer size, technical skill and experience. At Sweaborg it had demonstrated that it was powerful enough to destroy any naval arsenal anywhere in the world. As it turned out, the war had not solved the Eastern Question permanently, but when the next Balkans crisis arose in 1875–9 (see Section 14.4), Alexander did not push things as far as another war with Britain.

(c) *Other results of the war*

1   Some improvements were made in the British army: the system of supply was modernized, training standards raised, a modern breech-loading rifle introduced, and the price of commissions was reduced by a third. But it was not until Edward Cardwell became Secretary for War in 1868 that a really thorough reform took place.
2   Following Florence Nightingale's work in the Crimea, nursing was taken more seriously in Britain. Using the £50 000 presented to her by the grateful public, Miss Nightingale set up a training school for nurses at St Thomas's Hospital, in London (1861). The idea soon spread over the country, bringing a marked improvement in standards, as well as improvements in medicines and hospitals.
3   Britain's poor performance in the early stages of the war probably encouraged Bismarck to risk ignoring Palmerston's warning and go ahead with his invasion of Denmark in 1864 (see Section 9.5(e)). Bismarck's success in this venture, together with the check on Russian power, prepared the way for the unification of Germany.

Questions

1   **The outbreak of the Crimean War**
    Study Sources A to G and then answer the questions which follow.

Source A

The Tsar Nicholas I of Russia speaking to the British ambassador about Turkey, early in 1853

We have a very sick man on our hands, and we need a frank discussion as to the fate of Turkey. I want to speak as a friend and a gentleman, and as one keenly interested in the fate of millions of Christians. . . . I cannot allow Britain to take Constantinople, but for my part, I am willing to undertake not to establish myself there as proprietor. . . . Constantinople must not belong to any Great Power; as to the Principalities, which are in fact an independent state under my protection, they might well remain so; I am quite ready that England should take Egypt and Crete in any partition.

Source: quoted in R. W. Seton-Watson, *Britain in Europe 1789–1914*, Cambridge, 1937.

— **Source B** —

A letter from Lord Aberdeen, the Prime Minister, to Lord John Russell, September 1854

The assurances of prompt and effective aid, given by us to the Turks, would in all probability produce war. These barbarians hate us all and would be delighted to take their chance of some advantage by getting us mixed up with the other powers of Christendom. It may be necessary to give them moral support and to try to prolong their existence, but we ought to regard as the greatest mischief any engagement which compelled us to take up arms for the Turks. . . . Britain ought to keep perfectly independent and free to act as circumstances may require.

Source: as for Source A.

— **Source C** —

A letter from Lord John Russell to Lord Clarendon, the Foreign Secretary, September 1854

The Emperor of Russia is clearly bent on accomplishing the destruction of Turkey, and he must be resisted . . . plainly I shall stand for the Turk against the Russian.

Source: as for Source A.

— **Source D** —

A letter from Lord Palmerston to Sidney Herbert, the Secretary for War, September 1854

Turkey is not in decay, and for the last thirty years has made greater progress and improvement than any other country. . . . If the Tsar wishes the Christians of Turkey to be safe from oppression, then let him relieve the Principalities of the miseries inflicted by his own armies. Beyond that, let him be satisfied, as we all are, with the progressively liberal system of Turkey. If he wants to interfere between the Sultan and his subjects, then let us manfully assist Turkey and let the fortune of war decide between the Emperor's wrong and the Sultan's rightful cause.

Source: as for Source A.

Source E

Cartoon showing Lord Aberdeen and the British lion

[*Reproduced by permission of the Proprietors of 'Punch.'*

WHAT IT HAS COME TO.

Aberdeen. " I MUST LET HIM GO ! "

Figure 10.1

Source: *Punch*, October 1854.

Source F

Extracts from speeches by John Bright in the House of Commons,
October–November 1854

War will not save Turkey if peace cannot save her; but war will brutalize our people, increase our taxes, destroy our industry, postpone the promised parliamentary reform . . .; as to the supposed Russian threat to India – in the light of past history, we are more likely to attack Russia from India than the Russians to attack us there, for our Asian policy, much more than Russia's, has been designed to increase our power . . .

Is it really necessary for us to interfere in a dispute between Russia and Turkey? The Turks declared war on Russia against the advice of the British and French governments, but the moment war was declared by Turkey, our Government openly applauded it. My doctrine would have been non-intervention in this case. The danger of Russian power was a phantom . . .; our love for civilisation when we subject the Greeks and Christians to the Turks, is a sham.

Source: quoted in Donald Read, *Cobden and Bright*, Arnold, 1967.

Historian D. R. Ward writes about the outbreak of the war

It has often been argued that British policy, or lack of it, allowed the Russo-Turkish War to occur and then failed to prevent Britain being dragged into it. On the one hand, a firmer British stand, the Palmerston–Russell policy, would have made it clear to Russia from the outset that Britain would not tolerate any interference with Turkey. On the other hand, it is claimed, if Britain had been more determined with Turkey, showing that she was not prepared to assist her against Russia, the Sultan would have been more ready for compromise. Aberdeen disliked the idea of assisting the Turks, especially when the Turks treated Christians harshly, and he tried to bring pressure on her to settle with Russia. . . . However, he was not able to pursue this policy throughout, because influential members of his cabinet – Palmerston and Russell – held contrary views.

However uncertain the government was, public opinion was perfectly clear: the press lambasted the government for not standing up to the Russians. When a Turkish flotilla cruising in the Black Sea was sunk at Sinope by the Russians, public opinion became almost hysterical. So the divided Cabinet, finding it increasingly difficult to resist popular demand, issued an ultimatum demanding a Russian withdrawal from the Principalities. When it was not complied with, war was declared on 27 March 1854.

Source: D. R. Ward, *Foreign Affairs 1815–1865*, Collins, 1972.

(a) In what ways do Sources A, B, C and D differ in their assessment of
   Turkey?   (5 marks)
(b) (i) In the *Punch* cartoon (Source E), what message is the cartoonist trying to
        put over?   (3 marks)
   (ii) Judging by the style and detail of the cartoon, explain whether you think
        the cartoonist is sympathetic to Lord Aberdeen or not.   (3 marks)
(c) How useful do you think this collection of sources is for explaining the causes
   of the Crimean War and deciding who should bear the responsibility for the
   war? Use the sources themselves and information from Chapter 10. (14 marks)
                                                                   (Total 25 marks)
2 'Britain's intervention in the Crimean War resulted in a reduction in, rather than an
   enhancement of, its position as an international power.' How valid is this
   judgement in respect of the period 1856 to 1870? (Use information from Chapters
   9, 10 and 13).   [NEAB]

Britain, India and the Mutiny of 1857

Summary of events

The British had been in India since the early seventeenth century, when *the East India Company* had established trading settlements (known as factories) at Surat (1612) and Madras (1640), and later at Bombay (1661) and Calcutta (1690). In the early days the Company was there purely for trade and not to take political control of India. In the early eighteenth century the central administration of India began to break down; the Mogul Emperor found it difficult to maintain his authority against ambitious local princes. In this situation the Company trading posts were forced to defend themselves both against hostile princes and against rival French trading companies. Both sides trained and equipped Indian soldiers, known as *sepoys*, to help defend their settlements.

By 1764, largely thanks to the work of Robert Clive, who successfully supported friendly princes against hostile ones, the French threat had been curbed, and Company control was established in Bengal and Bihar and in the areas around Madras and Bombay. The job of running these areas was fast becoming too much for the East India Company, so *the 1784 India Act* gave the British government overall authority; this was to be exercised through the Governor-General, based in Calcutta, who would decide the political policy to be followed in the British parts of India, while the Company continued to control trade. During the Franco-British wars (1793–1815) the Company got itself into financial difficulties and the British government gradually took over most of its functions.

Successive Governors-General after 1800 were anxious to extend the area of British control. By 1857, partly through a series of bloody wars and partly by devious political manoeuvring, the vast majority of India and Burma was either directly controlled by the British government or had accepted British protection.

The British became careless and failed to read certain danger signals. British complacency suffered a painful jolt when, in May 1857, the Bengal sepoys suddenly mutinied and murdered all Europeans they could lay hands on. There were at least five times more Indian troops than Europeans, and for a time it seemed as though the British might lose control of the whole of India. Fortunately for them, however, only the Bengal sepoys mutinied; those in Madras, Bombay and the Punjab remained loyal. Even so there was a bitter struggle and terrible atrocities were committed on both sides; it took the British until the end of September to regain control, and it was another full year before all resistance ended. Relations between British and Indians were never quite the same again.

11.1 How was British power in India extended between 1800 and 1857?

After the 1784 India Act there was a long line of Governors-General appointed by the British government. The office of Governor-General carried with it enormous personal power and prestige, and every one of them made a contribution to the extension of British power in India. It was not always a case of sheer aggression by the British; sometimes native princes were persuaded to sign alliances with them; sometimes neighbouring tribes raided British territory and had to be subdued, giving the British an excuse to annex new areas. As well as initiating military campaigns, some of the Governors-General introduced reforms to improve administrative efficiency and social conditions.

(a) *Lord Wellesley (1798–1805)*

He began by attacking the ruler of Mysore, Tipu Sahib, who was supporting the French and had sworn to drive the British from India. Tipu was defeated and killed (1799) and Mysore came under British control, soon to be followed by the Carnatic. Wellesley's attitude towards the remaining independent Indian princes (who were known by various titles such as nawab, rajah, maharajah, nizam (in Hyderabad) and peshwa (in Maratha areas) which meant 'ruler', or 'prince' or 'governor') was to persuade them to sign *subsidiary alliances* with the British: the native ruler could run the internal affairs of his state while British troops would 'protect' him from attack. In return for protection, the ruler had to pay towards the expenses of the troops who would be based in his territory, accept a British resident (an adviser representing the British government) and promise not to sign treaties with other princes. The nizam of Hyderabad was the first to accept British 'protection', followed by the nawab of Oudh and by three Maratha chiefs. In seven years Wellesley had transformed the British position in India. Less impressive, however, were his superior attitude towards the Indians, especially Hindus (Indians were not allowed in top administrative posts and could not attend social events organized by whites), and his excessive vanity, which, so reliable reports had it, caused him to wear his medals and other decorations even in bed.

(b) *Lord Minto (1806–13)*

Minto did not find life as quiet as might have been expected following Wellesley's exploits: some sepoys had mutinied near Madras and the Maratha chiefs resented their treatment by the British. The Sikhs of the Punjab, led by Ranjit Singh from his capital at Lahore, had already captured Kashmir from the Afghans and now had designs on neighbouring British territory across the Sutlej river. Minto, however, was soon able to restore internal order, and persuaded Ranjit Singh to sign an agreement at Amritsar promising not to cross the Sutlej river.

(c) *Lord Hastings (1813–23)*

Like Minto, Hastings had to face possible attacks from tribes outside British territory. Most troublesome were the Gurkhas of Nepal to the north of Bengal. It took a difficult 18-month campaign (1814–16) in the Nepal mountains to persuade the Gurkhas to abandon their claim to British territory. Most of Nepal was left as an independent state and the Gurkhas have remained friendly to Britain ever since. Meanwhile the Pindaris, robber bands of Maratha tribesmen, were causing trouble in central India. When

Map 11.1 India

Hastings sent troops against them, several of the Maratha chiefs, including the rajah of Nagpur, rose against the British. In the large-scale campaign which followed, the British deployed over 100 000 troops against more than twice that number, and the Marathas were finally defeated at the Battle of Kirkee (1817). Feeling that subsidiary treaties with such rulers were a waste of time, Hastings decided to annex their territories; the Deccan became part of the province of Bombay and the rajah of Nagpur lost some of his territory. Hastings must take the credit for stabilizing the northern frontiers of British India, and after his annexations, the only significant parts of India not under British control (either directly or indirectly) were the Punjab and Sind in the north-west. He even found time for internal improvements such as the introduction of irrigation schemes and the building of new roads and schools.

(d) *Lord Amherst (1823–8)*

He was hoping for a peaceful time, but like his predecessors, he found himself harassed by raids; this time they were on the eastern frontier of Bengal where the aggressive king of Ava on the Irrawaddy river, occupied British territory near Chittagong (1824).

Reluctantly Amherst dispatched an 11 000-strong expedition by sea, which sailed up the Irrawaddy, capturing Rangoon and Prome. As the British approached Ava itself, the king promised to abandon his claims and to hand over to the British the coast of Burma from Chittagong down to the Irrawaddy delta. However, the cost had been heavy: the British troops had inadequate supplies and were hampered by monsoons and floods. Over half the force perished, most of them from tropical diseases.

(e) *Lord William Bentinck (1828–35)*

Thanks to the energy of his predecessors, Bentinck was able to enjoy a period of peace in which he put the country's finances on the road to recovery after the enormous expense of the military campaigns, and distinguished himself as a social reformer. It was during his time in India that *two conflicting British attitudes towards the Indians became apparent*:

- An increasing readiness to accept much of the Indians' own laws and customs and to respect the Indians themselves. *The India Act (1833)* stated that 'the interests of the Native subjects are to be consulted in preference to those of Europeans, whenever the two come into competition; and that therefore laws ought to be adapted rather to the feelings and habits of the natives than to those of Europeans'. It added that 'no native of India ... should be disabled from holding any place, office or employment by reason of his religion, place of birth, descent or colour'. Bentinck's own motto was 'British greatness is founded on Indian happiness'.
- The belief that western culture and methods must be introduced before India could become fully developed.

In fact India was so backward that *the drive towards westernization became dominant*:

1 Bentinck decided that English should be the language of instruction in all state-aided schools; the government would provide money to set up more schools and colleges of higher education. Thus began the process of imposing on educated Indians a European culture which was probably not appropriate for them, though it can also be argued that the use of English as a common language helped to unite India.

2 He began to stamp out two ancient but barbaric customs:
- *suttee* – the practice of burning Hindu widows on the funeral pyres along with their dead husbands.
- *thuggee* – sacrificial murders by members of a secret society called thugs.

3 He deposed the unpopular rajah of Coorg for cruelty to his subjects and the maharajah of Mysore for incompetent government.

4 Bentinck was influenced by *a new motive – fear of Russian ambitions* in the north-west, through Afghanistan. This led him to renew the alliance with Ranjit Singh of the Punjab signed originally during Minto's time, while the rulers of Sind were persuaded to sign an agreement allowing merchants to trade along the Indus river, on condition that no weapons or armaments were carried.

(f) *Lord Auckland (1835–42)*

He was the least successful of the Governors-General before the Mutiny; in fact his stay in India ended in disaster – British defeat in *the First Afghan War (1839–42)*. Auckland decided that Britain must gain control of Afghanistan in order to keep the Russians out. In 1839 he launched an invasion of Afghanistan with the intention of removing Dost Mahomed, the amir based at Kabul, and replacing him with Shah Suja, who had previously been driven out by the Afghans themselves.

Auckland's actions are difficult to defend: He had earlier assured Dost Mahomed that he had no intention of interfering in Afghan affairs; Dost was anxious to keep on good terms with him and much preferred the British to the Russians. Shah Suja was extremely unpopular and would never be accepted back by the Afghans. And finally, the British army, which lacked sufficient transport and supplies, went into Afghanistan through Sind, thereby breaking Bentinck's agreement.

The army captured Kabul and set up Shah Suja, but the outraged Afghans rose in revolt and besieged the British forces in Kabul and Kandahar. It was decided to retreat into India, but, in January 1842, 4500 British troops were caught in a narrow pass between Kabul and Jellalabad and were completely annihilated; only one survivor struggled through to Jellalabad.

(g) *Lord Ellenborough (1842–4)*

He arrived in India soon after the massacre. He sent a large relief expedition which forced its way through the Khyber Pass, recaptured Kabul (September 1842) and rescued the British prisoners still being held. However, the country was too rebellious to hold down for long, so the British withdrew to India. British prestige had been restored to some extent, but they had failed to achieve their original objective: Dost Mahomed was back in power in Kabul, Shah had been murdered, and the Afghans had to be left severely alone.

Carried away by the success of his expedition, Ellenborough sent troops into Sind, defeated the rulers and annexed the territory. This was a totally unjustified and unprovoked attack which the British government strongly disapproved of. Ignoring their protests, Ellenborough next launched an invasion of the state of Gwalior, which was soon defeated and taken under British 'protection'. Peel's government felt that this was going too far, and Ellenborough was dismissed; he was replaced by his brother-in-law.

(h) *Lord Hardinge (1844–8)*

Hardinge had no sooner arrived in India than he had to deal with a Sikh invasion from the Punjab across the Sutlej into British territory. So long as the capable and popular Ranjit Singh had been alive, the Sikhs had been friendly, but since his death in 1839 the Sikh army had dominated the country. Deeply suspicious of the British because of the activities of Auckland and Ellenborough, the Sikhs were convinced that the Punjab was next on the list for annexation, and decided to strike first. They were savage fighters, but after a series of bloody and costly engagements, the British captured Lahore, the Sikh capital (February 1846). The young maharajah Duleep Singh was placed on the throne, with Sir Henry Lawrence as resident; though the Punjab was not annexed, it seemed firmly under British control. As Hardinge left India in January 1848 he pronounced that 'it will not be necessary to fire a gun in India for seven years to come'. He was wrong.

(i) *Lord Dalhousie (1848–56)*

Dalhousie, who had been a successful President of the Board of Trade in Peel's government until 1846, was still only 36 when he arrived in India. His period in power was packed with incident: he was responsible for extending British power still further (though not always by design) and for introducing important reforms.

1   Three months after his arrival the Sikhs of the Punjab rose in revolt again, and another costly campaign was needed to restore order. This time Dalhousie decided to annex the Punjab, and Duleep Singh was deposed and sent to Britain. This enabled much needed and, on the whole, popular reforms to be introduced, with such success that the Sikhs remained loyal even during the Mutiny.

2   More of Burma came under British control after the Burmese had broken the agreement signed with Amherst (1826) by harassing British traders on the Irrawaddy river. In 1852 the Burmese attacked some British ships; Dalhousie felt strong action was needed to discourage similar anti-British moves in India. A carefully organized expedition was sent, avoiding Amherst's mistakes; with only 377 casualties, Rangoon and Pegu were captured, bringing the Burmese coast as far south as Tenasserim under British control.

3   Within India, Dalhousie was responsible for bringing under British rule a number of states which until this point had been governed by native rulers. This was achieved by using what was called *'the doctrine of lapse'*: Hindu tradition allowed a childless man to adopt an heir, and this applied to native rulers as well. However, Dalhousie decided that in certain cases of political succession, this should not be allowed to happen – if a native ruler died without an heir, his family's claim to the throne lapsed, and the state reverted to the British. By this method Dalhousie managed to annex seven states, of which the most important was Nagpur with a population of four million (1853). He also annexed the large northern state of Oudh after removing the nawab who had been notoriously incompetent and cruel for many years.

4   There were important advances in administration, communications and education. Dalhousie created a central legislative council and set up a Public Works Department to carry out his ideas. Two thousand miles of road were built, including the Grand Trunk Road from Calcutta to Peshawar; 18 000 miles of irrigation canal were completed, the showpiece being the spectacular Ganges Canal, opened by Dalhousie himself in 1854. He began the construction of railways to link Bombay, Calcutta and Madras, and introduced the Indian telegraph service. 753 post offices were built and a uniform postal rate adopted. An engineering college which eventually became a university was founded at Roorkee; hundreds of village schools were started, and the education of women encouraged.

All this was a tremendous achievement, but Dalhousie knew that he had offended many people; at the end of his stay in India he warned the British government to remain alert: 'No prudent man would ever venture to predict a long continuance of peace in India.' The government took little notice and only just over a year had passed when the Mutiny broke out.

11.2 What were the causes of the Mutiny?

In general, the reforms of Bentinck and especially Dalhousie, though well-intentioned and beneficial in many ways, were too quick and far-reaching for the conservative and traditionally minded Indians. They disliked the drive towards westernization and the attempt to impose an alien culture on them. Dalhousie left behind a number of individuals and groups nursing grievances and a sense of injustice, for political, economic and religious reasons:

(a) *Indian rulers resented Dalhousie's recent annexations*

Dalhousie's annexations using the 'doctrine of lapse', and especially the annexation of Oudh in 1856, alarmed other Indian rulers who began to feel that it was the beginning of a British plan to expel them all. They regarded the British behaviour as dishonourable, since in some cases it broke existing treaties. The dispossessed rulers and their supporters were left smarting and eager for revenge. Dalhousie realized how risky the annexation of Oudh would be, but decided it was essential for the welfare of the population. In fact, many ordinary people were as outraged as the nawab himself. One loyal sepoy, writing about his experiences, was certain that 'this seizing of Oudh filled the minds of the sepoys with distrust, and led them to plot against the Government'. Unfortunately for the British, many of the sepoys in the Bengal army came from Oudh.

(b) *There were economic grievances in both town and countryside*

● The British flooded India with all kinds of cheap, mass-produced goods, which were gradually putting Indian urban craftsmen out of business; one Indian complained that 'the introduction of English articles into India has thrown the weavers, spinners, cotton-dressers, the carpenters, the blacksmiths and the shoemakers, etc. out of employ, so that every description of native artisan has been reduced to beggary'.
● In the countryside the British tried to make the land more efficient by introducing European practices such as individual ownership of land and fixed money rents. But this caused enormous problems because both peasants and landlords, unaccustomed to making regular cash payments, got into debt and had to sell their land. According to Bernard Porter,

> the pattern of rural life was breaking up in many areas; families were forced to abandon lands they had tilled for generations; the old familiar feudal masters were replaced by new ones, sometimes unsympathetic with rural ways; and the loss of the old *elites* was regretted, apparently, by their faithful peasantry.

This was particularly true in Oudh.

(c) *There were religious differences among civilians and among sepoys*

1 The Brahmins (Hindu priests) objected to the abolition of suttee, though to Europeans it seemed a sensible and humane reform. To add insult to injury, in 1856 Dalhousie permitted Hindu widows to re-marry, a further breach of Hindu custom.
2 Much of the resentment arose because of *the caste system*: Hindu society is divided into four castes or classes, which make up the social scale. At the top are the priests, and below them the next caste – rulers and soldiers; third in the social scale are traders and farmers, and fourth artisans (craftsmen). People outside these groups were known as 'untouchables' who were regarded as the dregs of society. Members of different castes did not mix socially. Thus innovations such as the railways on which all classes were expected to travel together, and the British practice of everybody being equal before the law, seemed to be an insult to the higher castes, and were taken to be an attack on the caste system. Similarly, the spread of education and especially the education of women seemed to threaten the structure of Hindu society. The increasing number of Christian missionaries arriving in India confirmed suspicions that the British were trying to destroy not only Hinduism but Islam and Buddhism as well.

3   In the Bengal army there were discipline problems caused by the caste system. Since 1830 many high-class Hindus had been allowed to join the army as ordinary private soldiers, but they thought themselves superior to some of their officers and were unwilling to take orders from somebody of a lower caste. When the government tried to improve matters by forbidding the wearing of caste marks, this further offended Hindu principles. A rumour went round that two regiments of sepoys were about to be sent on operations to Burma, and this would involve sailing across the Bay of Bengal to get there. The Hindus were afraid that they would lose caste by crossing water; in fact there had already been a mutiny for the same reason at Barrackpore (1824) which had quickly been put down by a few well-directed cannon blasts. The British had failed to learn the obvious lesson.

(d) *The Indians began to realize that the British were not invincible*

British defeats in Afghanistan (1839–42) together with their recent less than impressive performance in the early part of the Crimean War (1854–6) showed the Indians that the British were not invincible. Also encouraging to the Indians was the obvious unpreparedness of the British: the arsenals at Delhi and Allahabad were inadequately guarded; some of the European troops had been withdrawn for service in the Crimea, Persia and Burma; there were scarcely 40 000 European troops in the whole of India, against 230 000 sepoys. In fact in Bengal itself, the most troubled area, there were only 5000 Europeans and nearly 55 000 sepoys. The British were far too careless and casual: they seemed unaware of the growing resentment and unconcerned at the prophecy that British rule in India would end on 23 June 1857 (exactly a hundred years after Robert Clive's famous victory at the Battle of Plassey).

(e) *The affair of the greased cartridges was the immediate cause of the Mutiny*

Cartridges for the recently introduced Enfield rifle had to be ripped open with the teeth before loading. A rumour spread that the grease for these cartridges was made from cow and pig fat. This caused consternation among both Hindus and Muslims, since the cow is sacred to Hindus and the pig considered unclean by Muslims. This united the two religious groups against the British; at Meerut the sepoys refused to touch the new cartridges, and 85 of them were given long prison sentences. The following day (10 May 1857) the Meerut sepoys mutinied and killed their European officers.

11.3 Events in the Mutiny

(a) *Fighting confined to the north*

After the initial shock at Meerut, the Mutiny spread rapidly through Bengal, Oudh and the North-West Provinces. The Punjab, only recently annexed and garrisoned by regiments of Bengal sepoys, might have been a danger area; however, the Sikhs remained loyal and helped the governor, John Lawrence, to disarm the Bengal regiments. After this the Punjab remained quiet, and there was very little trouble elsewhere, as the Madras and Bombay armies remained mostly loyal. Hyderabad was a critical area with its large Muslim population, but the nizam turned out to be completely reliable, and so did the king of Nepal who allowed his Gurkha soldiers to fight for the British. *The main centres of fighting were Delhi, Cawnpore and Lucknow:*

(b) *Delhi captured by the rebels*

Delhi was crucially important since it was regarded by the northern Indians as the seat of power. The Meerut rebels quickly marched on Delhi and were joined by the Indian regiments based there. They soon captured the city and slaughtered all the British they could lay hands on. A small British force of 3500 set out to relieve Delhi and fought its way to the Long Ridge just outside the city. It could make no headway against 40 000 sepoys with 114 cannons mounted on the walls. In fact the British did well to survive until August when a relief force from the Punjab, under John Nicholson, arrived on the Ridge. In September the British blasted their way into Delhi with heavy artillery, and after a further week's fierce fighting, the city was recaptured, though Nicholson himself was killed. The British shot three local princes as a reprisal for the slaughtering of European women and children.

(c) *Siege and massacres at Cawnpore*

At Cawnpore, early in June 1857, a tiny British force of less than 700 was besieged by 3000 rebel sepoys commanded by the Nana Sahib, who had had his large pension stopped by Dalhousie (he was the adopted son of the peshwa of Poona who had been deposed by the British). After three weeks the British were almost out of food and water, and since there were about 400 women and children with them, they decided to surrender and accept the Nana Sahib's offer of a safe-conduct by boat down the river to Allahabad. As the crowded barges were about to push off, the Nana Sahib turned his cannons on them and sprayed them with grapeshot at point blank range. Only four soldiers and about a hundred women and children survived, and they were held as prisoners. When a British relief force under Sir Henry Havelock was within two days of Cawnpore, the Nana Sahib had the prisoners hacked to death and their bodies thrown down a well. The city was taken on 17 July; the British were horrified at the remains of the massacre and took terrible revenge. Captured sepoys were made to lick up the blood from the floors of the prison huts before being hanged. The one British regret was that the Nana Sahib escaped and was never captured.

(d) *Lucknow besieged*

At Lucknow, the capital of Oudh, there were only about a thousand European troops holding out against 60 000 rebels, though only 10 000 of these were trained sepoys. Havelock advanced from Cawnpore, but although he managed to force his way into Lucknow (25 September), there were still not enough British troops to drive the rebels off. The siege lasted another two months before Lucknow was relieved by Sir Colin Campbell's force advancing from Calcutta (17 November). However, with over 100 000 rebels still in the area, there remained much for Campbell still to do. Lucknow was not finally secured until March 1858. At this point, the Governor-General, Lord Canning, in an attempt to end resistance in Oudh, announced that all the landowners should forfeit their land. But in an area where hatred of the British was stronger than anywhere else in India, this had the opposite effect to what Canning had intended; it was not until the end of 1858 that the Oudh rebels were finally subdued.

(e) *Why did the Mutiny fail to achieve its objectives?*

There is some disagreement about what the objectives of the rebels were. Some Indian historians see the Mutiny as a national revolution with the ultimate aim of expelling the British from India; it is sometimes called *the First National War of Independence.*

However, this was probably not the case. If it had been a war of independence, the whole country would have risen, with the civilian population joining in as well. If this had happened, the Indians would have stood a good chance of success. British historians therefore see the Mutiny as a spontaneous response to frustrations and grievances. *The rebels' aims* were to restore their old rulers, customs and institutions; beyond that they were vague – there were certainly no plans for a united India. *The Mutiny failed because*:

1   It was not a national rising: fewer than half the sepoys actually mutinied, and many important native rulers, for example in Hyderabad, Gwalior and Rajputana, stayed loyal. Some of them even supplied troops to help the British.
2   Except in Oudh, the civilian population was hardly involved, either because they had not been affected by British reforms, or because they had done well out of them. Many upper-class Indians had benefited from an English education and were playing an important part in the commercial life of the big cities. Very few Muslims took any part in the Mutiny.
3   No outstanding Indian leader emerged; there was no co-ordination between the different centres of unrest and no overall plan of campaign. Fatal mistakes were made: for example, at the beginning of the Mutiny, while the British in Delhi were still stunned with shock, the sepoys waited around for three weeks wondering what to do next.
4   Though individual British commanders made mistakes, the British had much better leadership than the Indians. The Governor-General, Lord Canning, was able to direct operations from Calcutta, while Havelock, Nicholson and Campbell distinguished themselves, though their forces were heavily outnumbered.

11.4 What were the results of the Mutiny?

(a) *The Government of India Act (1858)*

The British government was forced to admit that something must have gone sadly wrong with the way India had been ruled, to cause such a serious outbreak of violence. In order to secure greater efficiency, Lord Derby's Conservative government (1858–9) introduced *the Government of India Act (1858)*. This abolished the East India Company which for years had been slack and easy-going, and transferred all its powers, properties and territories to the Crown. A Secretary of State and a Council of 15 members were created to look after the running of India, and the Governor-General had his title changed to *Viceroy* (meaning 'in place of the king') to show that he represented the British monarch in India. The Indians were promised that there would be no further interference with their religions (a promise which was largely kept) and that they would have equality of opportunity with the British (which was not kept – see Section (d) below).

(b) *Lord Canning tries a policy of moderation and reason*

Lord Canning was Governor-General from 1856 until 1858 and then Viceroy until 1862. He followed a policy of moderation towards the Indians. He refused to carry out wholesale executions, to the annoyance of much of the British public which nicknamed him 'Clemency Canning'. Though reforms were continued, the pace was much more slow, and care was taken not to offend religious and local customs. The doctrine of lapse was abandoned and the British went to great pains not to offend native rulers and princes in other ways. This policy was successful, and on the whole, the Indian upper classes, realizing that it was impossible to get the British out by force, remained loyal well into the twentieth century.

(c) *No more annexations*

The British abandoned their policy of expansion for the time being. In 1863 when civil war broke out in Afghanistan, they wisely refused to become involved, preferring to concentrate on improving the vast territories they already held.

(d) *Legacy of ill-feeling between British and Indians*

As a result of the atrocities committed by both sides during the Mutiny, there remained considerable ill-feeling between British and Indians, in spite of Canning's efforts. The British felt they could never trust the Indians again: they sent more troops to India, disarmed the civilian population, and increased the proportion of Europeans in the army. The artillery was kept wholly in British hands. Equality of opportunity was never a reality; for example, although entrance to the Indian Civil Service was thrown open to anyone who could pass an examination, this had to be taken in London, which involved the problem of a candidate losing caste if he crossed the sea. Consequently only one Indian took the examination before 1871; Indians were relegated to low-level positions. In fact a much deeper gulf than ever before had come between the British and Indians, and this gulf was never bridged.

Questions

1   The Indian Mutiny of 1857
Study Sources A to E and then answer the questions which follow.

> **Source A**
>
> *An article in* The Times, *8 June 1857*
>
> *To bring high-caste Hindoos into contact with lard is, of course, a mistake*, but we doubt if it would in itself lead to disloyalty extending over several months. Those who know India well are not unprepared for the appearance of a restless, sullen, disorderly feeling on the part of the millions whom we rule, and especially of the troops.... By education, by a glimpse of history and natural science, by the spectacle of railways and telegraphs, and by the great events which have lately passed in Europe, the Hindoo had been roused from his sluggishness. In the old times when the *sepoys* had no knowledge and no ambition, there was pretty nearly always something for them to do. An enemy was always on our frontier, and there were tribes of robbers, murderers or fanatics to be put down. But now we have conquered all enemies within and without. There is no activity, no excitement beyond monotonous routine duties. We cannot help feeling that this dull and aimless existence is too much even for the apathy of the Hindoos.
>
> We can well imagine the effect on the quick, suspicious temper of a Hindoo of all that is passing in India. Everything around him is in a state of change. But the sepoy has time to brood over imaginary wrongs and to suspect that he is subjected to cunning temptations. It may be that this ill-feeling is the last stand made by the

Hindoo mind against the growing influence of European culture. It is not impossible that at a time when widows are marrying and men of all castes are sitting together in a railway carriage, the last efforts of those utterly resistant to change should be made.

Source: *The Times*, 8 June 1857.

Source B

A soldier's account of the relief of Cawnpore

When we reached the Bibigarh and saw the horror inside, none of us could speak. It looked as though cattle had been slaughtered in there. The walls were covered with bloody handprints and on the floor were pieces of human limbs, clothing, bibles, shoes, trinkets and lockets.... Looking into a well, I saw that the severed heads, limbs and mangled bodies had been thrown into it and it was full to within six feet of the top. I have faced death in every form, but I could not look down that well again.

Source: quoted in J. Harris, *The Indian Mutiny*, Hart-Davis MacGibbon, 1973.

Source C

Letter from Lord Canning, Governor-General of India, written shortly before the end of the Mutiny

One of the greatest difficulties which lie ahead will be the very violent bitterness of a very large proportion of the English community against every native Indian of every class. There is a raging and indiscriminate vindictiveness, even amongst many who ought to set a better example, which it is impossible to contemplate without something like a feeling of shame for one's fellow-countrymen. Not one man in ten seems to think that the hanging or shooting of forty or fifty thousand mutineers can be anything else but right; nor does it occur to them that it is simply impossible for the Sovereign of England to hold and govern India without employing and trusting natives. There are some who entirely refuse to believe in the faithfulness or goodwill of any native towards any Europeans.

Source: quoted in A. C. Benson and Viscount Esher, *The Letters of Queen Victoria*, John Murray, 1907.

The hanging of mutineers after the Indian Mutiny, 1857

Illus. 11.1

Source: The British Library.

Contemporary drawing of mutineers about to be blasted from cannons

Illus. 11.2

Source: Mansell Collection, Katz Pictures Ltd.

(a) Explain what the writer of Source A means by the following:
  (i) sepoys (1 mark)
  (ii) 'To bring high-caste Hindoos into contact with lard is, of course, a mistake.' (3 marks)
(b) On the basis of the evidence in Source A, suggest some possible causes of the Indian Mutiny. (7 marks)
(c) How useful is Source A as evidence of the British attitude towards the Indians *before* the Mutiny? (5 marks)
(d) How can it be inferred from these sources that Lord Canning's attitude towards the Indians was different from the attitude of the vast majority of the British people? (14 marks)
(e) Using the sources and the information in Chapter 11, analyze the results of the Indian Mutiny. (20 marks)
(Total 50 marks)

2 One of the mottos of Lord Bentinck (Governor-General of India 1828–35) was: 'British greatness is founded on Indian happiness'. To what extent did the British look after the happiness of the Indians during the period 1800 to 1862?

12 Social reform: factories, mines, public health and education

Summary of events

For the great mass of people in early-nineteenth-century Britain, the quality of life, the conditions in which they lived and worked and spent what little leisure time they had, left a lot to be desired. There has been some disagreement among historians about how bad conditions really were. Arnold Toynbee and J. L. and Barbara Hammond, writing before 1920, gave the left-wing view – that as a result of the industrial revolution, workers were shamefully exploited and lived in squalid slums. Sir John Clapham thought that this was a gross exaggeration and produced statistics which, he claimed, proved that the living standards of the poor were actually improving. More recently it was shown that life for the workers *before* the industrial revolution was not the bed of roses which some writers had seemed to suggest: long working hours, slum conditions and families living on the verge of starvation were just as common in rural Britain as they were in the new industrial towns. More recently still, the work of E. P. Thompson (*The Making of the English Working Class*, 1963) has questioned Clapham's findings. In spite of the disagreements, it is probably fair to say that

- in a majority of factories and mines, men, women and children had to work excessively long hours;
- many workers lived in disease-ridden slums and cellars;
- education for the working classes was almost non-existent, apart from that provided by voluntary groups and societies.

In an age of *laissez-faire*, the instinct of governments was to ignore these problems; the development of the industrial society which had given rise to this situation had taken place without any intervention from the state, and so it was assumed that individuals would find their own solutions, also without interference from the state. *Self-help* was a virtue much prized by the Victorians.

It was only very gradually that governments began to pay attention to the mass of evidence being placed before them about the unacceptable conditions endured by so many workers. After considerable debate, some sections of the ruling classes accepted that only through state intervention could the worst excesses be eliminated. However, even after the principle was accepted, there was determined opposition from industrialists and others who resented state interference; effective reform was therefore slow to come, and when it did, it often took the form of a compromise between the opposing factions.

12.1 Factory and mine reform: why was reform necessary?

(a) *There were no restrictions or controls*

The factory system, particularly mills and workshops driven by steam, were still comparatively new, and there were no restrictions, controls or checks of any kind. Factory owners were completely free to treat workers as they wished; fierce competition led employers to pay as little as possible for as much work as possible, and to take insufficient safety precautions. With nobody to protect the interests of the workers, it was inevitable that exploitation and abuses of all kinds would creep in.

(b) *Many factories were dangerous and unhealthy*

Machinery was not properly fenced off and textile-manufacturers often used small children to clean spinning machines and looms while they were still in motion. An adult spinner might use two or three children working as 'piecers'; their job was to crawl under machinery no more than a foot above the floor to tie broken ends. Serious accidents were common; *the 1840 Royal Commission Report* mentioned a case at Stockport where a girl had been caught by her clothing and carried round an upright shaft: 'her thighs were broken, her ankle dislocated, and she will be a cripple for life'. The Report went on to say that in the Stockport area 'fatal accidents generally happen from want of boxing-off; there has been a considerable number of accidents and loss of life within the last three months'.

The long-term effect of bending and standing for long periods was that children developed weak, curved legs and arched backs. Sometimes there were respiratory diseases caused by working for so long in the hot and humid atmosphere of a textile mill, where the air was contaminated by clouds of microscopic cotton dust.

There was danger in other industries too: the Staffordshire potteries were notoriously bad for health. Though some employers, like the Wedgwoods, were enlightened and caring, one Stoke-on-Trent doctor wrote: 'the potters as a class are as a rule stunted in growth and frequently deformed in the chest; they become prematurely old and are certainly short lived'. Workers in match factories often developed a disease known as 'phossy-jaw' which caused the teeth to fall out and the jawbone to rot away.

(c) *Mines had special problems*

There were frequent gas explosions since the Davey safety lamp was not compulsory. Small children, both boys and girls, sometimes as young as four years of age, were employed underground hauling trucks full of coal along passages which were too low for adults; or opening and closing ventilation doors (see Illus. 12.1), or filling coal trucks. *The Royal Commission Report which came out in 1842* revealed some appalling details: a 12-year-old girl had to carry a hundredweight of coal on her back, stooping and creeping through water in a low tunnel; children had to climb dangerous ladders up the pit shaft with huge baskets of coal strapped to their backs. The Report also expressed outrage that naked and semi-naked men, women, girls and boys all worked together, which had a demoralizing effect on the women and girls.

(d) *Long hours in textile factories*

Both adults and children had to work excessively long hours in textile factories. A parliamentary committee of enquiry in 1832 produced evidence to show that thousands of

Illus. 12.1   *Children working down a mine (sketch from the 1842 Royal Commission Report)*

small children, especially girls, were working from six in the morning until half-past eight in the evening, with only half an hour allowed for eating. Towards the end of the shift, they began to drop off to sleep, and depending on the foreman, had to be shaken or beaten with a strap to keep them alert. It was just as bad in other industries: Charles Shaw, a Tunstall potter who started work as a mould-runner at the age of six, recalled that 'my wage was a shilling a week. For this I had to work from between five and six o'clock in the morning and work on till six, seven or eight o'clock at night.' His job was to light the fire in the stove-room and spend the rest of the day rushing backwards and forwards bringing the raw clay to the potter and then running to take the plaster moulds (each bearing a soft plate) into the hot stove-room where the plates were hardened off.

(e) *Growing pressure for government intervention*

Pressure grew steadily for some government action. The main leader in the early days was a Leeds Tory Evangelical, Richard Oastler, who, after the failure of his career as a merchant, became estate manager at Fixby Hall, near Huddersfield. He was shocked by the horrifying conditions he saw in the Bradford woollen mills. A deeply religious man (he was brought up as a Wesleyan), he was moved to write a letter to the Leeds *Mercury* (1830) in which he claimed that child workers were being treated worse than slaves. 'Thousands of our fellow creatures, both male and female, the miserable inhabitants of a Yorkshire town, are this very moment existing in a state of slavery, more horrid than are the victims of that hellish system "colonial slavery".' Soon famous throughout the North, Oastler found himself the leader of a huge movement, publishing pamphlets and organizing public meetings and demonstrations demanding factory reform. Typical of the campaign were the mass marches which converged on York on Easter Monday 1832; the result was a petition containing over 130 000 signatures which was handed to parliament.

Inside parliament, the movement found an effective voice in another Tory Evangelical, Michael Sadler, who demanded a maximum working day of 10 hours for children. He was supported by other Tories and by humanitarians, who between them made up a formidable alliance. Their case was simple; as Derek Fraser puts it: 'it was a moral or religious crusade against an intolerable evil ... it simply could not be right for these things to persist'. However, there was bitter opposition to *the Ten Hour Movement* from most factory and mine owners.

12.2 What arguments were used by the opponents of reform?

- Benthamite Radicals (see Section 2.1(c)), many of whom were factory owners, believed that any state intervention was bad because it tampered with the natural working of the economic system. *Laissez-faire* was all-important. (However, there were exceptions, notably John Hobhouse, who was a Radical supporter of factory reform.)
- A shorter working day for children would mean restricting adult working hours, therefore causing a reduction in output. This in turn would mean lower profits and lower wages. One economist, Nassau Senior, Professor of Political Economy at Oxford, argued that the entire profit of industry was made in the last hour's work each day; therefore to reduce the working day even by one hour, would destroy profits. This theory had already been shown to be nonsense by Robert Owen, a progressive manufacturer who had reduced working hours in his textile mills in New Lanark, and had continued to make a comfortable profit; but many still clung to the argument.
- Better working conditions would push production costs up, making British goods more expensive on foreign markets. British exports would decline, causing unemployment. Apparently the British working classes had only a miserable choice available to them – to endure exhausting working hours and appalling conditions, or to suffer total poverty in unemployment.
- Some argued that children working long hours in industry was acceptable because it had gone on for centuries in agriculture without any protest. It was even suggested that child labour was to be encouraged since it gave them something to do and kept them out of mischief; too much leisure for the poor could be dangerous.

12.3 What improvements were made and why did it take so long for the Acts to become effective?

Before 1833 there were no fewer than six attempts by Act of Parliament to improve conditions in textile mills, but every single one was a failure. The most important were:

(a) *The Health and Morals of Apprentices Act (1802)*

This was the work of the elder Sir Robert Peel, who was influenced by the reports of a group of Lancashire doctors who were concerned at the exploitation of children in industry. The Act was designed to help workhouse children who were being used as apprentices in textile mills:

1 Apprentices were not to work more than 12 hours a day and must not work after 9 p.m.
2 They should be given two suits of clothes a year and sleep no more than two to a bed, with separate sleeping quarters for boys and girls. This was to regulate those manufacturers who had their workhouse children sleeping at the mill.

The weaknesses of this Act were that it did not apply to 'free' children, and no inspectors were appointed to make sure that it was enforced; instead it was left to local magistrates who might be relatives or friends of the mill-owner. Even Peel himself acknowledged that it was hardly ever enforced.

(b) *The Factory Act of 1819*

Again this was the work of the elder Peel, who was influenced by his discussions with Robert Owen (see Section 19.2). Owen's cotton mills at New Lanark, with their model villages and model schools for workers, had shown that reasonable profits could go hand in hand with humane living and working conditions. Peel's bill began its passage through parliament in 1815, but by this time the opponents of reform were well organized, and they were able to delay it and water it down in the House of Lords. *The final terms applied only to cotton mills*:

1   No children under the age of nine could be employed (Peel and Owen had wanted it to be under ten).
2   Young people aged nine to 16 must not work more than 12 hours a day (the original bill passed by the Commons said 11 hours); the work was to be done between 5 a.m. and 9 p.m. with one and a half hours off for meals.

Again the weaknesses of the Act were the same: no inspectors were appointed and magistrates were expected to enforce the new regulations. Peel apparently hoped that the offer of rewards would encourage informers, but very few workers dared risk the wrath of the mill-owner by reporting him to a magistrate. On the whole the Act was ignored, and in any case it did not apply to children in other industries. On the other hand *it was an important step* because it established the principle that parliament could interfere with parents' decisions about their children: no parent could now choose to send an eight-year-old to work in a cotton factory (at least in theory).

(c) *The Factory Act of 1831*

This was a good example of the alliance between different political groups. It was introduced by Sir John Hobhouse, a Radical, and was carried with Tory support. It extended the 12-hour limit to include 17- and 18-year olds, but was as disappointing as previous Acts because there were still no inspectors; in addition there was the problem of deciding a child's age, since there was, as yet, no official registration of births. Though these first three Acts were disappointing, nevertheless they *were* important because they showed that governments were prepared to depart from *laissez-faire*.

(d) *The Factory Act of 1833*

This was the first really effective piece of factory legislation. It was introduced by the Whig Chancellor of the Exchequer, Lord Althorp, though in fact all the credit was due to the Tory Evangelical, Lord Ashley (later the 7th Earl of Shaftesbury). The background was quite complicated:

Oastler and the Ten-Hour Movement, bitterly disappointed by Hobhouse's Act, redoubled their efforts to achieve a statutory ten-hour day, with Sadler leading the campaign in the Commons. However, in the 1832 general election (the first after the Reform Act) Sadler was defeated at Leeds and never managed to get back into parliament again. This seemed a fatal blow, but the leadership of the movement was taken over by Ashley, who turned out to be just as impressive and as dedicated as Sadler. Ashley introduced Sadler's Bill proposing to limit the working day of all textile operatives aged nine to 18 to ten hours. The hope was that by restricting young people's hours in this way, the factories would have to close after ten hours, giving adult workers too the benefit of a ten-hour day. The Whig government, under pressure from mill-owners, delayed the bill until a Royal Commission had investigated the situation. Dominated by the Benthamite Edwin Chadwick, the commission was efficient, detached and unemotional. It recommended (June 1833) that although ten hours was too long for young children, by the age of 14 they were almost adults and were strong enough to work a longer day. Vitally important was its suggestion that paid inspectors should be appointed to supervise the new regulations.

Impressed by Chadwick's report, the Commons immediately defeated Ashley's Ten Hour Bill (July 1833). Althorp introduced a Whig bill based on Chadwick's recommendations, which quickly became law (August 1833). In some ways the new Act fell short of what Ashley wanted, while in other ways it went far beyond what he and Sadler had in mind. It applied to all textile mills except those making silk and lace:

- No child under nine could be employed.
- Children from nine to 13 were limited to an eight-hour day, and were to receive at least two hours of education a day.
- Young people from 14 to 18 were limited to a 12-hour day, to be worked between 5.30 a.m. and 8.30 p.m.
- Four inspectors were appointed at an annual salary of £1000 each, to supervise the working of the Act; they had the power to enter any mill.

This was obviously a great advance on previous legislation, applying as it did to woollen and worsted as well as to cotton mills, and at long last introducing an inspectorate. *But it was still a disappointment for the Ten Hours supporters*:

- Most mill-owners responded by using a relay system of child labour, so that factories could be kept open for the whole time between 5.30 a.m. and 8.30 p.m., and so adults still had to work in excess of 12 hours.
- There still remained the problem of establishing a child's age; many parents needed the extra wages and often claimed that their 10, 11 and 12-year-old children were really 13-year-olds. However, this difficulty was soon overcome by the compulsory registration of births, marriages and deaths, introduced in 1836.
- The education clauses turned out to be ineffective: no money was provided for building schools, and only the most progressive factory owners complied.
- Four inspectors were not enough to cover the whole country adequately. After one had died of overwork in 1836, assistants were appointed. Their reports showed that although many manufacturers complied with the regulations, it was still easy for the unscrupulous ones to evade them. However, as historian Edward Royle points out, to dwell on the weaknesses of the Act is to miss the point of its real significance:

> The inspectors were working in a totally new area of legislation; their aim was not to make the factory masters into criminals, but to protect the workers; and they had to be confident of a successful prosecution before bringing a case. . . . But the Inspectors did their work conscientiously and made some impact. In the first five full years of the Act in the major textile districts of England, an average of nearly 600 charges were laid each year, with success in three out of every four cases. Moreover the Inspectors' experience in working the Act led them to demand further legislation. Their reports to the Home Office became propaganda for further reform and the Inspectors gave their full backing to Ashley's efforts in the 1840s. (Source: E. Royle, *Modern Britain: A Social History 1750–1985*, Arnold, 1988, p. 194)

Ashley certainly had no intention of giving up. In 1840 he persuaded parliament to appoint a committee with himself as chairman to investigate the working of Althorp's Act. It was able to use evidence from the Inspectors and it soon produced its own report (which included the details about Stockport mills in Section 12.1(b)) showing that factory work was still extremely dangerous. This led to:

(e) The Factory Act of 1844

In 1841 the Whig government was replaced by the Conservatives under Peel, who was not in favour of a 10-hour day; 12 hours was as far as he would go. Even so, *the Act was a great advance*:

- Children could start work at the age of eight (instead of nine), which seemed to be a backward step, but ...
- Children aged eight to 13 could only work a six-and-a-half-hour day.
- Women over the age of 13 were limited to a 12-hour day.
- Dangerous machinery had to be fenced and meals were to be eaten in a separate place.

(f) The Mines Act of 1842

Meanwhile Ashley had been active in other areas; he was equally concerned about conditions in mines, and he pestered parliament so much that a Royal Commission on the Employment of Women and Children in Mines was appointed. Its report (published in 1842) contained sketches showing some of the dangerous and unpleasant jobs which young children had to do. Until now mining conditions had received much less publicity than those in factories, and the public was deeply shocked by what the report revealed. Ashley's Mines Bill passed the Commons comfortably but ran into trouble in the Lords, which contained many aristocratic mine-owners. Led by Lord Londonderry, they were determined to weaken it as much as possible. *In its final form the Act*:

- Forbade the employment of women and girls in the mines, and of boys under the age of ten. (Ashley's original bill said no boys under 13 to be employed.)
- Appointed one inspector to enforce the regulations, but this was obviously inadequate.

(g) Fielden's Factory Act (1847) – the Ten Hours Act

The Ten Hour Movement lost its leader in parliament when Ashley resigned (1846) over Peel's decision to abolish the Corn Laws (see Section 7.5). His place was taken by John Fielden, the Radical MP for Oldham and a progressive owner of cotton mills in Todmorden. He introduced a bill to limit the working day of all women and young people up to the age of 18 to ten hours. At the same time Oastler made sure there were massive demonstrations and marches throughout the North of England, and to the intense jubilation of the movement, the bill passed without amendment, only three years after the Commons had decisively rejected similar proposals. *Reasons for the change in attitude were*:

- Peel, who had insisted on a 12-hour day, had now fallen from power and the Conservative party was split. Many Tories who sympathized with Ashley and Fielden but had been unwilling to go against Peel's orders in 1844, were now free to vote for the Ten Hours Bill.
- Some Tory landowners, infuriated by the Repeal of the Corn Laws, may have voted for the bill as a way of revenging themselves on the manufacturers, who had supported the Corn Law repeal.
- In 1847 there was a trade depression during which demand for British textiles was reduced. For this reason most factories were only working a ten-hour day, which seemed to upset the mill-owners' argument that they would be forced out of business if a ten-hour day was brought in.

The triumph was short-lived: as trade revived, manufacturers began to use the relay system, keeping their mills working from 5.30 a.m. until 8.30 p.m., so that adult males were still required to work over 12 hours. Ashley, back in parliament, kept up the agitation for a limit on factory opening hours, and eventually he agreed to a compromise with the mill-owning interests. This was passed into law as:

(h) *The Factory Act of 1850*

- Factories should only be open for 12 hours, of which an hour and a half must be for meals.
- The working day for women and young people was to be ten and a half hours.
- On Saturdays the factories must close at 2 p.m. and women and young people must only work seven-and-a-half hours.

Although some of Ashley's supporters were annoyed with him for agreeing to the extra half-hour, the Act was nevertheless a great achievement. As well as a ten and a half hour day and the half day off for women and children, it meant that in most cases the men's working day was also limited, even though this was not specifically mentioned in the Act. The shorter working day did not cause a fall in production as many manfacturers had feared. Gradually the health and efficiency of the textile workers improved and serious accidents were almost eliminated.

As yet these laws only applied to textile mills; it now remained to extend government control and regulation to those trades and industries where workers were still unprotected. Ashley (who became Earl of Shaftesbury in 1851) could not rest until all workers had been brought under some sort of protection. There were other reformers of course – he was not personally responsible for all subsequent improvements; but it was usually Shaftesbury who stole the limelight. As late as 1884, at the age of 83, he was still making speeches in the Lords and giving evidence to Royal Commissions (he died in October 1885).

(i) *More mining legislation*

The 1842 Mines Act had said nothing about safety in mines and there continued to be regular explosions and disasters.

- *The Coal Mines Inspection Act (1850)* provided more inspectors to enforce the earlier Act and to produce detailed reports on conditions and safety standards. However, it was a slow and difficult job to get even these modest advances, since the coal-owners in the Lords bitterly opposed all attempts at legislation; Lord Londonderry thought the 1850 Act was 'infernal'.
- *The Mines Regulation and Inspection Act (1860)* increased the number of inspectors and said that no boys under 12 must work underground.
- In 1862 it was laid down that every mine must have at least two shafts to improve the chances of escape if there was an explosion. By this time, *the Royal School of Mines* (opened in 1851) was doing invaluable work training inspectors and developing new and safer techniques.
- *The Coal Mines Regulation Act (1872)* insisted on the introduction of some of these safer methods: fan ventilators, stronger timbering, wire ropes, improved winding machinery and better safety lamps.
- Finally *the 1887 Mines Act* introduced stringent regulations about blasting precautions and the provision of first-aid and ambulance facilities.

(j) *More factory and workshop legislation*

In 1862 Shaftesbury secured the appointment of the Children's Employment Commission to investigate conditions in the other industries. As a result of the Commission's Reports, *two vitally important Acts were passed in 1867* by the Conservatives: one extended the mill legislation to all other workshops employing more than 50 people (such as iron and steel works, potteries, glass and paper mills and printing works). The other extended the regulations to workshops and ordinary houses where fewer than 50 people were employed.

This was a tremendous victory for Shaftesbury; but he had not quite finished yet – in 1871 he made a moving speech in the Lords about conditions in brickfields. 'I saw little children, three-parts naked, tottering under the weight of wet clay, some of it on their hands and some on their shoulders, and little girls with large masses of wet, cold and dripping clay pressed on their abdomens. They had to endure the heat of the kiln, and to enter places where the heat was so intense that I was not myself able to remain more than two or three minutes.' As a result, brickfields were brought under the Factory Act regulations.

Disraeli's Conservative government (1874–80) introduced further improvements:

1 *The Factory Act of 1874* reduced the working day to ten hours (instead of ten and a half). No child could be employed until he was ten (instead of eight); no young person could work full-time until he or she was 14 (instead of 13).

2 *The Factory and Workshops Act of 1878* put right a weakness of the 1867 legislation, which had placed the responsibility for inspecting workshops employing under 50 people on to the shoulders of local authorities, many of which had failed to make regular inspections. The new Act brought these premises under government inspection. This was an important advance, although there were still problems in making sure that the regulations were kept in private houses.

Another Conservative measure, *The Factory Act of 1891*, raised the minimum age at which children could be employed in factories to 11 (see Section 16.5(b)).

12.4 Public health: what were the main problems in industrial towns?

(a) *The rapid increase in the population*

This was at the root of most of the problems. Between 1801 and 1851 the population of England, Wales and Scotland more or less doubled, from 10.5 million to 20.8 million. Much of the increase was concentrated in industrial towns and cities, which had grown too quickly for the influx of people to be housed satisfactorily. During the same period – 1801–51 – the population of Glasgow increased from 77 000 to 357 000, Edinburgh from 83 000 to 202 000, Liverpool from 82 000 to 376 000, Manchester from 75 000 to 303 000, Birmingham from 71 000 to 233 000 and Leeds from 53, 000 to 172 000. Even more spectacular was the case of Bradford whose population increased eightfold during the same period, from only 13 000 to 104 000.* In the late 1840s the cities of northern England absorbed thousands of starving Irish fleeing from the potato famine. At first empty cellars and attics were pressed into use; later, cheap accommodation was

---

* Statistics from *Britain 1987*, London, HMSO, pp. 7, 22; B. R. Mitchell & P. Deane, *Abstract of British Historical Statistics*, Cambridge, 1962, pp. 6–7, 24–7.

built so that workers could live near the factories. Since there were few building regulations, this tended to consist of rows of cramped back-to-back houses (in northern England) or huge tenement blocks (in Scotland). Everywhere there was the problem of overcrowding – in 1847 a typical street (Church Lane) in the East End of London had 1095 people living in only 27 houses – an average of 40 people to a house, and probably eight to a room.

(b) *Lack of proper amenities*

Almost without exception in the rapidly growing industrial towns and cities there was a complete lack of what we, at the end of the twentieth century, consider to be the basic amenities – a pure water supply, drainage and sewage disposal, and street cleansing.

1 In working-class houses there was no such refinement as the water closet type of lavatory; usually there was an outside privy which might have to serve as many as 20 houses; these privies were not connected to sewers, but drained into cesspits which had to be emptied manually. A doctor who visited a particularly bad part of Liverpool reported: 'I found the whole court inundated with fluid filth which had oozed through the walls from two adjoining ashpits or cesspools and which had no means of escape in consequence of the court being below the level of the street, and having no drain. . . . The court had remained for two or three years in the state in which I saw it.' A Manchester doctor wrote about 'streets full of pits, brimful of stagnant water, the receptacle of dead cats and dogs'. In Nottingham 'the courts have no back yards, and the privies are common to the whole court; they present scenes of surpassing filth . . . the refuse is allowed to accumulate until, by its mass and its advanced putrifaction, it shall have acquired value as manure'.

2 Drinking water was usually supplied by private companies, but only the wealthiest people had water piped to their houses. The rest had to use stand-pipes, taps or pumps outside in the street, which would probably only be turned on for part of the day. Many towns had to use river water which was always polluted. London's water supply came mostly from the Thames into which no fewer than 237 sewers were emptied. In 1841 a Leeds newspaper described the River Aire (which supplied much of the city's drinking water) as being 'charged with the contents of about 200 water closets and similar places, a great number of common drains, the draining from dunghills, the Infirmary (dead leeches, poultices for patients), slaughter houses, pig manure, old urine wash and all sorts of decomposed animal and vegetable substances'.

3 There were unsatisfactory arrangements for funerals and burials which added to the general health hazards. Corpses were often kept in the house for a week or more (to give the family time to raise cash for the funeral expenses), even when death was due to an infectious disease such as cholera or typhoid. Cemeteries and churchyards were grossly overfilled; according to Edwin Chadwick's report on burial (1834), in London, 'on spaces of ground which do not exceed 203 acres, closely surrounded by the abodes of the living, layer upon layer, each consisting of a population equivalent to a large army of 20 000 adults and nearly 30 000 youths and children is every year imperfectly interred'. Some graveyards contaminated the district's water supply.

(c) *High death-rate from infectious diseases*

The appalling fact was that in 1840, one child in three died before reaching the age of five. Cholera was perhaps the most terrible of all these diseases. It first appeared in

Britain in Sunderland in 1831 and rapidly reached epidemic proportions, killing 21 000 people in England and Wales, 9000 in Scotland and 20 000 in Ireland. An even worse epidemic followed in 1848–9 which at its height was killing 2000 people a week in London alone; altogether 90 000 died in that outbreak, and there were further epidemics in 1854 and 1867. It was not known at the time that the cholera bacillus is carried in water that may otherwise be pure, which is why it affected the rich with their piped water supplies as well as the poor. The stages of the disease were horrifying: beginning with vomiting, the skin then turned blue, purple and finally brown or black; eventually the patient was afflicted with severe breathlessness, followed by rigid spasms of the legs and thighs, and almost invariably by death. Much more common were diseases such as typhus (usually referred to simply as 'the fever'), typhoid and tuberculosis (consumption), scarlet fever, diphtheria, measles and even ordinary diarrhoea, all of which were caused by contaminated water and lack of proper sewage disposal. Though they were all killers, the most lethal was tuberculosis, which caused between a quarter and one-third of all deaths during the first half of the century.

The national death-rate increased as the industrial towns mushroomed; before 1831 the figure was in the region of 19 per thousand, but during the 1830s it rose steadily to 22.4 (in 1838) and reached a peak of 25.1 in 1849. However, this was the average figure; in crowded urban areas the death-rate was usually around 30 per thousand, and in Glasgow during the 1830 cholera epidemic it hit 49 per thousand.

All of these problems were highlighted by Edwin Chadwick's *Report on the Sanitary Condition of the Labouring Population of Great Britain (July 1842)*. A fanatical Benthamite, always striving for greater efficiency, Chadwick had already been involved in the 1834 Poor Law Commission Report (see Section 5.3) and with the Royal Commission on Factory Conditions (1833) (see Section 12.3(d)). After the Poor Law Amendment Act of 1834 Chadwick was Secretary to the Poor Law Commissioners, and he became interested in the causes of disease. In Chadwick's way of looking at things, sickness cost money and caused people to become paupers, which cost more money. He hoped therefore, by controlling disease, to reduce the expenses of supporting the sick. What his report did was to hammer home the point that filthy conditions were the main causes of disease. He produced some startling statistics of life expectancy which shocked the public; whereas a lawyer in a rural county such as Rutland could expect to live (on average) to be 52, a labourer in a Manchester slum would be lucky to survive until 17, while in Liverpool his average life expectancy would be only 15. Unfortunately there was no organization or body either locally or nationally with the expertise or the funds necessary to tackle such enormous problems, except of course the government.

12.5 What advances were made in public health during the nineteenth century?

In his report Chadwick suggested a number of measures which would improve public health. These included providing all houses with piped water, which could be used for flushing sewage away from the houses into main sewers; instead of being large square tunnels built of porous brick, sewers ought to be smaller, tube-shaped and made of non-porous (glazed) pottery. The new system should be organized and controlled centrally, like the New Poor Law. But improvements were very slow to come, mainly because of the enormous expense involved. How, for example, did one set about supplying cities the size of Glasgow and Manchester with a system of pure, piped water? In addition, Chadwick's emphasis on compulsion and centralization was completely alien to Victorian *laissez-faire* principles. When progress did take place, it was due partly to government action, but more to advances in medicine, and to some great engineering projects.

(a) *Government action*

Before 1848, any action to improve sanitary conditions was taken on a local basis without any central direction. Liverpool had its own Sanitary Act (1846) which made the town council responsible for drainage, sewerage, cleansing and paving, and it was the first city to have a permanent Medical Officer of Health. But the nature and efficiency of these local *Improvement Committees* as they were called, varied widely. Chadwick's report had made it obvious that legislation was needed to cover the country as a whole, and after tremendous pressure and agitation, Russell's government introduced the first in a series of new measures:

1 *The Public Health Act of 1848* gave local authorities the power to appoint Boards of Health whose work was to be supervised by the General Board of Health, headed by Chadwick himself and including Lord Shaftesbury. Unfortunately the Act had a fatal weakness: there was no compulsion on local authorities to set up Boards; by 1854 only 182 Boards had been appointed in England and Wales, covering only two million people out of a population of 18 million. Most of those set up were ineffective; only 13 of them had started large-scale water and sewage works. Meanwhile the government continued to pass local acts; for example:
2 In 1858 three million pounds was provided to prevent sewage from being pumped into the Thames above London. Even this did not prevent 10 000 Londoners from dying in the 1866 cholera epidemic, and the national death-rate was still running at over 23 per thousand.
3 *The Sanitation Act of 1866* recognized that the 1848 Act had been a failure, and it therefore compelled local authorities to improve local conditions and remove nuisances. According to *The Times*, this 1866 Act 'introduces a new sanitary era'.
4 *The Public Health Act of 1872* (introduced by Gladstone's Liberal government) clarified the position by dividing England and Wales into districts under specific health authorities, each of which was to have its own Medical Officer and staff. Unfortunately this Act was another failure because it was not clear what the duties of the health boards were, and most of them were reluctant to spend the cash necessary for radical health reform.
5 *The Public Health Act of 1875*. It was left to Disraeli and the Conservatives to rationalize and consolidate the complicated patchwork of health legislation. The Act was the work of Disraeli's Home Secretary, R. A. Cross, and has been rated by some historians as one of the greatest pieces of legislation in the nineteenth century. It laid down in clear detail *what the compulsory duties of local authorities were*: they had to ensure that there was adequate water supply, drainage and sewage disposal; nuisances were to be removed, offensive trades regulated, and contaminated food to be sought out, confiscated and destroyed. Cases of infectious disease were to be notified to the Medical Officer, who had to take appropriate action. Other regulations dealt with markets, street lighting and burials.
6 *The Artisans' Dwellings Act (1875)*, also the work of Cross, attempted to deal with the problem of slum housing. Local authorities were given the power, if they wished to use it, to buy up and demolish insanitary property and replace it with modern, healthy accommodation. It was the violent opposition of many of his own party, who thought the bill a blatant invasion of landlords' rights, that caused Cross

to abandon the idea of making slum clearance compulsory. This seriously weakened the Act, but at least a start had been made. Birmingham, under its mayor, Joseph Chamberlain, was one of the first cities to begin a massive slum clearance programme (see also Section 14.2(a)).

7   *The Housing of the Working Classes Acts (1890 and 1900)* were two more Conservative measures which remedied the deficiencies of the 1875 Act. Now local authorities were *compelled* to demolish unhealthy housing and to provide other accommodation for those made homeless. Owners of slum property could be compelled to sell it to the council for demolition. What was needed next was legislation to carry slum clearance a step further by regulating the planning of towns. Unfortunately a great opportunity to encourage careful and systematic planning of new building schemes and new towns was missed in the next major piece of legislation . . .

8   *The Housing and Town Planning Act (1909).* This Liberal measure allowed local authorities to introduce town planning schemes in order to avoid piecemeal building, if they wished. But there was no compulsion, and the Act was so complicated that only one major scheme was started in the whole country before 1914.

(b) *Medical improvements*

Already in the late 1790s Edward Jenner had introduced his vaccination technique which controlled smallpox, though the disease was still dangerous. About the same time Humphry Davy (who was later to invent the miners' safety lamp) had used nitrous oxide (laughing gas) as a partial anaesthetic for use during operations. But it was another half a century before any further advances were made:

● The introduction of chloroform (late 1840s) as a general anaesthetic gave surgeons more time to perform operations, though there was still the problem of how to avoid infection in the wound.
● A major breakthrough came in the early 1860s when Louis Pasteur, a French chemist, put forward the germ theory of disease: that decay and putrefaction as well as infectious diseases are caused by micro-organisms or bacteria, not just by filth and bad smells, as Chadwick thought. A Glasgow surgeon, Joseph Lister, building on Pasteur's work, developed an antiseptic technique using carbolic acid; this reduced infection after operations and helped to bring down the death-rate.
● Standards of nursing improved steadily thanks to the work of Elizabeth Fry, who founded the Institute of Nursing Sisters, and of Florence Nightingale, who developed the Nightingale School of Nursing in St Thomas's Hospital, London.
● There were improvements in the education of doctors, and in 1858 the Medical Act set up the General Council for Medical Education and Registration, whose function was to supervise standards of efficiency among doctors.

(c) *Engineering achievements*

This might seem a strange topic to include in a chapter on public health, but in fact the provision of large-scale water, sewage and drainage schemes required some remarkable feats of civil engineering. One of the first cities to attempt such a scheme was Manchester, which in 1847 began work on its huge Longdendale waterworks, which was to cost in the region of three quarters of a million pounds. When it was completed ten years later, it could supply the city with thirty million gallons a day, whereas the previous private companies had managed no more than two million gallons a day. As soon as a continuous supply of water was available, work could go ahead on laying sewers. Liverpool soon followed with a massive water scheme supplied from reservoirs near Rivington Pike, which by 1857 could hold 3000 million gallons; by 1875 most of the city's housing had water closets connected to sewers. London's system of waterized sewers was completed by 1866. Most cities and towns of any size had followed suit by 1900.

In spite of the beginnings of improvement, the death rate was still hovering around 24 per thousand in 1870. Slowly but steadily over the next 30 years Britain became a healthier place to live in; the 1901 census showed that overcrowding was beginning to thin out and the death-rate had dropped to below 18 per thousand. Even so, every now and again, some sort of epidemic occurred which upset the growing late-Victorian complacency – a typhoid epidemic in Blackburn in 1881, cholera in London in 1893, and smallpox in several ports in 1902. The investigations of Charles Booth in London (1889–1903) and Seebohm Rowntree in York (1901) showed that there was still some way to go to the achievement of the final victory over filth and infectious diseases (see Section 20.1(b)).

12.6 Education: what kinds of school were there before 1870 and why was there no state system of elementary education?

(a) *A confusion of different types of school*

Before 1870 there was hardly anything which could be described as an educational 'system' in Britain. The government took very little interest in education and gave no financial support to education before 1833. Existing schools were run by private individuals and religious groups, and sometimes by companies of the City of London. Consequently there was a confusing hotch-potch of different sorts of school:

1 *Public schools.* There were nine major ones (Eton, Harrow, Westminster, Charterhouse, Rugby, St Paul's, Shrewsbury,Winchester and Merchant Taylors) and lots of minor ones. Although called 'public' schools, they were in fact only open to those members of the public who could afford the fees – wealthy aristocrats, landowners and industrialists. The education they provided was based on the classics (Latin and Greek), and in the early part of the century did not even include mathematics. It was only very gradually that the public school curriculum was modernized, thanks to the work of progressive Headmasters such as Thomas Arnold (Headmaster of Rugby, 1828–42) who insisted on mathematics and French being taught regularly. He also introduced the prefect system and encouraged the ideal of Christian duty.

2 *Grammar schools.* Many of these were ancient foundations going back to the sixteenth century. Unlike public schools, they did not take boarders, but the subjects taught were similar – heavily weighted towards Latin and Greek. Fees were charged, though most grammar schools provided some free places for poor children.

3 *Private schools.* Also fee-paying, these were newer schools started by people who were impatient with the old-fashioned curriculum of the public and grammar schools. One of the earliest was the Liverpool Royal Institution School (1819) which taught mathematics, modern languages and science.

All these schools were completely outside the reach of the great mass of the population, who were lucky to receive a few years of elementary education – basic reading, writing and arithmetic – in what were known as *Voluntary Schools*. These included Sunday Schools (Robert Raikes had founded the Sunday School Union in 1780), dame schools run by elderly ladies and often no more than child-minding establishments, and charity schools like those set up by the Society for Promoting Christian Knowledge (SPCK). After the 1833 Factory Act, a number of factory schools were set up, and during the 1840s large numbers of Ragged Schools were started in deprived areas, with Ashley as president of the Ragged Schools Union. The most widespread and best organized of the Voluntary Schools were those run by the Church of England (Anglican) and the Nonconformist churches:

● The Church of England organized its schools through *the National Society*, founded in 1811 by Andrew Bell.
● The Nonconformists worked through *the British and Foreign Schools Society (1814)*, whose leading light was Joseph Lancaster, who ran his own school for a thousand pupils in Borough Road, London.

There was bitter rivalry and hostility between these two groups, though their teaching methods – based on *the monitorial system* – were similar. In order to save money, and because of the shortage of teachers, older pupils (known as monitors) taught small groups of children. According to Lancaster: 'the whole system of tuition is almost entirely conducted by boys; the school is divided into classes, and to each of these a lad is appointed a monitor; he is responsible for the morals, improvement, good order and cleanliness of the whole class. To be a monitor is coveted by the whole school.'

There was wide variation in the quality of elementary education provided, and in some industrial areas there were no schools at all for working class children. In 1818 only one in 17 of the population was receiving any elementary education.

(b) *Why was there no state system of education?*

Many people felt that the only way to secure an efficient education system was for the government to organize it. Jeremy Bentham thought it would eliminate the dangerous rivalry between different religious denominations. In 1820 a Whig politician, Henry Brougham, introduced a bill which would have set up schools in parishes where there were none already in existence, but it was easily defeated.

Reasons for lack of progress:
1   The same *laissez-faire* outlook which delayed government intervention in the other problem areas applied equally to education; if the poor wanted education, they must see to it themselves; it was no part of a government's function to provide such an expensive service.
2   There was a strong belief that education of the working classes was unnecessary; all they needed were the skills of the job for which they were destined, and these could be learned perfectly well by simply doing the job. And if children spent their time being educated, industrialists would lose their source of cheap labour.
3   An educated working class could be dangerous: one MP, Davies Giddy, told parliament in 1807 that education would teach workers 'to despise their lot in life instead of making them good servants in agriculture and other laborious employments to which their rank in society had destined them'. He added that it would enable them to read seditious pamphlets and 'render them insolent to their superiors'. In 1825, another MP, afraid of revolution, delivered himself of the view that 'whenever the lower orders of any great nation have obtained a smattering of

knowledge, they have generally used it to produce national ruin'. Two years later a Tory MP argued that 'as education has increased amidst the people, vice and crime have increased . . . the majority of criminals consist of those who have been educated'.

12.7 Show how and why the government intervened in education

(a) First government action on education

Gradually those who were in favour of government intervention gained the ascendancy in parliament. The Whig government which came to power in 1830 was under pressure from its Radical Benthamite wing, and at last in 1833 the first breakthrough was made. However, *in the period 1833–70* the government did not provide any schools itself; it merely made some cash available and tried to make sure that the voluntary societies used it efficiently:

1   In 1833 the government gave a total of £20 000 to the Anglican and Nonconformist societies to help them to provide more school buildings. £10 000 was voted for building schools in Scotland.
2   In 1839 the grant was increased to £30 000, on condition that a committee of the Privy Council was set up to supervise how the money was spent. The secretary of the committee was Sir James Kay-Shuttleworth, who had been a doctor in the slums of Manchester; later, as a Poor Law commissioner, he developed workhouse schools and set up his own training college for teachers. At his suggestion, school inspectors were appointed; they soon began to produce disturbing reports about the inefficiency of the monitorial system.
3   In the 1840s teacher training colleges were established by the religious societies, following the example of Kay-Shuttleworth's Battersea College. He also introduced *the pupil-teacher scheme* by which able students were apprenticed to good voluntary schools at the age of 13 for five years, after which, with the help of government grants, they could go on to teacher training colleges. To finance this new scheme, which gradually replaced the monitorial system, the annual government grant was increased to £100 000 (1847). Within 10 years it had reached £500 000 and in 1856 the government set up the Department of Education to look after its administration.
4   *The Newcastle Commission* reported (1861) that although one in seven of the population was now receiving some education, the majority were still unable to read a newspaper or write a letter. It recommended that grants to schools and teachers' salaries should depend on how well pupils performed in examinations.
5   Robert Lowe, head of the Education Department in Palmerston's Liberal government of 1859–65, accepted this recommendation and introduced a *'payment by results' system (1862)*. School inspectors tested the pupils in reading, writing and arithmetic (known as the '3Rs'), and the number who passed determined both grants and salaries. The system aroused tremendous criticism because although it made schools more efficient and saved money, it led to a great deal of mechanical cramming and reciting of lists of facts learned off by heart. It also meant that the curriculum tended to become narrowed to the '3Rs', and it caused considerable nervous strain among teachers. Even so the system lasted until 1897.

The year 1870 saw the beginning of a new era: Gladstone's Liberal government (1868–74) decided that it was up to the state to make sure that every child received some education; if necessary, it would provide schools itself.

(b) *Why did the government decide that a state system of elementary education was needed?*

1   The 1867 Reform Act, which gave the vote to industrial workers living in the boroughs, meant that they needed some education to enable them to decide how to vote. According to Lowe himself: 'from the moment you entrust the masses with power, their education becomes an imperative necessity; you have placed the government of this country in the hands of the masses and you must therefore give them an education'.
2   Britain was lagging well behind Prussia and the northern states of the USA in the provision of education, and both seemed to be doing well militarily and economically. Prussia had easily defeated Austria–Hungary in 1866 and the North had turned out the eventual winner in the American Civil War (1861–5); it was already clear that both would soon be challenging Britain's industrial lead. These developments helped to swing opinion in Britain in favour of education for the masses.
3   The rapid population growth meant that the Voluntary Societies were unable to keep up; in fact they were losing ground – in some large industrial cities less than one in ten of the child population was receiving any education.
4   The supporters of education for the masses were waging a more vigorous campaign than ever before; spearheading the movement was Joseph Chamberlain's National Education League started in Birmingham in 1869.
5   Gladstone was anxious for greater efficiency and believed in 'equality of opportunity' for everybody.
6   Finally, Britain's economy was booming, so that the government felt able to provide the extra cash that would be needed to finance a full state system of education.

(c) *Forster's Education Act (1870)*

W. E. Forster, MP for Bradford and Gladstone's head of the Education Department, had a difficult problem: he had to find a way of including the existing religious voluntary schools within the new legislation; since there were so many of these schools, they could not simply be ignored, and certainly not abolished. Also he had to try not to seem to be favouring either Anglicans or Nonconformists. The result was bound to be a compromise:

1   The existing Anglican and Nonconformist voluntary schools were allowed to continue with increased grants from the government.
2   In areas where there was no voluntary school or where the existing schools could not provide enough places, a locally elected School Board was to be set up. Its function was to organize Board Schools for children aged five to twelve. These schools were to receive government grants as well as extra finance from a special local rate to be collected by the Board.
3   As an attempt to sidestep the religious problem, it was left to each Board to decide whether religious education was to be given in their schools. If so, it should be restricted to Bible study, and this should be 'undenominational' (it should not be taught with an Anglican or Nonconformist bias).
4   Attendance was not made compulsory (because as yet there were not enough school places for every child) and it was not made free. However, Boards could pay the fees for poor children either in the new Board Schools or in the voluntary schools.

Forster's Act caused a great political row: the religious bodies resented the fact that their schools received no money from local rates, and that the new schools might provide no religious teaching at all. Nonconformists were particularly annoyed because they had hoped that Forster would abolish Anglican schools, whereas he had actually strengthened the already strong Anglican position in many areas. To add insult to injury, Nonconformists now found themselves having to pay the local education rate, much of which might be used to finance 'godless' Board Schools. Equally galling was the possibility that some Boards would use their rates to pay the fees of poor children being educated in Anglican schools. This unfortunate situation led to bitter struggles in which the different religious groups fought for control of their local School Board.

The Act can also be criticized on the grounds that it resulted in a dual system of education – in which church schools were handicapped by a shortage of money. However, it achieved what Forster and Gladstone had in mind – 'to complete the present voluntary system ... to fill up the gaps'. B. H. Abbott claims that the Act 'remains a remarkable piece of social legislation, playing a vital part in civilizing the masses in the nation's vast industrial cities'. Certainly between 1870 and 1880, the number of children receiving elementary education had more than doubled to almost three million, as the new Board Schools sprang up all over the country.

(d) *Further developments in elementary education*

● *Sandon's Education Act (1876).* Lord Sandon, head of the Education Department in Disraeli's second government (1874–80), decided that local School Attendance Committees should be set up to encourage as many children as possible to take advantage of educational opportunities; parents were to be responsible for making sure that children received basic instruction, and committees *could* help parents who were too poor to pay the school fees, though this was not compulsory.
● *A. J. Mundella's Education Act (1881)* was a Liberal measure which *made attendance at elementary school compulsory* for all children between five and ten. There was still the problem of fees, which worked out at around three pence per child per week; this was far too much for poor families to afford, if they had several children.
● *The Fee Grant Act (1891).* This was a Conservative measure which meant that in practice *elementary education was now free*.
● During the 1890s Lowe's payment by results system was gradually phased out, thanks to recommendations made by *the Cross Commission (1888)*. Grants to schools were now based on attendance, and 'bald teaching of facts' was replaced by 'the development of interest and intelligence'.

By the end of the nineteenth century the vast majority of children were receiving some basic instruction, and the quality of that education was improving.

(e) *The Balfour Education Act (1902)*

This was the next major landmark, the work of A. J. Balfour, Conservative Prime Minister from 1902 until 1905. He decided that radical changes were needed in the way elementary education was being organized, and that some government policy was needed to deal with secondary education. *His reasons were*:

● Because of a shortage of money, the Voluntary Schools (of which the great majority were run by Anglicans) were much inferior in every way to the Board Schools.
● *The Bryce Commission reported (1895)* that there was a chronic shortage of suitable technical education, while Britain's industrial competitors – USA, Germany and Belgium – were far ahead in this field.

The details of the new Act were worked out by R. L. Morant, Balfour's educational adviser:

1 The School Boards were abolished; county councils and county borough councils were to run both Voluntary and Board Schools and were made responsible for organizing secondary and technical education.
2 For the first time Voluntary Schools were to receive money from the rates to enable them to bring their standards up to those of the Board Schools.
3 Local authorities, working through their own education committees, could help existing secondary schools (mostly old grammar schools) with money from the rates; they were also directed to set up their own fee-paying secondary schools.

The Balfour/Morant Act was vitally important: it meant a general raising of the standards of elementary education and more uniformity, though it perpetuated the dual church/state system. It also meant that the state was going to see to it that secondary education was more widely available; this caused the appearance of a new phenomenon – the state grammar school. Unfortunately these at first tended to model themselves on the old private grammar schools with their concentration on Latin and Greek and with insufficient attention to technical and scientific subjects.

At the time the Act caused another religious controversy, bitterly disappointing the Nonconformists again. They had hoped that Balfour would abolish Anglican and Roman Catholic schools, which were mostly teetering on the verge of bankruptcy. Instead they were rescued by money from the local rates (to which the Nonconformists themselves had to contribute). In some country areas, especially in Wales, the only school available was an Anglican one, which Nonconformists had to allow their children to attend.

(f) *Further steps towards secondary education for all*

● In 1906 Campbell-Bannerman's Liberal government introduced what in effect became *the 11-plus system*. All secondary schools which were receiving government grants had to reserve 25 per cent of their places for children coming up from elementary schools; they would be awarded scholarships on the results of a special entrance examination.

● *H. A. L. Fisher's Education Act (1918)* was passed by the Lloyd George government shortly before the end of the First World War. It raised the school-leaving age from 12 to 14 and required local authorities to provide what it called 'day continuation classes' or part-time education to the age of 18 for those children who left school at 14. Grants to secondary schools were increased so that more scholarships could be awarded, and State Scholarships were introduced so that secondary school pupils could go on to University.

Education had clearly come a long way since 1833, but there was still much to be done. In fact very little was done about Fisher's day continuation classes, because after the war, governments claimed to be short of the necessary funds. Although much was made of the fact that an 'educational ladder' had been established, it was still very rare for a child from a working class home to get to University. As J. A. Hobson (a well-known Edwardian expert on politics and economics) put it: 'What is needed is not an educational ladder, narrowing as it rises, to be climbed with difficulty by a chosen energetic few ... it is a broad, easy stair that is wanted ... one which will entice everyone to rise.'

(Later developments included the 1926 Hadow Report, see Section 20.4(e) and the 1944 Butler Act, see Section 28.7(b).)

Questions

1 The Case for Factory Reform

Study Sources A to E and then answer the questions which follow.

Source A

Evidence given by Samuel Coulson to the Parliamentary Commission on Factory Children's Labour, 1831–2

At what time, in the brisk time, did those girls go to the mill?
  In the brisk time, for about six weeks, they have gone at three o'clock in the morning, and ended at ten or nearly half-past at night.
What interval for rest and refreshment were allowed during those nineteen hours of labour?
  Breakfast a quarter of an hour, dinner half an hour and drinking a quarter of an hour.
Had you not great difficulty in awakening your children to this excessive labour?
  Yes: in the early time we had to take them up asleep and shake them when we got them on the floor to dress them, before we could get them off to their work; but not so in the common hours.
What time did you get them up in the morning?
  In general at two o'clock to dress them.
So that they had not above four hours of sleep at this time?
  No, they had not.
The usual hours of work were from six in the morning till half-past eight at night?
  Yes.
Did this excessive term of labour cause much cruelty also?
  Yes, with being so much fatigued the strap was frequently used.

Source B

Evidence given by John Hall to the Parliamentary Commission on Factory Children's Labour, 1831–2

Do you live at Bradford?
  Yes.
Are you the overlooker of Mr John Wood?
  I am.
Will you have the goodness to state the present hours of working in your factory?
  Our present hours are from six until seven.
With what intervals for rest and refreshment?
  Half an hour for breakfast and forty minutes for dinner.
Do you believe that the children can endure the labour you have been describing without injury?
  No, I do not.
When your hands have been employed for some time, do you see any alteration in their appearance?
  In the course of a few weeks I see a paleness in their faces, and they grow spiritless and tired.
Have you remarked that cases of deformity are very common in Bradford?
  They are very common. I have the names of, I think about 200 families I have visited myself that have deformed children, and I have taken particular care not

to put down one single case where it might have happened by accident, but only those whom I judge to have been thrown crooked by the practice of piecening ...

Source C

Evidence of William Forster of Plomton Mill near Knaresborough to the Parliamentary Commission on Factory Children's Labour, 1831–2

I often wish that Michael Sadler and Richard Oastler had my mill hands to govern. If they had they would, I am persuaded, soon abandon their visionary opinions. If the hours of child labour are reduced, mills will be unable to work a full twelve hour day, with a consequent reduction in the earnings of the adult workers as well as the profits of the mill-owners. The youngest child employed by me is never exhausted by 12 hours labour, which they clearly show by playing and romping when the hours of labour terminate.

Source D

An illustration from The Life and Adventures of Michael Armstrong the Factory Boy *by Frances Trollope, published in 1840. Michael, who has been put to work at the 'mules' repairing broken threads, is greeted by a former playmate*

Illus. 12.2

Extracts from a letter written by a Lancashire mill-owner in 1845

As to the conclusions I have come to from the working of my ... mill ... for 11 hours instead of 12 hours each day ... I am quite satisfied that both as much yarn and cloth may be produced at quite as low a cost in 11 as in 12 hours. . . . It is my intention to make a further reduction to ten and a half hours, without the slightest fear of suffering loss ... I find the hands work with greater energy and spirit; they are more cheerful and happy ...

About 20 years ago ... we had about 30 young women in our Manchester warehouse. I requested that they would work 12 hours (a day) instead of 11. At the end of the week, I found that they had not a mere trifle more work done; but supposing there was some incidental cause of this I requested that they would work 13 hours (a day) the following week, at the end of which they had produced less instead of more work. They were exhausted and making bad work and little of it. Since then I have been an advocate of shorter hours of labour.

Source: all these sources are taken from a Northern Examining Association Specimen Question.

(a) Compare and contrast Sources A.B,C and E and the evidence they provide about factory working conditions and their effects. (8 marks)
(b) Which of the Sources A,B and C does the illustration in Source D appear to support? (4 marks)
(c) What reasons can you suggest for the contradictions in these sources:
    (i) between the mill-owner (Source C) and the other two men who gave evidence to the Commission (Sources A and B): (4 marks)
    (ii) between the two mill-owners (Sources C and E). (4 marks
(Total 20 marks)

2 Robert Lowe, Liberal Head of the Education Department from 1859 until 1865, said in 1867: 'You have placed the government of this country in the hands of the masses and you must therefore give them an education'. In the light of this statement:
  (a) Why did it take so long for the state in Britain to introduce a satisfactory system of elementary education?
  (b) To what extent can Forster's Education Act of 1870 be seen as a turning point in the provision of elementary education?

13 Gladstone's first ministry 1868–74

Summary of events

Following the Second Reform Act (1867), the Liberals won the 1868 general election (see Section 8.5(b)), taking 387 seats to the Conservatives' 271. W. E. Gladstone became Prime Minister for the first time (December 1868), taking over from his great Conservative rival, Benjamin Disraeli, whose first government had only lasted since February 1868. During the late 1860s and the 1870s, the confusion in British politics, which had lasted since the Conservative party split in 1846, resolved itself. Politics became a well-defined struggle between two more or less united parties – Liberals and Conservatives – who alternated in government until the Liberals split in 1886 over the question of Irish Home Rule.

Parliament was dominated by the two party leaders, Gladstone and Disraeli. They came from vastly different backgrounds – Gladstone the son of a wealthy Liverpool merchant of Scottish ancestry, Disraeli the son of a comfortably off Jewish writer and novelist whose family had come over to England from Italy. Both were brilliant speakers and debaters, and they heartily detested each other, losing no opportunity to attack each other's policies, sometimes with thrilling oratory. Disraeli once described Gladstone as 'a sophisticated rhetorician, inebriated with the exuberance of his own verbosity', and later, more directly, as 'that unprincipled maniac'. Gladstone had something to say about Disraeli's principles, too: 'his doctrine is false, but the man is more false than the doctrine'. It was a real 'duel of the giants' which lasted for almost 20 years. As historian M. R. D. Foot puts it: 'To the popular imagination, in the days before the entertainment industries had distracted so much attention from politics, Disraeli and Gladstone appeared a pair of Titans, locked in colossal combat.'

Whatever Disraeli thought about Gladstone's principles, or lack of them, Gladstone now had his chance in this first ministry, to put into practice what he saw as the principles of Liberalism. There was a rush of long overdue reforms, which so dismayed Queen Victoria that she referred to Gladstone as 'that half-mad firebrand'. Much of his time was taken up with his largely unsuccessful attempts to solve the problems of Ireland. As so often happens when a government introduces radical changes, so many different people had been offended by the reforms that the Liberals were soundly beaten in the 1874 election, and the Conservatives were back in power with a majority for the first time in almost 30 years.

13.1 What were Gladstone's principles and aims?

(a) *A committed Christian*

Gladstone was deeply religious, and for a time when he was a young man, he thought of becoming an Anglican priest. Throughout his career, politics and religion were closely related and his policies were often dictated by what he thought was morally right. He saw politics as a means of carrying out God's will. During his years as a Tory, he believed that the Anglican Church, as the official (established) state church, had an important part to play in directing the moral life of the nation, and that its special position and privileges must be defended at all costs. However, although he remained a committed Anglican himself, his attitude gradually softened, and he was prepared to be tolerant towards Nonconformists and Roman Catholics. He even came to accept that in Ireland, where the vast majority of people were Roman Catholics, it was unreasonable to have a state church which was Anglican. Not all historians accept that religion *was* Gladstone's great driving motive: A. B. Cooke and John Vincent argue that political expediency usually came first, especially as regards his Irish policy.

Illus. 13.1   William Ewart Gladstone

(b) *Equality of opportunity*

He believed that the government should try to make sure that everybody had 'equality of opportunity'. He was determined, as he put it, to 'liberate' people from outdated restrictions, and he aimed to abolish special privileges which he considered unjust, wherever they existed, whether in the army, the Civil Service, the universities or in religious matters.

(c) *Free trade and laissez-faire*

Gladstone was committed to the principles of free trade and *laissez-faire*, and the idea that free enterprise was the best way to encourage economic growth and prosperity. However, this did not mean that the state had no role to play – he believed in a strong state whose function was to foster the Benthamite virtues of efficiency and economy, even though the two might be contradictory. According to his biographer, Philip Magnus, Gladstone 'loathed waste because he regarded all money as a trust committed by God to man'. One of his favourite words was 'retrenchment', which meant cutting back on government expenditure, and keeping taxation low.

(d) *Lukewarm on social reform*

Oddly enough his religious beliefs did not convince him of the necessity of practical social reform to improve working and living conditions and public health. Apart from the expense involved, too much government help might destroy the moral fibre of the nation. It was for the individual to make the best of his circumstances. The 1872 Public Health Act was Gladstone's only reform to improve actual material conditions, and that was not a success.

(e) *Peace and tranquillity in foreign policy*

In foreign affairs Gladstone's religious views led him to favour a policy of peace and tranquillity and to respect the rights of other countries. This was in great contrast to Lord Palmerston's methods of conducting overseas affairs which Gladstone saw as far too aggressive (as well as too expensive). However, there was a risk that foreign governments might interpret Gladstone's methods as a sign of weakness, though he did protect Britain's interests in Egypt and the Sudan during his second ministry.

(f) *A desire to pacify Ireland*

Gladstone had a burning desire, which became almost an obssession during his later ministries, to find solutions to the problems of Ireland.

(g) *Build up support for the Liberals*

Gladstone aimed to win support for the Liberals among the prosperous working classes (who had just been given the vote in the 1867 Reform Act) and the religious Nonconformists. He deliberately aimed to make himself into a 'populist' leader, making full use of all the available publicity. He toured the country, addressed mass meetings, especially in industrial areas, and won over many of the leading newspaper editors, so that he always got plenty of favourable press coverage. Gladstone was largely successful in this group of aims, and his success goes a long way towards explaining the big Liberal election victories of 1868 and 1880.

(h) *Hold the Liberal party together*

Gladstone's relationship with the Liberal party was never straightforward. It is important to remember that he began his political career in 1832 as a Tory, and opposed nearly all the Whig reforms of the 1830s.When the Conservatives split over Peel's repeal of the Corn Laws in 1846, Gladstone supported Peel and remained a Peelite for many years. He only really committed himself to the Liberal party in 1859 when Palmerston persuaded him to become Chancellor of the Exchequer. Although he had been Liberal for over 30 years when he retired in 1894, Gladstone never quite succeeded in breaking away from some of his early Tory principles. Many of the Liberals never fully understood Gladstone or his motives. The party was a difficult coalition of several different groups which didn't see eye to eye: aristocratic Whig landowners, Benthamite radicals, Nonconformists and Anglicans; they had also split over the need for further parliamentary reform in 1866 (see Section 8.4). Gladstone was constantly on the lookout for some cause which would unite the different factions; this was probably one of the reasons which led him to disestablish the Anglican church in Ireland (see below 13.3).

13.2 Gladstone's domestic reforms: necessary but unpopular

Every single one of the Liberal reforms succeeded in upsetting at least one influential group of people, and sometimes more. But Gladstone pressed on in spite of all protests, fortified by the belief that he was carrying out God's will.

(a) *Forster's Education Act (1870)*

By the late 1860s it was clear that the patchwork of elementary schools provided by the religious voluntary societies was totally unable to cope with the rapidly increasing population. The Forster Act was a creditable attempt to 'fill the gaps' and 'cover the country with good schools'; there could never be 'equality of opportunity' unless the whole population had the benefit of elementary education. Equally important in Gladstone's eyes was that education would enable the working classes to read the scriptures for themselves. However, the Act aroused tremendous opposition from the Nonconformists (for full details see Section 12.7(b–c)).

(b) *The University Tests Act (1871)*

This was a clear case of Gladstone removing a glaring injustice and promoting equality of opportunity in the universities. Action was needed because there was an ancient statute still in operation which allowed only Anglicans to become teachers or members of the administration, or to hold fellowships at Oxford and Cambridge Universities.

The new Act abolished this special privilege of the Church of England and threw these posts open to all suitable candidates, whatever their religion. Nonconformists were pleased but not sufficiently to make them drop their opposition to the Education Act. Many of Gladstone's fellow Anglicans acknowledged that it was a just reform, but others resented their loss of privilege; Lord Salisbury, the future Conservative Prime Minister, led a bitter but unsuccessful attack on the bill in the House of Lords.

(c) *Civil Service reform (1871)*

The problem with the Civil Service was that appointments were still made according to recommendations from an MP or a peer. It depended on who the aspiring candidate knew and what strings he could pull, and even sometimes how much he could afford to pay for the post. Inevitably many of the men appointed in this way were lazy or incompetent. As the administration of the country became more complex, a more efficient Civil Service was needed.

Gladstone, with the strong support of his Chancellor of the Exchequer, Robert Lowe, another efficiency fanatic, introduced the principle that recruitment must be by examination. This was a first-rate reform which opened up the Civil Service to the best brains in the country, and its efficiency and professionalism increased accordingly. However, many of the aristocracy, who had previously dominated the Civil Service, were bitterly opposed; in fact the Foreign Office had to be excluded from the reform because Gladstone's own Foreign Secretary, Lord Granville, flatly refused to agree to it for his department.

(d) *Trade Union reform (1871)*

The legal position, privileges and powers of trades unions had never been precisely defined; the Liberals came up with two measures, both in 1871, to clarify this state of affairs:

- *The Trade Union Act* recognized unions as legal bodies with rights to own property and funds, to protect their property and funds at law, and to strike. Trade unionists greeted the Act with delight, but almost immediately, this turned to disgust at the second measure:
- *The Criminal Law Amendment Act*. This stated that although unions could organize strikes, picketing of all types, even peaceful, was forbidden. In practice, it would be impossible to make a strike effective.

Some historians believe that this Act was Gladstone's most serious miscalculation in home affairs, since it lost it him much working-class support. His religious views probably explain his attitude: he was utterly against any kind of force to sway opinion, and picketing could easily lead to violence.

(e) *The Public Health Act of 1872*

This was a half-hearted attempt to deal with Britain's chaotic health problems. It was a great disappointment to those who were looking to the government for positive leadership and a large-scale injection of cash. Gladstone was not sufficiently interested, and the people who ran the local boards of health seemed to think that their most important function was to keep expenditure to a minimum. It was a classic example of the Benthamite contradiction – efficiency being sacrificed to economy (see Section 12.5(a)).

(f) *The Ballot Act (1872)*

Voting in elections was still carried out in public by a show of hands, a system which lent itself to bribery, corruption and intimidation of all kinds. *Gladstone's Act made voting secret*, but although it made elections more orderly affairs, it did not completely remove bribery and corruption: there were still ways of buying votes – free beer in pubs, and free transport for voters being the most obvious. It was not until the Corrupt Practices Act (1883), passed during Gladstone's second ministry, that corruption was successfully brought under control.

Although it was a necessary measure leading to more efficient electoral processes, the Ballot Act was highly unpopular with landlords and employers, who could no longer control the way their tenants and workers voted. Lord Hartington, leader of the right-wing Liberals, was one of the severest critics of the bill.

(g) *The Licensing Act (1872)*

Widespread drunkenness was one of the most striking features of mid-nineteenth-century Britain. Gladstone and his Home Secretary, Henry Bruce, looked on this as a moral issue; they felt that there were too many public houses and that the massive profit made by brewers ought to be controlled. Bruce was forced to tone down the original version of his bill, so fierce was the outcry from the brewers. The final version was a very mild measure:

- It gave magistrates the power to issue licenses for the opening of public houses, so that in areas where it was felt there were already too many, magistrates would be able to close some pubs down.
- Pubs must close at midnight in towns and at 11 o'clock in country areas.

- The adulteration of beer was forbidden; one of the most common practices was to add salt to the beer, which increased the thirst and therefore sales as well.

Though mild, the Act was highly unpopular with the working classes, and there were a number of near riots when police tried to enforce closing hours. Brewers resented what they saw as an attack on their independence and profits; others disliked the Act because it interfered with personal liberty. The Bishop of Peterborough, attacking the bill in the Lords, voiced his opinion that he would prefer to see 'England free better than England sober'. Some historians believe that the liquor trade became solidly Conservative because of the Licensing Act, which was consequently a major cause of the Liberal defeat in 1874.

(h) *The Judicature Act (1873)*

The British legal system was in an unbelievable muddle. It had developed piecemeal from medieval times, with new courts being created to meet specific demands. By the nineteenth century there were seven major courts, including Queen's Bench, Common Pleas and Exchequer, and the legal processes were slow and inefficient. Lord Selborne (Gladstone's Lord Chancellor) prepared the successful Act which greatly simplified the situation, uniting the seven courts into one Supreme Court of Judicature.

This was the least controversial of the Liberal reforms, though there were some objections to the clause which deprived the House of Lords of its right to act as the final court to which people could appeal, if they were dissatisfied with any verdict in a lower court. In 1876 Disraeli's government restored this right.

(i) *Edward Cardwell's army reforms*

The glaring faults and inefficiencies of the army had been exposed by the Crimean War (1854–6) and the Indian Mutiny (1857). The root cause of the trouble was that the army, like the Civil Service, acquired its officers not on merit, but by the purchase of commissions. Any wealthy young man could buy himself into the officer class, whether he knew anything about military matters or not. For example, a lieutenant-colonelcy could be bought for between £4500 and £7000; the price variations were because commissions were often auctioned to the highest bidder. An officer was free to sell his commission whenever he chose; money, not brains was what counted in the promotion stakes. The Commander-in-Chief was the Duke of Cambridge, a cousin of Queen Victoria, who often referred to him as 'poor George'; this was apparently because he had the reputation of being an expert at making bad situations even worse. He was slow-witted and against all change. For the Liberals, army reform was essential as an attack both on inefficiency and on privilege (the army was considered the natural preserve of the aristocracy). It was made more urgent by the Prussian victories over Austria (1866) and France (1870–1) which revealed a new, highly professional and potentially dangerous military power.

Edward Cardwell, the Secretary for War, was responsible for planning the reforms, which were introduced at intervals throughout the ministry:

- Troops were withdrawn from Britain's self-governing colonies, which were encouraged to raise their own forces.
- Flogging was abolished in peacetime.
- The Commander-in-Chief was made subordinate to the Secretary for War.
- The purchase of commissions was abolished – selection and promotion of officers was to be on merit.

- The different sections of the war department were all combined under one roof in the War Office.
- The regiments, which had previously been known only by numbers, were reorganized. Cardwell divided Britain into 69 districts, each with its own county regiment of two linked battalions, one on active service overseas, the other at home in Britain. The new regiments were given the name of their home county (e.g. Durhams, Gloucesters).
- The length of service was reduced from 12 years overseas followed by a period in the reserves, to six years overseas and six in the reserves. This was a more sensible arrangement since many men ended up broken in health after 12 years in India.
- The Martini-Henry breech-loading rifle was introduced as the main infantry weapon.

The reforms inevitably aroused a lot of opposition from the aristocracy, whose privileges were being threatened, and who believed that the main qualification for an officer was to be a gentleman and a sportsman rather than a professional. The Duke of Cambridge was suspicious of officers who had been to Staff College; 'Brains!' he said, 'I don't believe in brains!' Faced with this sort of mentality, it was not surprising that Cardwell's bill to abolish the purchase of commissions was defeated in the Lords. It was only when Gladstone showed that he was prepared to bypass the Lords by persuading Queen Victoria to issue a royal warrant to the same effect, that the Lords decided they had better pass the bill. This was quite an achievement by Gladstone, since Victoria herself considered the army reforms 'unwise'.

Cardwell's work was an outstanding success. The more humane and civilized conditions of service encouraged a better type of recruit and made possible a large and efficient reserve (increased from only 3500 to almost 36 000). The artillery received an extra 5000 men and 156 large horse-drawn guns (bringing the total to 336). In fact, thanks to Cardwell, Britain had the beginnings of an efficient modern army which made possible successful overseas campaigns like the one in Egypt in 1882 (see Section 16.2(c)).

On the other hand, *Cardwell would have gone much further if the opposition had been less violent*:

- He failed to create a permanent General Staff of the type already in existence in Prussia and France; this was one of the causes of the disasters in the early part of the Boer War.
- Incredibly, artillery officers preferred to continue using old-fashioned muzzle-loading cannon, even though recent Prussian victories had been achieved with breech-loading artillery.
- He had failed to get rid of the Duke of Cambridge who continued with his stubborn blocking of all further change until his retirement in 1895.

Though he was one of the most brilliant men in the Liberal party, Cardwell was so exhausted and disillusioned by his long struggle that he retired from active politics in 1874.

13.3 Gladstone and Ireland

(a) *Ireland since 1846*

The plight of Ireland can probably best be illustrated by simply looking at the population figures: from a peak of 8.2 million in 1841, the population fell dramatically over the next decade to 6.5 in 1851, and it continued to fall until by 1911 the figure was only 4.4 million.

The Irish suffered the utmost miseries during the famines of 1846–8; at least a million people died of starvation and cholera, and in desperation another million emigrated to the USA and Canada. During the 1850s and early 1860s, Ireland slipped from the forefront of the British newspapers, but that did not mean that the basic problems of Irish society had disappeared. The majority of the poverty-stricken Irish were still engaged in a grim struggle for survival. Occasionally their frustrations broke out in acts of violence against the property of wealthy landlords. British governments responded by ignoring the root causes of the problem and merely sent more troops to hold the Irish down.

A new phase in Irish affairs opened in 1867 when a society known as *the Fenians* (formed in the USA in the 1850s) began operations in Britain. They were pledged to revolution and wanted an Irish republic completely separate from Britain. There were several risings in Ireland in 1867. Manchester was the scene of a violent incident in which a group of Irishmen rescued two Fenians from a prison van; a policeman was killed and three of the rescuers were later hanged. An attempt to free two Fenians from Clerkenwell Gaol in London by blowing a hole in the prison wall with gunpowder went sadly wrong: 12 people were killed and over a hundred seriously injured. The Fenians had limited support in Ireland itself, but their activities were important because they helped to convince Gladstone that something must be done to help the Irish. Apart from anything else, he was acutely conscious of the cost of keeping Ireland under control – there were more troops stationed in Ireland than in India.

(b) *What were the grievances of the Irish in 1868?*

They fell into three main areas – *religious, economic and political.*

1 *The Protestant Church of England (Anglican) was the official state or 'established' church in Ireland*. However, about 88 per cent of the Irish were Roman Catholics (just over 5.3 million out of a population of 5.8 million, according to the 1861 census). They had to pay tithes (a tax amounting to 10 per cent of their annual income) to the Protestant church, even though they never attended its services, and since they also had to support their own churches and priests, the burden was heavy.

2 *There was intense poverty*, especially in the west of Ireland, because of the lack of industry and the land situation. Until the Act of Union (1800) there had been a prosperous Irish linen industry. But the Act introduced free trade between Ireland and England, and competition with the more advanced British ruined the Irish linen industry, causing widespread unemployment. Another problem was the partial collapse of the herring fishing industry along the west coast of Ireland, caused by the mysterious disappearance of the herring. These problems forced more and more people to rely on farming, and the Irish economy came to depend very much on agriculture being organized efficiently. However, most of the land was owned by wealthy Anglo-Irish landlords, many of whom lived in England, leaving agents to manage their property in Ireland. Irish people could only obtain land by renting it from absentee landlords.

As the population grew rapidly during the nineteenth century, demand for land increased and original tenants sub-let part of their holding; sometimes holdings were subdivided several times, so that by 1841, at least half the agricultural land of Ireland consisted of plots of less than five acres. The potato was the staple crop because it was possible to produce enough from one acre to keep a family of eight alive, whereas two acres would be needed to provide wheat for making bread. If tenants improved their holdings (by ditching, fencing or hedging) so that the value was enhanced, landlords would increase rents.

The whole system was uneconomic; many landlords were only interested in profits, and being dissatisfied with their paltry income from rents, took to evicting tenants so that small plots could be consolidated into large farms, on which modern methods of agriculture could be introduced. Between 1860 and 1870 the number of people seeking poor relief almost doubled, and desperate people could only retaliate against evictions by joining secret societies and indulging in acts of violence.

3   *There was a feeling of separateness among the Irish* who looked on the English as aliens. Many Irish people blamed the English for the decay of their country, which was obviously not regarded as an equal partner in the Union. Such was the English lack of sympathy for the hardships of the Irish, and the lack of understanding of Ireland's problems, that the feeling grew among the Irish that only when they were allowed to manage their own affairs would the country recover and prosper. *The Home Rule League*, formed in 1870 by Isaac Butt, a Protestant barrister, campaigned for a separate Irish parliament in Dublin to look after Irish internal affairs. At this stage the majority of the Irish were not thinking in terms of a complete break with Britain, and would have been happy for the Dublin parliament to be subordinate to Westminster for foreign affairs.

(c) *What measures did Gladstone take and how successful were they?*

Gladstone was anxious to solve the religious and land problems, though at this stage he was not interested in Home Rule. He was the first British politician to show a real understanding of Ireland's problems and a genuine desire to do something constructive about them instead of simply holding the Irish down by force. His concern sprang from his religious conviction that all people have certain basic rights of freedom and fair treatment; it seemed to him that in both religious and economic matters, the Irish were being denied these rights. When the news was brought to Gladstone in 1868 that he was about to be called on to form the next government, he was busy felling a tree on his Hawarden estate. The story goes that he laid down his axe and announced: 'My mission is to pacify Ireland.' That's not to say that political tactics didn't come into it as well; one of his biographers, Edgar Feuchtwanger, points out that when Gladstone introduced his first great Irish reform, the Irish Church Bill, 'he was acting largely for tactical political reasons. It was the issue which enabled him to pull the warring factions of the Liberal party together after the split over parliamentary reform.'

Gladstone did not have a great deal of success with his Irish policies, either during his first ministry or later. One of his difficulties was that Irish demands kept changing, becoming step by step more extreme; so Gladstone found that each of his concessions came too late and had already been overtaken by events. This was not necessarily the fault of the Irish: in fact the situation demanded the sort of drastic remedies which Gladstone was not prepared to take. This was not always because he was unwilling; more often than not he had to face deeply entrenched opposition from groups in the British parliament – such as Anglican bishops and the Anglo-Irish landlords – whose interests were threatened.

1   *The Irish Church Act (1869)* disestablished the Anglican Church in Ireland. This meant that although the church still existed in Ireland, Anglicanism was no longer the official state religion, and Roman Catholics no longer had to pay tithes to it.

Much of its property and wealth were taken away and used to improve hospitals, workhouses and schools. There was strenuous opposition to it in the Lords, and the bill only passed after Queen Victoria had intervened.

The Act was the first major breach in the Union between Ireland and Britain, and was naturally well received by the Catholics. However, its effect on the general situation was slight, since the other grievances still remained. It won Gladstone some popularity with the Roman Catholic Church leaders, but this was later lost by the failure of his attempt to convert Trinity College, Dublin, into a University which could be attended by both Catholics and Protestants (Catholics were refusing to attend the College in its existing form because it was a Protestant institution). However, Catholic leaders wanted their own University, while Protestants objected to Catholics being admitted. In the end the bill pleased nobody and it was defeated in the Commons (1873).

2   *The First Irish Land Act (1870)* was an attempt to give some sort of protection to tenants.

- The courts were to make sure that landlords did not charge exorbitant rents;
- Evicted tenants who had improved their holdings were to receive some compensation even if they had been evicted for non-payment of rent.
- A scale was introduced showing how much damages people could claim for having been evicted. The amount to be paid varied according to the size of the holding, but no damages would be paid if the tenant had been evicted for failure to pay his rent.

Unfortunately the Act was an almost total failure. It did not define how high an exorbitant rent was, and so landlords raised rents to ridiculously high levels which tenants could not possibly afford, and then evicted them for non-payment of rent. The courts, which were intended to protect tenants, almost always supported landlord against tenant. In such cases, although he might receive a little compensation if he had improved his plot, the evicted tenant would get nothing on the scale of damages. What the Irish tenants most wanted – security of tenure (i.e. to be safe from eviction) – was therefore not provided by the Act.

Why did Gladstone allow such an obviously ineffective measure to be introduced? The main reason was probably opposition in his own cabinet from Whig landowners like Clarendon and Argyll, who held strongly to the view that the state should not be able to interfere with the rights of property-owners, who should be free to do exactly as they wanted on their own estates; a more radical bill, for example, one specifying a fair rent and forbidding evictions, would not have passed the House of Lords. The Act, far from solving the land problem, only served to dash expectations and arouse more ill-feeling. Frustration led to further violence and outrage in the countryside.

The situation became so serious that Gladstone introduced a *Coercion Act (1871)* giving the police extra powers of arrest and imprisonment. In spite of his good intentions, Gladstone had been forced back on the old policy of repression. This was a tragedy: if only he could have somehow produced an effective Land Act, all the bitterness might have been taken out of the situation. In that case, as Karl Marx suggested, Ireland might have been more docile than Wales, and the demand for Home Rule would have been limited.

3   *The demand for Home Rule left Gladstone unmoved during his first ministry,* though he was to change his mind later (see Sections 16.1(e) and 16.8(b)). There was hardly any support for it among English MPs, though nobody could have been more reasonable in his demands and his approach than Isaac Butt. When it became clear that the Irish were making no progress using reasoned arguments

and gentle persuasion, Butt was cast aside in favour of more extreme leaders, like Charles Stewart Parnell, who were prepared to use less gentlemanly tactics.

13.4 How did Gladstone's foreign policies cause him to become unpopular?

Gladstone was hampered in his foreign policies by his desire to protect Britain's interests while at the same time respecting the rights of other nations and avoiding foreign entanglements that might involve Britain in war. He felt that war must be avoided at all costs: Britain's army, even with Cardwell's improvements, was not in the same class as the German professional army. There were also the financial considerations: Gladstone had been very critical of Palmerston whose aggressive overseas policies had been expensive. Unfortunately for the Liberals, these considerations caused Gladstone to follow reasonable and realistic policies, which often appeared weak and spineless, in marked contrast to Palmerston's general approach.

(a) *Britain and the Franco-Prussian War (1870–1)*

The British government decided to remain neutral in this struggle which began in July 1870. There was no clear-cut reason why she should support one side or the other, and indeed there was no other realistic possibility: the Germans already had nearly half a million troops in the field, whereas Britain, at a pinch, could have managed to get ten thousand across the Channel. However, British interests were involved in the war in two ways:

• *There was a danger that Belgium might be invaded*, and it was well known that Napoleon III of France hoped to annex it sooner or later. Britain had traditionally been concerned to make sure that no major power controlled this stretch of European coastline, strategically placed as it was, so close to the British coast and the Thames estuary. In August Gladstone persuaded both Prussia and France to sign an agreement with Britain guaranteeing Belgian neutrality. This was seen as a triumph for Gladstone: both countries kept the agreement, Belgian neutrality was preserved and British interests safeguarded.

• After France had suffered crushing defeats at Sedan (September) and Metz (October), *the Russian government, with the support of Bismarck, announced that she no longer considered herself bound by the Black Sea clauses of the 1856 Treaty of Paris* (see Section 10.3): she would patrol the Black Sea with her fleet, build bases and fortify the coastline. This destroyed one of the main British advantages gained from the Crimean War and provoked a storm of anti-Russian feeling in Britain. But the Russians had timed their announcement to perfection: with France, Britain's ally in the Crimea, on the verge of collapse, there was very little that she could do about it. After some diplomatic manoeuvring, a conference of the powers was held in London (January 1871) to review the situation.

Britain suffered a clear diplomatic defeat: it was agreed that the Black Sea clauses were cancelled, though Lord Granville, the British Foreign Minister, saved face to some extent by securing a general agreement that from now on, no government must break parts of a treaty unless all the other signatories agreed. The British government probably did as well as could be expected in the circumstances; A. J. P. Taylor (in *The Struggle for Mastery in Europe*) believed that the Russians signed the general agreement in all good faith and that because of it, they were prepared to agree to a renegotiation of the Treaty of San Stefano in 1878 (see Section 14.4(e)). But the British public felt that Gladstone had acted weakly in allowing the Russians to steal a march over Britain – he had somehow let Britain down in a way which Palmerston would never have allowed.

(b) *Gladstone and the* Alabama *case*

Ever since the American Civil War (1861–5), the American government had claimed compensation from Britain for the damage caused by the *Alabama* and other ships built in Britain (see Section 9.5(c)). In 1868 Disraeli's government had expressed Britain's readiness to submit to arbitration, but it was Lord Granville, the Liberal Foreign Minister, who represented Britain at the arbitration conference in Geneva. It was decided that Britain should pay the USA £3.25 million in compensation, a decision which Gladstone accepted (1872). This was probably the sensible and moral thing to do, but coming after the Black Sea affair, it seemed to confirm the impression that Gladstone lacked backbone. There was a widespread feeling that the amount was unjustifiably high and that Gladstone should have said so. There is no doubt that the incident contributed to the Liberals' growing unpopularity. One Conservative MP remarked that they showed 'a strange mania for eating dirt'. Shortly afterwards, Gladstone was booed as he entered St Paul's for a thanksgiving service for the recovery of the Prince of Wales from typhoid; when Disraeli came along, there was tumultuous applause.

13.5 Why did the Liberals lose the 1874 general election?

In January 1874 Gladstone decided that the time was ripe for a general election (though the Liberals had lost seven by-elections during 1873) and parliament was dissolved. His main programme was a pledge to abolish income tax, which he confidently asssumed would be enough to swing the electorate. He was astonished and dismayed at the result: a decisive Conservative victory. The figures were: Conservatives 342, Liberals 251, Irish Home Rulers 59. The latter appeared in parliament for the first time because the 1872 Ballot Act made it possible for Irish tenants to vote as they wished without fear of reprisals from landlords. The Liberals were defeated partly because Gladstone's policies had offended so many influential people, and because the Conservatives, for the first time for many years, appeared to offer a realistic alternative to the Liberals.

(a) *Unpopularity of the Liberal reforms*

Many of the Liberal reforms outraged *the upper and wealthy classes*, whose special privileges had been attacked, for example, the Civil Service and army reforms (especially abolition of the purchase of commissions). Many Anglicans resented the disestablishment of the Irish church and the University Test Act; some industrialists were annoyed at the legal recognition of trades unions. The Ballot Act was unpopular because it reduced landlords' influence at elections.

The working classes were offended by Gladstone's apparently contradictory behaviour of offering help to the unions with one hand and taking it back with the other, when he made picketing illegal. There was disappointment that the Liberals had introduced so little effective social reform and no further extension of the franchise.

Gladstone himself thought that the Licensing Act was the decisive cause of his defeat: 'We have been borne down in a torrent of gin and beer', he told his brother, though Robert Blake believes that although it may have cost him some votes, it was not the main reason for the defeat.

Nonconformists were still smarting over the Forster Education Act; they vented their disapproval by abstaining rather than by voting Conservative, but it was still damaging, since traditionally Nonconformists were the mainstay of Liberal support. And there was widespread dissatisfaction in all classes with Gladstone's handling of foreign affairs. For a combination of reasons therefore, Gladstone had lost the support of the two big groups – working classes and Nonconformists – most responsible for the Liberal victory in 1868.

(b) *The Conservatives present a new image*

The Conservatives, ably led by Disraeli, had been mounting an effective attack on the government since April 1872 when Disraeli addressed a huge meeting in Manchester's Free Trade Hall. In a blistering speech lasting over three hours, during which he fortified himself with two bottles of white brandy, Disraeli ridiculed the Liberals as 'a range of exhausted volcanoes – not a flame flickers on a single pallid crest'. He went on to give the Conservative party a new image – a party which stood for building up the British Empire and which aimed to improve 'the condition of the people'. Disraeli was seeking to cash in on Gladstone's areas of weakness, and his popularity grew appreciably.

During the election itself the party had the benefit of a highly efficient organization built up by John Gorst and his new Conservative Central Office. Finally, Robert Blake makes the point that many householders who had been enfranchised by the 1867 Reform Act voted for the first time in 1874, and voted Conservative – a belated thankyou to Disraeli.

Questions

1   **The Liberal government and foreign affairs**
    Study Sources A to F and then answer the questions which follow.

Source A

Historian B. H. Abbott writes about Britain and the Franco-Prussian War

The first task with which Gladstone had to deal was the seeming threat to Belgian neutrality with the outbreak of the Franco-Prussian War in 1870. It has been suggested that energetic action by Gladstone could have averted the outbreak of war between France and Prussia ... Britain could perhaps have prevented war, but only by committing herself to intervention on one side or the other, and to this, public opinion was certainly opposed. It was also clear to Gladstone that Britain had not the military means at her disposal. ... The threat to Belgium, however, could not be ignored, and by August both belligerents had signed a treaty with Britain guaranteeing Belgian neutrality. An important British interest was successfully safeguarded.

Source: B. H. Abbott, *Gladstone and Disraeli*, Collins, 1972.

Map of Europe in 1878

Map 13.1   Europe in 1878

Source: James Joll, *Europe Since 1870*, Penguin, 1976.

Speech by Gladstone in the House of Commons, 10 August 1870

What is our interest in maintaining the neutrality of Belgium? It is the same as that of every great power in Europe. It is contrary to the interests of Europe that there should be uncontrolled increase in the size of any one state. Is there any man who hears me who does not feel that if, in order to satisfy a greedy appetite for expansion, Belgium was absorbed, by no matter which power, the day that absorption took place, would hear the death knell of public right and public law in Europe?

Source: *Hansard Parliamentary Debates, 1870.*

Source D

Speech by Disraeli in the House of Commons, in reply to Gladstone's speech

I infer from the statement of the Right Honourable Gentleman that Her Majesty's Government have taken decided steps to maintain and defend the neutrality of Belgium. I accept this as a wise and spirited policy, in my opinion, not the less wise because it is spirited.... Viewing it from a very limited point of view, it is of the highest importance to this country that the whole coast from Ostend to the North Sea should be in the hands of free and flourishing communities.

Source: *Hansard Parliamentary Debates, 1870.*

Source E

Comments from a contemporary historian, Lewis Apjohn, in a biography of Gladstone published in 1884

The war introduced a new element of disturbance into English politics: Russia took advantage of the crippling of France to repudiate the clause of the Treaty of Paris of 1856 which neutralised the Black Sea and excluded foreign vessels from the Bosphorus. *Many Englishmen were greatly worried by this unceremonious action*, which they regarded as humiliating for themselves.... The English government soon found that they would be practically alone in Europe if they were to attempt to bind Russia down to the treaty, so they invited the Powers to send representatives to a conference in London. The conference met and Russia was released from her engagement ...

The critics of the government tried to make capital out of this, maintaining that we might have done more to keep the treaty in operation by taking up a firmer attitude to Russia. Mr. Disraeli on two occasions brought the matter before the House of Commons, saying that the conference had been called together merely to record the humiliation of this country. On many later occasions Mr. Gladstone has been blamed for his alleged lack of spirit in this business, as well as in the case of the *Alabama*. However, an impartial review of all the circumstances have led me to the conclusion that England could not help herself at that moment, and that the action of the Czar was perfectly natural.

Source: L. Apjohn, *William Ewart Gladstone: His Life and Times*, Walter Scott, 1884.

Speech by Disraeli at Manchester, 3 April 1872

As I sat opposite the Treasury Bench, the Ministers reminded me of one of those marine landscapes not very unusual on the coasts of South America. You behold a range of exhausted volcanoes. Not a single flame flickers on a single pallid crest.... *It would have been better for us all if there had been a little more energy in our foreign policy, and a little less in our domestic legislation.*

Source: quoted in B. H. Abbott, *Gladstone and Disraeli*, Collins, 1972.

(a) How may it be inferred from Sources A, B, C and D that the Franco-Prussian War posed a threat to the neutrality of Belgium, and therefore to Britain's interests? (8 marks)

(b) From the evidence of the sources and your own knowledge, explain the meaning of the passage in Source E: 'Many Englishmen were worried by this unceremonious action . . .' (4 marks)

(c) Using information from Section 13.4 and the evidence of the sources, explain the criticisms being made of the conduct of foreign affairs by Gladstone and his government. (5 marks)

(d) From the information in Section 13.4 and the evidence of the sources, do you think that Disraeli's claim, shown in italics in Source E, is a fair one?
(13 marks)
(Total 30 marks)

2 Consider the view that 'Gladstone was more of a liability than an asset to the Liberal party in the period 1865–1894'. (See also Chapter 16.) [AEB]

14 Disraeli and the Conservatives in power 1874–80

Summary of events

This was the first Conservative government to have real power since the collapse of Peel's ministry in 1846. The Conservatives were now more or less united under Disraeli's leadership and enjoyed a comfortable majority over the Liberals and Irish Home Rulers, who usually voted with the Liberals. The results of the election were: Conservatives 342, Liberals 251, Home Rulers 59.

It was an eventful ministry: Lytton Strachey, in his biography of Queen Victoria, called it 'six years of excitement, of enchantment, of felicity, of glory, of romance'. Disraeli was much more to the Queen's liking than Gladstone; the Liberal leader exhausted her with complicated documents and explanations – she complained that 'he speaks to me as if I were a public meeting'. Disraeli on the other hand was careful to charm and flatter her; 'everyone likes flattery', he said, 'and when you come to royalty you should lay it on with a trowel'. In 1876 Disraeli accepted a peerage, taking the title *Earl of Beaconsfield*.

In keeping with his ideas of *'Tory Democracy'* or *'New Conservatism'*, the early part of the ministry saw *important social reforms* dealing with housing, public health, factories, education and trades unions. *In overseas affairs* he was determined to restore Britain's prestige which was felt to have waned under Gladstone. When *the Eastern Question* flared up again, Disraeli took a firm stand against the Russians, culminating in *the Congress of Berlin in 1878*; this was hailed as a great triumph for Britain and a resounding diplomatic defeat for the Russians. He did all he could *to defend and strengthen the British Empire*, in Egypt, India, South Africa (Zulu War) and Afghanistan.

In the meantime *all was not well with the British economy*: in the late 1870s, industry ran into a serious depression, while agriculture suffered a near-disaster because of rapidly growing foreign competition. Even so, most people were surprised when the general election of March 1880 reversed the situation in parliament, bringing Gladstone and the Liberals back with an overall majority of around 50. Disraeli took his defeat well, but his health was deteriorating, and he died just over a year later (April 1881).

14.1 Disraeli's earlier career and his political outlook – Tory Democracy

(a) *Background and earlier career*

Benjamin Disraeli was the son of a Jewish writer and scholar whose family had come to England from Venice in the middle of the eighteenth century. The young Disraeli was educated at an obscure private school; he did not go to university, and when he left school, he worked as a solicitor's clerk. He wrote several novels and tried unsuccessfully to get into parliament – as a Whig. At the fourth attempt he was elected as MP for Maidstone (1837), having changed his allegiance to the Tories. He already had a reputation as something of a gambler and a flashy dresser. He had appeared at one society dinner dressed in green velvet trousers, a canary coloured waistcoat, low shoes with silver buckles, lace at his wrists, and his hair in tightly curled ringlets. His maiden speech in parliament was a disaster: he used such flowery language that he was shouted down with catcalls and shrieks of laughter. He soon improved his technique and was furious

Illus. 14.1   Benjamin Disraeli

when Peel refused to offer him a place in his government in 1841. Perhaps because of this *he led the attack on Peel over the Corn Law repeal in 1846* (see Section 7.5(d)). After that his career ran as follows:

- He was Chancellor of the Exchequer in the Conservative governments of 1852, 1858–9 and 1866–8.
- He was largely responsible for the 1867 Reform Act (see Section 8.4), though apart from that he had achieved nothing of great significance.
- He was Prime Minister for a few months in 1868 after Lord Derby's retirement. This in itself was a remarkable achievement, given his unconventional background and the fact that he was viewed as an outsider. Although he had been baptised a Christian (Anglican) at the age of 13, he had to put up with a great deal of anti-Semitic feeling. It speaks volumes for his brilliance as a politician that in spite of all his disadvantages, he was able, as he put it, to 'climb to the top of the greasy pole', leader of a party still dominated by wealthy landowners.

(b) *Tory Democracy/New Conservatism*

By the time he became Prime Minister for the second time in 1874, Disraeli seemed to have clear ideas about the direction he wanted the Conservative party to take. He spoke about this new approach in two famous speeches which he made while in opposition in 1872, one in Manchester and the other at the Crystal Palace; the ideas are sometimes referred to as *Tory Democracy* or *New Conservatism*:

1 He believed that there was value in privilege and tradition and wanted to preserve the power of the long-established institutions – the Anglican Church, the aristocracy and above all, the monarchy. But it was essential that these institutions used their power wisely and unselfishly, for the good of the whole community.

2 It was vitally important for the government and the privileged classes to help working people. In his novel *Sybil* (1845) Disraeli had written that there were really two separate nations living in Britain – the Rich and the Poor; though he had no intention of upsetting the class structure, he believed that something must be done to improve the conditions of the poor. He said so in his Manchester speech in 1872: 'Pure air, pure water, the inspection of unhealthy habitations, the adulteration of food . . . it is impossible to overrate the importance of the subjects; after all, the first consideration of a Minister should be the health of the people.' This was a paternalistic approach, that is, treating the poor kindly, like a benevolent father looking after his children. It became known as 'one nation Toryism' and was followed by some later Conservative leaders, notably Baldwin, Macmillan and Heath.

3 Disraeli hoped that social reform would lead to an alliance between the privileged classes and the mass of the population, which would strengthen the monarchy and aristocracy; as he remarked revealingly: 'the Palace is unsafe if the cottage is unhappy'.

4 The Conservative party must, in other words, adapt itself and come to terms with the new democratic and industrial age. If it failed to win working-class support, it would be condemned to remain a permanent party of opposition. Disraeli was highly critical of the Liberals because of their attack on privilege and their weak foreign policy. He called them an 'anti-national' party and despised them because they seemed to look after the interests of the middle class at the expense of the workers. This, he said, made them 'odious to the English people'.

5 He took up imperialism as a positive Conservative theme and hoped to develop the British Empire as a powerful economic and political union under the

monarchy. Only in this way, he believed, could Britain continue to compete successfully with the great continental empires of the USA, Germany and Russia.

(c) *Disraeli's motives have aroused some controversy*

He has been accused of not genuinely caring about social problems and of taking up social reform simply to score points over Gladstone who neglected it. Political hard-headedness probably did come into it: it was an obvious way to attract and hold on to working-class support. On the other hand Disraeli had talked and written sympathetically about the conditions of the poor as far back as the 1840s; it was not something he had suddenly taken up in 1872 because of Gladstone's failings.

Recently historian T. A. Jenkins has argued that too much has been made of the so-called *New Conservatism* based on social reform and imperialism. He suggests that this was 'part of the mythology that developed around Disraeli's memory after his death ... in reality Disraeli's comments about social reform were vague and non-committal, and his criticisms of what he alleged was the Liberals' hostile attitude towards the British empire were entirely negative and did not anticipate a new era of imperial expansion'. Insofar as Disraeli was interested in social reform, it was because he saw it as a less controversial alternative to the kind of 'harassing legislation' forced on the country by Gladstone. According to Jenkins, this is why Disraeli's social reforms were so cautious, and why he never produced a blueprint for social reform.

Whether this is true or not, it seems clear that the working class had certainly come to expect great things from the Conservatives – in Lancashire, the heart of the new industrial England, the Conservatives won 18 out of the 25 seats in the 1874 general election.

14.2 What did Disraeli's government do for working people?

(a) *Improvements in public health and living conditions*

- *The Public Health Act* and *the Artisans' Dwellings Act*, whose details were worked out by Richard Cross, Disraeli's Home Secretary, were passed in 1875 (see Section 12.5(a)).
- *The Sale of Food and Drugs Act* (also 1875) laid down stringent regulations about the preparation and adulteration of food.
- *The Enclosures Act* (1876) was designed to protect the public's right to use the common pasture land; landowners were restricted from absorbing such land into their estates, so that it would be kept free from building. Thus the idea of the green belt was born.
- It was made illegal to tip solid industrial waste into rivers (1876) and liquid could only be discharged if it was non-poisonous.

All these Acts met with success, although the Artisans' Dwellings Act would have made more impact if it had been compulsory. Even so, as B. H. Abbott points out, 'the legislation of those years laid the foundations of modern public health so thoroughly and lastingly that no major changes were required for over 60 years'.

(b) *The Factory Acts of 1874 and 1878*

These introduced important new limitations on working hours (see Section 12.3(j)).

(c) *Labour relations and trades union legislation*

1   *The Conspiracy and Protection of Property Act* (1875). Trades unionists had been bitterly disappointed by their treatment at the hands of the Liberals in 1871: although unions had been given legal recognition, picketing, even if was peaceful, was not allowed, which meant that it was more or less impossible to make a strike effective. This new measure, again introduced by Cross, made peaceful picketing legal and allowed unions to carry out as a group whatever actions an individual was permitted to take, in support of their case; unions could not be charged with conspiracy for taking such action.

2   *The Employers and Workmen Act* (1876), another Cross measure, put both employer and worker on an equal footing in cases of breach of contract. Previously, if a workman broke his contract, it was treated as a criminal offence, whereas if an employer did it, it was regarded only as a civil offence, for which the penalties were much lighter. Now both were treated as civil offences.

These two Acts mark a vitally important breakthrough in the development and recognition of trades unions as acceptable and respectable bodies (see Section 19.3(c)). Union leaders were delighted, and so was Disraeli who remarked that these laws 'will gain and retain for the Conservatives the lasting affection of the working classes'.

(d) *Sandon's Education Act (1876)*

This was less effective than it might have been because it lacked the element of compulsion (see Section 12.7(d)).

(e) *The Merchant Shipping Act (1876)*

This was passed after a vigorous campaign by its author, Samuel Plimsoll. The problem was that there were no regulations governing the loading and repair of merchant ships. It was not unknown for unscrupulous shipowners to overload decrepit and over-insured vessels so that they could make a handsome profit if the ships sank. Plimsoll's bill was designed to prevent this scandalous sacrifice of seamen's lives, but the shipowning interests in parliament delayed it as long as they could. Plimsoll became so exasperated that he caused a scene in the Commons, literally jumping up and down with rage and shaking his fist at Disraeli. This produced results and the bill passed. A line (known as the Plimsoll Line) was to be painted on the side of every ship to show the maximum loading point. However, the shipowners had the last laugh, for the time being, because the Act allowed *them* to paint the line where they thought fit. Only in 1890 did Board of Trade officials begin to apply the regulations as Plimsoll had intended.

14.3 What is meant by the term 'imperialism' and how successful was Disraeli in pursuing it?

(a) *Imperialism and the British Empire*

Imperialism has existed throughout history, and in many different continents. British imperialism in the nineteenth century was just one in a long succession of systems of imperialism which came and went. Imperialism involves the domination and exploitation of a weaker people by a stronger power. The dominant people, or colonisers, run the territory of the weaker people to suit their own interests, as sources of raw materials or markets; the wishes of the exploited peoples always take second place.

Britain had already had one empire founded in the early seventeenth century, on the east coast of North America. By the time the Americans broke away from British rule in their war of independence (1775–83), Britain already had a second empire in the making; by the end of the wars with France in 1815, the British controlled a large collection of territories in India, Africa, Australasia and the Caribbean.

Disraeli added a new dimension to the idea of Empire: it should not simply be a case of Britain making use of her overseas possessions; she had a duty to bring the benefits of British civilization – 'courage, discipline, patience, reverence for the public law, and respect for national rights' – to primitive peoples. Kipling later described this duty as 'the white man's burden'. Other European countries acted in the same way. Late-nineteenth-century imperialism therefore carried with it the false assumption that Europeans were racially superior to all other peoples, and the idea that European culture, religion and systems of government should be forced on other peoples, for their own good. Disraeli also had in mind that the empire could be called on for military help if Britain became involved in a major war.

Later, 'imperialism' became a term of abuse; Gladstone was one of the first critics who claimed that imperialism was not to be encouraged because it interfered with the rights and freedom of overseas peoples. In addition, it was expensive – a waste of British wealth and manpower; defence of the empire would be a constant strain on Britain's resources. The other major criticism made by historians is that imperialism was motivated by sheer greed – weaker peoples and their resources were exploited simply so that the British (and other Europeans) could make big profits. However, in a recent controversial article ('The British Empire', in *History Today*, February 1996), historian Max Beloff put forward a spirited defence of British imperialism, arguing that historians should 'search out the positive factors both in what was attempted and in what was done'. He believes that the profit motive was very much a secondary one: 'there were many easier ways of making money than acting as the overseas representative of the Crown at any level from royal governor to local magistrate'. The real motive, according to Beloff, was the British desire to bring other parts of the world under their rule so that they could be given the benefits of law and order; 'the core of Empire was not profit but governance'.

In fact Disraeli had no specific plans for pursuing imperialism, but in the early years of his ministry he made excellent use of circumstances. This, together with his successful stand against the Russians at the Congress of Berlin in 1878 (see next section), coming after six years of Gladstonian 'weakness' in foreign affairs, dazzled the public. Towards the end of his term, however, the imperialist adventures in South Africa and Afghanistan, though they both ended successfully, were badly mishandled along the way.

(b) *Disraeli and Egypt: the Suez Canal shares (1875)*

● The Suez Canal (opened in 1869) was controlled jointly by the French and the Khedive Ismail, the ruler of Egypt. In 1875 the Khedive, who was in serious financial difficulty, decided to sell his shares, which amounted to seven-sixteenths of the total. There was a strong possibility that a French company would buy them, posing the threat of complete French control of the canal, which had already proved itself a vital link between Britain and India.

● The Khedive was asking for four million pounds which the French company had difficulty in raising. Disraeli seized the opportunity: after securing the approval of the

cabinet, not without difficulty, he stepped in and bought the shares for the British government, using four million pounds lent by the banking house of Rothschilds.
● It is difficult to imagine any other politician of the time acting with such flair and panache, and there is no doubt that it was a splendid piece of opportunism. Although Britain had fewer than half the shares in the canal, the important point was that France had been prevented from gaining exclusive control, which would have given them great bargaining power over the Khedive; in addition, the shorter trade route to India had been safeguarded. The British were soon able to get the tolls reduced, and the ownership of the shares turned out to be profitable; by 1898 they were valued at over £24 million. The cost of transporting cargo to and from Australia and New Zealand was reduced by 75 per cent.
● Gladstone was highly critical of the purchase, calling it 'a ruinous and mischievous misdeed'. He believed that it would lead to an eventual British occupation of Egypt, and although Disraeli denied any such intention, Gladstone was later proved to be right (see Section 16.2(c)).

(c) *Victoria becomes Empress of India (1876)*

This was not Disraeli's idea; it had been discussed on and off since the Mutiny in 1857, and the Queen herself was eager for it. Disraeli was anxious to oblige, and *the Royal Titles Act* duly passed through parliament, though only after surprisingly strong resistance in both houses. Gladstone called it 'theatrical bombast'. However, there seemed good reasons for Victoria to take the title:

1   It demonstrated that the British had every intention of staying in India, and it was hoped that the new personal link with the Queen would mean more to the Indians than their relationship with an impersonal parliament.
2   It was a symbolic gesture to warn off the Russians who were extending their influence into Persia and Afghanistan, and who, it was feared, had designs on India.

(d) *South Africa: the Zulu War (1879)*

Again this was not part of Disraeli's intentions; it was forced upon him by the actions of the men on the spot and Disraeli was furious when the situation turned into war.

● *The background was complicated*: the Cape of Good Hope was originally colonized by Dutch settlers, but as a result of the Congress of Vienna (1815), ownership passed to Britain. Many of the Dutch farmers, known as Boers (or Afrikaners), disliked British rule, and in 1836 many thousands of them left the Cape in what was called *The Great Trek*. They founded two new states of their own, Transvaal and the Orange Free State. The British still claimed sovereignty over them, and for many years, relations between the new Boer republics and the two British colonies – the Cape and Natal – remained strained. Tension eased after the British recognized the independence of the Transvaal (by the Sand River Convention, 1852) and the Free State (by the Convention of Bloemfontein, 1854) (see Map 17.1).
● A constant threat to both the British and the Boers was the presence on the Transvaal/Natal border of the large and aggressive Zulu tribe under their king, Cetawayo. The Boers had already had one major clash with the Zulus at Blood River (1838) in which 3000 Zulus were slaughtered. Cetawayo was eager to avenge this defeat, though he was not unfriendly to the British.
● Disraeli's Colonial Secretary, Lord Carnarvon, who in 1867 had been responsible for uniting the four provinces of Canada into a single federation (see Section 18.1(e)),

had similar plans for South Africa. He hoped to bring the Transvaal and the Orange Free State under British control in a union with the Cape and Natal. The snag was that the circumstances in South Africa were completely different from those in Canada: the Boers were hostile to the idea, and the Cape and Natal, where lots of Boers had remained, were unenthusiastic.

● Carnarvon decided that the Boers, who were also being harassed by another tribe, the Bapedi, as well as by the Zulus,would be glad of British protection. He sent Sir Theophilus Shepstone, an ex-governor of Natal, to the Transvaal to sound the Boers out. He found them extremely nervous about Cetawayo's intentions, and also nearly bankrupt with only twelve shillings and sixpence in the treasury. Reluctantly president Burgers of the Transvaal agreed to a British annexation of the republic (though he was allowed to protest in public); Shepstone promised the Boers self-government later.

● Carnarvon also appointed Sir Bartle Frere as High Commissioner for South Africa with instructions to set up a federation. Frere was a well-known supporter of expansionist policies and was indignant when he discovered that Shepstone had promised the Boers self-government. He decided that the Zulu threat would have to be destroyed before a peaceful federation of South Africa could be achieved. Disraeli and the cabinet did not want a war in South Africa at this time, as they were preoccupied with the situation in the Balkans, and the British were already involved in hostilities in Afghanistan. Frere was given strict instructions not to start a native war, but he deliberately disobeyed orders and took it upon himself to launch an invasion of Zululand (January 1879).

● The beginning of the war was disastrous for the British: the commander, Lord Chelmsford, and his section of the invading army, were surprised by a 20 000-strong Zulu army at Isandhlwana. Chelmsford had ignored advice from the Boers to *laager* his wagons (arrange them in a circle) and suffered a crushing defeat, losing over a thousand men. The same night a much smaller force which had *laagered* correctly, held out against the Zulus at Rorke's Drift, though casualties were heavy. In June there was a further blow when the Prince Imperial (son of the former French emperor Napoleon III), who had volunteered to fight with the British, was killed by a Zulu raiding party. These events caused a public outcry in Britain.

● Disraeli was intensely angry with Frere, but felt he had to send reinforcements to South Africa. In the end Chelmsford redeemed himself by decisively defeating the Zulus at Ulundi, Cetawayo's capital (July 1789). Cetawayo was captured and deported and the Zulu threat was finally removed.

● However, much criticism had been aroused; the Liberals enjoyed themselves complaining about the unprovoked attack on the Zulus, the loss of life and the expense involved; although Carnarvon and Frere were to blame, Disraeli had to take the responsibility. Even the victory left a new problem: now that the Zulu threat had been removed, the Transvaal demanded its independence again. It was clear that a more subtle approach would have been to delay or even abandon altogether the complete destruction of Zulu power, so that the continuing menace would frighten the Transvaal into remaining under British protection. It was a problem which Gladstone inherited in his next ministry (see Section 16.2(b)).

(e) *The Second and Third Afghan Wars (1878–80)*

The British were interested in what happened in Afghanistan because they looked on it as a buffer state to protect India from Russian attentions. An earlier British attempt to control the country (the First Afghan War, 1838–42) had been thwarted by the Afghans. Now Disraeli wanted to build up good relations with the Amir of

Afghanistan, Sher Ali, in the hope that he would have nothing to do with the Russians, who also had thoughts of bringing Afghanistan within their 'sphere of influence'.

● Disraeli appointed Lord Lytton as Viceroy of India, with instructions to persuade Sher Ali to accept a British mission at his capital, Kabul. Lytton, like Sir Bartle Frere, was a well-known advocate of expansionist or 'forward' imperialist policies, and as it turned out, he too could not be relied on to obey orders. According to Robert Blake, 'he was curiously unbalanced in judgement' and became dangerously impatient when he failed to make progress with Sher Ali. It was not a wise appointment.

● In July 1878 a Russian military mission arrived in Kabul. Disraeli ordered Lytton to take no action until the situation had been discussed with the Russians through proper diplomatic channels. However, the Viceroy, itching to get the Russians out, ignored this and sent 35 000 troops under Sir Frederick Roberts into Afghanistan. The Russians withdrew, Sher Ali was driven out and his son Yakub Khan was placed on the throne. In May 1879 he signed a treaty of friendship with Britain; a British minister and staff took up residence in Kabul. Although Disraeli was secretly displeased with Lytton, this Second Afghan War seemed to have been completely successful.

● The achievement did not last long: in September 1879 the British minister and the entire mission were murdered by rebel tribesmen, and a Third Afghan War was needed to re-establish British control. Roberts again took Kabul, but it was now clear that a large section of the Afghans resented British interference, and serious fighting broke out in the south of the country. Before order was restored, Disraeli's government had been defeated (April 1880), and it was left to Gladstone to preside over the final stages of the problem. Roberts carried out a brilliantly executed 300 mile march from Kabul to Kandahar, the main centre of resistance, and in August, completely annihilated the rebel army. Again British control was complete.

● The Liberals criticized the 'wanton invasion' of an independent nation, and even Lord Salisbury, the Conservative Foreign Minister, thought that Disraeli should have kept tighter control over Lytton. The Gladstone government removed Lytton and withdrew British troops and the British mission from Afghanistan. It looked as though all Roberts's efforts had been a waste of time. However, the new Amir, who owed his position to Roberts, remained friendly to Britain for the next 20 years, and the Russians refrained from interfering in Afghanistan again, except for the Penjdeh incident in 1885 (see Section 16.2(e)). It is possible to argue therefore that Disraeli's policy had been a success after all – British military efficiency made a deep impression both in Afghanistan and in Russia.

(f) *Disraeli and Ireland*

In general, Disraeli had no understanding of small nations, such as those in the Balkans, who were struggling for independence. He saw Ireland in the same light – a troublesome possession trying to break away from Britain in the same way that the Balkans peoples were trying to win freedom from Turkey. Given his desire to consolidate the empire, he naturally did not see Home Rule as the solution to Ireland's problems. Towards the end of his government, the situation in Ireland deteriorated further because of a severe agricultural depression; an increasing number of tenants failed to pay their rents and landlords evicted them on a larger scale than ever before. But Disraeli was unmoved; according to Blake, 'he was at heart wholly out of sympathy with the Irish ... and he never did or said anything helpful to them'. One of his last pronouncements before the general election of 1880 was to warn the British government of the dangers of Home Rule.

14.4 The Eastern Question and the Congress of Berlin 1875-8

(a) Background to the Balkans crisis

The crisis which erupted in the Balkans in 1875 was a recurrence of the Eastern Question which had plagued international relations since early in the nineteenth century. For a full explanation of its origins see Section 3.3(b)(4). It was hoped that the Eastern Question had been solved by the Treaty of Paris (1856) which ended the Crimean War: the Russians were not allowed to have warships on the Black Sea – a severe check to their ambitions in the Balkans and Near East. The Sultan of Turkey had promised to treat his Christian subjects fairly, so that the usual Russian excuse for intervention in the Balkans – that they wanted to protect the Christians living under Turkish rule – would no longer be available. But British calculations were upset in two ways:

1   In 1870 (during the Franco-Prussian War) the Russians announced that they no longer felt bound by the Black Sea clauses (see Section 13.4(a)).
2   The Turks ignored their promises and continued to over-tax and generally to persecute their Balkan Christians. This led to a rebellion in Bosnia and Herzegovina, which soon spread to Serbia, Montenegro and Bulgaria.

The main European powers – Germany, Austria–Hungary, Russia, France and Italy (but excluding Britain) – sent the Berlin Memorandum to the Turks, protesting about their harshness and calling on them to make peace and behave themselves.

(b) What was Disraeli's attitude?

1   He was deeply suspicious about Russian intentions – if she intervened to help the Balkan Christians, there seemed every chance that the whole of the Balkans, perhaps even Constantinople and the Dardanelles, would fall under Russian control.
2   He also mistrusted the motives of the Austrians and Germans and suspected them of scheming with the Russians to partition the Ottoman Empire.
3   He therefore wanted to preserve Turkish power as the best way of maintaining British interests in the Near East. He had no sympathy with the peoples of the Balkans in their struggle for independence.
4   For these reasons he refused to support the Berlin Memorandum, but this refusal encouraged the new Sultan, Abdul Hamid, to think that he could rely on British support no matter what happened. The Turks redoubled their efforts to crush the rebels, and in Bulgaria some terrible atrocities were committed. Turkish irregular troops, known as Bashi-Bazouks, took vicious reprisals on Bulgarian peasants, slaughtering at least 12 000 men, women and children. This was embarrassing for Disraeli: he felt bound to condemn the Turks, though he did not change his determination to support them against Russia if necessary.

(c) Gladstone's attack on the Turks

Gladstone's attitude was the direct opposite of Disraeli's. He saw it as a purely moral issue – the threat from Russia paled into insignificance besides the appalling Turkish massacres of innocent Christians. He was so incensed that he published a pamphlet, *The Bulgarian Horrors and the Question of the East* (September 1876), which rapidly became a best-seller. It contained a blistering attack on the evils of Turkish rule, their 'abominable and bestial lusts', and the foul deeds by which women had been violated, roasted and impaled. He hoped that the Turks 'one and all, bag and baggage, shall clear out from the province they have desolated and profaned', and he went so far as to urge the Russians to expel them from Bulgaria as soon as possible.

As a result, much of British public opinion turned against the Turks, making it more difficult for Disraeli to maintain an anti-Russian front. He retorted that Gladstone was worse than any Bulgarian Horror, and relations between the two men became irretrievably embittered. In fact many Liberals thought Gladstone had over-reacted and was tempting fate by encouraging the Russians.

(d) *War between Russia and Turkey*

- The Russian Tsar Alexander II, possibly influenced by Gladstone's attitude, announced that he could no longer stand by and allow Turkish atrocities to continue (November 1876). Frantic negotiations followed during which the Russians gave assurances that they would not capture Constantinople and the Dardanelles, and that they had no intention of interfering with the Suez Canal and India; consequently Britain agreed to remain neutral.
- The Russians declared war on Turkey (April 1877); their forces marched southwards into the Balkans and beseiged the fortress of Plevna which held out from June to December. The Russians did not perform particularly well and progress was painfully slow against unexpectedly strong Turkish resistance. However, by January 1878 they had reached Adrianople, not much more than 100 miles from Constantinople.
- Doubts began to creep in – would the Russians keep their promises? Now that Constantinople was threatened, British public opinion veered round to become pro-Turkish; mobs hooted Gladstone in the streets and smashed his windows.
- Disraeli acted promptly: he demanded an armistice and ordered British warships to Constantinople where they arrived in February 1878. By now Russian troops were in San Stefano on the outskirts of Constantinople. Disraeli warned that if they captured it, Britain would declare war. Tension was high and a European war seemed imminent as the British prepared an expeditionary force.
- The attack on Constantinople never came. The Russian commanders realized that the Turks would throw everything into the defence of their capital; the Russian troops were nearing exhaustion and there were not enough of them to defeat 100 000 Turks. Disraeli claimed, perhaps with some justification, that the British threats had also influenced the Russians. Peace negotiations opened and eventually agreement was reached . . .

(e) *The Treaty of San Stefano (March 1878)*

This was signed between Russia and Turkey and naturally the terms were very favourable to Russia. As soon as the details became known, *there was an immediate outcry from Britain and Austria–Hungary*. The terms were:

1   Serbia, Montenegro and Romania were recognized as independent of Turkey.
2   Russia took Bessarabia from Romania, giving her control of the Danube mouth. This alarmed the Austrians who depended on the Danube as a vital trade outlet into the Black Sea; there was no mention of Bosnia and Herzegovina being given to Austria–Hungary, which the Russians had mentioned as a reward for Austria remaining neutral.

Map 14.1   Balkan frontiers after the Congress of Berlin 1878

3   A large independent state of Bulgaria was set up; referred to as 'Big Bulgaria', it
stretched right across the Balkan Peninsula and had a coastline both on the Black
Sea and the Aegean Sea. For 'an initial period', Bulgaria would be administered by
Russian army officers. This was the most sensational clause of all; the British and
Austrians were convinced that 'Big Bulgaria' would be a satellite of Russia, giving
her the use of a port on the Aegean, so that she would be able to bypass the
Dardanelles. It seemed that the Balkan peoples had exchanged rule by Turkey for
rule by Russia.

Britain and Austria protested in the strongest possible terms: Disraeli called up the
reserves and sent 7000 Indian troops to Malta. Moderate opinion prevailed in Russia
and it was decided not to risk a conflict with both Britain and Austria–Hungary.
Bismarck, the German Chancellor, offered to act as 'honest broker', and the Russians
agreed to attend an international Congress in Berlin to renegotiate the peace terms.

(f) *The Congress of Berlin (June–July 1878)*

Many of the issues had been settled at preliminary discussions, but there were still some important points to be decided when the representatives met. Disraeli himself led the British delegation, ably assisted by the new Foreign Secretary, Lord Salisbury. Disraeli dominated the Congress with his vitality and the force of his personality, though most of the detailed work was carried out by Salisbury. Between them they achieved nearly everything they wanted, and still had time to enjoy the incessant receptions, parties and banquets. *The terms of the new agreement were*:

1   The idea of a 'Big Bulgaria' was dropped; it was divided into three:

- a small independent state of Bulgaria in the north ('Little Bulgaria');
- in the centre an area known as Eastern Roumelia, belonging to Turkey but having self-government under a Christian governor;
- the rest – Macedonia – was to remain part of the Turkish Empire, with no Christian governor.

2   The Austrians were allowed to occupy and administer Bosnia and Herzegovina, though nominally it still belonged to Turkey.
3   The Turks allowed Britain to occupy Cyprus in return for military help if Russia should attack again; there were more Turkish promises of fair treatment for the Christians.

(g) *How successful was the Congress?*

At the time it was thought of as a great British victory, and a personal triumph for Disraeli, who drove from the station to Downing Street through cheering crowds. 'We have brought back peace with honour', he declared. It was the crowning achievement of his career: not only was he a successful Prime Minister, he was also now a highly respected statesman who had achieved most of what he hoped for at Berlin:

- Russia had been checked in her advance through the Balkans towards the Dardanelles, and British interests in the Near East had been safeguarded – and all without war.
- The association of Austria, Germany and Russia (the *Dreikaiserbund* – League of Three Emperors) which Disraeli had so mistrusted, had been destroyed. Russia was now on poor terms with Austria, and her relations with Germany (which had failed to support her at Berlin) were never the same again.
- Turkey had been bolstered up against further Russian expansion attempts and Britain had a strong position in the eastern Mediterranean with the acquisition of Cyprus.

Robert Blake believes that Disraeli deserves immense credit because the Congress gave Europe over 30 years of peace. However, some other historians have emphasized the drawbacks of the settlement:

- Bulgaria, far from becoming a Russian puppet state as expected, was determined to maintain her independence and turned out to be strongly anti-Russian. Salisbury later admitted that he and Disraeli had 'backed the wrong horse', meaning that from the British point of view it would have been better to have kept 'Big Bulgaria'.
- The Austrian occupation of Bosnia aroused resentment in Serbia which had hopes of expanding in that area. In the words of A. J. P. Taylor, this 'contained the seeds of future disaster'; it was the beginning of the friction between Austria and Serbia which was to culminate in the outbreak of the First World War in 1914.
- The Turks again failed to keep their promises and made no attempt to reform or strengthen their state. Many of the Balkans people remained under Turkish rule which

was therefore unacceptable to them. Thus the Eastern Question had still not been solved permanently and there would be further disturbances and crises.

In the autumn of 1878, though, none of this was apparent, and if a general election had been held then, there is little doubt that Disraeli and the Conservatives would have won easily.

14.5 Why did the Conservatives lose the 1880 general election?

After a surprise by-election victory in which the Conservatives won the Liberal strong-hold of Southwark, Disraeli judged that the tide was running in his favour. The general election of April 1880 showed that he had miscalculated badly; the results were: Liberals 353, Conservatives 238, Irish Home Rulers 61. Yet it was less than two years since Disraeli's triumph at Berlin. *What had gone wrong?*

- There was disappointment and criticism about some events overseas, *after* the Congress of Berlin, which spoiled Disraeli's image of the international diplomatic master – the mishandling of the Zulu War and the fiasco in Afghanistan which had not been resolved when the election took place.
- The lack of social reform aroused growing disapproval. Although the government had begun well, after 1876 no major reforming measure was introduced. This was partly because Disraeli was occupied with foreign affairs and partly because the 59 Irish MPs, having failed to secure Home Rule by reasoned argument, resorted to tactics of obstruction; more than once they kept the Commons up all night talking about Irish affairs, and the government could find no way of dealing with them.
- There was an industrial slump which caused unemployment to shoot up rapidly. In 1872 only about one per cent of trade union members were out of work, but by 1879 the figure was as high as 11 per cent. In some trades the situation was even worse – 22 per cent of registered engineers were without work. It was the first taste of foreign competition which was to oust Britain from her economic leadership of the world, and the beginning of what became known as *The Great Depression* (see Sections 15.2 and 15.4).
- There was an even more severe agricultural depression caused by a massive influx of cheap corn from North America and by a series of wet summers. Hundreds of farmers went bankrupt and thousands of farm labourers were put out of work. Most other European countries introduced tariffs, but Disraeli refused to do so, and was naturally criticized for this by the farming interests; ironically his argument (which he had opposed in 1846) was that free trade in corn would keep down the cost of living for the workers.
- Gladstone, who had retired from the Liberal leadership after their defeat in 1874, re-emerged as the real Liberal leader and conducted a stunning campaign, starting in his constituency of Midlothian and travelling the length of the country. He attacked Disraeli's policies as 'immoral and iniquitous': the Afghan War was 'a crime against God', and Cyprus was 'a valueless encumbrance'. Perhaps his most successful speech was the one in St Andrew's Hall, Glasgow, to a crowded audience of over 6000. For a man of over 70, *The Midlothian Campaign* (November–December 1879) followed by a repeat performance just before the election, was a remarkable achievement. Disraeli, approaching 80 and in failing health, was unable to provide an effective answer.
- Finally the Liberal party organization had reached peak efficiency under the guidance of Joseph Chamberlain (see Section 17.2(b)), whereas the Conservative organization had stagnated since 1874 and was caught unprepared for an election.

14.6 Assessment of Disraeli

Soon after Disraeli's defeat, Gladstone crowed: 'the downfall of Beaconsfieldism is like the vanishing of some vast magnificent castle in an Italian romance'. Did Disraeli's career have any lasting effect on British politics, or was Gladstone right? Opinions are divided:

● Robert Blake, probably Disraeli's best-known biographer, and historian of the Conservative party, believes that Disraeli's great and lasting achievement was to hold the Conservative party together through a difficult period and then to demonstrate that it was still capable of forming an effective government. After all, when a political party has failed to win a general election for over 30 years, even its staunchest supporters could be forgiven for writing it off. He also made it the party of the Empire and the party with a strong foreign policy, i.e. the party of British nationalism. By showing concern for the social conditions of the poor, Disraeli enabled the Conservatives to attract a large enough slice of the working-class vote to keep them in existence as a major party.

Disraeli's most recent biographer, T. A. Jenkins, believes that Disraeli's greatest contribution was to make the Conservatives into a genuinely national party, able to attract support from all classes in society. Although this might not have seemed clear in 1880 at the time of the big Conservative election defeat, 'in fact the image of a national party promoted by Disraeli was soon to stand the Conservatives in good stead, especially after Gladstone's Liberal party split over the question of Irish Home Rule in 1886. Already, by that time, the belief was gaining ground that Disraeli had laid the foundations for a "Tory Democracy", an idea that was to inspire the Conservatives for generations to come.'

● Some other historians feel that Disraeli's impact has been overestimated. Paul Smith claims that Peel had already made the Conservatives into a modern party when they won the 1841 general election, and that Disraeli actually retarded its development by leading the attack on Peel over the Corn Laws. The next leader of the party, Lord Salisbury, abandoned the social reform policy, so that aspect of Beaconsfieldism certainly did not survive long.

Whichever view one accepts, there is no escaping the fact that Disraeli was a first-rate parliamentarian; Blake calls him 'an impresario, an actor manager ... there is a champagne-like sparkle about him which has scarcely ever been equalled and never surpassed among statesmen'.

Questions

1 **Disraeli and Conservative policies**
   Study Sources A to E and then answer the questions which follow.

Source A

Extracts from a speech by Disraeli at the Crystal Palace, 24 June 1872

I have always been of the opinion that the Tory Party has three great objects. The first is to maintain the institutions of the country, especially the monarchy.... The second great object is to uphold the Empire of England. If you look at the history of this country since the arrival of Liberalism – forty years ago – you will find that there has been no effort so continuous, so subtle, and supported by so much

---

energy, as the attempts of Liberalism to bring about the disintegration of the Empire . . .

Gentlemen, another great object of the Tory Party is the improvement of the condition of the people. . . . The health of the people is the most important question for a statesman. . . . It involves the state of the dwellings of the people, the regulation of their industry, the inspection of their toil, the purity of their provisions, and it touches on all the means by which you may wean them from habits of excess and brutality.

A leading member denounced these policies the other day as a 'policy of sewage'. But to one of the labouring multitude of England, *it is not a policy of sewage, but a question of life and death* . . . and moreover, *the Palace is unsafe if the cottage is unhappy.*

Source B

From the memoirs of R. A. Cross, Disraeli's Home Secretary 1874–80

When the Cabinet came to discuss the Queen's Speech [in 1874], I was, I confess, disappointed at the lack of originality shown by the Prime Minister. From all his speeches, I had quite expected that his mind was full of legislative schemes; but this did not prove to be the case. On the contrary, he had to rely on the various suggestions of his colleagues, and as they themselves had only just come into office, there was some difficulty in framing the Queen's Speech.

Source C

From a speech by Gladstone at Dalkeith, 26 November 1879, during the Midlothian Campaign

Go from South Africa into the lofty hills of Afghanistan, as they were last winter, and what do we see? I fear a yet sadder sight than was to be seen in the land of the Zulus. You have seen during last winter from time to time that from such and such a village, attacks had been made upon the British forces, and that in consequence the village had been burned. Those hill tribes had committed no real offence against us. We, in the pursuit of our political objects, chose to establish military positions in their country. . . . The meaning of the burning of the village is that the women and children were driven forth to perish in the snows of winter. . . . Does this not arouse in you horror and grief, to think that England should be associated with such consequences, not for any political necessity, but for a war as frivolous as any ever waged in the history of man.

Source: sources A, B and C are quoted in P. Adelman, *Gladstone, Disraeli and later Victorian Politics*, Longman, 1983.

Source D

A modern historian, A. J. P. Taylor, writes about Disraeli

Disraeli had a flighty mind which drifted from smart triviality to adolescent day-dreaming and back again. . . . He was first and last a great actor, watching his own performance and that of others with ironic detachment. He cared for causes only as a means of combat. . . . His novel *Sybil* is supposed to contain a profound social analysis. In fact it says no more than that the rich are very rich and the poor very poor – by no means a new discovery. His own policy, when he came to power, turned out to be nothing more startling than municipal wash-houses. . . . His only genuine emotion in politics sprang from personal dislike – of Peel in his early career, of Gladstone even more strongly towards the end.

Source: A. J. P. Taylor, 'Dizzy', in *Essays in English History*, Penguin, 1976.

Source E

Comments from Robert Blake (now Lord Blake, a Conservative peer), Disraeli's biographer

Disraeli lacked the administrative and legislative ability of Peel, Gladstone and Balfour. His mind was like a catherine wheel shooting out sparks – most of them fell on damp earth. . . . Where he excelled was in the art of presentation. He was an impresario and an actor manager. He was a superb parliamentarian, one of the half dozen greatest in our history . . . but another side of him was a slightly mocking observer surveying with sceptical amusement the very stage on which he himself played a principal part. To him, more than to most, politics was 'the great game'.

Source: R. Blake, *Disraeli*, Methuen, 1969.

(a) Explain what you think Disraeli meant by the following two statements in Source A:
  (i) 'It is not a policy of sewage, but a question of life and death'.
  (ii) 'The Palace is unsafe if the cottage is unhappy'.   (6 marks)
(b) From the evidence of the sources and the information in Chapter 14, explain to what extent you think Disraeli's concern for the working classes was genuine.
     (10 marks)
(c) How can it be inferred from Sources A and C that Gladstone and Disraeli had differing views about the Empire?   (4 marks)
(d) How far do you think Sources D and E disagree in their assessment of Disraeli?   (5 marks)
(e) Comment on the strengths and weaknesses of each of these sources A to E.
     (10 marks)
     (Total 35 marks)

2 'The domestic reforms of Disraeli and the Conservative government of 1874 to 1880 brought major advances in modernising Britain'.
How far do you agree with this judgement?   [NEAB]

15 Victorian prosperity and depression

Summary of events

During the first few years of Queen Victoria's reign – from 1837 until about 1844 – industrial prosperity seemed variable, and there were several short trade depressions. The situation began to stabilize with a great surge of railway building from 1844 to 1847, and after that, industry moved into *a period of remarkable prosperity which lasted until 1873*. Agriculture enjoyed a similar 'Golden Age', usually known as the period of *High Farming*; this demonstrated that all the prophets of doom, who had forecast that the repeal of the Corn Laws in 1846 would ruin British farming, were wrong, at least for the time being.

The period from 1873 to 1896 is usually referred to as the Great Depression, though there is some controversy among historians about exactly how serious this so-called depression was. British industry went through a difficult period: although exports of most commodities continued to increase, prices and profits were falling, mainly because of overseas competition. There was something of a recovery between 1896 and 1914, but by the outbreak of the First World War in 1914, it was clear that the USA and Germany had toppled Britain from her position as the world's leading manufacturing nation. In agriculture the depression was much more severe, and although there was a slight recovery around the turn of the century, it was only during the war years (1914–18), when foreign wheat was difficult to obtain, that British farming began to revive.

15.1 Illustrate and account for Britain's industrial prosperity in the mid nineteenth century

(a) *The Great Exhibition of 1851*

This is probably the best illustration of Britain's prosperity during the mid nineteenth century. The suggestion for it came from the Royal Society of Arts, whose president, Prince Albert, was full of enthusiasm for the idea. The exhibition was housed in *the Crystal Palace*, a vast construction of glass and cast iron, designed by Joseph Paxton and erected in Hyde Park. One-third of a mile long and over 100 feet high, it contained a display of every conceivable type of British machinery (much of it working) and manufactures: railway engines, steam ploughs, steamship engines, cranes, steam hammers for heavy industry, printing machines, screw-making machines, Lancashire cottons and

Illus. 15.1   The Great Exhibition, in the Crystal Palace, 1851

Nottingham lace; there was even a silent piano (made out of papier-maché) and an unsinkable deckchair. To demonstrate that Britain was a free trade country, exhibits were included from foreign countries – Dresden china, and silks and tapestries from France. There were over six million visitors during the five months the exhibition was open, many of them from abroad, and lots of new export orders followed. Britain was regarded as 'the workshop of the world'.

(b) *The great export boom*

Over the next 20 years British industry enjoyed a remarkable export boom the like of which had never been experienced before. This can best be illustrated by looking at the export figures in Table 15.1. Table 15.2 shows how the total value of exports from Britain increased.

Another way in which prosperity showed itself was that the wages of the industrial working class increased, on average, by about 50 per cent in the period 1850–75. Prices also rose, but only by about 20 per cent on average; this meant that workers enjoyed a rise of about 30 per cent in *real wages* (what they could actually buy with their money).

(c) *Reasons for the prosperity*

1   The basis was that Britain was still enjoying the advantage of having been the first nation to industrialize. As yet there was no real competition from abroad, and the countries which were to become serious competitors later were still lagging far behind, for one reason or another. The USA was having difficulty supplying its

Table 15.1 Export figures for the main manufacturing industries
(a) Annual average for each five-year period

Year	Iron and steel (in thousand tons)	Coal (in million tons)
1845–9	458	2.50
1850–4	1225	3.20
1855–9	1411	5.99
1860–4	1536	7.83
1865–9	2027	9.86
1870–4	2965	12.31

(b) Annual average per decade

Year	Cotton textiles (in million yards)	Woollen goods (including carpets) (in thousand yards)
1840–9	978	93 316
1850–9	1855	161 563
1860–9	2375	236 267
1870–9	3573	311 601

Source: P. Mathias, *The First Industrial Nation* (Methuen, 1969) pp. 481–7.

own rapidly increasing population and was held back by the Civil War (1861–5); Germany did not become a unified state until 1871. Both these countries were important buyers of British manufactures.

2　Further inventions were made which helped to keep Britain in the forefront; most important were the new processes in the metal industry which resulted in mild steel taking over from malleable iron as the most popular metal.

　　Henry Bessemer patented a converter system which could produce steel in large quantities at much lower prices (1856); this caused railways and shipping-lines to change to steel for rails and metal plating. William Siemens, a German engineer working in Britain, patented his open-hearth process (1867) which could produce a stronger type of steel.

3　The population growth increased the demand for manufactured goods at home. Between 1851 and 1871 the population of Britain rose from 27.4 million to 31.5 million, and this acted as a stimulus to industry.

4　Gladstone as Chancellor of the Exchequer (1853–5 and 1860–5) made an important contribution to the prosperity by removing almost all the remaining tariffs (see Section 8.2). This meant that there were no artificial restrictions on trade: Britain could obtain cheap raw materials and flood the world with cheap manufactured goods.

5　The spread of railways contributed to the boom in many ways. In 1843 there were less than 2000 miles of track, but the rest of the decade saw an enormous investment of cash in railway building. This 'Railway Mania' as it became known,

Table 15.2 Total value of exports from Britain

Year	£ million
1840–9	124.5
1860–9	159.7
1870–9	218.1

Source: C. Cook and J. Stevenson, *Handbook of Modern British History* (Longman, 1988) p. 194.

resulted in the construction of a further 5000 miles of track by 1850, and in 1875 a total of 14 510 miles of track was open. Thousands of extra jobs were provided, as well as a large market for the iron industry, for rails, locomotives, coaches and wagons. Railways became an important consumer of coal, and railway towns like Crewe and Swindon mushroomed as workshop and repair centres. The cheap, fast transport provided by the railways enabled new inland coalfields to be developed, together with the iron ore mines in North Yorkshire. Most important of all, they made it possible to transport manufactured goods of all kinds to the ports much more quickly. This, together with the rapid spread of steam-power in merchant shipping after 1850, played a vital part in increasing British exports.

6   There was plenty of capital available for investment in industry. There were more reliable banking and credit facilities since the 1844 Bank Charter Act (see Section 7.2(c)). Once industrial progress had got under way, the vast profits which were earned from, for example, exports of cotton textiles, provided a continuous flow of capital which was used to finance further expansion. There was even some left over to be invested abroad – in 1875 at least £12 000 million of British capital was invested in railway and factory projects overseas. Much of this cash was used by foreigners to buy British goods. The discovery of gold in California (1849), Australia (1851) and New Zealand (1861) added to the capital available and further increased the demand for British manufactures.

15.2 In what ways and why can Britain be said to have suffered an industrial depression after 1873?

(a) No serious industrial slump

Although the last quarter of the century is often described as the time of the Great Depresssion, there was no serious industrial slump with sharply falling exports, as there was in the depression of the early 1930s (see Section 25.4). In most industries the general trend of production and exports was still rising. The steel industry enjoyed a massive expansion during the so-called depression; in coal and cotton textiles, output and exports continued to increase, though *the rate of growth was slowing down*; although production of iron decreased, this was only to be expected as steel became more widely adopted. One economic historian, S.B. Saul, even went so far as to call his book about the period *The Myth of the Great Depression*. However, economists described it as a depression because:

• Prices were falling, and therefore although exports continued to increase, they were worth less in cash; this is shown by the statistics in Table 15.3:
• Consequently profits were declining; as the economists put it, profit margins were being squeezed.
• Employers often tried to cut down costs and maintain profit levels by laying off workers, causing periodic bursts of unemployment. In the 20 years before 1874, the

Table 15.3   Exports of cotton textiles after 1870

Year	Cotton cloth exported (in million yards)	Value (£ million)
1870–9	3573	71.5
1880–9	4675	73.0
1890–9	5057	67.2

Source: P. Mathias, *The First Industrial Nation* (Methuen, 1969) pp. 468, 486.

average rate of unemployment among trades union members was 4.6 per cent, but during 1875–95 the average was 5.4 per cent. Some individual years were serious: the 1879 figure was 11 per cent and 1886 10 per cent. However, it was not a period of sustained unemployment: 1882–3 and 1888–90 were good years when no more than 2 per cent were out of work.

Pressure from businessmen, never slow to voice their concern when profits take a turn for the worse, caused the government to appoint a Royal Commission in 1886 to investigate the problem. Its conclusion merely stated the obvious: there was 'a diminution, and in some cases, an absence of profit, with a corresponding diminution of employment for the labouring classes'.

(b) *What caused the depression?*

Some historians have tried to explain it in terms of a single cause: falling prices were the result of the world economy running short of gold. Another favourite single explanation was that the depression was the inevitable down-turn in the economy following a boom. While there is probably some truth in both theories, the generally accepted view nowadays is that *the depression was produced by a complex combination of factors*:

1   There was a reduction in railway building: between 1845 and 1870 an average of 2000 miles of new track was opened in each five-year period. After 1850 the figure fell by half, and between 1885 and 1900 an average of only 750 miles of track were built in each five-year period. Thus there was a gradual falling-off in demand for metals, and a loss of jobs.
2   Britain was beginning to suffer serious competition from abroad, especially from the USA and Germany. This was probably inevitable: once other countries learned the techniques for themselves and began to industrialize, they were bound to challenge Britain's lead. The USA had enormous natural resources and a growing labour force (thanks to immigration). The statistics in Table 15.4 show how the USA and Germany were overtaking Britain and how Britain's growth rate was much smaller than theirs:

Table 15.4   Coal, pig-iron and steel production of the three leading powers

Coal production (in million tons)

	1850	1860	1870	1880	1890	1900	1910	1914
Germany	6.0	12.0	34.0	59.0	89.0	149.0	222.0	277.0
USA	–	3.4	10.0	64.9	143.0	244.0	350.0	455.0
Britain	57.0	81.0	112.0	149.0	184.0	228.0	268.0	292.0

Pig-iron production (in million tons)

	1850	1860	1870	1880	1890	1900	1910	1914
Germany	–	–	1.3	2.5	4.1	7.5	9.5	14.7
USA	–	0.8	1.7	3.9	9.4	14.0	27.0	30.0
Britain	2.2	3.9	6.0	7.8	8.0	9.0	10.0	11.0

Steel production (in million tons)

	1850	1860	1870	1880	1890	1900	1910	1914
Germany	–	–	0.3	0.7	2.3	6.7	13.8	14.0
USA	–	–	–	1.3	4.3	10.0	26.0	32.0
Britain	–	–	0.7	1.3	3.6	5.0	5.9	6.5

Source: A. J. P. Taylor, *The Struggle for Mastery in Europe 1848–1918* (Oxford, 1971) pp. xxix–xxx.

3   The British were now experiencing the disadvantages of having been the first nation to industrialize: their machinery and equipment were old and in some cases obsolete, whereas the Americans and Germans could start with the latest technology available. The Germans, for instance, were able to install the Siemens furnaces for making steel; they also took full advantage of a later invention by the cousins Percy Gilchrist (a Welsh steelworks chemist) and Sydney Gilchrist-Thomas (a clerk in a London law-court), who in 1878 discovered how to manufacture steel from iron-ore which had a high phosphorous content. The British were saddled with the earlier Bessemer converters, which the Germans had abandoned and which were more expensive to run than the Siemens and Gilchrist-Thomas methods.

Similar advances had been made in other industries: in the American cotton industry there was the introduction of ring-spinning instead of the slower and more expensive mule-spinning still used in Lancashire. America pioneered new machines like the typewriter and the sewing-machine. The Belgians made advances in the glass industry, enabling them to produce better quality glass more cheaply than the British. Over the whole range of industry the British were therefore suffering in two ways: they were being gradually pushed out of their markets in Europe and America (most states introduced tariffs to protect their developing industries); and foreign imports were making an increasing impact on the British market. The British government, still committed to *laissez-faire*, would not introduce tariffs.

4   There was a failure of management to respond positively to the new challenges:

- The most common unit was the family firm; top management tended to be chosen not because of ability but because of family connections; unfortunately, inspiration and interest often deteriorated by the time a firm had reached its third or fourth generation of owners. In the USA and Germany recruitment depended much more on ability.
- There was not enough effort to develop new industries, with the result that the British export trade relied too heavily on a few staple products. The Germans meanwhile surged ahead in the 'new' industries such as electrical engineering, chemicals and dyestuffs.
- There was not enough effort to improve designs and reduce costs by introducing the latest machinery; this might have enabled the British to hold on to their European and American markets. However, they preferred to switch exports to India, to other parts of the Empire and to China; this was especially true of the cotton industry. Management was too complacent, preferring to repair the old machinery rather than invest profits in new premises and equipment; in fairness though, the fall in profits during the 'depression' probably goes some way towards explaining the lack of investment.
- Even when they were prepared to invest, industrialists sometimes made the wrong decisions: between 1896 and 1914 there was a boom in cotton exports, and hundreds of new mills were built in Lancashire; but instead of taking the opportunity to install the latest automatic looms already widely used in the USA and Germany, manufacturers on the whole decided to invest in the traditional type looms.
- Too little attention was paid to the importance of science, especially in chemicals and electrical engineering.

5   Trade unions may have held up the introduction of some new machines and

processes in an attempt to make sure that skilled workers were not pushed out of their jobs.

6   Britain's education system was not geared to producing academically trained scientists and engineers. The public schools concentrated on the classics and worked on the assumption that gentlemen did not go in for practical training. A nationally organized system of elementary and secondary education was very slow in arriving (see Section 12.6) and even when it did, the science taught was not designed to prepare students for top-level technological training. In the 1870s science was scarcely taught in British universities except to medical students; yet in 1872 there were already 11 purely technical universities and 20 other universities in Germany, all organized and financed by the government.

If we accept these arguments, it seems clear that British industry was already suffering, long before 1914, from many of the major weaknesses which were to afflict it after the First World War and which were to cause Britain's long economic decline. However, not all historians go along with this interpretation. J. B. Saul argued that the depression was largely a myth (see Source D in question 1 at the end of the chapter). Professor Theo Barker, in an article in *History Today* ('Workshop of the World 1870–1914', June 1994), challenges many of the traditional arguments. He points out that Britain, though apparently lagging behind the USA in the 'new' industries such as electric lighting, electric traction and car manufacture, was later able to take advantage of the delay by introducing, before 1914, improved and more efficient techniques, which had been developed abroad by trial and error. Professor Barker also claims that:

●   the old industries like cotton and shipbuilding *were* showing a willingness to introduce changes;
●   the argument that heads of family firms lacked the drive and ability shown by their founders does not fit the facts;
●   there was ample opportunity to study science at grammar schools, technical schools and colleges, and at the expanding redbrick universities.

In fact, according to Professor Barker, on the eve of the First World War, all was set fair for the continuing growth of British industry. What threw everything off course was the First World War: 'the war accelerated trends with which, given the slower pace of peace, British manufacturers could have coped as they had been doing before 1914. Does anyone believe that Lancashire cotton in the 1920s would have been suffering as it did if there had been no war? Or British shipbuilding? Yet it has been after looking back from this side of the 1914–1918 war that historians have reached their gloomy conclusions about Britain's industrial performance on the other side of that disastrous conflict.' (See Section 22.5(j) for the effects of the war on the British economy.)

15.3 What is meant by the term 'High Farming' and why was the period 1846–74 one of prosperity for British agriculture?

(a) *High Farming*

High Farming was the title of a pamphlet written by a Wigtownshire farmer, James Caird, and published in 1849. In it he explained his ideas about how farmers should respond to the threat of foreign competition following the abolition of the Corn Laws in 1846. They should farm their land more intensively, using all the latest techniques and inventions, in order to increase yield and lower costs; it would thus be possible to cope with the lowering of prices which cheap foreign imports would bring, while still maintaining profits. According to F. M. L. Thompson, the early part of this period (1846–53) was one of only faltering prosperity, and it was only in 1853 that prices of farm produce stabilized at an encouraging level. The period of 'High Farming', the real Golden Age of British agriculture, lasted only about 20 years after 1853; it was when farmers with money to spare 'opened their purses and embarked on the new course in a big way'. It was a period of prosperity for farmers, whose incomes probably doubled; even farm labourers were becoming slightly better off as far as wages, housing and food were concerned.

(b) *What were the reasons for the prosperity?*

1   The new 'High Farming' techniques resulted in much greater productivity. Widespread use of clay piping improved land drainage; there was an increase in 'mixed farming', that is, growing wheat and root crops, *and* raising cattle, sheep and pigs as well. Artificial fertilizers – nitrate of soda, superphosphates, sulphate of ammonia, Peruvian guano and German potash – came into use. Pedigree breeds of cattle – Hereford, Aberdeen Angus, Ayrshire and Channel Island – were improved; by the early 1870s the major profit for most farmers came from their livestock. There were also improvements to ploughs and hoes, and the spread of the horse-drawn reaper. More spectacular were the steam threshing-machines and steam ploughs, though these were not so important; Thompson calls them 'the white elephant of high farming, a plaything of rich landowners with money to spare for anything new in farm gadgetry'.
2   Scientific farming was encouraged by the Royal Agricultural Society of England (founded 1838) which published a journal and organized agricultural shows. An experimental station was set up in 1842 at Rothamsted to carry out research into soils and fertilizers.
3   Britain's growing population meant an ever-increasing demand for the farmers' products, and therefore it meant higher prices and profits. Although wheat prices remained steady, the prices of all types of meat, butter, cheese and wool (for clothing) rose by close on 50 per cent.
4   Vitally important was the fact that because of the lack of fast shipping and of refrigeration facilities, there was very little competition from foreign produce, except Russian and American wheat. Imports of wheat gradually increased during the 1860s, which explains why wheat prices were steady while prices of meat and dairy produce rose.
5   Railways enabled livestock and perishable goods such as meat, milk and market garden produce to be transported quickly and cheaply over long distances for sale in the cities. Farmers who had previously been too far away from towns and cities now had a whole new market at their disposal. Counties such as Norfolk and Herefordshire could produce milk for London, and Aberdeenshire was supplying meat to industrial Lancashire and London.
6   Finally, even the weather was kind to the farmers with a run of mostly good summers and good harvests between 1850 and 1873.

15.4 Why and with what results was there a depression in agriculture after 1873?

The Golden Age changed quite suddenly into a depression which was especially severe in areas which relied heavily on wheat and cereal production. Prices and profits fell, harvests were smaller and many fields went out of cultivation. However, livestock and dairy farming were not so badly affected; the boom in this area of farming lasted well into the 1880s, when foreign imports began to bring down prices.

(a) *Reasons for the depression*

1   Bad weather played an important role; the summer of 1873 was wet and the harvest poor; the autumn of 1875 was exceptionally wet, and after that came 12 years of above average rainfall and below average temperatures. Crops were ruined and harvests disappointing. Worse still, the wet weather helped to spread pneumonia and foot and mouth disease among livestock; there were also epidemics of liver rot among sheep, and swine fever, causing farmers to suffer heavy losses.

2   The most important cause of the depression was the import of cheap foreign food which was now available to make up the shortages. The building of the trans-continental railways opened up the fertile prairies of North America as vast wheat-growing areas, and the development of large merchant steamships enabled American, and later Canadian, Indian, Australian and Argentinian wheat to be transported swiftly and cheaply to Britain. For example, in 1868 the cost of transporting a ton of wheat from Chicago to Liverpool was 65s.; in 1882 it had fallen to only 24s. Consequently the price of wheat fell, on average, by half; at one point it hit a record low level of 17s. 6d. a quarter. These trends are illustrated in Tables 15.5 and 15.6.

Table 15.5   Imports of wheat and flour into the UK (average per decade)

Year	(in thousand of cwt)
1840–9	10 667
1850–9	19 326
1860–9	33 697
1870–9	50 406
1880–9	70 282
1890–9	85 890
1900–9	102 85

Source: P. Mathias, *The First Industrial Nation* (Methuen, 1969) pp. 472–5.

Table 15.6   Wheat prices (annual average for 5-year periods)

Year	(shillings per quarter)
1840–4	57.85
1845–9	54.00
1855–9	57.62
1865–9	53.62
1870–4	55.00
1875–9	47.67
1885–9	31.58
1895–9	27.82
1900–4	27.37
1910–14	32.93

Source: P. Mathias, *The First Industrial Nation* (Methuen, 1969) pp. 472–5.

3   Disraeli's government (1874–80), despite intense pressure from farming interests, took the decision not to protect British agriculture by the reintroduction of tariffs.

In the 1880s the introduction of refrigeration ships brought frozen mutton from Australia and New Zealand and chilled beef from Argentina. At the same time, according to Thompson, 'the traditional English breakfast of Danish bacon and eggs was being established'.

(b) *Results of the depression*

● Farmers who relied heavily on wheat and cereal growing, particularly in southern and eastern counties, had a hard time; many went bankrupt, some tenant farmers fell into arrears with rents, and landowners suffered reduced profits from rents. The area of land producing cereal crops fell substantially from 9.6 million acres at the height of the Golden Age in 1872, to 6.5 million acres in 1913. On the other hand, in the Midlands, in Lancashire and Cheshire, and in Scotland, where mixed farming was common, the depression was comparatively mild.

● Many farmers survived by turning arable land over to pasture, and switching to livestock, dairy and poultry farming. Others turned to orchards and market gardening, producing fruit, vegetables, flowers and bulbs. The area under pasture increased from 17.1 million acres in 1872, to 21.5 million in 1913. Although it is true that meat, butter and cheese prices fell during the late 1880s and the 1890s in the face of foreign imports, this was not as disastrous as the fall in cereal prices. There were three reasons for this:

1   The price of animal feed fell substantially;
2   British meat was of a higher quality than imported frozen and chilled meat;
3   The growing demand for milk in the industrial towns and cities could only be met by British cattle.

● There were important social effects. In areas where arable farming was abandoned, many agricultural labourers were thrown out of work, and there must have been considerable hardship for a time. In 1871 there were close on one million farm labourers in Britain, but by 1901 the number had fallen to just over 600 000. Some had moved to London, others had emigrated to the USA, Canada, Australia and New Zealand.

● The depression brought the benefit of cheaper food, so that people who were lucky enough to have jobs could enjoy a slightly higher standard of living. For the remaining agricultural labourers, falling prices meant that although their money wages fell, their real wages probably remained steady.

(c) *Agriculture recovers slightly after 1900*

By 1914 total output of agriculture had increased by 5 per cent, and prices, even of wheat, were rising again. This apparent recovery took place because the blast of foreign competition had forced farmers to adapt and become more efficient, or go under. *The Eversley Commission (1893–7)* urged more people to take up dairy and poultry farming or turn to market gardening. Many took the advice, further slimming down the less profitable cereal producing sector. The government helped by forbidding the import of live cattle (1892); although the prime purpose of this move was to control cattle diseases, it removed an important element of competition. In the end, therefore, it was not so much a recovery as that the survivors had learned to live with world-wide foreign competition.

Questions

1 The industrial depression

Study Sources A to D carefully and then answer the questions which follow.

___ Source A _____

Cartoon in Punch, 1896, entitled 'Caught Napping'

(*Tenniel*, 1896, *reproduced by permission of the Proprietors of 'Punch'*.)

CAUGHT NAPPING.

'There was an old lady as I've heard tell, she went to market her goods for to sell | She went to market on a market day and she fell asleep on the world's highway | By came a pedlar—German— and stout, and he cut her petticoats all round about.'

Figure 15.1

Source: *Punch*, 1896.

In Sources B, C and D, three modern economic historians write about the causes and nature of the depression:

___ Source B _____

It might be questioned whether all Britain's losses can be attributed simply to the emergence of new industrial competitors; perhaps they stemmed from internal deficiencies. A country whose industrial structure is too narrowly based on a few traditional industries is obviously going to be more restricted as regards trading opportunities.

Source: D. H. Aldcroft, *The Development of British Industry and Foreign Competition*, Allen & Unwin, 1968.

Source C

If Britain was behind the times in technique and methods of production, she was even further behind the times in her selling methods ... a frequent complaint was scarcity of British trade representatives abroad ... poor packing of goods and inadequate credit facilities.

Source: D. H. Aldcroft and H. W. Richardson, _The British Economy 1870–1939_, Macmillan, 1969.

Source D

It is important to remember, however, that Britain retained a wide lead in many industrial sectors to 1914. Most of these had their roots in the industrial revolution; cotton textiles and textile machinery, heavy machine tools, locomotives, ships and steam-engines.

Source: S. B. Saul, _The Myth of the Great Depression 1873–1896_, Macmillan, 1969.

(a) How does the _Punch_ cartoonist of 1896 try to explain the causes of the industrial depression?　(4 marks)

(b) In the light of Sources B and C, how adequate is Source A as an explanation of the depression?　(6 marks)

(c) From the evidence of the sources and Section 15.2, how far do you think S. B. Saul (Source D) was correct when he claimed that the industrial depression after 1873 was a myth?　(15 marks)

(Total 25 marks)

2　Read the following extract about the agricultural depression in the late nineteenth century from _British Economic and Social History_ by C. P. Hill, and then answer the questions which follow.

> Wheat prices ... reached rock bottom in 1894. In 1874 there had been 3,630,000 acres under wheat in Great Britain; by 1900 the total was only just over half that figure. ... In thirty years some 300 000 agricultural labourers had left the countryside.

(a) Why was British agriculture in depression between the late 1870s and the early 20th century?　(8 marks)

(b) 'Far more people benefited from than were harmed by the agricultural depression'. Examine the validity of this claim.　(12 marks)

(Total 20 marks) [NEAB]

3　How accurate is it to describe the period c.1875–c.1914 in Great Britain as one of economic decline?　[AEB]

Gladstone and Salisbury 1880–95

Summary of events

This period was very much dominated by events in Ireland; governments of both parties usually tried to solve the problems by a combination of coercion and pacification, but without any lasting success. Of the six governments which held office, four were directly brought down by Irish affairs.

Governments 1880–95		
Party	*Prime Minister*	*In office*
Liberal	W. E. Gladstone (2nd ministry)	1880–June 1885
Conservative	Lord Salisbury (1st ministry)	June 1885– February 1886
Liberal	W. E. Gladstone (3rd ministry)	February– August 1886
Conservative	Lord Salisbury (2nd ministry)	1886–92
Liberal	W. E. Gladstone (4th ministry)	1892–March 1894
Liberal	Lord Rosebery	March 1894– June 1895

Gladstone began his second ministry with a large majority, but very little went right for him. His *Second Irish Land Act (1881)* failed to satisfy the Irish Nationalists and their leader, Charles Stewart Parnell, who would settle for nothing less than Home Rule. Disraeli had left Gladstone several problems abroad – in Afghanistan, Transvaal, Egypt and the Sudan. Gladstone's handling of these situations aroused criticism, and though his policies resulted in Egypt in effect becoming part of the British Empire, he was also held responsible for the death of the popular General Gordon in the Sudan. Though there was time for a few domestic reforms, notably *the Parliamentary Reform Act of 1884*, the Radicals felt that there ought to have been many more.

Believing that there was more to be gained for Ireland from the Conservatives, Parnell had no hesitation in using Irish Nationalist votes to turn Gladstone out and put Salisbury and the Conservatives in (June 1885). When it was revealed that Gladstone had been converted to Home Rule, despite the opposition of many of his own party, Parnell switched his support back to the Liberals. However, Gladstone's *1886 Home Rule Bill* was defeated in the Commons, when 93 Liberals voted against it. The Liberal party, deeply split over Ireland and other matters, was defeated in the following general election.

During the six years of Conservative rule there were several important developments: Ireland was given firm treatment along with some modest concessions; in foreign affairs Salisbury was concerned to keep Britain aloof from binding agreements with other powers – a policy which became known, misleadingly, as *'splendid isolation'*; and there were the early stages of the *'Scramble for Africa'*, during which the powers of western Europe somehow managed to divide Africa between them without a war. This was not exciting stuff for ordinary working people who were more concerned with the unemployment situation and the cost of living; the attentions of many of them were turning towards trades unions and events such as the successful dockers' strike of 1889.

In the 1892 election the Liberals won just enough seats to form a government with Irish Nationalist support. The main aim of the 83-year-old Gladstone was to secure Home Rule for Ireland; but his *Second Home Rule Bill*, although it passed the Commons, was defeated by the Conservative-dominated House of Lords, and Gladstone resigned. Lord Rosebery's short government was notable for the way in which the Lords continually prevented Liberal bills from becoming law. This was the beginning of the growing confrontation between the two houses, which was to reach its climax with *the Parliament Act of 1911*. With Gladstone's retirement, the Liberals had lost their main attraction for the electorate, and were heavily defeated in the election of 1895. Ten years of unbroken Conservative rule followed.

16.1 How did Gladstone try to pacify Ireland between 1880 and 1886 and why did he fail?

(a) *The deteriorating situation in Ireland*

The situation in Ireland had deteriorated during Disraeli's government. The agricultural depression, caused by cheap American corn, made farming in Ireland even less profitable than before. Many landlords reacted by evicting more tenant-farmers in order to consolidate holdings; violent incidents were common as desperate tenants retaliated. To make matters worse, the potato crop failed again for several years in succession, especially in Connaught in the west. All over Ireland a series of wet summers helped to cause epidemics among farm animals and ruined hay crops. Nor was there much industry for the farmers to fall back on; the once flourishing domestic textile industry had been killed off even before the famine by competition from cheap factory-produced cloth made in England and Scotland. For some reason, probably lack of suitable coal resources, the Irish had failed to develop their own textile mills.

Smallholders and tenant-farmers combined to form *the Irish Land League (1879)* under the leadership of Michael Davitt. He was an Irish Catholic whose family had been evicted from their land when he was a child; he had spent seven years in Dartmoor after being convicted of involvement in Fenian outrages. The League soon gained massive support throughout Ireland, and it demanded three concessions which, it was thought, would ease the situation. *Known as the 'three Fs', these were*:

- a fair rent;
- fixity of tenure (a guarantee that tenants would not be evicted provided they paid the rent);

- free sale (the right to sell their land, or their interest in a holding, without interference from the landlord, so that they could get the best possible price).

According to historian Michael Winstanley, the traditional view of these demands, that they were 'the reaction of a poverty-stricken peasantry to mounting landlord exploitation, excessive rents and widespread evictions', has now been discredited. He argues that during the prosperity of the previous thirty years, rents had actually lagged behind profits; the Land League's motive therefore was to force landlords to reduce rents still further so that smallholders and farmers could hang on to their gains. The League's official tactic was for farmers to refuse to pay rents, though in some areas they resorted to violence – maiming of cattle and burning of landlords' haystacks.

Whatever its exact motives were, the League was soon working closely with the Home Rule Movement and its formidable leader, Charles Stewart Parnell, a Protestant landlord with an Anglo-Irish father and an American mother. Aloof, icily disdainful and withdrawn, he detested the English. He had been MP for County Meath since 1875 and had organized the Irish Nationalist obstruction campaign in the Commons.

(b) *Gladstone tries to give the Irish concessions*

Gladstone was determined to be reasonable and go as far as he could towards giving the Irish what they wanted. At this stage, however, he was not prepared to consider Home Rule. He was hampered all along the way by opposition from the House of Lords, from the Land League, and from a section of his own party which felt he was being too lenient with the Irish.

1   A Bill was introduced (1880) to give compensation to Irish tenants who were evicted, but the Lords, many of whom owned land in Ireland, rejected it by a huge majority (282 to 51). Over 10 000 people had been evicted in that year alone, and there was widespread misery and desperation. The Land League retaliated by boycotting anyone who took over a farm from which the previous tenant had been evicted; he should be 'isolated as if he were a leper'. The first person to be dealt with in this way was Captain Boycott, the agent of a wealthy landowner in County Mayo; after evicting a tenant for non-payment of rent, Boycott found that servants, shopkeepers, labourers, in fact everybody, would have nothing to do with him, and troops had to be sent in to protect his property. A new word was thus added to the language, and the boycott idea spread rapidly.
2   The government replied with a *Coercion Act (1881)* which suspended Habeas Corpus (see Section 2.4(b)).
3   Gladstone would not be content with repression alone, and he was soon responsible for *the Second Irish Land Act (1881)*, which gave the Irish what the League wanted – the three Fs, plus Land Courts to decide fair rents. The Act was a remarkable achievement and shows how genuinely committed Gladstone was to easing the misery of the Irish. It took 58 sittings in the Commons and all Gladstone's tremendous skill and experience to pilot it through. The Lords only passed it thanks to Queen Victoria's influence. Unfortunately it did not solve the Irish problem, though there was very little wrong with the Act itself, except that it was ten years too late. Parnell decided that since his campaign had squeezed such a great concession out of Gladstone, then continued pressure might bring the ultimate prize – Home Rule. The Land League therefore boycotted the new Land Courts, ordered a non-payment of rent campaign, and did all it could to sabotage the working of the Act. Evictions and violence continued.

(c) *Gladstone, Parnell and Irish Nationalism*

While Isaac Butt was leader of the Home Rule League (formed in 1870) its campaign for a separate Irish parliament in Dublin to look after internal affairs, was moderate and respectable. Poverty and the land problem were probably behind the growth of nationalism during the last 30 years of the century, but there was much more to it than that. There was a deep feeling of separateness from the English, and the Home Rulers talked about 'the inalienable right of the Irish people to self-government'. Charles Stewart Parnell (who became leader in 1877) was much more aggressive than Butt. He pointed out that 'Ireland is not a geographical fragment of England; she is a nation'. The fact that New Zealand had been given self-government in 1856 and Canada dominion status in 1867 encouraged the Irish to hope for something similar. In the 1880 general election the Irish Nationalists won 61 seats and their success in pressurizing Gladstone to come up with the Second Land Act was a great boost to their confidence.

However, Gladstone was shocked and disgusted by their refusal to co-operate with the Act, and he had Parnell and other leaders arrested and imprisoned in Kilmainham Gaol, Dublin. This solved nothing, violence increased and a rash of secret extremist societies broke out.

1   After six months both Gladstone and Parnell were anxious to break the stalemate; Parnell was afraid that he might lose control of the movement while he was absent in gaol. An understanding (sometimes known as *the Kilmainham Treaty*) was reached, through intermediaries (April 1882). Parnell agreed to call off the rent strike and control the violence, and in return Gladstone promised an Arrears Bill to let tenants off their rent arrears which had accumulated during the recent campaign. Parnell was released. This agreement was an admission by Gladstone that only Parnell could control the Irish. It was probably around this time that Gladstone realized that Home Rule would have to come sooner or later.

2   *The Phoenix Park murders* ruined chances of immediate progress. Only four days after Parnell's release, Lord Frederick Cavendish, the new Chief Secretary for Ireland (and brother of Lord Hartington, leader of the Whigs), who had only been in the country a few hours, and T. E. Burke, the Permanent Under-Secretary, were attacked and stabbed to death with surgical knives, while they were walking in Pheonix Park, Dublin. The murderers were members of an extremist group known as the 'Invincibles'. Parnell was shocked and he denounced the group, but more murders followed, and it seemed as though Parnell's influence was declining. The English public was now convinced that the Irish were impossible to deal with and opinion hardened against Home Rule.

3   Gladstone bowed to pressure and an even more severe Coercion Act was passed which enabled the government to track down and arrest the 'Invincibles', five of whom were hanged.

4   Gladstone and Parnell tried hard to make the Kilmainham agreement work. The Arrears Act was passed and the Second Land Act began to operate, resulting in a general reduction of rents by an average of 20 per cent. During 1883 affairs in Ireland gradually settled into a period of comparative calm which lasted until June 1885. This must be seen as a partial success for Gladstone, but it was not a permanent solution.

(d) *Parnell puts the Conservatives in power*

Parnell still wanted Home Rule and still controlled a powerful group of 60 Nationalist MPs. He decided that instead of obstructing the government, there might be more to be gained by co-operation with one of the major parties. There seemed little prospect of the Liberals giving him what he wanted, since there was strong right-wing opposition to any further concessions. However, Lord Randolph Churchill, a brilliant up-and-coming young Conservative, eager to gain Irish votes, seemed to be offering major concessions. It made no difference to Parnell which party helped him, so he decided to take a chance with the Conservatives. In June 1885 the Nationalists voted with the Conservatives to defeat the Liberal government on an increase in the beer and spirit duties. Gladstone resigned and a Conservative government took office with Robert Cecil, Marquis of Salisbury as Prime Minister. He was totally dependent on Irish votes to stay in office, and consequently gave them two major concessions:

- The Coercion Acts were dropped.
- *Lord Ashbourne's Act (1885)* introduced a scheme which provided £5 million for loans to enable tenants to buy holdings from their landlords. During the following six years about 25 000 Irish farmers took advantage of this offer, and more and more landlords were prepared to sell holdings since their income from rents was declining. The terms for borrowers were quite generous – an interest rate of 4 per cent and 49 years to pay back the loan.

A general election was held in November 1885, and Parnell, delighted with his gains so far, instructed all Irishmen living on the mainland to vote Conservative. The election result was a strange one: the Liberals lost 18 seats but still had a majority of 86 over the Conservatives (335 Liberals to 249 Conservatives). By a strange coincidence the Irish Nationalists won 86 seats, which meant that if the Parnell–Salisbury alliance continued, the result was a dead heat. The Conservative government carried on with Parnell holding the balance: he could keep the Conservatives in office, or he could withdraw his support and allow the Liberals back in. By now Gladstone realized that only Home Rule would pacify the Irish, though he kept his feelings to himself. He hoped that the Conservatives would be the ones to introduce it, since they would have a better chance of getting the approval of the Lords. By early December, it was clear that Salisbury was not prepared to go so far as Home Rule; it was only a matter of time before Parnell removed him.

(e) *Gladstone and the First Home Rule Bill (1886)*

Gladstone decided in favour of Home Rule during the summer of 1885. *There were several reasons for his change of mind*:

- Violence was on the increase again following the Conservatives' removal of the Coercion Acts, and Gladstone was afraid the campaign would spread to England.
- Some leading British officials in Dublin, including Sir Robert Hamilton (successor to the murdered Burke), who knew the situation at first hand, believed that Home Rule was the only way to get consistent government in Ireland.
- Above all Gladstone realized that Irish nationalism, like Italian and Belgian nationalism (both of which the British government had supported) was such a deeply felt desire that the only just and reasonable course was to satisfy it.

Gladstone did not reveal his conversion to Home Rule because he hoped that the Conservatives would introduce it and because he was afraid of splitting the Liberals, many of whom were opposed to the idea and would require gradual persuasion. Lord Hartington, brother of Lord Frederick Cavendish and leader of the Liberal right wing (Whigs), was a bitter opponent of any further concessions to the Irish. However, a series of sensational developments took place:

1   On 15 December 1885, Gladstone's son Herbert, leaked the news of his father's conversion to the press. Having the news sprung upon them so suddenly outraged Hartington and his supporters and made Gladstone's job of winning them over almost impossible. Hartington announced that he would never support Home Rule, but Gladstone was determined to go forward. The Conservative government was defeated by the combined Liberal and Irish votes, and Gladstone became Prime Minister for the third time (January 1886).

2   *The First Home Rule Bill* was introduced in April. It proposed that Ireland should have its own parliament in Dublin and no Irish MPs would sit at Westminster. The Dublin parliament would control all internal affairs; foreign affairs, defence and trade would remain under the direction of Westminster. The bill met bitter opposition in the Commons from the Conservatives. Lord Randolph Churchill stirred up religious prejudices with the argument that the Protestant minority in Ulster would not be well treated by a Dublin government dominated by Catholics, and that Ulster should therefore oppose Home Rule by every means possible. His slogan was 'Ulster will fight and Ulster will be right'. There was also opposition to the bill from the Hartington faction, and from Joseph Chamberlain, leader of the Radical wing of the Liberal party. In June the bill was defeated by 343 votes to 313; 93 Liberals voted against it.

3   Gladstone decided to appeal to the country, but in the following general election the Liberals lost heavily and were reduced to only 191 seats against 317 Conservatives. The mainland electorate had given its verdict – decisively against Home Rule, and once again Irish affairs had brought down a British government. More than that, the Liberal party was now deeply divided; the anti-Home Rule Liberals remained as a separate group of 77 MPs (in addition to the 191 Gladstone supporters) and, under the leadership of Chamberlain, were known as *the Liberal Unionists* (because they wanted to preserve the union between England and Ireland). Many later joined the Conservatives and it was 20 years before the Liberal party recovered. (See Section 16.6 for Ireland under the Conservatives, 1886–92.)

(f) Why did Chamberlain oppose Home Rule?

There has been disagreement about his motives:

- Irish historians put it down to sheer ambition; it was widely expected that Gladstone would resign the leadership if Home Rule was defeated; this would leave the way clear for Chamberlain to become Liberal leader. His English biographers feel this is unfair on Chamberlain.
- Chamberlain believed that improved administration and social conditions would pacify the Irish, and felt that these could be achieved by a system of county boards, which would be a less drastic solution than complete Home Rule. Gladstone rejected this idea.
- Chamberlain, who was a great supporter of imperialism and the British Empire, disliked Home Rule because it meant the separation of Ireland from the rest of Britain; this might cause other British territories to demand independence, leading to the disintegration of the Empire.
- He was annoyed, with some justification, that Gladstone had not consulted him at any stage during the drawing up of the bill, and he felt that the government's time would have been better spent on introducing social reform.

16.2 The Liberals and the Empire

Gladstone's views on imperialism were well known – he disapproved of it because it interfered with the rights and freedom of overseas peoples to govern themselves; also it would be expensive – the Empire would have to be defended, causing a constant drain on British resources. He had criticized Disraeli unmercifully (see Section 14.3), but once back in office, he found to his annoyance that he was saddled with several imperial problems left by Disraeli. Gladstone wanted to disentangle Britain, but it was not so easy as he had expected.

(a) *Withdrawal from Afghanistan*

Gladstone reversed Disraeli's policy (see Section 14.3(e)) by withdrawing British troops from Afghanistan. This was regarded by the Conservatives as a typical example of Liberal weakness abroad, but in fact relations with Afghanistan remained good for the next 20 years.

(b) *The Transvaal wins independence*

Shortly before the outbreak of the Zulu War in 1879, the Transvaal, recently annexed by Britain, had been promised self-government once the Zulu threat had been removed. Since this had been achieved by the Zulu War, the Transvaal Boers expected immediate independence, given Gladstone's powerful condemnation of the annexation. However, nothing happened, partly because Gladstone was busy with financial affairs and because he was beginning to think about setting up a South African federation, to include the Transvaal and the Orange Free State. In January 1881 he told the Transvaal that immediate self-government was out of the question. The Boers rose in revolt and in February defeated a tiny British force of 359 men at *Majuba Hill*; a hundred of the British were killed, including the commander, Sir George Colley. Gladstone was in a dilemma, faced with two possible courses of action:

1   He could send out more troops to avenge the defeat and crush the Boers, which public opinion, the Queen and the Conservatives demanded.
2   He could make peace and concede independence to the Transvaal.

Showing great courage, Gladstone took the unpopular second course: *the Pretoria Convention (August 1881)* recognized the Transvaal's independence, 'subject to the suzerainty [overlordship] of her Majesty'. When the Boers protested at the suzerainty clause, Gladstone agreed that it should be dropped. There was an angry public outcry at this 'surrender', and Queen Victoria sent Gladstone a strongly worded letter of protest. But Gladstone was unrepentant – he had no intention of involving Britain in an expensive colonial war. It was probably the right decision in the circumstances, but he had handled the situation badly, with unfortunate consequences:

● He had given way to force, whereas if he had allowed independence earlier, British prestige would have been preserved.
● The Boers took it as a sign of British weakness, and became more arrogant in their relations with Britain. Their attitude was a contributory cause of the Boer War which broke out in 1899 (see Section 17.3).

(c) *The British occupy Egypt*

Gladstone had to accept that Britain was deeply involved in Egypt because of her ownership of almost half the Suez Canal shares (see Section 14.3(b)). Events compelled him, against his will, to intervene in Egypt to safeguard British interests. The Egyptian government was in worse financial difficulties than before as it tried to pay the interest on massive French and British loans which had been made to finance railways, roads, docks and agricultural projects. When an epidemic of cattle plague broke out in 1878, the country was brought to the verge of bankruptcy.

1 Britain and France, concerned about their financial interests, tried to force the ruler, the Khedive Ismail, to allow European advisers to control his country's finances. When he refused, they prevailed upon his overlord, the Sultan of Turkey, to replace Ismail with his son Tewfik (1879).

2 There was widespread resentment in Egypt at this foreign interference, and a strong anti-foreign Egyptian Nationalist party emerged led by an army officer, Arabi Pasha, who by May 1882, seemed on the point of deposing Tewfik. There was every chance that Arabi would seize the Canal and repudiate Egypt's debts.

3 Gladstone, acting jointly with the French, sent a fleet to Alexandria as a warning gesture, but this provoked serious anti-European rioting in Alexandria in which about 80 Europeans were killed. Arabi, far from overawed by the presence of the foreign fleets, began to fortify Alexandria. At this point the French decided to take no further action, but Gladstone authorized the bombardment of Alexandria's defences. A 12-hour artillery battle followed which ended with British troops occupying the city (July 1882).

4 Gladstone asked parliament for £2.3 million for an expedition 'to substitute the rule of law for that of military violence in Egypt'. The money was granted, and 16 400 British troops under Sir Garnet Wolseley were soon *en route* for Egypt. Having landed at Alexandria, they destroyed Arabi's army at *the Battle of Tel-el-Kebir* (September) and captured Cairo. Arabi was exiled to Ceylon and Tewfik restored to the throne.

5 Sir Evelyn Baring (later made Lord Cromer) was appointed Consul-General of Egypt, and virtually ruled the country for the next 23 years. He was a highly efficient administrator: as early as 1888 he had balanced the Egyptian budget, and he went on to introduce irrigation schemes and other reforms. Egypt had all the appearance of being a British colony, though Gladstone did not annex it and claimed that the British occupation was only temporary. The British stayed in Egypt until 1954.

Gladstone's decisive action astonished the public and boosted his popularity. He might have been expected to sympathize with the Egyptian nationalists, and yet it was a more 'forward' policy than anything Disraeli had initiated. It shocked the veteran pacifist John Bright who resigned from the cabinet, remarking that Gladstone's intervention was 'simply damnable – worse than anything ever perpetrated by Dizzy'.

Why did Gladstone agree to the occupation of Egypt?

The reason was simply that financial and strategic considerations outweighed sympathy for the nationalist movement. The possibility of Arabi repudiating Egypt's debts horrified Gladstone; if Arabi seized the Suez Canal, British shipping would be at a disadvantage and the route to India threatened. It was Britain's duty 'to convert the present interior state of Egypt from anarchy and conflict to peace and order'.

The policy was viewed as an outstanding success: British interests had been safeguarded and British prestige abroad enhanced. However, some imperialists felt that Gladstone ought to have annexed Egypt outright or at least declared it to be a British protectorate.

(d) *General Gordon and the Sudan*

There was soon another opportunity for Britain to seize territory, in the Sudan, but this time Gladstone acted predictably and did not take it. The affair was so badly mishandled that it turned out to be the most spectacular failure of the entire ministry. The Sudan had been ruled by Egypt since 1823, and the Sudanese, especially in the north, resented Egyptian rule because it was corrupt, it had abolished the profitable slave-trade, and it had close connections with Europeans, who were non-Islamic. Muhammed Ahmed, a local religious leader, proclaimed that he was the *Mahdi* – the saviour of Islam from foreign influence. He roused most of the country against the occupying Egyptian troops.

1   Tewfik, the newly restored ruler of Egypt, sent an Egyptian army commanded by a British officer, Hicks Pasha, to subdue the rebels, but the force, Hicks Pasha included, was slaughtered by the Mahdi and his Dervishes (November 1883).

2   Gladstone was faced with a difficult decision: should he send a British army to conquer the Sudan or should he leave it to the Mahdi? He decided against sending a British expedition, partly because Sir Evelyn Baring advised that the only reasonable course was to withdraw, so great was the Mahdi's popular support. Gladstone also sympathized with the Sudanese in their nationalist struggle against the Egyptians.

3   However, there were still a number of Egyptian garrisons in the Sudan, commanded by British officers, who could not be left to the mercy of the Mahdi. The government therefore sent out General Charles Gordon with orders to organize the evacuation of the garrisons as quickly as possible. This was where the first mistake lay: Gordon was not the sort of man to be relied on to organize a retreat. He had made himself famous through military exploits in China, Africa, India and the Crimea. In the words of Philip Magnus (one of Gladstone's biographers), 'fearless, erratic, brilliant, perverse, always notoriously undisciplined, he exercised an extraordinary fascination over his fellow-countryment'. Gordon had already been governor of the Sudan (1877–9), and early in 1884 he told the press that he considered it quite feasible to resist the Mahdi.

4   Gordon arrived in Khartoum, the Sudanese capital, in February 1884, but instead of hurrying on with the evacuation while there was still time, he decided to stay put; a fanatical Christian, he believed it was his duty to save the country from the Mahdi, and he asked for British troops to be sent to keep open the Nile route from the Sudan into Egypt. This request was refused. By the end of March the Mahdi's forces had closed in and Gordon was besieged in Khartoum.

5   Public opinion and the Queen demanded that help be sent immediately, but Gladstone, furious with Gordon for disobeying orders, hesitated. All through the summer the cabinet argued about what action to take, and it was not until October that a relief force under Wolseley left Cairo on its 1600 mile journey up the Nile. It arrived at Khartoum on 28 January 1885 only to find that the city had fallen to the Mahdi two days earlier. Gordon was dead.

The nation was stunned and Gladstone was blamed. Angry crowds hooted and jeered in Downing Street, and instead of being the 'GOM' ('Grand Old Man') he became the 'MOG' – murderer of Gordon. In April Gladstone outraged public opinion further by withdrawing Wolseley's forces and leaving the Sudan to the Mahdi. Although Gordon had brought disaster on himself by disobeying orders, there is no doubt that the cabinet could and should have sent help much sooner, and the Liberals were deeply unpopular.

Illus. 16.1   General Charles Gordon

(e) *The Penjdeh incident (1885)*

This crisis in Anglo-Russian relations was well handled by Gladstone. On 30 March 1885, encouraged by British embarrassment over the Sudan, the Russians seized the Afghan village of Penjdeh, a few miles from the Russian frontier. Gladstone responded vigorously, warned the Russians that Britain would not tolerate such aggression, and called up the reserves. The Russians withdrew and agreed to submit their claim for Penjdeh to arbitration. Gladstone had shown that he could be firm when international morality had been violated; unfortunately the effect was spoiled when the arbitrators awarded Penjdeh to the Russians; but this was after Gladstone's government had fallen.

Gladstone's record in imperial and foreign affairs during this ministry was not particularly impressive. Contemporaries found it difficult to understand his motives, and his actions seemed contradictory: he had abandoned the Transvaal and tried to give Ireland Home Rule with one hand while occupying Egypt with the other. All these situations were to cause further trouble later. Worst of all he had allowed the national hero, Gordon, to get himself killed in Khartoum.

16.3 What were the domestic achievements of the Liberal government?

There were several important domestic reforms:

(a) *The repeal of the Malt Tax (1880)*

This removed a long-standing grievance of farmers, who had campaigned against it more vigorously than ever as they began to feel the pinch of the agricultural depression. Disraeli had disappointed the farmers, but Gladstone obliged, even though he had to increase income tax by a penny in the pound to make up the lost revenue.

(b) *The Married Women's Property Act (1882)*

This was designed to protect the property of married women. When a woman married, her husband became the owner of all her worldly goods; he could spend her savings and sell her house, and the system was an open invitation for unscrupulous fortune-hunters to take advantage of innocent and unsuspecting, wealthy, young ladies. The new Act gave a married woman the right to continue as the separate owner of property of all kinds.

(c) *The Corrupt Practices Act (1883)*

This went a long way towards removing abuses and corruption during general elections. It specified the amount of money a party could spend on the campaign in each constituency, the sum being based on the number of voters. It also introduced rules about the type and number of carriages that could be used to take voters to the polls.

(d) *The Parliamentary Reform Act (1884) and the Redistribution of Seats Act (1885)*

These two Acts were the major domestic achievement of Gladstone's second ministry.

The demand for further parliamentary reform came from Joseph Chamberlain and the Radical wing of the Liberal party, who were disappointed with Gladstone's reforms to date in this ministry. Their case was unanswerable: the 1867 Reform Act had given the vote to householders in towns, but in the counties, the voting qualification was still high enough to prevent agricultural labourers and other workers from voting; thus the power of wealthy farmers and landowners was preserved. This was undemocratic, and Chamberlain was bitterly critical of the landowners; he described them as a class 'who toil not, neither do they spin ... whose fortunes have originated by grants made in times gone by ... and have since grown and increased while they have slept'. Another anomaly of the system was that the distribution of seats was still unfair, with many small towns having the same representation – two MPs – as large industrial cities (see Section 8.5(a)). Chamberlain carried a majority of the cabinet with him and a Reform (or Franchise) Bill passed the Commons comfortably (June 1884).

There was strong opposition from the Conservatives in the Lords who demanded that a Redistribution Bill should be passed first. They hoped that this would cause so many local difficulties that both bills would be delayed indefinitely. Chamberlain retaliated with a series of violent speeches warning the Lords of dire consequences if they continued to block Liberal legislation; his rallying cry was 'the Peers versus the People'. The Queen, worried about a constitutional crisis, suggested that Gladstone and

Salisbury should meet for tea and have talks. After secret negotiations between Liberal and Conservative leaders, an acceptable compromise was worked out:

- *The Reform (Franchise) Act* gave the vote to all householders in the counties, adding over two million voters to the list. Altogether 5.7 million people now had the vote. The same system was extended to Ireland.
- *The Redistribution Act* took away both MPs from boroughs with less than 15 000 inhabitants, while those with less than 50 000 lost one MP. This released 142 seats which were redistributed among more densely populated areas. The system was reorganized so that 647 out of 670 constituencies were represented by one MP each (these were known as single-member constituencies). The exceptions were large cities well in excess of 50 000, the Scottish universities, and Oxford and Cambridge Universities.

These Acts did not quite complete the transition to full democracy: it still remained to give the vote to women and to abolish plural voting (the right of a man to vote in every constituency where he owned property).

There were two other important results: the disappearance of most of the two-member constituencies put a stop to the Liberal practice of running one Whig and one Radical candidate in each constituency. This meant that fewer Whigs could gain acceptance as candidates: the aristocratic Whig section of the party began to shrink and the Radicals became the dominant wing of the party. In Ireland the changes meant that Parnell's nationalists swept the board and could always guarantee winning at least 80 seats.

These domestic reforms, though excellent in themselves, were disappointingly few for a government with a large majority, which lasted for over five years. Part of the trouble was that Irish affairs and Irish obstruction consumed far too much of the government's time; another reason was that the Liberal party was deeply divided over a number of issues, and these are examined in the next section.

16.4 Why were there so many tensions within the Liberal party 1880–6?

(a) *Divisions between the left (Radical) and right (Whig) wings of the party*

The Whigs, mostly aristocratic landowners like Lord Hartington (later Duke of Devonshire), Lord Granville, Lord Spencer and the Duke of Argyll, were much less progressive than the Radicals, whose main figures were Joseph Chamberlain, Sir Charles Dilke and John Bright. Gladstone, careful to please the Whigs, gave them all but two of the cabinet posts, and of the Radicals, only Chamberlain and Bright were included. The Radicals felt slighted and the two wings did not work smoothly together.

(b) *Gladstone difficult to work with*

Gladstone caused problems by his methods of running the government. As well as being Prime Minister, he took on the office of Chancellor of the Exchequer (1880); this meant that he was overwhelmed with a mass of financial details which prevented him from giving sufficient attention to other matters (such as independence for the Transvaal). Although he resigned the Chancellorship in 1882, much damage had been done. He often acted on impulse without consulting the cabinet, and was generally a difficult man to work with.

(c) *The Bradlaugh case an embarrassment for the government*

Charles Bradlaugh was elected Liberal MP for Northampton in 1880. A Radical of somewhat unorthodox views (for the time), he was an outspoken atheist and an advocate of contraceptives. The trouble started when he refused to take the normal oath of allegiance because it included the words 'So help me God'. After a Commons select committee decided that he must take the oath, Bradlaugh agreed, but a group of young Conservative MPs led by Lord Randolph Churchill (father of Winston) stirred the Commons up to vote for Bradlaugh's expulsion. He was obliged to stand for re-election, but after he had again won Northampton, the same procedure was repeated when he tried to take his seat. Churchill and his friends (nicknamed 'the Fourth Party') exploited the situation to divide the Liberals. Gladstone and many Radicals supported Bradlaugh, but the Nonconformist Liberals were outraged at the presence of such an avowed atheist, and Bradlaugh was again expelled. He was re-elected and expelled a further three times, but was prevented from taking his seat until the next parliament in 1885.

(d) *Disagreement over social reform*

Chamberlain was keen on social and local government reform, but these matters bored Gladstone, while Hartington was positively hostile. Before the 1885 election Chamberlain launched a campaign for reform – *the Unauthorized Programme*, so called because Gladstone had not approved it. Amid mass meetings and processions, Chamberlain outlined his programme:

- free primary education;
- payment of MPs;
- county councils to look after rural areas;
- a graduated income tax to make the wealthy foot the bill.
- With one eye on the new county voters, he also proposed that agricultural labourers should be given smallholdings; this became known as 'the three acres and a cow' policy.

In one of his speeches Chamberlain declared:

> I am told if I pursue this course that I shall break up the Party ... but I care little for the party ... except to promote the objects which I publicly avowed when I first entered parliament. In this rich country, an honest, a decent, an industrious man should be able to earn a livelihood for himself and his family, and should be able to lay aside something for sickness and old age. Is that unreasonable? Is that impossible?

Chamberlain and his programme were largely responsible for the Liberal success in the 1885 election, yet Gladstone made no concessions to him and ignored the case for social reform. 'Chamberlain's socialism repels me', Gladstone noted in his diary.

(e) *Mixed reactions to foreign and imperial policies*

Gladstone's foreign and imperial policies – especially independence for the Transvaal and the disaster in the Sudan – made the government unpopular with the public. Yet when he scored a success with the occupation of Egypt, some of the Radicals objected and Bright resigned from the cabinet.

(f) Irish affairs a major cause of tension

Whatever Gladstone did, he offended one section or another of the party. When he tried to make concessions to the Irish, the Whigs objected; Chamberlain's plan for Irish local self-government on a county basis was defeated in cabinet because all the Whigs (except Granville) opposed it (May 1885). Shortly afterwards, when Gladstone tried to take a hard line by stepping up coercion, the Radicals objected, and Chamberlain and Dilke resigned from the cabinet. Gladstone's determination to secure Home Rule at all costs during his 1886 government was disastrous for the Liberals: most of the Whigs and the main Radical leaders opposed it and the party split; Chamberlain led the breakaway group of Liberal Unionists. Without Chamberlain the Liberals had little to offer and the voters turned to the Conservatives. Some historians believe that the Liberal party never fully recovered from the split over the First Home Rule Bill (see Section 23.4(a)).

16.5 What contribution did the Conservatives make to domestic reform 1886–92?

(a) Lord Randolph Churchill and Tory Democracy

When Salisbury's Conservative government (317 seats) took office they could usually rely on the support of the 77 Liberal Unionists, which gave them a big majority over the 191 Liberals and 85 Irish Nationalists. At first it seemed as though it might turn out to be a great reforming ministry. The Chancellor of the Exchequer was the 37-year-old Lord Randolph Churchill, who had made a name for himself with his brilliant attacks on Gladstone; he seemed to have a gift for making the Liberal leader look ridiculous. He was easily the most exciting and dynamic personality in the government, and he aimed to follow the Disraeli brand of Conservatism – reform and modernization – in order to retain working-class support. In his famous *Dartford Speech (October 1886)* he announced his programme of Tory Democracy:

- improvement of public health and housing;
- compulsory national insurance;
- smallholdings for agricultural labourers;
- reform of parliamentary procedure;
- provision of parks, art galleries, museums and public baths and wash-houses.

However, Churchill soon left the government after a disagreement over his controversial Budget proposals. These included increases in death duties and house duties, and reductions in income tax and in tea and tobacco duties, to be paid for by cuts in defence expenditure. W. H. Smith, the War Minister, naturally objected strongly, and when Salisbury supported Smith, Churchill suddenly resigned from the Exchequer (December 1886). He apparently thought that he was indispensable and that his action would force Salisbury to bring him back and overrule Smith. But Churchill had completely miscalculated: he had shown himself to be far too radical for the right wing of the party, and Salisbury was probably relieved to be rid of such an embarrassment. He did not ask Churchill to withdraw his resignation and instead appointed Sir Edward Goschen, a Liberal Unionist, as Chancellor. With Churchill's departure, any chance of

Illus. 16.2 Robert Cecil, third Marquis of Salisbury

Illus. 16.3 Lord Randolph Churchill

far-reaching reform disappeared. He never again held cabinet office, and he died in 1895 at the early age of 45. His biographer, R. F. Foster, and Robert Blake, the historian of the Conservative party, both feel that the whole concept of Tory Democracy has been exaggerated, and that as far as Churchill was concerned, it amounted to little more than opportunism – he wanted to be Conservative leader and Prime Minister.

(b) *Salisbury's reforms*

The Conservative reforms were few in number for a government which lasted six years. Salisbury believed that the function of government was to preserve and extend individual freedom, with a minimum of interference by the state in social and economic matters. He was a strong advocate of self-help: 'No men ever rise to any permanent improvement in their condition of body or of mind except by relying upon their own personal efforts.' He was not a complete reactionary though, and in a speech at Exeter early in 1892 he claimed that the greatest service a government could render for a poor man was 'so to shape matters that the greatest possible liberty for the exercise of his own moral and intellectual qualities should be offered to him by law'. Measures which attempted to 'shape matters' in this way were:

● *The Labourers' Allotment Act (1887)*. This gave local authorities the power to acquire land for allotments, so that the working classes could 'elevate themselves into a position of manly independence by their industry'. The results were disappointing: since the Act was not compulsory, many local authorities ignored it.

● *The Mines Regulation Act (1887)* was more successful, extending legal protection for miners while they were at work.

● *The Tithe Act (1890)* made tithes (the annual tax, which amounted to one-tenth of income or produce, paid to support the Anglican church) payable by the owner of land and not by the occupier. This removed a long-standing cause of friction by ending the practice of seizing tenants' cattle and other possessions in lieu of cash payment.

● *In education* the government was responsible for the appointment of *the Cross Commission* (see Section 12.7(d)) and for *the Fee Grant Act (1891)* which abolished fees for elementary education.

● *The Factory Act (1891)* raised the minimum age at which children could be employed in factories to 11, and specified that the maximum working day for women was to be 12 hours with one and a half hours for meals.

(c) *The Local Government Act (1888) – The Conservatives' major reform*

This was the work of C. T. Ritchie (President of the Local Government Board) and Sir Edward Goschen. A change was necessary because the 1835 Municipal Corporations Act had only reformed the boroughs; in the counties local government was carried out by about 27 000 different boards, which dealt separately with matters such as sanitation, drainage and street-lighting. Goschen called it 'a chaos of authorities, a chaos of jurisdictions, a chaos of rates, a chaos of franchises, a chaos, worst of all, of areas'. Unlike the town corporations, these bodies were not directly elected; local Justices of the Peace, usually landowners, appointed their members. In 1884 agricultural labourers had been given the right to vote for their MPs, so it was only logical that they should be able to choose the people who governed them at local level. *The terms of the Act were*:

● The old boards were abolished and replaced by 62 elected county councils. They had wide compulsory powers over matters such as the maintenance of roads and bridges and the provision of police, and they took over the administrative functions of the JPs.

- Over 60 towns of more than 50 000 inhabitants were made into county boroughs: they were to have elected councils with the same powers as county councils.
- London was regarded as a county in its own right; subdivided into 28 Metropolitan boroughs, its overall government was to be in the hands of the London County Council.
- An important feature of the voting rules for these new councils and for the borough councils was that *unmarried women were given the vote*, though they were not allowed to be members of councils.

The following year (1889) this new system was extended to cover Scotland.

After a slow start the new councils gradually took over more and more functions. There was a marked improvement in the quality of local government, and the powers and influence of the landowing gentry were reduced. Further refinements were added by the Local Government Act of 1894 (see Section 16.8(a)).

Although these reforms were worthy enough, in one sense they were irrelevant to the main social and economic problem of late Victorian Britain – that a large proportion of the working class were living in conditions of extreme poverty. In February 1886 mobs smashed shop windows in the West End of London and set fire to cabs and carriages, as some of them put it, 'to frighten the idle rich'. Many workers were turning towards the Labour movement and the formation of unions for unskilled workers (see Section 19.4). In 1889 the London dockers came out on strike, and public support for their demand for a standard wage of sixpence an hour was so great that after four weeks the dock companies gave way. Salisbury was worried by these developments, but although he acknowledged that they arose from genuine hardship, he could see no cure for the problems, beyond self-help. Under his leadership the Conservatives took up an anti-trades-union stance.

16.6 How did the Conservatives deal with the problems of Ireland 1886–92?

This period saw a mixture of firm government and mild concessions; there was also high drama with the downfall and ruin of Parnell in a divorce case. Evictions of tenants were still continuing, and the Irish retaliated with *the Plan of Campaign*, organized by William O'Brien and John Dillon. All the tenants on an estate would offer what they considered to be a fair rent; if the landlord disagreed, they would refuse to pay any rent and put the money into a 'fighting fund'. The plan spread rapidly, but inevitably provoked more mass evictions and violence. It was the job of Arthur Balfour (Salisbury's nephew), the new Chief Secretary for Ireland, to deal with this situation.

(a) 'Bloody' Balfour

The government's first response was a new *Crimes Act (1887)* which gave police and magistrates extra powers to deal with offenders, including the right to suspend trial by jury. Balfour applied the Act rigorously, jailing anyone who broke the law. An ugly incident occurred at Mitchelstown in which police shot and killed three members of a crowd demonstrating against some evictions. Balfour ignored all protests and went calmly on, earning himself the nickname 'Bloody' Balfour.

b) *Parnell: triumph and downfall*

he next developments in Irish affairs concerned Parnell. *The Times* newspaper, lways strongly anti-Irish, ran a series of articles to try and discredit Parnell by showing 1at he was deliberately encouraging violence in Ireland. In April 1887 it published a :tter reputed to have been written by Parnell to a friend, expressing his approval of 1e Phoenix Park murders. Parnell protested that the letter was a 'barefaced forgery', ut very few people in England believed him. In 1888, during a libel action against *The 'imes*, more alleged Parnell letters were produced. The government appointed a spe- ial commission of three judges to investigate the charges. The enquiry dragged on for 1onths, but eventually it emerged that all the letters had been forged by an Irish jour- alist called Pigott whose motive had been to make money by selling them. Before he ould be arrested for perjury, he fled to Spain and shot himself in a Madrid hotel March 1889). Parnell was shown to be completely innocent; he was given a standing vation when he appeared in the Commons, and there was a rush of public sympathy oth for him and for Home Rule. It was the climax of his career; he was 'the ncrowned king of Ireland'.

However, disaster soon followed in 1890 when Parnell was named as co-respon- ent in a divorce case. For nine years he had been living with Katherine O'Shea, who ad separated from her husband, Captain W. H. O'Shea, before she met Parnell. The ffair was conducted so discreetly that the general public knew nothing about it.

Illus. 16.4   Charles Stewart Parnell

O'Shea kept quiet, hoping for political advancement from Parnell, and also for
share of the large fortune which his wife was expecting to inherit from a wealth
aunt. Although the aunt died in 1889, there was a legal wrangle over the will, and the
fortune was not forthcoming. O'Shea grew tired of waiting, started proceedings agains
his wife, naming Parnell as co-respondent, and in November 1890 was granted
divorce.

The news that Parnell was an adulterer came as a bombshell. The Victorian mora
code was such that affairs were acceptable provided they were conducted discreetly
But once they became public in the divorce courts, the guilty parties were disgraced
Overnight Parnell was shunned by many of his supporters. Nonconformist Liberal
refused to co-operate with the Nationalists unless they changed their leader; the Irish
Roman Catholic Church turned against him, and 44 of the Nationalist MPs deserte
him. Yet he refused to resign the leadership and damaged his health trying to re-estab
lish his authority. He died in October 1891, leaving the Nationalist party hopelessl
split.

(c) More concessions for the Irish

Parnell's disgrace and the chaos in the Nationalist party turned English opinion agains
Home Rule, and the government seized the opportunity to introduce some improve
ments. A *Land Purchase Act (1891)* extended the earlier Ashbourne Act and enable
thousands more Irish farmers to buy land, with government help. *The Congeste
Districts Board* was started (1891) to help over-populated areas. Using governmen
money, it introduced a variety of improvements such as draining and fencing of land
better farming methods, training schemes, railways and harbours. Living condition
gradually improved, and since Irish leaders were preoccupied with attacking each othe
instead of organizing protest campaigns against the English, Ireland became compara
tively calm.

16.7 Foreign and imperial affairs under the Conservatives

Salisbury's main interest was in foreign affairs; for most of the time he acted as Foreig
Secretary as well as Prime Minister, and often remarked that he would willingly ste
down from the premiership so that he could concentrate on diplomatic affairs.

(a) Salisbury's aims in foreign policy

● He would do his utmost to maintain peace and regarded war as 'the final and
supreme evil'.
● He wanted to protect British interests and 'to uphold England's honour steadily
and fearlessly and always be prone to let actions go along with words rather than to let
it lag behind them'.
● He expected the main threats to British interests to come from France and Russia,
and he hoped to use diplomatic means to counter these threats. However, he shrank
from the idea of binding alliances, because these might involve Britain in war. This
attitude has sometimes been described as a policy of 'splendid isolation', but this is a
misleading phrase. Salisbury was quite happy to sign agreements with other countries,

as he did with Germany, Italy and Portugal, provided they did not commit Britain to military action. Robert Taylor calls it a policy of 'limited liability' – seeking to influence events, without commitment, rather than initiating new policy.

- He recognized the value of Britain's colonies but, unlike Joseph Chamberlain, he was not anxious to expand the Empire further, and was unhappy about the British occupation of Egypt which he regarded as 'a disastrous inheritance'. 'However strong you may be, there is a point beyond which your strength will not go: . . . it is madness and ruin if you allow yourself to pass it.'

The main events during this Conservative government (1886–92) were:

(b) *The Balkans crisis and the Mediterranean Agreements*

1 Almost immediately Salisbury was faced with a serious international crisis. In 1885 Eastern Roumelia had declared itself united with Bulgaria, a clear breach of the 1878 Berlin Settlement (see Section 14.4(f)). Now that Bulgaria had turned out to be hostile to Russia, the Russians wanted Eastern Roumelia returned to Turkey; they even went to the lengths of organizing the kidnapping of the Bulgarian king Alexander, in an attempt to control the country. However, this misfired when the Bulgarians, with Austrian and Italian support, chose as their new king the anti-Russian Ferdinand of Saxe-Coburg.

2 At the same time relations between France and Germany were strained. General Boulanger, the French War Minister, was calling for revenge and the recovery of Alsace-Lorraine taken by the Germans at the end of the Franco-Prussian War (1871). Bismarck, the German Chancellor, had formed the Triple Alliance of Germany, Austria–Hungary and Italy, and was hoping for a breach between Britain and France, so that France would be completely isolated. The prospects for peace did not seem good. Salisbury had to try and influence the Triple Alliance powers to take some action to curb Russian designs in the Balkans, while at the same time avoid involving Britain so closely that she would be drawn into a war against France. Events worked out quite successfully for Britain, although at no stage did Salisbury take the initiative . . .

3 He supported Germany and Austria in their decision to oppose Russian demands for the return of Eastern Roumelia to Turkey and for the removal of King Ferdinand from the Bulgarian throne. The Russians had to accept this check to their Balkan ambitions.

4 Responding to a suggestion from the Italian government, Salisbury signed *the Mediterranean Agreement* with Italy (1887). Britain would help Italy maintain the *status quo* in the Aegean, Adriatic and Black Sea areas. Italy would support British interests in Egypt, and the British navy would protect the Italian coast, though only in the event of an *unprovoked* French attack on Italy. Six weeks later Austria–Hungary also signed the Mediterranean Agreement. Bismarck was pleased that the British were moving towards the Triple Alliance, and promised Salisbury unofficially that Germany would support British interests in Egypt.

5 Bismarck proposed a formal alliance with Britain (1889), intending it to have a strong anti-French flavour. Salisbury wanted it to include a promise of German assistance in case of Russian aggression, but Bismarck, hoping to remain on good terms with Russia, would not commit himself. Salisbury therefore declined the offer. Nevertheless relations between Britain and the Triple Alliance remained excellent right up to the resignation of Bismarck (March 1890) and while his successor, Caprivi, was in power (1890–4).

(c) Salisbury and the 'Scramble for Africa'

The 'Scramble for Africa', lasting roughly from 1881 to 1900, was the operation in which the European powers established control over most of the parts of Africa which had not already been claimed. *Their motives were mixed*:

● sometimes governments were forced to act to protect trading companies against local rulers or against rival companies;
● it was hoped that there would be economic advantages – cheap raw materials and large markets;
● sometimes, as in the case of Egypt, European investments needed protection;
● some people genuinely believed it was their duty (the 'white man's burden') to Christianize and civilize the African natives;

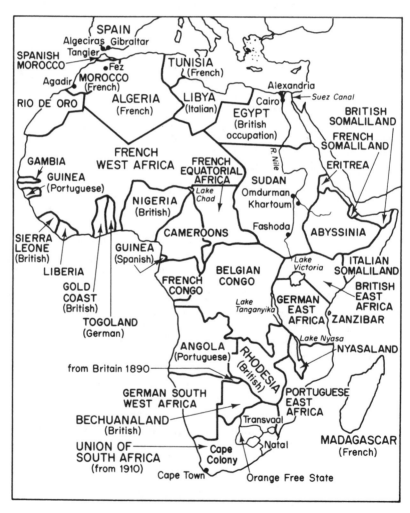

Map 16.1 The 'Scramble for Africa'

- there was the question of national prestige and the need to protect areas already taken by extending control into a neighbouring area (the British decided to subdue the Sudan in order to consolidate their hold on Egypt) (see Section 14.3(a) for more about the motives behind imperialism).

The operation was well under way when Salisbury came to power; the French (who already owned Gabon and Algeria) started the Scramble in 1881 by declaring a protectorate over Tunisia. Britain (who already controlled Cape Colony, Natal, Gambia, Sierra Leone and the Gold Coast) occupied Egypt (1882) and added Somaliland (1884) and Bechuanaland (1885) as protectorates. The Germans took South West Africa and the Cameroons (1884), followed by Tanganyika (1885), while the Italians acquired Eritrea (1885). In an attempt to avoid friction, *the Berlin Conference (1884–5)* had laid down rules of procedure which powers should follow. Each government was to inform the others which areas it was planning to settle and develop as colonies.

Nevertheless disputes did occur and Salisbury was worried in case these led to war.

- *The French* were highly indignant at the British occupation of Egypt where French interests were involved with the Suez Canal.
- *The Italians* were aggrieved at the French occupation of Tunisia, which they had been hoping to control.

Salisbury was unwilling to get involved: as Robert Taylor puts it, 'his aim was not to splash Africa with the red of the British Empire'. But he was driven to intervene by the need to protect British interests in Egypt and along the Nile, and to protect the trading companies in other parts of Africa – the Royal Niger Company clashed with the French who were trying to control the same area. The British East Africa Company was having problems with both German and French rivals, while Cecil Rhodes's South Africa Company was extending its operations northwards into what became known as Rhodesia, causing friction with the Transvaal Boers and the Portuguese.

In 1890 Salisbury signed a series of remarkable agreements which did much to reduce friction:

- The frontier between Portuguese East Africa (Mozambique) and the British areas was fixed, leaving Britain in control of Nyasaland and Rhodesia.
- The French accepted British control of Zanzibar in return for French control of Madagascar, and the northern frontier between Nigeria and French West Africa was agreed.
- The Germans recognized British control of Zanzibar, Uganda and Kenya (British East Africa); in return Britain accepted German control of German East Africa (Tanganyika), the Cameroons and South West Africa; Britain also gave Germany the North Sea island of Heligoland, which she had taken from Denmark in 1807.
- The Italians and British agreed on the frontier between Eritrea and the Sudan.

(d) *The Franco-Russian alliance*

A new and potentially dangerous problem appeared during the last year of Salisbury's government: Russia and France, the two powers most hostile to Britain, began to draw together in the friendship which was to lead to a full treaty of alliance in 1894. Salisbury was anxious to improve Britain's relations with France, but before he could do much about it, the Conservatives were thrown out of office.

16.8 The last of Gladstone (1892–4)

In the election of July 1892 the Conservatives lost 48 seats, but this was not enough to give the Liberals a decisive majority. There were 272 Liberals to 268 Conservatives; in addition there were 46 Liberal Unionists, who would vote with the Conservatives, and 80 Irish Nationalists. This meant that Gladstone was able to form a government, but only with the support of the Irish Nationalists. The Liberals were disappointed by the smallness of their majority, since they had been hoping to attract massive support with their *Newcastle Programme*; this included Home Rule for Ireland, a general election every three years, allotments for workers, employers to be held liable for accidents to workers, and payment for MPs. However, Philip Magnus calls the programme 'a hotch-potch which had been hastily compiled with the object of attracting as many votes from as many different sources as possible'. The Conservative defeat was probably due as much to the electorate's boredom with their record over the previous six years as it was to the Newcastle Programme.

(a) *The Local Government Act (Parish Councils Act) of 1894*

This was the major achievement of Gladstone's Fourth Ministry. The problem needing attention was that most of the county councils set up by the 1888 Act were finding it difficult to cope with the mass of detail involved, since the counties were so large. This new Act:

- subdivided the counties into urban districts and rural districts, each with its own elected council;
- rural districts were further divided so that each village had its own parish council;
- married as well as single women were allowed to vote in elections for these councils, and also *to stand as candidates*, an important new step.

The district councils gradually developed into efficient units looking after public health, roads and education. But the parish councils were never very important because the Lords insisted that their powers should be kept to a minimum. This framework of county and district councils remained the basis of local government until a new system came into operation in 1974, following the 1972 Local Government Act. (See Section 30.6(f)).

(b) *Gladstone and the Second Irish Home Rule Bill*

This was Gladstone's final attempt to solve the Irish problem. Introduced in February 1893, it was similar to the 1886 Bill, except that Irish MPs were to be allowed to sit at Westminster. There was a tremendous struggle to get the Bill through the Commons. Chamberlain led the attack on it, and Gladstone himself, 'alert and tireless, hardly ever left the House; he gloried in every episode of the battle, and his performance, at the age of 83, must be ranked among the supreme achievements of his life' (Magnus). Once, fighting broke out on the floor of the House, and it was not until September that the Bill finally passed (by 309 votes to 267). However, it was rejected overwhelmingly by the Lords (419 votes to 41). Gladstone wanted the government to resign and force a general election, so that he could appeal to the country on the grounds that the unelected Lords were thwarting the wishes of the democratically elected Commons. The rest of the cabinet refused, and after further disagreements about naval spending, Gladstone resigned (March 1894) and retired from politics. He died in May 1898.

(c) *Assessment of Gladstone*

Although his first ministry (1868–74) was impressive, looking at his achievements after that, it is sometimes difficult to see what all the fuss is about. Was he a great statesman or just a self-righteous bigot? He certainly had his faults – he was self-opinionated and his reluctance to discuss policies fully with his colleagues made him difficult to work with. His religious convictions led him into the irritating habit of claiming that he was at all times trying to carry out the will of God. More serious, in the words of R.T. Shannon, was that 'he had no real awareness of what the masses thought and did not care very much what they wanted ... he was moving not from right to left in the conventional manner, but rather into a lofty station of his own, remote from the main political course'.

But he also had qualities which made him the outstanding figure of Victorian politics: he was prepared to fight on behalf of fair play and freedom of the individual against traditional attitudes and restrictions; this led to the great reforms of the first ministry. Above all there was his determination to stick to a course of action if he thought it was morally right and necessary, hence his obsession with Ireland and Home Rule, where his attitude was far ahead of his time. This was unfortunately his greatest failure, and the tragedy was that if the Lords had passed the Second Home Rule Bill in 1893, all the problems and calamities of Ireland since that date might have been avoided.

Another area of controversy in Gladstone's career is his role in the rise and fall of the Liberal party. Many historians, like Paul Adelman, believe that Gladstone did the Liberal party a great service by winning the support of the skilled working classes, thus helping to make it a national and classless party (see Section 13.1(g)). Adelman goes on to argue, however, that by continuing as leader of the party until 1894 when he was well into his eighties, his resistance to radical social reform prevented the Liberal party from devoting itself to improving social and economic conditions, and so it was never able to fulfil the expectations of the working classes. 'It is no coincidence therefore,' argues Adelman, 'that two years after the death of Gladstone in 1898, a new political party was formed which, unlike the Liberals, did claim to be a class party. That party was the Labour party; and its formation is an instructive comment on the weaknesses and failures of the last phase of Gladstonian Liberalism.'

Jonathan Parry, in a recent book, also suggests that Gladstone's leadership had unfortunate long-term effects on his party, but for different reasons. He claims that it is misleading to talk about 'Gladstonian Liberalism', as if it was something invented by Gladstone. He points out that Gladstone did *not* invent Liberalism and he argues that the aristocratic Whig section of the party carried the real Liberal tradition; Gladstone was the outsider, the former Tory, who soon upset the traditional Liberals by his approach to foreign policy. His support for Irish Home Rule in 1886 completely undermined the Whig–Liberal tradition, and brought about the disastrous split in the party, so that it was never again the 'natural' party of government.

16.9 The Liberals in decline: Lord Rosebery's ministry (1894–5)

(a) *Rosebery's government an anti-climax*

It was probably inevitable that, immediately after all the brilliance of the larger-than-life Gladstone, a Liberal government led by anybody else would seem to be an anti-climax. Very little was achieved because:

1. Rosebery, though able and popular with the public, had never sat in the Commons and lacked experience of leadership and party management. The fact that he was a wealthy aristocrat who owned racehorses made him unpopular with the Radicals and especially with Nonconformists (he owned the winner of the Derby in 1894 and 1895, while he was Prime Minister).
2. The Lords rejected almost all the government's measures, with the excuse that the Liberal majority in the Commons was too small for them to claim that they had a mandate from the electorate.

Their only achievement was *the introduction of death duties on all forms of estate*. This was designed to raise an extra four million pounds a year, mainly to pay for increased naval building. The Conservatives were highly critical of the new duties, which penalized the rich, but the Lords did not reject them because they were included in Sir William Harcourt's 1894 budget, and it was the tradition that the Lords never interfered with finance bills.

In June 1895 Rosebery resigned, hoping that public disapproval of the Lords' actions would produce a big Liberal victory in the following general election. Instead they suffered a crushing defeat: they slumped to 177 seats against 340 Conservatives and 71 Liberal Unionists. There was the usual contingent of Irish Nationalists (82 this time) who would vote with the Liberals, but even so, Salisbury, with Liberal Unionist votes, could count on a majority of around 150.

(b) *Why did the Liberals lose so decisively?*

● The Liberal party was still suffering from the split over Home Rule; there was a widespread feeling that the government should have resigned after the failure of the Second Home Rule Bill, so that instead of sympathy for their treatment at the hands of the Lords, there was only impatience.

● The election coincided with a surge of public enthusiasm for imperialism which the Conservatives and Unionists seemed to stand for.

Questions

1. **Irish Home Rule**
   Study Sources A to E and then answer the questions which follow.

Cartoon by Sir John Tenniel which appeared in Punch *at the time of Gladstone's Second Irish Land Act in 1881. The figures represent from left to right: Parnell's Land League, Ireland, and Gladstone*

(*Tenniel, 1881, reproduced by permission of the Proprietors of 'Punch'.*)

THE RIVALS.

Figure 16.1

Source: *Punch*, 1881.

Speech by Charles Stewart Parnell in Cork, 21 January 1885

We shall never gain anything from England unless we tread on her toes; we will never gain a single sixpennyworth from her by conciliation ... In 1880 I pledged myself that I should form one of an independent Irish party to act in opposition to every English government which refused to concede the just rights of Ireland (applause). ... Every Irish politician must be forcibly driven back to the question of national self-government for Ireland (hear, hear). I do not know how this great question will be eventually settled ... but we cannot ask for less than the restitution of the parliament which was stolen from us at the end of the last century (loud cheers).

Source: quoted in L. Evans and P. J. Pledger (eds), *Contemporary Sources and Opinions in Modern British History, vol. 2*, Warne, 1967.

Source C

Speech by Gladstone in the House of Commons during the debate on the First Irish Home Rule Bill, 8 April 1886

Our ineffective coercion is morally worn out. ... Something must be done, something is demanded from us to restore to Ireland the first conditions of civilised life – the free course of law, the liberty of every individual in the exercise of every legal right, the confidence of the people in the law. ... The principle I am laying down is not just for Ireland ... years ago England tried to pass good laws for the Colonies; but the Colonies said – 'We do not want your good laws; we want our own'. We admitted the reasonableness of that principle. We have to consider whether it is applicable to Ireland. We stand face to face with what is termed Irish nationality, which demands complete self-government in Irish affairs. Is this an evil in itself? Is this a thing which we should view with horror? Sir, I believe that it is not.

Source: Hansard, *Parliamentary Debates*, 8 April 1886.

Source D

Extract from a book by A.V.Dicey, an opponent of Home Rule

Englishmen will find to their disappointment that they have not achieved the object which from an English point of view was the principle inducement to grant Home Rule to the Irish people, that is, freedom from the difficulty of governing Ireland. Home Rule is not separation, and nothing short of Irish independence would greatly lessen English responsibility. ... Britain remains responsible for the maintenance of peace and order. Home Rule cannot remove the causes of Irish discontent. It cannot tempt capital towards Ireland, but it may easily drive capital away. It cannot diminish poverty; it cannot soften religious bigotry; it cannot of itself remove agrarian discontent.

Source: A. V. Dicey, *England's Case against Home Rule*, John Murray, 1886.

Extract from a book by J. Tyndall published in 1887

In relation to Ireland, Mr Gladstone has proved an evil-doer. The predicted friendship between England and Ireland is pure moonshine. Give her Mr Gladstone's Home Rule and disloyal Ireland will hit befooled England with redoubled strength and bitterness. She will work for complete separation, and will win it. The hatred which has been nursed so long has only been intensified by untimely concession. ... On the other hand an empire still manned by Britons will not die without a fight. ... Mr Gladstone is a calamity to Britain. What has converted him into a traitor to his country? Mainly of course, the unsteadiness of his own character.

Source: J. Tyndall, *Perverted Politics*, Blackwood, 1887.

(a) From the evidence of Sources A and B, why did Gladstone's Second Irish Land Act fail to pacify Ireland? (6 marks)

(b) How useful are Sources C, D and E in helping the historian to understand the arguments for and against Irish Home Rule? (14 marks)

(c) In June 1886 Gladstone's First Irish Home Rule Bill was defeated in the Commons. Using information from Chapter 16, explain what effects, both short-term and long-term, this defeat had on:

    (i)   the Liberal party; (10 marks)

    (ii) the situation in Ireland. (10 marks)

(Total 40 marks)

2 'A combination of exaggerated hope and over-heated anxiety.' How adequate is this interpretation of the reasons for British Imperial expansion in the period 1880–1902 (see also information in Chapter 17)? [AEB]

17 Ten years of Conservative rule 1895–1905

Summary of events

Lord Salisbury was Prime Minister from 1895 until 1902 and also acted as Foreign Secretary until 1900 when Lord Lansdowne took over the Foreign Office. When Salisbury retired in July 1902, his nephew, Arthur James Balfour, became Prime Minister. The Liberal Unionists were now almost indistinguishable from the Conservatives, and two of their leaders, the Duke of Devonshire (formerly Lord Hartington) and Joseph Chamberlain, were members of Salisbury's cabinet. In fact the Conservatives and their Liberal allies were often referred to simply as *Unionists* to denote their commitment to maintain the full union between Ireland and the rest of the United Kingdom.

Joseph Chamberlain, the Colonial Secretary, was an outstanding figure in the government, often seeming to eclipse the Prime Minister himself. He chose to be Colonial Secretary because of his belief that it was important to build up the British Empire as a great political and economic unit; this period is therefore regarded as the heyday of *imperialism*. British influence was extended in China, and the Sudan was successfully reconquered (1898). In southern Africa, Britain became involved in *the Boer War (1899–1902)* against the Transvaal and the Orange Free State; though the war eventually ended successfully, the British victory did not come easily, and they were made painfully aware that they lacked friends. The policy misleadingly known as *splendid isolation* was therefore transformed into a search for allies. Two important agreements were signed, one with Japan (1902) and the other – the famous Entente Cordiale – with France (1904). The following Liberal government completed the transformation by signing an agreement with Russia in 1907 (see Section 20.7(c)2). As Britain's relations with France and Russia improved, those with Germany deteriorated because of economic and naval rivalry.

Queen Victoria, who had always exercised a restraining influence on her grandson, the German Kaiser Wilhelm II, died in January 1901. She had reigned since 1837 and had lived long enough to celebrate both her Golden and Diamond Jubilees (1887 and 1897). She was succeeded by her son, the 59-year-old Edward VII.

Ireland remained comparatively quiet and during Balfour's government some important concessions were made, including *Wyndham's Land Act (1903)*. In home affairs, social reforms were very few, though *Balfour's Education Act (1902)* was an important measure. In spite of the investigations of Charles Booth and Seebohm Rowntree which revealed serious poverty among the working classes, nothing much was done to help them, and many people began to be attracted to the newly formed Labour party (see Section 19.8).

Yet at the half-way stage of the period, the Conservatives still retained their popularity; in the general election of October 1900 they won an overall majority of around 130, probably thanks to a great surge of *jingoism* (aggressive or excessive patriotism) during the Boer War. It was during Balfour's premiership that public opinion began to grow tired of the Conservatives. In the election of January 1906 the Liberals won an astonishing victory, with 400 seats against the Conservatives' 157. One reason for the Conservative defeat was Chamberlain's controversial campaign in favour of *tariff reform*, which fatally divided the party. It was to be 1922 before the Conservatives were able to form another government.

17.1 Lord Salisbury and the Conservative dominance

(a) *Salisbury: the last of the great aristocrats?*

Robert Cecil, the third Marquis of Salisbury, like Gladstone, was Prime Minister of four governments: 1885–6, 1886–92, 1895–1900 and then after the 'Khaki' election of 1900, held during the Boer War, from 1900 until his retirement in 1902. In fact he was Prime Minister for slightly longer than Gladstone during a 20-year period when the Conservatives, with Liberal Unionist support, dominated the British political scene. Yet somehow, compared with Disraeli, Gladstone and Joseph Chamberlain, Salisbury remains a rather shadowy figure to later generations, and historians have paid less attention to him than to these other more charismatic figures.

The general feeling seems to have been that the Conservative domination during these 20 years had very little to do with any initiatives taken by Salisbury, but was the result of circumstances, mainly the fact that the Liberals were split over Home Rule for Ireland, and the anti-Home Rule Liberals supported the Conservatives. Unflattering things have been written about Salisbury: according to Paul Smith, for example, he was 'the last great aristocratic figure of a political system that died with Victoria, or even before, a great whale irretrievably beached on the receding shore of the nineteenth century'.

He never accepted that democracy was a fair and proper way to govern a country, and always did his best to minimize the effects of change and to maintain the status quo. Although he was a committed Christian (Anglican), this did not encourage him to try and improve working-class conditions, and he remained a staunch supporter of self-help. When Lord Randolph Churchill came out with a programme of social reform, Salisbury was quite happy to let him resign (see Section 16.5(a)). When Joseph Chamberlain brought his radical proposals into the Conservative government in 1895, Salisbury succeeded in limiting them to the Workmen's Compensation Act (1897).

(b) *A positive contribution to the Conservatives' dominance?*

In 'Lord Salisbury and Late Victorian Conservatism' (an article in the *Modern History Review*, February 1996), Dr Graham Goodlad suggests that Salisbury deserves more credit for the long period of Conservative dominance than historians have given him. He argues that Salisbury did much more than just passively enjoy the advantages of favourable circumstances, and that his role was a positive one in several ways:

- Although he disapproved of democracy, he took the trouble to appeal to the new urban voters and developed an effective speaking style addressing large audiences in the Midlands and North.
- It was Salisbury who did a deal with Gladstone over parliamentary reform in 1884 (see Section 16.3(d)): in return for the Conservative majority in the Lords passing the Franchise Act (giving the vote to rural workers), Gladstone agreed to a Redistribution Act which left the vast majority of seats represented by one MP. This worked to the advantage of the Conservatives in suburban areas, because it meant that Conservative supporters in 'respectable' middle-class London suburbs, and later in the suburbs of other cities, could elect their own Conservative MPs instead of being swamped in large multi-member constituencies. Salisbury described this new development as 'Villa Toryism'.
- Salisbury encouraged the development of efficient, professionally organized Conservative associations in the constituencies, run by full-time agents. These were complemented by the Primrose League (founded by Lord Randolph Churchill in 1881) which also had branches in every constituency, and which attracted members in large numbers with it social programmes of fetes and concerts, used to spread the Conservative message to all social classes.
- Salisbury did all he could to widen the split in the Liberal party; for example, in the 1886 election the Conservatives did not run candidates against sitting Liberal Unionist MPs.
- Above all, as Dr Goodlad points out, Salisbury showed great skill in managing and holding together a Conservative party which itself had the potential for serious divisions. Within little over a year after Salisbury's retirement in 1902, Joseph Chamberlain had split the party disastrously over the question of tariff reform.

Clearly then, Lord Salisbury led the party with great authority and did make a positive contribution to the long period of Conservative dominance. On the other hand, it seems inescapable that the direction in which he pointed the party during those 20 years was firmly backwards. As Dr Goodlad himself concludes: 'politics for Salisbury had been a slow, stubborn rearguard action against change'.

17.2 Joseph Chamberlain and imperialism

Born in 1836, the son of a prosperous London boot and shoe manufacturer, Chamberlain went to Birmingham at the age of 18 to become a partner in a screw-making factory owned by his uncle, J. S. Nettlefold. With his acute business sense, he quickly became the driving force behind the enterprise and developed it into a highly profitable firm. In 1876 he was able to retire and live on his personal fortune, devoting most of his time to politics. The appalling conditions in Birmingham led him to stand for the town council in 1869; he spent the rest of his life deeply involved in local and national politics, though after a severe stroke in 1906 he remained an invalid. He died in July 1914.

(a) *Chamberlain's work in Birmingham*

In the mid-1860s the people of Birmingham were suffering all the evils of a new industrial city: child labour, long working hours in dangerous conditions, overcrowded slums, and no proper disposal of sewage and refuse. The town council, reluctant to spend

Chamberlain's career	
1869–76	Member of Birmingham council; Mayor 1873–6
1876–86	Liberal MP for Birmingham; President of Board of Trade 1880–6
1885	Publishes his *Unauthorized Programme*
1886	Opposes Home Rule for Ireland and votes against Liberal government; at least partly responsible for Liberal split; Leads breakaway group of Liberal Unionist MPs
1886–95	Liberal Unionist MP for Birmingham
1895	Joins Salisbury's Conservative government
1895–1910	Conservative/Unionist MP for Birmingham
1895–1903	Colonial Secretary
1903	Resigns from cabinet to lead the campaign for tariff reform Conservative party splits between supporters and opponents of tariff reform

money, had ignored opportunities for improvement. Chamberlain was determined on action: 'The town,' he declared, 'shall not, with God's help, know itself.'

● Using his business skills and methods, he organized the Birmingham Liberal Association which enabled him and some of his friends to win seats on the council. By 1873 the Liberals were in a majority.

● He gave £1000 to the Birmingham (later the National) Education League, and soon became its chairman. The League campaigned for free, compulsory and undenominational education for all. Chamberlain felt that after the 1867 Reform Act, it was essential to educate the new working class borough voters. The League played a part in the passing of Forster's Education Act in 1870 (see Section 12.7(c)), though it far from satisfied them.

● The council bought up the town's two gas companies and its waterworks, which were then modernized and expanded. A Medical Officer of Health was appointed and a new hospital built. A Drainage Board was set up to deal with the proper disposal of drainage and refuse. Street paving and lighting were extended and six public parks opened. Chamberlain even organized a national conference in Birmingham to encourage other authorities to follow Birmingham's example.

● His most remarkable achievement was *the Improvement Scheme* made possible by the 1875 Artisans' Dwellings Act (see Section 12.5(a)). About 90 acres of slums in the town centre were demolished and replaced by a fine new shopping area – Corporation Street – and by high-quality housing for workers.

● New libraries, museums and art galleries were opened and in 1900 Chamberlain founded the University of Birmingham. Thanks to Chamberlain, Birmingham was recognized as a city in 1889 and was widely regarded as a model of progressive local government.

(b) *Chamberlain as a Liberal MP*

Right from his first appearance in the Commons, Chamberlain was full of self-confidence; he was an excellent speaker and soon established a reputation as 'Radical Joe', the champion of the working classes. He was not afraid to criticize anyone or any thing which stood in the way of social reform, whether it was the monarchy, the House of Lords, or other members of the Liberal party. He believed that the party could only survive if it dropped its Whig elements, and he was impatient with Gladstone for his lack of interest in social questions and his obsession with Ireland. He wanted the government to 'intervene on behalf of the weak against the strong, in the interests of labour against capital, of want and suffering against luxury and ease'. Gladstone never understood or liked Chamberlain, who was not exactly a modest man and was as difficult to work with as Gladstone himself. It was with the greatest reluctance that Gladstone made Chamberlain President of the Board of Trade in 1880. Working closely with his friend Sir Charles Dilke, another Radical, Chamberlain was able to make a valuable contribution:

● In 1877 he had formed *the National Liberal Federation* with the aim of helping Liberal candidates fight elections. Using the same techniques as his local party 'caucus' in Birmingham, the Federation provided efficient organization in many constituencies – producing pamphlets and posters, collecting subscriptions, attracting new members and holding public meetings and social events. This contributed to the Liberal victory in the 1880 general election.
● Pressure from Chamberlain and the Radicals resulted in the introduction of the *Third Parliamentary Reform Bill in 1884* (see Section 16.3(d)).
● Before the 1885 election Chamberlain produced his *Unauthorized Programme* of social reform (see Section 16.4(d)). Lloyd George later paid him a handsome compliment: 'I am convinced that our victory [in the 1885 election] is all due to Chamberlain's speeches. Gladstone had no programme at all that would draw.'
● He was concerned at the growing unemployment and he urged the Poor Law Guardians to use their powers to provide work for the unemployed (1886).

Chamberlain was the most dynamic of the leading Liberals; he was ambitious, and was viewed in many quarters as the most likely leader when Gladstone eventually retired. However, this was not to be: serious trouble began when Chamberlain, a passionate imperialist, opposed Gladstone's decision to give Home Rule to Ireland (see Section 16.1(e)), thereby splitting the Liberal party.

(c) *Chamberlain as Colonial Secretary*

When Chamberlain joined Salisbury's government in 1895 there was an hysterical chorus of criticism from Liberals; they said he was inconsistent, a turncoat, a traitor, a Judas. 'It seems to me,' remarked Gladstone, 'that Chamberlain is the greatest blackguard I have ever come across.' However, Chamberlain believed that he was being perfectly consistent; he was convinced that the best way of curing the trade depression was by developing and expanding the British Empire – the larger the Empire, the more profitable British commerce would become; this would reduce unemployment and help the workers. He also believed in Britain's 'national mission' to take the benefits of peace and civilization to backward peoples. This was the heyday of the *Pax Britannica*, a phrase at its most popular during the 1890s. Since the Conservatives were more committed to imperialism than the Liberals, it was only logical that Chamberlain should eventually join them. So strongly did he feel about imperialism that he chose to be Colonial Secretary instead of Chancellor of the Exchequer.

Nor had he abandoned his radicalism: he hoped to push the Conservatives towards social reform, and was responsible for the *Workmen's Compensation Act (1897)* which enabled workers to claim compensation for injuries suffered at work. The Act had its weaknesses – seamen, domestic servants and agricultural labourers were not included; but at least the government had accepted the principle that employers must bear the responsibility for accidents; eventually, by 1908, all categories of workers were included. Chamberlain also urged Salisbury to introduce *Old Age Pensions*, but nothing came of it, partly because the expenses of the Boer War used up all the available funds. Chamberlain's main energies were lavished on his imperial policies:

1   In 1896 Chamberlain negotiated a successful conclusion to a dispute with
    Venezuela about her frontier with British Guiana. The American President
    Cleveland resurrected the Monroe Doctrine (see Section 3.3(b)), threatening war
    if Britain tried to seize any Venezuelan territory. Tension was high, but Salisbury
    allowed Chamberlain to visit the USA, where he persuaded the Americans to
    submit the case to international arbitration. The verdict awarded Britain almost
    the entire territory she had claimed.
2   An expedition under Wolseley was sent to the Gold Coast to deal with the Ashanti
    tribesmen who were constantly raiding areas claimed as British. Early in 1896 the
    Ashantis were defeated and British control assured.
3   In 1897 a dispute arose with France about the frontier between the French colony
    of Dahomey and the British territory of Nigeria. French troops occupied two small
    towns, Busa and Nikki, claimed by the British. Chamberlain retaliated by
    organizing the West African Frontier Force commanded by Sir Henry Lugard.
    This firm action resulted in a compromise (June 1898) by which France kept Nikki
    but gave Busa to Britain.
4   The Sudan was reconquered (1898), and the Fashoda incident, another dispute
    with the French, was successfully concluded (see Section 17.4(a)5–6).
5   Britain leased the Chinese port of Wei-hai-wei (1898) in response to the German
    seizure of Kaiochow and the Russian occupation of Port Arthur.
6   As a result of the Boer War (see next section), the Transvaal and the Orange Free
    State were brought under British control, and in 1910 they became part of the new
    Union of South Africa.
      It was not simply a case of acquiring as much territory as possible; Chamberlain
    tried to improve the British possessions. 'We are landlords of a great estate', he
    remarked; 'it is the duty of a landlord to develop his estate'.
7   He encouraged the formation of Joint Stock Companies, which, in return for a
    monopoly of trade in an area, undertook to develop it by providing amenities such
    as harbours and railways.
8   Government money was sometimes given directly to finance projects like, for
    example, a railway in Uganda. *The Colonial Loans Act (1899)* provided £3 million
    which was spent on a variety of projects – railways in Sierra Leone, Lagos
    (Nigeria) and the Gold Coast, irrigation and railway systems in Cyprus, harbours
    and railways in Jamaica.
9   Chamberlain's initiative led to the founding of Two Schools of Tropical Medicine,
    one in London, the other in Liverpool, to investigate the causes of the diseases
    which were holding up progress.
10 He was responsible for organizing *the Colonial Conference of 1897* where he
    explained his ideas for an empire customs union. He wanted the colonies to
    remove the duties by which they protected their industries against imported British
    goods, but they would only agree if Britain promised to give preference to their
    goods on the British market. This would require Britain to place tariffs on goods

imported from countries outside the Empire, but since Britain was a free trade country, this was not possible. At the 1902 Colonial Conference, attended by members from Australia, New Zealand, Newfoundland, Cape Colony and Natal, the result was the same, and Chamberlain also failed to persuade them to join in an imperial federation.

Although his imperial policies had a great deal of success, Chamberlain was deeply disappointed at his failure to organize the Empire into a great customs union. Consequently he took the disastrous decision to campaign for a return to tariffs, which would enable a system of imperial preference to be introduced. He resigned from the cabinet so that he could devote himself fully to the campaign. This was to be his greatest failure, splitting the Conservatives and contributing to their crushing defeat in 1906. Peel had also split the Conservatives, and Lloyd George was to do the same to the Liberals during the First World War; but Chamberlain is the only politician to have split two major parties.

17.3 The Boer War 1899–1902

(a) *What caused the war?*

Since the First Boer War of 1881, after which the Transvaal was granted independence (see Section 16.2(b)), her relationship with Britain had not been a comfortable one, although the Orange Free State remained friendly towards Britain. Relations gradually deteriorated; by 1897 the Orange Free State had joined the Transvaal and events escalated into war. The reasons were:

1   *President Paul Kruger of the Transvaal wanted to extend his country's boundaries*, but was continually frustrated by the British who occupied Bechuanaland on the Transvaal's western frontier in 1885. Cecil Rhodes, head of the British South Africa Company, was granted a charter which enabled him to develop Rhodesia (1888–91), hemming the Transvaal in to the north.

2   *Cecil Rhodes was the central figure in British South Africa.* Sent out to his brother in Natal on a health cure (for tuberculosis) in 1870 when he was only 17, Rhodes became involved in the diamond mining recently opened up at Kimberley. By 1881 he had secured control of virtually all the Kimberley mines for his company, the de Beers Corporation, and he was immensely rich. His burning ambition was to use his wealth to extend the Empire until Britain controlled the whole of southern Africa. He had grandiose plans to build a railway linking the Cape with British-controlled Cairo in the north. A confrontation between Rhodes and Kruger was inevitable: if Rhodes had his way, the Transvaal must become part of the British Empire.

3   *The discovery of gold in the Transvaal in 1886 complicated the situation.* From being a poor agricultural country, the Transvaal was suddenly transformed into one of the wealthiest areas in Africa. By 1894 it seemed to Rhodes that it was becoming richer than Cape Colony; it was also becoming less dependent on the Cape, since the Boers could now import and export goods along a new railway to Delagoa Bay in Portuguese East Africa, and there was no need to pass through British territory at all. Kruger began to buy armaments from Germany and there were rumours that he was planning to take over the whole of South Africa. This was not as unlikely as it might sound: there were thousands of Boers living in the Cape, and if they co-operated with Kruger, such a plan would have been perfectly

Frontier of the Union of
South Africa formed in 1910

feasible. More than ever it seemed essential to Rhodes that some action must be taken against 'Krugerism'.

4 *Rhodes, who became Prime Minister of Cape Colony in 1890, decided on direct intervention.* Thousand of settlers, many of them Cape British, had moved into the Transvaal to work in the goldmines. By 1895 these *uitlanders* (outsiders) as the Boers called them, outnumbered the Boers themselves. Kruger, afraid of being swamped and anxious to preserve the character of his country, refused them all political rights and taxed them heavily. Rhodes decided to stir up uitlander unrest into revolution which, with some outside help, might be strong enough to overthrow Kruger. The result of his efforts was . . .

5 *The Jameson Raid (December 1895).* Dr Leander Starr Jameson, an associate of Rhodes, was to lead an invasion of the Transvaal from Bechuanaland to coincide with an uprising of uitlanders in Johannesburg. However, uitlander unrest, genuine though it was, was too disorganized to produce revolution, and when Jameson rode into the Transvaal at the head of only 500 troops, he was easily defeated by the Boers. Chamberlain, the Colonial Secretary, claimed that he knew nothing about the raid, but historian Elizabeth Longford has shown that he was deeply implicated and suggests that the probable understanding was that if the exploit failed, Rhodes should take the responsibility, which he did by resigning as Cape Prime Minister. *The results of the affair were disastrous*: to the rest of the world it seemed that Britain had authorized the unprovoked invasion of a foreign state, and the German Kaiser sent a telegram to Kruger congratulating him on successfully defending his country. The raid offended the Orange Free State and the Cape Boers; it confirmed all Kruger's fears about British intentions and he

continued to arm heavily. War was not inevitable at this stage though, provided the British abandoned their designs on the Transvaal.

6   *Sir Alfred Milner, appointed High Commissioner for South Africa in 1897, must bear much of the responsibility for the outbreak of war.* A passionate imperialist, Milner suspected that Kruger might try to expand the Transvaal southwards, with backing from the Germans and the Cape Boers. In order to destroy Kruger, he deliberately set about provoking a crisis which could be turned into war. Given Kruger's belligerent attitude, this was not too difficult, though in fact the old man was prepared to make some concessions. The uitlanders sent a telegram to Queen Victoria protesting about their 'frightful' treatment at the hands of the Boers. This prompted the British government to demand that some improvement be made in the uitlanders' position. Kruger agreed to meet Milner at Bloemfontein, the capital of the Orange Free State, in June 1899. He offered to give the uitlanders the vote after a residential qualification of seven years, and there seemed a good chance of a peaceful compromise. However, Milner rejected this and demanded a five-year qualification which Kruger would not hear of; the meeting broke up without progress. Chamberlain, genuinely hoping to avoid war, attempted to reopen negotiations, but without satisfactory response. British troops now began to move up to the Transvaal frontiers.

7   *The Boers, also moving troops, responded by sending an ultimatum to the British government.* This suggested independent arbitration, but demanded the withdrawal of British troops from Boer frontiers and the return home of all British forces which had recently arrived in South Africa. When this was rejected, the Transvaal and Orange Free State Boers immediately attacked Natal and the Cape. Kruger had therefore played into Milner's hands, and as Salisbury put it, he had 'liberated us from the necessity of explaining to the people of England why we are at war'.

(b) *Events in the war*

1   The Boer armies moved swiftly and beseiged Ladysmith in Natal, and Mafeking and Kimberley (where Rhodes himself was trapped) in the west. Sir Redvers Buller, British Commander-in-Chief, split his troops into three divisions in an attempt to relieve all three towns. But in the same week in December 1899 – Black Week as it became known to the British public – all three armies were defeated:

- Buller himself, advancing to relieve Ladysmith, was checked by Louis Botha's troops at Colenso;
- the division moving along the road to Kimberley was heavily defeated by Cronje's forces at Magersfontein;
- the third division, attempting to relieve Mafeking, was driven back at Stormberg.

In January 1900 Buller tried again to relieve Ladysmith but failed more disastrously than before, losing 1700 men at Spion Kop.

2   The British failures were not difficult to explain. The Boer forces outnumbered the British by two to one, they were all mounted and they were excellent marksmen who knew the country well; they had superior German Krupps artillery and rifles. The War Office had not studied the situation properly and sent too many unmounted troops who had to operate at great disadvantage in unfamiliar territory where the local population was hostile. Most historians have blamed the incompetence of the generals, particularly Buller, but Thomas Pakenham in his book about the Boer War defends Buller, claiming that he was learning fast under

Illus. 17.1 The first Welsh regiment make camp during the Boer War

the most difficult circumstances, and would eventually have been just as effective as Roberts and Kitchener, the men sent out to supercede him. What was needed was large numbers of extra troops.

3   As vast reinforcements poured in, Lord Roberts, with Kitchener as his Chief-of-Staff, outmanoeuvred Cronje and relieved Kimberley (February). Soon afterwards Cronje was forced to surrender at Paardeberg. After that things happened quickly: Buller relieved Ladysmith (February), Roberts captured Bloemfontein (March), Mafeking was relieved (May) after a siege lasting 217 days, and finally Johannesburg and Pretoria (capital of the Transvaal) were captured (June). Kruger escaped to Europe and the Boer republics were taken over by Britain. It seemed as if the war was over, and Roberts returned home. British successes at this stage were a result partly of the fact that they now had many more troops at their disposal, including some from Canada, Australia and New Zealand, and partly because the Boers made the mistake of keeping too many of their troops tied up in the sieges of Ladysmith, Kimberley and Mafeking.

4   The Boers, however, refused to surrender or negotiate, and continued to fight in small guerrilla groups, constantly harassing the British forces. Helped and sheltered by the friendly local populations, they raided Natal and Cape Colony, destroying crops and attacking railways. Kitchener found these tactics difficult to deal with and eventually he resorted to a drastic policy of 'scorched earth': farms and crops were destroyed to deny the guerrillas food; forts or blockhouses were built to protect railways; the civilian population, including women and children, were rounded up into concentration camps to prevent their helping the guerrillas. Kitchener's methods were effective: the Boer leaders agreed to negotiate and a peace treaty was signed at Vereeniging in 1902.

5   British tactics aroused world-wide criticism, since the concentration camps were

overcrowded and badly mismanaged; epidemics broke out which killed over 20 000 people during 1901. Sir Henry Campbell-Bannerman, the Liberal leader, denounced government policy as 'methods of barbarism'.

(c) *Results of the war*

● *The Treaty of Vereeniging was reasonable and generous in its terms*: although the two Boer republics were annexed, they were promised eventual self-government; English was to be the official language but Afrikaans (the language of the Boers) was to be allowed in schools and law-courts. Three million pounds was given by the British government to help the Boers repair damage and re-stock farms. On the whole this settlement was satisfactory to both sides, though some Boer leaders demanded more money and doubted whether the promise of self-government would ever be kept. In fact, Campbell-Bannerman's Liberal government did carry it out in 1906, and as relations between British and Boers steadily improved, the Transvaal and the Orange Free State agreed to join the Union of South Africa, along with Cape Colony and Natal, in 1910 (see Section 21.2).

● The war revealed Britain's isolated position in the world: the other major European powers – Germany and Austria–Hungary, France and Russia – all sympathized with the Boers. Consequently the British made determined efforts to find new allies.

● As the war dragged on through 1901 and into 1902, the public tended to grow disenchanted with it. It had cost at least £200 million and over 20 000 British lives, and people began to question whether it had all been worth it. The effect was to turn a large section of public opinion against the Conservatives and against imperialism, which became discredited.

17.4 Foreign affairs 1895–1905

For the sake of simplicity it is usual to divide this period into two phases:

● 1895–1900 when Britain continued the policy known as '*splendid isolation*';
● 1900–1905 when Britain looked for, and found, allies – Japan (1902) and France (1904).

(a) *'Splendid isolation'*

Salisbury had started the 'splendid isolation' policy during his previous government of 1886–92. His aims in foreign policy are set out in Section 16.7(a). But in fact it is a misleading term: it was not that Britain deliberately refused to have anything to do with the rest of the world – Salisbury signed the Mediterranean Agreements and negotiated boundary settlements in Africa. However, Britain *was* isolated in the sense that Salisbury kept her aloof from binding alliances in case they committed her to military action.

By the time Salisbury came to power again in 1895, an important change had taken place: the two countries he most feared, *France and Russia, had signed an alliance with each other in 1894.* Germany, Austria–Hungary and Italy were already bound together in *the Triple Alliance*, so that left Britain as the only major European country not associated with an alliance bloc. Nor was Salisbury anxious to commit Britain to either of the blocs. He preferred to try and revive the old Concert of Europe in which *all* the powers would co-operate together in times of crisis, but he had little success. He was getting old – he was 66 in 1895 – and his health was deteriorating; he came under increasing pressure from some of his cabinet, particularly Chamberlain, Goschen and Lansdowne, for a more positive policy. Chamberlain was full of enthusiasm for an alliance with Germany, but Salisbury did all he could to avoid it. The main events illustrate the different strands:

1   *The Venezuela dispute (1895–6)* was settled in Britain's favour (see Section 17.2(c)), but not before it had demonstrated the lack of support for Britain.

2   *New problems arose in Turkey in 1896* when the Turks, breaking their promise made at Berlin (1878), began wholesale massacres of Christian Armenians. Salisbury tried to persuade the European powers to take joint action to restrain the Turks, but the Germans, who were cultivating the Sultan as an ally, would not co-operate and the attempt failed.

3   *British intervention in the war between Greece and Turkey (1897–8)* was one of Salisbury's successes. The Greeks tried to capture the Turkish island of Crete in the Mediterranean, but the Turks were too strong for them and retaliated by occupying a large part of Thessaly in mainland Greece. Salisbury managed to get the Concert of Europe to bring about a Turkish withdrawal from Thessaly, but Germany and Austria–Hungary would take no action in Crete itself. This time, however, the British fleet could be brought into play; Salisbury used it to expel Turkish troops from the island, after which Prince George of Greece was appointed governor.

4   *Britain's position in China and the Far East was being threatened both by Russia and Germany*. In 1894 the Japanese had surprised Europe by sending troops into the Chinese territory of Korea, ostensibly to help put down revolution, and then by defeating Chinese forces which tried to prevent them. China was forced to agree to *the Treaty of Shimonoseki (1895)* which gave Japan the Liaotung Peninsula, including the first-class harbour of Port Arthur. This was too much for the Russians who themselves had designs on Port Arthur which was ice-free; with the support of France and Germany, they forced Japan to hand back Liaotung. The following year the Russians signed a treaty with the Chinese promising to defend China and receiving in return the right to build a railway across the Chinese province of Manchuria, bordering on Russia. Then suddenly in 1897 the Germans seized the Chinese port of Kiaochow; ignoring Salisbury's attempts to dissuade them, the Russians followed this up by forcing the Chinese to grant them a 25-year lease on Port Arthur. It seemed as though China was about to be carved up, much against the wishes of Salisbury, who preferred an 'open-door' policy – to keep China open for trade but politically independent. The best Britain could do was fall in with the trend and lease Wei-hai-wei.

5   *The reconquest of the Sudan* was achieved by an army under the command of Sir Herbert Kitchener. Salisbury agreed to the campaign for several reasons. Since Gordon's death (1885) the Sudan had been controlled by the Dervishes. Although the Mahdi died soon after Gordon, his successor, known as the Khalifa, was a constant threat to Egypt itself. In 1889 his forces had invaded Egypt and Kitchener had played an important part in repelling the attack. The Dervishes were also threatening the Italian colony of Eritrea, and the Italian government, with German support, urged Britain to destroy the Khalifa. Salisbury was suspicious of French ambitions in southern Sudan: in June 1896 the French Captain Marchand had set out from French West Africa with a small force, heading for Fashoda on the Nile, above Khartoum; thus it was important to assert British control of the Sudan before the French became established (see Map 16.1 on p. 244).

Setting out in 1896, Kitchener's expedition advanced slowly up the Nile, building a railway as they went and fighting off repeated Dervish attacks. Other hazards included cholera outbreaks, and torrential rain which washed away a section of the newly constructed railway. The climax came in September 1898 when the Khalifa's army was heavily defeated at *Omdurman* just outside Khartoum. Dervish power was destroyed and British control of the Sudan was assured, though the French still had hopes in the area.

6   *The Fashoda incident (1898) seemed likely to bring war between Britain and France.* Only a few days after the Battle of Omdurman, news was brought to Kitchener that Marchand had arrived at Fashoda, claiming the Upper Nile for France. Kitchener moved southwards to Fashoda and invited Marchand to withdraw, pointing out with perfect courtesy that if it came to a showdown, his force was much larger than Marchand's. The two governments negotiated, and although the press in both countries adopted warlike attitudes, good sense prevailed. The French government ordered Marchand to withdraw from Fashoda. They had decided not to risk war because:

- they could not compete with the British fleet which was cruising in the Eastern Mediterranean;
- their Russian ally was unable to help;
- they were afraid that the Germans might profit in some way if France became embroiled in a war with Britain.

This was viewed as a personal triumph for Salisbury, though he hated confrontations of this nature and immediately began to look for ways of improving relations with the humiliated French.

7   *The Boer War (1899–1902)* was the climax of the Salisbury period in foreign affairs (see previous section).

8   *Britain's relations with Germany* were generally good while Bismarck and his successor, Caprivi, were in power. But after Caprivi's resignation in 1894, the Kaiser Wilhelm II began to play a leading role in the conduct of German foreign affairs. He wanted to build Germany up into a great colonial and world power. His attitude towards Britain was difficult to understand. Envious of her naval power and at the same time full of grudging admiration, he was sometimes belligerent and arrogant, sometimes co-operative. Some historians think that he really wanted an alliance with Britain and was hoping to frighten her into joining the Triple Alliance by a show of strength:

- In January 1896 Wilhelm sent his famous telegram to Kruger congratulating him on defeating the Jameson Raid (see Section 17.3(a)). Whether the Germans intended to take any action is doubtful, though three German cruisers were in Delagoa Bay off Portuguese East Africa. In case they were intending to act, Salisbury despatched a small fleet described as a 'flying squadron', and Wilhelm realized he had gone too far. The incident had important effects: coming so soon after the Franco-Russian alliance (1894), it shocked the British to find the Germans so hostile. On the German side it justified an expansion of the German navy, so that any future British flying squadrons could be dealt with. Britain had 33 battleships and 130 cruisers whereas Germany had only six and four respectively. Tirpitz, the Minister of Marine, was responsible for the 1897 Navy Laws which provided for the building of seven battleships and nine cruisers. In 1900 it was proposed to build three new battleships a year for the next 20 years.
- Twice, in 1898 and 1899, Chamberlain proposed an alliance with Germany,

but the Germans refused on the grounds that Britain wanted to use the Germans to check Russian expansion in the Far East.

- During the Boer War Wilhelm behaved correctly and refrained from interfering; when Kruger arrived in Germany, the Kaiser refused to meet him.
- *The Boxer Rising in China (1900)* brought Britain and Germany together in close co-operation. The Boxers, a Chinese nationalist group, besieged the foreign legations in Peking in protest against the increasing outside intervention in their country. Britain played an important role in organizing an international expedition to relieve the legations. At the suggestion of the British, a German officer was placed in overall command; the besieged foreigners were rescued and order restored.
- At the Kaiser's suggestion, an Anglo-German convention was signed (October 1900), sometimes known as *the Yangtze Agreement*. Both promised to maintain the 'open-door' in China to the trade of all nations and to check foreign aggression.

(b) *Why and with what results did Britain look for allies after 1900?*

The reasons why Britain began to search for allies with more urgency after 1900 (most of them already mentioned) can be summarized briefly:

1   All the other major European powers had allies, whereas British isolation had been clearly demonstrated by the Jameson Raid, the Venezuela incident and the Boer War. It had been difficult to defeat the Boers; what would happen if Britain were to be attacked by one or more of the great powers?
2   France was still hostile, smarting over diplomatic defeats in Nigeria and at Fashoda, and resenting the British presence in Egypt and the Sudan.
3   Russia was viewed as a likely enemy, with designs on India and northern China.
4   Though Germany was seen as the most probable ally, the Kaiser himself was unpredictable and the Navy Law of June 1900 suggested that the Germans were setting out to match Britain's naval power. Naval rivalry was later to become the main cause of Anglo-German friction.
5   In October 1900 Salisbury at last gave up the Foreign Office and Lord Lansdowne took his place. Lansdowne, like Chamberlain, had long been in favour of a more positive approach to finding Britain an ally.
6   The matter became urgent with the growth of Russian power in northern China. Towards the end of 1900 Russian troops occupied the northern part of Manchuria, and in January 1901, the details of a Russo-Chinese agreement became known; this meant that in practice, Manchuria was now part of Russia. Lansdowne was determined to form some sort of alliance to check Russian ambitions.

The search for allies:

1   Lansdowne first tried to arrange a joint Anglo-German action under the Yangtze Agreement, but the Germans refused to co-operate, arguing that this only applied to the Yangtze Valley and not to Manchuria. The real reason was that they were happy for the Russians to be occupied in Manchuria, since that kept them out of the Balkans, where they might clash with Germany's ally Austria–Hungary. Yet another attempt at a formal agreement with Germany had failed; the Germans were convinced that Britain would be unable to find allies elsewhere.
2   *The Anglo-Japanese Alliance was signed in January 1902.* Lansdowne realized that the power which had the closest interest in checking the growth of Russian power in the Far East was Japan. The Russians were already turning their attention

towards Korea, and the Japanese were determined not to allow Russia to control Korea as well as Manchuria. The terms of the agreement were:

- Japan recognized Britain's interests in China and the Pacific, and Britain recognized Japan's rights in Korea.
- If Japan was involved in a war with Russia, Britain would remain neutral, but if another power (presumably France) joined in to help Russia, Britain would help Japan.

The alliance had important results: the position of both powers in the Far East was greatly strengthened; if Russia continued to press her ambitions, there was now a much greater chance that Japan would resist by force. This in fact is what happened – war between Russia and Japan followed in 1904–5 and it was Japan which emerged victorious. The alliance also played a part in gaining Britain her second ally:

3   *The Anglo-French Entente Cordiale* (friendly understanding) was signed in April 1904. On the face of it, it was a highly unlikely development: for years relations had been strained over colonial matters; during the Boer War the French press had been violently anti-British and extremely rude about Queen Victoria and Edward VII. But pressures for an understanding had built up on both sides: though the French resented British colonial power, they did not want a war with Britain, and still viewed Germany as their main enemy. They were alarmed at the Anglo-Japanese alliance and the growing danger of war between Japan and their ally, Russia. The Russians would expect help from France, but this might also provoke British help for Japan, and the French would find themselves involved in war with Britain.

Delcassé, the French Foreign Minister, worked hard to improve relations. On the British side it was Chamberlain who made the first move; his motive was a desire to sort out the colonial squabbles. Lansdowne was probably thinking in terms of a counter-move against the build-up of German naval strength, though the government denied that it was an anti-German agreement. Edward VII helped the process of reconciliation by paying an official visit to Paris (May 1903) during which he went to great lengths to show Britain's readiness to co-operate. The outbreak of the Russo-Japanese War (February 1904) made an agreement urgent and speeded up the final negotiations. *The terms were*:

- France would give Britain a free hand in Egypt and the Sudan while Britain recognized French interests in Morocco.
- France gave up her claim to the Newfoundland coast in exchange for land in Gambia (West Africa). Agreement was reached in disputes over Siam, Madagascar and the New Hebrides.

Results of the Entente: It had the desired effect of limiting the Russo-Japanese War. There was one tense incident in October 1904 when the Russian Baltic fleet fired on some British trawlers near the Dogger Bank, apparently mistaking them for Japanese torpedo boats. The French mediated and the Russians apologised and agreed to pay compensation. The Entente was just a settling of differences, not a military alliance. However, the Kaiser soon began to view it as an anti-German move and announced that Germany too had interests in Morocco. This was clearly a challenge to the new Entente; over the next few years the German attitude pushed Britain into a closer commitment to France and away from the German camp. The next move was to be a similar agreement with France's ally Russia in 1907 (see Section 21.7(c)).

17.5 Ireland under the Conservatives

Although the situation in Ireland was comparatively calm, the basic problem was still there – the majority of the Irish were still without land of their own and were living in extreme poverty. George Wyndham, who became Chief Secretary for Ireland in 1900, believed that the best solution was to enable as many tenants as possible to buy land; the more content they were, the more likely they would be to forget their desire for Home Rule. *Wyndham's Land Purchase Act (1903)* lent money to tenants who wanted to buy farms of their own in cases where a reasonable price could be agreed with the landlord. The loans were at a low rate of interest – only three and a quarter per cent – and the repayments were spread over 68 years. All parties involved approved and by 1910 some 250 000 tenants had taken advantage of the measure. Earlier the administration of the country had been improved by the introduction of elected county councils on the same lines as those in Britain.

17.6 What were the achievements of Balfour's government (1902–5) and why had it become so unpopular by 1905?

Arthur James Balfour had had a distinguished career – a successful Chief Secretary for Ireland (1887–91) (see Section 16.6) and First Lord of the Treasury (1895–1902). As Salisbury's health deteriorated, Balfour took on more and more of the burden of government. He was able, cultured and witty, though he often seemed to lack a strong commitment in any particular direction. Lloyd George dismissed him contemptuously as 'just like the scent on a pocket handkerchief'. He remained leader of the Conservative party until 1911, but his reputation is tarnished by the fact that he led the Conservatives into the crushing electoral defeat of 1906 and then lost two further general elections in 1910. No party leader could survive that record. Yet during his short period as Prime Minister, there were some important achievements.

(a) *Balfour's achievements*

1 *The Education Act of 1902* was probably his greatest achievement (see Section 12.7(e)).
2 *Wyndham's Land Purchase Act of 1903* (see previous section).
3 *The Licensing Act of 1904* dealt with the problem of whether or not brewers should be compensated when a public house was closed down by having its licence withdrawn. The brewers naturally felt that they were entitled to compensation in cases where licences were withdrawn because there was an excess of public houses; but in 1891 the House of Lords had decided that liquor licences were to last only for one year and that there should be no compensation for licences not renewed. The situation became urgent in 1902 when magistrates in certain areas launched what seemed to be a determined effort to reduce the number of public houses – in Birmingham alone over 50 had their licences withdrawn. Balfour felt that his Act achieved a masterly compromise:

- If a public house was closed because there were too many in the area and not because of any misconduct, the brewer should receive compensation.
- However, the compensation would come, not from public money, but from a fund paid into by the brewers themselves.

Opposition was therefore aroused on both sides: the anti-drink movement objected to the payment of any compensation, no matter where it came from, while the brewers were not happy at having, in effect, to compensate themselves.

4   *Measures to improve defence.* Balfour, like other politicians, had been profoundly disturbed by Britain's poor military showing in the early stages of the Boer War. There was also the realisation that the navy, although more efficient than the army, might well have to face a challenge from Germany within a few years.

- The Prime Minister became Chairman of the Committee of Imperial Defence, and a thorough investigation was started into the Empire's military requirements. This had made little progress when the government fell, but at least a beginning had been made for Lord Haldane, the subsequent Liberal War Minister, to build on (see Section 21.7(b)).
- Sir John Fisher was appointed First Sea Lord and Lord Cawdor First Lord of the Admiralty. They took two crucial decisions: they created a third fleet – the Atlantic Fleet based at Gibraltar – in addition to the existing Channel and Mediterranean Fleets; and they authorized the building of a revolutionary new battleship, the *Dreadnought*, launched in February 1906. Weighing 17 900 tons, equipped with eight 12-inch guns, driven by steam turbines and capable of reaching a speed of 21 knots, the *Dreadnoughts* made all other battleships obsolete. The plan was to build four *Dreadnought* type battleships every year.

5   *The Anglo-French Entente of 1904* (see Section 17.4(b)).

(b) *Why did Balfour's government become unpopular?*

Balfour was unfortunate: though some of his own policies aroused criticism, he and the Conservative party paid the price for the shortcomings and mistakes of Salisbury's governments:

1   *There had been an almost complete absence of major social reform from the Conservatives for the previous 20 years.* This was because both Salisbury and Balfour, unlike Disraeli, had very little conception of the problems and needs of the working classes; strong believers in self-help, they were not prepared for the state to take on responsibility for the problems of old age, sickness and unemployment. And yet there was an example to follow – in Germany the conservative Bismarck had introduced successful schemes for sickness insurance (1883) and old age pensions (1889).

2   *The trade union movement was hostile to the Conservatives* because of the Taff Vale case, in which the House of Lords, acting as the final court of appeal, had ordered the railway workers' union to pay heavy damages following a strike (1900). This made it impossible for any union to hold a strike without at the same time risking bankruptcy (see Section 19.6(b)). This decision, and the failure of Balfour's government to take any action to reverse it, caused a surge of support for the Labour party.

3   *There was a reaction after the Boer War*, against the shortcomings of the government and the military, against the 'methods of barbarism' in Kitchener's concentration camps, and against imperialism itself.

4   *Balfour's Education Act (1902) and the Licensing Act (1904)* were vote losers.

5   *The 'Chinese slavery' affair caused a political storm.* Balfour made a serious mistake by allowing thousands of Chinese labourers to be brought into the Transvaal to work in the gold mines. They were not treated as free people, and were confined in barrack-like compounds even in non-working hours. There were

around 50 000 of them by the end of 1905, working for very low wages. There were protests from Canada, Australia and New Zealand, and the trade union movement was outraged at this inhuman treatment of fellow labourers. The Liberal opposition made the most of it, but again Balfour showed his lack of awareness and tact, merely claiming that the situation had been exaggerated.

6 *The tariff reform controversy split the Conservative party.* It was clear that Britain's period of industrial and commercial predominance was rapidly coming to an end. Most other countries had introduced tariffs, but since Britain persisted in remaining a free trade country, British manufacturers and farmers were suffering intense competition from abroad. German and American manufactured goods were doing most of the damage to British industry. Joseph Chamberlain was convinced that the time had come to abandon free trade and return to a policy of tariffs. This would have two advantages:

- It would protect British industry against cheaper foreign imports and would therefore help maintain full employment.
- It would make possible the introduction of a system of imperial preferences; this would encourage a closer union of the Empire by having low tariffs or perhaps no tariffs at all on imports from the Empire, and comparatively high tariffs on imports from foreign countries outside the Empire.

Chamberlain announced his policy in May 1903, and although there was a lot of support for him in the party, most of the cabinet was against his ideas. He therefore resigned from the cabinet and launched a propaganda campaign backed by *the Tariff Reform League.* Balfour tried to produce a compromise but this only annoyed both sides. The row in the Conservative party enabled the Liberals to forget their differences and spring to the defence of free trade. Their argument was that free trade guaranteed 'cheap food', whereas tariffs would put up the cost of living for the workers.

(c) *The Conservative defeat*

Early in December 1905 Balfour suddenly resigned, but did not ask for parliament to be dissolved. This was a gamble on Balfour's part. If he asked for a dissolution, there would have to be an immediate general election in which Conservative prospects could not be too bright. However, if the Liberals formed a minority government, there was a chance that disagreements in the Liberal party between imperialists and anti-imperialists might suggest that they were still unfit for government.

Sir Henry Campbell-Bannerman formed a Liberal government, not without some difficulty; but it soon became clear that Balfour had miscalculated. The leading Liberals were far too shrewd to waste such a golden opportunity. They patched up their differences and began to campaign for a general election in mid-January 1906. The election result was a massive Liberal victory; the figures were: Liberals 400, Conservatives and Unionists 157, Irish Nationalists 83 and Labour 29. No doubt all the issues mentioned above played a part in the Conservative defeat, but possibly the question of tariff reform was the crucial one. Liberal election posters showed a large loaf representing the cheap food provided by free trade, and a small loaf representing the more expensive food which would result from tariffs. Even Balfour lost his seat at Manchester which he had held for 20 years, though Chamberlain's popularity in Birmingham was so great that he held his seat with an increased majority.

Questions

1. The outbreak of the Boer War, October 1899

Study Sources A to F and then answer the questions which follow.

__ **Source A** __

> *Speech by Joseph Chamberlain in the House of Commons, 19 October 1899*
>
> From the first day I came into office I hoped for peace, I strove for peace and I have believed in peace.... After that extraordinary *ultimatum* which was addressed to the government, it is impossible for us to do any other than fight with all energy the war which has been thrust upon us.... We are going to war in defence of the principles upon which this Empire has been founded. The first principle is that if we are to maintain our position in regard to other nations, if we are to maintain our existence as a great power in South Africa, we are bound to show that we are able to protect British subjects everywhere when they are made to suffer from oppression and injustice.... The second principle is that in the interests of South Africa and the British Empire, Britain must remain the paramount power in South Africa. *We are now at war because Kruger and the government of the Transvaal has placed British subjects in the Transvaal in a position of distinct inferiority.*

Source: quoted in L. Evans and P. J. Pledger, *Contemporary Sources and Opinions in Modern British History, vol 2*, Warne, 1967.

__ **Source B** __

> *Speech by Sir Henry Campbell-Bannerman (Liberal leader) in the House of Commons, 5 February 1904*
>
> It was on June 20, 1899. The right hon. gentleman [Chamberlain] came to my room. He told me that he wished to submit to me certain proposals that the government were contemplating. The first was to send out 10 000 men to the Cape ... he went on to say, 'You need not be alarmed. There will be no fighting. We know that those fellows' – that was the Boers – 'won't fight.... We are playing a game of bluff.' I think I ventured to express frankly to the right hon. gentleman my opinion that such a policy was unworthy of the country. I said it was a rash and dangerous policy to begin a course of bluff when you did not know what it might lead to.

Source: quoted in J. Wilson, *A Life of Sir Henry Campbell-Bannerman*, Constable, 1973.

__ **Source C** __

> *Letter from Lord Selbourne, one of Chamberlain's Colonial Office Ministers, to Lord Milner, British High Commissioner in South Africa*
>
> DOWNING STREET, 22/3/98 (Confidential) ... Our object is the future combination of South Africa under the Union Jack.... Our first object is to avoid war if it can be done safely, but if it is to come, what are the conditions under which we must manoeuvre for it to come? It must command the practically unanimous consent of the British in South Africa, and the approval of as large a proportion as possible of our own Dutch in South Africa, and the action must have the unanimous consent of public opinion at home.

Source: as for Source A.

Remark by Milner to Mr J. T. Molteno, a member of the Cape parliament, 3 October 1899, reported to the Daily Chronicle *by Mr Molteno*

Well, Mr Molteno, it is no use; I am determined to break the dominion of Afrikanerdom.

Source: as for Source B.

Source E

Speech by Lloyd George at Carmarthen, 27 November 1899

I do not mean to say that there are no circumstances which would compel us to fight, but I would say that the case must be an overwhelming one indeed before we do so. In this particular instance war could have been avoided. We were negotiating, and the Boers had conceded our demands, which we then withdrew. In the meantime we sent tens of thousands of soldiers to South Africa with artillery and munitions for war.... We are fighting for a franchise in the Transvaal which we do not give our own subjects at home.... I do not believe the war has any connection with the franchise. It is a question of 45 per cent dividends.

Source: quoted in P. Rowland, *Lloyd George*, Barrie & Jenkins, 1975.

Source F

Bernard Porter, in The Lion's Share, *gives a historian's view of the outbreak of war*

Milner could not imagine the Afrikaners of the Cape being loyal to the Empire while there remained an independent nation of their 'race' to the north to divert their loyalties, and he could not see the Transvaal forfeiting her independence without war. In any case she should be pushed to the limit, mainly on the issue of the *uitlander franchise* – because it was a genuine grievance, and because if Kruger did give satisfaction on it, Britain's position in South Africa would be automatically secured: uitlanders outnumbered Boers, most of them were British, and it was assumed that if Britons were given the vote, they would use it imperially. Consequently from the beginning of 1898 Milner devoted his energies to bringing on a crisis which could be exploited to this end.... He did all he could to prevent a reconciliation with the Boers, and his constant fear was that Kruger would make reasonable concessions which he would have to accept, which would take from him the excuse for grabbing all he wanted. At a conference with Kruger at Bloemfontein in June 1899 he had to work hard to avoid a peaceful settlement. But he succeeded and the war he desired at last broke out.... In the event, the fact that it was the Boers who issued the *ultimatum* and not the British, made it easier (the British had one prepared in case the Boers failed to).... Though it was Milner who forced the pace, the government's aims were no different from his. All ministers agreed on the importance of bringing the Transvaal to heel in order to uphold British supremacy. Where Milner and his political masters disagreed was over tactics – Milner wanted to rush in, but the ministers had to be sensitive to the reactions of public opinion; Salisbury was concerned to get the boards clear of other troubles first.

Source: B. Porter, *The Lion's Share: A Short History of British Imperialism 1850–1970*, Longman, 1975.

(a) Using information from Section 17.3(a) and the sources, explain the following words in the sources:

  (i) ultimatum (sources A and F); (2 marks)

  (ii) *uitlander* franchise (source F). (3 marks)

(b) What evidence do Sources A,B,C and F provide about Joseph Chamberlain's political aims and methods? (7 marks)

(c) 'We are now at war because Kruger ... has placed British subjects in the Transvaal in a position of distinct inferiority' (Source A). Using information from Section 17.3 and the evidence of the sources, explain how far you think this is an adequate analysis of the causes of the Boer War. (18 marks)

(Total 30 marks)

2 To what extent did the British government abandon 'splendid isolation' in the period 1895 to 1905 through fear of Germany?

The Dominions: Canada, Australia and New Zealand before 1914

Summary of events

At the 1907 Colonial Conference it was decided to use the word *'dominion'* instead of 'colony' to describe all the parts of the British Empire which were self-governing – Canada, Australia, New Zealand, Newfoundland and South Africa (from 1909). In the early days of overseas settlement, the theory was that colonies existed simply for the benefit of the mother country. After Britain lost her American colonies in the American War of Independence (1775–83), the idea gradually became accepted that colonies with predominantly European and British populations would eventually be allowed to rule themselves. *Lord Durham's Report on the Affairs of British North America (1839)* played a vitally important part in persuading the British government that this was the only way to hold the Empire together.

Canada, Australia and New Zealand passed through similar stages of development:

1 Direct rule by a Governor with a council chosen by himself.
2 Representative government – an elected council which could advise the Governor but had no real power itself.
3 Responsible government – an elected assembly which had the power to appoint and dismiss ministers and control internal affairs.
4 Federal government – the separate colonies or provinces united in a federation, keeping their own separate parliaments, but also joining in a central, federal parliament.

Canada achieved independent federal dominion status in 1867 and Australia in 1901. New Zealand became a federal self-governing state in 1856, and then in 1876 decided to abandon the federal system in favour of a single parliament at Wellington. South Africa had a rather different and more troubled history, which eventually resulted in the Union of South Africa in 1910 (see Sections 17.3 and 21.2(b)).

Dominion status was rather a vague term, since it had never been precisely stated how much control the British government had in the last resort over the dominion governments. In 1926 a definition was produced which seemed to satisfy all concerned: in effect the dominions were completely free from British control, but they retained a link with Britain through the monarchy.

18.1 Canada

(a) *The early settlement of Canada*

Representatives of rival French and British trading companies were the first European settlers in Canada. The French were defeated in the Seven Years' War (1756–63), and by *the Treaty of Paris (1763)* Canada, with its considerable French population, became British.

- *The Quebec Act (1774)* was designed in part to placate the French settlers. Canada (still called Quebec at this point) was to be ruled by a British governor who would choose a council of up to 23 members to advise him. There was no elected parliament. French civil law was recognized, but English criminal law was introduced. The French Roman Catholics were given freedom of worship. At this time, the Maritime Provinces of modern Canada – Nova Scotia, Prince Edward Island, Newfoundland and New Brunswick (founded 1784) – were treated as separate colonies.
- *Pitt's Canada Act (1791)* arose from the changing situation brought about by the American War of Independence (1775–83). Many Americans, wanting to remain loyal to Britain, left the USA and moved into Canada. Known as *United Empire Loyalists*, some stayed on the coast in New Brunswick, while others travelled inland and settled along the northern shores of Lake Ontario. At the same time immigrants were flocking in from Britain, especially from Scotland and Ireland. With the influx of English-speaking settlers, Quebec began to split into a French-speaking east and an English-speaking west. Pitt's Act therefore recognized this by dividing Quebec into two provinces:

1   *Upper Canada* (Ontario) for the British
2   *Lower Canada* (Quebec) which was overwhelmingly French.

Each had its own Lieutenant-Governor with an elected assembly which could advise the Lieutenant-Governor and his nominated council, but had no legislative powers and could not dismiss the Lieutenant-Governor. There was also a joint governor for both provinces together. Canada had secured representative government, but there was over half a century to wait before responsible government was achieved.

(b) *Unrest and the rebellions of 1837*

During the Napoleonic Wars the USA fought against Britain (1812–14). American forces attacked Canada and burnt down the Upper Canada Assembly building in York (later called Toronto). The Canadians and British retaliated by setting fire to the American presidential residence in Washington. Gradually, however, both Upper and Lower Canada became impatient with British rule for a variety of reasons:

- In British Upper Canada there was still a feeling that the Lieutenant-Governor and his advisory council gave preferential treatment in matters such as allocation of land and in civil service and political appointments, to United Empire Loyalists and their families. Another grievance was that large areas of land – known as clergy reserves – were controlled by the Church of England.
- In French Lower Canada the elected assembly was naturally predominantly French, but the Lieutenant-Governor and his advisory council, who had the final say in politics, were British. The French became more suspicious of British motives in 1833 when a new company, calling itself the British American Land Company, began to sell land to British non-Catholic immigrants.

Map 18.1 Canada before 1914

- There was a demand in some quarters, particularly among commercial interests, for a union of the two provinces, since it was felt that the existence of two separate customs systems was hampering the smooth flow of trade along the St Lawrence River.
- During the 1830s the major issue in both provinces was the demand for responsible government, so that the elected assemblies could enforce their will over the Lieutenant-Governors. In 1834 Lord Grey's Whig government sent out a commission of enquiry, but when it became clear that it was not prepared to recommend any major concessions, extremists in both provinces could restrain themselves no longer.

In 1837 there were two separate rebellions. The one in Lower Canada was led by Louis Papineau, a French-Canadian member of the assembly. The one in Upper Canada was organized by a Scottish-Canadian journalist, William Lyon Mackenzie. Both were easily suppressed, but they acted as a warning to the British government that they must treat Canadian grievances seriously.

(c) *Lord Durham and the Canada Act (1840)*

Melbourne decided to send out Lord Durham, the leading Radical Whig, to investigate and report on the situation. Durham, who took with him as adviser his imperialist friend, Edward Gibbon Wakefield, had vague ideas about a federation of *all* the Canadian colonies, but was disappointed to find that the maritime colonies were very cool towards the idea. He was only in Canada from May until November 1838, when he was recalled because his dictatorial attitude made him unpopular; but it was long enough for him to size up the situation.

Lord Durham's Report, published in 1839, was an important document, often regarded as setting the guidelines not just for Canada, but for the whole of the Commonwealth. He believed that representative government was not enough to keep the colonists happy and loyal; they would have to be given responsible government, otherwise there was likely to be a Canadian War of Independence. He suggested that the two Canadas should be reunited, in the mistaken hope that the French Canadians would eventually be absorbed into the language and culture of the British population, so making a completely united people. There should be one Governor with his advisory councils, and an elected assembly which would control internal affairs, defence and foreign policy. This last proposal was too radical for Lord Melbourne, but most of Durham's other suggestions were carried out in *the Canada Act of 1840*:

- Upper and Lower Canada were united under a Governor-General;
- He was to have an advisory council whose members were nominated for life;
- There was to be an elected House of Assembly containing equal numbers of members from each province.

This was a disappointment for supporters of responsible government, since the Assembly still had very little power. However, Lord Elgin, who became Governor-General in 1847, was a liberal Scotsman (and Durham's son-in-law). He came to an agreement with the parties in the Assembly, that provided they maintained the connection with Britain, he would accept laws proposed by them. In effect therefore, Canada had responsible government. At about the same time Nova Scotia, New Brunswick and Newfoundland were also given responsible government.

(d) *Canada's relations with the USA*

Since the birth of the hostile USA, Canadians had been worried about the threat to their largely undefended frontiers. The events of 1812–14 had shown that their fears were justified and it seemed that the Americans were trying to outdo the Canadians at every opportunity. The Canadians retaliated effectively:

- In 1825 the Americans opened the Erie Canal joining Lake Erie to the Hudson River, and threatening to take trade away from the St Lawrence. The Canadians retaliated by building the Welland Canal joining Lakes Erie and Ontario. This proved to be a great success, but commercial rivalry continued.
- A dispute about the frontier between Canada and Maine was settled by *the Ashburton Treaty (1842)*. Called after the British negotiator who worked it out with the Americans, the treaty was unpopular with Canadians who felt it had given too much away.
- More popular was *the Oregon Treaty (1846)* which solved a dispute about possession of the Pacific coast. The Americans claimed the whole of the coastline right up to Alaska (owned by Russia until 1867 when it was bought by the USA for $7 million) which would shut Canada out completely from the Pacific. There was considerable tension between Britain and the USA, whose extremists wanted war. President Polk gave way and the treaty fixed the boundary to Canada's advantage along the 49th parallel, with a detour so that the whole of Vancouver Island could be included in Canada.

(e) *The move towards federation and the Dominion of Canada (1867)*

In the early 1850s the idea of a federation of all the Canadian colonies began to be widely discussed. There were different motives:

- Time showed that Lord Durham had been wrong in thinking that the French Canadians would be assimilated into their British surroundings. In fact they became more determined to preserve their French customs and language, and more worried as English-speaking immigrants continued to flood in. When gold was discovered in the Fraser River canyon in the far west in 1858, there was the prospect of thousands more flocking into the west, tipping the balance even more heavily against the French. In 1830 the English-speaking population of Upper Canada totalled only half the population of French Lower Canada; by 1861, because of massive immigration, there had been a dramatic turnaround – there were now 1.4 million people in Upper Canada and 1.1 million in Lower Canada. The Upper Canadians were protesting that they ought to have more MPs than the Lower Canadians. The French Canadians decided that a federal system might be the best way of saving themselves from being submerged: Upper and Lower Canada could be separated again and they would at least have their own assembly for internal affairs.
- All the colonies realized the need for a railway to link Halifax (Nova Scotia) with Quebec. This intercolonial scheme received very little support from London and the separate colonies seemed unable to agree on a joint policy. The idea spread that only if British North America became united would the railway be built.
- The colonies had economic problems. As Britain moved towards complete free trade, Canada lost its preferential rates for timber exported to Britain. The American Civil War (1861–5) adversely affected Canada's trade. The Canadians realized that the only way to survive was by closer co-operation between the provinces.
- The American Civil War gave a decisive impetus to federation in another way. The Northern States and Britain were close to war, and British troops shipped out to Halifax had to travel by sleigh through New Brunswick to Quebec. This convinced the British government that a united defence and an inter-colonial railway were needed.

The Canadians began discussions at the Quebec Conference (1864). This broke up without agreement, but the matter became urgent in 1866 when the Fenians (see Section 13.3(a)) attacked from the USA and captured Fort Erie in Upper Canada. British troops were able to drive them back, but the constant threat from the USA convinced all the colonies that unity was essential. Talks were resumed and the Canadians produced their own plan which the British government accepted in *the British North America Act of 1867.*

Upper and Lower Canada were separated again and became the provinces of Ontario and Quebec; they joined New Brunswick and Nova Scotia to form the Dominion of Canada. It was understood that other provinces would join later as they became more populated and developed. Manitoba joined in 1870, British Columbia in 1871, Prince Edward Island in 1873, and Alberta and Saskatchewan in 1905. The last to join was Newfoundland (1949) which had been a dominion in its own right. Each province had its own parliament (which pleased the French in Quebec) which had certain specific powers over local affairs. There was a federal parliament containing representatives from all the provinces, which was to sit at Ottawa, the new Canadian capital; this controlled matters such as defence, taxation and overseas trade. The Act also contained provision for the long needed railway to link all the provinces. The word *dominion* was chosen to solve the problem of what title to give the new confederation. 'Kingdom' of Canada offended many people, so Samuel Tilley of New Brunswick suggested a text from Psalm 72: 'He shall have dominion also from sea to sea'. Thus the Dominion of Canada came into existence.

(f) *Important developments since 1867*

• The first Prime Minister of Canada was Sir John A. Macdonald who had played a leading part in drawing up the details of the 1867 Act. He went on to point the new state towards successful development, the first step in which was the completion of the Intercolonial Railway from the St Lawrence to Halifax in 1876.

• After initial problems, Macdonald was able to promote the building of the Canadian Pacific Railway linking Montreal with Vancouver on the Pacific coast. When this was completed in 1885, it enabled more and more pioneer farmers to move out west and made possible the vast expansion of wheat farming.

• There was one unpleasant episode in 1885. The Federal Government had in 1869 bought up the territory of the Hudson's Bay Company which had been trading in furs for the past 200 years. These huge Northern Territories came under Federal control, but the government had been surprised when Louis Riel, a French Indian, led a rebellion of buffalo hunters who farmed along the banks of the Red River. Macdonald agreed that their settlements should become the province of Manitoba, and calm was restored. However, in 1885 Riel appeared again, leading a rebellion along the Saskatchewan River. This was quickly suppressed by troops rushed from the east along the new railway. Macdonald made himself unpopular by having Riel hanged, which reawakened much of the resentment between French and British, and helped to keep alive Quebec nationalism which has survived until the present day.

• Macdonald encouraged the development of Canadian industries by introducing high protective tariffs against American goods, though British goods were given preference.

• The link with Britain remained strong. During the Boer War Canada unhesitatingly sent troops to help the British, while during the First World War no fewer than 650 000 Canadian troops played an important role in the eventual defeat of the Central Powers.

18.2 Australia

(a) *New South Wales: the first Australian colony*

The first European settlers, 750 convicts, arrived at Botany Bay in 1788, under the command of Captain Arthur Phillip. Australia was already peopled by the native Aborigines, whose ancestors are thought to have reached the country from Java or South East Asia some 40 000 years ago. It was estimated that in 1788 there were between 300 000 and a million Aborigines living in Australia, but the discovery of a huge burial site in New South Wales in 1994 has led archaeologists to revise that figure upwards to something like three million.

The first European settlement was at Port Jackson and soon afterwards Sydney was founded. The first free settlers arrived in 1793, but the early years were violent ones: the convicts had to be kept in order by troops, and floggings and executions were common. Under pressure from the free settlers, the British government stopped the transportation of convicts to New South Wales in 1840, though the penal settlements remained open until 1866 when the last convicts finished their sentences. Convicts continued to be sent to Western Australia until 1868.

Sheep farming was the vital factor in the early prosperity of New South Wales and of the other colonies as well. The Spanish merino sheep had been introduced from South Africa in 1796 by Captain John Macarthur. At first sheep farmers stayed in the coastal area, but in 1813 an expedition led by William Lawson, Gregory Blaxland and W. C. Wentworth crossed the Blue Mountains and discovered the rich pastureland of the Bathurst plains. A rapid expansion of sheep farming followed and by 1850 Australia, producing high quality wool, was the world's largest wool exporter. The British woollen industry came to rely heavily on supplies from Australia.

Gold became the other mainstay of Australian prosperity. It was first discovered at Bathurst in New South Wales in 1851, and soon afterwards at Ballarat and Bendigo in Victoria, which had separated from New South Wales the previous year. It was in Victoria that the largest deposits were found.

(b) *The other Australian colonies*

Explorers began to move into the interior and around the coasts. Midshipman Samuel Flinders and Surgeon George Bass sailed round Van Diemen's Land (later called Tasmania) in 1798, and by 1803 Flinders had sailed all the way round Australia, mapping the entire coastline.

- *Tasmania* was the second colony to be founded, taken by the British in 1803 to prevent the French claiming it. Hobart was the capital, but in the early days it was used as a penal settlement for the worst type of convicts. The free settlers distinguished themselves by their brutal treatment of the Aborigines who were eventually placed on Flinders Island in the Bass Straits. By 1869 all the Aborigines of Tasmania had died.
- *Victoria* began as a sheep-rearing settlement around the village founded in 1835 and known as Melbourne after the British Prime Minister. Development was rapid: by 1850 there were 77 000 settlers and five million sheep in Victoria, and in that year it was recognized as a separate colony. When gold was discovered the following year, there was a frantic rush of immigrants both from the other colonies and from Britain. 19 000 people arrived in Melbourne in one month – September 1852, while the total for the year was around 84 000. There were enormous problems of administration and law and order, but eventually the industry settled down and the mining was taken in hand by large companies.

Map 18.2 Australia and New Zealand before 1914

- *South Australia* was the other important colony (see below). *Queensland* was first used in 1824 as another dumping-ground for convicts; it became a separate colony in 1859 though its population was only 25 000. The first settlers arrived at Perth in *Western Australia* in 1829, but development was slow and difficult because of the way the land was distributed. The government sold it at less than a shilling (5p) an acre, so colonists bought far more than they needed and lacked sufficient labour to work the land. They even petitioned the government to send them convicts who could work as labourers. The government gratefully obliged, sending 10 000 between 1850 and 1868. Another boost to the colony's development was the discovery of gold at Coolgardie (1892) and Kalgoorlie (1894).

(c) *Edward Gibbon Wakefield and South Australia*

Edward Gibbon Wakefield came from a Quaker and Radical background, his father having been a close friend of Bentham and Place. The young Wakefield was wild and undisciplined. He eloped with one rich heiress and later kidnapped another who happened to be under age; this earned him three years in Newgate Prison, London. Here he had plenty of time to ponder about the plight of criminals and convicts, particularly those in Australian penal settlements. He developed a theory about how overseas colonization should be organized; this was explained in his *Letter from Sydney* written in 1829 while he was still in prison.

The idea was that if emigration was properly organized by the government, *it could be the perfect solution for unemployment and poverty in Britain.* As things were at present in Australia, he believed it was too easy to get land and too difficult to find labourers to cultivate it. The government should therefore sell land at a 'sufficient price', which would be high enough to ensure that only responsible people acquired it and acquired only a workable area. The money raised would be used to pay the passages of more immigrants who would have to work as labourers until they had saved enough money to buy farms for themselves. The purchase money could then be used to bring out more immigrants, so that the balance between the demand for and supply of labour would always be kept. Convicts would no longer be needed.

- In 1830, as soon as he emerged from prison, Wakefield started a *Colonial Society*, and almost immediately many of his ideas were adopted in the existing colonies. Between 1832 and 1842, 7000 free settlers arrived in New South Wales; since land was priced at five shillings (25p) an acre, and by 1842 at £1 an acre, most of the new arrivals had to do their stint as labourers to begin with. Transportation of convicts was duly stopped in 1840. This was in marked contrast to what happened in Western Australia where land was sold too cheaply (see above).
- Wakefield, wanting to found a colony of his own, started *the South Australia Association (1834)* and persuaded the government to agree to the setting up of South Australia. The first settlers arrived in 1836 and work began on the capital, Adelaide (named after William IV's Queen). Land was offered at 12 shillings (60p) an acre. Soon, however, the problems of starting a new colony from scratch under Wakefield's system became apparent. The government allowed no cash; this was expected to materialize from land sales and loans. Twelve shillings an acre proved to be too expensive to attract enough buyers, but not enough to raise sufficient cash. And a great deal of cash was needed, since there was a complete lack of facilities and not even a reasonable harbour. Wakefield quarrelled violently with the other members of the governing body – he wanted to raise the price of land to 72 shillings an acre, but they rightly felt this was unrealistic. He withdrew from the whole project and started a New Zealand Association instead.

South Australia was saved from disaster when G. F. Angas floated a company which raised £320 000, enough to provide most of the vital facilities. Progress was slow even then, but by 1850 the colony was well and truly launched. It had a population of 63 000 with around a million sheep and 60 000 cattle. The land proved to be fertile enough for wheat growing, so that the new colony developed into the granary of Australia. The discovery of copper in 1846 brought an added boost to the economy and in 1850 total exports were valued at £570 000. The success of South Australia had little to do with Wakefield, but at least his was the inspiration that founded it.

(d) *Political developments: the move towards a united Australia (1901)*

The colonies moved towards responsible government without the agitations and disturbances which characterized Canada. New South Wales became a Crown colony in 1826 under a Governor-General who nominated his own advisory council. In 1842 it was allowed that two-thirds of the members of the council could be elected. The other colonies followed a similar pattern until in 1855 responsible elected assemblies – with the power to decide policies – were granted in New South Wales, Victoria, Tasmania and South Australia. Responsible government came to Queensland in 1859 and to Western Australia in 1890.

For many years there was little interest in federation. The six colonies had developed separately and communications between them were so poor that any sort of union seemed impractical, at least until after 1870. It was only after 1890 that federation began to be discussed seriously. The reasons were:

- *External threats began to worry many Australians.* Both Germany and Japan had ambitions in the Pacific. After 1890 the Germans began to follow an aggressive policy of expansion wherever possible, and the Japanese showed their potential by defeating the Chinese decisively in 1894. A strong and united defence was essential to dissuade any foreign ambitions of expansion into Australia.
- *The early 1890s were a time of economic difficulty* culminating in the crisis of 1893. In fact South Australia had been in difficulties since around 1880 because of drought and plagues of rabbits which ruined the wheat harvests. In 1886 a sudden fall in world wool prices threw many farmers into debt in all the colonies. Though Australia had experienced an industrial revolution after 1850, much of the new industry was inefficient and in 1890 a depression set in, bringing widespread unemployment. In 1893 the crisis worked its way through to the banks as people rushed to withdraw deposits. Panic followed, and of the 32 major banks in Australia, 22 had to suspend payments. Although prosperity gradually returned, the crisis had been a profound shock for the Australians and was probably the main stimulus to the federation movement. Union would remove the troublesome customs barriers between the states; the increased confidence would enable Australians to borrow from abroad. Improved communications made the idea feasible: Melbourne and Sydney were linked by rail in 1883, Melbourne and Adelaide in 1887 and Sydney and Brisbane (Queensland) in 1889.

The Commonwealth of Australia Act passed the British parliament in 1900 and came into operation on 1 January 1901. The Federal parliament was to control defence, foreign policy and treaties, trade and customs duties, postal services, marriage and divorce, banking and currency and immigration. Everything not specifically mentioned in the list, was left to the state parliaments. These had more power than their counterparts in Canada, controlling social services, health, education, labour and industry, agriculture, mines, police, rivers and railways. To avoid inter-state jealousies, a new federal capital was to be built at Canberra, between Sydney and Melbourne.

(e) *The Dominion or Commonwealth of Australia*

The new state did not become prosperous overnight, but by 1914 the policies of the Federal government had stabilized the economy and the depression had disappeared. Important measures of the Federal parliament were:

- *The Immigration Restriction Act (1901)* in effect allowed only whites to enter the country. This was because Australians were afraid that Asian and Pacific labourers would work for very low wages, forcing down wages paid to white Australians. There was also the fear that the whites would be swamped if unrestricted immigration was allowed from such countries as Japan and India.
- *An Arbitration Court was introduced (1904)* to fix 'fair and reasonable' wages and to mediate in industrial disputes. The novelty of this was that the court's decisions were binding on all parties.
- Old age pensions (1908), invalid pensions (1911) and maternity allowances (1912) were introduced.
- In defence matters, conscription was introduced (1911) and the first ships of the Australian navy were launched in 1913. Australia played an important part in the First World War, sending over 300 000 troops to Europe.

18.3 New Zealand

(a) *Early colonization*

When the first Europeans arrived, New Zealand was already inhabited by the Maoris, a Polynesian race with light brown skins. Captain James Cook had mapped both the North and South Islands in 1769, and had claimed them for Britain. The British government had ignored their existence and there was no large-scale attempt to colonize New Zealand until well into the nineteenth century. The only European settlers were missionaries – the first of whom arrived in 1814 – trying to convert the Maoris, and there were some whalers and escaped convicts.

Edward Gibbon Wakefield was responsible for the first organized settlement. After he had washed his hands of the South Australia project, he formed *the New Zealand Association (1837)* which, the following year, was allowed by the British government to become a chartered company. The first expedition of 1200 people arrived and four settlements were started – Wellington, Wanganui and New Plymouth on North Island and Nelson on South Island. The British government announced that it had annexed the colony, just in time to forestall a French colonizing party which was off the coast.

The first Governor, William Hobson, signed *the Treaty of Waitangi (1840) with the Maoris of North Island*. It was agreed that:

- the Maoris would regard Victoria as their queen;
- in return the British guaranteed the Maoris in the possession of their land;
- the British government would buy any Maori land offered for sale, provided the whole tribe agreed. This was designed to prevent settlers acquiring land cheaply from individual Maoris.

Unfortunately many settlers and officials of the company broke the treaty and simply evicted Maoris from their lands. The Maori tribes retaliated and there was some spasmodic fighting sometimes referred to as the *First Maori War (1842–6)*. By 1845 the new colony was not a success: the Maoris were hostile, the settlements were not expanding and exports were non-existent.

(b) The New Zealand Federation (1852)

Sir George Grey became Governor of New Zealand in 1845, and immediately matters took a turn for the better. Aged only 33, he had already made a reputation as a successful governor of South Australia. He quickly subdued the Maoris, mainly by a show of military strength, but then showed great sympathy and understanding and made a study of Maori language and literature. He stopped the private sale of land and negotiated the purchase of almost the whole of South Island, where there were only about 2000 Maoris. He developed a close friendship with many of the chiefs and spent money on schools, hospitals, law-courts and agricultural advice. The farmers began to prosper as exports of foodstuffs and livestock to Australia increased in the early 1850s because of the rush to the Australian goldfields.

As the numbers of settlers increased, they began to campaign for self-government, though Grey wanted to postpone it until the land and Maori problems had been settled completely. The first major step was taken in 1852, while Grey was still Governor: *The New Zealand Federation was established by an Act of the British parliament.* The six main settlements – Auckland, New Plymouth (later called Taranaki), and Wellington in North Island, and Nelson, Canterbury and Otago in South Island – were given their own elected councils, and there was a central federal assembly. Although this was representative government, it was not yet responsible government, since in the last resort the Governor was still in charge. Grey ended his first period as Governor in 1853, and the British parliament agreed that the New Zealanders could have full responsible self-government in 1856.

(c) Relations with the Maoris deteriorate again

- There was a great influx of new settlers after self-government was achieved. In 1856 there were still no more than 60 000 Europeans in New Zealand, but the number soared to 350 000 by 1878. There was tremendous pressure for land, causing settlements to spread from the coastal towns into the interior of North Island where the Maoris had previously been left undisturbed. Now they gathered themselves for the final desperate defence of their lands, and the *Second Maori War (1860–71)* broke out.
- The Maoris fought bravely, but against the superior military strength of the Europeans there was no chance of a Maori victory. Grey was recalled for a second term as Governor (1861–8), and though he did his best to bring peace, he had very little power since the introduction of self-government. However, he managed some concessions: the Maoris were allowed to have at least four representatives in the federal assembly (1867) and an agreement was reached which allowed them to live undisturbed in an area amounting to about one-third the size of North Island. Fighting gradually fizzled out, but the fact remained that the Maoris had been deprived of much of their most fertile land, sometimes by purchase, but more often by straightforward confiscation.

(d) The united New Zealand (1876)

In the early 1870s a group of leading politicians, including Julius Vogel of Otago, became convinced that the provincial assemblies were largely inefficient and lacking in vision, and that government could be carried on more effectively without them. An Act to abolish them passed the federal legislature and came into operation in 1876. There was to be a single parliament in Wellington.

Economically New Zealand went through a difficult period until the mid-1890s. Then prices of foodstuffs and wool began to recover and farmers enjoyed a period of great prosperity, lasting right through the First World War. The development of refrigerator ships enabled them to export lamb to Britain.

The Liberal governments of Richard John Seddon (1893–1906) introduced some remarkable reforms: votes for women (1893), old age pensions, cheap loans to farmers, improved working conditions and a system of compulsory arbitration of industrial disputes (the first country in the world to have such a system).

During the First World War a remarkably high proportion of New Zealand's population served in the armed forces. About 100 000 men served overseas, and many distinguished themselves, and lost their lives, in the Gallipoli Campaign of 1915 (see Section 22.1(d)).

Questions

1 Lord Durham and the development of Canada

Study the extract from Lord Durham's *Report on the Affairs of British North America (1839)* and then answer the questions which follow:

> Throughout the whole of the North American Provinces there prevails among the British population affection for the Mother Country which a wise policy on the part of the Imperial government may make the foundation of a safe and enduring connexion. But I must warn that a blind reliance on the all-enduring loyalty of our countrymen may be carried too far. It is not wise to waste and cramp their resources and to allow the backwardness of the British provinces to present a melancholy contrast to the progress and prosperity of the United States ...
>
> The influence of the USA surrounds him on every side and is for ever present. It stamps, on all the habits and opinions of the surrounding countries, the thoughts, feelings and customs of the American people. ... The system which I propose would place the internal government of the colony in the hands of the colonists themselves. I know of no respect in which it is desirable that we should interfere with their internal legislation in matters which do not affect their relations with the Mother Country. The matters which concern us are very few – regulation of foreign relations, trade with the Mother Country, other British colonies and foreign nations ... are the only points on which the Mother Country requires a control.

Source: quoted in D. Holman, *Portraits and Documents – Earlier Nineteenth Century 1783–1867*, Hutchinson, 1965.

(a) Using the extract and your own knowledge, explain the circumstances which had caused Lord Durham to write this report. (10 marks)

(b) To what extent were Durham's recommendations carried out in the Canada Act of 1840? (8 marks)

(c) Why did the provinces of Canada become a federation in 1867, and how successfully did the Dominion of Canada develop up to 1914? (12 marks)

(Total 30 marks)

2 New South Wales was the first Australian colony to be founded, in 1788; it was followed by Tasmania (1803), Western Australia (1829), South Australia (1836), Victoria (1850) and Queensland (1859).

(a) Show how sheep-farming and gold-mining were important in the early development of the Australian colonies. (6 marks)

(b) How important was the work and influence of Edward Gibbon Wakefield in the development of Australia? (5 marks)

(c) What problems delayed the development of Western Australia, and how were similar difficulties avoided in New South Wales? (4 marks)

(d) Why, during the 1890s, did the six colonies begin to think about joining together, and what arrangements were made by the Commonwealth of Australia Act of 1900? (10 marks)

(Total 25 marks)

The growth of the trade unions and the Labour party to 1914

Summary of events

Between 1799 and 1824 the *Anti-Combination Laws* made trade unions (and employers' associations) illegal. Although they were given legal recognition in 1824 (see Section 2.6(b)), their powers were more or less non-existent. Between 1829 and 1834 various attempts were made to form national unions, culminating in *Robert Owen's Grand National Consolidated Trades Union of 1834*. All the attempts failed, and it was to be the last quarter of the century before there were any serious efforts to form unions for the lowest paid workers.

In the 1850s associations known as *'New Model' trade unions* were successfully founded for skilled workers. The first was *the Amalgamated Society of Engineers (1851)*. After a long campaign, the Trade Union Act of 1871 granted legal protection for union funds and in 1875 peaceful picketing was allowed.

As Britain moved into depression during the late 1870s, the low-paid workers were driven to form trade unions. These so-called *'New Unions'*, unlike the Model Unions, contained some socialists, although just how great the differences were between the two types of union has been the subject of some debate among historians. The first major triumph of the New Unionism was the successful *dockers' strike of 1889*. From 1900 to 1913 the unions were involved in legal wrangles – *the Taff Vale case (1900) and the Osborne Judgement (1909)* – with the courts and the House of Lords. Both were eventually resolved in a way satisfactory to the unions, but for a number of reasons there was considerable bitterness in labour relations, resulting in a wave of strikes in the years 1910 to 1913.

During the 1890s the Labour party began to develop; in 1900 representatives of several socialist groups and of some trade unions, came together to form *the Labour Representation Committee*, which is usually taken as the beginning of the Labour party. Working closely with the trade unions, Labour won 29 seats in the general election of 1906, and 42 seats in 1910.

19.1 Early trade union developments and failures

(a) *Repeal of the Combination Laws*

There had been unions of labourers and workmen for centuries in the form of local trade associations. Towards the end of the eighteenth century, the industrial revolution caused skilled tradesmen to combine together to protect their interests. It was unfortunate that these early combinations happened to coincide with the French Revolution, so in the eyes of the ruling classes, unions were dangerous and revolutionary.

- *The Combination Acts* introduced by Pitt's government in 1799 and 1800 made it illegal for workers to form Combinations 'for obtaining an Advance of Wages ... or for lessening ... their Hours of working'. These Acts remained in operation throughout the wars with France and the period of unrest which followed after 1815.
- A campaign for the repeal of the Acts, led by Francis Place and Joseph Hume, was eventually successful in 1824 (see Section 2.6(b)), but so great was the resulting crop of new unions and strikes that the government immediately introduced an *Amending Act (1825)*: trade unions could exist to negotiate about wages and hours of work, but were forbidden to obstruct or intimidate. Although some progress had been made, it was still almost impossible to hold a strike without breaking the law.

(b) *The attempt to form nationwide unions (1829–33)*

The year 1825 saw the beginning of a trade depression which made it difficult for trade unions to have any impact. There were many attempts at local strikes, usually in protest at wage reductions, but employers broke them by bringing workers (blacklegs) in from nearby areas. The idea therefore grew that, instead of having separate local unions, it was essential to form nationwide unions of all the workers in a particular trade. Only in this way could the interests of the workers in that trade be protected. Beyond that, some leaders were already thinking in terms of uniting these national unions into a single national union for all trades.

- *The National Union of Cotton Spinners (1829)* was the first effective national union in a single trade. Founded by John Doherty in Manchester, it soon gained massive support, encouraging Doherty to go one step further and set up a *National Association for the Protection of Labour (1830)*. This attracted the support of 150 trade unions throughouth the North and Midlands, but both unions had died out by 1832 because of cash shortages, a failure to co-ordinate their activities, and an improvement in trade.
- An *Operative Builders' Union* was founded in Manchester (1832), bringing together all the various crafts in the building trade. Headed by a Grand Lodge and publishing its own journal, the new union seemed stronger than Doherty's creations, but it too had faded out by the end of 1834.
- The climax of this phase of trades unionism was the formation of Robert Owen's *Grand National Consolidated Trades Union* in 1834.

19.2 Robert Owen and the Grand National Consolidated Trades Union (GNCTU)

Born in Newtown, Montgomery, in 1771, Robert Owen became one of the most remarkable industrialists and reformers of the nineteenth century. From a modest background – his father was a postmaster – he was apprenticed to a draper in Stamford, and after a spell in London, he became a draper's assistant in Manchester. At the age of 18 he went into partnership with a mechanic to produce the recently introduced spinning machines, and he soon became manager of a large spinning mill of 500 workers. In 1794 he set up his own factory in Manchester where he introduced the spinning of American Sea Island cotton, the first British manufacturer to do so.

(a) *Owen as an enlightened manufacturer*

In 1800 Owen moved to Scotland and became a partner in the New Lanark cotton mills. Before long he had factories of his own where he put into practice his advanced theories, so that the New Lanark mills and community facilities became a showpiece. His ideas were later published in a pamphlet, *A New View of Society*, in 1813.

● He believed that people's characters were a product of their environment; if miserable living and working conditions and grinding poverty drove people to crime, it was wrong to blame them. It was the duty of men with power and influence to improve the environment.
● He turned New Lanark into a vast experiment to prove his theories. He enlarged the factories, making them lighter and more airy, and reduced working hours. All this was in marked contrast to the usual practices. He built new cottages for the workers and a school for the local children where there was an emphasis on outdoor activities – rambling and botany. He had parks and gardens laid out for the workers and introduced a scheme enabling them to buy goods at cost price.
● He believed that capitalists should take only limited profits and that surplus profits should be used on services and facilities for workers – a theory which he certainly put into practice. He astonished his fellow manufacturers by continuing to pay wages when trade was slack and when cotton supplies were cut off during the war with the USA (1812–14). He was a strong supporter of the movement to limit children's working hours and played an important part, along with Sir Robert Peel senior, in securing the 1819 Factory Act, though he was bitterly disappointed with its terms (see Section 12.3(b)). Although this Act was not a success, the effects of Owen's methods at New Lanark were vitally important: he had demonstrated that a manufacturer could still make a reasonable profit, while at the same time reducing working hours and caring for his employees instead of exploiting them.

(b) Owen and the Co-operative movement

Although his ideas were arousing a great deal of interest and attracting supporters and followers, Owen was disappointed at the lack of response from government and from other industrialists. Consequently he carried his logic further, influenced by a theory of David Ricardo, a leading economist of the time. Ricardo argued that the value of a manufactured article depended entirely on the amount of labour put into it, and that workers were therefore not receiving a just reward for their labours. If Ricardo was right, then capitalists were not necessary; society should be reorganized to rid it of landowners and capitalists. *Co-operative communities of workmen*, jointly owning the means of production, would produce the goods and fix prices according to the relative quantity of labour in each product. Sometimes they might exchange their products for the goods they wanted. He thought up a scheme for co-operative villages laid out in quadrangles, some producing food, others manufacturing goods. Oddly enough, Owen did not see this scheme as an attack on the rich, and he disapproved of strikes and violence to achieve it. Like the later Fabians (see Section 19.8(b)), he tried to appeal to the employers' better nature; he hoped that as they realized the attractions of this new 'socialism', they would voluntarily give up their property and join in the experiment.

● As a preliminary experiment, a 'Labour Exchange' was set up in Gray's Inn Road, London, for the exchange of goods. Workers brought their products and received certificates stating how much each article was worth in hours' work. The certificates entitled them to other goods of equivalent value. This was not a success, mainly because there proved to be too much of some items and not enough of others – particularly food; the experiment was abandoned in 1834.

● He started the London Co-operative Society (1824) which opened several co-operative shops. These had only limited success but the idea was taken up with spectacular results by the Rochdale Pioneers in 1844 (see Section 19.2(d)).

● Owen himself went to the USA in 1824 to set up an experimental co-operative village at New Harmony in Indiana, but this collapsed in 1828 and he returned to Britain.

(c) *Owen and the trades unions*

When he arrived back in Britain Owen found that his co-operative ideas had great appeal among workers, and some union leaders were attempting to put them into practice. In 1833 the Derby silk-throwers declared that the factories which they worked were now co-operatives; the employers, not sharing Owen's enthusiasm, announced that they would not employ any labourer who was a member of a trade union, and proceeded to lock out their workers. Union leaders looked to Owen for guidance; his response was to set up *the Grand National Consolidated Trades Union* towards the end of 1833. All existing trade unions were invited to join, and within a few weeks it had attracted over half a million members. On paper it had an impressive organization; in every district there was to be a branch of each separate trade together with a joint branch linking the different trades. In central control was a Grand Council meeting twice a year. Members were to pay a shilling a year, and co-operative workshops were to be set up. Schools, recreational facilities and other services would be provided on the New Lanark model. When these were established, the next step, as Owen himself explained, would be 'the union of master traders and manufacturers with the operatives and manual producers'. Finally 'the Government will not only feel the necessity of uniting with them, but it will also discover the advantages to the whole empire of this national bond of union'. What Owen was aiming for was a complete reorganization of society in which workers' control replaced private ownership and in which ultimately, the GNCTU would control the government. He hoped it could be achieved voluntarily and without violence. If not, there would have to be a general strike, or 'sacred month' as it was called. However, the problems were enormous, and by August 1834 the GNCTU had more or less collapsed. *Reasons for its failure*:

● Four of the most important unions – builders, potters, spinners and clothiers – decided not to join; they were apparently afraid of losing their separate identities. In fact skilled workers tended to remain aloof.

● There were problems of communication between one district and another; it was impossible to make sure that all branches knew what action they were supposed to be taking, and to discipline branches which failed to co-operate.

● There were disagreements between different trades and branches, some wanting immediate strikes, others wanting to wait until a nation-wide general strike could be organized. Some leaders merely wanted to improve conditions, others wanted a revolution.

● Employers everywhere reacted with hostility. The Derby silk-throwers were soon defeated and so were the London tailors and the Leeds clothiers. Some employers insisted on their workers signing a statement known as 'The Document', swearing that they were not members of the GNCTU. Anybody refusing to sign it was sacked.

● Probably most important was that the Whig government, alarmed at the wave of rick-burning and machine-breaking in the southern counties, decided to support local magistrates who dealt harshly with trade unionists. The most famous example occurred at the village of Tolpuddle in Dorset, where there was a branch of the Friendly Union of Agricultural Workers. Although there had been no violence or even strike action, the union leader, George Loveless, who was also a Methodist preacher, was arrested and convicted, along with five other men, on a charge of 'administering illegal oaths'. For this, the five *Tolpuddle Martyrs* were sentenced to seven years' transportation to Tasmania (1834). Lord Melbourne, the Home Secretary, upheld the sentence. In the face of such harsh measures by government and employers, trade unionists became discouraged, and although many individual unions survived, the GNCTU collapsed.

Owen himself and his group of supporters continued to publicize his ideas. Calling themselves socialists (what *they* meant by the word were people who believed that capital and land should not be held in private hands) they founded the co-operative settlement of Queenwood (East Tytherly) in Hampshire (1839) which survived until the mid-1840s. Although none of Owen's ideas had much success outside New Lanark, he was important because he was the first person to publicize socialism.

The immediate results of the failure of the GNCTU were to turn workers towards Chartism and the Anti-Corn Law League. One of Owen's ideas which *was* taken up seriously later was the co-operative shops experiment.

(d) *The Rochdale Pioneers and the Co-operative movement*

In 1884 two Rochdale weavers, G.J.Holyoake and Charles Howarth, persuaded five fellow-weavers to join them in setting up a co-operative store. It was partly an act of self-help and a defence against the ineffectiveness of the 1820 Truck Act (see Section 2.4(c)). They pooled their savings, bought their goods in the usual markets like any other shopkeeper, and sold them at normal retail prices. The difference was that most of the profits, instead of remaining in the hands of a single shopkeeper, were shared out among the people who had bought at their shop, in proportion to their purchases. By the end of 1844 the Pioneers, as they became known, had attracted 28 members who shopped regularly at their store. The following year the store became well established and other co-operative societies began to spring up, so that by 1850 there were over a hundred. In 1863 all the stores joined together to form the *Co-operative Wholesale Society (CWS)*, which bought goods in bulk for sale in the local shops. In 1873 the society began to open its own factories and by 1900, when there were over two million members, it had even bought its own tea plantation in Ceylon.

19.3 Show how the 'New Model' unions were established in the 1850s and how they gained legal recognition

After the collapse of the GNCTU in 1834, the unions went through a difficult period which lasted into the early 1840s; there was a serious trade depression, unemployment and wage reductions. Yet many unions of skilled workers survived, and as the country moved into the prosperity of the 1850s there were new and more successful attempts, mainly by skilled workers, to form large national unions.

(a) *The 'New Model' Unions*

1   In 1851 William Allan and William Newton formed *the Amalgamated Society of Engineers*. Its aim was not to change society, but simply to improve the position of

its members within the capitalist system, by securing better wages and better conditions. They were prepared to negotiate and to co-operate with employers; they were desperately keen to be respectable and looked on strike action as very much a last resort. With 11 000 members each paying the high membership fee of a shilling (5p) a week, it had an income of over £500 a week, and was rich enough to provide unemployment and sickness benefits for its members. It had its own headquarters and paid officials.

2   Other national unions soon followed, deliberately modelling themselves on the ASE, hence the phrase 'New Model' unionism. In 1860 appeared *the Amalgamated Society of Carpenters*, which really became a national organization in 1862 when Robert Applegarth was appointed general secretary at a salary of £1.10s. (£1.50) a week. Much smaller than the ASE to begin with, Applegarth built it up into an effective craft union; in 1870 it had over 10 000 members and 230 branches, and it was financially sound. Other amalgamated societies were the Shoemakers and Tailors, while in the North, the National Union of Miners was revived, and the Union of Lancashire Cotton Operatives was formed to deal with the problem of fixing piece-rates.

3   The secretaries of these unions became powerful men; some of them – Allan, Applegarth, George Odger (Shoemakers) and Daniel Guile (Iron Founders) – used to meet regularly for consultations, and were nicknamed *the Junta* (a word usually used for a group of army officers running a country) by critics who resented their influence. The Junta, who seemed to see their members as a kind of 'labour aristocracy', superior to ordinary unskilled workers, went to great lengths to convince society that their New Model unions were moderate and respectable, and in no way revolutionary. The 1867 Royal Commission Report (see below) was a great help in this respect. Applegarth was particularly successful, winning respect from politicians and the press. The Junta was also responsible for the first *Trades Union Congress (TUC)* which met in 1868; this turned into an annual meeting and soon became a permanent organization, guiding and advising individual member unions and even having contacts with government ministers.

(b) *The unions run into difficulties, 1866–7*

Although it was now accepted that unions had the right to negotiate with employers, there were two areas of trade union activity which had never been specifically settled: one was whether striking and picketing were to be legalized or not; the other was the question of the legality of a trade union's funds. Although the Junta disapproved of strikes on the whole, every union had its firebrands who were eager for action. Many employers were waiting for an excuse to mount an attack on the unions, whether the leaders were moderate or not:

●   The so-called *Sheffield outrages* gave the unions' opponents their opportunity. Union extremists sometimes used crude intimidation to force workers to join or make members pay their dues, and a number of unsavoury incidents occurred in Sheffield. Workers' tools and equipment were smashed, a small workshop was blown up, and in 1866 a can of gunpowder exploded in the house of a workman who had just withdrawn from the local Saw Grinders' Union. The culprit, the union treasurer, was arrested, and it emerged that he had been responsible for a whole string of similar outrages in several other towns. The employers demanded a Royal Commission to enquire into the conduct of trade unions, and the government obliged.

●   A further crisis arose for the unions in 1867 when the Boilermakers' Society sued the treasurer of its Bradford branch who had pocketed £24 of union funds. It was thought that union funds were protected by the 1855 Friendly Society Act, but when the case (known as *Hornby* v. *Close*) came before the Court of Queen's Bench, it was ruled that a trade union was not a Friendly Society, it was an organization 'in restraint of trade', and therefore its funds were not protected.

● The Royal Commission, to the disgust of the employers, came out in grudging support of the unions (1868–9). Applegarth had presented a skilful defence of their activities, emphasizing their disapproval of strikes, and pointing out the financial and social benefits gained by members. The Commission decided that outrages were on the decline and that union funds should be protected by law. This was a major triumph, preparing the way for the complete legalization of trade union activities which came during the 1870s.

(c) *Legal recognition for the unions (1871–6)*

Two considerations probably influenced the governments' thinking:

● Following the Royal Commission Report, unions were widely considered to be 'respectable';
● Many union members had been given the vote by the 1867 Reform Act, and both parties were anxious to win this new working-class vote.

The vital measures were:

1 *Gladstone's Trade Union Act (1871)* recognized unions as legal bodies with the right to strike and to protect their funds at law. However, Gladstone followed this up with *The Criminal Law Amendment Act (1871)* which made picketing illegal (see Section 13.2(d)), so that strikes were impossible to enforce.
2 *Disraeli's Conspiracy and Protection of Property Act (1875)* made peaceful picketing legal, while the *Employers and Workmen Act (1876)* put both employer and worker on an equal footing in cases of breach of contract (see Section 14.2(c) for full details).

19.4 The 'New Unionism' for unskilled workers

(a) *Why did the 'New Unionism' emerge?*

Though trade unions had achieved full legal recognition by 1876, most of them represented skilled workers; the vast majority of unskilled workers were still unorganized and unprotected. During the 1880s an increasing number of semi-skilled and unskilled labourers began to show an interest in forming their own unions. The main reason was the depression of the last quarter of the century: during the serious slumps of 1879 and 1886, it was always the unskilled labourers who were laid off first and who seemed to be exploited most. The spread of education meant that intelligent labourers were literate, and they were perfectly well aware of the advantages that members of the 'Model' unions enjoyed. It was only logical that they should try to follow their example. The spread of the factory system meant that there were greater concentrations of unskilled labour than ever before, which tended to encourage working-class solidarity. Joseph Arch had already formed the *National Agricultural Labourers' Union (1872)* which soon attracted 100 000 members. But when it asked for a wage increase from 13s. to 14s. for a 54-hour week, the farmers in Suffolk reacted decisively, locking out 10 000 labourers. The union went almost bankrupt paying out over £20 000 in strike pay, and the agricultural depression killed it off completely. Eventually, however, the 'New Unionism' had some successes:

- *In 1888 there was a strike of 700 girls working in the Bryant & May match factory in London.* Encouraged by the Fabian socialist, Annie Besant, they were protesting about having to work in an atmosphere full of choking, poisonous phosphorous fumes. Amid great public sympathy, the match girls won their case.
- In 1889 Will Thorne, a stoker at Beckton gasworks, East Ham, formed a *Gasworkers' Union*. When the union demanded an eight-hour day, the owners granted it without argument.

(b) *The London dockers' strike of 1889*

This was the most spectacular success of the 'New Unionism'. Encouraged by the success of the gasworkers and the match girls, Ben Tillett, Tom Mann and John Burns formed a *General Labourers' Union*, and asked for a minimum wage for dockers of 6d. an hour (the dockers' tanner). In fact there was more behind the strike than simply wanting more money: the dockers wanted the right to work more hours a day, and they objected to having to hang around the docks at all hours of day and night on the offchance that they might be taken on. A further objection was that more often than not they had to bribe the hirer to get any work at all. The dock owners refused to negotiate, so the entire dock labour force came out on strike (14 August 1889). The dispute lasted almost five weeks and the employers tried to break the strike by bringing in blackleg labour. In the end, however, they gave way and agreed to allow the men their tanner. *A number of reasons contributed to the dockers' victory:*

- They received solid support from skilled stevedores and watermen who had their own unions, and there were soon about 100 000 men on strike; the entire port of London was paralyzed and cargoes were rotting in the hot weather.
- The strike was conducted in a peaceful way with huge processions and mass meetings to publicize the justice of their claim. These won over public opinion and brought a rush of donations from sympathizers. This was vitally important since the union had no funds of its own for strike pay.
- Just when it seemed that the cash would run out, the dockers received an unexpected gift of £30 000 from the Australian trade unions which enabled them to continue.
- Finally, Cardinal Manning, head of the Roman Catholic Church in Britain, supported the dockers, and together with the Lord Mayor of London, he persuaded the employers that the men's demands were reasonable.

The dockers' strike was a vital turning point in trade union development. It showed that even the lowest paid and most exploited and despised labourers could take on their employers and beat them, provided their demands were reasonable and provided they conducted their strikes in an orderly fashion. 'New Unionism' received an enormous boost, as all types of unskilled workers formed new unions or rushed to join existing unions which had been struggling to find their feet. There was also an increase in the membership of the older 'Model' unions.

19.5 The unions run into problems during the 1890s

1889 – the year of the dockers' strike – was a year of triumph for the unions. Yet within a very short time 'New' unionism ran into all sorts of difficulties which slowed up development. Many strikes took place, often involving dockers and seamen, during the years 1890–3, usually to try and enforce the 'closed shop' (this would take the form of an agreement with the owners that they would only employ union members). All the strikes were unsuccessful.

(a) *What were the problems?*

● The country moved into another period of depression, when unskilled workers were always the first to be laid off. It was impossible to run a successful strike when there was unemployment, since the owners could simply sack the strikers, knowing that they would be able to fill the vacancies with unemployed men who were desperate for a job.
● Employers also began to fight back by taking on non-union labour, with police protection where necessary. This applied mainly to dockers and seamen, and was the main reason for the failure of their strike at Hull in 1893; as *The Times* put it: 'At Hull, as elsewhere, the New Unionism has been defeated, but nowhere has the defeat been so decisive, or the surrender so abject.'
● There were quarrels within the trade union movement between the older 'Model' unions and the 'New' unionism.

(b) *What were the differences and similarities between the 'Model' and 'New' unionism?*

There is some debate among historians about how great the differences actually were. Superficially there seemed to be some fairly obvious differences, at least in the 1880s and 1890s:

1 The 'New' unions were much poorer, since their membership fees – usually about 1d. a week – had to be lower than those for the skilled unions. Nor did they undertake Friendly Society benefits and pensions, believing instead that the state ought to provide them.
2 They tended to be more militant than the 'Model' unions, which seemed reluctant to face up to the problems of unemployment. According to Mann and Tillett, writing in 1890: 'A kind of deadly stupor covered them and they really appeared to be dying of inanation' (lack of nourishment).
3 Many of the leaders of the 'New' unions were socialists who wanted political action as well as industrial action. They believed that it was the duty of the state to provide a decent standard of living for everybody by the introduction of social benefits. In the early years of the twentieth century some of these unionists threw their weight behind the Labour Party. Tillett and Mann complained that the leaders of the old 'Model' unions 'do not recognize, as we do, that it is the work of the trade unionist to stamp out poverty from the land. ... A new enthusiasm is required, a fervent zeal. ... The cause we have at heart is too sacred to admit of time being spent quarrelling amongst ourselves' (see Source A in question 1 at the end of the chapter).

These quarrels used to be seen as the struggle between the reactionary 'old-guard' leaders who were trying to cling on to power, and the brash new unionists, many of them socialists, who were trying to hi-jack the trade union movement. However, many historians now recognize that this interpretation is too simplistic: the 'old-guard' were not as conservative as used to be thought. Paul Adelman points out that between 1885 and 1887 the three presidential speeches at the TUC all spoke in support of two of the favourite aims of 'New' unionism:

- the eight-hour maximum working day
- nationalization of land.

They also criticized the existing capitalist system. Henry Pelling is of the same opinion, believing that the differences have been exaggerated: 'It is clear that Marxist historians have completely got the wrong end of the stick: militancy was much more likely to be found among the better-off than among the poorer workers' (see Source B in question 1).

Whatever the differences, there is no doubt that the 'New' unionism found it hard going during the 1890s. As J. Savile points out, 'outside the highly skilled trades, to win even an approximation to the closed shop or to ensure that blackleg labour did not swamp a strike, militant tactics were demanded which the older unionists ... believed they no longer needed; the employers' first reaction was to smash these new upstart organizations' (see Source C in question 1). By 1900 the total membership of the 'New' unions was at most only 200 000, whereas membership of all unions was about two million. Even the 200 000 was only a tiny fraction of the total unskilled labour force of perhaps 15 million. However, 'New' unionism survived and struggled on into the twentieth century.

(c) *How did 'New' unionism manage to survive the problems of the 1890s?*

- Workers in some industries which were expanding – such as gas, water and electricity – coped better than the dockers and seamen. These expanding industries were often owned by the local councils who might be held accountable by voters if there were constant gas and electricity cuts. Thus the workers had more power; employers needed to have a good relationship with them, since industrial action would affect the customer more immediately than a dock strike would.
- Unions of gas, water and electricity workers tended to be better led than the dockers' and seamen's unions, and they gradually became more like the old craft unions in organization and general outlook. For example, the Gasworkers' Union aimed to build up its strength in certain large works rather than over the industry as a whole.
- They also concentrated on building up the idea that they were 'specialized' workers and therefore indispensable, and this helped them to pressurize employers to recognize their union. Many employers did so; once this had been achieved, 'collective bargaining' would follow; this was when the union would negotiate for better conditions of work for the entire industry.

As 'New' unionism gradually won the battle for survival, according to Paul Adelman, 'the frontiers between 'old' and 'new' unionism began to become blurred'. For example in 1892 the Amalgamated Society of Engineers (an 'old' union) relaxed its rigid qualifications for membership, so that unskilled workers in the engineering industry could join. Between 1891 and 1893 the TUC adopted the eight-hour day as one of its policies.

What was the real significance of the 'New' unionism in the 1890s?

If this question had been put in 1889 immediately after the dockers' strike, the answer would have seemed obvious – it was going to have great industrial importance. But in fact this industrial significance did not develop in any big way before 1914. However, it did have great political significance. According to Ben Tillett, 'it marked the beginning of that close alliance in thought and purpose between the Trade Union Movement and the Socialist Movement which produced, in due time, the Labour Party'. Both agreed on the need for working-class solidarity and state action against poverty. The alliance became closer because of legal problems facing the unions.

19.6 What legal problems faced the trade unions in the early years of the twentieth century and how were they overcome?

Most manufacturers and men of property were genuinely afraid of trade unionism and some were determined to smash the movement. The Federation of Engineering Employers, for example, refused to discuss a workers' demand for an eight-hour day. The men were locked out from July 1897 until January 1898, while the management moved blackleg labour in. The employers won, and although the unions survived, there was great bitterness. Even more serious for the unions was that the law courts seemed biased against them; several adverse judgements had serious implications for both skilled and unskilled unions:

(a) *The Lyons* v. *Wilkins case (1899)*

In a dispute between the Society of Fancy Leather Workers and a workshop owner named Lyons, the Appeal Court issued an injunction which prevented union members from picketing Lyons' premises. This could be interpreted as reversing the 1876 Trade Union Act if the same thing was to happen every time there was a strike. It prompted the TUC to vote (with a small majority) for a meeting with the various socialist societies; it was this meeting which set up *the Labour Representation Committee* (February 1900). Its purpose was to run independent Labour candidates for parliament. Many trade unionists had come to the conclusion that if strikes were failing and the law was against them, the only option left was to work through parliament. However, at this stage there was only lukewarm support – only ten unions affiliated to the Labour Party out of a total of over 1300 unions.

(b) *The Taff Vale case (1900–1)*

This arose from a strike by the workers of the Taff Vale Railway Company in South Wales. They wanted better working conditions and the right to join the Amalgamated Society of Railway Servants, which recognized the strike as official. The company refused to negotiate and broke the strike by bringing in blackleg labour. After two months the men had to return to work on the old terms (August 1900). The company decided to press home its advantage by suing the ASRS for damages suffered through loss of profits during the strike. After months of argument the House of Lords judged in favour of the company, and ordered the ASRS to pay £23 000 damages, plus costs, making a grand total of £42 000. This was a disastrous decision for the trade unions, since it meant that no union could call a strike without risking bankruptcy; strike action was virtually impossible.

The only way to defeat the Taff Vale decision was for the government to pass an

Act changing the law in the unions' favour. The unions had therefore to concentrate on political means to restore their powers. The Conservatives declined to co-operate, so many union leaders advised their members to support the Labour party. By the end of 1903 a further 168 unions had affiliated to Labour, which won 29 seats in the 1906 general election. Twenty-four trade unionists were elected as Liberal MPs and one of the first measures of the new Liberal government was *the Trade Disputes Act (1906)*. This said that unions could not be sued for damages and accepted that peaceful picketing was legal. This Act, possibly the most important in trade union history, left the unions more powerful than ever before, and made possible the strike wave of 1910–14.

(c) *The Osborne Judgement (1909)*

This was another legal decision which displeased the unions, though it was the Labour Party which suffered directly from it.

1   The situation was that the unions charged their members what was called *the political levy* – a small weekly payment on top of their normal union subscription, which was mostly used to provide financial help for Labour members of parliament, since at that time MPs were not paid a salary. Not all union members were supporters of the Labour party, and W. V. Osborne, a Liberal, and secretary of the Walthamstow branch of the Amalgamated Society of Railway Servants, challenged the right of his union to demand the political levy. The House of Lords ruled that it was illegal for unions to demand such a payment for the purpose of helping a political party. This was a serious blow for the Labour party which was chronically short of funds and could not afford to pay the salaries of around sixteen of its MPs. The Osborne Judgement drove many trade unionists towards syndicalism (see next section).

2   Again, it was only by parliamentary means that the Osborne Judgement could be defeated, and the unions and Labour launched a campaign to pressurize the Liberal government into action. This was slow to materialize, since the government was beset by many other serious problems (see Section 21.3–5), but eventually the Liberals gave satisfaction:

●   In 1911 an annual salary of £400 was introduced for MPs. This fulfilled one of the Chartists' demands and eased the difficulties caused by the Osborne Judgement. But union pressure continued, and the result was:

●   *The Trade Union Act of 1913*, which, in effect, reversed the Osborne Judgement. The political levy was legal, but any individual who objected to contributing to the Labour party could 'contract out'. Since this required some personal effort and filling-in of forms, the vast majority of trade union members did not bother to 'contract out', and Labour party funds accordingly received a life-saving boost.

On the eve of the First World War, therefore, trade unions had overcome all legal obstacles; they had the power to strike, to picket, and to play an important role in politics.

19.7 Syndicalism and trade union militancy

In the years 1910–14 many of the 'New' trade unions became much more militant and violent, influenced by French and American syndicalism or revolutionary trade unionism (*syndicat* is the French word for a trade union).

(a) *Syndicalist ideas*

- The trade union movement, not the state, was destined to become the main democratic organization of the future, owning industries and land and controlling the country's economic and social policies.
- This could be achieved, not by political action through parliament, but by direct action outside parliament. Syndicalists introduced the idea of the 'sympathetic' strike – if a union was conducting a strike, other unions in different industries would strike in sympathy, so that maximum pressure could be brought on employers and government. Ultimately they hoped to disrupt the country by a general strike so that the capitalist system would be overthrown and the trade union movement would take charge. There was some similarity to Robert Owen's ideas, though he never liked the idea of violence.

(b) *Why did Syndicalism develop in Britain?*

There was serious labour unrest because of unemployment and the fact that while prices were rising, wages were actually falling in real terms. As usual, it was the unskilled, low-paid workers who suffered most. The results achieved by the skilled unions and by the Labour Party in parliament were disappointing. The Osborne Judgement seemed deliberately designed to cripple the Labour Party. Some historians see the rejection of Lloyd George's budget by the House of Lords in November 1909 (see Section 21.3) as an important stimulus: 'if the peers can sabotage the constitution for their own ends, why can't we?' was the question on the lips of many trade unionists. If parliamentary action was impossible, there remained only direct action outside parliament.

(c) *The strike wave, 1910–14*

The wave of strikes began in July 1910 with action by railway workers, soon followed by Lancashire cotton workers, boilermakers and Welsh miners. In 1911 there was a successful dock strike which affected all ports, and in Liverpool there was a transport strike during which troops were moved in and two men were killed. There seemed to be a lull in the strikes on the mainland during 1913, though there was a major syndicalist strike in Dublin lasting over six months.

In fact the unskilled workers were gathering themselves together for another onslaught. Several small railway unions united to form the National Union of Railwaymen (NUR), and in 1914 the powerful *Triple Alliance* was formed, consisting of the new NUR, the Transport Workers' Federation and the Miners' Federation. The outbreak of the First World War may have prevented a massive Triple Alliance strike in 1914, but the Alliance survived and moved into action later during the general strike of 1926.

19.8 Examine the causes which led to the rise of the Labour party and trace the main stages in its development to 1914

It is an oversimplification to talk about the rise of the Labour Party as if it were a single homogeneous body. In fact it was an amalgamation of three different socialist groups – the Social Democrat Federation, the Fabians and the Independent Labour Party – with some trade unions. Although all these groups were described as socialist, their aims and methods were not always the same. The word 'socialist' meant different things to different people. One thing which all the members did agree on though, was that their aim was to represent working-class interests in parliament, and to do their best to improve life for the workers. The origins of the party lay in the conditions and circumstances of late Victorian Britain.

(a) *Poverty and poor social conditions*

During the last quarter of the nineteenth century at least 30 per cent of the working class were living close to starvation level. Agricultural and industrial depressions had worsened the situation, bringing unemployment. Often wages were so low that families were living in dire poverty even when the breadwinner was in full-time employment. Many people were becoming disturbed at the striking contrast between this poverty and the comfortable existence enjoyed by the upper and middle classes.

- *Progress and Poverty*, a book by an American economist, Henry George, published in Britain in 1881, focused attention on the tremendous contrasts of wealth and poverty. George blamed the problems on the greed of the landowners and advocated a massive land tax as the cure for all ills. In a time of severe agricultural depression, the book was bound to have an impact both on middle-class intellectuals and on the working classes. Thanks to the spread of education following Forster's Education Act (1870), working people could read George's book and other socialist propaganda, such as Robert Blatchford's influential newspaper, *The Clarion*.
- There was growing impatience among Radicals with Gladstone's second government (1880–5) which virtually ignored their suggestions for social reform. This was ill-advised, since many workers had been given the vote by the 1867 Reform Act, and Gladstone himself had extended the franchise to many more in 1884.

(b) *Two important socialist groups were formed in 1884*

1 *The Social Democratic Federation (SDF)* was set up by an old-Etonian, H. M. Hyndman, and also included John Burns and Tom Mann. Advocating violent revolution to overthrow the capitalist system, they achieved publicity by organizing marches and demonstrations. The most famous one, held in Trafalgar Square in 1887, was broken up by police and is remembered as *Bloody Sunday* because of the violence on both sides.
2 *The Fabian Society* was a group of middle-class intellectuals which included Sydney and Beatrice Webb and George Bernard Shaw. They believed that land and industrial capital should be owned by the community, but unlike the SDF, they did not believe in violence. They took their name from Fabius, the Roman general who defeated Hannibal by waiting patiently and avoiding battle, knowing that time was on his side. The Fabians believed that society would gradually change from capitalism to socialism and that their function was to persuade the political parties to accept socialism. At first they preferred this policy of 'gradual permeation', instead of creating a separate Labour party, but they changed their minds when it became clear that the Liberals and Conservatives were not impressed by their ideas.

(c) *A slump in the Yorkshire woollen industry leads to the formation of the ILP*

The Independent Labour Party (ILP) was formed by James Keir Hardie, secretary of the Scottish Miners' Federation, in 1893. He had already formed *the Scottish Labour*

James Keir Hardie, the Ayrshire miners' leader, who was destined to become the first leader of the Labour Party.

Illus. 19.1   Keir Hardie (1856–1915)

Party in 1888 because he was disgusted with the complacency and ineffectiveness of the Liberal party. He became the first Labour MP in 1892 (for West Ham South) and soon played a crucial role in the formation of the Labour party. He was convinced that the needs of working people could only be properly satisfied by a Labour group completely independent of other parties.

A slump in the Yorkshire woollen industry in the early 1890s, caused by foreign competition and American tariffs, gave Hardie and his associate, John Burgess, who ran a newspaper called *The Workman's Times*, the chance to form a new party. In the winter of 1890–1, the whole woollen area was badly hit by unemployment and wage reductions, and the unions were weak. Woollen workers at Manningham Mills in Bradford went on strike in protest against wage cuts, but they found themselves up against the combined forces of mill-owners, local politicians and police, who prevented them from holding public meetings. Although the strike failed, the treatment of the workers and the hostile attitude of local Liberals (many of whom were mill-owners) gave great impetus to the idea of a separate Labour party. The area was bristling with Labour clubs – 23 of them in Bradford alone, where the old Chartist tradition lingered on. Hardie organized a conference in Bradford in 1893 which led to the formation of *the Independent Labour Party*.

Its ultimate aim was *the collective ownership of the means of production*, in other words, the state should own land, gas and electricity, water, railways, and important industries such as coal, iron and steel. Hardie knew that this was a highly controversial programme, so to begin with, the new party aimed to concentrate on improving social conditions. The ILP was a northern working-class organization, but Hardie wanted a Labour party which was a national body with middle-class support.

(d) *The growth of trade unions contributed to the formation of the Labour Party*

The trade unions gradually moved towards the idea of a Labour Party, following incidents such as the great engineering lock-out of 1897–8 and the *Lyons* v. *Wilkins* case of 1899 (see Section 19.6(a)). The TUC proposed a meeting with the socialist groups. Representatives of some unions, the SDF, the Fabians and the ILP attended the meeting at the Memorial Hall, Farringdon Street, London (February 1900) and decided to form a distinct Labour group in parliament. *The Labour Representation Committee* was appointed to organize their election campaign, and James Ramsay MacDonald, later to become the first Labour Prime Minister (1924), was its unpaid secretary. This is usually taken as the beginning of the Labour party. Its aim was simply to represent working class interests in parliament. About socialism, it was very vague.

There has been some argument about what part Marxism played in the formation of the Labour Party. Karl Marx (1818–83) was a German Jew who spent most of his life after 1848 in Britain. His economic and political ideas were explained in *The Communist Manifesto (1848)* and *Das Kapital (Money) (1867)*. He believed that economic factors are the real cause of historical change and that workers (the proletariat) are everywhere exploited by capitalists. This must inevitably lead to a struggle between the classes, to revolution and to the setting up of a classless society. His ideas certainly appealed to syndicalists and became the basic doctrine of communism. However, it is easy to exaggerate his influence on politics in Britain. *Das Kapital* did not appear in English translation until 1887; Hyndman had read it in a French translation in 1880–1 and the SDF was the most Marxist of the socialist groups. The ILP, which was more important than the SDF in the emergence of the Labour party, arose out of the practical problems of the working class, in Scotland, in the Yorkshire woollen towns and in Lancashire, though Marx's theories may have had an indirect influence.

(e) *Stages in Labour Party development, 1900–14*

The major priority after the formation of the LRC was to get Labour MPs elected. Already in 1892 Keir Hardie and two other Labour MPs had been successful, but all three lost their seats in 1895. The immediate impact of the new party was disappointing. In spite of the interest shown by the TUC, there was only lukewarm support; only ten unions decided to affiliate (associate themselves with, and give financial support) to the Labour party, and their members numbered only about 200 000, only one-tenth of total union membership.

● In the election of October 1900 the LRC ran 15 candidates, but only two were successful – Hardie himself at Merthyr Tydfil and Richard Bell at Derby. It was unfortunate for the new party that the election came so soon after its formation, when it was suffering from a severe cash shortage and had very little union support.

● *The Taff Vale case (1900–1)* changed the situation dramatically (see Section 19.6(b)). Ramsay MacDonald wrote to all trade unions stressing the need for a large

Labour representation in parliament, and this produced a surge of trade union support. By the end of 1903, a further 168 unions had affiliated to Labour; this brought an immediate improvement in the financial situation, thanks to the political levy.

- *The electoral pact between the LRC and the Liberals, agreed in 1903*, brought an important boost in terms of seats in parliament. MacDonald came to an arrangement with the Liberals, who agreed that at the next election, they would not run candidates in certain constituencies, thus giving Labour a straight fight against the Conservatives. The Liberal motive was not to help Labour, but to avoid three-cornered contests in constituencies where the Conservatives were not thought to have much chance of winning. If both Labour and Liberal candidates ran, this would split the anti-Conservative vote, and allow the Conservatives to win. It was this electoral pact which allowed Labour to make the first breakthrough: in the 1906 election Labour ran 50 candidates, 30 of whom were not opposed by Liberals. 29 were successful, and when they took their seats in parliament they decided to call themselves simply the Labour Party.
- At first Labour had some success in parliament. *The Trade Disputes Act (1906)* which reversed the Taff Vale decision, was based on the Labour Party's own bill, and they were able to add small improvements to the Workmen's Compensation Act and to the School Meals and Medical Inspections Act (see Section 20.3(a–b)). However, after 1907 they had very little influence on the government; they seemed to have run out of ideas and simply accepted the Liberal reforms.
- Important developments were taking place outside parliament: the unions were grateful to Labour for the Trade Disputes Act and more of them decided to affiliate to the Labour party instead of to the Liberals. Another reason for the move to Labour was that the steady fall in real wages and the increasing number of disputes with employers (who often happened to be Liberals) made socialist ideas seem more attractive. The most important catch for Labour was *the National Union of Mineworkers* in 1909, one of the largest unions in the country. If all the miners voted Labour instead of Liberal, this could swing as many as 60 seats to Labour. This is what actually happened after 1918 when the electoral pact was no longer in operation.
- *The Osborne Judgement of 1909* (see Section 19.6(c)) damaged the party financially and their funds were further strained by the fact that there were two general elections in 1910. In January Labour won 40 seats and this increased to 42 in December. However, only two of these had defeated Liberal candidates; the other 40 were successful because of the continuing electoral pact.
- By 1914 the Labour party, though making some progress in local council elections, had failed to break away from its dependence on the Liberals. Convinced socialists were disappointed with Labour's showing, particularly when MacDonald claimed in 1911 that the party was 'not socialist', but was a federation organized for 'immediate political work'.

Was the rise of the Labour Party inevitable?

This question, along with the parallel one – Was the decline of the Liberal party inevitable? – has been the subject of long debate among historians. Henry Pelling and Ross McKibbin believe that by 1906 the rise of Labour was more or less inevitable.

Pelling stresses that long-term social changes – the growth of large industrial cities and the greater concentration of industry, together with the steadily rising cost of living, were gradually turning large sections of the working class towards the Labour party. McKibbin attaches special importance to the growth of trade unionism, which he thinks had already undermined Liberal strength before 1914. He argues that the reasons why the Labour party did not do better before 1914 were that:

- the party was financially handicapped by the Osborne Judgement and this prevented it from improving its organization and campaigning;
- in spite of the Reform Acts of 1867 and 1884, voting was still restricted, and many working men did not qualify to vote; this meant that Labour was deprived of many of its 'natural' supporters. *If all workers had been able to vote before the First World War,* the rise of Labour and the decline of the Liberals would have been obvious in 1914. *The Representation of the People Act (June 1918)* was therefore the crucial factor in the Labour breakthrough. By trebling the electorate, it brought the industrial working classes into a majority for the first time.

However, other historians like P. F. Clarke and Trevor Wilson do not go along with this 'inevitable rise of Labour' theory. Clarke argues that with the coming of 'New Liberalism', there was still plenty of life left in the Liberal party before 1914. Wilson believes that the First World War was the crucial factor, because it split and discredited the Liberal party and opened the way for Labour to step in. Without the war, there was no way that Labour could have become the main opposition party to the Conservatives.

Two more recent writers, Duncan Tanner and Martin Pugh, also reject the idea that the Labour party would inevitably take over from the Liberals. Martin Pugh thinks this view is the product of hindsight; he argues that before the First World War it was difficult for Labour to project itself as a party radically different from the Liberals, except by advocating socialism, which was not popular with the vast majority of the working class nor with the Labour MPs at that point. He also highlights the weakness of Labour's constituency organizations and the fact that in the elections of 1910, although the Liberals lost many seats gained in 1906, these went back to the Conservatives, not to Labour. The Liberals held on to most of their seats in the industrial North, Midlands, Scotland and Wales (for a further discussion of Labour's rise and the Liberals' decline, see Section 23.4).

Questions

1 The 'Old' and the 'New' unionism

Study Sources A to C and then answer the questions which follow.

Source A

Tom Mann and Ben Tillett write about the 'New' unionism in 1890

We repeat that the real difference between the 'new' and the 'old' is that those who belong to the latter, and delight in being distinct from the policy endorsed by the 'new', do so because they do not recognise, as we do, that it is the work of the trade unionist to stamp out poverty from the land. They do not contend, as we contend, that existing unions should exert themselves to extend organisations where they as yet do not exist. They know the enormous difficulties under which hundreds of thousands labour, and how difficult it is for them to take the initial steps in genuine trades unionism and how valuable a little 'coaching' would be from those who have had experience in such matters; but they have not done what they might to supply this – we shall. A new enthusiasm is required, a fervent zeal that will result in the sending forth of trade union organisers through the length and breadth of the country. Clannishness in trade matters must be superseded by a cosmopolitan spirit, brotherhood must not only be talked of but practised. And that real grit exists in the 'new' unions is evident, not only from the manner in which they are perfecting their own organisations, but also from the substantial way in which they have contributed to the support of other trades, such as the bargebuilders, whose strike balance sheet shows that the 'new' unions were much more prompt in rendering monetary aid than the 'old' ones. Nevertheless, what we desire to see is a unification of all, a dropping of all bickerings. . . . The cause we have at heart is too sacred to admit of time being spent quarrelling amongst ourselves . . . we are prepared to work unceasingly for the economic emancipation of the workers. Our ideal is a Co-operative Commonwealth.

Source: T. Mann and B. Tillett, *The 'New' Trades Unionism*, 1900.

Source B

Comments from historian Henry Pelling

The concept of the *labour aristocracy* has had its value in drawing attention to the differences within the working class; but if it implies the existence in the late nineteenth and early twentieth century of a labour elite distinctly separated from lower strata and *marked by political behaviour of an acquiescent type*, then it is a concept that does more harm than good to historical truth. To be sure, in some industries the craftsmen did manage to perpetuate, sometimes even to extend, a tight control over entry into their trades. But the number of industries in which this was possible was constantly in decline after the onset of the industrial revolution. The growth of the factory and mining population in the nineteenth century meant the growth of a more homogeneous working class than had existed previously, and in this working class there was no aristocracy, unless we think of foremen, who, although they often appeared in wage statistics, did not normally belong to trade unions. As for politics, it is clear that Marxist historians have completely got the wrong end of the stick: militancy was much more likely to be found among the better-off than among the poorer workers . . . recruitment to the Communist Party, both in this country and in other countries of Europe, has been much more successful among more highly paid manual workers than among those of lesser income.

Source: H. Pelling, *Popular Society and Politics in Late Victorian Britain*, Macmillan, 1968.

Source C

Professor John Savile gives his view of the 'New' unionism, published in 1971

It was the special characteristics of new unionism that made it the immediate target of ruling class fury. Recent research has modified the picture of new unionism that has been generally accepted, and today it is recognised that 1889 was less of a break with the past than was formerly believed. Nevertheless, when all the necessary qualifications have been added to the traditional interpretation of old and new unionism, it is important not to underestimate the climacteric [crucial event] of 1889. The economic problems of the unskilled and semi-skilled trade unionists were very different from those of the skilled workers, and their industrial methods and tactics were also different. While the old unions were able to rely on the skill of their members as a crucial bargaining weapon, the new unions were at all times, even in the years of good trade, subject to the pressures of an overstocked labour market. Picketing, for instance, was rarely a major problem in the strike action of many sections of skilled workers . . . among the cotton spinners of Lancashire, or the boilermakers on the north east coast, or the coalminers in well-organised districts, both sides to an industrial dispute knew that when work was resumed the same men would have to be taken on. . . . The position was very different in the ports employing dock labour, where only a proportion of those applying for work on any one day would be accepted. In such circumstances, and these were familiar in many other industries, it was immensely more difficult to make a strike solid or to achieve stable unions. Outside the highly skilled trades, to win even an approximation to the closed shop or to ensure that blackleg labour did not swamp a strike, militant tactics were demanded which the older unionists had pioneered decades before but which, by the end of the 1880s, they believed they no longer needed.

Source: J. Savile, 'Trade Unions and Free Labour: The Background to the Taff Vale Decision', in
Essays in Labour History 1886–1926, ed. A. Briggs and J. Savile, Macmillan, 1971

(a) On the basis of the evidence in Source A, explain why there was some friction between the 'Old' and 'New' trade unions. (8 marks)

(b) Using information from Sections 19.3–5 and the evidence in Source B, explain why the writer of Source B, Henry Pelling, rejects the idea of the existence of a 'labour aristocracy . . . marked by political behaviour of an acquiescent [non-protesting] type'. (12 marks)

(c) How useful is Source C in helping you to reach a conclusion in the debate about how deep the differences were between the 'Old' and 'New' unions? (10 marks)

(Total 30 marks)

2 Examine the influences which (a) encouraged, and (b) limited, the growth of the Labour party to 1914. [AEB

3 How far can the London Dock Strike (1889) be considered a turning-point in the history of trade unions in the period 1871–1914? [AEB

20 The state and the people from the 1890s to 1939

Summary of events

Summary of events

For most of the nineteenth century, the state did very little to organize society in Britain. The government did provide some cash for education, and several Acts of Parliament were passed to organize and improve education. The state had also introduced regulations dealing with health matters and working conditions (see Chapter 12). But there were many problem areas which the state made no attempt to deal with: it did nothing, for example, to try to plan the nation's economy; it did very little to help the poor, except to provide workhouses for them to live in when they could no longer cope at home. However, this gradually changed, and one of the major themes of British history in the twentieth century is *the development of the Welfare State*. This means a state in which the government tries to provide the best possible services for everybody, in health care, education, housing, pensions and unemployment benefit. It is also accepted that in a Welfare State the government does its best to make sure that everybody has a job.

The Welfare State was not achieved without a great deal of debate and struggle. There was never any overall plan or blueprint for setting up such a system, and it happened in a piecemeal fashion, in fits and starts. The first big steps were taken under the Liberal governments of 1905–15, and another important 'surge' took place between 1940 and 1948, mainly as a result of the Second World War (see Section 28.7 and Chapter 29).

In 1900 there was a great debate going on about whether or not the state – the government – should be expected to do anything to help the poor. Was it the function of the state to introduce old age pensions, health insurance and unemployment benefit? There were two opposing views:

- *Individualism or self-help* – this was the traditional Victorian view which went hand-in-hand with the theory of *laissez-faire*: the belief that the government should interfere as little as possible with people's lives and activities; they should be left alone with the freedom to organize their own lives. The poor should be encouraged to help themselves and not expect to be helped out by the state.
- *Collectivism* – this was gradually becoming more widespread after about 1870, and was the belief that the state had a duty to look after the welfare of its people and to do its best to improve things for the poor.

The Liberal governments of 1905–15 were partially converted to the idea of collectivism, and though they could never fully tear themselves away from their *laissez-faire* background, they did introduce some important social reforms. During the period between the wars (1919–39) politicians of all three parties (though not *all* politicians) came to accept that it *was* the state's job to provide social services. The social reforms of the Liberals were gradually extended, but not without difficulties, mainly because of the enormous cost of financing unemployment benefit, which was far greater than anybody had expected. These problems led some politicians, especially those in the Labour party, to suggest that the government should play a part in planning and organizing the economic life of the country; in other words, there should be *a managed economy*. This, in theory, would help to reduce unemployment and keep costs under control.

20.1 Individualism v. collectivism: the main arguments in the debate

(a) *The case for individualism or self-help*

1   Throughout the nineteenth century there was a strong feeling that the state should interfere as little as possible with the lives and activities of individual people, who should be left in freedom to act as they wanted, without any government directions or restrictions. As early as 1776, Adam Smith, in his book *Wealth of Nations*, put forward the theory that the economy would function most efficiently if people were free to pursue their own self-interest. He thought this applied to individuals as well as to nations, and so it followed that individual people were more likely to be successful at making money if the government kept out of it.

2   One of the supreme Victorian virtues was thought to be self-help. This was the belief that, given complete freedom, everybody had an equal chance to do well; initiative and hard work would always be rewarded. Samuel Smiles was one of the best-known supporters of self-help and he published a book about it in 1859. 'Heaven helps them who help themselves', he wrote. 'Even the best institutions can give a man no active help. Perhaps the most they can do is to leave him free to develop himself and improve his individual condition.' And in fact Victorian Britain was full of examples of men who, by their own determination and dedication, had pulled themselves to the top from modest or poor backgrounds. Nor did Smiles believe in unemployment benefit: 'every working man should strive, in times of prosperity and good wages, to save something and accumulate a fund in case of bad times'. Friendly Societies were a good example of workers helping themselves; they were insurance schemes run by workers to provide burial expenses, sickness and unemployment benefits, and even old age pensions.

3   There was also the question of cost – who would foot the bill for old age pensions and other benefits? If the government was expected to provide funding, that would mean increased taxation, which would be unpopular with electors. If cash was to come from local authorities, that would mean higher rates – another certain vote-loser. One of the main motives behind the new Poor Law of 1834 had been to reduce rates. There was another possible source of cash – tariffs (import and export duties); but these were also out of the question – the Liberals were committed to free trade, and the Conservatives were split on the issue (see Section 17.6(b) 6).

4   If success was due to self-help, it must follow (so the theory went) that poverty occurred when people failed to help themselves because of some character defect such as laziness, drunkenness, a weakness for gambling, or just a general inability to cope with life's stresses. This was the belief underlying the new Poor Law system under which conditions in workhouses were made as unattractive as

possible, so that the poor would make every effort to find work, and only come to the workhouse as a last resort. Life in the workhouse was deliberately made more miserable than the existence of the poorest labourer outside. The idea was known as the *'less eligibility' principle*, and it was expected to encourage self-help and prevent the poor from looking on workhouses as havens of refuge (see Section 5.3).

5 Finally it was thought that state help for the poor was not a good idea because it would destroy the initiative of the working class; they would stop trying to help themselves and expect the state to do everything for them. Samuel Smiles was convinced of this: 'whatever is done for men ... takes away the stimulus and necessity of doing for themselves ... and the inevitable tendency is to render them comparatively helpless'. Individualism was therefore the best way of dealing with the working class because it encouraged people to work hard, live a moral life and save money.

(b) *The case for collectivism – state intervention to help the poor*

1 During the final quarter of the nineteenth century there was a great deal of unemployment – this was the time of the so-called 'Great Depression' caused mainly by increasing competition from Germany and the USA (see Section 15.2). Things improved around the turn of the century, but 1904 and 1905 were years of high unemployment. With no unemployment insurance to support them, many workers and their families had to endure severe hardship. This was where the self-help theory seemed to be breaking down – often, no matter how hard a man tried to find work, there were simply no jobs available. Freedom was useless if circumstances beyond his management had caused him to lose control of his life. The 'freedom' that he really wanted was freedom from unemployment and freedom from poverty.

2 There was a growing realization that the Poor Law was completely inadequate in a situation like this. Able-bodied poor who could not support themselves were expected to move into workhouses run by local authorities, which received no financial help from the government. As the population of mainland Britain increased from 29.7 million in 1881 to 37 million in 1901, so the number of paupers (poor people) grew, and the burden on the local rates became heavier. In 1900 working people still viewed workhouses with fear and suspicion. Inmates were treated almost like criminals, losing their personal freedom and their right to vote. Many families, especially in London and the industrial cities, were living close to starvation level, trying to survive as long as possible before entering the dreaded workhouse. It was clear that in times of high unemployment this system was inappropriate; something more was needed to support the overburdened Poor Law.

3 There were plenty of charity organizations and the churches did a lot to help, but they could not cope in a systematic enough way with the unemployment of the 'Great Depression' period. Charity had another drawback – it tended to be degrading to those receiving it, producing the feeling that they were inferior beings humbly accepting crumbs of comfort passed down by their wealthy superiors.

4 Poverty received more publicity in the last quarter of the nineteenth century than ever before:

- Recruitment for the Boer War (1899–1902) drew attention to the problem of poverty when it was found that almost half the men who volunteered for the army were physically unfit for military service. This convinced many people that the time had arrived for government action to help the poor, otherwise Britain might be unable to defend her Empire adequately in the event of a major war.

- Between 1886 and 1903, Charles Booth, a Liverpool shipowner and manufacturer who was a Christian and had a social conscience, carried out a series of investigations which showed that over 30 per cent of the population of London were living in serious poverty. Among old people the situation was worse: possibly 45 per cent of the old people of London were living in dire poverty. Booth also showed that in a time of depression, a worker might be unable, through no fault of his own, to find a job. Another point revealed by the survey was that some men were living in poverty because they were too ill to work. These discoveries were important because they probably did more than anything to explode the Victorian myth that poverty was always the result of laziness or some other character defect.

- Seebohm Rowntree, a Quaker and a member of the famous York chocolate and cocoa manufacturing family, found it difficult to believe that London's poverty level would be repeated over the rest of the country. So he carried out his own survey in York. His findings, published in 1901, showed that 28 per cent of the population of York were living in serious poverty. 'We are faced with the startling possibility,' he wrote, 'that from 25 to 30 per cent of the town population of the United Kingdom are living in poverty.' And he discovered something worse – that in York wages were so low that even men in full employment, working long hours every day, were forced to live close to starvation level. The work of Booth and Rowntree was vitally important because it provided the hard statistical evidence needed to boost the case for state intervention.

5   It followed that if nearly one-third of the population needed help, only the state could afford the necessary cash, and only the state had the necessary powers to provide what was needed. The next question for those who accepted that some state intervention was required was: *what was the best way to help the poor?*

Charles Booth suggested a pension of five shillings (25 pence) a week at the age of 65. Another of his ideas was for the state to take care of the poorest 10 per cent of the population, which he described as 'the incapable'. He believed that this would remove them as competitors to the other 20 per cent of poor people, so enabling them to get work and earn a reasonable living. He described this as 'limited socialism' and he said that if the state intervened in the lives of this small percentage of the population, it would be possible 'to dispense with any Socialistic interference in the lives of all the rest'.

Seebohm Rowntree suggested that the state should introduce a minimum wage, and he recommended that 21s.8d. (£1.08p) a week was needed to keep a couple with three children in what he called 'Spartan physical efficiency'.

The most drastic suggestions came from the various socialist groups (see Section 19.8) which wanted *a redistribution of wealth*. They all agreed on *the collective ownership of the means of production*. This means that important sources of wealth such as land, coal-mines, heavy industries like iron and steel, industries producing power (gas and electricity) and transport should all be jointly owned by the people. The state should organize and run these industries and take all the profits, which would be shared out among all the people, possibly in the form of lower prices, instead of going into the pockets of a few wealthy industrialists. In this way, wealth would be spread more fairly and poverty should disappear. However, suggestions like this were enough to strike terror into the hearts of the wealthy, and so . . .

6 *Fear of socialism* became an important argument in favour of some less drastic state action. Many ordinary working people had been given the vote in 1867 and 1884, and might well be attracted to socialist ideas if the Liberals and Conservatives failed to do something about poverty. Moderate social reform would improve conditions for the workers sufficiently to turn them away from socialism. This would kill off the infant Labour party which had been formed in 1900, and would preserve the capitalist system. This had been the motive of Bismarck, the German Chancellor: when he introduced state old age pensions, and sickness and unemployment benefit schemes in the 1880s, he too was hoping to put a stop to the growth of German socialism.

(c) *What was the government response to the growing pressure for state intervention?*

Arthur Balfour's Conservative government (1902–5) (see Section 17.6) responded to the arguments and suggestions with two pieces of action. First came *the Unemployed Workmen Act (1905)* which allowed local committees to be set up to provide work for the unemployed, using voluntary subscriptions. This was a failure because the government had missed the point that some state help with financing was necessary. More important was *the Royal Commission on the Poor Law set up in 1905*. This was a committee of experts, including Charles Booth and Beatrice Webb (a leading Fabian), who were to investigate the shortcomings of the Poor Law system and suggest ways of improving it. Unfortunately the committee took a long time to reach any conclusions, mainly because of disagreements among the members, which reflected the individualism v. collectivism debate. Beatrice Webb, George Lansbury (a future Labour MP) and two other members wanted to abolish the Poor Law system altogether and set up a national system for helping the poor, to be run by a new Ministry of Labour. There would be labour exchanges, re-training schemes and public works programmes to provide jobs in times of depression. Another department would look after people who were unable to work because of ill-health. However, the chairman, Lord George Hamilton, and 14 other members of the committee merely wanted to extend the Poor Law system and make more use of charities. They found it difficult to tear themselves away from their belief in individualism, and there was no way in which the two groups would ever agree. In the end they brought out two separate reports:

1 *The Minority Report* was written by Beatrice Webb and her three supporters. They argued that basically problems brought about by the state of the national economy (such as depression and unemployment) were the main causes of poverty, and that consequently poverty should be dealt with on a national level by state intervention.
2 *The Majority Report* was produced by Hamilton and his 14 supporters. They pointed out that in their view 'the causes of distress are not only economic and industrial; in origin and character they are largely moral'; in other words, it was very much a man's own fault if he found himself in poverty.

The arguments dragged on so long that it was 1909 before the Reports were published. The Conservative government which had appointed the Commission had been replaced in December 1905 by a Liberal government. By 1909 this Liberal government had already done something to deal with the problem of poverty.

20.2 Why did the Liberals introduce social reforms, 1906–14?

The Liberal governments which were in office from December 1905 until May 1915 were the first governments in Britain to do anything in a systematic way for the poor, apart from providing them with workhouses. Starting in 1906, they introduced a series of social reforms: measures to help children, old age pensions, new laws to help people at work, and labour exchanges to help people find jobs. Lloyd George's National Insurance Act of 1911 provided health and unemployment insurance for many workers.

Given the strength of support for individualism and self-help, it is astonishing that the Liberals did so much, and it should be no surprise that the reforms can hardly be described as fully collectivist. In fact the Liberals had no master plan for reform prepared when they came to power. Each reform was a response to a particular problem or situation, and politicians had mixed motives in acting as they did:

(a) *The New Liberalism*

In the last 20 years of the nineteenth century, many Liberals on the left wing of the party realized the need for more social reform, especially to help the unemployed, the old and the sick. Influenced by the economist J. A. Hobson and the sociologist L. T. Hobhouse, they accepted that the time had come for the Liberal party to turn away from laissez-faire; only when the state intervened could these nationwide social problems be effectively tackled. These New Liberals were a minority at first, but they gradually influenced and won over the moderate centre of the party (see Section 21.1 for more details about New Liberalism).

(b) *Compassion and a desire for justice and fairness*

Many Liberals felt that it was simply not right for a third of the population to be living in such misery at a time when the country as a whole was enjoying a fair degree of prosperity. It did not seem fair that when the profits of most industrialists were showing a healthy increase, the wages of those who were helping to earn those profits were hardly keeping up with the rise in prices. Statistics showed that half the total national income was going into the pockets of one-ninth of the population, and it seemed that prosperity and good times were passing the working class by. However, if this had been the only consideration, it is doubtful whether much would have been done.

(c) *The need for a healthy working class for military and economic purposes*

This was probably a more important motive. The poor physical condition of many working-class volunteers for the Boer War (1899–1902) had shocked the nation. If Britain were to be involved in a major war, an efficient army would be necessary to defend the Empire, and so it was vital that Britain's children should be properly fed and cared for. This was why the Committee on Physical Deterioration in 1904 suggested school meals and regular medical inspections. The Birmingham Chamber of Commerce called for health insurance on the grounds that a healthy workforce would be more efficient and more profitable. It was a question of national survival.

(d) *Pressure from the Labour Party and the trade unions*

29 Labour MPs had been elected in January 1906 and 24 Liberal MPs were trade unionists; they were now able to make their demands for free school meals and old age pensions heard in the House of Commons. When the Liberals began to lose by-elections to Labour, they decided that a limited amount of social reform would attract voters away from socialism and so defeat the challenge from the infant Labour party. This was certainly one motive for the introduction of old age pensions in 1908 – Lloyd George remarked: 'it is time we did something that appealed straight to the people – it will, I think, help to stop this electoral rot and that is most necessary'. This became even more urgent after the two general elections of 1910 which left the Liberals with only 272 seats instead of the 400 won in 1906. Labour had gone up to 42, the Irish Nationalists to 84, and with the Conservatives also on 272, the Liberals were dependent on Irish and Labour support to stay in office. The need to 'steal Labour's thunder' was one motive for Lloyd George's National Insurance Act of 1911.

(e) *The need for policies to distinguish the Liberals from the Conservatives*

Some Conservatives, for example, had wanted to introduce free school meals, but Balfour refused because of the cost, which would have to be met by increasing taxes or local rates. Here was an excellent chance to show that the Liberals had something different to offer.

(f) *Liberal politicians wanting to make a name for themselves*

Both Lloyd George and Churchill, who were responsible for most of the reforms, were ambitious politicians who were keen to make a name for themselves. They genuinely wanted to help the poor, but they wanted to further their own careers as well. As historian Derek Fraser puts it, writing about the campaign to get National Insurance introduced: 'it had always been Lloyd George's intention to make a great stir, to do something really big that would attract public attention'. An observer wrote of Churchill in 1908: 'He is out for adventure; he follows politics as he would follow the hounds. I wonder whether he has any driving motive save ambition.'

20.3 What were the Liberal reforms and how far did they go towards creating a Welfare State?

(a) *Trade union legislation*

- *The Trade Disputes Act (1906).* Since 1901 the trade unions had been agitating for some action to reverse the Taff Vale decision (see Section 19.6(b)) which made it almost impossible for a union to conduct a strike without risking bankruptcy. The cabinet agreed that something ought to be done to protect trade union funds and thus keep the support of organized labour, but it got into a tangle trying to draw up a bill which gave the unions only limited powers. The Labour party had its own bill prepared, so Campbell-Bannerman decided to accept it as it stood, to save time. The resulting Act was therefore more drastic than many Liberals intended: unions could not be sued for damages, and peaceful picketing was allowed. Critics felt that this gave far too much power to the unions, which were now more or less immune from the law.

- *The Trade Union Act (1913)* remedied the situation caused by the Osborne Judgement of 1909 (see Section 19.6(c) for full details). It was prompted by the desire to soothe union militancy, and, given the Liberals' much weaker position following the 1910 general elections (see Section 21.3(c)), by the need to keep the support of the Labour MPs, now 42 in number.

(b) *Measures to help children*

1   Local education authorities were given the power, if they wished to use it, to provide free school meals for needy children (1906). This developed from a Labour bill, but its immediate effects were not as great as had been hoped, since *it was not compulsory*. By 1914 less than half the education authorities in England and Wales were providing meals, so in that year the government made it compulsory and provided some funds to help towards the cost.

2   There were to be compulsory medical inspections in schools, and education authorities could provide free medical treatment (1907). Again this was a hesitant measure since many authorities ignored the second part of the Act. However, in 1912 government grants were made available to provide treatment, and school clinics began to be set up.

3   Child offenders were to be tried not in ordinary lawcourts but in special juvenile courts, and were to be sent to corrective schools (borstals) instead of to ordinary prisons. Probation officers were to be appointed for after-care. There were to be stiff penalties for people ill-treating children or selling them cigarettes and tobacco, or alcohol in unsealed bottles or jugs (1908).

4   The Liberals took action on the academic side of education. Already by 1900 the state had taken over the responsibility for financing and organizing elementary education which was free and compulsory for all children. Secondary education was a different matter. Balfour's Education Act of 1902 gave local authorities power to help existing voluntary secondary schools with money from the rates; they were also directed to set up their own secondary schools. However, these were fee-paying, and very few working-class parents could afford the fees. The Liberals therefore introduced the 'free place' system – all secondary schools had to reserve 25 per cent of their places free of charge for children from elementary schools; they would be awarded scholarships on the results of a special entrance examination.

In spite of its weaknesses, this *Children's Charter*, as it became known, was important because it was the first time any government had intervened so directly in the lives of ordinary people. It was providing help not as a charity as the Poor Law did, but as a right, and it was a service to which all were entitled. The state was at last beginning to admit that it had a responsibility to look after the poor.

(c) *Old age pensions*

These were introduced at the rate of five shillings (25p) a week at the age of 70, not at 65 as Charles Booth had suggested. It was a non-contributory pension (people did not have to pay anything towards it). It was to be financed by the government out of taxation, and it would be paid out at post offices. No one could receive the pension if his income from other sources exceeded £21 a year or if he had a conviction for drunkenness or some other offence. The Labour Party complained that five shillings was too little and that many people would not survive until 70 to enjoy it. Nevertheless, the pension was enormously popular and Lloyd George gained credit for it. However, it left the strange situation that Britain had two parallel systems for dealing with the poor; the new system was growing up alongside the Poor Law.

(d) *Measures to help working people*

1 A *Workmen's Compensation Act (1906)* extended the earlier Conservative Act of 1897 to include all categories of worker, and also allowed compensation for injury to health caused by industrial conditions as well as for injury caused by accidents.

2 *The Merchant Shipping Act (1906)* introduced stringent regulations covering standards of food and accommodation for crews on British registered ships. This was the work of Lloyd George who was already showing considerable drive at the Board of Trade, where he was also responsible for a *Patents Act* which gave inventors more protection.

3 *The Mines Act (1908)* introduced a maximum eight-hour working day for miners. This was a remarkable milestone since it was the first time the British government had intervened to regulate the working hours of adult males. In 1912 came *the Minimum Wage Act* which set up local boards to fix minimum wages in each district in order to help miners working in difficult seams. This sounds impressive, but the Act was an emergency measure forced through parliament to end the damaging coal strike which had lasted from February to April. Nor did it fully satisfy the miners who had been campaigning for *a national minimum wage* of five shillings (25p) a day for a man and two shillings for a boy.

4 *Labour Exchanges* were set up (1909) by Churchill and William Beveridge at the Board of Trade. This was an idea pressed on the government by Beatrice Webb and recommended in her Minority Poor Law Report. With unemployment rising steeply in 1908 and 1909 – in some trades it was double the 1907 figure – Churchill decided to act. Employers with vacancies were to inform the Labour Exchanges so that unemployed workers could easily find out what jobs were available. By 1913 there were 430 exchanges in Britain and the system was working well; but again it could have gone further – it was only voluntary at this stage.

5 *The Trade Boards Act (1909)* was another of Churchill's achievements; it dealt with the problem of low-paid and depressed workers in what were called the 'sweated' industries. These usually employed female and child labourers working excessively long hours in their own homes for outrageously low wages. Described by Charles Booth as 'a body of reckless, starving competitors for work', their plight had been publicized by the National Anti-Sweating League, since the nature of their work made trade union organization impossible. Churchill's Act set up boards to fix minimum wages in four occupations: tailoring, lace-making, box-making and chain-making. In 1913 this was extended to cover six more 'sweated' trades, so that now almost 400 000 workers were protected and were ensured a reasonable wage. This certainly broke new ground, showing that the state was prepared to make some move towards establishing a minimum wage, as Seebohm Rowntree had suggested; but it was a pity that only a small fraction of the total workforce was affected.

6 *The Shops Act (1911)* gave shop assistants a statutory half day holiday each week, but unfortunately it did not limit hours of work. This meant that assistants were often required to make up for the half day off by working later at other times during the week.

(e) *The National Insurance Act of 1911*

This was the most important of the Liberal measures to help working people and it was

Lloyd George's greatest achievement before 1914. It was a compulsory scheme in two parts: one provided some health insurance, the other unemployment insurance. The Act introduced a new principle – unlike old age pensions which were non-contributory, this was to be *a contributory insurance scheme* into which workers themselves had to pay. The Labour party wanted the scheme to be non-contributory but Lloyd George believed it would be far too expensive to finance the whole thing from the treasury, especially as the cost of old age pensions had turned out to be much higher than anybody had expected. It had been partly to offset the high cost of pensions and other future reforms that Lloyd George had introduced his controversial budget of 1909, which taxed the rich in order to help the poor; in that sense this was a collectivist action by Lloyd George (see Section 21.1). The reason for the introduction of health insurance was very much the drive for greater national efficiency, though Lloyd George was genuinely concerned at the large number of deaths from tuberculosis – estimated at 75 000 a year. Unemployment insurance was a response to Labour party and trade union pressure. Both were an attempt by the Liberals to head off socialism.

- *Health insurance* was provided by a fund into which the worker paid fourpence, the employer threepence and the state twopence a week. When he was off work ill, the worker would receive ten shillings (50p) a week sick pay for 13 weeks, and was entitled to free medical attention and medicines, a maternity grant of 30 shillings and a sanatoria allowance if he fell ill with tuberculosis. The obvious drawback was that benefits (apart from the maternity grant) did not apply to the worker's wife and children, nor to those earning more than £160 a year.

The whole scheme caused bitter controversy: although Labour moderates accepted the contributory principle, strong socialists like Keir Hardie were against it and they demanded even higher taxes on the wealthy so that the scheme would be a genuinely collectivist solution to the problem of poverty. Another complaint, bearing in mind the small state contribution, was that instead of providing sickness benefit, the state was merely forcing workers to provide their own.

The Conservatives succeeded in turning many workers against it by arguing that the government had no right to force people to pay into the scheme directly from their wages. There was also opposition from doctors who feared they would lose their independence, and from friendly societies and insurance companies who were afraid of losing business. It was here that Lloyd George showed his skill in reconciling all the conflicting interests; it was decided, for example, that the scheme would be operated by 'approved societies', usually insurance companies, as it turned out, which workers would join. However, these would be under state supervision.

- *Unemployment insurance* applied only to workers in certain trades where the demand for labour fluctuated most; these were building, shipbuilding, mechanical engineering, iron-founding, vehicle construction and sawmilling. Worker and employer both paid two and a half pence into the fund and the state twopence. The unemployment benefit was seven shillings a week up to a maximum of 15 weeks in any 12-month period. Soon 2.25 million men were protected by this scheme, though its obvious drawback was that it covered only a small handful of trades. There was also the question of what would happen after 15 weeks if the worker was still unemployed; and there was the criticism that again, as with health insurance, the state's contribution was too small. It is important to remember though, that Lloyd George intended both parts of the Act to be an experimental beginning, to be extended as soon as possible; but unfortunately the First World War intervened. Nevertheless it was an important extension of state aid and it established the principle that health and unemployment schemes should be contributory.

(f) *The Housing and Town Planning Act (1909)*

This introduced compulsory slum clearance schemes and gave local councils the power to build council houses. New regulations specified that houses should not be built more than 12 to an acre and banned the building of back-to-back houses. Again this Act had its faults – although it resulted in the demolition of some of the country's worst slums, very few councils took up the option to build new houses to replace them, because there was no government cash forthcoming to help with the cost.

(g) *How successful were the reforms?*

Although individual reforms had varying degrees of success, taken together they must have done something to relieve the worst effects of poverty. However, in 1914 there were still some areas which had not been touched by any of this legislation. For example, hardly any of the recommendations of the Poor Law Commission Reports (apart from Labour Exchanges) had been carried out, leaving the country with an unsatisfactory dual system in which the new state aid was being provided alongside the old Poor Law, with its stigma of charity, which continued until 1929. Nothing had been done for agricultural labourers who remained the worst paid of all workers. Between 1900 and 1914 real wages rose very little, and the trade unions were not impressed by the reforms, as they showed by their increasing militancy between 1910 and 1914. Another disturbing fact was that in 1914 the percentage of army volunteers rejected as physically unfit was almost as high as it had been in 1900. However, this was only to be expected; there was bound to be a time-lag before the benefits of the new state aid made themselves felt.

It is easy, with the benefit of hindsight, to be critical of the Liberals for being too cautious. But it is important to remember that they had to face determined opposition from the Conservatives and sometimes from the right wing of the Liberal Party itself – in the election of January 1910 about 25 Liberal MPs stood down rather than support a programme which they saw as too left-wing. Given the strong support still around for individualism and self-help, the Liberals deserve credit for going as far as they did. The vitally important point was that the government had laid the foundations on which Lloyd George and Churchill intended to build later. They weren't to know that, following the First World War and the rapid rise of the Labour party, there would never be another Liberal government after May 1915.

(h) *How far had Britain moved towards a Welfare State by 1914?*

There are differing opinions about this:

● Jo Grimond (Liberal leader from 1956 until 1967) claimed that the Liberal reforms were so novel for the times that they established all the necessary basic principles and therefore as good as created the Welfare State.
● Historian Arthur Marwick believes that the full Welfare State was not created until after the Second World War by the Labour governments of 1945–51.
● Another historian, Donald Read, came up with a good compromise conclusion: he suggests that what the Liberals had achieved – and it *was* a new departure – was the beginnings of a *social service state* rather than a *welfare state*. The difference is this: a *social service state* is one in which certain minimum standards are ensured by the government; a *welfare state* is one where the government provides the best possible services for everybody.

20.4 State social policy between the wars: problems and successes

(a) *Effects of the First World War*

Historians disagree about how profound the effects of the First World War were on British society. Some, like Martin Pugh, feel that the war merely speeded up developments which had already started. Others, like Arthur Marwick and Derek Fraser, believe the effects were more dramatic. There can be no doubt that the war did have important effects on the role of the state in British society. Whether it wanted to or not, the government was forced to abandon *laissez-faire* so that the war could be fought more efficiently. The government controlled and directed the life of the nation in a way which would have been unthinkable before the war. Coalmines and merchant shipping were taken over directly by the state, factories were told what to produce, strikes and lockouts were prohibited, farmers were obliged to cultivate more land, wages and prices were controlled and food was rationed. Although most of this was abandoned at the end of the war, people had become used to the idea of state intervention (see Section 22.5 for more about the effects of the war on British society).

As the war dragged on, people began to talk about post-war 'Reconstruction'. In July 1917 the government set up a Ministry of Reconstruction and a Ministry of Pensions; it seemed to be taken for granted that the state would plan and carry out this reconstruction. Clearly state collectivism was much more widely accepted than it had been before the war.

The idea began to spread that working-class people deserved some rewards for their sacrifices during the war; Lloyd George talked about building 'homes fit for heroes'; H. A. L. Fisher, the Minister for Education, wanted better education for everybody. Other areas mentioned for improvement were unemployment insurance and health. In a speech in 1917 Lloyd George said: 'the country will be prepared for bigger things immediately after the war ... it will be in a more enthusiastic mood'. Improvements were certainly made in all four areas mentioned: education, housing, health, unemployment insurance, and in health insurance and pensions as well, as the following sections (c) to (h) show. However, the amount of legislation introduced up to 1939 may seem disappointing, given all the brave talk of 1917–18. The truth is that a variety of problems arose which limited the extent of state intervention in the inter-war years.

(b) *Problems limiting state intervention – slump, economic decline and unemployment*

- Soon after the end of the war, starting at the beginning of 1921, there was a severe slump which threw about two million people out of work by the end of the year. There was a reduction in government revenue (money flowing into the treasury from taxation) caused partly by the general falling-off of trade, and partly by the enormous expense of unemployment benefit. It meant also that there was less government money to be spent on other social welfare policies like education and health.
- Some parts of British industry went into a slow but permanent decline which became apparent during the 1920s, causing a steady rise in unemployment. This is known as *structural unemployment* – people were unemployed because there was something wrong with the structure of the economy. Unemployment caused by a slump is known as *cyclical unemployment*, since it is caused by the operation of the trade cycle – trade flows in a fairly regular cycle of boom followed by a slump, which gradually

develops into another boom. People in cyclical unemployment tend to be out of work for short periods until the next boom arrives, but people in structural unemployment are likely to be out of work for much longer periods because there is something seriously wrong with the structure of the economy. This was the case in Britain in the 1920s and 1930s when unemployment in certain areas refused to go away. These areas were Scotland, Tyne-Tees, Cumberland, Lancashire, Northern Ireland and South Wales, where the older export industries – coal, textiles, shipbuilding, iron and steel – were situated.

Reasons for Britain's economic decline:

● Even before the First World War these older industries had begun to suffer competition from abroad; after the war, many countries did not resume buying British goods because they had found alternative sources. There was fierce competition from more highly mechanized and more efficient foreign industries and cheaper foreign goods, such as Japanese and East European textiles. India, the main market for British textiles before the war, was rapidly developing her own industry. Coal exports were badly hit by cheap coal from Germany, Poland and Holland and the world demand for coal was decreasing anyway as oil, gas and electricity came into wider use. By 1939 over half the world's merchant ships were using oil instead of coal. More efficient rival shipyards had opened in the USA, Japan, Holland and Scandinavia. Many foreign countries introduced tariff barriers to protect their home industries; some governments began to subsidize their industries to enable them to compete more successfully. However, in Britain, very little was done to modernize these struggling industries and there were no state subsidies. There were far too many small coal-mines which were expensive to operate and therefore uncompetitive; the cotton industry was slow to adopt automatic looms and electric power; the more profits fell, the less cash was available for reinvestment in new techniques and equipment. Worse still was that foreign rivals were gaining a foothold in the British market: there were textiles from India as well as foreign ships, iron and steel.

● The World Economic Crisis, which began in the USA with the Wall Street Crash in October 1929, made unemployment in Britain much worse. As the world moved into a slump, demand for British goods declined, throwing more people out of work in the areas already depressed, and causing cyclical unemployment in other areas. By 1932 almost 23 per cent of the insured workforce was unemployed; in the old staple industries in the depressed areas the figures were appalling – 59.5 per cent in shipbuilding, 48.5 per cent in iron and steel and 41.2 per cent in coal (see Section 25.4 for full details). Unemployment benefit was costing the treasury well over three times the amount it was getting from contributions.

● The governments were constantly having to wrestle with the problem of how to finance unemployment benefit and other social policies. From 1930 onwards, no matter how well-intentioned a government was, its first priority was always to restrict expenditure so that it could balance the budget without having to raise taxes. Often it tried to deal with this problem by pressurizing local authorities to pay more towards the cost of social services. Another device was to keep benefits lower than wages and to make them *means-tested*; this is when the total income and assets of the household were taken into account in deciding the level of benefit to be paid. This aroused considerable resentment among respectable working people who felt they were being cheated out of what was rightfully theirs.

(c) *Unemployment and poverty*

Governments spent more time and energy on this area of social welfare than on any other, which was not surprising since unemployment was the most pressing problem of the inter-war years.

1   *The Unemployment Insurance Act of 1920* brought in a great expansion of Lloyd George's 1911 scheme to include most workers with incomes under £250 a year (except agricultural labourers, domestic servants and self-employed people). Contributions were increased, but so were benefits – from seven shillings to fifteen shillings a week for up to fifteen weeks per year. In 1921 extra allowances were made for an unemployed man's wife and family. These were admirable steps forward: not far short of two-thirds of the entire labour force were now insured against unemployment. Unfortunately there were problems almost immediately: the scheme was expected to be self-supporting, but unemployment rose so sharply during 1921 that it was soon running deeply into debt.

2   Lloyd George's coalition government (1918–22) accepted that the state would have to contribute more, since many workers had still failed to find jobs at the end of the fifteen weeks. In theory, any worker still unemployed after he had exhausted his fifteen weeks' benefit would have to apply to the local Poor Law for further relief. This was an intolerable prospect for most workers, and anyway the Poor Law would hardly be able to bear the additional cost. There was unrest in industrial areas, and the danger of riots and perhaps even revolution if nothing was done to help. It was under these pressures that Lloyd George extended the benefit to two sixteen-week periods per year, with a gap between (1921). The extra payments were called 'uncovenanted' benefits (meaning that the worker had not contributed anything towards them), and they later became known as the 'dole'. Because the dole was in a sense a 'gift' from the treasury, it was means-tested; careful checks were made into family circumstances to make sure that the unemployed man did genuinely need the extra payments. Lloyd George had accepted a new principle: *unemployment benefit was no longer just an insurance scheme; it was in many cases long-term maintenance by the state.* The first Labour government (1924) removed the gap between the two periods of benefit.

3   *The Unemployment Insurance Act of 1927* (the work of Neville Chamberlain, Minister of Health in Stanley Baldwin's Conservative government) abolished the distinction between 'covenanted' and 'uncovenanted' benefit. Benefit would be paid for an unlimited period, provided an unemployed person could show that he had genuinely been seeking work. The extra benefit over and above what he would have received as 'covenanted' benefit (which he had paid for by his contributions), was now known as 'transitional' benefit. Here the Conservatives were accepting *the principle of long-term maintenance by the state*, though workers' contributions were increased and benefits decreased.

4   The Conservatives were also responsible for another major step forward – *the end of the Poor Law (1929–30)*. Although Beatrice Webb had been advocating this since 1904, all governments had shied away from such a daunting problem. It was still the last resort for people not covered by state welfare provision. According to historian John Stevenson, 'between one third and one fifth of those dying in the larger cities and towns could expect to end their days in the workhouse or Poor Law infirmaries'. At times of high unemployment, as many as one and a half million people were claiming financial help from the Poor Law, and the burden on the local rates was becoming unbearable. Neville Chamberlain (as part of his 1929 Local Government Act) abolished the entire Poor Law system and handed all the workhouses and other buildings over to the county and county borough councils,

which were expected to appoint Public Assistance Committees (PACs) to be responsible for the care of the poor. Local authorities were to receive a grant from the government towards the cost of these services. The new system was much more efficient, but it was still not perfect; one drawback was that the local authorities still had to use the same buildings, and though the names and the administration had changed, the poor still thought of them with loathing as the workhouse. It was only very gradually that this attitude changed.

5 *Unemployment benefit was cut by 10 per cent in 1931*, bringing it down to 15s. 3d a week. This was the result of the financial and political crisis which in August 1931 brought down the second Labour government (1929–31). The world economic crisis sent unemployment shooting up to over two and a half million, causing a massive increase in 'transitional' benefits from the treasury. In 1931 the state paid out £120 million in benefits, but only took in £44 million from contributions. Foreign bankers would only make new loans to the government on condition that expenditure was reduced, and this included unemployment benefit. The Labour government resigned rather than comply (see Section 25.2), but the National government which took over from Labour had no hesitation in introducing the 10 per cent cut.

6 *The Unemployment Act of 1934* (the National government's next attempt to deal with the problem) introduced yet another new scheme distinguishing between 'covenanted' benefit paid from insurance contributions, and 'unemployment assistance', paid by a new *Unemployment Assistance Board (UAB)* financed by the treasury. Branches of the new UAB all over the country would pay out means-tested 'assistance', taking over this function from the PACs. This aroused massive protests in some areas when it was discovered that the new 'assistance' rates were less than the old relief rates paid locally by the PACs. There were demonstrations in South Wales, and eventually the government gave way and allowed payment of whichever rate was higher. The 10 per cent cut was restored and benefit was payable from the age of 14. In certain areas the assistance rates were actually higher than some wages – so the 'less eligibility' principle had gone at last. However, the means test was bitterly resented, especially when a man was refused benefit because other members of his family were working, or because he had some savings. It could be demoralizing when a man seemed to be penalized because he had been careful and thrifty, or when he had to be supported financially by his own children.

7 *Agricultural workers were insured for the first time in 1936.* By this time the pressure on the treasury was beginning to subside, and by 1937 unemployment was down to 1.4 million, the lowest level since the end of 1929.

Provision for the unemployed was probably the most successful of the state's welfare policies during the inter-war period, though the amounts paid were perhaps inadequate and the means test unsatisfactory. Some historians believe that Lloyd George's extension of the scheme in 1920–1 saved the country from revolution. Later developments, though haphazard and unplanned, did at least get rid of the old Poor Law and the 'less eligibility' principle. Most important of all, the state had accepted responsibility for financing 'transitional benefits'.

(d) *Housing*

This was an area in which great things were expected of the government, bearing in mind Lloyd George's promises to build 'homes fit for heroes'. Very few new houses had been built during the war and it was estimated that 600 000 were needed.

1   *The Addison Housing Act of 1919* (the work of Christopher Addison, Minister of Health in Lloyd George's coalition government) provided government cash for local authorities to build houses for the working classes. This was an important milestone: the principle was now established that provision of reasonable housing was the responsibility of the state. By the end of 1922 over 213 000 new houses had been built, but the scheme was abandoned in 1922 as part of the government's economy drive during the slump.

2   *The Wheatley Housing Act of 1924* was an attempt by the first Labour government to get house building moving again. It provided grants of £9 million a year to local authorities to build council houses, which would be for rent only. Rents were to be at pre-war levels so that working people would be able to afford them. This scheme ran successfully until 1933 when over half a million new houses had been built under the Act.

3   *The Greenwood Housing Act of 1930*, another Labour measure, provided government subsidies to local authorities to clear slums and to build new houses to replace them. The National government suspended the scheme from 1931 to 1934 when the slump was at its worst, though in fact thousands of jobs could have been created if the scheme had continued. It also decided to end the subsidy provided by the Wheatley Act, believing that private enterprise ought to build working-class houses that were not direct replacements for demolished slums. When the worst of the slump was over, the scheme was started up again and by 1939 over 700 000 council houses had been built to rehouse slum dwellers.

Clearly housing conditions improved considerably between the wars, with the building of well over a million new council houses (plus about three million built by private enterprise). The new council houses tended to be far superior to the houses they replaced: they were brighter, more spacious and easier to clean, and had more bedrooms and better sanitary facilities. Between 1918 and 1939 the government spent over £208 million on housing and slum clearance – a staggering amount for those days, bearing in mind the economic difficulties. The average number of people per house was reduced from 5.4 to 3.5. But there was still a long way to go – many of the new houses only replaced those which had been demolished. There was still serious overcrowding in some areas, especially Scotland where in 1936 almost a quarter of all houses were overcrowded.

(e) *Education*

●   *Fisher's Education Act of 1918* was a product of the war. Fisher believed that the working class deserved a better education in order to avoid 'intellectual wastage'. There was to be full-time compulsory education for all up to the age of 14, and more free places at secondary schools for bright children from poor backgrounds. Teachers' salaries were made uniform throughout the country. Local authorities could provide 'continuation schools' for young people up to the age of 16, as well as nursery schools for under-fives. Unfortunately only the first part of the Act was carried out. From 1921 government attempts to economize fell heavily on education; hardly any continuation or nursery schools were built.

●   The Labour Party deplored the fact that the vast majority of working-class children did not receive any education beyond the age of 14. C. P. Trevelyan, Labour's Minister of Education, was a strong believer in *'Secondary Education for All'*, and he appointed a committee chaired by Sir Henry Hadow to look into how this might be achieved (1924). *The Hadow Report (1926)* was an important milestone in education: it recommended the break between primary and secondary education at the age of 11, and a school-leaving age of 15. There should be two types of secondary school:

1   the existing ones, now to be called 'grammar schools', were to provide an advanced academic education;
2   'modern schools' which most children would attend until the age of 15.

Although these recommendations were generally accepted, very little was done in the immediate future because of economic difficulties. No government legislation followed, and by 1939 only a tiny fraction of working-class children were getting any 'advanced' secondary education; this was not seen as a priority area.

(f) *Pensions*

1   The non-contributory old age pension of five shillings a week at 70, first introduced in 1908, was increased to ten shillings a week in 1919 by the Lloyd George coalition government. Many socialists pressed for it to be paid at 60, but all governments thought that a non-contributory pension for so many extra people would be an impossible burden on the treasury.
2   *The Widows', Orphans' and Old Age Contributory Pensions Act (1925)* was the main development – another Conservative measure steered through by Neville Chamberlain. It was a compulsory insurance scheme into which both workers and employers paid, and to which the state would also contribute. It provided a worker with a pension of ten shillings a week from 65 to 70 (without means test), £1 for a married couple, ten shillings a week for a widow, extra payments for children (five shillings for the first child and three shillings each for other children) and seven shillings and sixpence a week for orphans. The scheme was extended to self-employed workers in 1937.

This was in many ways a welcome extension of pensions, *but there was much controversy over the principle behind it*. The Labour party complained that workers were really paying for their own pensions, and that if the Conservatives had not kept on reducing income tax, the whole scheme could have been financed from the treasury; and in fact under Chamberlain's scheme the treasury contributions were quite small. According to R. C. Birch, Chamberlain 'had neither the resources nor the imagination to practise generosity'. Another criticism was that the system of pensions was now unnecessarily complicated: the old non-contributory pension at 70 still continued, and the insured worker had to transfer to this scheme when he reached the age of 70.

(g) *Health insurance*

This was the most disappointing area of state welfare activity between the wars, with *no major change in the 1911 health insurance provision*. The weekly payment was raised from ten to fifteen shillings in 1919, but in 1926 the state reduced its contribution. A Royal Commission on National Health Insurance (1926) recommended that it should be extended to cover a worker's wife and children. Another point made was that some of the 'approved societies' which administered the scheme were offering better services than others; it was suggested that the insurance companies should pool their resources in order to provide wider and better services for all. However, the larger and more wealthy companies (such as the Prudential and the Pearl) objected to being expected to subsidize the smaller ones. They were in business primarily for profit, not to improve the nation's health. So powerful was their influence that the system survived without any improvements or extensions until after the Second World War. *The most glaring criticisms were:*

- no provision for workers' families to have medical treatment;
- no payments towards the cost of hospital treatment;
- not enough hospitals provided by local authorities. This was because the new

Ministry of Health set up in 1919 had taken no action to *compel* local authorities to provide hospitals.

(h) *How effective were government social policies by 1939?*

There can be no doubt that the average citizen was much better provided for in 1939 than in 1914 in the areas of housing, unemployment insurance and pensions. State spending on social services increased dramatically from £22 million in 1913–14 to £204 million in 1935–6, though one striking point about these statistics is that the actual proportion of government expenditure devoted to the social services remained almost exactly the same – about one-third.

The most obvious areas of failure were in health insurance and education. Left-wingers deplored the acceptance of the insurance principle, believing that this was not a genuine state collectivist solution to the problem of poverty, but merely a device to shift the responsibility for decent social services onto the workers themselves and their employers.

Although most people were in work and enjoying an increase in real wages after 1935, there was still some appalling poverty in the depressed areas which could have been given more help. Seebohm Rowntree carried out another survey of York which was reasonably prosperous in the late 1930s. His conclusion, published in 1941, was that the standard of living of the workers in York was about 30 per cent higher than in 1899, thanks to smaller families, the increase in real wages, and 'the remarkable growth of social services'. But he went on to point out that 'there is no cause for satisfaction in the fact that in a country so rich as England, over 30 per cent of the workers in a typical provincial city have incomes so small that it is beyond their means to live even at the basic subsistence level ... nor in the fact that almost half the children of working-class parents spend the first five years of their lives in poverty'. In 1939 there was still no generally planned social policy and certainly no planned economy.

20.5 Why was the idea of a planned economy discussed between the wars and what plans were suggested?

(a) *Why was the idea discussed?*

During the 1920s many people began to feel that *something was seriously wrong with the British economy.* The main symptom was the persistently high level of unemployment which never fell below a million between the wars. There had been spells of unemployment during the nineteenth century, but these had usually been fairly short-lived – most workers found jobs again when the next boom came along. However, after the First World War, the next boom was very slow to arrive in the old established industries (coal, iron, steel and shipbuilding) which were now clearly seen to be in decline. Reasons for the decline are explained in Section 20.4(b).

Structural unemployment therefore seemed to be here to stay. To make matters worse, the depression in world trade from 1929 to 1933 affected most British industries, adding cyclical unemployment to the existing structural unemployment. British exports in 1932 were only half what they had been in 1913, and unemployment reached a new peak at 2.8 million. The economy recovered gradually and unemployment began to fall; by 1937 the Midlands and the south were prosperous again, with only 7 per cent of the workforce unemployed; but in the north of England, Wales, Scotland and Northern Ireland, structural unemployment lingered stubbornly on with, on average, 20 per cent of the insured workers out of a job.

Some people believed that unemployment had become a permanent feature and was an unavoidable evil of modern economies. They concentrated on trying to work out the best way of caring for the unemployed. A more imaginative approach was to argue that it ought to be possible to defeat unemployment by careful planning or managing of the economy; a wide variety of suggestions appeared both from the right and the left of politics.

(b) *What policies were suggested?*

1   *The Liberals put forward some good ideas in their 1929 election manifesto*, written with the guidance of John Maynard Keynes, a leading economist and Liberal supporter. Keynes believed that the vast amounts of government money being paid out in unemployment benefit would be far better spent financing works schemes and new industries which would create lots of new jobs. The workers in these new jobs would receive wages instead of unemployment benefit and would be able to afford to buy more than if they had been unemployed; this in turn would help to revive trade. What Keynes was suggesting was that *a government should spend its way out of a depression* instead of following the usual practice of cutting government expenditure and wages, which, Keynes thought, would only reduce people's purchasing power and so make the depression worse. The Liberals therefore proposed spending £250 million on public works – building new roads and houses, and extending electricity to all homes.

2   *Many Conservatives had similar ideas*; one of their leading thinkers was Harold Macmillan, MP for Stockton-on-Tees. They produced a document called *Peace and Reconstruction* (1935) setting out detailed public works schemes which could be organized by government and local authorities, using cash which would have been spent on unemployment benefit.

3   *A group known as Political and Economic Planning (PEP)* involved a wide cross-section of people – Liberal and Conservative politicians, businessmen, bankers, economists, architects and town-planners. They believed that the needs of industry and the social services should be investigated carefully so that things could be planned well in advance instead of in the haphazard fashion of the 1920s. Starting in 1931, they produced a flood of reports on every conceivable subject from housing and the health service to the reorganization and relocation of industry.

4   *The Mosley Memorandum (1930)* was an interesting plan worked out by Sir Oswald Mosley (Chancellor of the Duchy of Lancaster in the second Labour government), after consultations with Keynes, to deal with the economic crisis of 1930–1. He suggested import restrictions, subsidies for farmers (to reduce food imports), government control of banks to ensure that industry was allowed more credit (to enable new industries to expand), old age pensions at 60 and the school-leaving age at 15 (instead of 14). These last two measures would have made an immediate impact on unemployment. Although there was much support in the Labour party for Mosley's plan, the leaders rejected it.

5   *Later there were other plans within the Labour party* which was gradually taking on

Keynes's ideas of a planned economy, together with a greatly expanded network of social services. The most radical cure suggested for the ailing economy was the socialist idea of *nationalization*. In a pamphlet entitled *The Theory and Practice of Socialism (1935)* John Strachey argued that boom, overproduction and slump were inevitable in an uncontrolled capitalist economy. Nationalization (taking into state ownership and control) of the main industries would enable careful forecasting and planning to take place so that production could be limited to need, and slumps and unemployment therefore eliminated.

(c) *Lack of government action*

Successive governments largely ignored all this good advice. Some action was taken but it was the usual piecemeal government approach and it failed to get to the root of the problem.

- *Free trade was abandoned in 1932* when a 10 per cent duty was placed on imports.
- *The Special Areas Act (1934)* appointed two unpaid commissioners and gave them £2 million to try to revive Scotland, Cumberland, Tyneside and South Wales. This had little effect because employers could not be compelled to move into depressed areas. Businessmen were much more attracted to the Midlands and South-East and the ready markets of the London area. Later the government offered rates, rent and income tax remission to encourage firms to move in. This resulted in the setting up of trading estates such as the ones at Treforest (South Wales) and Larkhall (near Glasgow); but these provided only a few thousand jobs, many of them for women.
- *An attempt was made to revive the steel industry* by imposing a tariff on foreign steel and setting up the British Iron and Steel Federation. Government pressure brought about the building of two new steelworks at Ebbw Vale and Corby, but the federation was bitterly criticized for refusing to allow one to be built at Jarrow where the unemployment rate was the highest in the country.
- From 1936 onwards *the rearmament programme helped to create extra jobs*.

But by 1939 there was still no sign of any long-term strategy emerging to plan the economy and eliminate unemployment.

(d) *Why was more not done?*

1   Although many of the ideas suggested were supported by people in all three political parties, there were never enough of them to form a majority. The Mosley Memorandum, for instance, had a lot of support in the Labour Party, and many Liberals would have voted for some of its proposals. But it was never even considered in the Commons because a majority of Labour MPs, including MacDonald (the Prime Minister) and Philip Snowden (Chancellor of the Exchequer), were against it.
2   A majority of MPs in all three parties were still convinced that unemployment was incurable and that the only way to deal with it was to try and make unemployment insurance as effective as possible.
3   All the proposals would cost money and the leading politicians were very cautious. They all felt, as did the Bank of England and the Treasury, that the most important requirement was to keep government expenditure as low as possible in a time of depression in order to balance the budget. Borrowing should also be kept to a minimum. They believed that Keynes's proposals to 'spend your way out of a depression' were far too risky – not sound economics. This was why MacDonald and Snowden refused to contemplate Mosley's plans in 1930, and why from 1931

until 1940 Chamberlain took very little notice of the suggestions put forward by PEP. For the next major steps, the country had to wait until after the Second World War (see Chapter 29).

Questions

1 Poverty and self-help

Study Sources A to F and then answer the questions which follow.

— **Source A** —————————————————————————————————————

A diagram and some of the findings from Seebohm Rowntree's investigation into poverty in York, first published in 1901

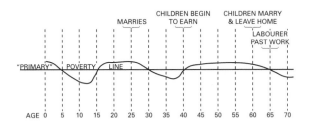

Every labourer who has as many as three children must pass through a time, probably lasting about ten years, when he will be in a state of 'primary' poverty; in other words when he and his family will be *underfed* . . .

The wages paid for unskilled labour in York are insufficient to provide food, shelter and clothing adequate to maintain a family of moderate size in a state of bare physical efficiency – a diet less generous than that allowed in the York workhouse. No allowance is made for any other expenditure. A family like this must never spend a penny on railway fare or omnibus. They must never buy a newspaper or a ticket for a popular concert. They must write no letters to absent children for they cannot afford to pay the postage. They cannot save, nor can they join a sick club or trade union. The children must have no pocket money for dolls, marbles or sweets. The father must not smoke or drink beer.

Source: S. Rowntree, *Poverty, a Study of Town Life*, Nelson, 1914 edn.

— **Source B** —————————————————————————————————————

An investigation into poverty by Arthur Ponsonby, 1910

The following is authentic information based on actual facts:

Man of 'no occupation'. Married. Two rooms; two children; parish relief; ill; incapable. Two little girls, one consumptive. The rooms are miserable, badly ventilated and damp. This house shares one closet with six other houses, and one water tap with three others.

Another man of 'no occupation'. Married. Two children. Four houses. The London house has 62 rooms and there are 36 indoor servants.

Source: A. Ponsonby, *The Camel and the Needle's Eye*, 1910, quoted in D. Read (ed.), *Documents from Edwardian England*, Harrap, 1973.

A letter written in 1897

I have known Mrs D— for ten years and have found her to be a thoroughly honest woman from a respectable family. But what with bad trade she was nearly brought to starvation some time ago, and I try as often as I can to help her. My father and some more of the citizens of this delapidated town got up a Relief Committee and we started a Bread and Tea Fund for the winter months.

Source: quoted in P. Keating (ed.), *Into Unknown England*, Fontana, 1976.

Source D

From a book by Helen Bosanquet published in 1902

It still remains true that the strength of the people lies in its own conscious efforts to face difficulties and overcome them. 'Difficulties to overcome, and freedom to overcome them,' is an essential condition of progress for human beings of whatever position in life. Any class or any individual which is either unconsious of difficulties, or unable to make the effort to master them, must stagnate and ultimately deteriorate ... the real solution will rest in the hands, or rather the minds of the people most nearly affected. If they cannot be made to care for it and seek for it, it can never be given to them from outside. ... We can do much on the one hand to provide opportunities. Freedom from self-indulgence and from tyrannous appetites and blind vacancy can only be attained by the interests which draw a man out of himself; and these he will find largely in the difficulties which he has to overcome in life, and in the education which we put within his reach. Freedom from excessive toil can only come from economic improvement; and that can best be attained by raising a larger number to the ranks of skilled workers. But the one thing to avoid in all our work, whether legislative, social or personal, is the risk of diminishing the saving interests in the life of an individual or a class by doing for them what they could do for themselves.

Source: H. Bosanquet, *The Strength of the People*, Macmillan, 1902, quoted in Read, as for Source B.

Source E

The view of Lord Hugh Cecil, a Conservative MP, in 1912

Care for the rights of property must take precedence over social reform. It is plain that to take what one man has and give it to another is unjust, even though the first man be rich and the second poor. The state should help the poor only for reasons of charity; but I am sure that the poor have no *right* to assistance. The cruel state that leaves a man to starve does not actually injure him. The only question is, does it withhold from him something to which he is entitled? I find it hard to agree that it does.

Source: quoted in Read, as for Source B.

Extracts from a speech by Lloyd George, the Liberal Chancellor of the Exchequer, at Limehouse, 30 July 1909

This Budget is introduced for raising taxes that will bring forth fruit . . . provision for the aged and deserving poor – it was time it was done. (Cheers.) It is rather a shame for a rich country like ours – probably the richest country in the world – that it should allow those who have toiled all their days to end in poverty and possible starvation. (Hear, Hear.) It is rather hard that an old workman should have to find his way to the tomb through the brambles and thorns of poverty. (Cheers.) There are many in the country blessed by Providence with great wealth, and if there are amongst them men who grudge out of their riches a fair contribution towards the less fortunate of their fellow-countrymen, they are shabby rich men. (Cheers.) We are raising money to provide against the evils that follow from unemployment. We are raising money to provide for the sick and the widows and orphans. . . . I do not believe any fair-minded man would challenge the justice and the fairness of the objects which we have in view in raising this money.

Source: quoted in J. H. Bettey (ed.), *English Historical Documents 1906–39*, Routledge & Kegan Paul, 1967.

(a) Explain in your own words the meaning of the 'primary poverty' diagram in Source A. (4 marks)

(b) What do these sources reveal about the attitudes of their authors towards the poor? How do you explain the different attitudes? (18 marks)

(c) Using the information in Section 20.1(b) and the sources, explain the different causes of poverty in early-twentieth-century Britain. Which do you think were the most important causes? (14 marks)

(d) Using the evidence of the sources and the information in Chapter 20, explain why it took so long for the state to intervene on behalf of the poor. (14 marks)
(Total 50 marks)

2 Why were the revelations of Charles Booth and Seebohm Rowntree about poverty at the turn of the century both surprising and significant for British government and society? [NEAB]

⟨21⟩ The Liberals in power 1905–14

Summary of events

The Liberal government which took office in December 1905 and then won a landslide victory in the general election of January 1906 (see Section 17.6(b–c) for statistics and reasons) in many ways marked the beginning of a new era. For the first time Britain had a government which was not dominated by wealthy landowners and aristocrats. The radical wing of the Liberal party had come to the forefront, and though there were some aristocrats in the cabinet (like Sir Edward Grey, the Foreign Secretary), most of the senior posts were filled by lawyers (Asquith, Lloyd George and Haldane), with a sprinkling of writers and journalists. As President of the Local Government Board there was John Burns, who had worked as an engineer, had helped to organize the 1889 dock strike and had for a time been a member of the SDF before joining the Liberals. Also in parliament were the 29 new Labour MPs and 24 Liberal MPs sponsored by the miners' unions, who usually sat with the Labour men.

This radical predominance has led historians to describe these years as the era of New Liberalism. The Prime Minister, the 69-year-old Sir Henry Campbell-Bannerman, was a successful Scottish businessman who had been Liberal leader in the Commons since 1898. Generally regarded as a radical and known affectionately in the party as C-B, he was level-headed, kindly and sympathetic, but he was also tough and determined. Though he was not a brilliant speaker and not in robust health, he turned out to be an expert at managing his cabinet, which was full of brilliant men. Herbert Henry Asquith was Chancellor of the Exchequer, and David Lloyd George, a fiery young Welshman from a modest background, was President of the Board of Trade.

Campbell-Bannerman died in April 1908, his greatest achievement having been *the settlement of the South African problem*. Asquith became Prime Minister, and a cabinet reshuffle made Lloyd George Chancellor of the Exchequer and brought Winston Churchill in as President of the Board of Trade.

The government had an enormous majority, and carrying its policies into effect should have been plain sailing. However, it was a period full of tensions and crises.

- The built-in Conservative majority in the House of Lords decided to block much of the Liberals' programme, which inevitably led to *a bitter confrontation between the two houses, settled eventually by the Parliament Act of 1911.*
- *The suffragettes* mounted a determined and violent campaign to secure the vote for women.
- From 1910 there was *serious labour unrest and a wave of strikes.*

- There was *new trouble in Ireland* where civil war was averted only by the outbreak of the First World War at the end of July 1914.
- Foreign affairs were characterized by Britain's growing friendship with France, and, in spite of Grey's efforts, the deterioration of relations with Germany, which brought Britain into the war in 1914.
- In spite of all these distractions, the Liberals found time to introduce *important reforms to help trade unions and working people* (see Section 20.2–3). Though in some ways their social reforms were disappointing, it is usual to regard them as the beginning of the welfare state.

The period from 1901 to 1914 is known as the Edwardian era, after Edward VII who reigned from the death of his mother, Queen Victoria, in 1901, until 1910. He was succeeded by his son, George V, who reigned until 1936.

21.1 The New Liberalism

During the last 20 years of the nineteenth century, many left-wing Liberals moved away from the old-fashioned Gladstonian Liberalism, which had concentrated on laissez-faire, and on cheap and efficient administration. They acknowledged the need, if the party was to survive and attract working-class votes, for the state to play a new and decisive role in bringing about social reform. The leading thinkers of New Liberalism were the economist J. A. Hobson and the sociologist L. T. Hobhouse, both of whom had been influenced by the Fabians. They argued that 'old' Liberalism had been too concerned with individual liberty, and that it was ridiculous to talk about liberty and freedom in connection with the poorest ranks of the working class, because their freedom of action had been taken away from them by their poverty. They proposed that the state should take the lead in introducing far-reaching social reforms such as old age pensions and a minimum wage, to be financed by increased taxes on the land and incomes of the wealthy. By redistributing wealth in this way, the purchasing power of the working class would be increased, and this would stimulate the economy and the general prosperity.

Both Hobson and Hobhouse were prolific writers and their ideas had enormous influence – men like Seebohm Rowntree and C. P. Scott (the editor of *The Manchester Guardian*) were committed New Liberals. The New Liberals gradually influenced the moderate centre of the party, though it would not be true to say that the *entire* party had been converted by 1906. Nevertheless the Liberal reforms of the next few years showed how deeply New Liberal thinking had penetrated, and so did Lloyd George's famous budget of 1909 which contained many elements of New Liberalism. When the Liberal government scored its big triumph over the House of Lords in 1912 (see Section 21.3(c–d)), it seemed that there was plenty of life left in the party, and it was the New Liberals who were at the forefront.

21.2 The Liberals and South Africa

Many of the New Liberals, and especially Hobson, were against imperialism. In his book *Imperialism* (1902), Hobson argued that imperialism held back the progress of social reform because it diverted both attention and financial resources away from the domestic scene, and only benefited the upper classes and capitalists, such as arms manufacturers and merchants. Campbell-Bannerman agreed and the New Liberals saw him as an ally. He had no hesitation in dealing decisively with two of the most pressing imperial problems, both in South Africa:

(a) *Chinese slavery*

This problem, which had embarrassed Balfour so much (see Section 17.6(b)5), was settled immediately. The government simply made it illegal to bring any more Chinese labourers into the Transvaal. The existing workers had to serve out their contracts, but when this was completed in 1910, the problem disappeared.

(b) *The Transvaal and the Orange Free State*

After their defeat in the Boer War, these two Boer republics had been annexed by the British government; however, in the Treaty of Vereeniging (1902) they were promised eventual self-government (see Section 17.3(c)). Campbell-Bannerman saw no sense in delaying it any longer: complete self-government was granted to the Transvaal (1906) and the following year to the Orange Free State. The Boer leaders were much impressed by the government's speed and had retained great respect for Campbell-Bannerman ever since he had described Kitchener's concentration camps as 'methods of barbarism'. For these reasons they decided to join Cape Colony and Natal to form *the Union of South Africa* which came into existence officially in 1910. Although this took place after C-B's death, the creation of the new dominion and the reconciliation of the Afrikaners and the British were very much his achievement. South Africa supported Britain in two world wars and stayed in the Commonwealth until 1961.

There was one major criticism: no provision was made to safeguard the rights of non-whites and no guarantee was given that they would eventually be allowed to vote. However, if the government had insisted on such guarantees being written into the new constitution, the Boers would not have agreed to join the Union. The Liberals hoped that in time the more progessive attitude of English-speaking South Africans would prevail and ensure that non-whites received equal treatment. Unfortunately this did not happen and the policy of *apartheid* was later introduced by the Boer-dominated South African government (see Section 32.6(d)); but it is hardly fair to blame Campbell-Bannerman and Asquith for this.

21.3 The Liberals and the dispute with the House of Lords

(a) *The House of Lords in 1906*

The House of Lords contained 591 members, known as 'peers of the realm', of whom 561 had inherited their seats from their fathers or from another male relative. The other 30, whose seats were not hereditary, consisted of four law lords, the two Archbishops (Canterbury and York) and 24 bishops. Roughly two-thirds of the peers were Conservatives, the rest were Liberals, and this gave the Conservatives a built-in, permanent majority in the Lords. New peers could be created by the sovereign on the advice of the Prime Minister.

In theory the powers of the Lords and Commons were equal: bills could be introduced in the Lords as well as in the Commons. In 1900 the Conservative Prime

Minister, Lord Salisbury, sat in the Lords, though he was the last Prime Minister to do so. However, two traditions had gradually developed during the nineteenth century:

> all bills dealing with finance and taxation started life in the Commons;
> the House of Lords did not reject finance bills.

b) *What were the causes of the dispute?*

Although the Commons was in the process of becoming the more important of the two houses, the Lords could still change bills radically and even prevent a government passing laws altogether if there seemed to be a good reason for doing so (see Section 4.1 for the stages in passing a bill through parliament). The basic cause of the dispute was that the House of Lords, with its permanent Conservative majority, continually rejected Liberal bills, although during the previous ten years of Conservative rule, it had not once interfered with a Conservative bill. The Liberal government, in spite of having been elected with a huge majority, was being prevented from carrying out its policies by a House of Lords which had not been elected; democracy was being denied. *The confrontation built up gradually:*

1. Gladstone's Second Irish Home Rule Bill had been rejected by the Lords in 1893 (see Section 16.8(b)) and this was followed by the defeat of most of Lord Rosebery's attempted measures (1894–5) (see Section 16.9). The Lords' justification was that the Liberals had only a tiny majority.
2. After lying dormant for ten years the House of Lords woke up and in 1906 defeated two of Campbell-Bannerman's most important bills – an Education Bill and a Plural Voting Bill (which would have removed the right of people owning premises in several constituencies to vote more than once). The following year two more important bills were rejected and two more were changed so drastically by the Lords that they turned out to be almost worthless.
3. In 1908 the Lords rejected the Licensing Bill designed to reduce the number of public houses, though Edward VII advised them to pass it. There could be no excuse that the Liberals had a flimsy majority, and Campbell-Bannerman warned the Conservatives that if this continued, an attempt would be made to restrict their powers. It seemed to the Liberals that the Conservative leaders, Balfour and Lord Lansdowne, were making blatant use of the Lords' powers to protect the interests of their own party and class. According to historian Robert Blake (who is himself now a Conservative peer), 'this was a denial of parliamentary democracy; ... many Conservatives behaved as if the verdict of 1906 was some freak aberration on the part of the electorate and that it was their duty, through the House of Lords, to preserve the public from the consequences of its own folly till it came to its senses'.
4. The Lords were also preparing to oppose old age pensions, but Asquith thwarted them by using an important loophole – *the tradition that the Lords never interfered with a finance bill, usually the annual budget.* Asquith shrewdly designated the pensions bill as a finance bill and it passed without controversy.
5. The dispute came to a climax in 1909 when the Lords *broke the constitutional tradition by rejecting Lloyd George's entire budget for that year.* It was Lloyd George's first budget and it was designed to raise an extra £15 million to pay for pensions, labour exchanges, and *Dreadnought* battleships. The wealthy were to foot the bill:

- income tax up from a shilling to 1s.2d in the pound on incomes over £3000;
- supertax of 6d in the pound on incomes over £5000;
- higher taxes on tobacco and spirits (a bottle of whisky went up from 3s.6d to 4s.), and higher charges for liquor licences;

- taxes on petrol and cars;
- taxes on mining royalties;
- most controversial of all – a 20 per cent tax on the increased value of land when it was resold.

6   The budget was debated in the Commons from April until November – much longer than usual. The Conservatives assaulted it viciously both in the Commons and outside, forming a Budget Protest League. They claimed that it was a deliberate attack on the wealthy, especially on landowners, and that it was the beginning of socialism: the new land tax would require all land to be valued, and this, they feared, could be the preliminary to the nationalization of land. The Duke of Beaufort said he would like to see Lloyd George and Churchill 'in the middle of twenty couple of foxhounds'; Lloyd George hit back in his famous Limehouse speech, accusing landlords of being selfish creatures whose sole function was 'the stately consumption of wealth produced by others'. In November 1909 the budget passed the Commons with a huge majority (379 to 149), but later the same month the Lords rejected it, even though Edward VII was anxious for it to pass. Lord Lansdowne, the Conservative leader in the Lords, justified this on the grounds that such a revolutionary measure ought to be put before the public in a general election. Balfour said that the Lords were merely carrying out their proper function as the 'watchdog of the constitution' (meaning that its function was to make sure that no irresponsible laws were passed and that all proper rules and procedures were kept to), but Lloyd George retorted that the Lords were acting as if they were 'Mr Balfour's poodle'.

It has been suggested that Lloyd George deliberately produced a controversial budget to trap the Lords into rejecting it, so that the Liberals would have a cast-iron case for restricting their powers. But there is little evidence of this; the government needed the money and were determined to make the wealthy pay a fair share. On the other hand the budget was cleverly framed to embarrass the Conservatives: if they did not oppose the tax increases, their landowning supporters would be furious; if they did oppose them, they would lay themselves open to charges of selfishness for refusing to contribute towards defence and help for the poor. Very few Liberals could have expected the Lords to break the tradition by rejecting the entire budget.

(c) *The constitutional crisis and the two elections of 1910*

The 'insane decision' (as Robert Blake calls it) of the Conservative Lords to reject the budget immediately caused a constitutional crisis. No government can continue unless its budget is approved by parliament, so that it can go ahead and collect taxes. If the Lords were allowed to get away with it, the basic principle of democracy which had developed in Britain would be overturned: the hereditary House of Lords and not the elected House of Commons would control government policy. Asquith declared that the Lords had breached the constitution and he prepared to do battle to reduce their powers. It was a long and bitter struggle which was only resolved in August 1911, over 18 months after the rejection of Lloyd George's 'People's Budget'.

1   Parliament was dissolved and a general election held (January 1910) on the issue of 'Peers v. People'. The results were disappointing for the Liberals who lost over 100 seats; the figures were: Liberals 275, Conservative and Unionists 273, Labour 40, Irish Nationalists 82. Liberal losses can probably be explained by the fact that some traditional Conservative seats which had fallen to the Liberals in the

landslide of 1906, now returned to the Tories. Many people who had voted Liberal in 1906 may have been frightened off by the government's radical policies.

2   In spite of their heavy losses the Liberals continued in government because they could usually count on Irish and Labour support. However, Asquith's dependence on the Irish meant that the constitutional crisis became mixed up with the Irish Home Rule question. The Irish Nationalist leader, John Redmond, agreed to vote for Lloyd George's budget (which now had to pass the Commons again), but at a heavy price – he demanded two rewards:

- another Irish Home Rule Bill;
- a bill to restrict the powers of the House of Lords so that it would not be able to throw out the Home Rule Bill, as it had in 1893.

3   April 1910 was therefore a busy month: a Parliament Bill designed to reduce the Lords' power passed the Commons easily, closely followed by the budget. The following day the Lords approved the budget, perhaps hoping to escape the Parliament Bill.

4   The next problem for Asquith was how to manoeuvre the Lords into passing the Parliament Bill which would significantly reduce their own powers. Asquith tried to persuade Edward VII to create about 250 new Liberal peers, enough to defeat the Conservatives in the Lords. The king would only agree if the Liberals could win another election on the issue, but Asquith dared not risk another one so soon. Edward died suddenly in May 1910, and the new king, George V, suggested a conference. This met and discussed the situation for the next six months. A compromise solution was almost reached but the conference broke down over the problem of Ireland. The Conservatives wanted special loopholes in any new bill, which would enable them to block Home Rule, but Asquith would not agree.

5   In November 1910 Asquith resumed battle by sending the Parliament Bill up to the Lords. When they refused to pass it, he met the king and secretly secured a promise that if the Liberals won another general election, George would create the required peers. Armed with this promise, Asquith went into the general election of December 1910 which had a remarkably similar result to the previous one: Liberals 272, Conservative and Unionists 272, Labour 42, Irish Nationalists 84. The Liberals and their allies had maintained their support, and the Parliament Bill again passed the Commons with a comfortable majority (May 1911).

6   In July 1911 Asquith announced in the Commons that the king had promised to create as many as 500 new Liberal peers if necessary, to get the bill through the Lords. The furious Conservatives led by Lord Hugh Cecil (Salisbury's son) howled Asquith down with shouts of 'Traitor!' and he was unable to complete his speech. It caused a split in the Conservative ranks between the outright opponents of the bill (nicknamed the 'Ditchers') and the moderates (the 'Hedgers'). The moderates decided that it would be better to accept a reduction of their powers rather than be permanently swamped by the Liberals, and many of them abstained when it came to the vote. But it was a close run thing – the bill was passed by 131 votes to 114 (August 1911). The Parliament Act became law and the constitutional crisis was over.

(d)   *Terms of the Parliament Act and its results*

1   The Lords were not allowed to amend or reject a finance bill and the Speaker of the House of Commons was to decide which were finance bills.
2   The Lords could still amend and reject other bills, but if a bill passed the Commons in three successive sessions of parliament and was rejected three times

by the Lords, it would automatically become law on its third rejection by the Lords. In simple terms, this meant that the Lords could delay a bill for two years.

3   There was to be a general election at least every five years instead of every seven.

The Act was of major importance in the development of the constitution. Democracy had been safeguarded – the Lords had no control over the country's finances; they could delay other legislation for two years, but could not prevent it becoming law eventually, provided the government remained in power long enough. There can be no doubt that it was a vitally important step in the reduction of the powers of the aristocracy, many of whom now began to withdraw from politics. The Duke of Northumberland remarked in 1917: 'I have almost abandoned politics as hopeless – at any rate for a peer.'

On the other hand the Lords still had the power, if they felt like using it, to paralyze a government for the last two years of its five-year term. As for immediate results, the Lords were so incensed at the Liberals that they used their remaining powers to the full: they rejected the Irish Home Rule Bill, a Welsh Disestablishment Bill (which would have meant that the Anglican Church was no longer the official state church in Wales) and another Plural Voting Bill; not one of these perfectly reasonable bills had passed into law when war broke out in 1914. Nor had the Parliament Act done anything to make the membership of the House of Lords more democratic – most peers still inherited their seats instead of having to win them in an election. For the next reduction of the Lords' powers in 1949 see Section 29.3(b).

21.4 Women's rights, suffragists and suffragettes

(a) *Early moves towards equal rights for women*

In the middle of the nineteenth century in Britain, women were still treated as second-class citizens in a number of ways. When a woman married, all her money and possessions became the property of her husband; if the marriage broke down, the husband was legally entitled to keep the children, even if he was responsible for the breakdown. Women were not expected to take up careers, were not allowed to take degrees at universities, and were barred from professions such as medicine, law and accountancy. Nor could they become magistrates, sit on juries, vote or become MPs.

Mary Wollstonecraft (1759–97) was one of the first to campaign for an improvement in the status of women. In her book *A Vindication of the Rights of Women* she argued that girls should receive the same education as boys, and she advocated free state education for everybody. As the nineteenth century progressed, a number of outstanding women began to make a breakthrough: Mary Somerville became an outstanding mathematician, Elizabeth Fry played an important part in prison reform, and Florence Nightingale elevated nursing as a recognized career for women. In the 1870s the first women doctors began practising, while school-teaching and office work became common occupations for women. Further important steps were:

- The legal status of women was improved by *the Married Women's Property Act (1882)* which allowed a woman to continue as the separate owner of her property when she married.
- *The Guardianship of Children Act (1886)* allowed a mother to claim custody of her children if her marriage broke up.
- Women's political rights were being advanced: in 1888 unmarried women were allowed to vote for the new county and borough councils. In 1894 both married and

unmarried women were allowed to vote for the new urban and rural district councils and could stand for election to these councils.

(b) *Suffragists and suffragettes*

These were basically middle-class movements, but they had strong working-class support especially in the North; they campaigned for women to be given the right to vote for MPs. This was nothing new – there had been women's suffrage societies since the late 1860s when the question of votes for women was raised during the debates on the 1867 Reform Act. They did not attract a lot of attention until the Edwardian period, when interest began to revive for several reasons: women had just been given the vote in New Zealand; the new Independent Labour Party, particulary Keir Hardie, were encouraging; and given that women could now vote for rural and district councils, and could stand for election to these councils, it was logical to expect that they would soon have the right to chose their MPs.

- *The National Union of Women's Suffrage Societies (NUWSS)*, formed in 1897, campaigned non-violently for votes for women on the same terms as men; they did not want the vote for *all* women. Historian Martin Pugh believes that by 1906 a majority of MPs had been won over to the general principle of votes for women by Mrs Millicent Fawcett, the suffragist leader, and her peaceful campaign. The problems were: finding time for legislation in a crowded parliamentary timetable, and deciding exactly which women should be given the vote – should it be given to all women or just to unmarried women and widows, since married women were not considered to be householders.
- A much more vocal pressure group than the suffragists was *the Women's Social and Political Union (WSPU)* founded in 1903 by Mrs Emmeline Pankhurst, helped by her daughters Christabel and Sylvia. She was the widow of a Manchester barrister and she believed that only when women had the vote would sufficient pressure be brought on governments to improve social conditions. The suffragettes, as *The Daily Mail* called them, had high hopes of the new Liberal government, since it was well known that Campbell-Bannerman and Lloyd George were sympathetic. Their hopes were further raised by *the Qualification of Women Act (1907)* which allowed women to become members of county and borough councils and to act as mayors.
- However, later the same year, a private member's bill to give women the vote was heavily defeated in the Commons. In fact both Liberals and Conservatives were divided on the issue; the Liberal government would not introduce a bill for women's suffrage, their excuse being the difficulty about which classes of women to include; the real reason was probably that Asquith, who became Prime Minister in 1908, was against the whole idea.
- *What were the arguments against votes for women?* The outright opponents argued that women, by their nature, were too emotional to have sound political judgement. It was not that they were thought to be inferior to men; it was simply that the women's role was seen as rearing children and looking after the home; politics and earning the family income was the role of the male. Even pro-suffragist supporters had to admit that there was a genuine problem about which women should be included. The pro-suffragist Liberals were undecided whether to give the vote to *all women* or to restrict it to women who owned property. They were not happy at the prospect of women voters outnumbering men if all women could vote. On the other hand, if only propertied women were included, that might benefit the Conservatives, since rich women might be more inclined to support the Conservatives. The increasing militancy of the suffragettes only served to strengthen the opposition by discrediting the whole women's rights movement for a time ...

- Faced with what they saw as the government's stubbornness, the WSPU became more militant. Since 1905 they had been disrupting meetings addressed by Liberal politicians; Christabel Pankhurst and Annie Kenney, a Lancashire cotton worker, spent a week in gaol after being ejected from the Manchester Free Trade Hall for heckling Sir Edward Grey. Next they turned to smashing windows, chaining themselves to the railings of Buckingham Palace and Downing Street, kicking and scratching policemen who tried to move them on, and holding massive demonstrations and processions.
- By 1912 Asquith and the cabinet had accepted the principle of women's suffrage, and to save time, made a late addition to the Plural Voting Bill which was already under discussion. The amendments gave the vote to certain categories of women. However, in January 1913 the Speaker ruled that the additions could not be allowed, since they changed the nature of the bill.
- This decision drove the suffragettes to desperate measures – they resorted to setting fire to post boxes, churches and railway stations, and there were physical attacks on cabinet ministers, particularly Asquith. Some extremists tried to tear his clothes off on the golf-course at Lossiemouth, and others beat him over the head with dog-whips. Lloyd George's new house, which he had fortunately not moved into, was badly damaged by a bomb explosion, for which Mrs Pankhurst was given a three-year gaol sentence. The most horrifying incident occurred at the 1913 Derby, when Emily Davidson was killed as she threw herself in front of the king's horse.

This extremism was not really necessary: the Liberals had accepted the principle of votes for women and had only failed to get it through the Commons on a technicality. It is more than likely that they would have tried again later in 1913 and that the Commons would have approved it by 1914. But the government hesitated to try again because it did not want to seem to be giving way to violence. The moderates of the NUWSS, which had played no part in the violence, were disgusted with the WSPU, because it was clear that their behaviour was delaying the granting of votes for women. Even within the WSPU itself the Pankhursts were losing support because of their dictatorial attitude.

- As the suffragettes became more militant, the government response became more unpleasant and insensitive. When suffragettes went on hunger-strike in prison, the government authorized them to be forcibly fed. When this provoked criticism the government responded with the farcical 'Cat and Mouse' Act of 1913; this permitted the release from prison of women who were in a weak physical state because of hunger-strike, and allowed them to be re-arrested when they had recovered.
- As soon as Britain entered the war in August 1914 the suffragettes called off their campaign, although they had failed to achieve their objective. Over the next four years women made such a vital contribution to the war effort that it appeared even more ludicrous that they were denied full political rights. In 1918 the Lloyd George government's *Representation of the People Act* gave the vote to all men at the age of 21 and to women at the age of 30. Women were also allowed to become MPs. The situation was not righted fully until 1928 when Baldwin's Conservative government gave the vote to women at 21. Historian Martin Pugh is not convinced that the role of women in the war was the vital factor in securing them the vote. He rightly points out that this theory ignores the changes of attitude which had already taken place before the war. 'During the war,' he writes, 'not surprisingly votes for women simply vanished from the agenda for some time. The issue returned only because the politicians grew anxious to enfranchise more men, many of whom had lost their qualification as a result of moving home for war service. It was this that led to the scheme of parliamentary reform in 1917 in which women were included.'

21.5 Why did the Liberals' attempts to settle the Irish question fail before 1914?

Since the rejection of Gladstone's Second Irish Home Rule Bill by the Lords in 1893, the issue had been pushed into the background, and there was no prospect of Home Rule during the ten years of Conservative rule from 1895 to 1905. However, it was a period full of important developments for the Irish people. *There was a growing emphasis on all things Irish, to keep alive the idea that Ireland was a separate nation with its own culture and heritage.* There was a revival of interest in Irish sports such as Gaelic football and hurling. *The Gaelic League,* founded in 1893, aimed to spread the Gaelic language and culture – folk music, dancing and literature. It culminated in a great Anglo-Irish literary movement involving outstanding writers like the poet W. B. Yeats and the playwright J. M. Synge. The new Abbey Theatre was opened in Dublin in 1904 and quickly became a centre of the Irish revival. The cultural revival affected politics as well: *in 1905 Arthur Griffith founded a new political group called Sinn Fein (Ourselves Alone).* Griffith believed in self-reliance – there was no reason why the Irish could not be economically prosperous provided they were given political freedom, which he hoped could be achieved by passive resistance to Britain.

The Irish Nationalists, led by John Redmond, were hopeful of quick satisfaction from Campbell-Bannerman and the Liberals, especially when he was so quick to give the Boers self-government. However, the most they were prepared to allow in the immediate future was *an Irish Executive Council* to look after certain affairs such as the Congested Districts Board and education. This was not a genuine Irish parliament, and the proposal was rejected by Redmond.

The situation changed dramatically with the general election of January 1910 which left Asquith heavily dependent on the Irish Nationalists to stay in office. As the price for their support for Lloyd George's budget, Asquith had to promise to reduce the powers of the House of Lords so that another Irish Home Rule Bill could be passed. The Parliament Act of August 1911 (see Section 21.3(d)) opened the way for the Third Irish Home Rule Bill which passed the Commons in 1912. It was immediately rejected by the Lords and the same thing happened again in 1913. However, under the terms of the Parliament Act, the bill only had to pass the Commons a third time to become law at some point during 1914; but things turned out not to be so simple. In August 1914 a solution to the Irish problem was as far away as ever, and the country was on the verge of civil war. *The reasons were complex:*

(a) *The Irish Nationalist Party was being eclipsed by Sinn Fein*

Irish opinion was bitterly disappointed by Redmond's failure to get anything like Home Rule from the Liberal government before 1910, and this caused more people to look towards Sinn Fein. Griffith wanted a similar solution to the one which had settled the problems of the Habsburg Empire where the Hungarians had been campaigning for independence from Austria. In 1867 Austria and Hungary became separate countries, each with its own parliament, but they kept the same ruler, Franz Josef, who was to be Emperor of Austria and King of Hungary. It was known as the Dual Monarchy. Griffith could see no reason why Ireland could not be treated like Hungary – having its own parliament with full powers, but keeping the monarchy as a link between the two. Eventually, as their ideas were ignored, Sinn Fein moved to the position of demanding an independent republic. Another group which was gaining support was the Irish Republican Brotherhood (IRB) or Fenians, which also wanted a complete break with Britain. This was not necessarily fatal for chances of a solution, but it meant that at the very time when Home Rule was imminent (thanks to the Parliament Act), a large section of the Irish wanted something which went much further.

(b) *The problem of Ulster was more serious than before*

At the time of the First Home Rule Bill (1886), Lord Randolph Churchill had tried to stir up the Ulster Protestants against the Bill with warnings that they would be swamped by the Catholics of Southern Ireland. At the time this was probably not a major issue: Parnell, the Nationalist leader, was himself a Protestant; but by 1912 the situation had changed. Ulster had developed industrially, especially shipbuilding at Belfast, and there was also linen manufacture and whisky distilling. Ninety per cent of all Ireland's manufactured exports were made in the area around Belfast, while the rest of Ireland remained largely agricultural and backward. Griffith's talk of introducing tariffs to protect Irish industries worried Ulster businessmen who were afraid that Home Rule would mean the loss of their valuable markets in the rest of Britain. The Protestant Ulstermen felt themselves to be a separate community both economically and in religious matters. Four counties – Antrim, Armagh, Down and Derry – had large Protestant majorities and they were strongly against becoming part of an independent Ireland in which, they feared, they would be dominated and discriminated against by a Catholic government in Dublin. They were determined to keep as much of Ulster as possible united with Britain.

Even before the Home Rule Bill was introduced into the Commons, *the Ulster Unionists* began to organize themselves to resist Home Rule. Appointing Sir Edward Carson, a prominent barrister and Unionist MP, as their leader, they held massive demonstrations and threatened to set up a provisional government if the bill passed. Hundreds of thousands of Ulstermen signed a Covenant swearing to fight any government which tried to force Home Rule on them.

(c) *The Conservatives (Unionists) intensified the crisis by encouraging the Ulster Unionists*

There is no doubt that the unfortunate Nationalists were the victims of the bitterness between Liberals and Conservatives in the aftermath of the 1911 Parliament Act. The Conservatives, still smarting from the Parliament Act and their failure to win three consecutive general elections were, in the words of Roy Jenkins, 'sick with office hunger'. The Ulster situation was the perfect weapon with which to embarrass Asquith and might even be used to bring the government down. When Carson openly organized a military force, the Ulster Volunteers, and held drills and parades, Andrew Bonar Law, the new Conservative leader, actually went over to Ireland to take the salute at a review. He told a Conservative party rally at Blenheim Palace in July 1912: 'I can imagine no length of resistance to which Ulster will go, which I shall not be ready to support.' In other words, the leader of the British Conservative party was encouraging armed rebellion against a law about to be passed by the legally elected British government. The Conservatives even called themselves Unionists at this time to show how strongly they felt about maintaining the union between England and Ireland.

(d) *Asquith and the Liberal government were partly to blame for the stalemate*

Asquith realized that the Conservatives were only using the Irish situation as a lever to get the government out, and he decided to let events take their course, or as he put it, 'wait and see'. He could have eased the situation from the beginning by discussing the possibility of a partition, allowing the four counties with a Protestant majority to remain under British rule. There would have been opposition from the Nationalists, but it was not out of the question for them to have accepted a compromise of this sort, and it would have avoided the formation of the Ulster Volunteers. Not until early in 1914 did Asquith show that he was prepared to exclude Ulster. By this time the Nationalists had also organized their private army, *the Nationalist Volunteers*. This was another fatal omission by Asquith: he should have taken immediate action to ban all private armies and arms imports. He took no action, and both sets of volunteers openly imported arms, built up their manpower and drilled their troops. Only in March 1914 did Asquith decide to send British troops into Ulster to guard arms depots and other strategic points.

(e) *The 'Curragh Mutiny' seemed to undermine the government's position*

This was not an actual mutiny, just the threat of one. When the government's intention to send troops to Ulster became known, about 60 army officers stationed at the Curragh in Dublin, threatened to resign if they were ordered to force Ulster into accepting Home Rule. The Secretary for War, J. E. B. Seely, assured them in an astonishing statement, that they would not be used to force Home Rule on Ulster. At this, Asquith insisted on Seely's resignation and took over the War Office himself. However, the damage had been done – the impression had been given that in the event of fighting breaking out, the government might not be able to rely on the loyalty of its own army; this could only encourage the Ulster Volunteers into bolder action.

(f) *The Larne gun-running incident inflamed the situation further*

The Ulster Volunteers were allowed to smuggle 30 000 rifles and three million rounds of ammunition into Ireland via Larne (April 1914) without any interference from the police, though by this time there was an official ban on arms imports.

(g) *The Home Rule Bill passed the Commons for the third time in May 1914*

However, it still contained no provision for a separate Ulster. Frantic negotiations followed culminating in an all-party conference (July). At one point, a solution seemed near, as Redmond, faced with civil war, was apparently prepared to agree to the exclusion of the four mainly Protestant counties from Home Rule, at least temporarily. But the Unionists stepped up their demands and insisted that Fermanagh and Tyrone, whose population was at least 50 per cent Catholic, should also be excluded. Redmond could not agree to this and the conference broke up.

On 26 July there was *the Howth incident* which showed how precarious peace was in Ireland. The Nationalist Volunteers smuggled in a large shipment of rifles, despite the efforts of troops sent to prevent them. A hostile crowd gathered, angry that the Nationalists should be treated differently from the Ulster Volunteers. Stones were thrown at the troops who opened fire, killing three people and wounding 38. Tensions ran high and Ireland seemed on the verge of civil war. A few days later Britain entered the First World War, and although the Home Rule Bill had been placed on the statute book, the government decided to suspend its operation until one year after the war was over. No solution had been found to the stalemate, but it was generally hoped that the Irish would remain quiet and support the war effort. Many did, but the convinced republicans had other ideas, as they showed at Easter 1916 (see Section 26.2).

Map 21.1   Ireland showing the provinces and counties

21.6 Why was there so much political and industrial unrest between 1909 and 1914 and how did Asquith's government deal with it?

Most of the information to answer the question has appeared earlier in the chapter, but it will be helpful to summarize the points briefly:

(a) *The Commons v. Lords conflict*

This was brought to a climax by Lloyd George's so-called 'People's Budget' of 1909; skilfully handled by Asquith, probably his greatest achievement.

(b) *The suffragette agitation*

This was not particularly well handled by the government, which ought to have introduced a women's suffrage bill before the situation got out of hand; Asquith, however, opposed votes for women.

(c) *The Irish situation*

This was made worse by the attitude of the Conservatives, but again ineptly handled by Asquith and his 'wait and see' approach.

(d) *The Osborne Judgement*

This contributed towards trade union unrest. The situation was put right by the Trade Union Act of 1913, though only after a delay of four years.

(e) *Industrial unrest*

This was sometimes caused by unemployment, especially in 1908–9, but more often by the fact that wage increases were not keeping pace with rising prices. Some statistics show that in 1908, 1909 and 1910, average real wages were lower than in 1900 (see Cook and Stevenson, p. 207), and the cost of living rose sharply in 1910–13. Syndicalism also played a part in causing the strike wave (see Section 19.7). The government tried to handle the strikes by a mixture of conciliation and firmness. Churchill sent troops to deal with a mining dispute at Tonypandy in South Wales (though they were not used). Asquith's attitude was that essential services must be maintained at all costs, and he authorized the use of troops during the 1911 railway strike, resulting in the deaths of two men at Llanelly. This sort of approach was an over-reaction and did nothing to calm the situation. Eventually Asquith handed the railway strike over to Lloyd George, who had developed considerable skill as a conciliator. Somehow or other he soothed tempers and within four days he had found a compromise. The 1912 coal strike was settled when the government manoeuvred both sides into accepting the Minimum Wage Act (see Section 20.3(d)3).

Historians have disagreed about how serious the threats to law and order were; the country seemed to be in total disarray, given the amount of violence and unrest. George Dangerfield, in his vividly written book *The Strange Death of Liberal England 1910–1914* (1936), argued that in 1914 Britain stood on the verge of anarchy and revolution. He believed that there would have been a massive general strike led by the Triple Alliance, probably in October, 'an appalling national struggle over the question of the living wage'. Coinciding with civil war in Ireland, this would have placed an enormous strain on the government's resources, and he clearly felt that the Liberals would not have been equal to the task. Only the outbreak of the First World War saved Britain from internal social catastrophe. One reason the cabinet was so ready to enter the war was to save the country from descending into total anarchy. However, most historians today feel that Dangerfield's theories are rather exaggerated, even though his book still provides a good read. True there were many problems for the Liberals to deal with, but they were steadily being overcome one by one. The worst of the strike wave was over by 1914, and even the big syndicalist strike in Dublin which had lasted over six months ended in January 1914. T. O. Lloyd points out that there were the beginnings of a trade depression early in 1914 which would have made a strike less likely. Although people were uneasy about what might happen, 'England in 1914 was not on the verge of plunging into disorder and chaos'.

21.7 Liberal defence and foreign policies 1905–14

(a) *Problems facing Sir Edward Grey*

Britain's foreign policy was conducted largely by Sir Edward Grey who was Foreign Secretary from December 1905 until December 1916. The period from 1905 until the outbreak of war was full of international tensions, and there were a number of incidents which seemed likely to cause a major European conflict; these were the Moroccan Crisis (1905–6), the Bosnia Crisis (1908), the Agadir Crisis (1911) and two Balkan Wars (1912 and 1913). When Grey took over at the Foreign Office, Britain had already moved a long way from her isolation of Salisbury's time, having recently signed an alliance with Japan (1902) and the Entente Cordiale with France (1904) (see Section 17.4(b)). *Grey's aims were to build on these alliances while at the same time working for good relations with the Germans*, who, as we saw earlier, viewed Britain' understanding with France as a hostile gesture against them.

Grey's task was difficult:

- The British were bound to see the build-up of the German fleet (which started with the 1897 Navy Laws) as a challenge to their naval supremacy.
- Although Britain was well ahead in numbers of ships, the problem was that whereas the British fleet was strung out across the world defending the Empire, the German fleet would be concentrated in the North Sea, where it might on occasion outnumber the available British ships.
- There was a need therefore for Britain to press ahead with her *Dreadnought* programme, and also to make some improvements in her army, which was pitifully small by European standards.
- Yet the more Britain increased her military strength and the closer she drew in friendship towards France, the more difficult it would be to improve relations with Germany.

On the whole Grey performed with great skill and steered Britain successfully through the crises. But the general trend of events was for Britain to find herself supporting France against Germany, and consequently Grey failed to reconcile Britain and Germany.

(b) *Britain's defences improved*

1 *In the army* very little had changed since the days of Cardwell's reforms during Gladstone's First Ministry (1868–74). Some reorganization was needed as the army's performance in the Boer War had shown. The Liberal Secretary for War, R. B. Haldane, had spent some time being educated in Germany at Gottingen and Dresden and was an expert on German affairs. He used his experiences to good effect in bringing the British army up to date. Beginning in 1907, he introduced a General Staff to give an efficient and co-ordinated direction to army leadership. An Expeditionary Force was organized consisting of six infantry divisions and a cavalry division, 160 000 troops in all, together with the necessary accessories – artillery, transport, medical units and reserves. All the various volunteer and part-time soldiers were organized into the Territorials – around 300 000 men who were to be fully equipped and trained so that they could compare in efficiency with the regulars. To improve the supply of officers, Haldane brought the Officers' Training Corps at the public schools under the control of the War Office. This was a fine achievement by Haldane; when he left the War Office in 1912 to become Lord

Table 21.1 Fleet sizes, 4 August 1914 (figures in brackets indicate ships under construction)

	Germany	Great Britain
Battleships	33 (+7)	55 (+11)
Battlecruisers	3 (+3)	7 (+3)
Cruisers	9	51
Light cruisers	45 (+4)	77 (+9)
Destroyers	123 (+9)	191 (+38)
Torpedo ships	80	137 (+1)
Submarines	23 (+15)	64 (+22)
Dreadnoughts	13	20

Source: R. Wolfson, *Years of Change* (Arnold, 1978) p. 137.

Chancellor, the only drawback was that the army was not large enough (see Table 21.2).

2 *The navy was Britain's great strength*, but it was also expensive to maintain. Campbell-Bannerman decided to reduce the Cawdor–Fisher Plan (see Section 17.6(a)4); instead of building four *Dreadnoughts* a year, only three were built in 1906 and two in 1907. C-B hoped this would induce the Germans to slow down their naval programme and prepare the way for disarmament, but it had the opposite effect – Tirpitz, the German Navy Minister, saw it as a chance to catch up, and the Germans built three ships in 1906 and four each year from 1907 to 1909. This caused a public outcry in Britain, and when the government announced a plan to build six *Dreadnoughts* in 1909, the First Sea Lord, still the forceful and determined Fisher, urged the press into mounting a campaign for eight; 'we want eight and we won't wait', ran the slogan. The public got their eight *Dreadnoughts*, though the expense was alarming and led to Lloyd George's controversial budget. A further five were built in 1910 and five more in 1911. Fisher and the government had already in 1906 created the Home Fleet based on the Nore (London). When he retired in 1912, Fisher left Britain with a marked superiority in numbers of ships and in gunpower, though it was discovered during the war that individual German ships were better equipped than their British counterparts.

(c) *Events leading up to the outbreak of war*

1 *The Moroccan Crisis (1905–6) was already under way when Grey arrived at the Foreign Office.* It began as a German attempt to test the new Anglo-French Entente, with the implication that France would soon add Morocco to her overseas empire. The Germans announced that they regarded Morocco as independent and

Table 21.2 Numbers of men in the armed forces, 1880–1914

	Germany		Great Britain	
	Army	Navy	Army	Navy
1880	401 650	7350	198 200	59 000
1891	511 650	17 000	209 000	97 600
1901	604 100	31 200	773 500	114 900
1911	622 500	33 500	247 000	128 000
1914	791 000	73 000	247 000	146 000

Source: Wolfson, as above, p. 138.

would assist its ruler to maintain that independence. They demanded an international conference to discuss Morocco's future. A conference was duly held at Algeciras in Spain (January 1906). Grey believed that if the Germans had their way it would be tantamount to acknowledging German diplomatic control of Europe and North Africa. At the conference he came out strongly in support of the French demand to control the Moroccan bank and police. Russia, Spain and Italy also supported France, and the Germans suffered a serious diplomatic defeat. This was an impressive start for Grey; he had shown that the Anglo-French Entente meant something, and he had helped to preserve the balance of power. The French were most grateful and Anglo-French 'military conversations' were started.

2 *The British agreement with Russia (1907) was another blow to Germany.* Britain's motive was not to build up an anti-German bloc; it was more a desire to settle differences with the Russians. For years the British had viewed Russia as a major threat to her interests in the Far East and India, but recent events had changed all that. Russia's defeat in the war with Japan had weakened her and she no longer seemed so much of a danger. The remaining area of dispute was Persia (Iran), and it seemed desirable to both sides, particularly the Russians who were anxious to attract British investment, to eliminate rivalry. Such an agreement was only logical, since Russia had signed an alliance with France, Britain's Entente partner, as far back as 1894. Persia was divided into 'spheres of influence'. The north was to be Russian, the south (bordering on Afghanistan and India) British, and the central area was to remain neutral. Unfortunately the Germans took the agreement as confirmation of their fears that Britain, France and Russia were planning to 'encircle' them.

3 *The Bosnia Crisis (1908) caused great tension.* The Austrians, taking advantage of a revolution in Turkey, annexed Bosnia (still technically Turkish territory) as a deliberate blow at Serbia which also hoped to acquire Bosnia. The Serbs appealed for help to their fellow-Slavs, the Russians, who called for a European conference, expecting French and British support. When it became clear that Germany would support Austria in the event of war, the French drew back, not wanting to become involved in a war in the Balkans, and Grey, anxious to avoid a breach with Germany, contented himself with a formal protest to Austria. Austria kept Bosnia; it was a triumph for the Austro-German alliance, *but it had unfortunate consequences*: Serbia remained bitterly hostile towards Austria and it was this quarrel which developed into the First World War. The humiliation stimulated Russia into a massive military build-up; and Grey and Asquith were now convinced that Germany was out to dominate Europe, an impression confirmed when Tirpitz seemed to be speeding up the naval building programme. The outcome was the hysterical 'we want eight' campaign and an intensification of the naval arms race.

4 *The Agadir Crisis (1911)* arose when French troops occupied Fez, the Moroccan capital, to put down a rebellion against the Sultan. A French annexation of Morocco seemed imminent; the Germans sent a gunboat, the *Panther*, to the Moroccan port of Agadir, hoping to browbeat the French into giving them some compensation, perhaps the French Congo. Grey was concerned in case the 'compensation' turned out to be the German acquisition of Agadir, a vital naval base which could be used to threaten Britain's trade routes. With the intention of strengthening French resolve, Lloyd George (with Grey's permission) made a famous speech at the Lord Mayor of London's banquet at the Mansion House, warning the Germans that Britain would not stand by and be taken advantage of 'where her interests were vitally affected'. Eventually the gunboat was removed,

Map 21.2 The Balkans in 1913 showing changes of territory from the Balkan Wars (1912–13)

and the Germans agreed to recognize the French protectorate over Morocco in return for two strips of territory in the French Congo.

This was seen as a further triumph for the Anglo-French Entente, but in Germany public opinion became intensely anti-British. Inevitably the French and British were driven into closer co-operation; a joint naval strategy was discussed, and to ease the burden on both, it was agreed (1912) that the British fleet would patrol the Atlantic and the Channel while the French would concentrate on the

Mediterranean. The French pressed for a definite written alliance with Britain, but Grey felt unable to agree for fear of committing Britain irrevocably against Germany.

5   *The Balkan Wars. The First Balkan War (1912)* began when Serbia, Greece, Montenegro and Bulgaria (calling themselves the Balkan League) attacked Turkey and captured most of her remaining territory in Europe. All the great powers felt their interests threatened: the Russians were afraid of the Bulgarians taking Constantinople, the Austrians feared that Serbia would become too powerful, the Germans thought that their hopes of controlling Turkey via the railway to Baghdad would be disappointed if the Balkan states became too powerful and the Turkish Empire collapsed. Grey seized the opportunity to show that Britain and Germany could still work together; *a peace conference met in London*, where it was decided which territories the Balkan states should take from Turkey. The Serbs were not pleased with the outcome, since they wanted Albania which would give them an outlet to the sea; but the Austrians, with German and British support, insisted that Albania should become an independent state. This was yet another attempt by Austria to prevent Serbia from becoming too strong.

   The Bulgarians were also dissatisfied: they were hoping for Macedonia, but most of it was given to Serbia. *Bulgaria therefore attacked Serbia, starting the Second Balkan War (1913)*, but her plan misfired when Greece, Romania and Turkey rallied to support Serbia. The Bulgarians were defeated, and by *the Treaty of Bucharest* lost most of their gains from the first war. Grey was pleased with the outcome, feeling that joint British and German influence had prevented an escalation of the wars by restraining the Austrians, who were itching to attack Serbia.

   Unfortunately Grey did not realize at the time the seriousness of the consequences:

●   Serbia had been strengthened and was now determined to stir up the Serbs and Croats inside the Austrian Empire; war between Austria and Serbia was only a matter of time.

●   Turkey was now so weak that she fell more and more under German influence.

●   The Germans took Grey's willingness to co-operate as a sign that he was ready to be detached from France and Russia.

6   *The naval race was still continuing.* From time to time the British proposed a joint slow-down in the naval building programme. In 1911, shortly after Agadir, Haldane went to Berlin, but although the Kaiser expressed an interest in a slow-down, he wanted Britain to promise not to intervene again in disputes between Germany and another state. This, of course, Haldane could not accept. The British tried again in 1912 and 1913, hoping that their joint action during the Balkan Wars would encourage the Germans to co-operate. Churchill proposed that there should be a 'naval holiday' during which all building of warships should stop; the Germans declined. However, right through 1913 Anglo-German relations were good. According to historian A. J. P. Taylor, the naval rivalry had lost its bitterness: 'the British had come to tolerate the German navy and were outstripping it without undue financial strain'. In June an Anglo-German agreement was reached over a possible partition of the Portuguese colonies of Mozambique and Angola which were being badly ruled by the mother country.

7   *The assassination of the Austrian Archduke Franz Ferdinand in Sarajevo (28 June 1914) was the event which sparked off the war.* The Archduke was the nephew and heir to the Habsburg Emperor Franz Josef. Against all advice, he paid a visit to

Sarajevo, the Bosnian capital. He and his wife were shot dead by a Serb terrorist, Gavrilo Princip. The Austrians blamed the Serbian government and sent them a stiff ultimatum. The Serbs accepted most of the points in it, and the Austrian government, its armies unprepared for war, was divided about whether to take military action or not. However, with German encouragement and promises of support, the Austrians declared war on Serbia (28 July). The Russians, determined not to let the Serbs down this time, ordered a general mobilization (29 July). The German government demanded that this should be cancelled (31 July), and when the Russians failed to comply, Germany declared war on Russia (1 August) and on France (3 August). When German troops entered Belgium on their way to invade France, Britain, who had promised (in 1839) to defend Belgian neutrality, demanded their withdrawal. When the Germans ignored this, Britain entered the war (4 August). Austria–Hungary declared war on Russia on 6 August, and other countries joined later.

(d) *What caused the war?*

It is clear that the Austrian quarrel with Serbia precipitated the outbreak of war. Austria was genuinely afraid that if Serbia acquired Bosnia (which contained about three million Serbs), all the other Serbs and Croats living inside the Habsburg Empire would want to join Serbia; other national groups such as Czechs, Poles and Italians would be encouraged to demand independence, and the result would be the collapse of the Habsburg Empire. For the Austrians, it was an essential 'preventive' war.

It is more difficult to explain why this should have escalated into a major war, and historians have still not managed to agree. Some blame Russia, the first country to order a general mobilization; some blame Germany for making Austria more aggressive with her promises of support; and some blame Britain for not making it clear that she would support France; this, it is argued, might have dissuaded the Germans from declaring war on France. Historians have suggested many other reasons and some of these have been rejected by other historians:

1   *The existence of the two opposing alliance systems or armed camps is thought by some to have made war inevitable.* The blocs were:

  - *The Triple Alliance* – Germany, Austria–Hungary and Italy;
  - *The Triple Entente* – Britain, France and Russia.

    But these had not proved binding earlier – Britain and France had not supported Russia during the Bosnia Crisis and Austria–Hungary kept aloof from Germany during the Agadir Crisis. It is just as arguable that the existence of two fairly evenly balanced power blocs acted as a deterrent to war during the 20 years before 1914.

2   *Colonial rivalry.* This had caused friction in the past, but in 1914 there were no specific quarrels; as late as June 1914 Britain and Germany had reached agreement about the future of the Portuguese colonies in Africa.

3   *Anglo-German naval rivalry.* This was probably no longer a major cause of friction, since Britain's lead was unassailable.

4   *Economic rivalry.* It has been argued that the desire for economic mastery of the world caused German businessmen to want war with Britain. However, Germany was already well on the way to economic victory; one leading German industrialist remarked in 1913: 'Give us three or four more years of peace and Germany will be the unchallenged economic master of Europe.'

More plausible suggestions are:

1   *The Russians should bear some responsibility for the escalation of the war.* They were deeply worried about the Balkans where both Bulgaria and Turkey were under close German influence. Russian existence depended on the free passage of merchant ships through the Dardanelles and this now seemed threatened. Once Austria declared war on Serbia, the Russians felt they must mobilize. There was also the need to maintain Russian prestige as leader of the Slavs. The Russian Tsar Nicholas II, though not exactly relishing the prospect of war, nevertheless was well aware that it could be useful to divert the public's attention away from domestic problems.

2   *German backing for Austria was vitally important.* In 1913 Germany had restrained the Austrians from attacking Serbia, yet in 1914 the Kaiser egged them on and promised German help without conditions – the so-called 'blank cheque'. This could mean that the Germans now felt ready for war and wanted to get on with it, for one of two reasons:

   ● either because they were set on world domination, as the German historian Fritz Fischer suggested;
   ● or because they felt encircled and threatened by British naval power and by the Russian military build-up. In this case a preventive war, a war for survival, was necessary before the end of 1914. After that, they thought, the Russians would be too strong.

3   *The mobilization plans of the great powers were blamed by A. J. P. Taylor.* He believed that there was very little evidence to show that Germany deliberately timed the war for August 1914, and suggested that all the countries involved became the victims of their own moblilization plans and timetables, and also of the belief that the opening battles would be the decisive ones – as had been the case in the Balkan Wars. The German *Schlieffen Plan* assumed that in the event of war, France would automatically join Russia; therefore the bulk of German forces were to be sent through Belgium to knock France out in six weeks, after which they would be rushed across Europe by train to face Russia. Once Moltke, the German Commander-in-Chief, knew that Russia had ordered a general mobilization, he demanded immediate German mobilization, which, under the Schlieffen Plan, required German troops to enter Belgium. The Kaiser suggested a partial mobilization just against Russia, hoping that Britain would stay neutral if Germany refrained from attacking France. But Moltke insisted on the full plan; he said there was no time to change all the railway timetables to send the troop trains to Russia instead of to Belgium. This suggests that even if Britain had announced on 31 July that she would definitely support France, it would have made no difference: it was the full Schlieffen Plan or nothing, even though Germany at that point had no specific quarrel with France.

Whatever the truth, it is clear that Germany must take much of the responsibility for the war. For years the Kaiser's aggressive attitude had alarmed Britain, France and Russia, and given the impression that Germany wanted to dominate Europe. Her encouragement of Austria and the invasion of Belgium were vital factors. At the present time the majority of historians, including many Germans, accept Fritz Fischer's theory as the most convincing one: that the outbreak of the war was deliberately provoked by Germany's leaders.

(e) Why did Britain enter the war?

- *Defence of Belgium?* The immediate British instinct on the outbreak of war was to remain neutral. The public knew little about Serbia, and Britain did not seem directly threatened. Grey tried to organize a conference to discuss Serbia, but the Germans refused, and events moved so quickly after 28 July that there was no time for negotiation. Grey warned the Germans not to count on British neutrality and warned the French and Russians not to count on British help. However, when German troops entered Belgium, Grey immediately sent an ultimatum to the Germans warning them to withdraw. Britain had promised in the 1839 Treaty of London, along with France and Prussia, to guarantee the neutrality of Belgium. When the ultimatum was ignored, Britain declared war on Germany.
- *Although the defence of Belgium was given as the official reason for Britain's entry, there was more to it than that.* There was the moral obligation to the French; having given them solid diplomatic support since 1904, to desert them in their hour of greatest need would have damaged Britain's international prestige. Probably more important, a German victory would endanger Britain's trading interests and ruin the balance of power in Europe. *The real reason for Britain's entry was therefore the need to resist German domination of Europe.* The attack on Belgium was convenient because it enabled Grey to unite the Liberals and so bring Britain in as early as possible.

Grey has often been accused of being too indecisive, and of not making it clear that Britain would support France. But this is probably unfair. It was hardly possible for him to have acted differently, because the cabinet was not united in favour of intervention until the last minute, and even then two leading members resigned. In any case, given the attitude of the German generals and the Schlieffen Plan, it is difficult to imagine anything that Grey could have done to prevent the war spreading. One thing is certain – the cabinet was extremely reluctant to commit Britain to war. As Grey looked out of the Foreign Office window late on the evening of 4 August, he made his most memorable remark: 'The lamps are going out all over Europe; we shall not see them lit again in our lifetime.'

Questions

1 The suffragettes

Study Sources A to D and then answer the questions which follow.

Source A

From Mrs Emmeline Pankhurst's book, My Own Story, *1914, describing the first major suffragette demonstration in London on 19 February 1906*

Those women had followed me to the House of Commons. They had defied the police. They were awake at last. They were prepared to do something that women had never done before – fight for themselves. Women had always fought for men, and for their children. Now they were ready to fight for their own human rights. *Our militant movement* was established.

From the speech of Mrs Emmeline Pankhurst when standing in the dock of the Magistrates' Court, Bow Street, London in 1908

We have tried every way. We have presented larger petitions than were ever presented before for any other reform, we have succeeded in holding greater public meetings than men have ever had for any reform. We have faced hostile mobs at street corners, because we were told that we could not have that representation for our taxes which men have won unless we converted the whole country to our side. Because we have done this we have been misrepresented, we have been ridiculed, we have had contempt poured upon us ...

Well, sir, that is all I have to say to you. We are not here because we are law-breakers, we are here in our efforts to become law-*makers!*

From Viscount Ullswater's book, A Speaker's Commentaries *(1925). Here he recalls suffragettes' activities when he was Speaker of the House of Commons in 1913*

The activities of the militant suffragettes had now [1913] reached the stage at which nothing was safe from their attacks. Churches were burnt, public buildings and private residences were destroyed, bombs were exploded, the police and individuals were assaulted, meetings broken up, and every imaginable device resorted to in order to inconvenience or annoy His Majesty's lieges.* When any offenders were caught and convicted they were sent to prison; but as they generally resorted to a hunger strike ... which would have resulted in death, they were released and immediately repeated their former offences. A Bill was introduced, called the Prisoners' Temporary Release Bill, soon nicknamed the 'Cat and Mouse Bill', the purport of which was to permit the release of offenders on licence, with the provision that in the event of a subsequent offence being committed the licence should be cancelled and the offenders re-arrested. The Bill passed without much difficulty, but proved valueless in preventing a continuance of the outrages. The feeling in the House, caused by the extravagant and lawless action of the militants, hardened the opposition to their demands.

(*lieges = subjects)

An opinion on the suffragettes expressed by the historian, R. C. K. Ensor in his book, England, 1870–1914 *(1936)*

The vote was not sought for any practical object, but as a symbol of equality. They were obsessed by an inferiority complex. And similarly upon politics at large their militancy had more effect than their suffragism. The means mattered more than the end, and indeed conflicted with it. For while the vote presupposes the rule of free persuasion, the WSPU leaders proclaimed, by word and deed, that the way to get results was through violence. Such doctrines are always liable to become popular, when a politically inexperienced class or classes come into the public life of a nation.

(a) Consult Sources A and C.

With reference to Sources A and C, and using your own knowledge, explain what was meant by the following phrases in the sources, as they applied to suffragette activity in the period 1906 to 1918.

(i) 'Our militant movement' (Source A)

(ii) 'Cat and Mouse Bill' (Source C). (6 marks)

(b) Consult Sources A, B and C.

On the basis of the evidence contained within these sources, suggest why suffragette militancy caused problems for the state. (4 marks)

(c) Consult all four sources and use your own knowledge.

'The suffragette movement was as difficult a challenge for the Liberal governments before the First World War as any other domestic challenge at the time'. How valid is this judgement? (10 marks)

(Total 20 marks)

[An NEAB question, June 1994]

2 'Ulster will fight and Ulster will be right'. Why was Unionist opposition to Irish Home Rule so strong during the period 1906–14, and to what extent was this responsible for the Liberals' failure to find a solution to the Irish problem before 1914?

3 How far can it be argued that Sir Edward Grey was a successful Foreign Secretary in the period 1906 to 1914?

22 Britain, the First World War and its aftermath

The two opposing sides in the war were:

The Allies or Entente Powers	*The Central Powers*
Britain and the Empire	Germany
France	Austria–Hungary
Russia (left December 1917)	Turkey (entered November 1914)
Japan	Bulgaria (entered October 1915)
Italy (entered May 1915)	
Serbia	
Belgium	
Romania (entered August 1916)	
USA (entered April 1917)	

Most people in Britain, and certainly the Germans, thought the war would only last a matter of weeks. In Britain there was a general feeling that 'it would all be over by Christmas'. But Lord Kitchener, the newly appointed Secretary for War, was not so sure; he dismayed the cabinet by telling them that it would last nearer three years than three months. Once the German Schlieffen Plan had failed to achieve the rapid defeat of France, Kitchener was proved right. Although the Germans penetrated deeply, Paris did not fall, and *stalemate quickly developed on the western front*, with all hope of a short war gone. Both sides dug themselves in and spent the next four years attacking and defending lines of trenches which were difficult to capture because the increased fire-power provided by magazine rifles and machine-guns made frontal attacks suicidal and rendered cavalry useless. The British, desperately looking for a way to break the stalemate, *opened up a new front by attacking Turkey at the Dardanelles (1915)*; but everything went wrong and the troops had to be withdrawn.

In eastern Europe there was more movement, with Russian successes against the Austrians, who constantly had to be helped out by the Germans, causing friction between the two allies. But by December 1917 the Germans had captured Poland (which was Russian territory) and forced the defeated Russians out of the war. Britain, suffering heavy losses of merchant ships through submarine attacks, and France, whose armies were paralyzed by mutiny, seemed on the verge of defeat.

Gradually the tide turned; the Allies, helped by the entry of the USA in April 1917, wore the Germans down. The last despairing German attempt at a decisive breakthrough in France failed in the spring of 1918. The success of the British navy in blockading German ports and defeating the submarine threat by defending merchant convoys, was also telling on the Germans. By the late summer of 1918 they were nearing exhaustion. An armistice was signed on 11 November 1918, although Germany itself had scarcely been invaded. A controversial peace settlement was signed at Versailles the following year.

The war had important effects on the political scene in Britain, causing the resignation of Asquith, the end of the Liberal government and the fatal split in the Liberal party, the move to coalition governments and the remarkable premiership of Lloyd George, remembered by many as 'the man who won the war'.

Main political changes during the war	
May 1915	End of the Liberal government. Asquith forms coalition, bringing Conservative leaders and Henderson (Labour leader) into government. Lloyd George becomes Minister of Munitions.
July 1916	Lloyd George becomes Secretary for War after death of Kitchener.
December 1916	Asquith resigns and Lloyd George becomes Prime Minister of second coalition government.
August 1917	Labour leader Henderson resigns from government after disagreements with Lloyd George.
May 1918	Maurice debate shows seriousness of Liberal split as 98 Liberals vote against government.
December 1918	Lloyd George's coalition wins landslide victory in 'coupon' election. He remains in power until October 1922 when Conservatives withdraw support.

22.1 Mons to the Somme 1914–16

(a) *The British Expeditionary Force (BEF)*

This was quickly mobilized under the command of Sir John French and sent to join the French army at Maubeuge. It was extremely small – only four divisions, compared with 70 French and 72 German divisions, but it made an important contribution towards slowing down the German push towards Paris. The Schlieffen Plan had already been held up by unexpectedly strong Belgian resistance, and it took the Germans over two weeks to capture Brussels. This was a vital delay, giving the French time to make full preparations, and leaving the Channel ports free for the BEF to land. Instead of sweeping around in a wide arc, capturing the Channel ports and approaching Paris from the west, the Germans found themselves making straight for Paris just east of the city. They penetrated to within 20 miles of the capital and the French government withdrew to Bordeaux. But the nearer they got to Paris, the more the German impetus slowed up; there were problems in keeping the armies supplied with food and ammunition, and the troops became exhausted by long marches in the August heat.

● *The first British engagement took place at Mons (23 August)* where the BEF suddenly found itself in the path of the advancing German 1st Army under von Kluck. The British distinguished themselves by fighting back the Germans who had been surprised to encounter any British troops. However, when the French army retreated to the River Marne, the British had no alternative but to move with them.

● *At the Battle of the Marne (September 1914)* the French under Joffre attacked the wilting Germans and drove them back to the River Aisne, where the Germans were able to dig trenches. The British played a valuable supporting role and suffered only a few casualties. The battle was vitally important; some historians have called it one of the most decisive in modern history. It ruined the Schlieffen Plan once and for all; France would not be knocked out in six weeks; hopes of a short war were dashed and the Germans would have to face full-scale war on two fronts. The war of movement was over; the trench lines eventually stretched from the Channel coast to the Alps and there was time for the British navy to bring its crippling blockade to bear on German ports.

● *The BEF was suddenly moved northwards into Flanders* to protect Ypres from the German advance following their capture of Antwerp. In the bloody *First Battle of*

Map 22.1   The Western Front

Ypres (October–November 1914) the British managed to hang on to the city, though it proved to be a vulnerable point right through the war. This is usually taken to mark the end of the BEF. Casualties were extremely high at Ypres; over half the force was wounded and about one-tenth killed. For its size, it made a remarkable contribution to the early stages of the war. Von Kluck paid it the highest compliment, claiming that it was British resistance which had prevented him from taking Paris.

(b) *Kitchener raises a new army but runs out of ideas*

Kitchener decided that Britain needed an army of 70 divisions, and since Asquith refused to introduce conscription (compulsory military service), Kitchener mounted a propaganda campaign to encourage volunteers. Soon Britain was bristling with huge posters of Kitchener pointing his finger, and the words: 'Your country needs You'. The response was amazing: 10 000 men volunteered within a few days, and by mid-September the total was 500 000. By the end of February 1915 a further 500 000 had been recruited. The dominions sprang to the call – Canada and Australia sent 30 000 men each and New Zealand 8500.

Having arrived at the front, the new troops found that they could make no headway against the German trench lines. The stalemate on the western front continued throughout 1915, though several attempts were made to break through. The British tried at *Neuve Chapelle in March 1915 and at Loos (September)* where they suffered heavy casualties. The Germans attacked again in Flanders *at the Second Battle of Ypres (April–May)*, but all attempts failed. *The reasons for these continued failures right through until 1918 were always the same:*

- There was no chance of a surprise attack because a massive artillery bombardment always preceded the infantry attack to clear the barbed wire away from no-man's land between the two lines of trenches, and generally to soften up the enemy.
- Reconnaisance aircraft and observation balloons could spot troop concentrations on the roads leading up to the trenches.
- Even when a trench line was breached, advance was difficult because the ground had been churned up by the artillery barrage and there was deadly machine-gun fire to contend with.
- Any ground won was difficult to defend since it usually formed a *salient* or bulge in the trench line; the flanks of a salient were always vulnerable.
- Another method of attack which turned out to be unpredictable was the use of poison gas. The Germans used it at Ypres, but when the wind changed direction it was blown back towards their own lines and they suffered more casualties than the Allies, especially when the Allies released some gas of their own.

Nevertheless when all possible allowances have been made, it is clear that Sir John French was not an outstanding commander. He was therefore replaced by Sir Douglas Haig. But French was not the only one to find himself at a loss in these new conditions: Kitchener commented to Grey: 'I don't know what is to be done. This isn't war.'

(c) *The eastern front*

The Russians, having mobilized more quickly than the Germans expected, made the mistake of invading both Austria and East Prussia at the same time, though they were successful against Austria, occupying the province of Galicia. The Germans called Hindenburg out of retirement and twice defeated the Russians *at Tannenberg (August 1914) and the Masurian Lakes (September)*, driving them out of Germany. Worse was to come: in 1915 the Germans occupied Poland, and the Turks began to blockade the

Dardanelles, severing the most convenient supply lines to the Russians and hampering their import and export trade.

(d) *The Gallipoli (Dardanelles) Campaign (1915)*

This was launched by the British partly to open up the vital supply lines to Russia. It was an idea strongly pressed by Winston Churchill (First Lord of the Admiralty) to escape the deadlock in the west by eliminating the Turks, who were thought to be the weakest of the Central Powers because of their unstable government. Success against Turkey would enable help to be sent to Russia and might also bring Bulgaria, Romania and Greece into the war on the allied side; it would then be possible to attack Austria from the south.

The campaign was a total failure. The first attempt, in March, was an Anglo-French naval attack through the Straits to capture Constantinople; this failed because the Turks had laid lines of mines across the channel. This ruined the surprise element, so that when the British attempted landings at the tip of the Gallipoli peninsula, the Turks had strengthened their defences and no advance could be made (April). Further landings by Australian and New Zealand troops (Anzacs) in April, and by British in August were equally useless and positions could be held only with great difficulty. In December the entire force was withdrawn.

The consequences were serious: besides being a blow to Allied morale, it turned out to be the last chance of relieving Russia via the Black Sea and probably caused Bulgaria to join the Central Powers. A Franco-British force landed at Salonika in neutral Greece to try and relieve Serbia, but it was too late. When Bulgaria entered the war in October, Serbia was quickly overrun by Bulgarians and Germans. The year 1915 therefore was not a good one for the Allies: casualties at Gallipoli had been heavy: 250 000 wounded and 43 000 British, Australians and New Zealanders dead.

On the other hand Turkish losses were even heavier and the Turkish army probably never recovered fully. So arguably Gallipoli weakened the Turks and made possible the later British victories against them in Palestine in 1917. But this was very much in the future, and there were more British disasters to come before then. A British army sent to protect Anglo-Persian oil interests found itself surrounded by Turks at *Kut-el-Amara in Mesopotamia*. After a siege lasting from December 1915 until April 1916, General Townshend surrendered with 12 000 men, of whom some 8000 later died in the dismal conditions of the Turkish prison camps.

(e) *The Battle of the Somme (1916)*

This was the major operation involving the British on the western front in that year. In February the Germans, under Falkenhayn, launched *a massive attack on the French fortress town of Verdun*, but the French defended stubbornly. It was partly to relieve pressure on the French that Haig decided to attack the German lines near the River Somme; he also hoped that by keeping the Germans fully committed, they would be unable to risk sending any more troops to the eastern front against Russia. The campaign began on 1 July with disastrous results: the preliminary artillery bombardment failed both to destroy the barbed wire in no-man's land and to soften up the Germans, who merely waited in heavily fortified dugouts. When the British troops left their trenches, under orders to advance at a slow walking pace, many were caught up in the wire and all came under murderous German machine-gun fire. *21 000 were killed and over 35 000 wounded on the first day, with no gains to show for it.* Yet incredibly, Haig continued with these attacks until November.

At the end of it all, the Allies had made only limited advances varying between a

Illus. 22.1   British casualties during the Somme offensive in July 1916

few hundred yards and seven miles along a thirty-mile front. *The real importance of the battle was the blow to German morale* as they realized that Britain (where conscription was introduced for the first time in May1916) was a military power to be reckoned with. Losses on both sides killed or wounded were appalling (Germans 650 000, British 418 000, French 194 000), and Haig came under severe criticism for persisting with suicidal frontal attacks. However, they probably helped to wear down the German armies: Hindenburg himself admitted in his *Memoirs* that the Germans could not have survived many more campaigns like Verdun and the Somme. The Somme also contributed to the fall of the Prime Minister, Asquith; as criticisms of British tactics mounted, Asquith resigned and was replaced by Lloyd George.

(f) *Asquith's failings as a war leader*

Asquith had been a competent peacetime Prime Minister, handling many problems well, particularly the clash with the House of Lords. However, his 'wait and see' attitude to the Irish and suffragette problems was not a good omen for his performance during the war. Unfortunately he continued his detached approach after hostilities had started. He believed it was the generals' job to run the war and was most reluctant to interfere even when French turned out to be incompetent and when there was a serious shortage of shells in 1915. There was a complete lack of urgency in all departments just at the time when decisive leadership was needed. As A. J. P. Taylor put it: 'Asquith was as solid as a rock, but like a rock, incapable of movement.' In May 1915 Asquith tried to counter the growing criticism by bringing some leading Conservatives – Bonar

Law, Lansdowne, Balfour, Carson and Lord Curzon – together with the Labour party leader, Arthur Henderson, into the cabinet. This was the end of a purely Liberal government and the beginning of government by coalition.

His most important move was *the appointment of Lloyd George as Minister of Munitions*. He soon emerged as the outstanding member of the cabinet, his vigour and panache contrasting sharply with Asquith's detachment and lack of energy. After Kitchener's death (he was drowned on his way to Russia when his ship, the *Hampshire*, struck a mine), Lloyd George took his place as Secretary for War (July 1916). Relations between Asquith and Lloyd George deteriorated steadily, the introduction of conscription being the main area of dispute. Lloyd George felt it was the only way to win the war, but Asquith was totally opposed, believing it to be against all Liberal principles. As news of the terrible casualties on the Somme became known, moves began to oust Asquith and replace him with Lloyd George. Asquith was manoeuvred into resigning, much against his will, and Lloyd George became Prime Minister of another coalition government (December 1916). However, he only had the support of about half the Liberal MPs, the other half remaining loyal to Asquith. It was the Conservatives who had put Lloyd George into power, because he seemed the only man with sufficient drive to win the war for Britain.

22.2 Lloyd George at the helm

(a) *Lloyd George as Minister of Munitions*

Lloyd George immediately began to show in his new job, as he had as Chancellor of the Exchequer, that he was a man who got things done instead of just talking about them. He sliced through all the official red tape in the most unconventional ways. He began by requisitioning a hotel to house his new ministry and appointed businessmen to important positions in the government because he thought they were more decisive than politicians. He made sure that the supply of shells increased and was responsible for the widespread adoption of the machine-gun. At the outbreak of war, each battalion had only two machine-guns, which, in Haig's view, was 'more than sufficient'. Kitchener thought four would be a good idea, but the British Army School of Musketry had recommended six. Lloyd George is reputed to have said: 'Take Kitchener's figure. Square it. Multiply it by two. Then double it again for good luck.' This figure was achieved. There were two further occasions on which Lloyd George superseded Kitchener (who was still Secretary for War):

● In January 1915 Wilfred Stokes demonstrated his new light mortar, but the War Office thought it was too dangerous. Lloyd George persuaded a wealthy Indian prince to finance the first thousand Stokes mortars and it soon proved to be one of the most effective weapons of the war.
●   Kitchener was apparently not impressed with the tank, which had been developed from an idea of Major E. D. Swinton, and first demonstrated in February 1916. Lloyd George was most enthusiastic, and the first order for 40 tanks was placed.

Lloyd George was also behind the Munitions of War Act, giving the government power to take control of factories responsible for armaments and other war work. Strikes and lockouts were prohibited and measures taken to combat drunkenness, so that the war effort would not be impaired. Most controversial of all, Lloyd George at last got his way over conscription which was introduced in May 1916 and applied to all males aged 18 to 45.

(b) *Lloyd George as Prime Minister*

Even after he became Secretary for War in July 1916 Lloyd George was prevented from doing all he wanted by the dithering Asquith. But as soon as he became Prime Minister, he began to run the country almost like a dictator. According to one of his biographers, K. O. Morgan, 'Lloyd George's war premiership was without parallel in British history. No previous Prime Minister had ever exercised power in so sweeping and dominating a manner.' Almost everything he did provoked controversy and offended somebody, but so great was the crisis facing the country that he was able to get away with it:

- He set up a small war cabinet of five men – himself, Bonar Law (the Conservative leader), Curzon, Henderson (the Labour leader) and Milner (the former governor of Cape Colony) – which took all the main decisions. He appointed men from outside parliament to head important ministries: Sir Joseph Maclay, a Glasgow shipowner, made an excellent ship-building organizer, Lord Beaverbrook, owner of *The Daily Express*, a brilliant Minister of Propaganda.
- He introduced the Cabinet Secretariat under Sir Maurice Hankey to organize cabinet business. This was so successful in co-ordinating the different departments and their advisers that it was kept after the war. Lloyd George also had his own private secretariat and advisers, including Waldorf Astor, owner of *The Observer*. This was known as the 'Garden Suburb' because it met at first in huts in the garden behind No. 10 Downing Street.
- More government controls than ever before were introduced. All merchant shipping was brought under government direction, to defeat the submarine threat.

Illus. 22.2   Lloyd George on a visit to the front – talking to British soldiers

Farmers were ordered to cultivate extra land to meet the food shortages, factories were told what to produce (for example, army blankets and khaki for uniforms), and the coal industry was taken directly under government control. The new Ministry of National Service decided which men would be called up, depending on whether their jobs were vital or could be done by women. Food was rationed and prices and wages controlled.

• Lloyd George was able to do less on the military side of the war. However, he was mainly responsible for the adoption of the convoy system (see Section 22.3(e)) which saved Britain from starvation in 1917. He disapproved of Haig's costly and unimaginative tactics but could find nobody better to replace him. However, he did manage to have the French Marshal Foch appointed as Supreme Allied Commander on the western front, which reduced Haig's influence to some extent.

Unfortunately for Lloyd George and his future in politics, his policies and the style in which he carried them out, made him many enemies. Asquith and his supporters never really forgave him for the way in which Asquith was removed from the premiership, causing a fatal split in the Liberal Party. Lloyd George has therefore been blamed for the decline of the Liberal Party; but it has to be said in his defence that, like Peel, he was never primarily a party man. For Lloyd George the paramount aim was to win the war, not preserve the Liberal Party. Most historians would agree that if Asquith had remained Prime Minister for another year, Britain would have lost the war.

22.3 The war at sea

The general public in Germany and Britain expected a series of naval battles rather like the Battle of Trafalgar, in which the rival Dreadnought fleets would confront each other. But both sides were cautious and dared not risk any action which might result in the loss of their main fleets. The British Admiral Jellicoe was particularly careful; as Churchill pointed out, 'he was the only man on either side who could have lost the war in an afternoon'. Nor were the Germans anxious for a confrontation because they only had 13 of the latest Dreadnoughts against 20 British.

(a) *The Allied blockade and the Battle of the Falkland Islands*

The Allies aimed to prevent goods entering or leaving the Central powers, thus cutting off their trade and slowly starving them out. At the same time trade routes had to be kept open between Britain, her Empire and the rest of the world so that the Allies themselves would not starve. A third function of the navy was to transport British troops to the continent and keep them supplied via the Channel ports. The British were successful in carrying out these aims, and they went into action against German units stationed abroad.

The most important battle in the early stages of the war took place off *the Falkland Islands (December 1914)*. Admiral von Spee with a squadron of two cruisers and three light cruisers was about to bombard the Falklands when he was attacked by a much stronger British squadron (which included two battle-cruisers) commanded by Admiral Sturdee. The Germans were no match for the superior fire-power of the British battle-cruisers, and von Spee's entire squadron was destroyed. By the end of 1914 most of the German armed surface vessels had been sunk or badly damaged and the Falklands engagement made the Kaiser unwilling to lose any more ships. One fleet continued to blockade the Baltic in order to cut off supplies to Russia, but the main German fleet did not venture out of port until the Battle of Jutland in 1916. The Kaiser had some idea of keeping his fleet intact as a bargaining counter in peace negotiations, and the British were happy with this situation which left them in control of the surface, though not of the submarines. The navy made an important contribution during 1915 to the Gallipoli campaign, though this was not one of its successes (see Section 22.1(d)).

(b) *The Allied blockade causes problems*

Britain was trying to prevent the Germans using the neutral Scandinavian and Dutch ports to break the blockade. This involved stopping and searching all neutral ships and confiscating any goods suspected of being intended for enemy hands. The USA objected strongly to this, being anxious to continue trading with both sides.

(c) *The Germans retaliate with mines and submarine attacks*

This was their only alternative since their surface vessels had either been destroyed or were being blockaded in port. At first they respected neutral shipping and passenger liners, but it was soon clear that the German U-boat blockade was not effective, partly because they had insufficient U-boats and partly because of problems of identification – the British tried to fool the Germans by flying neutral flags and by using passenger liners to transport arms and ammunition. In April 1915 the British liner *Lusitania* was sunk by a torpedo attack. In fact the *Lusitania* was armed and carrying vast quantities of arms and ammunition, which the Germans knew all about; hence their claim that the sinking was not just an act of barbarism against defenceless civilians. *The sinking had important consequences*: out of the thousand dead, 118 were Americans. Woodrow Wilson, the US President, found that the USA would have to take sides to protect her trade. Whereas the British blockade did not interfere with the safety of passengers and crews, German tactics certainly did. For the time being, however, American protests made the Germans tone down their submarine campaign, rendering it even less effective.

(d) *The Battle of Jutland (31 May 1916)*

This was the only time in the war that the main battle-fleets emerged and engaged each other; the result was indecisive. The German Admiral von Scheer tried to lure part of the British fleet out from its base, so that that section could be destroyed by the numerically superior Germans. However, more British ships came out than he had anticipated. After the two fleets had shelled each other on and off for several hours, the Germans decided to retire to base, firing torpedoes as they went. On balance the Germans could claim that they had won the battle since they lost only 11 ships to Britain's 14. But the real importance of the battle lay in the fact that the Germans had failed to destroy British sea power. The German High Seas Fleet stayed in Kiel for the rest of the war, leaving Britain's control of the surface complete. In desperation at the food shortages caused by the British blockade, the Germans embarked on a campaign of 'unrestricted' submarine warfare.

(e) *'Unrestricted' submarine warfare (January 1917)*

The Germans had been concentrating on the production of U-boats since the Battle of Jutland, and so this campaign was extremely effective. They attempted to sink all enemy and neutral merchant ships in the Atlantic, and although they knew that this was bound to bring the USA into the war, they hoped that Britain and France could be starved into surrender before the Americans could make any vital contribution. They almost did it: the peak of German success came in April 1917 when 430 ships were lost. Britain was down to about six weeks' corn supply, and although the USA came into the war in April, it was bound to be several months before their help became effective. However, the situation was saved by Lloyd George, who insisted that the Admiralty adopt the convoy system – a large number of merchant ships sailed together so that they could be protected by escorting warships. This dramatically reduced the losses, and the German gamble had failed.

In an attempt to finish off the U-boat threat completely, the navy carried out daring raids on the captured Belgian ports of Ostend and Zeebrugge, which the Germans were using as submarine bases. On the night of 22 April 1918, under cover of smoke-screens, ships loaded with cement were brought in and sunk to block the exits from the ports. The operation at Zeebrugge was the more successful one, and although not as much damage was inflicted as had been hoped, Zeebrugge was rendered almost useless as a German base. This, together with extra defences at the Straits of Dover, made it almost impossible for the Germans to attack the Straits, and increasingly difficult for submarines to slip through.

The German 'unrestricted' submarine campaign was important because it brought the USA into the war. By mid-1918 the British navy, helped by the Americans and the Japanese, had achieved their three aims mentioned under (a) and played a vitally important role in the defeat of the Central Powers.

22.4 Vimy Ridge to the armistice 1917–18

(a) *The failure to get a negotiated peace*

One reason why the war continued to drag on for so long, apart from the difficulties of breaking the stalemate of trench warfare and the fact that both sides were so evenly balanced, was the failure of all attempts at negotiation. By the summer of 1915, when it was clear that it would not be a short war, there were people on both sides who felt that the cost in men and money had already been too high, and that it should be possible for intelligent, civilized people to get together and negotiate peace terms that would be acceptable to both sides. After the terrible slaughter at Verdun and the Somme in 1916, several serious attempts were made to start negotiations, but all failed. The reasons were:

- There were people on both sides who thought outright victory was still possible. In Germany the generals were more powerful than the politicians. Chancellor Bethmann-Hollweg was ready to negotiate, but General Ludendorff wanted to fight on.
- In Britain Lord Lansdowne and the Labour party were keen to negotiate, but Lloyd George was a hard-liner who still believed in the 'knock-out' blow.
- Negotiations would mean compromise, and neither side was prepared to make sufficient concessions. The Germans, for example, insisted on keeping some sort of control over Belgium and parts of Poland.

Woodrow Wilson tried all through 1916 to get talks started before the USA was drawn into the conflict. When Bethmann-Hollweg eventually agreed to talk in December 1916, Britain and France rejected the offer. They took it as a sign that Germany was weakening; it later emerged that German demands would have been too high anyway.

After the overthrow of the Tsar Nicholas II in March 1917, the Russian socialists proposed 'peace without annexations or indemnities' and suggested a conference in Stockholm to be attended by socialists from all countries involved in the war. However, the British and French governments would not allow their socialists to attend.

Henderson was told that he would be a traitor if he went, because he would have to talk to Germans. This was the major reason for Henderson's resignation from the government.

The Pope also proposed a peace conference (August 1917), but this came to nothing when the Germans refused to attend. The German generals had persuaded the Kaiser to dismiss Bethmann-Hollweg on the grounds that he was too weak. With that, all chances of a negotiated peace disappeared. The German armies were doing well at that point, and Russia was on the verge of collapse; Ludendorff was determined on a fight to the finish.

(b) *Limited Allied successes on the western front during 1917*

In April the Canadians captured Vimy Ridge, north of Arras. This was an impressive achievement, though at the time it was not followed up. In March 1918 allied possession of the ridge turned out to be a serious obstacle in the way of the German spring offensive. The allied campaign at Vimy was accompanied by a massive French offensive under their new commander, Nivelle, on the Aisne. It achieved absolutely nothing and provoked the French army to mutiny. Nivelle was replaced by Petain who successfully calmed the situation.

From June to November the British fought *the Third Battle of Ypres*, usually remembered as *Passchendaele*, in appallingly muddy conditions. British casualties were enormous – 324 000 compared with 200 000 Germans for a four-mile advance. More significant was *the Battle of Cambrai* which demonstrated that tanks, properly used, might break the deadlock of trench warfare. 381 massed British tanks made a wide breach in the German line, but lack of reserves prevented the success from being followed up.

However, the lesson had been observed: Haig realized that the best tactic was to stop the advance once a breach had been made in the German line and to start another attack at a different point. The technique was therefore a series of short, sharp jabs instead of a prolonged push at one point. This avoided creating a vulnerable salient and would force the enemy to fall back at several points, eventually withdrawing the whole line.

Meanwhile the Italians were heavily defeated by Germans and Austrians at *Caporetto (October 1917)* and retreated in disorder. This unexpectedly proved to be an important turning point. Italian morale revived, perhaps because they were faced with having to defend their homeland against the hated Austrians. The defeat also led to the setting up of an Allied Supreme War Council. The new French premier Clemenceau, a great war leader in the Lloyd George mould, rallied the wilting French.

(c) *The eastern front*

Disaster struck the Allies when the Russians withdrew from the war (December 1917). Continuous defeat by the Germans, lack of arms and supplies in the right places and incompetent leadership caused two revolutions (March and November 1917), and Lenin and the Bolsheviks, who seized power in November, were willing to make peace. This meant that in 1918 the entire weight of German forces could be thrown against the west; without the Americans, the Allies would have been hard pressed.

On the other hand, encouragement was provided by British victories against the Turks. More troops and supplies were sent out, and Kut was taken at the end of February 1917. The capture of Baghdad (March) encouraged the Arabs of Syria and Palestine to revolt against Turkish rule, which was an important reason for the Turkish defeat. The British supplied the Arabs with arms, and T. E. Lawrence (Lawrence of

Arabia), an archaeologist working with the Arab bureau, helped to organize an Arab campaign which captured the port of Aqaba and ruined Turkish communications by constantly blowing up railway lines. Allenby captured Jerusalem (December 1917) and after a delay during the first half of 1918, when some of his forces were rushed to the western front to help stem the German spring offensive, he entered Damascus (October 1918). The way was clear to Constantinople, and the Turks signed an armistice with Britain on 30 October.

(d) *The USA enters the war (April 1917)*

This was provoked partly by the German U-boat campaign, and also by the discovery that Germany was trying to persuade Mexico to declare war on the USA, promising her Texas, New Mexico and Arizona in return. The Americans had hesitated about siding with the autocratic Russian government, but the overthrow of the Tsar in the March revolution removed this obstacle. The USA made an important contribution to the Allied victory: they supplied Britain and France with food, merchant ships and credit. Actual military help came more slowly. By the end of 1917 only one American division had been in action, but by mid-1918 over half a million men were fighting. Most important was the psychological boost which the American potential in resources of men and materials gave the Allies, and the corresponding blow it gave to German morale.

(e) *The German spring offensive (1918)*

This was launched by Ludendorff in a last desperate attempt to win the war before too many US troops arrived, and before discontent in Germany led to revolution. It almost came off: throwing in all the extra troops released from the east, the Germans broke through on the Somme (March). By the end of May they were only 40 miles from Paris and the Allies seemed to be disintegrating. However, under the overall command of the French Marshal Foch, they managed to hold on as the German advance lost momentum and created an awkward bulge. Lloyd George, helped by Sir Joseph Maclay, organized the recall and transportation to the front of 88 000 British troops who were at home on leave, and others were brought from Palestine.

(f) *The Allied counter-offensive*

This began on 8 August 1918 near Amiens. With Haig using his new tactics, hundreds of tanks attacked in short, sharp jabs at many different points and forced the Germans to withdraw their entire line. Slowly but surely the Germans were forced back until by the end of September the Allies were through the Hindenburg Line. Though Germany itself had not yet been invaded, Ludendorff was convinced that they would be defeated in the spring of 1919. He insisted that the German government ask President Wilson for an armistice (3 October) hoping to get less severe terms based on Wilson's 14 points (see Section 22.6(a)). By asking for peace in 1918, he hoped to save Germany from invasion and preserve the army's reputation. Fighting continued for another five weeks, but eventually an armistice was signed on 11 November.

(g) *Why did Britain and her allies win the war?*

The reasons can be summarized briefly:

1 Once the Schlieffen Plan had failed, removing all hope of a quick German victory,

it was bound to be a strain on their resources. They had not intended to fight a long war nor a war on two fronts.

2 Allied sea power was decisive, enforcing the crippling blockade which caused desperate food shortages, while at the same time keeping Allied armies fully supplied.

3 The German submarine campaign was defeated by the use of convoys protected by British, American and Japanese destroyers. The campaign itself was a mistake because it brought the USA into the war.

4 The entry of the USA brought the Allies vast new resources of men and materials.

5 Allied political leaders at the critical time – Lloyd George and Clemenceau – were more competent than those of the Central Powers. The unity of command under Foch in 1918 probably helped, while Haig learned lessons from his 1917 experiences about the effective use of tanks and the avoidance of salients.

6 The continuous strain of heavy losses told on the Germans – they lost their best troops in the 1918 offensive and the new troops were young and inexperienced. An epidemic of deadly Spanish 'flu did not help the situation, and morale was low as they retreated.

7 Germany was badly let down by her allies and was constantly having to help out the Austrians and Bulgarians. The defeat of Bulgaria by the British (from Salonika) and Serbs (29 September 1918) was the final straw for many German soldiers, who could see no chance of victory after that. When Austria was defeated by Italy at Vittorio-Veneto and Turkey surrendered (both in October), the end was near.

The combination of military defeat and dire food shortages produced a great war weariness, leading to mutiny in the navy, destruction of morale in the army and a revolution in Germany which forced the Kaiser to abdicate (9 November).

22.5 Effects of the war on British society

The whole question of the ways in which major wars have affected societies is a fascinating and a controversial one. Some historians believe that 'total' wars, like the First and Second World Wars, were bound to have profound effects on the countries involved. Arthur Marwick has made a special study of the ways in which these two major conflicts have affected British society. Although he concludes that the effects of the Second World War were more drastic, he nevertheless argues in his book *The Deluge: British Society and the First World War* (1965; second edition 1993) that the Great War had vitally important political, social and economic consequences for Britain. Derek Fraser goes along with this: 'The war quite simply swept away a whole world and created a new one,' he writes, 'and the Edwardian epoch became a vision of the distant past.' However, Martin Pugh, in his recent book, *State and Society* (1994) is more cautious. 'On investigation,' he writes, 'many of the trends and innovations attributed to the great war turn out to be not so much the direct product of war as the outcome of long-term developments whose origins lie in the pre-1914 period.'

It is possible to find evidence to support both points of view. Some changes have to be seen in the context of long-term trends already well under way, which were perhaps accelerated by the war: the move towards more complete democracy in the 1918 Representation of the People Act falls into this category. Other changes do seem to have been largely the result of the war – the sudden decline of the Liberal party may be the best example of this (though some historians believe that the party was already in decline *before* the First World War).

(a) *Important effects on the political parties*

The war sent the Liberal party into a disastrous decline. The party had not enhanced its reputation with its fumbling conduct of the first nine months of war, and then came the split between the Lloyd George and Asquith supporters. The seriousness of the Liberal divisions was demonstrated in May 1918 in the House of Commons during what was called the Maurice debate. General Maurice had accused the government of holding back army reserves at the critical moment when they were needed to stem the German spring offensive. Lloyd George defended himself and his government in a brilliant speech, but the opposition insisted on a vote being taken (the only time this happened during the entire war). Lloyd George won easily, having shown that Maurice's statistics were wrong, but 98 Liberals voted against the government. The split continued after the war was over, keeping the party fatally divided and demoralized.

This allowed the Labour party to become the viable alternative opposition to the Conservatives. The war helped the Labour party in other ways – it gave at least two of its members cabinet experience and caused it finally to assert its independence from the Liberals. While he was a member of the War Cabinet, Henderson had more than once been offended by Lloyd George's high-handed attitude. He decided it was time for Labour to establish its identity as a separate party. He resigned from the government (August 1917) and gave Sidney Webb the job of producing the new and attractive manifesto, *Labour and the New Social Order*, which included the following points:

- common ownership of the means of production – nationalization of mines, iron, steel, railways, canals, armaments, shipping, gas, electric and land; (this was the famous Clause 4);
- a statutory basic wage for men and women;
- full employment, unemployment insurance and abolition of the Poor Law;
- the development of health services;
- a special tax on capital;
- abolition of conscription;
- freedom for Ireland and India.

Henderson himself was responsible for encouraging the formation of party organizations at constituency level (see Section 23.4 for a full discussion of the Liberal decline and the rapid rise of Labour).

The war also benefited the Conservative party which had been in such disarray before the war, after losing two elections in 1910 and having to concede the 1911 Parliament Act. As early as May 1915 some Conservatives were back in government after Liberal failures forced Asquith to form a coalition. The Liberal split meant that there was no strong party of the left or centre to oppose them. So dominant did they become that for the next 30 years after 1915 there were only three years (1924 and 1929–31 when Labour was in power) when there were no Conservatives in the government.

(b) *Greater government intervention and control than ever before*

Section 22.2(b) showed how there was much greater government control of industry and labour than had ever been known in Britain, and ordinary people found that the government interfered with their lives as never before:

- From May 1916 conscription meant that most men aged 18 to 45 were compelled to join the armed forces, and this was later extended to 51. Consequently the majority of wives were left struggling on inadequate army pay, while children often missed their father's discipline and there was an increase in child crime.

• Early in the war, trade unions were not happy about the regulations which prevented workers leaving jobs in munitions factories and other vital industries. However, Lloyd George won them over by guaranteeing reasonable minimum wages and by favouring firms which used union labour. This encouraged more workers to join trade unions, which generally enhanced their reputation with their responsible attitude throughout the war. The unions did not have things all their own way; although strikes were illegal under the Munitions of War Act, there were several strikes, mostly about wage rates. In July 1918 during a strike of munitions workers in Coventry, Churchill, who was now Minister of Munitions, gave them a choice – either return to work or be called up for military service; they returned to work. An important feature of the wartime industrial unrest, particularly in engineering and shipbuilding, was the emergence of a new type of union leadership – the shop-steward, who organized workers in individual factories and workshops.

• The food situation caused problems. At first there were no real shortages, but prices increased substantially: in June 1916 food prices on average were 59 per cent above the level of July 1914. Towards the end of 1916, supplies of imported goods began to dwindle and long queues formed outside shops. In some areas local rationing schemes were started and worked extremely well. The government adopted the idea nationally in 1918, rationing meat (to one pound per head a week), sugar (half a pound), bacon, ham and jam. This eased the situation and the queues disappeared. One highly unpopular government policy was its interference with drinking habits. It was felt that much absenteeism from work was caused by drunkenness; in 1915 therefore, opening hours of public houses were restricted (normally from midday to 2.30 pm and from 6.30 to 9.30 pm), and beer was made weaker and more expensive.

Most of these changes came to an end when the war was over, but the 'afternoon gap' in public house opening hours survived into the 1990s.

(c) *Important steps forward in the emancipation of women*

As more and more men joined the army, women began to fill the vacancies in a wide variety of jobs which had previously always been done by men. Girls worked in munitions factories, on farms and on the buses, railways and docks. Even more remarkably, women were to be found as police, window cleaners, blacksmiths, and quarry workers; some did very heavy work in gasworks and foundries, carrying sacks of coal and coke and stoking furnaces. 'Many is the time,' recalled one lady, 'that the girls would be affected by the gas, the remedy being to walk them up and down in the fresh air and then drink a bottle of Guinness.' Middle-class women went into banking and took clerical jobs in administration, commerce and education.

Many became nurses and worked both at home and in Europe, like Vera Brittain, who wrote a moving account of her experiences in *Testament of Youth*. Women had made such a vital contribution to the war effort that their whole position in society was changed. Many men were amazed at what women had proved themselves capable of, and women's confidence in themselves increased accordingly. True, as Martin Pugh points out, most of these women were forced to leave their wartime jobs once the men came home from the war; but the fact remains that their role had been an indispensable one, and although there was still a long way to go, the war marked an important step forward in the emancipation of women and their acceptance as the complete equals of men.

(d) *Huge step forward in the move towards full democracy*

In 1914, in spite of three parliamentary reform Acts and the 1911 Parliament Act,

Britain was still not a genuinely democratic country, since no women were allowed to vote for MPs, and about 40 per cent of all adult males were still without the vote. The war gave an enormous boost to the development of full democracy. By 1918 a general election was long overdue (under the terms of the 1911 Parliament Act there should have been an election no later then December 1915) and the government felt it was important to hold one as soon as the war was over. Voting rights were widely discussed during the war and the government was influenced by two points:

- Many men serving in the armed forces had lost their right to vote because they were out of the country; this was because there was a rule that you had to live in a constituency for one year before an election to be entitled to vote.
- Many working-class men who had never had the vote had made an indispensable contribution to the war effort, fighting in the armed forces or working in vital industries.

It was widely felt that both groups must be given the right to vote in recognition of their contribution. It was also felt, in view of *their* vital role in the war effort, that women could not be left out if there was to be another extension of voting rights. All these points were taken into consideration in *The Representation of the People Act (July 1918)*. The vote was given to all males at the age of 21 and to women at the age of 30 (it was 1928 before women were given the vote at 21). Voting in general elections was to take place on the same day instead of being spread over several weeks. The idea of the 'deposit' was introduced: in order to exclude the lunatic fringe from standing in elections, every candidate had to pay a deposit of £150; if he failed to win one-eighth of the total votes cast, he forfeited his deposit.

(e) *Important effects on education*

The Education Act of 1918 was a product of the war. Lloyd George's Minister of Education, historian H. A. L. Fisher, believed that the war had create an 'increased feeling of social solidarity' and that the contribution of the working class to the war effort entitled them to a better education (see Section 20.4(e) for full details).

(f) *Important effects on housing*

The war caused an almost complete stoppage of house building, which affected the working class most of all. In 1913 it had been calculated that 120 000 new houses were needed, and by the end of the war the figure was in the region of 600 000. Lloyd George talked of providing 'homes fit for heroes' and during the 20 years following the end of the war, great progress was made with council-house building (see Section 20.4(d)).

(g) *Stimulus to aviation and broadcasting*

Apart from the obvious effects of stimulating scientific and technological research in order to produce better weapons, the war did not have a great impact on pure science. However, it led to two striking developments which otherwise might not have taken place so quickly: aviation and broadcasting. Commercial companies soon realized their potential and began to exploit them for profit. The first regular commercial passenger flight was introduced between London and Paris in July 1919. Also important was the growth of the mass media – there were soon six private companies broadcasting for profit; in 1922 these amalgamated to form the British Broadcasting Company. The government decided that radio had far too great a potential to be left in private hands, and in 1926 the Conservatives made it into a public corporation – the British Broadcasting Corporation (BBC) (see Section 24.2(a)).

(h) *Repercussions in Ireland*

At Easter 1916 the Irish Republican Brotherhood decided to turn Britain's preoccupation with the war to their own advantage (see Section 26.2(a)).

(i) *Appalling loss of life and limb – the 'lost generation'*

Something like 745 000 British men were killed and 1.6 million wounded, many so severely that they could never work again. Between the wars, people talked about the 'lost generation' and the shortage of young men. Marwick suggests that one of the reasons for the political weakness of Britain during the inter-war years was the loss of so much young talent during the war. Recent demographic research has shown that in fact there was no great shortage of men in the 1920s and 1930s, because the war caused an almost total stoppage of emigration from Britain; after 1918 emigration never returned to its pre-war levels of several hundred thousand men every year. But as Peter Clarke points out in his latest book, *Hope and Glory: Britain 1900–1990* (1996), 'It was not the demographic but the human impact of the losses which burned so deep ... it is the sheer cumulative impact of the losses, week by week and month by month which is staggering.... Women at home bore this special burden, dreading the arrival of a telegraph boy on his bicycle – in working class streets telegrams were only received from the War Office, with their invariable bad news.... The "lost generation" was an emotional and psychological reality which made a life-long impact on its surviving members.' The sheer horror of life in the trenches and the atmosphere of wartime life in general are admirably caught in Robert Graves's *Goodbye to All That*, and in the trilogy of novels by Pat Barker, *Regeneration, The Eye in the Door* and *The Ghost Road*.

(j) *Serious economic effects on Britain's world position*

Britain had lost some 40 per cent of her merchant shipping and run up enormous debts, mainly to the USA, which had to be repaid with interest. While Britain was preoccupied with the war, many other countries either developed their own industries or bought goods from elsewhere; consequently Britain never regained many of the export markets which had been closed to her during the war. Compared with the USA and even Germany, Britain's economic position had deteriorated sharply; this was one reason for the high unemployment between the wars.

(k) *Economic effects on the different social classes*

Increased taxation to help finance the war fell most heavily on the aristocracy and the middle classes. The landowning aristrocracy were especially badly hit; many were forced to sell their estates, so that, although they were still wealthy, they had lost their position as the dominant political and landowning class. The middle classes found that their living standards fell; for example, they were unable to maintain such large households. Fewer servants were needed, and the number of domestic servants fell by about 50 per cent over the whole country.

The working class, on the other hand, benefited from government intervention. Wage rates on average doubled, the average working week was reduced from 55 hours to 48 hours, and food rationing actually meant that some working-class families could afford meat for the first time. Admittedly some of these changes were not permanent, but as Marwick puts it, 'the working class in 1914 was large and it was poor. In the early 1920s it was not quite so large and it was not quite so poor.'

(l) *Less respect for authority*

Before the war, people who criticized society and the establishment were only a small minority. But partly as a result of the war, people had less respect for, and became more ready to challenge, authority and were less willing to accept propaganda from the government. This was especially true among working-class men who had fought in the trenches and had experienced at first hand the incompetence and lack of imagination of many of the generals and officers. After the war there was a marked decline in church attendance; there seemed to be a reaction especially against the Anglican church because it had supported the government line and the war so solidly.

22.6 Britain and the peace settlement

A peace conference met at Versailles in January 1919 to decide what should be done with the defeated powers. The three most important people at the conference turned out to be Lloyd George, Clemenceau (representing France) and the American President Woodrow Wilson. It quickly emerged that, depending on their war aims, they had rather different ideas about how to treat the Central Powers, and Germany in particular.

(a) *War aims of the Allied leaders*

Britain's war aims had been vague at the outset. The public was told that the intention was to defend Belgium. In January 1918, probably to encourage the troops by presenting them with some clear objectives to fight for, Lloyd George spelled out Britain's war aims in more detail. They included the defence of democracy and the righting of the injustice done to France in 1871 (in other words, the return of Alsace and Lorraine which the Germans had taken from France at the end of the Franco-Prussian War), the restoration of Belgium and Serbia, an independent Poland, democratic self-government for the nationalities of Austria–Hungary, self-determination for the German colonies and an international organization to prevent war.

In an off-the-cuff speech made in December, which he later regretted, Lloyd George said that Germany should be made to pay the whole cost of the war. Sir Eric Geddes, one of the businessmen brought into the government by Lloyd George, suggested that Germany should be 'squeezed until you can hear the pips squeak'. These were popular slogans in preparation for the election which the Lloyd George coalition won with an overwhelming majority in December 1918 (see Section 23.1(a)). Once the election was safely over, Lloyd George toned down his language, and at the conference argued that a lenient approach to Germany was essential so that she would not become embittered, and so that international trade could settle down to normal again. On the other hand, he now felt that Britain ought to be given Germany's African colonies, and should be allowed to keep the Turkish territories in the Near East with their valuable oil supplies.

Clemenceau and the French wanted the harshest possible treatment of Germany in revenge for France's defeat in the Franco-Prussian War of 1870–1 and in payment for all the damage inflicted by the Germans over the previous four years. Germany must be completely crippled so that she could never again invade the sacred soil of France.

Woodrow Wilson's peace aims were set out in his 14 Points, also issued in January 1918. They were similar to Lloyd George's aims but emphasized the idea of national self-determination – peoples should have democratic governments of their own nationality. It was difficult to reconcile these conflicting aims, but eventually a settlement was hammered out.

(b) *The Treaty of Versailles dealt with Germany*

The Germans had to lose territory in Europe: Alsace and Lorraine to France; Eupen, Moresnet and Malmédy to Belgium; North Schleswig to Denmark (after a plebiscite); West Prussia and Posen to Poland, though Danzig, the main port of West Prussia, was to be a free city under League of Nations administration, because its population was wholly German. Memel was given to Lithuania; the Saar was to be administered by the League of Nations for 15 years, when a plebiscite would decide whether it should belong to France or Germany. In the meantime France was to have the use of its coalmines. Germany's African colonies were taken away and became 'mandates' under League supervision. This meant that various member states of the League 'looked after' them. In particular it meant that Britain acquired Tanganyika, and Britain and France divided Togoland and the Cameroons between them. German armaments were strictly limited: a maximum of 100 000 troops and no conscription; no tanks, armoured cars, military aircraft or submarines, and only six battleships. The Rhineland was to be permanently demilitarized (this meant that German troops were not allowed in the area). The War Guilt clause (Article 231) fixed the blame for the outbreak of the war solely on Germany and her allies. Germany was to pay reparations for damage done to the Allies; the actual amount was not decided at Versailles, but announced later (1921) after much argument and haggling as £6600 million. A League of Nations was set up, its aims and objectives being set out in the League Covenant; its main aim was to settle international disputes by discussion, and so prevent war.

(c) *Treaties dealing with Germany's defeated allies*

Germany's defeated allies were each dealt with by a separate treaty. When Austria was on the verge of defeat, the Habsburg Empire disintegrated as the various nationalities declared themselves independent. Austria and Hungary separated and declared themselves republics, but both lost huge areas, some of which went to make up the new states of Czechoslovakia and Yugoslavia; some was given to a much-enlarged Romania, and the rest went to make up the newly reconstituted state of Poland. By the Treaty of Sèvres (1920) Turkey was allowed to keep Constantinople but was forced to hand the rest of her European territory and the area around Smyrna in Asia Minor to Greece. Her Arab territories were taken away; Iraq, Transjordan and Palestine became mandated territories supervised by Britain, and Syria became a French mandate.

(d) *Lloyd George was reasonably satisfied with the terms*

Both Lloyd George and the general public seemed happy with the terms, and Lloyd George was given a hero's welcome on his return from Paris. However, it gradually emerged that there were many faults with the settlement. The most common charges are that it was too hard on the Germans and that some of the terms – especially reparations payments and German disarmament – were impossible to carry out. There was much controversy about the size of the reparations bill: J. M. Keynes, a British economic adviser at the conference, argued that £2000 million was a more realistic figure

Key:

- Territory lost by Germany
- Former territory of tsarist Russia
- Austria-Hungary until 1918

Curzon Line — proposed by Britain (Dec. 1919) as Poland's eastern frontier. Russian territory east of the line was seized by Poland in 1920.

Map 22.2 European frontiers after the First World War and the peace treaties which the Germans could afford to pay without bankrupting themselves. On the other hand, some of the British and French extremists were demanding £24 000 million, so the final figure of £6600 million was kinder to the Germans than it might have been.

The settlement had the unfortunate effect of dividing Europe into the states which wanted to revise it (Germany being the main one) and those which wanted to preserve it, and on the whole, even they turned out to be lukewarm in their support of the settlement. The US Senate failed to ratify it, much to the disgust of Woodrow Wilson, and the USA never joined the League of Nations. This in turn left France completely disenchanted with the whole business because the Anglo-American guarantee of her frontiers could not now apply. Italy felt cheated because she had not received the full territory promised her in 1915, and the Russians were ignored because they were now under communist rule. All this tended to sabotage the settlement from the beginning, and it became increasingly difficult to apply the terms fully. Worst of all, it *did* embitter the Germans, yet did not weaken them enough to prevent further aggression. Only 20 years were to pass before Hitler's armies invaded Poland, beginning the Second World War.

Questions

1 **Munitions and change during the First World War**
  Study Sources A to D and then answer the questions which follow.

Source A

From The Decline of the Liberal Party, 1910–1931, *by Paul Adelman, 1981, describing the consequences of the formation of a coalition government in May 1915*

The one great success of the new government was Lloyd George's work at the *Ministry of Munitions*. There his energy, confidence and dynamism infused a new spirit into war production. The Ministry was run like an up-to-date business concern. 'Men of push and go' were brought in from outside to get things moving, and Lloyd George himself dealt ruthlessly with the problems of labour, red tape and inefficiency that impeded the output of munitions. Within a year the task had been virtually completed. As the *Official History of the First World War* stated: 'He laid the foundations of the Ministry's productive capacity on a scale so vast that it was almost sufficient . . . to carry the country to the end of the war.'

Source B

From a speech made by Lloyd George at Liverpool on 14 July 1915, calling for the co-operation of trade unions and workers in producing munitions

I am not saying a word about Trades Union regulations during a period of peace. I have no doubt they were essential safeguards to protect labour. . . . But . . . Government regulations have to be suspended during the period of the war because they are inapplicable in a time of emergency. The same thing applies to many *Trade Union regulations and practices*. . . . I should like to call attention to those rules which had been set up, for very good reasons, to make it difficult for unskilled men to claim the position and rights of men who have had training. . . . If all the skilled engineers in this country were turned on to produce what is required, if you brought back from the front every engineer who had been recruited, if you worked them to the utmost limits of human endurance, you would not have enough labour even then to produce all we are going to ask you to produce during the next few months. Therefore we must appeal to the patriotism of the unions to relax these particular rules in order to eke out, as it were, the skill ... to enable us to turn out the necessary munitions of war to win a real and speedy triumph.

___ **Source C** _____

From the topical and humorous magazine, Punch, *August 1916*

THE BIG PUSH

Munition Worker: "Well, I'm not taking a holiday myself just yet, but I'm sending these kids of mine for a little trip on the Continent."

Figure 22.1

> *From* Britain in the Century of Total War, *1968, by Arthur Marwick, commenting on improved pay and status for working-class women*
>
> Of great significance was the escape from ill-paid, life-diminishing drudgery as dress-makers and domestic servants or low-grade industrial labour into work which gave both economic status and a confidence in the performance of tasks once the preserve of skilled men. At the end of the war female munitions workers were earning well over 40s.* per week, while other women factory workers could count on about 25s. a week. In his report for 1916 the Chief Factory Inspector made a point of what he called 'the new self-confidence engendered in women' by these various transformations,
>
> (*s. = shillings. 20 shillings equalled £1.00)

(a) Consult Sources A and B.

With reference to Sources A and B, and using your own knowledge, explain what was meant by the following phrases in the sources, as they applied to changes made during the First World War.

(i) 'Ministry of Munitions' (Source A)

(ii) 'Trade Union regulations and practices' (Source B). (6 marks)

(b) Consult Sources A, B and C.

What evidence do these three sources provide that the need to give priority to armaments production had been fully understood in the early years of the war?
(4 marks)

(c) Consult all four sources and use your own knowledge.

'The demands of war required not only a fundamental change in the role of government, but also significant changes in social and economic life'.

On the evidence of these four sources, and using your own knowledge, how far do you agree with this judgement? (10 marks)
(Total 20 marks)
[NEAB]

2 How decisive were the land campaigns of 1918 in bringing about the defeat of the Central Powers in the First World War? [AEB]

3 Given that most people expected the war to be over by Christmas 1914, why did it take Britain and her allies until 1918 to defeat Germany and her allies?

23 Politics in confusion 1918–24

Summary of events

At the end of the war, politics did not return immediately to the normal two-party system. Lloyd George was still Prime Minister of the wartime coalition consisting of his own section of the Liberal party supported by most of the Conservatives under the leadership of Andrew Bonar Law. The coalition won an overwhelming victory in the election of December 1918 and stayed in government for the next four years.

The problems of peacetime Britain proved to be as difficult to deal with as the problems of war, and Lloyd George was unable to find permanent solutions for the post-war depression and for the chronic difficulties encountered by the coal industry. His popularity gradually ebbed away, and when his Conservative supporters decided to withdraw from the coalition to fight the next election on normal party lines, Lloyd George was left with less than half a party to lead, as the Liberal split continued. This enabled the Labour party to make a major breakthrough, coming in second place to the Conservatives in the election of November 1922.

Although the Conservatives seemed set to rule for the next five years, the revival of the old tariff reform problem caused another general election only a year later. The Labour party won enough seats to form a government, with James Ramsay MacDonald as the first Labour Prime Minister (January 1924). Lacking a majority, this government proved to be only a short-lived experiment, and yet another election followed (October 1924). This was won decisively by Stanley Baldwin and the Conservatives who remained in office for the next five years. The Liberals slumped badly at that election, confirming that Labour was now the alternative party of government to the Conservatives.

23.1 The Lloyd George coalition 1918–22

(a) *The election of December 1918*

This was the first general election since December 1910, and it must have been confusing for the voters, especially those who were voting for the first time – some six million women and two million extra men who had been enfranchised by the recent *Representation of the People Act* (see Section 22.5(d)). The confusion arose because the election was not fought on normal party lines; Lloyd George, as the successful leader of the wartime coalition of Liberals and Conservatives (Labour had withdrawn in 1917),

A summary of the different governments December 1918–June 1929		
Date	*Government*	*Prime Minister*
December 1918–October 1922	Coalition	David Lloyd George
October 1922–January 1924	Conservative	Andrew Bonar Law (October 1922–May 1923) Stanley Baldwin (May 1923–January 1924)
January–October 1924	Labour	James Ramsay MacDonald
November 1924–June 1929	Conservative	Stanley Baldwin

decided to continue the coalition, but since the Liberal Party was still split, it meant that in most constituencies there were two Liberal candidates – a Lloyd George coalition Liberal and an Independent or Asquith Liberal. It became known as the 'coupon election' because Lloyd George and Bonar Law issued coupons (signed letters) to their candidates, so that the electors would know which were genuine coalition candidates.

The coalition won easily, mainly because of Lloyd George's popularity as the man who had led Britain to victory, and his promises to create 'a fit country for heroes to live in' and to make Germany pay 'the whole cost of the war'. The coalition won 478 seats, made up of 335 Conservatives, 133 Lloyd George Liberals and 10 Labour and other supporters. The main opposition consisted of 63 Labour members, 28 Asquith Liberals and 48 Conservatives who refused to support the coalition. There were also 73 Sinn Feiners, but they refused to take their seats at Westminster and set up their own parliament in Dublin. The election result was a disaster for the Liberals whose representation in parliament was almost halved; even Asquith lost his seat. Though in one sense it was a triumph for Lloyd George, he was left very much dependent on the Conservatives, who had enough seats to form a government of their own. However, this was out of the question for the time being since their leader, Bonar Law, was a great admirer of Lloyd George and he acknowledged that the Conservatives owed their success to Lloyd George's popularity.

(b) *What problems faced Lloyd George and how successfully did he deal with them?*

The situation in the aftermath of the war was chaotic, and all Lloyd George's brilliance was needed to bring the country through such a difficult period:

1   Difficulties arose with demobilization of the troops from the army. The government began by releasing holders of key civilian jobs first, leaving the ordinary rank-and-file troops until last. Some alarming protest demonstrations broke out and the government smartly changed its tactics, adopting a 'first in, first out' policy. This worked well and by the autumn of 1919 over four million troops had been successfully 'demobbed'. Most of them found jobs, thanks to the post-war boom – an encouraging beginning.

2   There was a sudden period of inflation at the end of the war partly caused by the removal of government wartime controls on prices, profits and guaranteed wage levels. Prices and profits rose but wages lagged behind. Trade unions were determined to protect their members, and during 1919 and 1920 there were over 2000 strikes. However, it was not simply a desire for higher wages; there were other reasons for labour unrest: there was serious disillusionment and bitterness among the working class caused by their experiences in the trenches; this seemed to emphasize the gulf between workers on the one hand, and on the other, capitalists and profiteers who had done well out of the war. The Russian Revolutions (1917) gave tremendous publicity to nationalization and worker control, and some of the strikes in 1919 threw the government into a panic in case they developed into something more serious.

In February and March 1919 a strike of Clydeside engineers and shipbuilders demanding a 40–hour week seemed ominously like the start of a revolution: huge demonstrations, rioting, and a red flag hoisted in George Square, Glasgow, caused the government to move in troops and tanks. Order was quickly restored and two of the leaders, Willy Gallacher and Emmanuel Shinwell, were sent to jail. The Miners' Federation threatened a national strike if their demands for a six-hour day, a 30 per cent wage increase and continued government control of mines through nationalization were not accepted. This time Lloyd George avoided a confrontation and played for time: he offered a seven-hour day, continued government control for the time being, and a Royal Commission (the Sankey Commission) to investigate the problem. The miners accepted his offer.

3   There was a slump beginning early in 1921 which threw about two million people out of work by the end of the year. The unemployment figure never fell below a million again until the Second World War. The slump had a variety of causes; in a sense it was the continuation of the slow decline of the British economy which had begun in the 1870s. The requirements of the war economy had stimulated the steel, coal and textile industries, but as soon as peace returned, this extra demand disappeared. Many foreign buyers who had been unable to obtain British goods during the war had found alternative sources of supply, or had developed their own manufacturing industries. Thus demand for traditional British exports – ships, textiles, coal, iron and steel – never revived to its pre-war level. Already in 1920 the government had extended the 1911 National Insurance Act so that unemployment payments were made, for not more than 15 weeks in any one year, to *all workers* earning less than £250 year (except agricultural labourers, domestic servants and civil servants). At that point, boom conditions still applied and mass unemployment was not expected. When it came in 1921, the new scheme could not cope: payments to the unemployed far outweighed contributions. However, having once conceded the principle of state benefit for the unemployed, the government could hardly do a U-turn simply because unemployment had increased. During 1921 therefore, benefit was extended to two 16-week periods in the year with a gap between (see Section 20.4(c)1–2 for more details). The government aid probably eased the situation and may even have prevented revolution. Nevertheless it was criticized by Labour because it only treated the symptoms and did nothing to remove unemployment. Labour MPs claimed that the benefits were too low and were 'mocking the poor', while Conservatives condemned them on the grounds that they would demoralize the workers.

4   The trouble in the coal industry over whether it should remain under government control or be returned to private ownership, had been simmering since the appointment of the Sankey Commission. Matters came to a head on 1 April 1921 when the entire industry came out on strike. This was because the Sankey

Commission had been unable to agree on a solution to the problems. Some members recommended nationalization and others recommended the return of the mines to private ownership. This bitterly disappointed the miners, who wanted nationalization, and it gave Lloyd George the opportunity to avoid permanent nationalization. The government announced that mines and railways would be handed back to private control on 1 April.

Mine-owners informed the men that wages would have to be reduced because of the slump in exports. For a time the miners' strike threatened to develop into a general strike, but on 15 April the miners' allies in the Triple Alliance – the railwaymen and transport workers – decided to abandon the idea. This the miners regarded as a betrayal, and the day was remembered as the 'Black Friday' of the trade union movement. The miners continued alone, and their strike lasted three months; but without support, their position was hopeless and they had to give way on all points. Soon afterwards, workers in other trades (engineering, shipbuilding, docks, building, textiles, printing and railways) had to accept wage reductions. Lloyd George had solved the problem in the sense that the strike had failed and a general strike had been averted, but he was fast losing his popularity with the workers.

5   There was a reduction in government revenue (money flowing into the treasury from taxation). This was caused partly by the general falling-off of business during the slump and partly by the enormous expense of unemployment benefits. A committee under Sir Eric Geddes recommended 'retrenchment' (drastic cuts in expenditure); the government took the advice, saving itself £64 million. The policy became known as *the Geddes Axe* and it involved greatly reduced expenditure on the army, navy, education, health services and council-house building. The economy measures were successful, but highly unpopular with the Labour Party who criticized the government for 'making the children pay while the ladies of Mayfair spend extravagantly on dresses and the rich betake themselves to St Moritz'. Left-wing or progressive Liberals were not happy either: it seemed to these critics that Lloyd George was no more than a prisoner of the Conservatives who were using him to do their dirty work for them.

6   Trouble flared up in Ireland immediately after the election when the 73 Sinn Fein MPs (who wanted Ireland to be independent from Britain) set up their own parliament (Dail) in Dublin and proclaimed the Republic of Ireland. The IRA began a campaign of terrorism against the police, and the government retaliated by using the Black and Tans. Although Lloyd George found a temporary settlement by partitioning Ireland (see Section 26.2(e) for full details), he had made enemies in doing so: many Liberals resented his use of the Black and Tans, whereas the Conservatives were furious at the way the union between Britain and Ireland had been destroyed. This was serious for Lloyd George because the survival of his coalition depended on continued Conservative support.

7   There were numerous problems in foreign affairs which took up a large proportion of the Prime Minister's time throughout the four years. Sometimes – at the Paris Peace Conference for example – he was successful; but there were also failures, and the overall impact of his foreign policies was to damage his reputation.

• Under strong pressure from his Conservative supporters, Lloyd George sent British troops to help the anti-Bolshevik forces in the Russian civil war. By the end of 1919 the Bolsheviks (later known as communists) were victorious and the British troops were withdrawn, having achieved nothing. The Russian communists, and many among the British working class who admired them, resented Lloyd George's intervention. In fact he was anxious for a reconciliation and consequently an Anglo-Russian trade treaty was signed (March 1921).

- *The Genoa Conference (1922)* took place on Lloyd George's initiative. There was growing tension between Germany and France over reparations, since the Germans were already complaining that they would not be able to afford the next instalment. Lloyd George hoped to calm the situation by persuading the French to reduce their demands. Other problems to be discussed were the need to resume diplomatic relations with Russia and Europe's war debts to the USA. The conference was a dismal failure: the French refused all compromise and insisted on full reparations payments; the Americans refused to attend; and the Russians claimed to be insulted at the suggestion that they should honour all debts owed by the Tsarist government. The Germans and Russians withdrew and signed a separate agreement at nearby Rapallo: Germany officially recognized the Soviet government and both countries wiped off their mutual debts. The other nations were alarmed at this reconciliation between two 'suspect' states, and blamed Lloyd George. To be fair though, the fault was more that of the French premier, the bitterly anti-German Poincaré, for his refusal to compromise.
- *The Chanak incident (1922), though successfully concluded by Lloyd George, was the event which triggered his downfall.* The Turks threatened to break the Versailles settlement by moving troops into a neutral zone, thereby clashing with the British occupying force based at Chanak on the Dardanelles (see Map 22.2). Lloyd George took a strong line, warning the Turks that if the neutral zone was violated, they would face war not only with Britain but with the British Empire as well. Eventually a compromise was reached by *the Treaty of Lausanne (1923)*, allowing Turkey to keep Eastern Thrace and Smyrna. The crisis passed, war was averted, and it seemed that Lloyd George had triumphed. Unfortunately he had made the mistake of not consulting the Commonwealth Prime Ministers before committing them to a possible war against Turkey. Many of the Conservatives were outraged at what they saw as his unforgivable rashness, and his days in power were numbered.

(c) *The coalition found time for some important political and social reforms*

1   *The Sex Disqualification Removal Act (1919)* allowed women to stand for parliament; the first woman to take her seat was Nancy Astor, the American-born wife of Viscount Waldorf Astor.
2   *The Addison Housing Act (1919)* (see Section 20.4(d)1).
3   The extension of unemployment insurance mentioned above (see Section 20.4(c)1–2).
4   Increases in old age pensions (see Section 20.4(f)1).
5   *The Rent Act (1920)* protected working-class tenants against exorbitant rent increases.

(d) *The fall of the Lloyd George coalition (October 1922)*

Unfortunately for Lloyd George his achievements were not enough to save the coalition. He had been losing working-class support steadily and it was significant that Labour won 13 by-elections between 1918 and 1922. Much depended on whether the Conservative MPs would continue to support him at the next general election which he intended to hold fairly soon. A meeting of Conservative MPs held at the Carlton Club

(29 October) was expected to endorse the decision to continue supporting the coalition. However, when a vote was taken it was 185 to 85 *in favour of ending their support of Lloyd George*. The main anti-Lloyd George speech which swayed the meeting was made by Stanley Baldwin. Lloyd George immediately resigned and Andrew Bonar Law became Prime Minister of a Conservative government.

The Conservatives decided to abandon him because he had outlived his usefulness. They resented his solution of the Irish problem and his handling of the Chanak incident, and they criticized him because he allowed the sale of knighthoods and other honours to unsuitable candidates. More than that, they were afraid that if the coalition continued much longer, Lloyd George would split the Conservative Party permanently (between those who supported the coalition and those who opposed it) in the same way that he had split the Liberal Party. This was the point made forcibly by Baldwin when he said that although Lloyd George was a dynamic force, such a force was 'a very terrible thing'.

He was still only 59, but he was never again to hold an important political office, though he remained an MP until the end of 1944 when he became Earl Lloyd George of Dwyfor. He died in March 1945. Historian A. J. P. Taylor calls him 'the most inspired and creative British statesman of the twentieth century'. If this is so, then it must be seen as a national tragedy that Lloyd George had to sit on the side-lines during the problems of the 1920s and 1930s, while in the words of C. L. Mowat, 'the pygmies, the second-class brains, frittered away Britain's power in the world'. However, as Kenneth Morgan, one of Lloyd George's many biographers, points out: 'Ideas were not enough. He needed also supporters, organization, a party base – above all, public trust. These were assets which Lloyd George, however fertile in ideas and initiatives, conspicuously lacked.'

23.2 The Conservatives and tariff reform again

(a) *The Conservative election victory, November 1922*

The Conservatives won a decisive victory: they had 345 seats and a majority of 75 over all other parties combined. It was a disaster for the Liberals who fought the election in two separate groups: the Asquith Liberals won 62 seats, the Lloyd George Liberals 54. The combined Liberal total of 116 seats was well behind Labour's 142, and it was clear that *Labour had emerged as the main opposition party to the Conservatives*.

However, the new Conservative government did not last long. After Bonar Law's resignation through ill-health in May 1923, Stanley Baldwin became Prime Minister. After only a few months in office he decided that another general election was necessary, though the Conservatives still had their comfortable overall majority.

(b) *Tariff reform again*

Joseph Chamberlain's cure for all ills, tariff reform (see Section 17.6(b) 6), was the question at issue. Baldwin had decided that Joseph Chamberlain was right after all – tariffs must be reintroduced. But since Bonar Law had earlier promised that this was exactly what the Conservatives would not do, Baldwin felt it was only fair to give the voters a chance to express their view. Many Conservatives thought it was a totally unnecessary exercise and Lord Curzon called it an 'idiotic' decision.

Baldwin's argument was that tariffs would make foreign goods more expensive in Britain and thus give a much-needed boost to British industry; the growing unemployment problems would be solved at a stroke. The two sections of the Liberal party reunited under Asquith's leadership and campaigned for free trade, the traditional Liberal policy. Together with Labour, they argued that continued free trade and foreign imports would keep down the cost of living for the workers. The results were: Conservatives 258, Labour 191 and Liberals 159, a clear defeat for protection, and a further confirmation that Labour had replaced the Liberals as the alternative party to the Conservatives.

23.3 The first Labour government (January–October 1924)

(a) *Formation of the Labour government*

When the election results were announced, it was not immediately clear what would happen next. Baldwin remained as Prime Minister for six weeks while discussions took place. The Conservatives could not remain in office for long, because although they were the largest single party, they had lost their overall majority; both Labour and Liberals would vote against a Conservative Bill to introduce tariffs. Some Conservatives felt they should patch up their differences with the Liberals over tariffs, and form a government of national unity to keep Labour out. But Baldwin was quite happy for a Labour government to go ahead: he knew that if MacDonald tried to do anything unacceptable, the Tories and Liberals between them could vote Labour out. When Asquith decided to promise Liberal support in the Commons for a Labour government, Baldwin encouraged him, because he knew it would outrage right-wing Liberals like Winston Churchill who were likely to join the Conservatives. Baldwin was right again, and this proved to be yet another nail in the Liberals' coffin. Therefore Labour, as the second largest party, formed a government on the understanding that Liberal support would be forthcoming, and James Ramsay MacDonald became the first ever Labour Prime Minister.

(b) *James Ramsay MacDonald*

It was an exceptional achievement for MacDonald to become Prime Minister. Born at Lossiemouth, the illegitimate son of poor parents, his only formal education was at the local board school and then as a pupil teacher. He went to London where he worked as a clerk and as a political journalist, and after joining the ILP (1893) he became secretary of the Labour Representation Committee (1900) and Labour MP for Leicester in 1906. After opposing Britain's entry into the war, he was forced to resign the leadership, and lost his seat in 1918. Re-elected to parliament in 1922, his prestige had recovered sufficiently for him to become leader of the party again.

There was near panic in some quarters when it was realized that there was going to be a Labour government. Some people thought that everybody's savings would be confiscated and that there would be a period of profound social revolution; but nothing spectacular happened: MacDonald's cabinet, with only two exceptions, consisted of moderates – Philip Snowden as Chancellor of the Exchequer, Arthur Henderson, J. H. Thomas and Sydney Webb. He even brought in three former Liberals including Haldane as Lord Chancellor. In fact this Labour government, and the one which followed in 1929–31, were a great disappointment to their socialist supporters.

(c) Why didn't the two Labour governments have more success?

1 Both were minority governments lacking an overall majority, and dependent on Liberal votes to stay in office. They had therefore to pursue moderate policies, and it was out of the question to introduce nationalization and disarmament even if MacDonald had wanted to. This meant that their policies were very little different from those of Liberal governments.

2 Labour had difficulty in projecting itself as a genuinely national party, since from the beginning it had claimed to be the party of the industrial workers, and was closely tied to the trade unions. It was distrusted by people of property who feared nationalization and the link with militant trade unionism.

3 Labour could not break its ties with the trade unions because they provided most of the party's funds. In return, the unions expected to be able to control the party, which caused serious friction because union leaders were preoccupied with furthering the interests of their members. They gave very little support to the 1924 Labour government and made no allowances for its dependence on Liberal support, criticizing its 'half-measures'. Almost immediately there was a dockers' strike in support of a demand for an extra two shillings a day. This was organized by Ernest Bevin, general secretary of the Transport and General Workers' Union. Following the success of this strike, London Transport workers also came out, and the situation became serious enough for MacDonald to proclaim a state of emergency, enabling the government to use armed lorries for moving essential supplies. In the end this was not necessary because the employers gave way and made an acceptable wage offer; but it was embarrassing for the government and left its relationship with the unions strained.

4 It proved impossible to work out a joint plan of action between the parliamentary Labour party and the trade unions. When some Labour intellectuals suggested that the two should co-operate to avoid a repitition of the 1924 fiasco, Bevin dismissed the idea, claiming that left-wing intellectuals and Fabians did not understand the working class.

5 Both governments were unfortunate enough to have to deal with serious economic problems: a million unemployed in 1924 and the world economic crisis in 1930–1. Labour had no answer beyond nationalization, and since that was out of the question, they were helpless.

6 The divisions between left and right in the party were shown up by MacDonald's attitude. He immediately offended the left by not giving them a fair representation in the cabinet, and affronted them by calmly accepting the limitations of a minority government. The Scottish Clydeside MPs and the ILP wanted him to bring in genuinely socialist measures; although these would be defeated in the Commons, it would give Labour a chance to appeal to the electorate. MacDonald had no intention of attempting such heroics; he wanted moderate policies to gain the confidence of the country, and he condemned strikes for wage increases as 'not socialism'. It wasn't long before the left decided that MacDonald himself was really no socialist.

(d) Social reforms of the first Labour government

The 1924 government could claim a few achievements in spite of the disappointments:

● *Wheatley's Housing Act* provided grants of £9 million a year for the building of council houses (see Section 20.4(d) 2).

● Old age pensions and unemployment benefit were increased and the gap between the two 16-week benefit periods was removed.

- The number of free places in grammar schools was increased and state scholarships to universities brought back. Sir Henry Hadow was appointed to work out the needs of education (see Section 20.4(e)).

(e) *Achievements in foreign affairs*

MacDonald acted as Foreign Secretary as well as Prime Minister, and had clear ideas about what he hoped to achieve. Like Lloyd George, he felt it was essential to improve relations between Germany and France which had deteriorated sharply during 1923. Following the German refusal to pay their reparations instalment, the French sent troops to occupy the Ruhr (the important German industrial region which includes the cities of Essen and Dusseldorf), in an attempt to force the Germans to pay. MacDonald was also anxious to resume normal diplomatic relations with Russia, to promote disarmament, and to support the new League of Nations as the best hope for the maintenance of peace. His policy produced quick and impressive results.

- *He was largely responsible for the Dawes Plan (1924)* which solved the problem of Franco-German relations for the time being. By the end of 1923 the French occupation of the Ruhr had succeeded in producing only galloping inflation and the collapse of the German mark. MacDonald invited Herriot, the new French premier, and Stresemann, the new German Foreign Minister, to a conference in London and persuaded the Americans to participate as well. The conference was chaired for part of the time by the American representative, General Dawes. No reduction was made in the total amount Germany was expected to pay, but it was agreed that she should pay annually only what she could reasonably afford, until she became more prosperous. A foreign loan of 800 million gold marks (about £40 million), mainly from the USA, was to be made to Germany. France, now assured of at least some reparations from Germany, agreed to withdraw her troops from the Ruhr. The plan was successful: the German economy began to recover on the basis of the American loans, and international tensions gradually relaxed. MacDonald was fortunate that the formidable Poincaré had fallen from office, and his successor, Herriot, was anxious for reconciliation. Nevertheless he made excellent use of the situation and showed that a Labour government could conduct a successful foreign policy, which many people had doubted.
- MacDonald gave full diplomatic recognition to the Soviet regime in Russia, signed a trade treaty and opened discussions about a British loan to Russia. This was a realistic policy, but the Conservatives and Liberals strongly disapproved.
- MacDonald made a serious effort to make the League of Nations work; he attended its meetings in Geneva, and tried to strengthen it by introducing *the Geneva Protocol*, a proposal which would have made arbitration of international disputes compulsory. Unfortunately the Labour government fell before the Protocol was accepted, and the Conservative government which followed felt unable to ratify it.

(f) *The fall of the first Labour government (October 1924)*

The end of the government came rather suddenly over *the Campbell Case*. J. R. Campbell, editor of the communist *Workers' Weekly*, was arrested and charged with incitement to mutiny, for writing an article urging soldiers not to fire on their fellow workers in the event of a strike. However, the Labour Attorney-General withdrew the prosecution, and both Conservatives and Liberals, already alarmed by MacDonald's opening of relations with Russia, accused the government of being sympathetic towards communists. The Liberal demand for an enquiry into the matter was carried in the

Commons by 364 votes to 198. MacDonald took this as a vote of no confidence and resigned.

The following election was complicated by the affair of *the Zinoviev Letter*. This appeared in the *Daily Mail* four days before polling; the paper claimed it was from the Russian Communist leader, Zinoviev; it was addressed to the British Communist Party, marked 'very secret', and contained instructions on how to organize a revolution. The fact that the Foreign Office protested to the Russians about this interference in British affairs made the letter appear genuine, though it seems fairly certain that it was a forgery. But it caused a sensation at the time and was taken to show that Labour sympathy towards Russia was encouraging the British Communists. Labour dropped to 151 seats, the Liberals lost disastrously, winning only 40 seats, while the Conservatives emerged triumphant with 419 seats.

Labour blamed their defeat on the Zinoviev Letter, but historians seem to agree that the Conservatives would have won anyway. Although short, the first Labour government was not without significance: it proved that a Labour government could work, which had been MacDonald's main aim in what was clearly going to be a short stay in power; and Labour had won respect both at home and abroad. This was probably also the point of no return for the Liberal party.

23.4 Why did the Liberal party decline so rapidly?

The decline of the Liberal party was one of the most dramatic developments in recent British history because of the speed with which it happened. At the time of the great Liberal landslide victory of 1906, very few people could have foreseen that within less than 20 years Labour would have formed a government and the Liberals would have slipped into a poor third place. Worse was to come: in the election of 1935 they could muster only 21 seats and 6.4 per cent of total votes cast. Historians have had a long debate about whether the Liberal party decline was inevitable as the Labour party began to grow, or whether different courses of action by the Liberal leaders could have kept them in contention and squeezed Labour out. Another point at issue is whether the Liberal decline began before the First World War or whether it was the war which caused the decline.

(a) *Some historians believe that the Liberal party was in serious difficulties long before 1914*

They had split over the question of Ireland in 1886 when 93 Liberal MPs led by Joseph Chamberlain voted against Gladstone's First Irish Home Rule Bill (see Section 16.1(e–f)). The Bill was defeated and the Liberal government fell, leaving the party weak, divided and out of office for the next ten years. A different split developed between the left or progressive wing of the party, which favoured the so-called New Liberalism (state action to bring about social reform – see Section 21.1), and the right wing which favoured old-fashioned Gladstonian *laissez-faire* (wanting government intervention kept to a minimum). George Dangerfield argued in his book *The Strange Death of Liberal England* (1935) that the many problems facing Asquith's government were too complex for the divided Liberals to cope with. The combination of the clash with the House of Lords, potential civil war in Ireland, the suffragette campaign and industrial unrest stretched the Liberals beyond the limits of their capabilities and, according to Dangerfield, left Britain in 1914 on the verge of anarchy and perhaps revolution. The Liberal decline was shown in the general elections of 1910 when they lost heavily and were only able to stay in office because the Irish Nationalists and Labour MPs supported them.

(b) *Other long-term causes are stressed by Henry Pelling and Ross McKibbin*

Pelling believes that long-term social changes – such as the growth of large industrial cities, the greater concentration of industry, and the steadily rising cost of living were gradually causing large sections of the working class to look towards the Labour party. McKibbin thinks that the growth of trade unionism was especially important and had already undermined Liberal strength before 1914 (see Section 19.8(e)). Between 1909 and 1913 trade union membership rose from something like 2.47 million to 4.13 million; unions were steadily switching support from the Liberals to Labour, and in 1913 the political levy became legal again, so that unions could use funds for political purposes. *The 1918 Representation of the People Act* can therefore be seen as a crucial factor in the Labour breakthrough. By trebling the electorate it brought the industrial working classes into a majority for the first time. It was this new mass electorate which the Liberals had to attract if they were to survive as a major party. Unfortunately for them, the Liberals did not produce sufficiently attractive policies and did not choose enough working-class candidates. Labour, on the other hand, with its new party organization and its new programme, successfully projected itself as the party of working people. In the elections of 1918 and 1922, Labour was much better organized than the Liberals, and in 1922, for the first time, won more seats than the Liberals (142 to 116).

(c) *Some historians reject the 'inevitable rise of Labour' theory*

Paul Adelman believes that Dangerfield's whole argument 'seems hopelessly exaggerated'. Peter Clarke argued in his famous book *Lancashire and the New Liberalism* (1971) that there was plenty of life left in the Liberal party in 1914; they had adapted to the social changes taking place and their social reform policies *were* attracting support among the workers. He based his conclusions on by-election results and local election results in Lancashire which showed that Labour was losing ground to the Liberals after 1910. Even where the Liberals did lose seats, it was often to the Conservatives, not to Labour. More recently, Duncan Tanner and Martin Pugh also reject the idea that Labour would inevitably take over from the Liberals (see Section 19.8(e)). If these historians are correct, and the Liberals were not already in a terminal decline before 1914, the question remains: why had they slumped into third place only eight years later?

(d) *The First World War was the key factor, according to another group of historians*

Trevor Wilson, in his book *The Downfall of the Liberal Party 1914–35* (1966), compares the war to a 'rampant omnibus', which first knocked down and then ran over the unfortunate Liberal party. First of all its prestige was ruined by the hesitant and inappropriate way in which it tried to run the war on traditional *laissez-faire* principles. Then Lloyd George split the party by the way in which he manoeuvred Asquith into resigning so that he could form a coalition government with the Conservatives and Labour (December 1916). Asquith's supporters never forgave Lloyd George for this 'betrayal' and the party remained divided. The split between the two was highlighted during the Maurice debate in the Commons (May 1918) when only 72 Liberals voted for Lloyd George and 98 voted against him (see Section 22.5(a)). The party entered the first two elections after the war – in 1918 and 1922 – still fatally divided just as the Labour Party was presenting a strong challenge.

While the war divided the Liberal party, it worked to the advantage of Labour. Arthur Henderson, the Labour leader during the war, gained cabinet experience as a member of the wartime coalitions. When he left the government after disagreements with Lloyd George, he concentrated on providing the party with a new constitution, a new manifesto and new constituency organizations. The war caused Labour to adopt a new foreign policy: they wanted a pacific approach to foreign affairs as well as what they called 'open dipomacy' – no more secret diplomacy, since this only led to misunderstandings and suspicions – plus an internationalist attitude to foreign policy. This attracted many converts from the left wing of the Liberal party, who also felt that there would be more chance of social reform from Labour than from the other two parties (see Section 22.5(a) for more details of Labour's new programme). Labour therefore entered the 1918 election united and better prepared than the Liberals, and was able to run over 350 candidates, as opposed to only 72 in December 1910. Another boost for Labour was the increase in trade union membership during the war from 4.14 million in 1914 to 7.9 million in 1919; this again damaged the Liberals because by this time most of the big unions had affiliated to the Labour party.

The real disaster for the Liberals came in 1922 when they were still divided into the Lloyd George and Asquith factions. For the first time Labour won more seats than the Liberals, and there seemed every chance that Labour would become the main opposition party to the Conservatives unless the Liberals were able to unite and produce the necessary policies.

(e) *The Liberal party leaders were a liability after 1918*

Although the Liberals did succeed in reuniting under Asquith's leadership for the general election of December 1923 (in defence of free trade), Asquith was now over 70 and out of touch with most of the electorate, while Lloyd George had lost his popularity with the workers. This was because of his close cooperation with the Conservatives, especially during the coalition of 1918–22, when on many occasions his policies had seemed unsympathetic towards the workers. Asquith did not retire from the leadership until 1926 when it was too late for the party to recover. If the party's leaders were not impressive, neither were its policies: all the important things which the Liberals had stood for were ceasing to be major issues: Irish Home Rule, for example, was no longer an issue after the 1921 partition. Nor could the Liberals compete with Labour's new social policies and their attractive leader, Ramsay MacDonald.

Even so, with all these disadvantages, the Liberals were not all that far behind Labour in the 1923 election, polling 4.31 million votes (29.6 per cent of votes cast) to Labour's 4.43 million (30.5 per cent). This gave Labour 191 seats to the Liberals' 159 (there were 258 Conservatives). Arguably all was not lost at this point: dynamic leadership, some new creative policies and the right decisions might well have tipped the balance back in favour of the Liberals. However, ...

(f) *The Liberals made fatal mistakes after the 1923 election*

Historian Chris Cook argues that Asquith and the Liberals made the fatal mistake of allowing MacDonald and the Labour party to form a government 'without any understandings or conditions, and without having considered how they would fare if Labour refused to cooperate'. This played into the hands of both MacDonald and Baldwin who each had strategies of their own:

- MacDonald was not interested in cooperation with the Liberals; his aim was to destroy them as the rival left-wing party. This could be done, he believed, by pushing them permanently into third place, so that the British electoral system, which always works against smaller parties, would work to the advantage of Labour.
- Baldwin encouraged the Liberals and their promises of support for Labour because he knew that many right-wing or middle-class Liberals would disapprove of the way Asquith was allowing Labour into office, and would switch to voting Conservative as the best way of keeping Labour out.

Both strategies worked perfectly: during the 1924 Labour government MacDonald ruthlessly rejected all suggestions of an alliance with the Liberals, even though Labour was totally dependent on Liberal votes to stay in office. At the next election (October 1924) the Liberals were crushed, winning only 40 seats and 17.6 per cent of the vote; their total vote fell by 1.4 million. Although the Conservatives won the election with 419 seats and Labour lost 40 seats, the Labour vote increased by well over a million, from 30.5 per cent to 33 per cent.

This was the end of the road for the Liberals: a precedent had been set – they had allowed Labour to show that it was capable of forming a government without the expected social upheaval. From now on, anti-Conservatives began to vote Labour as the best way of keeping the Tories out. The loss of their right-wing, middle-class and business support was serious for the Liberals because it deprived them of much of their financial backing. Four expensive election campaigns between December 1918 and October 1924 left them short of funds, while Labour could rely on financial support from the trade unions. With the benefit of hindsight it is clear that Asquith had missed an opportunity which was never to come the Liberals' way again: he could have insisted on a coalition government with Labour which might have been able to introduce a pro-portional representation system of voting.

(g) *The Liberals were at a disadvantage because of the electoral system*

With three parties contesting many seats, a high proportion of MPs won their seats on a minority vote; many Liberals came second and their votes were not reflected in the Commons. The 1924 election revealed how unfair the system was. The percentages of votes polled were: Conservatives 48.3, Labour 33 and Liberals 17.6; under the 'first past the post system' this gave the Conservatives 419 of the 615 seats, Labour 151 and Liberals 40. Under some kind of proportional representation system which would have given a fairer distribution of seats, the result might have been something like: Conservatives 312, Labour 205 and Liberals 98.

The 1929 election is usually regarded as the Liberals' last chance: Lloyd George led a united party with an attractive programme, but they could scrape together only 59 seats (23.4 per cent) to Labour's 288 (37.1 per cent); the Conservatives actually polled more votes than Labour (38.2 per cent) which gave them fewer seats (260). There was a lack of confidence in Lloyd George and a feeling that Baldwin and MacDonald, though less exciting, were more solid and reliable. Again the electoral system worked against the Liberals; under a different voting system they could have had as many as 140 seats, while the Conservatives would have been the largest party in the Commons. Many peo-ple now stopped voting Liberal, believing it to be a 'wasted vote'. The election of 1935 saw the Liberal share of the vote slump to only 6.4 per cent, giving them 21 seats.

Perhaps the simplest conclusion is that given the circumstances after the First World War, with the Conservatives firmly established as the party of the property-own-ers and the ratepayers, and Labour in alliance with the trade unions as the party of the workers, there was no remaining interest group large enough to keep the Liberal party going as a serious contender for power. On the other hand it has to be remembered that if the Liberals could have come up with the right policies and the right leader to attract working-class votes, there may well have been nothing inevitable about their decline.

Questions

1 **The decline of the Liberal Party**
   Study Sources A to G and then answer the questions which follow.

___ Source A _____

General election results and statistics

Year	Conservatives MPs	%	Liberals MPs	%	Labour MPs	%	Total votes cast
1910 (Jan)	273	46.9	275	43.2	40	7.6	6.6m
1918(Dec)	335	32.6	161	25.6	63	22.2	10.7m
			133	13.5			
			(coalition)				
			28	12.1			
			(independent)				
1922(Nov)	345	38.2	116	29.1	142	29.5	14.4m
			62	11.6			
			(Asquith)				
			54	17.5			
			(Lloyd George)				
1923(Dec)	258	38.1	159	29.6	191	30.5	14.5m
1924(Oct)	419	48.3	40	17.6	151	33.0	16.6m
1929(May)	260	38.2	59	23.4	288	37.1	22.6m

Source: C. Cook and J. Stevenson, *The Longman Handbook of Modern British History 1714–1987*, Longman, 2nd edn,1988.

___ Source B _____

Memorandum by Herbert Gladstone, director of Liberal Headquarters, written in November 1924

The results of the 1918 election broke the party, not only in the House of Commons, but in the country. Local associations perished, or maintained an existence in name only. Masses of our best men passed away to Labour. Others drifted to Conservatism or independence. Over and over again our remnants in the constituencies declined even to hold meetings. In the election of 1922, many constituencies actually refused to fight, even though candidates and funds were available.

Source: quoted in C. Cook, *The Age of Alignment 1922–29*, Macmillan, 1975.

Extracts from the diary of C. P. Scott, Liberal editor of the Manchester Guardian, *1921*

What struck me most about Asquith was his immobility. He had not moved – did not really know about things. He could see no good in Lloyd George or anything he did. All the time he (Asquith) laid down the law with great positiveness. Altogether a somewhat grumbling and very old old man ...

Sir Donald Maclean [an Asquith Liberal MP] told me, 'I have done with Lloyd George. I could never work with him or under him'. Of Asquith himself, though entirely loyal, Maclean said that he was not gaining but losing ground in the country. He had missed a great and unique opportunity by his failure to make any impact in Parliament since his return, mainly because of laziness.

Source: T. Wilson (ed.), *The Political Diaries of C. P. Scott 1911–28*, Collins, 1970.

Letter written by Sir Charles Hobhouse, a 'New' Liberal journalist and former MP, to C. P. Scott, 7 November 1924

I doubt if the Liberal Party any longer stands for anything distinctive. My reasons are on the one side that moderate Labour – Labour in office – has represented essential Liberalism better than the organized party since Campbell-Bannerman's death. The Liberal Party never seems agreed within on essentials. Part leans to the Tories, part leans to Labour, part has nothing distinctive. Tradition and class distinctions kept many good Liberals outside Labour. Now Labour has grown so much that it tends to absorb them and to leave only the 'bad' Liberals who lean towards the Tories.

Annual Report of Home Counties Liberal Federation, May 1924

All through our areas the revival of Liberalism continues. ... Political activity is greater than at any time since the outbreak of the Great War. ... Liberalism has never been more active in this area except in the years preceding the landslide of 1906.

Statement by the Secretary of the Midland Liberal Federation, 5 September 1925

It has become a very difficult thing since the war to secure candidates, because in dark times like these when there are so few decent chances to offer a candidate, it has become exceedingly difficult to find men and women who are prepared to face a contest and provide all the money.

Sources: D, E and F are quoted in C. Cook, *The Age of Alignment 1922–29*, Macmillan, 1975.

Historian Chris Cook writes about the decline of the Liberals

The problems stemmed, not from the split of Asquith and Lloyd George, but from the fundamental and long-term weaknesses in the structure, social composition and outlook of the party in the industrial areas. . . . It was a middle class party which failed to accomodate working class candidates or to produce a relevant industrial policy. Perhaps the war accelerated these factors. But they were quite clearly at work before 1914. . . . After the war, a succession of body-blows coming on top of the changing social structure reduced the party from supremacy to powerlessness. . . . [The final blow was] *the folly of the Liberal course of action in the months of 1924, . . .*

There was a lack of consultation between Asquith and Lloyd George. No Liberal leader really thought about the possibility that the party, though supporting Labour in parliament, might find itself constantly under attack in the constituencies. . . . The Liberals voted Labour into office without any understandings or conditions, and without having considered how they would fare if Labour refused to co-operate. . . . Either the Liberals would have to support Labour measures or vote against them. To vote against meant an election which, for financial reasons, the Liberals did not want.

Source: C. Cook, *The Age of Alignment 1922–29*, Macmillan, 1975.

(a) Source B says that 'the result of the 1918 election broke the party'. Using the statistics in Source A, show how the 1918 election was a serious blow to the Liberals in the House of Commons. (3 marks)

(b) Using the statistics in Source A, show how the 'first past the post' electoral system works to the disadvantage of smaller parties. (5 marks)

(c) Source G mentions 'the folly of the Liberal course of action in the months of 1924'. Using Source G and your own knowledge, explain what the writer means by this statement. (4 marks)

(d) Sources B, C, D, E and F were all written by Liberals. What do you think are the advantages and disadvantages of each of these sources for the historian trying to reach a conclusion about why the Liberal Party declined? (15 marks)

(e) Historian Trevor Wilson argues that the First World War was mainly responsible for the decline of the Liberals, because of the way in which it split the party between Lloyd George and Asquith supporters. Using the evidence from these sources and the information in Chapter 23, explain whether you agree or disagree with Trevor Wilson. (18 marks)

(Total 45 marks)

2 'An interlude of sheer futility'. Do you think this is a fair verdict on the Labour government of 1924?

Baldwin, the Conservatives and the General Strike

Summary of events

With a massive overall majority in excess of 200, the reunited and revitalized Conservative party was in a powerful position. The rebel wing of the party, which included Austen Chamberlain (Joseph's son) and Lord Birkenhead, which had wanted to continue supporting the Lloyd George coalition, was now safely back in the fold. Chamberlain was Foreign Secretary, and Winston Churchill, who had drifted back to the Conservatives after 20 years as a Liberal, became Chancellor of the Exchequer. Neville Chamberlain, another of Joseph's sons, was one of the most successful members of the government; as Minister of Health, he was responsible for steering no fewer than 21 bills through parliament. The government lasted for almost its full term of five years, introducing a mass of solid, if unspectacular legislation. The only dramatic incident was the General Strike of 1926, which aroused considerable emotion, fears and excitement, though it lasted less than two weeks. Throughout the period, with his image of a plain and honest man puffing contentedly at his pipe, Stanley Baldwin presided over the country's fortunes.

24.1 The Conservative revival

The party had gone through a difficult period after its disastrous defeat in 1906, failing to win the general elections of 1910 and suffering a further split over the Parliament Bill of 1911. However, signs of recovery were there before the First World War:

(a) *Organizational improvements*

Balfour set up a committee to improve party organization (1910) which resulted in two major changes:

- A new post was invented to help the Conservative Chief Whip – this was
Chairman of the Party Organization. Previously the Chief Whip had been responsible for all organization both inside and outside parliament, and the job had become too much for one person. The Chairman was now responsible for all matters outside parliament.
- Conservative Central Office was found to be inefficient, with no proper accounts

or records being kept. This was put right and there was to be much closer contact between Central Office and the National Union of Conservative Associations.

Another important change was that by 1914 local constituency branches had gained the right to control propaganda and speakers and to choose their own candidates instead of being told what to do by Central Office.

(b) *A new party leader – Bonar Law*

Balfour, having lost three consecutive elections, resigned as leader in 1911. There were two candidates for the leadership – Austen Chamberlain, from the 'progressive wing' of the party, and Walter Long from the 'die-hards'. Since support seemed to be evenly divided, the choice of either of them would have been unacceptable to the other camp, and the party split would have been perpetuated. In the end both agreed to stand down in the interests of party unity, and Andrew Bonar Law, who was acceptable to both camps, was chosen. Bonar Law had been born in Canada; his father was a Scottish Presbyterian minister and there were family connections with Ulster. Robert Blake calls him 'a melancholy teetotal widower', but he had great fighting qualities – he was 'a hard-hitting debater' and was full of 'bluntness, vigour and invective'. In addition, he was passionately against Irish Home Rule, and was prepared to go to almost any lengths to keep Ulster British. It was fortunate for the party that the Ulster issue came to the forefront at this point, because it gave them a cause they could all agree on. For the first time since 1900 the party was able to unite, under the leadership of Bonar Law, and the tariff issue slipped into the background (see Section 21.5(c)).

(c) *First World War benefits the Conservatives*

Liberal failures and splits during the war led to some Conservatives being included in the Asquith and Lloyd George coalitions (1915–18) (see Section 22.1(f)). According to Robert Blake, 'on almost every issue that came up, Conservative tradition and ideolology was better suited than Liberal to meet the needs of the hour'. They were the party who stood for patriotism, strong defence and conscription; although Lloyd George was recognized as 'the man who won the war', the Conservatives could claim some of the credit too, and this was reflected in the fact that 335 coalition Conservatives were elected in the 1918 'coupon' election. The continuing Liberal split after the war meant that there was no strong party of the left or centre to challenge the Conservatives.

(d) *The changed Irish situation helps the Conservatives*

When the Anglo-Irish Treaty partitioning Ireland came into operation in 1922 (see Section 26.2(e)), it meant that there were no longer any Irish Nationalist MPs in the Commons. Up to 1918 there had always been at least 80 Irish Nationalists who had almost always supported the Liberals, and had kept the Liberals in office after the 1910 elections. Now the only Irish MPs in the Commons were mostly Ulster Unionists who always voted Conservative.

(e) *Another new leader – Stanley Baldwin*

Baldwin was the son of a wealthy Worcestershire iron and steel manufacturer. After leaving Cambridge, he worked in the family business and was over 40 when he first became an MP (1908). He was President of the Board of Trade in Lloyd George's coalition (1921–2), but grew to dislike Lloyd George's methods; it was his speech at the

Carlton Club (October 1922) attacking Lloyd George which established him as one of the leading Conservatives, and Bonar Law made him Chancellor of the Exchequer when the party took office at the end of 1922. When Law resigned in 1923, Baldwin was the surprise choice as next leader and Prime Minister. The obvious candidate, Lord Curzon, was unpopular with the party because he was pompous and arrogant. When told of the choice, Curzon is reported to have described Baldwin as 'a person of the utmost insignificance'. In fact he was an extremely able politician and a much better manager of people than Lloyd George, who offended many of his colleagues. He gave the impression of being honest and lacking in deviousness, unlike Lloyd George, whom Baldwin regarded as 'a corrupter of public life'. Baldwin wanted a return to 'clean government', and donated to the Exchequer a large slice of the profits he had made from the manufacture of armaments during the war. He believed essentially in a moderate consensus, utterly rejecting the idea of a class war; treating his own workforce with sympathy and understanding, he applied the same methods to national labour relations (though at the time of the General Strike the more extreme members of the cabinet gained the upper hand) and was highly respected by Labour MPs whom he could often be seen chatting to in the smoking-room of the House of Commons. In the atmosphere of industrial unrest between the end of the war and the General Strike, it could have been disastrous if the Conservatives had adopted anti-working-class policies. In a splendid Commons speech in 1925, he killed off a 'die-hard' Conservative private member's bill to reduce trade union powers, and ended with the plea: 'Give peace in our time, O Lord'. He was certainly a popular figure in the country and a great electoral asset; even in the 1929 election which was won by Labour, the Conservatives polled more votes than Labour. Probably his greatest achievement was in helping to reunite the Conservative Party and holding it together until his retirement in 1937. On the other hand he was later blamed for neglecting Britain's defences in the face of the threat from Nazi Germany, especially when he was Prime Minister of the National Government (1935–7). His main failing, apart from his lack of originality, was his reluctance to take the initiative. According to John Charmley, the most recent historian of the Conservative party, Baldwin was 'an idle man who disliked work, and he had what amounted to a chronic inability to take decisions until they were forced upon him. As chairman of the Cabinet he would listen to his colleagues but give little, if any, indication of his thoughts; he may not have had any, but his colleagues had to assume that he did, and were thus left in a state of uncertainty whilst trying to divine them.' Neville Chamberlain was the real driving force behind most of the domestic achievements of the government.

Why has the Conservative Party remained such a dominant force in British politics?

For well over a hundred years now – since the first Liberal split over Irish Home Rule in 1886 – the Conservatives have been the most consistently successful party on the British political scene. Many people see them as the natural party of government. By the time of the Conservative defeat in 1997, they had been the largest party in the House of Commons for 76 out of the 111 years that had passed since 1886, over two-thirds of the time – a remarkable record. The previous section analyzed how the party successfully recovered from its disaster of 1906. There were other general factors which played a part in making the Conservatives such a dominant force:

● They could always rely on the support of the majority of the upper classes and the upper middle classes – broadly speaking, people of wealth and property – as well as much of the lower middle class; all these sections of society felt that the Conservative Party could best be relied on to safeguard their interests. These were people who had the education, the financial resources, the influence and the press support needed to keep a political party at the forefront.

● The Conservatives also proved to be adept at winning sufficient working-class support – probably in the region of a third of working-class votes – to tip the overall balance in their favour. It wasn't until 1945 that Labour actually polled more votes than the Conservatives in a general election.

● One reason for the party's continuing popularity was its readiness to adapt to changing circumstances. Its basic principles were quite vague: provided the existing capitalist power structure was preserved, so that political power was kept in the hands of the wealthy property-owning class, the Conservatives were prepared to introduce important reforms. Disraeli took the initiative by introducing the 1867 Reform Act, which was followed by various social reforms. Under Baldwin and Neville Chamberlain, the party again showed its readiness to pursue social reform, and even moved towards collectivism (the idea that the state should intervene directly to guide social policy and plan the economy). This trend continued during and after the Second World War in the period of consensus politics, when the Conservatives largely accepted the social and nationalization policies of the Attlee Labour governments (1945–51).

24.2 Conservative achievements 1924–9

(a) *Important domestic achievements*

1 *The Widows, Orphans and Old Age Contributory Pensions Act (1925).* See Section 20.4(f)2 for full details and criticisms of the Act.

2 The vote was extended to women at the age of 21. Labour objected strongly because the plural vote was not abolished.

3 *The Unemployment Insurance Act (1927)* increased contributions and reduced benefits, but had the great advantage that benefit would be paid for an indefinite period, provided an unemployed person had been genuinely seeking work. The Conservatives had accepted the principle of long-term maintenance by the state (see Section 20.4(c)3 for more details).

4 *The Local Government Act (1929)* was Neville Chamberlain's greatest achievement. It provided a complete overhaul of local government organization, rates and provision for the poor: Poor Law Unions and their boards of guardians, who had provided relief for the poor since 1834, were abolished, and their functions taken over by county and county borough councils (see Section 20.4(c)4 for full details). Agricultural land and farm buildings were to be exempt from payment of rates, and industrial property and railways were to pay only one-quarter of the previous rate. This was designed to encourage farmers and industrialists to expand operations and provide more jobs. Local councils would receive a block grant from the government to cover the cost of services to the poor and of other functions such as public health, slum clearance, roads, and town and country planning. This was a much fairer system because expenses were being shared by the whole body of taxpayers in the country, instead of poor areas with high unemployment having to foot the bill from rates collected locally. However, the Labour Party protested bitterly that it was an attack on the independence of local councils, since the government could now cut off grants to local councils which did not follow their wishes. Many Labour-controlled councils had been running up huge debts paying wages and benefits well above the approved levels;

Illus. 24.1   Neville Chamberlain (left) and Stanley Baldwin
arriving at the House of Commons

this was known as 'Poplarism' after the London borough where the practice originated. Now these councils would have to obey the rules.

5   *The Central Electricity Board* appointed by the Minister of Transport was made responsible for the distribution of electricity. The National Grid was started with its thousands of pylons connecting the generating stations; it was completed in 1933.

6   *The British Broadcasting Company* became a public corporation, to be controlled by governors appointed by the Postmaster-General. John Reith, the first governor-general of the BBC, was determined that it should provide more than just light entertainment. He built the BBC up into an important educational and cultural influence, with its own symphony orchestra. There were regular news bulletins and educational programmes, and leading politicians were invited to broadcast. Baldwin and Philip Snowden soon developed an excellent radio technique but Lloyd George and MacDonald, used to addressing huge live audiences, never mastered the new medium.

7   Depending on one's viewpoint, it is possible to argue that the government's handling of the General Strike was an achievement. The strike lasted less than two weeks, and has never been repeated. The 1927 Trade Disputes Act reduced the powers of the trade unions (see next section).

(b) *Overseas affairs*

These were in the hands of Austen Chamberlain, the Foreign Secretary.

1 He made an important contribution to the signing of *the Locarno Treaties (1925)*, a number of different agreements involving Germany, France, Britain, Italy, Belgium, Poland and Czechoslovakia. The most important one was that *Germany, France and Belgium promised to respect their joint frontiers*; if one of the three broke this agreement, Britain and Italy would assist the state which was being attacked. Germany signed agreements with Poland and Czechoslovakia providing for arbitration over possible disputes. The agreements were greeted with wild enthusiasm all over Europe, and the reconciliation between Germany and France was referred to as the 'Locarno honeymoon'. Later, historians were not so enthusiastic about Locarno: there was one notable omission from the agreements – *no guarantees were given about Germany's eastern frontiers with Poland and Czechoslovakia.* By ignoring this problem, the signatories at Locarno were also ignoring the fact that by signing the League of Nations Covenant they had already undertaken to guarantee all members against aggression. Locarno gave the impression that no action need necessarily be taken if Germany attacked Poland and Czechoslovakia, and that Britain had turned her back on eastern Europe. Indeed Chamberlain talked of Poland's frontier with Germany as something 'for which no British government ever will or ever can risk the bones of a British grenadier'.

   The Conservatives continued to be cool towards the League of Nations; Chamberlain had already rejected MacDonald's Geneva Protocol; this latest slight made the League even less realistic than before, and can be interpreted as the beginning of appeasement (see Section 27.1). For the time being though, as the world enjoyed a period of great economic prosperity, any uneasy thoughts were pushed into the background; Germany was admitted to the League in 1926 and Stresemann and Briand (the French Foreign Minister from 1925 to 1932) met regularly and had friendly discussions; often Austen Chamberlain joined them. The 'Locarno spirit' culminated in:

2 *The Kellogg–Briand Pact (1928).* This originated in an idea of Briand, who proposed that France and the USA should sign a pact renouncing war. Frank B. Kellogg, the American Secretary of State, suggested that the whole world should be involved; eventually 65 states, including Britain, signed the pact, agreeing to renounce war as an instrument of national policy. This sounded impressive but was completely useless because no mention was made of sanctions against any state which broke its pledge. Japan, for example, signed the pact, but was not prevented from waging war against China only three years later.

3 No attempt was made to develop the new relationship with Soviet Russia, started by the 1924 Labour government. The Conservatives had no love for the Communists. Chamberlain immediately told the Russians that Britain would not keep to the treaties which the Labour government had signed with them. The British attitude became even more hostile when evidence appeared that Russian propaganda was partly responsible for the unrest in India (see Section 26.4(b)). Police raided the British Communist Party headquarters in London (1925) and the premises of Arcos, a Soviet trading organization based in London (1927), and claimed to have found evidence of Russian plotting with British Communists to overthrow the capitalist system. The government expelled the trading mission and broke off diplomatic relations with the Russians, who replied by arresting some British residents in Moscow. It has been argued that conciliation would have been a more rational approach, which might have persuaded the Russians to emerge from their isolation.

4   The way was prepared for *the Statute of Westminster* (eventually signed in 1931) which defined the relationship between Britain and the rest of the Commonwealth (see Section 26.1(b)). Baldwin also set up *the Simon Commission (1927)* to report on the situation in India (see Section 26.4(b)2).

24.3 What caused the General Strike of 1926?

As usual there was a combination of long-term causes which had been building up for several years, and short-term causes which triggered the whole thing off:

1   In the background was the post-war economic depression which brought falling exports and mass unemployment.

2   On the whole, industrialists failed to promote greater efficiency and more mechanization which would have enabled them to compete better with other countries. They tended to blame declining profits on higher wages, and their attempts to reduce wages caused strained relations with their workforces.

3   The problems of the coal industry were important because it was here that the stoppage began. Coal sales were probably worse hit than those of any other industry, partly because more gas, electricity and oil were being used, and because there was stiff competition from Germany and Poland which had more modern mechanized pits. In 1925 only 20 per cent of British output was produced by coal-cutting machines; the rest was produced by hand-picks. In addition, France and Italy were receiving free coal from Germany as part of reparations.

4   The government had refused to nationalize the mines, though it was widely believed that only government control could bring about the essential modernization that would enable the industry to survive. Mine-owners were unwilling to take any initiative.

5   The return to the gold standard in April 1925 worsened the export position of all British industries, not just coal. According to the economist J. M. Keynes, Churchill, the Chancellor of the Exchequer, though acting on the best available advice, had over-valued the pound by 10 per cent, making British exports that much more expensive.

6   The situation worsened in June 1925 when there was a sudden drop in coal exports, following a brief revival while the German mines in the Ruhr were closed during the French occupation. The owners announced that they would have to lower wages and increase hours. The miners protested and threatened action; Baldwin saved the situation for the time being by providing a government subsidy for nine months to keep wages at the existing levels until a Royal Commission under Sir Herbert Samuel could come up with a solution. This was viewed by the miners as a victory, and the day the subsidy was announced became known as 'Red Friday'. Some of the more militant trade unionists took Baldwin's sympathetic action to mean that the mere threat of a strike would be enough to get what they wanted; however, the government began to make preparations so that it would not have to give way if the miners tried the same tactic again.

7   Meanwhile the Trades Union Congress (TUC) made it clear that they would support the miners, because if miners' wages were reduced, it was more than likely that wages of other workers would soon follow. This stiffened the attitude of the miners, but the TUC, relying on the Samuel Commission to find a way out, made no special preparations for a general strike.

8   Everything hinged on whether the Samuel Commission could find a solution. Its report appeared in March 1926 and was an eminently sensible document. It recommended that mine-owners should press ahead with reorganization and modernization, should not insist on longer hours (which would lead to over-production) and should not reduce wages (which would simply enable them to avoid reorganization). The government should not continue the subsidy. For the time being, until the crisis had passed, miners must accept some wage reductions. Neither the owners nor the miners would accept the report, though the TUC welcomed it and tried to keep negotiations going because they were still not prepared for a general strike. The government made no attempt to force acceptance of the report, though one moderate mine-owner, Sir Alfred Mond, urged Baldwin to do so.

9   The mine-owners brought a showdown one step nearer by announcing that wages would be reduced on 30 April, to which the miners replied that they would strike on 1 May. The owners got in first and staged a lock-out on Friday 30 April. The coal strike had begun. Ernest Bevin announced that a general strike would begin on 3 May if a settlement was not reached.

10   The TUC General Council, hoping that the threat of a general strike would bring results, continued to negotiate with the government on behalf of the miners. However, negotiations between cabinet and TUC were hampered all through 2 May because the miners' leaders had gone home, leaving the TUC to handle the talks. Baldwin heard that the *Daily Mail* compositors had refused to print an article which claimed that a general strike would be a revolutionary action. He described this as an 'overt act', a sign that the general strike had begun; in fact it was an unofficial action by the printing workers. Baldwin called off the negotiations, and although TUC representatives went to Downing Street in the early hours of 3 May to protest about the abrupt ending to the talks, they found that the cabinet had dispersed and Baldwin had gone to bed. No solution had been found and so the General Strike began.

Why did it prove impossible to prevent the General Strike?

Left-wing historians have no hesitation in laying the blame for this on Baldwin. They argue that he should have followed Mond's advice and insisted on all parties accepting the Samuel Report; nor should he have broken off negotiations so abruptly when the TUC was prepared to go on talking. There is a lot of evidence to suggest that many members of the government wanted a showdown so that they could deal with the trade union threat once and for all; they were well prepared and they knew that the TUC had made very few plans. On the other hand, the miners were completely inflexible, their favourite slogan being 'not a minute on the day, not a penny off the pay'. The mine-owners (with a few exceptions) were equally inflexible, insisting on district wage agreements (instead of a national wage rate), longer hours and lower wages. Even Lord Birkenhead, no friend of the miners, remarked that he thought the miners' leaders were the stupidest men in the country until he had the misfortune to meet the owners.

24.4 The General Strike and its aftermath

The strike was an impressive show of working-class solidarity. In the industries called out (road, rail, docks, printing, gas, electricity, building, iron, steel and chemicals), the response was almost a hundred per cent, which seemed to show how alienated workers had become from employers and government. Over one and a half million men were on strike, and it soon affected other industries too, as factories ran out of raw materials and workers had to be laid off. Since the aim was to paralyze industry, workers in essential service industries such as sewage, rubbish collection and domestic electricity were not called out, so that the general public would not be inconvenienced more than was necessary. It was hoped that once industry was at a standstill, the government would soon be forced to intervene and make the mine-owners see reason. The TUC made it clear that it was not a political strike: they did *not* want to bring the government down; they did *not* want to run the country; what they *did* want was to force the government to defend miners' wages and jobs.

However, by 11 May there was no sign that the government would give way. When Sir Herbert Samuel offered to act as mediator, the TUC accepted. He produced *the Samuel Memorandum* suggesting a short-term renewal of the subsidy to maintain wage levels, no wage reductions until reorganization was assured, and a National Wages Board. On 12 May the TUC called off the General Strike, hoping that the Memorandum would be accepted, though it was strictly unofficial and Baldwin had given no guarantees. The strike lasted unofficially until 14 May, but the miners refused to go back. Since the mine-owners refused to compromise, the coal strike dragged on until December. In the end the miners had to give way and go back to longer hours and lower wages. There was much bitterness about the TUC's 'betrayal'.

(a) *Why did the TUC call the General Strike off so soon?*

They were dismayed when at the end of the first week there was no sign of a softening in the government's attitude; in fact the extremists in the cabinet were talking about 'unconditional surrender'. The TUC, completely unprepared for a general strike, was anxious to end it before provocative government actions caused events to take a more violent turn (see below). There were doubts about the legal position – Sir John Simon, a Liberal MP who was also a lawyer, said in the House of Commons that the strike was 'an illegal proceeding', not an industrial dispute, and that the leaders were liable to be sued for damages – 'to the utmost farthing' of their possessions – and then sent to jail. The Labour Party's attitude was unhelpful – MacDonald was against sympathetic strikes and was afraid that they would simply lose the party votes. The strike was proving too expensive – the TUC had already used £4 million out of their total strike fund of £12.5 million.

(b) *How well did Baldwin handle the strike?*

This question has evoked sharply contradictory views:

● The critical view is that Baldwin acted in his usual indolent way, scarcely 'handling' the strike at all. Worse still, he allowed the right-wing 'fire-eaters' in his cabinet (Churchill and Sir William Joynson-Hicks, the Home Secretary) to take aggressive actions which might have provoked the strikers into violence. There is plenty of evidence to support this view. Baldwin put Churchill in charge of the *British Gazette*, the government emergency newspaper, which printed uncompromising articles and fighting exhortations to the police and special constables, though the TUC had given strict orders that all violence was to be avoided. The tone of the *British Gazette* became so strident that King George V, who showed himself in a very favourable light throughout the strike, protested to Baldwin, and the *Gazette* became more restrained. It was Churchill's idea to use armoured cars to protect food convoys; 'we are at war', he declared; 'we must go through with it; either we crush the strike or the strike will crush us'. In fact, the special constables had been protecting the food convoys perfectly adequately.

● The sympathetic view is that Baldwin played a skilful waiting game, knowing that the TUC had no stomach for a prolonged strike. He took the view that the strike was an attack on the constitution and not an ordinary industrial dispute; therefore he refused to negotiate until the strike was called off. He concentrated on operating emergency plans prepared months earlier, and these worked efficiently. Volunteers kept food supplies moving, unloaded ships and drove trains and buses. Food convoys were organized and protected by special constables (and later by Churchill's armoured cars) while the navy manned power stations. At the same time Baldwin was usually conciliatory in tone – in a broadcast on 8 May he told the country that he was a man of peace and appealed to the strikers to trust him to secure a fair deal for everybody.

Whichever view one accepts, the fact remains that the General Strike failed, and the government claimed the credit.

(c) *What were the results of the strike?*

Historians and trade unionists are still divided in their views about the significance of the General Strike in trade union and labour history. Some see it as a watershed, a turning-point, the climax of the last period of labour militancy, when the failure of the strike caused the working classes to concentrate on political action through parliament. Others feel this is exaggerated; Margaret Morris, for example, believes that it is difficult to isolate the effects of the General Strike from those of the coal strike. As she points out, although important developments did take place in working-class attitudes, these might well be the product of other factors such as mass unemployment and structural changes in industry, as old industries declined and contracted and new industries expanded. However, here are some of the developments which can be at least partly attributed to the General Strike and the coal strike:

● There was a good deal of working-class disillusionment with the TUC for its 'betrayal' of the miners. Membership of unions dropped from over 5.5 million before the strike to 4.9 million in 1927, reaching a lowest point of 4.4 million in 1933. After that it began to recover and had reached 6 million in 1938. In fact there had been a much bigger fall in union membership following 'Black Friday', when the railwaymen and transport workers failed to support the miners' strike (April 1921) – from a peak of 8.3 million in 1920, membership fell to 5.6 million in 1922.

● The TUC abandoned the idea of a General Strike, convinced that one could never succeed.

● There was no solution to the problems in the coal industry and no modernization. The industry continued in slow decline with exports falling steadily. 73 million tons had been exported in 1913; by 1929 the figure had fallen to 60 million tons, and even more disastrously, to 39 million tons in 1932.

● The government introduced the *Trade Disputes Act of 1927* which was designed to make another general strike impossible. Sympathetic strikes and intimidation were illegal and union funds could be seized during a dispute. Trade union members were not required to contribute to the union's political fund (the political levy paid to the Labour Party) unless they chose to do so and gave written notice of their intention. This was known as 'contracting-in', which now replaced 'contracting-out' introduced by the 1913 Trade Union Act. The new Act placed the responsibility on the member; many did not bother to contract in, and this caused a fall of over 25 per cent in the Labour Party's income.

The Act seems to have been largely unnecessary since the TUC had had enough of general strikes. Baldwin gave way to pressure from the Conservative right-wingers who had been trying since the war to get trade union rights limited. It was bitterly resented by the unions, but was not repealed until 1946.

● The working classes realized that parliamentary action offered the best chance of achieving their aims. Bitterness at the Trade Disputes Act and unemployment standing at over a million helped to bring trade unionists and the Labour party together again; there was a big surge in support for Labour, which must have been partly responsible for the Labour victory in the 1929 general election.

● The strike was not without some beneficial effects for the workers. It acted as a warning to other employers who, on the whole, were more reasonable than the mine-owners and avoided drastic wage reductions. Some employers made genuine efforts to improve labour relations; for example, Sir Alfred Mond, founder of Imperial Chemical Industries (ICI), began a series of talks with Ernest Bevin of the Transport and General Workers' Union, and with other leading trade unionists.

(d) *The general election of 1929*

The election was a strangely quiet affair with no dramatic issues under debate. The main Conservative slogan was 'Safety First', while the Labour programme played down full socialism and concentrated on immediate reforms. Much the most interesting was the new Liberal manifesto, *We Can Conquer Unemployment*. Liberal politicians had been having long consultations with leading economists such as J. M. Keynes and William Beveridge and had taken on many of their ideas. Under the leadership of Lloyd George, the party proposed a series of far-reaching reforms for agriculture, town-planning, housing, road-building and railway modernization; these were to be financed by state spending and could be expected to create at least half a million new jobs. The Conservatives lost over 140 seats and slumped to 260. Labour, though winning fewer votes than the Tories, emerged with 288 seats, while the Liberals, in spite of having the best ideas, were bitterly disappointed to reach only 59 seats.

Why did the Conservatives lose? The government had done nothing to solve unemployment, which, though lower than when they took office, still stood at over a million. The coal-mining industry continued to decline and the balance of payments was unhealthy (this means that the value of goods imported was greater than the value of goods exported, causing a drain on gold and foreign currency reserves to make up the difference). The government – Neville Chamberlain excepted – seemed dull and lacking in inspiration and energy. Probably the main reason for the swing to Labour was the aftermath of the General Strike: the 1927 Trade Disputes Act backfired on the government by giving the trade unions and the Labour party a common cause. The government's attitude towards the miners probably alienated much of their normal support among working men. In a sense, though, it was an indecisive result: Labour lacked an overall majority, and more people had voted Conservative (8.6 million) than Labour (8.4 million). The Liberal vote of 5.3 million was not fairly reflected in their 59 seats. Over 60 per cent of the electorate did not want a Labour government, but there was no possibility of a coalition between Conservatives and Liberals because Baldwin detested Lloyd George so much.

Questions

1   Read the following extract about the General Strike of 1926 from *Empire to Welfare State: English History 1906–1976* by T. O. Lloyd and then answer the questions which follow.

> The miners' stand was not flexible: 'not a minute on the day, not a penny off the pay'. Nor were the owners more helpful: district agreements, longer hours, and lower wages was their answer.

(a) How far was the General Strike caused by lack of flexibility on the part of both mine-workers and mine-owners? (12 marks)

(b) Why did the General Strike fail? (8 marks)

(c) How important was the General Strike in the development of trade union and working-class history between the wars? (5 marks)

(Total 25 marks)

[based on an NEAB question]

2 Why did the Conservative Party have such a dominant position in British politics in the inter-war period (see also Chapter 25)?

25 The second Labour government (1929–31), the world economic crisis and the National governments

Summary of events

Labour was again in a minority, though this time the government was slightly stronger, since Labour was the largest single party. With 288 seats to the Conservatives' 260, they needed the support of the 59 Liberals to get any contentious legislation through the Commons. This time MacDonald did not attempt to combine the premiership with the Foreign Office, which went to Arthur Henderson. The cabinet was again solidly moderate, with a sprinkling of ex-Liberals; it contained one left-winger, George Lansbury, in a minor post, and for the first time ever in Britain, a woman, Margaret Bondfield, who became Minister of Labour.

The government's main achievements were in foreign affairs, but its promise was blighted by *the world economic crisis (sometimes known as the Great Depression)* which began with *the Wall Street Crash*, a dramatic fall in share prices on the New York Stock Exchange (October 1929). By May 1931 the unemployment figure in Britain had risen to 2.5 million and there was a financial crisis. The Labour cabinet could not agree on what measures to adopt, and consequently MacDonald handed in the government's resignation (August). However, he himself stayed on as Prime Minister of a coalition government of Labour, Conservative and Liberal MPs, to the intense fury of the majority of the Labour movement, which accused him of betraying the party. The new *National Government* as it was called, introduced emergency measures and then won an overwhelming victory in a general election held in October 1931. After more emergency measures, the country began to recover gradually from the worst effects of the depression, though unemployment remained a serious problem in certain areas.

MacDonald was Prime Minister until his retirement in June 1935, when Baldwin took over. The following November, the National Government won another election, which proved to be the last one until July 1945. Baldwin was Prime Minister until May 1937, and was succeeded by Neville Chamberlain who was premier until May 1940, when he was replaced by Winston Churchill. The main issues of these last years were the question of rearmament in the face of the worsening international situation (see Section 27.2–3), and the abdication crisis of 1936.

25.1 Labour policies at home and abroad

(a) *Domestic achievements*

These included *the Housing Act of 1930*, the work of Arthur Greenwood, the Minister of Health. It renewed the government subsidy for council-house building and organized the speeding-up of slum clearance. The Act was suspended during the financial crises of 1931–4, but then the National Government began to apply it later in 1934, and by 1939 vast slum areas had been cleared. Another advantage of the Act was that it created extra jobs. *The Coal Mines Act (1930)* reduced the miners' working day from eight hours to seven and a half. But there was little else to show; an attempt to repeal parts of the 1927 Trade Disputes Act was defeated by the Liberals, and an Education Bill to raise the school-leaving age to 15 was rejected by the House of Lords, showing its remaining teeth again after slumbering for five years.

(b) *Overseas affairs*

1 Henderson was anxious to continue Britain's conciliatory attitude towards Germany and was involved in *the Young Plan (1929)*. This aimed to settle the remaining problem of reparations – the Dawes Plan (1924) had left the total amount payable uncertain. The French were willing to compromise, and a committee chaired by an American banker, Owen Young, decided to reduce reparations from £6600 million to £2000 million, to be paid on a graded scale over the next 59 years. This was the figure that Keynes had urged at Versailles, and its acceptance ten years later was an admission of error by the Allies. The Plan was welcomed in Germany, as was the withdrawal of Allied troops from the Rhineland five years ahead of schedule, at Henderson's suggestion.

   Unfortunately there was hardly time to put the Young Plan into operation before a series of events following in rapid succession destroyed the fragile harmony of Locarno:

   - the death of Stresemann, the German Foreign Minister (October 1929), removed one of the outstanding 'men of Locarno';
   - the Wall Street Crash in the same month soon developed into the world economic crisis, bringing mass unemployment in Germany. Hopes of peace and tranquillity were kept alive by the Lausanne Conference (1932), at which Britain and France released Germany from most of her remaining reparations payments.
   - In January 1933 Hitler became German Chancellor, and after that, international tension mounted.

2 Relations with Russia improved again when the Labour government, encouraged by the new pro-western Foreign Minister, Maxim Litvinov, resumed diplomatic relations in 1929 and signed another trade agreement the following year; but the improvement was only short-lived since the Conservative-dominated National government cancelled the trade agreement in 1932.

3 Henderson was an enthusiastic supporter of the League of Nations and was highly respected by foreign governments. He worked unceasingly for disarmament and was rewarded by being chosen as president of the World Disarmament Conference which was planned to open in Geneva in 1932. Bitter disappointment was to follow though: by the time the conference met, Henderson was out of office, and the proceedings ended in failure when the Germans walked out (October 1933).

4 MacDonald scored a personal triumph with his visit to the USA (1929) when he

became the first British Prime Minister to address the US Congress; his visit did much to heal the rift caused by disagreements over Britain's war debts to the USA. MacDonald followed this up by organizing a conference in London (1930) attended by the Americans and Japanese, at which the three states re-affirmed the 5 : 5 : 3 ratio of cruisers, destroyers and submarines which had been agreed at an earlier conference in Washington (1921–2). This was successful in re-establishing friendship between the USA and Britain, but the Japanese soon exceeded their limits.

Less successful were Labour's attempts to deal with the problems in India (see Section 26.4(b)3), Palestine (see Section 26.5(c)) and Egypt. Most serious of all were the economic problems which led to the downfall of the government.

25.2 How did the economic crisis bring down the Labour government in 1931?

It was the financial crisis resulting from the world economic crisis which caused the government's resignation.

Illus. 25.1   Labour cabinet meeting, June 1929. (From left to right) Ramsay MacDonald, Arthur Henderson and Sydney Webb

a) *Why was there an economic crisis?*

1   The root of the problem lay in the USA, where American industrialists, encouraged by high profits and helped by increasing mechanization, were producing too many goods for the home market to absorb, at a time when foreign countries were becoming increasingly reluctant to buy American goods. This was partly because the Americans had introduced tariffs to keep foreign goods out; this prevented European states from making the profits they needed, both to buy American goods and to pay their war debts to the USA. The result was a general stagnation of trade which began to show itself during 1929, and which caused some of the better-informed American investors to sell their shares. Confidence in the future was shaken, and in a panic, thousands more investors rushed to sell their shares. However, with the future now so uncertain, very few people were prepared to buy shares, and share prices tumbled on the New York Stock Exchange in Wall Street. One especially bad day was 24 October 1929 – Black Thursday – when nearly 13 million shares were 'dumped' on the stock market at depressingly low prices. This was the so-called Wall Street Crash which ruined millions of investors and almost half the country's banks. As the demand for goods of all types fell away, men were laid off and factories closed. By 1933 almost 14 million Americans were out of work.

2   The crisis in the USA affected most European countries. Europe's prosperity since 1924 (particularly in Germany) had much to do with American loans under the Dawes Plan, which enabled Germany to revive her industries and pay reparations to Britain, France, Belgium and Italy. This in turn enabled these countries to pay their war debts to the USA, and thus Europe and America were closely linked in a circle of loans and repayments. Disaster in one part of the circle inevitably had repercussions elsewhere. The USA ceased to import goods from Europe, stopped all further loans to Germany and called in the short-term loans already made. The effects were most serious in Germany, where in 1931 unemployment was approaching four million. Austria and Hungary were badly affected and a number of banks collapsed; the Austrian government had to ask for loans from the League of Nations to get through the crisis.

(b) *Unemployment in Britain*

The effects of the world economic crisis in Britain were not as sudden or as dramatic as in the USA and Central Europe. This was partly because in Britain there had been nothing like the same boom in the late 1920s as had been experienced in the USA, and certainly nothing like the same speculation in shares. Britain was spared the disastrous bank collapses which ruined so many people in the USA and Europe. But the effects were serious enough: unemployment was already standing at over a million when the Labour government took office; by December 1930 it had shot up to 2.5 million, and in the depths of the depression in 1932, exports had fallen by a third from the 1928 figure, and unemployment had passed the three million mark; this was about 23 per cent of insured workers.

   The government seemed stunned by the enormity of it all, and took no action to try to reduce unemployment. There was no shortage of advice: economic radicals among both Labour and Liberal supporters proposed that the government should create jobs by spending money. Sir Oswald Mosley (Labour's Chancellor of the Duchy of Lancaster) produced a plan, after consultations with J. M. Keynes, suggesting import restrictions, subsidies for farmers (to reduce food imports), bulk purchase from the Dominions, government control of banks to ensure that industry was allowed more credit (to enable new industries to expand), old age pensions at 60 and the school leaving age at 16 (instead of 14). The last two measures would be expensive but would have made an immediate impact on unemployment (see Section 20.5(b) for other ideas put forward at the time).

MacDonald and Snowden were far too cautious; they ignored all advice, and cut expenditure as much as possible, hoping that trade would revive. The government's minority position was no excuse for its inaction, since the Liberals would have voted for a big programme of government investment to create jobs. There was much support for Mosley within the Labour party, but when the leaders rejected his proposals, he left Labour and launched the New party. This had no success and Mosley later founded the British Fascist party.

(c) *The financial crisis and the fall of the Labour government*

Payment of unemployment benefit was placing a severe strain on the government's finances, with nothing to show for it. A committee was appointed under Sir George May to investigate national expenditure; its report, published in July 1931, was an extremely gloomy document. It forecast that by April 1932 there would be a budget deficit of £120 million. To stave off the crisis it proposed a general reduction of salaries in public sector jobs (such as the armed forces, civil servants, judges and police). Teachers were singled out for the largest cut of all – 20 per cent, and the report recommended that unemployment benefit should be cut by the same amount.

Unfortunately foreign bankers were extremely nervous at this time, following the recent collapse of the largest bank in Austria, the Credit Anstalt. The May Report led them to the conclusion that Britain must be on the verge of bankruptcy, and they rushed to withdraw gold, plunging the country into a deeper financial crisis. The Bank of England informed the government that immediate economies were needed to restore confidence in sterling; American and French bankers said that further loans could be made if unemployment benefit was cut by 10 per cent. MacDonald and Snowden were prepared to implement most of the May Report's recommendations, together with the 10 per cent reduction in unemployment benefit. However, this was too much for some of their colleagues: after a fierce argument in cabinet, the cut in benefit was approved, but only by 11 votes to 9.

MacDonald claimed that the minority was too large for the government to continue; there was nothing else for it but to resign. He went to Buckingham Palace to hand in the government's resignation to George V, but to the amazement of almost the whole of the Labour party, he stayed on as Prime Minister of what was called a National Government, with a cabinet consisting of Conservatives, Liberals and just three other Labour MPs (24 August 1931).

(d) *Did MacDonald betray his party?*

The majority of the Labour party was furious with MacDonald; they condemned him as a traitor to the Labour movement and expelled him from the party. They accused him of being vain, ambitious and out of touch with the grass-roots of the party, and claimed that he had been planning to ditch them for some time, so that he could remain in power. There is no solid evidence to support this view; his biographer, David Marquand, believes that George V and Baldwin persuaded MacDonald to stay on as Prime Minister of an all-party government as the best way of restoring confidence and avoiding a general election. Robert Skidelsky suggests that MacDonald's real betrayal of the party occurred not in August 1931, but in the earlier part of his government, when he ignored advice and failed to take actions which might have avoided the crisis of 1931. More recently, Philip Williamson has put forward a slightly different interpretation: he suggests that Neville Chamberlain proposed a National Government in preference to a Conservative government, because 'this would shield their party from the electorally damaging accusations that it was a rich man's party cutting the incomes of the poor' (see Source C in question 1 at the end of the chapter).

25.3 The National Government and its attempts to promote recovery

The new government had a small cabinet of only ten – four Labour (MacDonald, Snowden, Thomas and Lord Sankey), four Conservatives (Baldwin, Neville Chamberlain, Sir Samuel Hoare and Sir Philip Cunliffe-Lister) and two Liberals (Sir Herbert Samuel and Lord Reading).

(a) *Emergency measures*

These were introduced by Snowden, the Chancellor of the Exchequer; his emergency budget implemented much of the May Report to try and restore confidence and save the pound. Income tax was raised from 4s. 6d to 5s. in the pound, and salaries of public employees and unemployment benefits were reduced by 10 per cent. These did not produce the desired effect, and foreign bankers continued to withdraw funds from Britain. Nor was the situation helped by *the Invergordon Mutiny* (September 1931) when naval crews protested against the proposed salary cuts, though this soon petered out when the government assured them that cuts would not exceed 10 per cent. In the end the government went off the gold standard (21 September), so that the value of the pound fell by about 25 per cent on the foreign exchanges. The National Government had failed in its original aim of staying on the gold standard, but at least the financial crisis was more or less over. Though the devaluation of the pound might have been expected to help British trade by making exports cheaper, there was no immediate revival: unemployment continued to rise and topped the 3 million mark during the winter of 1932–3.

(b) *The general election of October 1931*

By October the leaders of the National Government had decided that a general election was necessary. The government was originally intended as a temporary expedient to deal with the immediate crisis. Now that the financial crisis was over, most people expected an election on normal party lines. However, MacDonald and Baldwin had worked well together; Baldwin seemed to like the arrangement which gave him (as Deputy Prime Minister) plenty of power, but left MacDonald to bear the final responsibility. The Labour members were prepared to go along with the Conservatives' main idea for dealing with unemployment – the introduction of tariffs; even some leading Liberals like Sir John Simon had been converted to protection. There seemed very good reasons for staying together and continuing the National Government, and MacDonald appealed to the country for 'a doctor's mandate' to do whatever was necessary for recovery, including the introduction of tariffs.

In the general election of October 1931 the National Government won a landslide victory with 554 MPs, which included 473 Conservatives, 13 Labour, 35 Simon Liberals (who supported tariffs) and 33 Samuel Liberals (who supported free trade). The opposition consisted of 52 Labour MPs led by Arthur Henderson, and 4 Lloyd George

Liberals. Although MacDonald was Prime Minister, it was in effect a thinly disguised Conservative government; Neville Chamberlain became Chancellor of the Exchequer, replacing Snowden who retired to the House of Lords.

Why did Labour do so badly in the election?

Probably the main reason was that the electors blamed the Labour government for the depression; unemployment had more than doubled since Labour came into office, and there was a feeling, rightly or wrongly, that the government had 'run away' from the crisis by resigning. Under Henderson's leadership the party had moved further to the left, and was suggesting that real socialism was the only way to cure Britain's economic problems. This enabled their opponents to wage an alarmist campaign just before the election: Snowden called Labour's programme 'Bolshevism run mad', and there were rumours that a Labour government would seize everybody's money in the Post Office savings bank. Against this, the National Government offered what seemed to be an attractive immediate solution to the country's economic problems – tariffs.

(c) *Further government measures to help the economy*

Free trade was abandoned when Neville Chamberlain fittingly introduced his father's policy, in the *Import Duties Act* of 1932. This placed a 10 per cent tariff on most imports, except those from the empire. As well as increasing sales of British goods at home, this brought in extra revenue, so that Chamberlain was able to avoid raising income tax again. However, an attempt at the Ottawa Conference to develop empire trade met with little success (see Section 26.1(c)). Defence expenditure and interest on war loans were reduced. Some attempt was made to reorganize iron and steel, ship-building, textiles and coal, and to persuade new industry to move into areas of high unemployment, though without much success (see next section 25.4(d)). Remaining off the gold standard made British goods cheaper abroad and led to an increase in exports. Bank rate was reduced from 6 per cent to 2 per cent, mainly to reduce debt charges; however, many local authorities took advantage of low interest rates to borrow money for house building. This provided extra jobs not only for builders but for all the allied trades, including gas and electricity.

These measures helped to boost the economy and to increase sales at home and abroad, though it can be argued that foreign manufacturers, deprived of markets in Britain by the new import duties, became competitors in export markets. Economic historian Derek Aldcroft points out that although by 1937 'Britain had achieved a strong cyclical recovery with income and production levels well above the former peaks of 1929 ... exports failed to regain previous levels. The recovery was very much a domestically-based one, being powered by housing and the newer industries'. Since this was a cyclical recovery, it seems likely that it was due more to increasingly favourable circumstances than to the efforts of the National Government, though to be fair their policies did have some unintentional, indirect benefits, like the boost to house-building provided by low interest rates.

(d) *Favourable circumstances*

These would probably have occurred anyway as part of the normal economic and trade cycle, whatever action the government had chosen to take:

● Prices of all products (both British and imported) fell during the depression, including the prices of raw materials, which reduced production costs for British industry and brought down the cost of house-building. The cost of living also came down, and even with wage reductions, there was an increase in real wages (what people could actually buy with the cash available).

● This enabled people in jobs to spend their extra cash on British consumer goods and even on luxuries such as radios and holidays, which stimulated the creation of jobs.

(e) *Signs of prosperity*

Unemployment gradually fell from a peak of over 3 million in late 1932 to around two million in 1935. This encouraged Baldwin to hold an election in November of that year. The election brought another convincing victory for the National Government with 432 seats; Labour recovered to 154 but the independent Liberals slumped to only 21. As the recovery continued after 1935, the economy in the Midlands and the South was booming, the most striking success being the expansion of new industries like motor-car manufacturing with its factories in Coventry and Oxford. The majority of the population began to enjoy a higher standard of living than ever before. New council houses were available and the sales of consumer goods increased rapidly – radios, electric cookers, refrigerators, modern furniture and telephones. Some workers were able to afford an Austin or Morris car – the number of private cars registered doubled between 1930 and 1939. Cinemas and dancehalls were packed and the annual holiday at the seaside became a national institution; the first Butlin's holiday camp was opened at Skegness in 1937. Higher real wages also meant an improvement in diet – more fresh fruit, vegetables and dairy produce were eaten, helping to improve the health of the nation.

However, there was one disturbing fact – although much of the country seemed to have recovered from the depression by 1937–8, unemployment would not go away completely. This was structural unemployment, something quite separate from the world economic crisis, which had caused cyclical unemployment, and it needs to be examined separately.

25.4 Unemployment in the 1930s

(a) *The two-economy problem*

There were really two economies in Britain: the Midlands and the South were, on the whole, prosperous and booming, once the effects of the world economic crisis passed; but the North of the country – Wales, the North of England, Scotland and Northern Ireland – remained depressed. Tables 25.1, 25.2 and 25.3 show the magnitude of the unemployment problem and how badly the North suffered in comparison with the Midlands and South.

Table 25.1   Total numbers registered unemployed, average over 12 months (in millions)

1927 = 1.08	1932 = 2.75	1937 = 1.48
1928 = 1.22	1933 = 2.52	1938 = 1.79
1929 = 1.22	1934 = 2.16	1939 = 1.51
1930 = 1.91	1935 = 2.04	1940 = 0.96
1931 = 2.63	1936 = 1.76	1941 = 0.35

Source: C. Cook and J. Stevenson, *The Longman Handbook of Modern British History 1714–1987* (Longman, 1988), p. 217.

Table 25.2 Percentage unemployed in staple trades compared to national average

	1929	1932	1936	1938
Coal	18.2	41.2	25.0	22.0
Cotton	14.5	31.1	15.1	27.7
Shipbuilding	23.2	59.5	30.6	21.4
Iron and steel	19.9	48.5	29.5	24.8
Average for all industries	9.9	22.9	12.5	13.3

Source: J. Stevenson, *British Society 1914–45* (Penguin, 1984), p. 270.

Table 25.3 Unemployed as a percentage of insured workers in different regions

	1929	1932	1937
London and S.E. England	5.6	13.7	6.4
S.W. England	8.1	17.1	7.8
Midlands	9.3	20.1	7.2
Northern England	13.5	27.1	13.8
Wales	19.3	36.5	22.3
Scotland	12.1	27.7	15.9
Northern Ireland	15.1	27.2	23.6

Source: J. Stevenson, *British Society 1914–45* (Penguin, 1984), p. 271.

In some towns in the depressed areas the individual figures were startling: Jarrow had 68 per cent of its total workforce unemployed in 1934; in Merthyr Tydfil the figure was 62 per cent, while in St Albans at the same time it was only 3.9 per cent. The Midlands and the South were much better off because they had the new industries – motor cars, aircraft and chemicals.

(b) *Why was unemployment so persistent in the depressed areas?*

These areas had specialized in the older export-based staple industries – coal, textiles, shipbuilding, and iron and steel – which had flourished until the 1880s, and then, for a variety of reasons, the export trade declined (see Section 20.4(b) for a full analysis of reasons for the decline). Sadly, very little was done to modernize these declining industries; machinery and techniques were out-of-date, and they were inefficient and over-staffed compared with their main foreign competitors; but as profits fell, there was less chance of re-investment to make them more competitive. Employers laid men off, and this is why unemployment was so high in the North of the country even before the world economic crisis. This is known as *structural unemployment* because it was caused by faults in the structure of the economy.

The depressed areas had concentrated exclusively on the staple industries, so that there was very little alternative employment to be had. Some historians have suggested that unemployment benefit took away the worst effects of unemployment and there-fore prevented people moving to more prosperous areas. But the evidence does not support this claim: in the first place many men moved from South Wales into the London area, and secondly, many of the new industries in the South wanted young men or women to work on production lines for comparatively low wages; married men with families simply could not afford to move long distances to low-paid jobs in areas where housing was expensive. So they were forced to stay put, and become part of the reservoir of long-term unemployed.

(c) *The effects of long-term unemployment*

The effects could be devastating. In areas of high unemployment, shops and other businesses were forced to close, and places like Jarrow and Merthyr became like ghost towns. Seebohm Rowntree carried out another survey in York, discovering that 31 per cent of working-class families were living in serious poverty. In Stockton-on-Tees the average income of families where the wage-earner was unemployed was less than £1.50 a week, and clearly, unemployment benefit was insufficient. Men had to resort to casual labour which brought very poor rewards. Families fell into debt and many were evicted for non-payment of rent. Diet suffered and health deteriorated. This was reflected in the infant mortality rate, which in 1935 in the South was 42 per thousand live births, while in South Wales it was 63 and in Durham and Northumberland it was 76. In Jarrow it was as high as 114. There was an increase in diseases such as rickets and anaemia, and prolonged unemployment could cause nervous depression and mental disorders.

(d) *Government action to deal with unemployment*

There was no shortage of suggestions for dealing with unemployment. These ranged from Keynesian ideas of state investment to stimulate new industries, through radical

Illus. 25.2 A hunger march to London in 1932

Conservative schemes for job creation, to the socialist solution of a planned economy (see Section 20.5(b) for full details). But like the Labour government before it, the National Government ignored most of the advice offered, partly because it shrank from spending any large amounts of cash, and partly because it refused to accept that the problem could be solved (see Section 20.5(d)). Its response was unimaginative and its measures failed to get to the root of the problem:

1   *The Unemployment Act (1934)* set up the Unemployment Assistance Board whose branches in every part of the country would pay out benefit after an unemployed man ran out of the normal period of insurance benefit. The way in which the Act was applied caused great bitterness among the unemployed, since it was based on the *'means test'* introduced in 1931 (see Section 20.4(c) 5–6).

2   *The Special Areas Act (1934)* appointed two unpaid commissioners and provided them with £2 million to try to revive Scotland, Cumberland, Tyneside and South Wales; they did not have a great deal of success (see Section 20.5(c)).

3   The Bank Rate reduction from 6 per cent to 2 per cent helped the housing boom and encouraged local authorities to embark on road-building. This was in fact a Keynesian measure, but it was unintentional: the goverment's prime motive was to reduce its own debt charges. It showed that it didn't really appreciate the potential of what it was doing, because it was constantly urging local authorities to economize.

4   An attempt was made to revive the steel industry by imposing a tariff on foreign steel and setting up the British Iron and Steel Federation (see Section 20.5(c)). By 1937 the steel industry was showing signs of revival.

5   Loans were provided to encourage shipbuilding, including the completion of the *Queen Mary*.

6   From 1936 onwards the rearmament programme helped in the creation of extra jobs.

Although by the end of 1937 total unemployment had fallen to 1.4 million, there had been little improvement in the depressed areas where most of the 1.4 million were concentrated. The government had failed to produce any positive strategy for planning the economy or reducing long-term unemployment. There was another recession in 1938 which sent unemployment over 1.8 million; only in 1940, as the war effort intensified, did the figure fall below one million.

25.5 Baldwin and the Abdication Crisis 1936

(a) *Popularity of Edward VIII*

George V died in January 1936 and was succeeded by his 41-year-old unmarried son, Edward VIII. The new king was popular and unconventional and seemed genuinely to care about the problems and hardships of his people. In November he paid a visit to some of the South Wales mining valleys where unemployment was still high. Appalled by the poverty, he is reported to have said, 'terrible, terrible, something will have to be done about this'.

Edward had fallen in love with Wallis Simpson, an American lady who had been divorced from her first husband and was now married to a London stockbroker. In October 1936 Mrs Simpson was granted a divorce from her second husband, and Edward intended to marry her; however, the story was not mentioned in the British press, and the general public knew nothing about it.

(b) *Objections to the marriage*

Baldwin decided, for once, that decisive action was needed. He pointed out to Edward that his marriage to a twice-divorced American lady would not be popular with the government or the British people, and tried to dissuade him from going ahead. There was the prospect of a serious constitutional crisis if Edward acted against his cabinet's wishes, since presumably Baldwin would resign and no other party leader would serve as Prime Minister under Edward. It was an agonizing dilemma for the king, especially when the whole affair was reported in the papers on 3 December. There was some support for him in the country; many people, including Churchill and Mosley, and the powerful newspaper-owners, Beaverbrook and Rothermere, believed that he ought to be allowed to marry whoever he wanted. But the majority opinion supported Baldwin and the government; the Archbishop of Canterbury, Dr Lang, was against the marriage on the grounds that the king, as Head of the Church of England, ought not to marry a divorcee. *The Times* announced self-righteously that the monarchy would be fatally weakened if 'private inclination were to come into open conflict with public duty and be allowed to prevail'.

(c) *Edward decides to abdicate*

Edward hoped that an arrangement could be made allowing Mrs Simpson to marry him and remain a private citizen, without becoming Queen (this is known as a morganatic marriage). When the cabinet refused to agree to this, Edward decided that he must abdicate the throne. This he did on 11 December, and was succeeded by his brother George VI. He took the title Duke of Windsor and married Mrs Simpson the following year. The Windsors spent most of their married lives in exile from Britain.

It was generally agreed that Baldwin had handled the situation well, and his popularity, which had waned considerably earlier in 1936 at the time of his limp conduct of foreign affairs (see Section 27.2(d–e)), was suddenly restored. He had avoided an awkward constitutional crisis, saved the monarchy from a damaging controversy and secured the smooth succession of George VI and his wife, Queen Elizabeth, both of whom became popular with the public. Baldwin retired to the House of Lords soon after the coronation in May 1938. Before long, however, his reputation lay in ruins: when the Second World War started (September 1939), Baldwin was blamed for having left Britain with inadequate defences.

Questions

1 Formation of the National Government, August 1931
Study Sources A to C and then answer the questions which follow.

___ **Source A** ___

The account by Philip Snowden, Chancellor of the Exchequer in the Labour Government (1929–August 1931) and in the National Government (August–October 1931)

Mr. MacDonald at the palace meeting on the Monday morning agreed to the formation of a National Government, with himself as Prime Minister, without a word of previous consultation with any of his Labour colleagues. . . . When the Labour cabinet as a whole refused to agree to a reduction of Unemployment pay, Mr. MacDonald assumed too readily that this involved the resignation of his government. He neither showed nor expressed any grief at this regrettable development. On the contrary, he set about the formation of the National Government with an enthusiasm which showed that the adventure was highly agreeable to him. . . . A meeting of the Parliamentary Labour Party was held on August 28th. Mr. MacDonald did not attend it, nor did he send any message or appeal. Taking all these things together, I think they give ground for the suspicion that Mr. MacDonald deliberately planned the scheme of a National Government, which would at the same time enable him to retain the position of Prime Minister and to associate with political colleagues with whom he was more in sympathy than he had ever been with his Labour colleagues.

Source: P. Snowden, *Autobiography*, Nicolson & Watson, 1934.

Source B

Memoirs of Emmanuel Shinwell, a junior minister in the 1929–31 Labour government

I prefer to take a tolerant view of MacDonald's activities at this time. On the personal plane it must be remembered that MacDonald was 65 and appeared much older. What I am bound to say is that MacDonald believed he was right. He felt he was doing his duty on behalf of the nation; this conviction was the motive rather than any personal ambition to hold on to office. What hurt him was through his actions he had been misunderstood and had lost the support and friendship of people like myself who had previously stood by him. To dismiss MacDonald as a traitor is nonsense.

Source: E. Shinwell, *I've Lived Through It All*, Gollancz, 1973, and *Conflict without Malice*, Odhams, 1955.

Source C

Historian Philip Williamson gives his interpretation

MacDonald, it was said, must have been seduced into 'betraying' his party by royal flattery. . . . That the king took an unusually active part during the August crisis is now beyond doubt. Once it became clear that the Labour cabinet would probably resign, in separate audiences with the party leaders and then at a Buckingham Palace conference with all three, the king did not so much seek advice as press for agreement with his own preference for a National government. . . . All party leaders understood that the national interest required the preservation of financial confidence, yet tax increases and expenditure cuts threatened severe difficulties for whichever party imposed them. Consequently, as the Labour cabinet disintegrated, party leaders sought to escape sole responsibility by spreading the burden to their rivals. With Baldwin absent on holiday, Neville Chamberlain proposed a national government in preference to a Conservative or Conservative/Liberal government, because this would shield their party from the electorally-damaging accusation that it was a rich man's party cutting the incomes of the poor. The acting Liberal leader, Samuel, and his colleagues supported the idea because they too feared an electoral backlash. MacDonald put the proposal to the Labour cabinet as a means to ensure 'equal financial sacrifices' from all classes. So even before the king became involved, Labour, Conservative and Liberal negotiators had discussed the formation of a National government.

Source: P. Williamson, 'The King, Politicians and the 1931 Crisis', in *Modern History Review*, November 1993.

(a) Using the evidence of the sources and your own knowledge, analyse the various theories which have been put forward about how the National Government came to be formed in August 1931.   (10 marks)

(b) What reasons can you suggest for the differences of opinion and contradictions between the sources?   (10 marks)

(c) How successful was the National Government in dealing with the financial and economic problems facing it over the next four years?   (20 marks)

   (Total 40 marks)

2 Why, and with what consequences for the main political parties, did National governments hold office between 1931 and 1939?   [NEAB]

3 'Increased consumption by individuals pulled Britain out of the slump'. In the light of this statement, examine the reasons for the recovery of the British economy in the 1930s.   [AEB]

26 Britain and the problems of Empire between the wars

Summary of events

Britain had the largest empire in the world; it included vast areas in Africa, Malaya, India, Burma, the West Indies, and the Arab territories of Iraq, Transjordan and Palestine; these last three areas had been acquired from Turkey as mandates at the end of the First World War. There was a special feature which no other empire could boast – the white dominions – Australia, Canada and New Zealand, and there was also South Africa. During and after the First World War, nationalist movements developed in some parts of the empire, aiming at independence from Britain; these were mainly in India, Egypt and the Arab mandates. The Irish did not wait until the end of the war – republicans staged the Easter Rising in 1916. Even the white dominions were unhappy about what the term 'dominion status' meant, and pressed for a clear definition.

The attitude of British governments was that territories would be allowed to proceed to independence in gradual stages, though it often seemed to the nationalists that these stages were so gradual that they could scarcely be detected. Southern Ireland was granted dominion status in 1922; Egypt took steps towards independence in 1922 and 1936; and Iraq gained full independence in 1932. *The Statute of Westminster (1931)* satisfied the dominions about their relationship with Britain and saw the formation of the British Commonwealth; however, progress in India was far too gradual for the nationalists' liking, and their relationship with Britain was uneasy. It was only in 1947 that India was granted independence.

26.1 Britain and her relations with the Commonwealth

(a) *Britain's white dominions*

Australia, Canada and New Zealand, as well as South Africa and the Irish Free State (since 1922), were already self-governing as far as internal affairs were concerned, but traditionally acted along with Britain for foreign policy, which was one of the reasons why they all fought on Britain's side in the First World War. By the end of the war, a desire to run their own foreign affairs had developed; this was partly because the war had made them more aware of their importance as separate nations (together they had put over a million men in the field); in addition they were encouraged by Woodrow Wilson's support for the principle of national independence, and they were worried in case Britain tried to drag them into another war. Consequently Canada and South Africa refused to help Britain during the Chanak incident in 1922 (see Section 23.1(b) 7), and they all refused to sign the Treaties of Lausanne (1923) and Locarno (1925) (see Section 24.2(b)). South Africa became increasingly hostile to Britain and seemed determined to leave the empire. Clearly some initiative was needed, and happily for the future of the Commonwealth, as it was beginning to be called, this was taken at:

(b) *The Imperial Conference of 1926*

Under the chairmanship of Arthur Balfour, the former Conservative Prime Minister, the conference showed that Britain was prepared to conciliate the dominions. Balfour produced a formula which defined the dominions as 'free countries, equal to each other and to Britain, and in complete control of their own internal and foreign affairs'; they were to be 'freely associated as members of the British Commonwealth of Nations'. This satisfied the dominions (even South Africa for the time being) and was passed through the British parliament as *the Statute of Westminster (1931)*. The Commonwealth was a unique experiment in international organization, but because of the degree of independence enjoyed by the dominions, the achievements of the new 'white man's club', as it was described, were often something of a disappointment. There was no Commonwealth parliament or other set machinery for co-operation to take place, though from time to time conferences were held.

(c) *The Imperial Conference in Ottawa, (July–August 1932)*

This met during the depression, soon after Britain had introduced tariffs. Baldwin and Chamberlain hoped that they could increase trade within the empire by offering preferential rates for Commonwealth goods in return for concessions by the dominions for British manufactured goods. The discussions were often heated, and more than once the conference almost broke up. Eventually 12 agreements were signed: among them Britain agreed to give preference to foodstuffs and certain other commodities from the empire; the dominions on the whole would not agree to lower tariffs on British goods, but they did raise tariffs on foreign goods. It was a kind of preference, but not quite what the British had hoped for, since the tariffs against British goods were already too high.

(d) *The Imperial Conference of May 1937*

This took place while the dominions' Prime Ministers were in London for the coronation of George VI. It was unremarkable except that they all expressed support for Britain's policy of appeasing Hitler (see Section 27.1–2). This was predictable since they had no wish to find themselves involved in another war.

26.2 Events leading up to the partition of Ireland in 1922

In the summer of 1914 the operation of the Third Irish Home Rule Bill, which had passed through all its stages in parliament, and which would have given self-government to Ireland, was postponed until the end of the war. Thus the future of Ireland and the dilemma of whether to include Ulster in Home Rule (see Section 21.5(g)) was put on ice for the time being. The British government hoped that Ireland would remain quiet for the duration of the war, but their hopes were dashed when violence broke out again at Easter 1916.

(a) *The Easter Rising 1916*

When Britain entered the war in August 1914, the majority of the Irish people *were* prepared to wait until the war was over for Home Rule to come into operation. Thousands volunteered to fight for Britain against the Germans, and the Nationalist leader, Redmond, pledged the full support of the Nationalist Volunteers. However, not all of them were happy about this, and a minority group led by Patrick Pearse split off to form the Irish Volunteers. Working with the revolutionary Irish Republican Brotherhood (IRB), they saw Britain's preoccupation with the war as a chance to seize Irish independence, perhaps with help from Germany. Plans were made for a rebellion to take place at Easter 1916, and Sir Roger Casement tried to persuade the Germans to send support. When it became clear that no German help would be given, some of the leaders tried to call the rebellion off, but others went ahead. On Easter Monday they proclaimed a republic and seized several key points in Dublin, including the General Post Office, hoping that the rest of the country would rise in sympathy and force the British to withdraw. However, no sympathetic rising took place and British troops soon put an end to the rebellion, which was militarily a complete failure. Most Irish people condemned it; one Nationalist called it 'this piece of criminal folly'.

(b) *British treatment of the rebels changes the situation*

Although the rebellion was over in a few days, British treatment of the rebels caused a wave of disgust throughout Ireland and the USA, which had a large Irish population. Sixteen of the leaders were executed; one of them, James Connolly, already dying of gunshot wounds and unable to stand, was shot sitting in a chair. This made them into heroes and caused a great outburst of anti-British feeling; more and more people were now wanting not just Home Rule, but complete independence from Britain. Nationalist influence was waning rapidly, and Sinn Fein won four by-elections in 1917.

However, there was still the problem of Ulster, with its Protestant majority, who wanted to remain under British rule. By now the British government had accepted that Ireland would have to be partitioned; Lloyd George was thinking in terms of excluding the six most Protestant counties of Ulster (Antrim, Armagh, Down, Derry, Fermanagh and Tyrone) from any further Home Rule legislation. The Ulster Unionists were prepared to sacrifice the other three counties of the historic Ulster (Donegal, Cavan and Monaghan) because Roman Catholics were in a majority in those counties. In a six-county Northern Ireland, the Protestants would have a 3 to 1 majority; if all nine counties were included, the Protestant majority would be much less secure.

(c) *The Irish Republic declared – January 1919*

In the British general election of December 1918 Sinn Fein won 73 out of the 105 Irish seats; the Nationalists were reduced to 6. Only in Ulster were things different: here the Unionists, committed to staying with Britain, won 26 seats. Nothing less than full independence would now satisfy a majority of the Irish people. Instead of going to the British parliament at Westminster, the Sinn Fein MPs proclaimed an independent Irish republic with their own parliament, *Dail Eireann* (Assembly of Ireland) in Dublin. They elected as President Eamonn De Valera, one of the few surviving leaders of the Easter Rising, who now became the symbol of Irish republicanism. Together with Michael Collins and Arthur Griffith, he organized an effective government which ignored the British and ran the country in its own way, collecting taxes and setting up law courts.

Lloyd George wanted a quick settlement of the Irish problem so that he could concentrate on Britain's many other problems. The government's Irish Committee came up with an ingenious compromise plan: it involved setting up two governments – one in Belfast for the nine counties of Ulster, one in Dublin for the rest of Ireland, and a Council of Ireland to act as a link between the two. Sinn Fein rejected this. Next Lloyd George introduced *the Government of Ireland Act* (February 1920) which he hoped would win moderate support back for the British. This was really a revised version of the Third Home Rule Bill: it involved partitioning the country, with a parliament in Belfast for the six most Protestant counties of Ulster, and a parliament for the rest of Ireland in Dublin. Ulster reluctantly accepted its parliament, but Sinn Fein rejected the entire Act because it only gave them control of certain domestic matters, whereas they were determined on a complete break with Britain; also they wanted control of Ulster.

(d) *Escalating violence*

The Irish Republican Army (IRA), which was formed in January 1919, carried out a campaign of terrorism against the police. Lloyd George retaliated by letting loose the notorious Black and Tans (recently demobilized British soldiers) against the IRA, and both sides committed terrible atrocities. One Sunday in November 1920, for example, 14 British officers living in Dublin were shot dead in their beds. Later the same day British troops retaliated by opening fire at a football match at Croke Park, Dublin (Dublin were playing Tipperary); 12 people were killed, including one of the Tipperary players, and about 70 injured. The Black and Tans especially went too far in their brutal reprisals; even the *Times* said that their cruelty was 'enough to make Englishmen hang their heads in shame', and Lloyd George had to admit that there had been 'deplorable excesses'.

(e) *The Irish Free State established, 1922*

By the spring of 1921 both sides were beginning to feel that the violence had gone on too long; after Lloyd George had put out peace feelers, a truce was agreed in July 1921 and talks began in London. *Why were they both prepared to negotiate?*

● King George V was very distressed by the situation in Ireland, and made a speech appealing for 'all Irishmen to forgive and forget and join in making for the land which they love, a new era of peace, contentment and goodwill'.
● The Liberal and Labour parties, many of the Conservatives and a majority of the general public in mainland Britain realized the strength of the Irish desire for independence. Although it might have been possible by sending somewhere in the region of 100 000 troops, to subdue Ireland, it would be impossible ever again to have the consent or the co-operation of the Irish people.
● On the Irish side, the IRA, who never had more than about three thousand men, were close to exhaustion.

An Irish delegation led by Michael Collins and Arthur Griffith, came to London, though De Valera refused to join the negotiating team. Lloyd George used all his skills as a negotiator and after both sides had made some concessions, agreement was reached on *the Anglo-Irish Treaty* which involved a partition of Ireland (December 1921):

● Southern Ireland was to become independent as *the Irish Free State*, with the same status as dominions like Australia and Canada. This gave the Irish much more than had been offered in the 1920 Government of Ireland Act, but on the other hand they had to drop the idea of a republic and they still had to recognize the British monarchy. In addition they had to allow the British navy to use three ports – Queenstown, Berehaven and Lough Swilly.

- To satisfy the Ulster Unionists, *Northern Ireland*, consisting of the six counties of Antrim, Armagh, Londonderry, Down, Fermanagh and Tyrone, remained part of Britain with its own parliament at Belfast. Here again the Irish had to make concessions: some were against the idea of partition and wanted Northern Ireland included in the Free State. Even many of those who accepted partition felt that some areas where Catholics were in a majority should have been in the Free State; these areas included south Fermanagh, south Armagh, south Down and much of Tyrone. However, *a Boundary Commission* was included in the treaty and it was hoped in the south that the necessary adjustments to the frontier would be made in due course (see Map 21.1 on p. 342). It has to be seen as a considerable achievement by Lloyd George, in the circumstances, that an agreement of any sort was reached, though in the last resort he had to threaten the Irish delegation with a renewal of the war to get them to sign.

Unfortunately the troubles in Ireland were still not over. A section of Sinn Fein, led by De Valera, refused to accept the treaty because of the partition and the remaining connection with Britain. A vicious civil war broke out between the two Sinn Fein factions, during which Michael Collins was killed. The war ended in April 1923 with a victory for supporters of the treaty. The Irish Free State came into existence officially in December 1922.

26.3 Relations between Britain and the independent Ireland

Relations between the two states were never easy. As historian A. J. P. Taylor put it: 'the Irish had won, but they were not reconciled or friendly. Their victory had come after terror and troubles, not as a work of conciliatory statesmanship, and they had nothing to be thankful for.' The vast majority of the people of the Free State resented the existence of a separate Northern Ireland just for the benefit of the Ulster Protestants. They felt that most of these Protestants were not genuinely Irish, since their ancestors had been moved in (or 'planted') from Scotland and England during the sixteenth and seventeenth centuries to 'civilize' the Catholics. Both main political parties in the Free State had as part of their programmes the ultimate unification of Ireland. On the other hand, British governments felt obliged by the strength of Protestant Unionist feeling in Northern Ireland, to maintain its union with Britain. No compromise seemed possible on either side and so relations could never be close. And yet some important ties remained. The Dublin parliament, the Dail, voted to recognize 'the common citizenship of Ireland with Great Britain'. This meant that Irish people were still British citizens and could still vote in British elections. There were close trade ties, with almost all Ireland's food exports going to Britain. The major landmarks after 1922 were:

(a) *The failure of the Boundary Commission*

The treaty had promised a Boundary Commission to consider possible changes to the frontier between the Free State and Northern Ireland. Hints had been dropped to the Irish during the negotiations (though nothing had been put in writing), that Britain might be prepared to give parts of Fermanagh and Tyrone to the Free State. However, when the Commission met in 1924, Lloyd George was out of office, and Baldwin's

Conservative government made it clear that it had no intention of making any major changes. The Commission folded up in 1925 after confirming the original frontier, leaving the Irish feeling cheated and doing no good at all for Anglo-Irish relations.

(b) De Valera cuts the links with Britain

Eamonn De Valera remained implacably hostile to Britain. He formed a new party, *Fianna Fail* (Soldiers of Destiny), which won the 1932 election largely because the slump and unemployment had made the government of William Cosgrave highly unpopular. De Valera served as Prime Minister for the next 16 years, gradually breaking all the remaining ties with Britain:

• Using the 1931 Statute of Westminster by which the British parliament ceased to have any control over the dominions' parliaments, De Valera abolished the oath of loyalty to the Crown, introduced separate Irish citizenship and took away all power from the governor-general (the representative of the Crown). This was perfectly legal, but the British government, instead of accepting the inevitable with dignity, placed trade sanctions on the Free State. De Valera responded by refusing to hand over money owing to the British government in the form of annual loan repayments from farmers who had bought land under the Land Purchase Acts after 1870. Trade between the two countries all but ceased, which did neither of them any good. Trade gradually resumed during 1935, but De Valera had made his point, and the Irish treasury benefited from the cash still owing to Britain.
• In 1937 De Valera took the chance offered by the abdication of Edward VIII to introduce a new constitution, making Eire, as it was now called, completely independent in practice.
• Neville Chamberlain (British Prime Minister 1937–40) made concessions in an attempt to win Eire's friendship. He accepted the new constitution, wrote off most of the cash still owing (about £100 million by 1938) and gave up the rights to use the three naval bases. However, Eire remained unco-operative. Chamberlain failed to realize how deeply De Valera felt about the situation: he would never be reconciled with Britain until Northern Ireland became part of Eire.
• Eire remained neutral during the Second World War and refused to allow the British navy to use ports on her west and south coasts. This left British shipping more vulnerable to German submarine attacks and contributed to their heavy losses in the Atlantic. This caused great bitterness in Britain, especially since the food convoys were bringing supplies to Eire as well as to Britain.
• In 1948 Eire refused to take part in the discussions which led to the formation of NATO (see Section 32.1(f)). She would only consider joining if Ireland became united.
• In 1949 Eire declared itself an independent republic. (For events in Northern Ireland after 1922, see Section 31.1.)

26.4 The Indian struggle for independence

(a) The growth of Indian nationalism

Nationalist feelings began in the late nineteenth century when many middle-class Indians, having received a British-style education, often at Oxford or Cambridge, felt frustrated that their country continued to be run by the British, while they were allowed no say in the government and only a very minor role in local affairs. They founded a party called *the Indian National Congress* (1885) to press for greater participation by Indians in government. They were encouraged by the Japanese victory over the Russians in 1905, which raised hopes that this new Asian power might help the Indians in their struggle against British colonialism. A decision by the British in 1905 to divide the huge province of Bengal into two, greatly upset the Hindus, because it split the Bengali-speaking Hindus right down the middle and reduced their potential power.

In response to the pressures, the British introduced the 1909 *Morley–Minto reforms* (Morley was the Secretary of State for India, Lord Minto the viceroy, who ruled India on behalf of the king). Indians were allowed to sit on the executive councils which advised the provincial governors; later the partition of Bengal was abandoned. This was not enough to prevent unrest increasing, and there was an attempt on the viceroy's life in 1912. After 1914 nationalist feeling intensified, probably encouraged by the important contribution made by the Indians to the war effort, and perhaps by the successful revolutions in Russia and by Woodrow Wilson's talk of self-determination for subject peoples.

(b) *How did British governments deal with demands for Indian independence?*

For years the British tried to ignore Indian nationalism, having apparently convinced themselves that there were too many differences in Indian society for the Indians ever to form a united movement; there were social, regional, and above all, religious differences, especially between Hindus and Muslims. However, during the war, Hindus and Muslims began to work together to pressurize the British, who were slowly coming round to the idea that India would have to be given a measure of self-government. In 1917 the Indians were promised 'the gradual development of self-governing institutions with a view to the progressive realization of responsible government in India as an integral part of the British Empire'. However, many Conservatives, including Winston Churchill and Lord Birkenhead (Secretary of State for India from 1924 to 1928), were utterly opposed to the idea. Seeing India as 'the brightest jewel in the imperial crown', they could not come to terms with the idea of 'giving it away'; Indian independence would be the beginning of the end of the British Empire. Not surprisingly, the pace was far too slow for the impatient nationalists, whose leaders, the Mahatma Gandhi and Jawaharlal Nehru, both lawyers educated in London, organized an anti-British campaign. The stages in the gradual move towards independence were:

1   In 1918 Edwin Montagu (Secretary of State for India 1917–22) and Lord Chelmsford (Viceroy) put forward plans which eventually became *the Government of India Act (1919)*. There was to be a national parliament with two houses; about five million of the wealthiest Indians were given the vote; in the provincial governments the ministers of health, education and public works could now be Indians; a commission would be held ten years later to decide whether India was ready for further concessions. Congress was bitterly disappointed because, although the new parliament had some powers, the really important decisions were still taken by the governor-general; the British also kept control of the key provincial ministries such as law and order and taxation.

In addition, the Indians were enraged at the slowness with which the British put even these limited advances into operation. Rioting broke out, and at Amritsar in the Punjab, after five Europeans had been murdered, General Dyer dispersed an excited crowd of over 5000 Indians with machine-gun fire, killing 379. Order was soon restored but the Amritsar Massacre was an important turning-point: it provoked so much fury that Congress was transformed from a middle-class party into a mass movement. 'After Amritsar', writes Martin Gilbert, 'no matter what compromises and concessions the British might suggest, British rule would ultimately be swept away.'

By this time Gandhi was the leading figure of Congress. He believed in non-violent protest and the equality of all classes. Always dressed as a simple peasant, he somehow managed, by sheer force of personality, to persuade Indians to refuse to work, stage sit-down strikes, fast, stop paying taxes and boycott elections. Unfortunately he was unable to control some of his more extreme supporters and violence often developed. In 1922 he called off his first non-co-operation campaign.

2 The next British move, apart from putting Gandhi in gaol, was that Baldwin, acting a year early, appointed *the Simon Commission* (1927), as the 1919 Act had recommended. In 1930 this proposed self-government for the provinces, but was treated with contempt by the Indians; they were not even represented on the commission and they were demanding immediate dominion status. As soon as he was out of gaol, Gandhi began his second civil disobedience campaign by breaking the law that only the government could manufacture salt. After a symbolic 250-mile march to the sea, he produced salt from sea-water; but again violent incidents developed and again Gandhi was arrested.

3 Lord Irwin (later Lord Halifax) (viceroy 1926–31) was a humane and enlightened politician, and was sympathetic to the Indians. Before the Simon Report appeared in 1930 he had expressed the view that dominion status must come; this is why the Indians had felt so let down when the report made no mention of it. Irwin was convinced that negotiations must take place, and he was fully supported in this view by Ramsay MacDonald who had just become Prime Minister. Consequently *two Round Table Conferences were held in London (1930 and 1931)*. The first was unsatisfactory because, although the Indian princes were represented and accepted the idea of an Indian federation, no Congress representatives were there, because most of them were in prison. Irwin had them released and prevailed upon Gandhi to travel to London to attend the second conference, much to the horror of Churchill, who refused to meet him and described him as 'this malignant and subversive fanatic'. Again little progress was made, this time because of disagreements about Muslim representation in an independent Indian parliament.

4 *The Government of India Act of 1935* was a major step towards independence. It was introduced as a result of co-operation between MacDonald and Baldwin, and in spite of bitter opposition from Churchill who called it 'this bogus act'. The elected Indian assembly was to have a say in everything except defence and foreign affairs; the eleven provincial assemblies were to have more or less full control over local affairs. The nationalists were still not satisfied: the Act fell short of dominion status (the white dominions controlled their own defence and foreign policies), and the princes who still ruled certain areas of India refused to co-operate; thus their areas remained outside the system. Another failure of the Act was that it ignored the religious rivalry between Hindus and Muslims. Roughly two-thirds of the Indians were Hindus, and the next largest group, the Muslims (who believed in the Islamic religion), were afraid that in a democratic India they would be dominated and unfairly treated by the Hindus. When Nehru's Congress Party, which was overwhelmingly Hindu, won control of eight out of the eleven provinces in the 1937 elections, the Muslim League, under its leader M. A. Jinnah, demanded a separate state of their own called Pakistan, while Congress and Gandhi were determined to preserve a united India. No further developments took place before the Second World War, but mounting Hindu/Muslim hostility boded ill for the future, and provided some justification for the British reluctance to grant full self-government. (For events leading to independence in 1947 see Section 32.2.)

26.5 Britain and the Middle East mandates

In 1916 the Arabs in the Turkish empire rose in revolt, and helped by the British colonel T. E. Lawrence (Lawrence of Arabia), and later by British troops under Allenby, they played an important part in liberating the Arab territories from Turkish control. As a bribe to win Arab support against Turkey, the British had made vague promises that when the war was over, the Arabs would be allowed to set up independent states; but about the same time (1916), the British had also made the contradictory *Sykes–Picot agreement* with France, whereby Turkey's Arab lands would be divided between the two of them. In 1919, therefore, to their intense disappointment, the Arabs found their territories handed over as mandates (to be 'looked after' and prepared for self-government) to Britain, which was given Iraq, Transjordan and Palestine, and France, which was put in charge of Syria and Lebanon.

Britain was reluctant to sever all connections with her mandates because of the Middle East oil resources, especially in Iraq, and wanted to be allowed to station troops there to guarantee a sure supply of oil. On the other hand, the British dared not offend the Arabs too deeply or her oil supplies might equally be threatened. Consequently steady progress towards independence was made in Iraq and Transjordan, though with strings attached; however, the situation in Palestine was complicated by the Jewish/Arab problem.

(a) *Iraq*

After some initial nationalist rioting in Iraq, the British set up an Iraqi national government in which each minister had a British adviser. The Amir Feisal (who had just been driven out of Syria by the French) was accepted as king. Although extreme nationalists did not approve, this set-up was agreed by *the Anglo-Iraqi Treaty of 1922* and seemed to work well. An elected parliament was introduced in 1924 and Feisal, a man of great personal charm and political ability, proved to be an excellent ruler. With British help, industry and agriculture were organized and an efficient administrative system was introduced. The British won Iraqi support by successfully opposing Turkish claims to the province of Mosul with its vast oil resources. In 1932 Iraq became fully independent, though Britain was allowed to keep two air-bases. According to one Arab nationalist, George Antonius, 'the modern state of Iraq owes its existence largely to the efforts and devotion of its British officials'.

(b) *Transjordan*

Here the British set up Feisal's brother Abdullah as king, and allowed him to run the country's internal affairs, which he did competently. However, Transjordan was a poor state, lacking in resources, especially oil, and was therefore dependent on Britain for subsidies and for defence. In 1946 it was given complete independence, though Abdullah kept on the British officers who led his army.

(c) *Palestine*

Palestine proved to be the most troublesome mandate because of the growing hostility between Jews and Arabs. The problem originated about two thousand years earlier, in AD 71, when most of the Jews were driven out of Palestine, their homeland, by the Romans. In fact small communities of Jews remained behind in Palestine, and during the following centuries there was a gradual trickle of Jews returning from exile, though until the end of the nineteenth century there were never enough to cause the Palestinian Arabs to feel threatened. However, in 1897 some European Jews founded *the World Zionist Organization* in Basle (Switzerland), an event which was to be of profound importance for the Middle East. Greatly disturbed by the recent persecution of Jews in Russia, Germany and France, the Zionists demanded a Jewish national home in Palestine. Even before they were given the mandate over Palestine, the British had become involved in the controversy, and must take much of the blame for the chaos that followed, especially after 1945.

How did Britain become involved and how did the situation develop up to 1939?

● During the First World War the British had made three contradictory promises, which were bound to lead to frustration and hostility. There were the two already mentioned: independent states for the Arabs, and the partition of Arab territories between Britain and France. The third was *the Balfour Declaration* (November 1917) in which the British Foreign Secretary pledged British support for a Jewish 'national home' in Palestine. The British motive, apart from genuine sympathy with the Zionists, was a belief that the Jews would help to safeguard the Suez Canal and provide a buffer between the canal zone and the French in Syria.
● Faced with bitter Arab protests both against the British failure to grant independence and against the arrival of increasing numbers of Jews, the British government stated (1922) that there was no intention that the Jews should occupy the whole of Palestine and that there would be no interference with the rights of the Arabs in Palestine. The British hoped to persuade Jews and Arabs to live together peacefully in the same state, and they failed to understand the deep religious gulf between the two.
● Jews continued to arrive, equipped with Zionist money, bought land from Arabs who were at first willing to sell, started industries and reclaimed land. It was soon clear that they intended to develop not just a national home, but a Jewish national state; by 1928 there were 150 000 of them. The Arabs rioted and began murdering Jews; in 1929 the British Labour government decided that Jewish immigration must cease for the time being. Now it was the turn of the Zionists to rage against the British, to such an extent that MacDonald felt obliged to allow immigration to continue.
● The situation took a turn for the worse after Hitler came to power in Germany (1933); Nazi persecution caused a flood of refugees, until by 1935 about a quarter of the total population of Palestine was Jewish. Arabs again began to attack Jews while British troops struggled to keep order.
● In 1935 the British *Peel Commission* suggested dividing Palestine into two separate states, one Jewish, one Arab, but the Arabs rejected the idea.
● As war loomed in 1939 the British felt the need to win Arab support, and in a White Paper they agreed to limit Jewish immigration to 10 000 a year and promised to set up an independent Arab state within ten years, thus guaranteeing an Arab majority in the new state. At this point, with nothing resolved, the British hoped to shelve the problem until after the war (see Section 32.3 for later developments).

Questions

1 The Amritsar Massacre (1919) and Indian independence
Study the two Sources and then answer the questions which follow.

Historian Bernard Porter writes about Indian nationalism and the Amritsar Massacre

The First World War made it less likely that the promise of reforms to India, when it did come, would be enough to stem the nationalist tide. Indian nationalism was fired enormously by the war, its grievances increased, its support expanded, its organization greatly improved and its expectations increased . . .

In April 1919 there was a rash of rebellions in the Punjab serious enough to convince at least one British general that the Indian Mutiny was about to be repeated; this persuaded him to open fire on a crowd of unarmed Indians in a public square in Amritsar, and to continue firing into their backs until his ammunition ran out, killing at least 380 and wounding 1200 . . .

General Dyer was mildly censured by the army and then vigorously defended by his superiors, by the House of Lords, by much of the press, by most Conservative MPs and by a large number of ordinary people who subscribed £26 000 in a month to a fund set up on his behalf by the *Morning Post*. The effect of all this on Indian nationalist opinion was disastrous. Gandhi made it the occasion for his first non-co-operation campaign, and repression only undid the gains made by the earlier policies of concession.

Source: B. Porter, *The Lion's Share: A Short History of British Imperialism 1850–1970*, Longman, 1975.

Source B

Another historian, Robert Rhodes James, writes about Churchill's attitude

The good effects of this modest advance – the Government of India Act (1919) – were spoiled by the Amritsar Massacre in April 1919, and perhaps even more spoiled by the strong support – official and unofficial – that General Dyer received in British India and Britain for his indefensible actions. . . . Churchill strongly supported the dismissal of Dyer after Amritsar, and in his speech in defence of the government's action, had stated firmly that 'our reign in India or anywhere else has never stood on the basis of physical force alone'. But his acceptance of the permanence of British rule over India was complete. While prepared to support policies that would calm nationalist ambitions, he was not prepared to contemplate equality in government between British and Indians and was outraged by the suggestion of any reduction of British supremacy.

Source: R. R. James, *Churchill – A Study in Failure 1900–1939*, Weidenfeld & Nicolson, 1970.

(a) From the evidence of the sources and your own knowledge, explain why there was a great increase in Indian nationalism during and after the First World War. (5 marks)

(b) From the evidence of the sources, why was the Amritsar Massacre so important in Anglo-Indian relations? (6 marks)

(c) What clues do the sources provide as to why the Indians had to wait until 1947 for their independence? (9 marks)

(Total 20 marks)

2 When and why did Partition become the only practicable solution to the Irish Question? [AEB]

27 Appeasement and the outbreak of the Second World War: foreign affairs 1931-9

Summary of events

British foreign policy during this period was dominated by one principle – *appeasement*. This was the practice of making what were thought to be reasonable concessions to aggressive foreign powers – Japan, Italy and Germany – in the hope that it would avoid war. The National governments of MacDonald (1931–5) and Baldwin (1935–7) followed this policy, and Neville Chamberlain, Prime Minister from 1937 until 1940, was its main exponent, though he did abandon it belatedly in March 1939. In one sense the policy failed completely since it culminated in the outbreak of the Second World War (1939–45); for this reason 'appeasement' came to be looked on as a dirty word, a term of abuse. On the other hand, Chamberlain himself claimed that his policy bought time for Britain to rearm and prepare for war.

Between 1924 and 1929, following the Dawes Plan (1924) and the Locarno Treaties (1925), international relations were harmonious. But the Great Depression plunged the world's industrial powers into severe economic crisis, with dwindling markets and mass unemployment. The Locarno spirit of sweetness and goodwill suddenly disappeared and it was a case of every country for itself. Three states – Japan, Italy and Germany – all of which had right-wing nationalist governments, tried to solve their economic problems by territorial expansion, which meant aggression against other states. The League of Nations, vainly trying to operate a policy of *collective security* (joint action to keep the peace), but lacking strong support, failed to curb the aggressors. Britain and France, instead of backing the League and collective security, preferred appeasement. Consequently all three aggressors successfully defied the League and the majority of world opinion until 1939.

●   Japan was the first aggressor with her successful invasion of the Chinese province of Manchuria (1931).
●   Adolf Hitler, who became German Chancellor in January 1933, began cautiously by announcing the reintroduction of conscription (March 1935), a breach of the Versailles Treaty.
●   Mussolini, the Italian fascist dictator, sent his troops to conquer Abyssinia (October 1935).
●   In 1936 German troops reoccupied the Rhineland, another breach of Versailles.
●   During the summer of 1936 the Spanish Civil War broke out, and Hitler and Mussolini sent help to General Franco, leader of the Spanish right wing in their revolt against the left-wing republican government. By 1939 Franco was victorious and a third fascist dictator was installed in Europe.

- Since the League of Nations was completely ineffective against these acts of aggression, Hitler was encouraged to carry out his most ambitious project to date – the annexation of Austria (known as the *Anschluss* or union – March 1938).
- Next he turned his attention to Czechoslovakia and demanded the Sudetenland, an area containing some 3.6 million Germans adjoining the frontier with Germany. When the Czechs refused Hitler's demands, Chamberlain, anxious to avoid war at all costs, attended a conference at Munich (September 1938) at which it was agreed that Germany could have the Sudetenland, but no more of Czechoslovakia. War seemed to have been averted.
- However, the following March Hitler broke this agreement and sent troops to occupy Prague, the Czech capital. At this Chamberlain decided that Hitler had gone too far and must be stopped.
- Hitler next demanded Danzig from Poland. The Poles rejected his demand, and Britain and France promised to help Poland if the Germans attacked. Hitler was not sufficiently impressed by these British and French threats and grew tired of waiting for Poland to negotiate.
- Having first secured a non-aggression pact with Russia (August 1939), the Germans invaded Poland on 1 September. Britain and France accordingly declared war on Germany.

27.1 What was appeasement and why did Britain follow such a policy?

(a) *The two phases of appeasement*

Appeasement was the policy followed first by the British and later by the French, of avoiding war with aggressive powers such as Japan, Italy and Germany by giving way to their demands, provided they were not too unreasonable. There were two distinct phases of appeasement:

1 From the mid-1920s until 1937 there was a vague feeling that it was vital to avoid war, and Britain and sometimes France, drifted along accepting the various breaches of the Versailles Treaty and the acts of aggression as *faits accomplis*.
2 When Neville Chamberlain became British Prime Minister in May 1937 he gave appeasement new drive. He believed in taking the initiative: he would find out exactly what it was that Hitler wanted, and show him that reasonable claims could be met by negotiation rather than by force.

The origins of appeasement can be seen in British policy during the 1920s with the Dawes and Young Plans, which tried to conciliate the Germans, and also with the Locarno Treaties and their significant omission: *Britain did not agree to guarantee Germany's eastern frontiers*, which even Stresemann, the 'good German', said must be revised. When Austen Chamberlain, the British Foreign Secretary (and Neville's half-brother), remarked at the time of Locarno that no British government would ever risk the bones of a single British grenadier in defence of the Polish Corridor, it seemed to the Germans that Britain had turned her back on Eastern Europe. Appeasement reached its climax at Munich, where Britain and France were so determined to avoid war with Germany that they made Hitler a present of the Sudetenland and so set in motion the destruction of Czechoslovakia. Even with concessions as big as this, appeasement failed.

(b) *Justifications for appeasement*

At the time appeasement was being pursued, however, there seemed much to commend it, and the appeasers, who included MacDonald, Baldwin, Sir John Simon (Foreign Secretary 1931–5), Sir Samuel Hoare (Foreign Secretary June–December 1935) and Lord Halifax (Foreign Secretary 1938–40), as well as Neville Chamberlain, were convinced of the rightness of their policies:

1 It was essential to avoid war which was likely to be more devastating than ever before, as the horrors of the Spanish Civil War showed. One of the most appalling incidents was the German bombing of the defenceless Basque town of Guernica in which at least 1600 people were killed. The fear was that in any future war British cities and the civilian population would be at risk, since 'the bomber will always get through'. Moreover Britain, still in the throes of the economic crisis, could not afford vast rearmament and the crippling expense of a major war. British governments seemed to be supported by a strongly pacifist public opinion. In February 1933 the Oxford Union voted that it would not fight for King and Country. In July 1935 the Peace Pledge Union organized a nationwide public opinion poll in which 92.5 per cent (10.05 million) of people questioned said they were in favour of all-round reduction of armaments by international agreement. In November 1935 Baldwin and the National Government won a huge general election victory shortly after he had declared: 'I give you my word of honour that there will be no great armaments.'

2 Many people felt that Italy and Germany had genuine grievances: Italy had been cheated at Versailles, Germany treated too harshly. Millions of Germans had been denied self-determination and found themselves living outside Germany's frontiers in Poland and Czechoslovakia. Therefore Britain should react with sympathy, and in the case of Germany, try to revise the most hated clauses of the Versailles Treaty. This would remove the need for German aggression and lead to Anglo-German friendship.

3 Since the League of Nations seemed to be helpless, Chamberlain believed that the only way to settle disputes was by personal contact between leaders; in this way he thought he would be able to control and civilize Hitler, and Mussolini into the bargain, and bring them to respect international law.

4 Economic co-operation between Britain and Germany would be good for both; if Britain helped the German economy to recover, the internal violence would die down.

5 Fear of Communist Russia was great, especially among British Conservatives, many of whom believed the Communist threat to be greater than the danger from Hitler. Many British politicians were willing to overlook the unpleasant features of Nazism in the hope that Hitler's Germany would be a guarantee against Communist expansion westwards; better still would be a war between Nazi Germany and Communist Russia ending in the destruction of Communism; in fact many British politicians admired Hitler's drive and achievements.

6 Underlying all these feelings was the belief that Britain ought not to take any military action in case it led to a full-scale war, for which the country was totally unprepared. British military chiefs told the government that Britain was not strong enough to fight a war against more than one country at the same time. Even the navy, which was still the strongest in the world apart from the American navy, would have been hard pressed to defend the far-flung empire and protect merchant shipping in the event of war against Germany, Italy and Japan simultaneously. The army chiefs were working on what they called the principle of 'limited liability'. This meant in simple terms that there was no question of

immediately sending a large army to France as they had done in 1914; at most there were only four divisions available. At the same time the USA stood firmly for isolation, while France was weak and divided. The air force was woefully short of long-range bombers and fighters.

Some British politicians thought there was an alternative to appeasement. Winston Churchill, for example, thought the government should make no concessions to the dictators and should concentrate on building up a Grand Alliance, including Russia if necessary. He was convinced that people like Hitler and Mussolini would only take notice of military force. On the other hand, given Britain's military difficulties, it is clear that Chamberlain's options were fairly limited. Historian John Charmley mounts a spirited defence of Chamberlain in his book *Chamberlain and the Lost Peace*, arguing that Chamberlain's policies were far more realistic that those suggested by Churchill and Eden. Philip M. Taylor also takes a sympathetic view in his article on appeasement in the *Modern History Review* (November 1989). He suggests that Chamberlain's real achievement was to prove to the world that Hitler would never be satisfied with concessions and was determined to achieve his aims by force.

27.2 Appeasement in action

(a) *The Japanese invasion of Manchuria (September 1931)*

This act of aggression brought a Chinese appeal for help to the League of Nations, which condemned Japan and ordered her troops to be withdrawn. However, there was a certain amount of sympathy in Britain for the Japanese, and Sir John Simon attempted to put both sides of the case at the League Assembly in Geneva. Unfortunately, according to A. J. P. Taylor, Simon had one serious defect which made him unfit to be British Foreign Secretary – he was 'too cool and rational'. He pointed out that Japan had been involved in the province since the 1890s and had been given a privileged position in south Manchuria as a result of the Russo-Japanese War. Since then the Japanese had invested millions of pounds in Manchuria in the development of industries and railways. China seemed to be growing stronger under the rule of Chiang Kai-shek and the Japanese were afraid that he would try to exclude them from Manchuria. They could not stand by and see themselves gradually squeezed out of such a valuable province with a population of some 30 million, especially when they were already suffering economic hardship because of the great depression.

At Simon's suggestion the League appointed an investigating commission under Lord Lytton which decided (1932) that there were faults on both sides and proposed that Manchuria be governed by the League. However, Japan rejected this and withdrew from the League (March 1933). The question of economic sanctions, let alone military ones, was not raised, because Britain and France had serious economic problems and were reluctant to apply a trade boycott to Japan in case it led to war, which they were ill-equipped to win, especially without American help. It is possible to argue that Simon's policy was the only realistic one, but it meant that Japan had successfully defied the League, a fact which was carefully noted by Hitler and Mussolini.

(b) *The failure of the World Disarmament Conference (1932–4)*

The final collapse of the conference came when the French refused to agree that the Germans should be allowed equality of armaments with France. This gave Hitler an excuse to walk out of the conference and to take Germany out of the League, marking the end of MacDonald's great hope – to maintain peace by disarmament and collective security, working through the League. This led to the publication in March 1935 of a government White Paper called *Statement Relating to Defence*, which announced that since Britain could no longer rely on collective security, her own military strength must be built up. It was, in fact, the decision to rearm; this new policy was put into operation, though very gradually at first.

The White Paper gave Hitler the excuse to announce that he intended to introduce conscription and build the German army up to 600 000 men; both actions were breaches of Versailles. In response MacDonald, now physically almost on his last legs, met Mussolini and Laval (French Foreign Minister) at Stresa in Northern Italy; they condemned Hitler's actions and promised to resist any further unilateral breaches of treaties which might endanger the peace of Europe. This agreement was known as *the Stresa Front* (April 1935); it was significant that both the British and French carefully avoided discussion of the Abyssinian crisis which was already brewing; Mussolini took this to mean that they would turn a blind eye to an Italian attack on Abyssinia, regarding it as a bit of old-fashioned colonial expansion.

(c) *The Anglo-German Naval Agreement (June 1935)*

The Stresa Front lasted only a matter of weeks before it was broken by the naval agreement. This astonishing move occurred when Hitler, shrewdly realizing how frail the front was, offered to limit the German navy to 35 per cent of the strength of the British navy. Britain eagerly accepted this offer and even went further, allowing Germany to build up to 45 per cent of Britain's total of submarines. This agreement was reached without any consultation whatsoever with the French and Italians; it meant that Britain was condoning German rearmament, which proceeded with gathering momentum. This was Sir Samuel Hoare's first action as Foreign Secretary; his justification was that since the Germans were already breaking Versailles by building a fleet, it would be as well to have that fleet limited. However, it convinced Mussolini of Britain's cynicism and self-interest and disgusted Laval who decided there was more to be gained from co-operation with Mussolini.

(d) *The Italian invasion of Abyssinia (October 1935)*

1   It had been obvious for months that Mussolini was preparing for an invasion of Abyssinia (Ethiopia), the last major African territory not subject to European control. Abyssinia was a member of the League, and Baldwin was in the difficult position of wanting to support the League in preserving Abyssinian independence while at the same time avoiding a confrontation with Italy. The British hoped that the Stresa Front still had some meaning and wanted to use Italy as an ally against Germany, which was now perceived as the real threat to the peace of Europe. This dilemma helps to explain Britain's apparently weak and sometimes contradictory policy throughout the crisis.

2   Sir Anthony Eden, Minister for League of Nations Affairs, was sent to Rome to make an offer to Mussolini – he could take part of Abyssinia and Britain would give Italy part of neighbouring British Somaliland as compensation. Mussolini rejected this, arguing that Italy ought to have a similar position in Abyssinia to that of Britain in Egypt – a difficult point for the British to answer.

3   Sir Samuel Hoare made what sounded like a fighting speech at the League Assembly in Geneva (September 1935). Hoping to warn Mussolini off, he affirmed that Britain would support the League against acts of unprovoked aggression.

Mussolini ignored the warning and went ahead with the invasion of Abyssinia (3 October). The League, responding to a moving appeal from the Abyssinian emperor, Haile Selassie, immediately imposed economic sanctions on Italy; these included a refusal to buy Italian goods and a ban on exports of iron ore, rubber, tin, scrap iron and other metals to Italy. Britain seemed to be taking the lead in support of the League and of collective security, and public opinion generally approved.

4   With collective security apparently working, Baldwin decided that this was a good time to hold a general election (November 1935). During the campaign he told the voters 'I give you my word of honour that there will be no great armaments'; he wanted a mandate simply to 'remedy the deficiencies which have occurred in our defences'. This was what the people wanted to hear at the time, and the National Government won a convincing victory (see Section 25.3(e)); later Baldwin was accused of having deliberately misled the country by keeping quiet about the need for rearmament.

5   By the time the election was over, it was clear that the sanctions were not working; Italy had not been brought to her knees. Chamberlain suggested further sanctions to stop the export of oil and coal to Italy, which Mussolini later admitted would have forced him to make peace within a week. The cabinet rejected this idea, fearing it would provoke Mussolini to declare war, for which Britain was unprepared. The League's prestige suffered a further blow when it emerged that Hoare had been to Paris and made a secret deal with Laval (December) to hand over a large section of Abyssinia to Italy, provided military action ceased. This was more than the Italians had succeeded in capturing at the time, and when news of *the Hoare–Laval Pact* leaked out, public opinion in Britain and France was so outraged that the plan had to be dropped. Hoare, who had made the agreement without cabinet approval, resigned in disgrace. No further action was taken and by April 1936 the Italian conquest of Abyssinia was complete. In June it was decided to discontinue the ineffective economic sanctions.

6   *The results were disastrous*: the League and the idea of collective security were finally discredited; Mussolini was annoyed by the sanctions and began to be drawn towards friendship with Hitler, who had not criticized the invasion and refused to apply the sanctions; in return Mussolini dropped his objections to a German takeover of Austria; Hitler took advantage of the preoccupation with Abyssinia to send troops into the Rhineland. Baldwin's popularity slumped dramatically.

(e) *German troops reoccupy the Rhineland (March 1936)*

Since this was another breach of Versailles, Hitler gave his troops orders to withdraw at the first sign of any French opposition. No resistance was offered beyond the usual protests. Hitler, well aware of the mood of pacifism among his opponents, soothed them by offering a peace treaty for 25 years. Baldwin and Eden (the new Foreign Secretary) judged that British public opinion would not have supported military action, since the Rhineland *was* part of Germany. Indeed, Lord Londonderry (a Conservative who was Secretary of State for Air from 1931 to 1935) was reported to have sent Hitler a telegram congratulating him on his success, while Lord Lothian remarked that the German troops had merely entered their own 'back garden'.

(f) *The Spanish Civil War (1936–9)*

In June 1936 an army revolt broke out against the Spanish left-wing republican government. General Franco soon assumed the leadership of the revolt, and a quick victory was expected. However, the repubicans controlled most of the south, including Madrid, and a bitter struggle developed in which both sides committed terrible atrocities. Most of the states of Europe, including Britain, France, Germany and Italy, signed an agreement promising not to interfere in Spanish affairs. Mussolini and Hitler broke the agreement and sent extensive help to Franco – some 50 000 Italian troops and many planes, together with hundreds of German planes and tanks. In Britain opinion was divided; some left-wing groups – the ILP and the Communist Party – wanted the government to support the republic against Spanish fascism; however, the Labour Party under its new leader Clement Attlee, did not want to become involved and shrank from any action which meant co-operation with Communists. Baldwin and Chamberlain were determined on non-intervention since most of the Conservatives disapproved of the Spanish republican government with its anarchist and Communist connections. Volunteers were allowed to go – about 2000 Britons, many of them unemployed miners, fought for the Spanish republic in the International Brigade; but no official help was sent. British policy reached rock bottom in April 1938 when the Foreign Secretary, now Lord Halifax, tried to resurrect the Stresa Front by agreeing to recognize Italian possession of Abyssinia in return for the withdrawal of Italian troops from Spain. However, Mussolini ignored his side of the bargain, and the British government had been made to look weak and treacherous, condoning Mussolini's aggression and betraying the efforts of the League of Nations. Eventually Italian and German help proved decisive in securing victory for Franco.

(g) *The German occupation of Austria (March 1938)*

This was Hitler's greatest success to date. Having first reached an understanding with Mussolini (the Rome–Berlin Axis of 1936) and signed the Anti-Comintern Pact with Japan, Hitler carried out the *Anschluss* (union) with Austria, a further breach of Versailles. Matters came to a head when the Austrian Nazis staged huge demonstrations in Vienna, Graz and Linz, which Chancellor Schuschnigg's government could not control. Realizing that this could be the prelude to a German invasion, Schuschnigg announced a plebiscite (referendum) about whether or not Austria should remain independent. Hitler decided to act before this took place, in case the vote went against union; German troops moved in and Austria became part of the Third Reich. It was a triumph for Germany: it revealed the weaknesses of Britain and France who again did no more than protest; it demonstrated the value of the new understanding with Italy, and it dealt a severe strategic blow at Czechoslovakia which could now be attacked from the south as well as from the west and north (see Map 27.1). All was ready for the beginning of Hitler's campaign to acquire the German-speaking Sudetenland, a campaign which ended in further triumph at the Munich conference in September 1938.

27.3 Munich to the outbreak of war: September 1938 to September 1939

(a) *Hitler's aims*

Hitler's most pressing aims in foreign affairs when he came to power were to destroy the hated Versailles settlement, to recover lost territory such as the Saar (this was returned to Germany by a plebiscite in 1935) and the Polish Corridor, and to bring all areas containing German people within the Reich. Much of this, culminating in the annexation of Austria, had already been achieved; the rest would require the acquisi-

North Sea

Baltic Sea Danzig

LITHUANIA

EAST PRUSSIA

GERMANY

Berlin

Polish Corridor

Memel from Lithuania 1939

Rhineland remilitarised 1936

Sudetenland from Czechoslovakia at Munich 1938

POLAND

U S S R

Bohemia occupied 1939 Moravia CZECHOSLOVAKIA Ruthenia Slovakia

Saar by plebiscite 1935

Munich

AUSTRIA annexed 1938

SWITZER-LAND

HUNGARY

RUMANIA

tion of territory from Czechoslovakia and Poland, both of which had large German minorities.

There is some disagreement about what, if anything, Hitler intended beyond these aims. Most historians believe that the annexation of Austria and parts of Czechoslovakia and Poland was only a beginning, to be followed by the seizure of the rest of Czechoslovakia and Poland and by the conquest and permanent occupation of Russia as far east as the Ural Mountains. This would give him what the Germans called *Lebensraum* (living space) which would provide food for the German people and an area in which the excess German population could settle and colonize. An additional advantage was that Communism would be destroyed. However, not all historians agree about these further aims; A. J. P. Taylor, for example, claimed that Hitler never intended a major war and at most was prepared only for a limited war against Poland.

(b) *Hitler, Chamberlain and Czechoslovakia*

It seems likely that Hitler had decided to destroy Czechoslovakia as part of his *Lebensraum* policy; he hated the Czechs for their democracy and for the fact that their state had been created by the Versailles Settlement. His excuse for the opening propaganda campaign was that the 3.6 million Sudeten Germans under their leader Konrad Henlein were being discriminated against by the Czech government. It is true that unemployment *was* higher among Germans, but apart from that, they were probably not being seriously inconvenienced. The Nazis organized huge protest demonstrations in the Sudetenland and clashes occurred between Czechs and Germans. The Czech president, Benes, feared that Hitler was deliberately stirring up trouble so that German troops could march in 'to restore order'. Chamberlain and Daladier, the French Prime Minister, both feared that war between Germany and Czechoslovakia was imminent.

It was now that Chamberlain took the initiative. He was determined to play a lead-ing role in international affairs, and felt it his duty to go to almost any lengths to pre-vent war. His aim was to prevail upon the Czech government to offer Hitler concessions which would make a German invasion unnecessary. Under pressure, Benes agreed that the Sudeten Germans might be detached from Germany. Chamberlain flew to Germany and had talks with Hitler at Berchtesgaden (15 September) explaining the offer. Hitler seemed to accept, but at a second meeting at Godesberg (22 September) he stepped up his demands: he wanted more of Czechoslovakia and the immediate entry of German troops to the Sudetenland. This Benes would not agree to, and he immediately ordered the mobilization of the Czech army.

When it seemed that war was inevitable, Hitler invited Chamberlain and Daladier to a four-power conference which met at Munich (29 September). Here a plan pro-duced by Mussolini (but drafted by the German Foreign Office) was accepted. The Sudetenland was to be handed over to Germany immediately, but Germany along with the other three powers guaranteed the remainder of Czechoslovakia. Neither the Czechs nor the Russians were invited to the conference; the Czechs were told that if they resisted the Munich decision, they would receive no help from Britain or France, even though at Locarno the French had guaranteed the Czech frontiers.

The following morning Chamberlain had a private meeting with Hitler at which they both signed a statement, 'the scrap of paper', prepared by Chamberlain, promising that Britain and Germany would renounce warlike intentions against each other and

Illus. 27.1   On his return from Munich, Neville Chamberlain waves the 'scrap of paper' containing Hitler's promise of peace

would use consultation 'to deal with any other question that may concern our two countries'. When Chamberlain arrived back in Britain, waving the 'scrap of paper' for the benefit of the newsreel cameras at Heston airfield, he received a rapturous welcome from the public, which thought war had been averted. Chamberlain himself remarked: 'I believe it is peace for our time'. However, not everybody was so enthusiastic: Churchill called Munich 'a total and unmitigated defeat', and Alfred Duff Cooper, the First Lord of the Admiralty, resigned from the cabinet saying that Hitler could not be trusted to keep the agreement. It is open to debate as to whether Chamberlain really understood the sort of man Hitler was; he persisted in treating him as a responsible statesman and ignored his ill-treatment of the Jews and the mass of evidence (for example, the way he increased his demands at Godesberg when he realized how committed Chamberlain was to maintaining peace at all costs) suggesting that Hitler was not reliable. On his return from Godesberg, Chamberlain told the cabinet that he had established some influence over Hitler, a man who would be 'rather better than his word'.

Duff Cooper and Churchill were right; Czechoslovakia was crippled by the loss of 70 per cent of her heavy industry and almost all her fortifications to Germany. Slovakia began to demand semi-independence, and when it looked as though the country was about to fall apart, Hitler pressurized President Hacha into requesting German help 'to restore order'. Consequently in March 1939 German troops occupied the rest of Czechoslovakia. Britain and France protested but took no action: according to Chamberlain, the guarantee of Czech frontiers did not apply because technically Czechoslovakia had not been invaded: German troops had entered by invitation. However, the German action caused a great outburst of criticism: for the first time the appeasers were unable to justify what Hitler had done – he had broken his promise and seized non-German territory. Even Chamberlain and Halifax felt this was going too far, and their attitude hardened.

(c) *Hitler, Chamberlain and Poland*

After taking over the Lithuanian port of Memel (which was admittedly peopled largely by Germans), Hitler turned his attentions to Poland. The Germans resented the loss of Danzig and the Polish Corridor at Versailles, and now that Czechoslovakia was safely out of the way, Polish neutrality was no longer necessary. At the end of March 1939, Chamberlain, still outraged at the German occupation of Prague, wrote to the Polish government promising that if their independence was threatened, Britain and France 'would at once lend them all the support in their power'. In April Hitler demanded the return of Danzig and a road and railway across the Corridor. This demand was, in fact, not unreasonable since Danzig was largely German-speaking; but coming so soon after the seizure of Czechoslovakia, the Poles were convinced, probably rightly, that the German demands were only a prelude to invasion. Already fortified by the British promise of help, the Polish Foreign Minister, Colonel Beck, rejected the German demands and refused to attend a conference, no doubt afraid of another Munich. Chamberlain now began to have second thoughts as the threat of war increased again. Britain urged the Poles to surrender Danzig, but Beck stood firm.

Meanwhile there was pressure from certain quarters in Britain for some sort of alliance with the USSR. The Labour party, Lloyd George and Churchill all pointed out that the promise of British help to Poland was meaningless without military help from the Russians, who could threaten Germany's eastern frontier. Stalin was anxious for an understanding with Britain and negotiations opened in April 1939. However, both Chamberlain and Halifax detested Communism and were sceptical of Russia's military strength. An added difficulty was that the Poles were as nervous of the Russians as they were of the Germans, and would not agree to Russian troops crossing Poland to take up positions on the frontier with Germany. The negotiations dragged on without any result, and in the end the Russians grew tired of British stalling and signed a non-aggression pact with Hitler (24 August). Also agreed at the same time was a partition of Poland between Germany and the USSR, though this was kept secret.

Hitler was now convinced that with Russia neutral, Britain and France would not risk intervention; when the British ratified their guarantee to Poland, Hitler took it as a bluff. When the Poles still refused to negotiate, a full-scale German invasion began early on 1 September 1939. Chamberlain had not completely thrown off appeasement and still shrank from committing Britain to war. He suggested that if German troops were withdrawn, a conference could be held – there was no response from the Germans. Only when pressure mounted in parliament and in the country did Chamberlain send an ultimatum to Germany. When this expired at 11 a.m. on 3 September, Britain was at war with Germany. Soon afterwards France also declared war.

(d) Britain's defences

Britain had never begun actively to disarm, though in the years before Hitler came to power, the government had been spending progressively less each year on armaments. For example the Conservatives had spent £116 million in 1926–7, Labour £110 million in 1930–1, and the National Government £103 million in 1932–3. As soon as Hitler became German Chancellor (January 1933) Churchill pressed the government to build up Britain's armaments, and especially her air defences. He warned that if war broke out, Britain would be subjected to heavy bombing: 'the crash of bombs exploding in London, and cataracts of masonry and fire and smoke will warn us of any inadequacy in our aerial defences'. The government responded, though slowly. In July 1930 it was announced that over the next five years an extra 820 planes would be built, bringing the strength of the RAF up to 1304 front-line planes. Churchill thought this inadequate; in May 1935 Hitler told Simon that his airforce was already larger than Britain's. This was an exaggeration, but it helped to speed up British rearmament, especially after German troops entered the Rhineland (March 1936).

Until Munich, German rearmament was much more rapid than Britain's; in 1937–8 Britain spent £350 million on armaments, whereas Germany spent £1600 million. At the end of that year Germany had 2800 front-line planes, Britain still fewer than 1000. After Munich Chamberlain was responsible for a dramatic surge in arms production, though it was only in the spring of 1940 that British aircraft production overtook that of Germany, and Germany was still in the lead at that point. There was also a fourfold increase in the numbers of anti-aircraft guns; perhaps the most vital of all in the air-defence system was the building up of a chain of 20 radar stations to track enemy planes.

However, there are still doubts about how committed Chamberlain really was. Cabinet papers and Chamberlain's letters show that he hoped Munich would turn out to be a permanent understanding with Germany, so that rearmament would be unnecessary. With unemployment approaching two million on the eve of war, Britain was certainly not rearming to full capacity.

27.4 Who or what was to blame for the war?

The debate is still going on about who or what was responsible for the Second World War.

- The Versailles treaties have been blamed for filling the Germans with bitterness and the desire for revenge, while at the same time leaving the states of central Europe (Czechoslovakia, Poland, Austria, Hungary) too weak and divided to be able to defend themselves against Hitler.
- The League of Nations and the idea of collective security have been criticized because they failed to secure general disarmament and to control potential aggressors.
- The world economic crisis has been mentioned, since without it, Hitler would probably never have come to power.

While these factors no doubt helped to create the sort of tensions which might well lead to war, something more was needed. It is worth remembering that by the end of 1938 many of Germany's grievances had been removed: reparations were largely cancelled, the disarmament clauses had been ignored, the Rhineland was remilitarized, Austria and Germany were united, and 3.6 million Germans had been brought into the Reich from Czechoslovakia. Britain had even offered some compensation for lost German colonies. Germany was, in fact, a great power again. So what went wrong?

(a) *Was Hitler to blame?*

During and immediately after the war there was general agreement outside Germany that Hitler was to blame. By attacking Poland on all fronts instead of merely occupying Danzig and the Corridor, Hitler showed that he intended not just to get back the German areas lost at Versailles, but to destroy Poland. Martin Gilbert argues that his motive was to remove the stigma of defeat in the First World War; 'for the only antidote to defeat in one war is victory in the next'. Hugh Trevor-Roper and many other historians believe that Hitler intended a major war right from the beginning. They argue that he hated Communism and wanted to destroy the USSR and control it permanently; this could only be achieved by a major war. The destruction of Poland was an essential preliminary to the invasion of Russia. The German non-aggression pact with Russia was simply a way of lulling Russian suspicions and keeping her neutral until Poland had been dealt with.

Evidence for this theory is taken from statements in Hitler's book *Mein Kampf* (*My Struggle*) and from the Hossbach Memorandum, a summary made by Hitler's adjutant, Colonel Hossbach, of a meeting held in November 1937, at which Hitler explained his plans to his generals. Another important source of evidence is Hitler's *Secret Book* which he finished around 1928 but never published.

If this theory is correct, appeasement cannot be blamed as a cause of war, except that it made things easier for Hitler. Hitler had his plans, his 'blueprint' for action, and this meant that war was inevitable sooner or later. Germans, on the whole, were happy with this interpretation too. If Hitler was to blame, and Hitler and the Nazis could be viewed as a kind of grotesque accident, a temporary 'blip' in German history, that meant that the German people were largely free from blame.

However, it seems certain that Hitler had no intention of starting a *world war*. He believed that Poland and Russia were weak and would be swiftly knocked out by lightning strikes (*Blitzkrieg*).

(b) *Were the appeasers to blame?*

Some historians claim that appeasement was equally to blame. Their theory is that Hitler was prepared to get what he wanted either by war or by diplomatic means. They argue that Britain and France ought to have taken a firm line with Hitler before Germany became too strong: an Anglo-French attack on western Germany in 1936 at the time of the Rhineland occupation would have taught Hitler a lesson and might have toppled him from power. By giving way to him, the appeasers increased his prestige at home; with each success Hitler's position became progressively stronger and he became increasingly contemptuous of the western powers. As Alan Bullock writes: 'success and the absence of resistance tempted Hitler to reach out further, to take bigger risks'. He may not have had definite plans for war, but after the surrender at Munich, he was so convinced that Britain and France would remain passive again, that he decided to gamble on war with Poland.

Chamberlain has also been criticized for choosing the wrong issue over which to make a stand against Hitler. It is argued that German claims for Danzig and routes across the Corridor were more reasonable than her demands for the Sudetenland (which contained almost a million non-Germans and had never been part of Germany). Poland was difficult for Britain and France to defend and was militarily much weaker than Czechoslovakia. Chamberlain therefore should have made his stand at Munich and backed the Czechs.

Chamberlain's defenders claim that his main motive at Munich was to give Britain time to rearm for an eventual fight against Hitler. Philip M. Taylor makes the point that it was only during the year after Munich that Hitler gave proof that he intended to achieve his aims by force: 'the forceful incorporation into Germany of Czechs and Slovaks in March 1939 demonstrated what kind of man Hitler was ... this proof was essential if a vulnerable British public was to enter the war united behind the government'. But Chamberlain's critics point out that if he had genuinely intended to curb Hitler, it would have been better for Britain and France to have fought alongside Czechoslovakia, which was militarily and industrially strong and had excellent fortifications.

(c) A. J. P. Taylor and his 'Origins'

A. J. P. Taylor, in his book *Origins of the Second World War* (1961), came up with the most controversial theory about the outbreak of the war. He believed that Hitler did not intend to cause a major war, and expected at the most, a short war with Poland. According to Taylor, Hitler's aims were similar to those of previous German rulers – Wilhelm II and Stresemann; only his methods were more ruthless. Hitler was a brilliant opportunist taking advantage of the mistakes of the appeasers and of events such as the crisis in Czechoslovakia in February 1939. Taylor thought the occupation of the rest of Czechoslovakia in March 1939 was not the result of a sinister long-term plan: 'it was the unforeseen by-product of events in Slovakia' (the Slovak demand for more independence from the Prague government). Whereas Chamberlain miscalculated when he thought he could civilize Hitler, Hitler misread the minds of Chamberlain and the British. How could Hitler foresee that the British and French would be so inconsistent as to support Poland (where his claim was much more reasonable) after giving way to him over Czechoslovakia (where his case was much less valid)?

Thus, for Taylor, Hitler was lured into the war almost by accident after the Poles had called his bluff. Many people in Britain were outraged at Taylor because they thought he was trying to 'whitewash' Hitler. But Taylor was not defending Hitler; just the opposite in fact – Hitler was still to blame, and so were the German people, for being aggressive.

> Hitler was the creation of German history and of the German present. He would have counted for nothing without the support and cooperation of the German people.... Many hundred thousand Germans carried out his evil orders without qualm or question.

(d) *Did the USSR make war inevitable?*

The USSR has been accused of making war inevitable by signing the non-aggression pact with Germany. It is argued that she ought to have allied with the west and with Poland, thus frightening Hitler into keeping the peace. On the other hand, it has to be remembered that *Stalin wanted an agreement with Britain*; it was the British who delayed and stalled and were most reluctant to ally with the Russians. Like the Poles, Chamberlain distrusted them (because they were Communists), and he thought they were militarily weak. Russian historians justify the pact on the grounds that it gave the USSR time to prepare its defences against a possible German attack.

What conclusion are we to reach? Today, well over 30 years after Taylor published his famous book, very few historians accept his theory that Hitler had no long-term plans for war. Some recent writers believe that Taylor ignored a lot of evidence which did not fit in with his own theory. Hitler *was* largely responsible for the war. As D. C. Watt puts it: Hitler's 'will for war was able to overcome the reluctance with which virtually everybody else approached it. Hitler willed, desired, lusted after war. No-one else wanted it.... The record of the British and French cabinets ... is neither a happy nor an edifying spectacle. But it is really open to doubt whether any alternative course would have made any difference.'

Questions

1   Munich and appeasement

Study Sources A to C and answer the questions which follow.

Source A

The memoirs of Hugh Dalton, a Labour MP in 1939 and a supporter of rearmament

There has been much propaganda on behalf of Chamberlain that 'he gained a precious year', that Britain was much stronger in September 1939 than in September 1938. I have little doubt that *we lost a precious year....* First we lost the Czechs who had a million and a half men behind the strongest fortress line in Europe, and equipped by a highly organized and powerful industrial machine. They also had a formidable Air Force. An attack on Czechoslovakia would have absorbed a large part of the German Army and Air Force, in addition to which, considerable German forces would have been needed on the French and Polish frontiers.... At that time the Germans were not well equipped with tanks and other armour. All that came later, much of it taken from the Czech Army and some produced in Czech arsenals.... The machines with which the Germans overran Poland and France were captured or constructed in the year 'gained' by Chamberlain at Munich or in the eight months of the 'Phoney War'.... Though the weakness of the British Air Force compared with the German was a terrible fact, yet the Germans were farther away in 1938 than in 1940 when they overran Holland and France. Their bombers attacking Britain would have had much farther to fly in 1938, and without fighter escort.

Source: H. Dalton, *The Fateful Years*, Muller, 1957.

The memoirs of Lord Halifax, the Foreign Secretary 1938–40

Once the Austrian *Anschluss* had taken place, *it was no longer possible to defend Czechoslovakia.* . . . When all has been said, one fact remains unchallengeable. When war did come a year after Munich, it found a country and Commonwealth wholly united and prepared, and convinced that every conceivable effort had been made to avoid war. And that was the big thing that Chamberlain did.

Source: Lord Halifax, *Fullness of Days*, Collins, 1967.

__ Source C __

Letter from Neville Chamberlain to Stanley Baldwin, 17 October 1940

Never for one single instant have I doubted the rightness of what I did at Munich. Nor can I believe that it was possible for me to do more than I did to prepare the country for war after Munich. I still further increased the programme for a larger Air Force and I began all the Air Raid Precaution measures which have developed since. I also introduced Conscription. In Sept. '38 we only had 60 fire pumps in London, which would have been burned out in a week. Some day these things will be known. My critics differed from me because they were ignorant, it is only fair to add, deliberately ignorant in many cases. So I regret nothing in the past.

Source: quoted in K. Feiling, *The Life of Neville Chamberlain*, Macmillan, 1947.

(a) From the evidence in Source B and the information in Chapter 27, explain why Lord Halifax thought it was no longer possible to defend Czechoslovakia.
(3 marks)

(b) On the basis of the evidence in the sources and your own knowledge, how valid is the judgement expressed in Source A that 'we lost a precious year' because of Munich? (10 marks)

(c) What do you think are the main strengths and weaknesses of these three sources for the historian? (6 marks)

(d) To what extent do you think appeasement helped to cause the Second World War? (11 marks)
(Total 30 marks)

2 (a) To what extent was the British policy of appeasement in the 1930s evident before Chamberlain became Prime Minister (May 1937)? (8 marks)

(b) How far was Chamberlain's policy of appeasement in 1937–8 defensible?
(12 marks)
(Total 20 marks)

Britain and the Second World War 1939–45

Summary of events

Though Britain had declared war on Germany ostensibly to help Poland, there was very little that Britain herself could do; her army was minute in comparison with those of Germany and France. It would be possible to send only a token force to the western front, until a larger army had been assembled. Until then it would be a question of defending Britain against whatever Hitler decided to throw against her; most people expected immediate bombing raids, as Churchill had prophesied in 1934. However, there was a long delay, and it was July 1940 before the expected onslaught on Britain arrived. There were other surprises too: unlike the 1914–18 war, the Second World War was a war of rapid movement and was altogether a more complex affair. Major campaigns took place in western and central Europe, in the heart of Russia, in Burma and the Far East and in the Pacific and Atlantic Oceans. *The war falls into four fairly clearly defined phases:*

1 Opening moves: September 1939 to December 1940

By the end of September the Germans and Russians had defeated and occupied Poland. After a five-month pause (known as the 'phoney war'), the Germans took over Denmark and Norway (April 1940). A British attempt to dislodge them failed and caused Chamberlain to be replaced as Prime Minister by Winston Churchill who proved to be an outstanding war leader, like Lloyd George in the First World War. In May the Germans attacked Holland, Belgium and France, which were soon defeated, leaving Britain alone to face the dictators (Mussolini had declared war in June just before the fall of France). Hitler's attempt to bomb Britain into submission was thwarted in *the Battle of Britain* (July to September 1940), but Mussolini's armies invaded Egypt and Greece.

2 The Axis offensive widens: 1941 to summer 1942

The war now began to develop into a world-wide conflict. First Hitler, confident of victory over Britain, launched an invasion of Russia (June 1941), breaking the non-aggression pact signed less than two years previously. Then the Japanese forced the USA into the war by attacking the American naval base at Pearl Harbor (December 1941) and followed this by capturing the British territories of Hong Kong, Singapore, Malaya and Burma, as well as the Philippine Islands. At this stage of the war there seemed to be no way of stopping the Germans and Japanese, though the Italians were less successful.

3 The offensives held in check: summer 1942 to summer 1943

This phase of the war saw three important battles in which Axis forces were defeated:

● In June 1942 the Americans drove off a Japanese attack on *Midway Island*, inflicting heavy losses.
● In October, the Germans, advancing into Egypt, were halted by the British at *El Alamein* and later driven out of North Africa.
● The third battle was in Russia where, by September 1942, the Germans had penetrated as far as *Stalingrad*. Here the Russians put up such a fierce resistance that the following February, the German army was surrounded and compelled to surrender.

Meanwhile the war in the air continued with both sides bombing enemy cities, and at sea, where, as in the First World War, the British and Americans gradually got the better of the German submarine menace.

4 The Axis powers defeated: July 1943 to August 1945

The enormous power and resources of the USA and the USSR, combined with an all-out effort from Britain and her empire, slowly but surely wore the Axis powers down. Italy was eliminated first and this was followed by an Anglo-American invasion of Normandy (June 1944) which liberated France, Belgium and Holland. Later Allied troops crossed the Rhine and captured Cologne. In the east the Russians drove the Germans out and advanced on Berlin via Poland. Germany surrendered in May 1945 and Japan in August, after the Americans had dropped two atomic bombs, one on Hiroshima and one on Nagasaki.

28.1 Early setbacks: Norway and Dunkirk

(a) *The defeat of Poland and the 'phoney war'*

The Poles were swiftly defeated by the German *Blitzkrieg* (lightning war); this consisted of rapid thrusts by motorized divisions and tanks (*Panzers*) with air support; the *Luftwaffe* (the German Air Force) put the Polish railway system out of action and destroyed the Polish Air Force. This was the first demonstration of the vital role which air support was destined to play in the war. Polish resistance was heroic but hopeless; they had no motorized divisions and attempted to stem the German advance by massed cavalry charges. Britain and France did little to help their ally directly, because French mobilization procedure was slow and it was difficult to transport sufficient troops to Poland to be effective.

The main British actions were to begin a blockade of German ports, as in the First World War, in the hope that Hitler would soon lose heart, and to send troops across to France. Chamberlain brought Churchill into his War Cabinet as First Lord of the Admiralty, and there were several successful naval actions, including the defeat of the German pocket battleship *Graf Spee* by three British cruisers. It was soon clear though that the submarine was to be just as much of a menace as in the previous war: in October a U-boat slipped through the defences at the Scapa Flow naval base in the Orkneys and sank the battleship *Royal Oak*. However, throughout the winter of 1939–40 there was no large-scale military action; this led American journalists to call it the 'phoney war'.

(b) *German victory in Norway*

On 4 April 1940, Chamberlain said that Hitler had 'missed the bus', but his complacency was rudely shattered a few days later when Hitler's troops occupied Denmark and landed at the main Norwegian ports. Control of Norway was important for the Germans because Narvik was the main outlet for Swedish iron ore bound for Germany, which was vital for her armaments industry. The British were interfering with this trade by mining Norwegian coastal waters, and the Germans were afraid that they might occupy some of Norway's ports, as they were indeed planning to do. Admiral Raeder, the German navy chief, realized that the fjords would be excellent naval bases from which to attack Britain's trans-Atlantic supply lines. When a British destroyer chased the German vessel *Altmark* into a Norwegian fjord and rescued 300 British prisoners who were on board, Hitler decided it was time to act. On 9 April the Germans landed at Oslo, Kristiansand, Stavanger, Bergen and Trondheim; although British and French troops arrived a few days later, they were unable to dislodge the Germans, who were already well established. After a temporary success at Narvik, all Allied troops were withdrawn by early June because of the growing threat to France itself.

The Germans were successful because the Norwegian forces were not even mobilized, and local Nazis, under their leader Vidkun Quisling, gave the invaders every assistance. In addition, the British had no air support, whereas the German Air Force constantly harassed the Allies.

The Norwegian campaign had important results: Germany was assured of her bases and her iron ore supplies, but had lost three cruisers and ten destroyers, which rendered the navy less effective at Dunkirk than it might have been. It showed up the incompetence of Chamberlain's government which, in the words of Churchill, had been 'forestalled, surprised and outwitted'. In the Commons debate on the campaign it became clear that a large section of the Conservatives was turning against Chamberlain and wanted a more decisive leader. Leo Amery, quoting Oliver Cromwell's remarks to the Long Parliament, told Chamberlain: 'You have sat too long here for any good you have been doing. Depart, I say, and let us have done with you. In the name of God, go.' In the division Chamberlain's majority dropped to 81 instead of the usual 240, and he resigned soon afterwards, expecting Lord Halifax, the Foreign Secretary, to succeed him. Halifax did not seem anxious for the job, and it was Churchill who formed a new government, on the same day (10 May) that Hitler's forces attacked Holland, France and Belgium.

(c) *Churchill as war leader*

Aged 65 when he became Prime Minister, Churchill was generally regarded as something of a failure in his parliamentary career so far. In 1970, when historian and Conservative MP Robert Rhodes James wrote his biography of Churchill covering the years 1900 to 1939, he subtitled it *A Study in Failure*. Churchill was blamed for using troops to disperse rioting Welsh miners at Tonypandy (1910), though in fact the troops were not used and the job was done by unarmed police. He was blamed for the failure of the Gallipoli campaign (1915), for his mistaken revaluation of the pound (1925), for his aggressiveness during the General Strike (1926), for his opposition to the India Act (1935) and for his support of Edward VIII (1936). For all these reasons, it was thought that his judgement was questionable. He had changed parties – from Conservative to Liberal and back to Conservative again – so that many regarded him as unreliable and inconsistent. However, two things he had always been consistent about were the need to rearm and the need to stand up to Hitler. His aggressiveness, which had so often seemed inappropriate in peacetime, was exactly the quality needed for an effective war leader. As A. J. P. Taylor put it, 'it was as if all his life had been an unconscious preparation for this hour'.

Churchill set up a War Cabinet of five men: himself as Prime Minister and Minister of Defence, Neville Chamberlain (who died in November 1940), Halifax, and from the Labour party, Clement Attlee and Arthur Greenwood. Churchill became leader of the Conservative party on Chamberlain's death; he later brought into the cabinet Beaverbrook as Minister of Aircraft Production, and Ernest Bevin as Minister of Labour. Other Labour men included were Herbert Morrison and Hugh Dalton, while the Liberal leader, Sir Archibald Sinclair, became Air Minister. It was a genuinely national government which turned out to be extremely effective, steering Britain through a very difficult year when she stood alone against Germany and Italy (June 1940 to June 1941), and organizing the entire nation, including the civilian population, to meet the demands of 'total war'. *The Emergency Powers Act (May 1940)*, which was rushed through parliament in one day, gave the government almost unrestricted power over all British citizens and their property; whatever action was thought necessary could be taken.

Some historians took the chance provided by the 50th anniversaries of key events in the war to offer reassessments of Churchill's war leadership, some of them not very complimentary. Andrew Roberts, in his book *Eminent Churchillians* (1993), makes much of Churchill's mistakes during the war, while John Charmley is even more controversially harsh in two books – *Churchill: The End of Glory* (1993), in which he outraged many people by suggesting that Churchill would have done better for Britain if he had secured a negotiated peace in 1940 (see Source G in question 1 at the end of the chapter), and *Churchill's Grand Alliance* (1995). A more balanced view is presented in a collection of 29 essays edited by Robert Blake and William Roger Louis, entitled *Churchill: A Major New Assessment of his Life in Peace and War* (1993). Eleven of the essays are devoted to aspects of Churchill's role during the Second World War. In their introduction the editors argue that the choice of Churchill as Prime Minister in May 1940 was one of the most crucial decisions in modern British history (see Source F in question 1). The general conclusion seems to be that although Churchill certainly made mistakes, in the end that does not detract from his 'greatness' as a war leader. David Reynolds (in chapter 14 of the collection – 'Churchill in 1940') claims that 'recognition of Churchill's remarkable role in 1940 must be balanced by acknowledgement that he was not always right in his decisions … [however] a sober examination of Churchill's performance as war leader in 1940 does not belittle his greatness. On the contrary, it makes him a more human and thereby a more impressive figure than the two-dimensional bulldog of national mythology. Churchill's greatness is that of a man, not an icon.'

Churchill dealt with general strategy and diplomacy; his mind was brimming with original ideas, some of which were impractical and even dangerous. The Chief of the Imperial General Staff, Sir Alan Brooke (from the end of 1941), spent much of his energy persuading Churchill to drop some of his wilder suggestions (see Source C). Even so, mistakes were made: possibly his most serious error was to completely underestimate the aggressiveness and the strength of the Japanese and he would not be swayed from his conviction that 'Fortress Singapore' was impregnable. He must therefore take much of the responsibility for the loss of Singapore, and he was at least partly responsible for the defeats in Libya. He was very slow to appreciate the importance of air support in naval operations and underestimated the deadliness of aircraft to large surface vessels – hence the disaster off Crete (see Section 28.3(a)).

On the other hand, the great advantage of Churchill's methods was that they kept all the military leaders constantly on the alert, so that failures became fewer as the war went on. According to Michael Carver (in chapter 20 of the collection – 'Churchill and the Defence Chiefs'), 'up to the end Churchill maintained his "ceaseless prodding", inveighing against the caution of generals ... in the last years of the war, the military leaders, not least Brooke, Alexander, Montgomery and Mountbatten, had learned how to deal with Churchill: never to complain about the "ceaseless prodding"; to stand firm but to keep him sweet by a constant stream of information and by an adroit balance of flattery, cajolery and frankness. They knew that they could not do without him, and did not want to, and he knew that they were indispensable to him.'

Churchill's greatest contribution to the war effort was the sheer impact of his larger-than-life personality and his will to win. He provided an all-important psychological boost to a country which, within a few days of his taking office, seemed on the verge of defeat. For a 65-year-old, he had remarkable physical vitality and mental energy; he was full of bulldog pugnacity, and everybody soon realized that with Churchill in command, decisive action would be taken. He actually seemed to be enjoying himself and this came over in his broadcasts. He had a brilliant command of words, and his speeches in the Commons and particularly over the radio were highly effective. He spoke in language ordinary people could understand, rallying the nation in one supreme co-operative effort – the Dunkirk spirit. He left people in no doubt about what to expect; three days after becoming premier he told them: 'I have nothing to offer you but blood, toil, tears and sweat.' Britain's war aim was simple: 'Victory – victory at all costs, victory in spite of all terror, victory, however long and hard the road may be; come then, let us go forward together with our united strength.' With a man like this in charge, the majority of people did not think about defeat.

(d) *Dunkirk and the fall of France (May–June 1940)*

German troops attacked Holland, Belgium and France simultaneously on 10 May, and again *Blitzkrieg* methods brought swift victories. The Dutch, shaken by the bombing of Rotterdam which killed almost a thousand people, surrendered after only four days. Belgium held out longer, but her surrender at the end of May left the British and French troops in Belgium trapped in a pincer movement as German motorized divisions swept across northern France; only Dunkirk remained in Allied hands. The British navy played the vital role in evacuating over 338 000 troops, two-thirds of them British, from Dunkirk between 27 May and 4 June. This was a remarkable achievement in the face of constant *Luftwaffe* attacks on the beaches; it would perhaps have been impossible if Hitler had not ordered the German advance towards Dunkirk to halt (24 May) probably because the marshy terrain and numerous canals were unsuitable for tanks.

The events at Dunkirk were important: a third of a million troops were rescued to fight again, and Churchill used it for propaganda purposes to boost British morale with the 'Dunkirk spirit'. In reality it was a serious blow for the Allies: the armies at Dunkirk had lost all their arms and equipment, so that it became impossible for Britain to help France. The British government unfairly tried to blame the disaster on king Leopold of the Belgians for his 'treachery' in surrendering when he did, and equally unfairly criticized the French for their 'panic and cowardice'.

Churchill flew to France several times to try and rally the government, and even offered them an Act of Union to turn Britain and France into one nation. But the position was hopeless. The Germans now swept southwards; Paris was captured on 14 June and France surrendered on the 22nd. At Hitler's insistence the armistice was signed at Compiègne, in the same railway coach which had been used for the 1918 armistice. The Germans occupied northern France and the Atlantic coast, giving them valuable submarine bases, and the French army was demobilized. Unoccupied France was allowed its own government under Marshal Petain at Vichy, but it had no real independence

Map 28.1 German attacks in May 1940

Illus. 28.1 British troops waiting to be rescued from the beach at Dunkirk

and collaborated with the Germans. The fall of France was the high-water mark of Hitler's achievements. Britain and her empire stood completely alone against the dictators, and Hitler immediately began to prepare for Operation Sealion – the invasion of Britain.

What the general public did not know at the time, but which is now clear from sources which have become available more recently, is that during the last week of May the British cabinet seriously discussed the possibility of opening peace negotiations with Nazi Germany. Churchill was determined to fight on, at least for a few months, but Halifax, who thought the war was already lost, wanted to appeal to Mussolini (who was still neutral) to act as a mediator. Chamberlain agreed with him about the need to put out peace feelers, but crucially, did not believe that an approach via Mussolini would bring 'decent terms'; so the war must continue for the time being. Attlee and Greenwood were in full agreement with Churchill, and Halifax had been outmanoeuvred. However, during the summer of 1940 Halifax continued to make unofficial soundings via the British embassy in Stockholm about what German peace terms might be. Eventually Halifax was dropped from the War Cabinet and sent as ambassador to the USA.

28.2 The Battle of Britain (August–September 1940)

(a) *Hitler prepares to invade Britain*

In July Hitler began to assemble an invasion fleet of barges to carry the first wave of 260 000 troops which would be landed between Brighton and Folkstone. But he had his problems: he had neglected the German navy, not really expecting a full-scale war with Britain; it was therefore up to the *Luftwaffe* to clear the British navy out of the Channel and destroy the RAF so that the invasion could go ahead unhindered. In one of his most stirring broadcasts, Churchill warned of the vital importance of what was about to happen:

> Hitler knows that he will have to break us in this island or lose the war. If we can stand up to him, all Europe may be free and the life of the world may move forward into broad, sunlit uplands. But if we fail, then the whole world, all that we have known and cared for, will sink into the abyss of a new Dark Age. . . . Let us therefore brace ourselves to our duties, and so bear ourselves that, if the British Empire and its Commonwealth last for a thousand years, men will say, 'This was their finest hour'.

Already in July the *Luftwaffe* was attacking convoys in the Channel, though without much success; the Germans lost twice as many aircraft as the RAF lost fighters. In August the *Luftwaffe* switched to bombing RAF aerodromes and communication systems. On 8 August there were the fiercest battles so far: the RAF shot down 31 German planes, and lost 20 themselves. On 12 August the radar station at Ventnor (Isle of Wight) was put out of action, but shortly afterwards Goering, head of the *Luftwaffe*, called off these attacks, underestimating the importance of radar. The Germans made their greatest effort on 15 August, believing that the British must soon run out of fighters; but again their losses were heavy – 75 to 34 British.

Illus. 28.2   Winston Churchill inspecting air-raid damage, September 1940

(b) *The failure of the Luftwaffe*

The crucial period of the battle was the fortnight from 24 August to 6 September. The RAF began to lose heavily – on 6 September alone they lost 161 planes against 190 German planes shot down. Many of the British fighters were bombed on the ground, and the aircraft factories could not keep up with losses of this magnitude. Also serious was the loss of pilots – during that fortnight 103 were killed and 129 wounded; again it was impossible to make up these losses with experienced pilots. Six out of seven major airfields in the south-east were badly damaged. Then, not realizing how close they were to victory, Goering switched to bombing London and other large cities, in retaliation, it was claimed, for a British raid on Berlin. He was hoping to destroy civilian morale and reduce industrial production; but although enormous damage was caused and thousands of civilians were killed, the German bombers suffered heavy casualties in daytime raids and were forced to change to night bombing.

After the shock of the first raids in the 'blitz' (over a thousand people were killed in the first three days in London), morale rallied well as the civilian population soon learned how to cope with the resulting chaos and disruption. On 15 September the Germans lost 60 aircraft to Britain's 26. The Germans had failed to gain air superiority, and two days later Hitler called off the invasion of Britain. Bombing raids continued until May 1941 when Hitler was almost ready to launch his attack on Russia. The Battle of Britain is usually taken as finishing at the end of September, when it was clear that Britain had been saved from a German invasion. There has been some dispute about exactly how many planes were lost by both sides during the battle. At the time the British claimed that between 12 August and the end of September the RAF destroyed

2700 German aircraft, while Goering claimed 3000 British planes shot down. It is now clear that both these figures, especially the German one, were exaggerated for propaganda purposes. The true figures were something like 1100 German planes destroyed against 650 lost by the RAF.

(c) *Reasons for the British victory*

Vitally important was the chain of 51 radar stations which gave plenty of warning of German attacks; this worked right through the battle and the Germans failed to realize the importance of disrupting the system. German bombers were poorly armed and German Messerschmitt fighters, though not significantly inferior to the British Spitfires and Hurricanes, were hampered by limited range; they carried enough fuel for 90 minutes' flight, which gave them only a few minutes over London before they had to head for home. The switch to bombing London was a major error, because although it caused great damage and loss of life, it relieved pressure on British airfields and fighters at the critical moment. British aircraft production was highly effective; monthly output of fighters had been running at 250 early in the war, but this increased to 325 in May 1940 and reached a peak of 496 in July; even in September at the height of the blitz, 467 were produced. The Germans could not match this, and Britain always had more reserves than the *Luftwaffe*. Finally there was the skill and spirit of the fighter pilots and the careful strategy of Air Marshals Dowding and Park. As Churchill remarked when he paid them tribute: 'Never in the field of human conflict was so much owed by so many to so few.'

(d) *Importance of the Battle of Britain*

For the first time in the war the Germans had been checked; this showed that they were not completely invincible, and was therefore probably the first major turning-point of the war. To the general surprise of the rest of the world, Britain was able to remain in the struggle and her prestige stood high. It meant that Hitler, who was poised to begin his invasion of Russia, would be faced with war on two fronts, a situation which had proved fatal to Germany in the First World War.

28.3 The Axis offensive widens

As the war developed into a world-wide conflict during 1941, Britain, having survived the immediate danger of invasion, now had to counter the threat to her empire – in Egypt and the Far East.

(a) *Greece and Crete*

Mussolini, who had already captured Albania, wanted a large Balkan empire. His forces invaded Greece (September 1940) but were soon driven back into Albania. Mussolini was clearly going to be an embarrassment to Hitler, who began 1941 by helping out his faltering ally. Churchill decided to support Greece as a matter of prestige, to encourage other countries such as the USA and Turkey to enter the struggle. 60 000 British, Australian and New Zealand troops arrived in Greece, only to be driven out immediately by a massive German invasion which soon overran the Greek mainland (April 1941). The Allies withdrew to the Greek island of Crete which had been under British occupation for six months. However, they had failed to fortify the island adequately, and it was captured by the Germans in a spectacular parachute attack, which forced the Allies to withdraw again, with heavy losses (June). They had no air protection, and lost some 36 000 men with their equipment. The government was criticized for intervening in Greece, but the Germans also suffered, losing a third of their troops and 220 aircraft; they did not attempt another operation of this sort again. It has also been argued that Hitler's involvement in Greece and Crete delayed his attack on Russia by about five weeks. It this was so, it may well have saved Moscow.

(b) *Mussolini invades Egypt*

Mussolini had opened hostilities in North Africa by invading Egypt from the Italian colony of Libya (September 1940). A mixed army of British, Indian, Australian, New Zealand, French and Polish troops commanded by Wavell, pushed the Italians out of Egypt and back into Libya, defeating them at Bedafomm and capturing 130 000 prisoners and 400 tanks. This was a great boost to British morale and helped to keep hopes of ultimate victory alive. Tobruk and Benghazi were captured, but in February 1941 the British advance was stopped on Churchill's orders, so that many of Wavell's troops and planes could be used in the Greek campaign. This was unfortunate since only a few days later Hitler sent Rommel, one of his best generals, to Tripoli with a large German army, to stiffen Italian resistance. By April 1941 Rommel had driven the British out of Libya, though they managed to hold on to Tobruk behind the German lines. The unfortunate Wavell was replaced by Auchinleck, who succeeded in relieving Tobruk (December) but made no further headway.

→ Allied advances and offensives 1942–4

Map 28.2 North Africa and the Mediterranean

(c) British difficulties in North Africa

The main problem was that the further westwards the British advanced, the more their lines of communication and supply with Egypt became strained. The other source of supply was from the sea across the Mediterranean. There was a constant battle for control of the Mediterranean, where Britain's vital naval base was Malta; this was subjected to the most intense German and Italian bombing and was in danger of being starved into surrender. Between January and July 1941, very few ships managed to get through to Malta, though the situation eased after Hitler withdrew most of the *Luftwaffe* for the attack on Russia. Even so the loss of the aircraft carrier *Ark Royal* was a serious blow, and for much of 1941 and 1942, British troops in Egypt had to be supplied by ships sailing round the Cape of Good Hope and up through the Suez Canal.

Additional problems were the extreme heat of the desert and the sandstorms, which made the job of the mechanics more difficult than usual. Moreover it seemed that the British position in Egypt was not secure; there was a large anti-British party which demanded the withdrawal of British troops and stores from Cairo and Alexandria. The British moved swiftly to deal with this problem: in February 1942 troops surrounded the royal palace and the Egyptian king was forced to accept a pro-British government. Crisis-point was reached in June 1942 when Rommel's forces suddenly struck, capturing Tobruk and penetrating deep into Egypt until they were only 70 miles from Alexandria.

(d) The Battle of El Alamein (October 1942)

This was the real turning-point in North Africa when Rommel's *Afrika Korps* was driven back by Montgomery's Eighth Army. This great battle was the culmination of several engagements fought in the El Alamein area: first the Axis advance was temporarily checked (July); when Rommel tried to break through he was halted again at Alam Halfa (September); finally, seven weeks later in the October battle, he was chased out of Egypt and almost out of Libya too by the British and New Zealanders. Tripoli was captured in January 1943. *The Allies were successful partly because* during the seven-week pause massive reinforcements had arrived, so that the Germans and Italians were heavily outnumbered – they had only 80 000 men and 540 tanks against 230 000 troops and 1440 tanks. Allied air power was vital, constantly attacking the Axis forces and sinking their supply ships crossing the Mediterranean, so that by October there were serious shortages of food, fuel oil and ammunition; at the same time the air force was strong enough to protect the Eighth Army's own supply routes. Montgomery's skilful preparations probably clinched the issue, though he has been criticized for being over-cautious and for allowing Rommel and half his forces to escape into Libya. However, there is no doubt that the *El Alamein victory was one of the three major turning-points in the war* (the other two were Midway Island and Stalingrad). It prevented Egypt and the Suez Canal from falling into German hands and ended the possibility of a link-up between the Axis forces in the Middle East and those in the Ukraine. More than that, it led on to the complete expulsion of Axis forces from North Africa; it encouraged landings of American and British troops in the French territories of Morocco and Algeria, to threaten the Germans and Italians from the west, while the Eighth Army closed in on them from Libya. Trapped in Tunisia, 275 000 Germans and Italians were forced to surrender (May 1943), and the Allies were well placed for an invasion of Italy. The desert war had been a serious drain on German resources which could have been used in Russia where they were badly needed.

(e) *The Far East: Malaya, Singapore and Burma*

Here there was nothing but disaster for Britain. The Japanese, after their successful attack on Pearl Harbor (7 December 1941), in which 19 American ships were sunk or disabled and over 2000 lives lost, went on to invade British territories in the Far East, all of which were inadequately defended. Hong Kong was taken, and Japanese troops landed on the coast of northern Malaya, capturing all the airfields. This deprived the British of air protection, and Japanese planes sank the *Repulse* and the *Prince of Wales* (10 December) with the loss of 600 lives. These were the two main capital ships which were intended to maintain control of the area. Meanwhile Japanese troops advanced down the Malay peninsula until by the end of January 1942 only Singapore remained in British hands. The Australians now seemed on the verge of panic, fearing that they were next in line for a Japanese attack; it was mainly to satisfy them that Churchill sent more troops to Singapore. But it was too late: the fortress was primarily a naval base and it was not equipped to withstand an assault from the land. On 15 February, with the supply of fresh water cut off, the British commander surrendered with 60 000 troops.

Though it was not the knock-out blow that Hitler hoped, it was a serious blow to Britain's prestige as an imperial power. For the first time Britain had suffered a major

Map 28.3   The war in the Pacific

defeat at the hands of an Asian power. This encouraged opposition to British rule in India, and it meant that after the war the Indians would be content with nothing less than full independence. Australia began to look towards the USA as her main defence against Japan. The loss of Singapore led to the Japanese occupation of Burma (March 1942), and the fall of India seemed imminent. However, although the British did not realize it at the time, they need not have worried: the Japanese were mainly concerned with the Pacific and had no immediate plans to conquer India. This came much later – in March 1944 (see Section 28.6(d)).

28.4 The war at sea

As in the First World War, the British navy had a vital role to play. This included protecting merchant ships bringing food supplies, sinking German submarines and surface raiders, blockading Germany, and transporting and supplying the Allied troops in North Africa and later in Italy. At first success was mixed, mainly because the British failed to understand the importance of air support in naval operations and had few aircraft carriers. Thus they suffered defeats in Norway and Crete where the Germans had strong air superiority. In addition the Germans had numerous naval bases in Norway, Denmark, France and Italy. British weakness in the Far East led to the fall of Hong Kong, Malaya, Singapore and Burma. However, there were some successes:

1 Aircraft from the carrier *Illustrious* sank half the Italian fleet at Taranto (November 1940); the following March five more warships were destroyed off Cape Matapan.
2 The threat from surface raiders was removed by the sinking of the *Bismarck*, Germany's only battleship at the time (May 1941).
3 The navy destroyed the German invasion transports on their way to Crete (May 1941), though they could not prevent the landing of parachute troops.
4 The navy provided escorts for convoys carrying supplies to help the Russians; these sailed via the Arctic to Murmansk in the far north of Russia. Beginning in September 1941, the first twelve convoys arrived without incident, but then the Germans began to attack them, until convoy 17 lost 23 ships out of 36 (June 1942). After this disaster, Arctic convoys were not fully resumed until November 1943, when stronger escorts could be spared. Altogether 40 convoys sailed: 720 out of a total of 811 merchant ships arrived safely, with valuable cargo for the Russians, including 5000 tanks and 7000 aircraft, as well as thousands of tons of canned meat.
5 The navy's most important contribution was their victory in *the Battle of the Atlantic*. This was the struggle against German submarines attempting to deprive Britain of food and raw materials. At the beginning of 1942 the Germans had 90 U-boats in operation and 250 being built. In the first six months of that year the Allies lost over 4 million tons of merchant shipping and destroyed only 21 U-boats; losses reached a peak of 108 ships in March 1943, almost two-thirds of which were in convoy. However, after that the number of sinkings began to fall, while U-boat losses increased. By July 1943 the Allies could produce ships at a faster rate than the U-boats could sink them, and the situation was under control. *Reasons for the Allied success were* that more air protection for convoys was provided by long-range Liberators, both escorts and aircraft protection improved with experience, and the British introduced the new centimetric radar sets which were small enough to be fitted into aircraft, so that submarines could be detected in poor visibility and at night. The victory was just as important as Midway, El Alamein and Stalingrad:

Britain could not have remained in the war for much longer if she had continued to sustain the heavy losses of March 1943.

6 Sea and air power together made possible the great invasion of France in June 1944 (see Section 28.6(b)).

28.5 The war in the air

1 The first significant achievement from the British point of view was the Battle of Britain (1940) when the RAF beat off the *Luftwaffe* attacks, causing Hitler to abandon his invasion plans.

2 In conjunction with the British navy, aircraft played a varied role: the successful attacks on the Italian fleet at Taranto and Cape Matapan, the sinking of the German battleship *Tirpitz* by heavy bombers in Norway (November 1943), the protection of convoys in the Atlantic, and anti-submarine operations. In fact, in May 1943 Admiral Doenitz, the German navy chief, complained to Hitler that since the introduction of the new radar devices, more U-boats were being destroyed by aircraft than by naval vessels.

3 The American air force, together with the navy, played a crucial part in winning the Pacific War against the Japanese. Dive-bombers operating from aircraft carriers won the Battle of Midway Island in June 1942. Later, in the 'island-hopping' campaign, attacks by heavy bombers prepared the way for landings by marines, for example at the Mariana Islands (1944) and the Philippines (1945). American and RAF transport planes kept up a flow of essential supplies to the Allies during the campaign to recapture Burma.

4 The RAF took part in specific campaigns which would have been hopeless without them; for example, during the desert war, operating from bases in Egypt and Palestine, they constantly bombed Rommel's supply ships in the Mediterranean and his armies on land.

5 British and American planes flew in parachute troops to aid the landings in Sicily (July 1943) and Normandy (June 1944) and provided air protection for the invading armies. However, a similar operation at Arnhem in Holland in September 1944 was a failure.

Allied bombing of German and Japanese cities

This was the most controversial action by the Allied air forces. The Germans had bombed London and other important British cities and ports during 1940 and 1941, but these raids dwindled during the German attack on Russia which required all the *Luftwaffe*'s strength. The British and Americans retaliated with what they called a 'strategic air offensive' – this involved massive attacks on military and industrial targets to hamper the German war effort. The Ruhr, Cologne, Hamburg and Berlin all suffered badly. Some raids seem to have been carried out to undermine civilian morale – about 50 000 people were killed during a single night raid on Dresden (February 1945).

Early in 1945 the Americans launched a series of devastating raids on Japan from bases in the Mariana Islands. In a single raid on Tokyo (March), 80 000 people were killed and a quarter of the city destroyed.

There has been some argument about how effective the bombing was in hastening the Axis defeat, beyond merely causing inconvenience. Critics also point to the heavy losses suffered by air-crews – over 158 000 Allied airmen were killed in Europe alone. Others argue that this type of bombing, which caused the deaths of so many innocent civilians (as opposed to bombings which targeted industrial areas, railways and bridges) was morally wrong. Estimates of German civilian deaths from Allied bombing vary between 600 000 and a million. German raids on Britain killed over 60 000 civilians.

The conclusion now seems to be that the campaign against Germany was not effective until the autumn of 1944. German industrial production continued to increase until as late as July 1944. After that, thanks to the increasing accuracy of the raids and the use of the new Mustang fighter escorts which could outmanoeuvre all the German fighters, synthetic oil production fell rapidly, causing acute fuel shortages. In October the vital Krupps armaments factories in Essen were put out of action permanently, and the war effort ground to a halt in 1945. By June 1945 the Japanese had been reduced to the same state.

In the end therefore, after much wasted effort early on, the Allied strategic air offensive was one of the decisive reasons for the Axis defeat: besides strangling fuel and synthetic oil production and destroying rail communications, it caused the diversion of many aircraft from the eastern front, thus helping the Russian advance into Germany.

28.6 The defeat of the Axis powers

(a) *The fall of Italy*

This was the first stage in the Axis collapse. British and American troops landed in Sicily from sea and air (10 July 1943) and quickly captured the whole island. This caused the downfall of Mussolini who was dismissed by the king. Allied troops crossed to Salerno, Reggio and Taranto on the mainland and captured Naples (October 1943), by which time Marshal Badoglio, Mussolini's successor, had signed an armistice and brought Italy into the war on the Allied side. However, the Germans, determined to hold on to Italy, rushed troops through the Brenner Pass to occupy Rome and the north. The Allies landed a force at Anzio, 30 miles south of Rome (January 1944), but bitter fighting followed before Monte Cassino (May) and Rome (June) were captured; Milan in the north was not taken until May 1945. The campaign could have been finished much sooner if the Allies had been less cautious in the early stages and if the Americans had not insisted on keeping many divisions back for the invasion of France. Nevertheless the elimination of Italy did contribute towards the final victory: it provided air bases for the bombing of the Germans in central Europe and the Balkans, and it kept German troops occupied when they were needed to resist the Russians.

(b) *The invasion of France – Operation Overlord (6 June 1944)*

Operation Overlord (also known as the 'Second Front') began on 'D-Day', 6 June 1944. It was felt that the time was ripe now that Italy had been eliminated, the U-boats controlled and Allied air superiority achieved; the Russians had been urging the Allies to start this second front ever since 1941 to relieve pressure on them. The landings took place from sea and air on a 60-mile stretch of Normandy beaches (codenamed Utah, Omaha, Gold, Juno and Sword) between Cherbourg and Le Havre. There was strong German resistance, but at the end of the first week 326 000 men with tanks and heavy lorries had landed safely.

It was a remarkable operation: it made use of prefabricated 'Mulberry' harbours which were towed across from Britain and positioned close to the Normandy coast, mainly at Arromanches (Gold beach), and of PLUTO – pipelines under the ocean – carrying motor fuel. Eventually over 3 million Allied troops were landed; within a few

Map 28.4   The D-Day landings – 6 June 1944

weeks most of northern France was liberated (Paris on 25 August), putting out of action the sites from which the German V1 and V2 rocket missiles had been launched with devastating effects on south-eastern Britain. In Belgium Brussels and Antwerp were liberated in September.

(c) *The assault on Germany*

The assault on Germany followed, but the end was delayed by desperate German resistance and by disagreements between the British and Americans. Montgomery wanted a rapid thrust to reach Berlin before the Russians, but the American General Eisenhower favoured a cautious advance along a broad front. The British failure at Arnhem in Holland (September 1944) seemed to support Eisenhower's view, though in fact the Arnhem operation (an attempt by parachute troops to cross the Rhine and out-flank the German Siegfried Line) might have worked if the troops had landed nearer the two Rhine bridges.

Consequently Eisenhower had his way and Allied troops were dispersed over a 600-mile front, with unfortunate results: Hitler was able to launch a last offensive through the weakly defended Ardennes towards Antwerp; the Germans broke through the American lines and advanced 60 miles, causing a huge bulge in the front line (December 1944). Determined British and American action stemmed the advance and pushed the Germans back to their original position. But *the Battle of the Bulge* as it became known, was important because Hitler had risked everything and had lost 250 000 men and 400 tanks, which at this stage could not be replaced. Early in 1945 Germany was being invaded on both fronts, from east and west. The British still wanted to push ahead and take Berlin before the Russians, but supreme commander Eisenhower refused to be hurried, and Berlin fell to Stalin's forces in April. Hitler committed suicide and Germany surrendered (7 May 1945).

Map 28.5 The defeat of Germany 1944–5

(d) *The defeat of Japan*

This took longer and was not achieved until August 1945. Since the Battle of Midway (June 1942) the Japanese had never recovered from their losses of aircraft carriers and strike planes. The Americans always maintained their lead. Under the command of General MacArthur, they began to recover the Pacific islands, beginning in August 1942 with the landings on the Solomon Islands. It was a long and bitter struggle which continued through 1943 and 1944 by a process known as 'island hopping'. The British contributed to the Japanese defeat by prising them out of Burma. The prelude to this operation came in March 1944 when the Japanese advanced into Assam and besieged the town of Imphal. They were resisted by a joint army of British and Indians under Mountbatten. Both sides had to endure appalling jungle conditions – intense heat, snakes and disease, mainly malaria. The Japanese were amazed at the ferocity of the resistance – since the fall of Singapore they had been contemptuous of British fighting power. After eight weeks they were forced to abandon the siege and withdraw into Burma. It turned into a humiliating defeat for the Japanese, who lost 53 000 of the 85 000 troops who had started the campaign.

The main reason for the British and Indian victory was that the RAF was able to fly constant supplies of food and ammunition into Imphal. The Japanese air force, under heavy pressure in the Pacific, was unable to supply the besieging armies who were short of food, ammunition and medical supplies. The Japanese in Burma now found themselves pressed by the British and Indians from the north-west, from landings on the south-west coast, and by the Chinese from the north. When the Japanese-trained Burmese army joined the British, the fate of the Japanese was sealed. Rangoon, the capital, was captured in April 1945, and soon afterwards the Japanese withdrew into Malaya.

The end came for Japan in August 1945. On 6 August the Americans dropped an atomic bomb on Hiroshima, killing perhaps as many as 84 000 people and leaving thousands more slowly dying of radiation poisoning. Three days later they dropped an atomic bomb on Nagasaki which killed perhaps another 40 000. After that the Japanese government surrendered (14 August).

The dropping of these bombs was one of the most controversial actions of the entire war. President Truman's justification was that he was saving American lives, since the war might otherwise drag on for another year. Many historians believe that the bombings were not necessary, since the Truman government knew that the Japanese had already put out peace feelers in June by sending an envoy to Russia. One suggestion is that the real reason for the bombings was to end the fighting swiftly before the Russians (who had promised to enter the war against Japan) gained too much Japanese territory which would entitle them to share the occupation of Japan. A demonstration of the awesome power of the bomb would help the USA to gain a diplomatic advantage over the USSR which did not possess any nuclear weapons. According to the American Admiral Leahy, 'the scientists and others wanted to make this test because of the vast sums that had been spent on the project – two billion dollars'.

(e) *Why did the Axis powers lose the war?*

The basic reason was that they simply took on too much; by attacking Russia before Britain had been eliminated, Hitler was facing two powerful enemies. The Allies learned how to check *Blitzkrieg* attacks and began to appreciate the importance of air support and aircraft carriers. Italian incompetence was a constant drain on German resources, and the longer the war went on, the more the strain began to tell. Italy and Germany suffered from a shortage of raw materials and even Germany was short of rubber, cotton, nickel and, after mid-1944, oil. On the other hand, the combined resources of the USA, the USSR and the British empire were potentially overwhelming. The Russians moved their industry east of the Ural Mountains and so were able to continue production even though the Germans had occupied vast areas in the west. By 1940 they had four times as many tanks as the Germans and could put twice as many men in the field. When the American war machine reached peak production it could turn out over 70 000 tanks and 120 000 aircraft a year, which the Germans and Japanese could not match.

(f) *East–West relations at the end of the war*

Towards the end of the war the harmony which had existed between Britain, the USA and the USSR began to show signs of strain, as the old mutual suspicions revived. The deterioration could be seen in two conferences, at Yalta and Potsdam (February and July 1945).

1   *The Yalta Conference (February 1945)* was held in Russia, in the Crimea, and it
    was attended by Churchill, Roosevelt and Stalin. At the time it was generally

thought to be a success, agreement being reached on several points: the United Nations Organization was to be set up; Germany was to be divided into zones – Russian, American and British (a French zone was included later); Berlin, which would be in the Russian zone, would be split into corresponding zones; similar arrangements were to be made for Austria. Free elections would be allowed in the states of eastern Europe. Stalin promised to join the war against Japan on condition that Russia received the whole of Sakhalin Island and some territory in Manchuria. However, there were ominous signs over Poland: when the Russians swept through Poland as they pushed the Germans back, they had set up a Communist government in Lublin, even though there was already a Polish government-in-exile in London. It was agreed at Yalta that some members (non-Communist) of the London-based government should be allowed to join the Lublin government, while in return Russia could keep the strip of eastern Poland which she had occupied in 1939; but Roosevelt and Churchill refused to agree to Stalin's demands that Russia should be given all German territory east of the Rivers Oder and Neisse.

2   *The Potsdam Conference (July 1945)* was held in Berlin and revealed a distinct cooling-off in relations. The main representatives were Stalin, Truman (replacing Roosevelt who had died in April) and Churchill (replaced by Clement Attlee after Labour's election victory). The war with Germany was over but no agreement was reached about her long-term future beyond what had been decided at Yalta; it was understood that she would be disarmed, the Nazi party disbanded and its leaders tried as 'war criminals'. Moreover Churchill and Truman were annoyed because Germany east of the Oder–Neisse Line had been occupied by Russian troops and was being run by the pro-Communist Polish government which expelled some four million Germans living there; this had certainly not been agreed to at Yalta. Churchill was given the latest information about the successful atomic bomb tests; but although Truman told Stalin that the USA had a powerful new weapon, he did not go into exact detail and did not tell Stalin that it was about to be used against Japan. A few days after the conference closed, the two atomic bombs were dropped on Japan, and the war ended quickly on 14 August without the need for Russian aid (though the Russians declared war on Japan on 8 August and invaded Manchuria). Though they annexed south Sakhalin, as agreed at Yalta, they were allowed no part in the occupation of Japan.

28.7 What were the effects of the war on Britain?

(a) *The civilian population experience 'total war'*

Civilians were more directly involved in this conflict than in the First World War. It was a 'total war' summed up perfectly by Churchill in one of his speeches:

> The whole of the warring nations are not only soldiers, but the entire population, men, women and children. The fronts are everywhere. The trenches are dug in the towns and the streets. Every village is fortified, every road is barred. The workmen are soldiers with different weapons but the same courage.

Immediate measures included the mass evacuation of children from cities and large towns to escape the expected bombings, the frantic digging of air-raid shelters and piling up of sand-bags, and the issue of gas-masks to civilians, in case of poison gas attacks. A complete blackout was imposed so that no chinks of light would remain to

Land taken by Poland from Germany: territory east of the *Oder–Neisse* Line and part of East Prussia

Land acquired by the USSR during the war

Occupation zones in Germany and Austria:
1 Russian   3 French
2 British   4 American

Map 28.6   Europe after 1945

guide the German bombers; this had the unfortunate effect of doubling the number of road accidents, and before the end of 1939, partial or 'glimmer' lighting of streets was allowed. Theatres and cinemas were closed and football matches banned, in case of bombing, but regulations were relaxed before Christmas and never reimposed.

In 1940, with the German invasion imminent, the government began to take more drastic action. *The Emergency Powers Act (May 1940)* gave the authorities full powers to do whatever was thought necessary. Signposts, place-names and station name-boards were removed to confuse the Germans (if they arrived). Rationing of bacon, butter, cheese and meat was introduced, and during 1941, as the German submarine campaign reached its peak, regulations were further tightened. The weekly rations per person were austere to say the least: eight ounces of meat, one ounce of cheese, four ounces of bacon or ham, eight ounces of sugar, two ounces of tea, two ounces of butter and two ounces of jam or marmalade. A 'points' system was introduced for other foods: each person was allowed 16 points for four weeks, so that the wealthy were prevented from buying up all the supplies. Goods available on the points system included tinned foods, rice, sago and tapioca, peas and tomatoes, breakfast cereals and condensed milk, and syrup, treacle and biscuits. Bread, beer and tobacco were never rationed, but beer was watered until it had no more than two-thirds its original alcohol content. Later, clothing and fuel were rationed. There were chronic shortages of all household goods as the war effort drew in most of the available raw materials. On the whole, people accepted the rationing without too much complaint because it seemed to be fair.

Conscription was immediately introduced and applied to women as well as men, if they were required. The government also called for local volunteers, aged 40 to 65, to act as a Home Guard in the event of an invasion; by mid-1940 over a million men had joined. Though their potential value as a fighting force has been questioned, they fulfilled a useful function in guarding the British coast, so that the professional army was free to undergo intensive training.

German bombing was the worst trial. Starting in early September 1940, London was bombed for 76 consecutive nights and the attacks continued through into May 1941. Other cities also suffered – Coventry, Liverpool, Manchester, Plymouth, Hull, Glasgow, Belfast and many more took a battering. About 60 000 people were killed, about half of them in London, and perhaps 100 000 seriously injured. Hundreds of thousands of people were made homeless and had to be housed in emergency centres – cinemas, theatres, schools, or whatever was convenient. In London thousands took refuge in the tube stations, since government preparations for civil defence were largely inadequate. This caused a great deal of resentment, particularly in London's East End, but on the whole morale stayed remarkably high, and American journalists were amazed at the calmness with which ordinary people tried to continue business as usual among the damage and disruption.

The war economy produced full employment for the first time since 1918, and the poorer working class groups probably benefited from this. The government tried to keep prices under control to avoid inflation, and although it did not succeed completely, wages rose faster than prices. At the beginning of the war, average weekly earnings were around 53s., while at the end they were 96s. Bevin had the power to direct workers where they were needed, and he did his job with such tact and sensitivity that with very few exceptions the workers were reasonably happy.

(b) *Long-term social effects of the war*

These are more difficult to be sure about. Some historians believe that the war caused a social revolution, while others, such as Angus Calder, think this is an exaggeration and that, at most, it hastened British society 'in its progress along the old grooves'. Henry

Pelling believes that society emerged from the war basically unchanged. The problem is that there were many different forces – political, economic and social – at work causing changes, and it is difficult to isolate which developments were caused solely by the war and which would probably have happened anyway. Arthur Marwick feels that although caution is desirable, 'in the end it does not do full justice to the complex range of human reactions touched off by war'. He argues that the war caused, if not exactly a social revolution, certainly some vital changes in attitudes:

1   The enormous cost of the war caused the government to follow Keynes's policies of high spending and high taxation to meet the war effort. This eliminated unemployment and demonstrated that such policies, admittedly in special circumstances, did actually work. The question was bound to be faced: why could these policies not be continued after the war?
2   The war increased the sense of social solidarity and created, as John Stevenson puts it, 'a climate of common endeavour, which blunted some of the pre-war objections to increased social spending'. As early as 1940 the state took the unprecedented step of introducing free school milk, and later free school meals and nurseries.
3   Middle and upper class families were appalled by the deprivation of many of the evacuee children from the big cities who came to stay with them. Often poorly-clothed and undernourished, these deprived children did a lot to arouse the nation to a realization that they deserved something better.
4   Even Calder admits that in a total war, 'the nation's rulers, whether they liked it or not, depended on the willing co-operation of the ruled, including even scorned and under-privileged sections of society, manual workers and women'. It was widely felt that the poor, by their co-operation and all-out efforts, had earned concessions – better education, a higher standard of living and better welfare services. There was the added incentive that if the workers were not given what they wanted, they might try and take it by revolution.

The new thinking showed itself in a number of ways:

●   The Christian churches began to speak out on matters of social concern. In 1942 William Temple, a socialist, became Archbishop of Canterbury, and his widely read book *Christianity and the Social Order* set out the minimum social standards which people ought to be able to expect in a Christian society and left no doubt that it should be the state's responsibility to enforce these standards.
●   *Political and Economic Planning (PEP)* produced a plan in July 1942, proposing a new Ministry of Social Security and a National Health Service, as well as a national minimum wage and family allowances for everybody.
●   *The Beveridge Report (1942).* The government appointed a committee under Sir William Beveridge, a Liberal, to investigate the problems of social insurance. His report claimed that *the five giant evils to be overcome were want, disease, ignorance, squalor and idleness*, and suggested that the government should fight them with insurance schemes, child allowances, more houses, a national health service, a policy of full employment and secondary education for everybody. The Report received widespread publicity and was debated in parliament in February 1943. The Labour party wanted to carry out its proposals immediately, but Churchill was more interested in finishing off the war successfully. This explains why so little was done immediately to implement Beveridge's proposals. Only one of its recommendations was introduced before the end of the war – payment of child allowances at the rate of 5s. a week for each child after the first. It was left to the Labour governments of 1945–51 to introduce a Welfare State (see Section 29.2). Arthur Marwick is convinced that the war *was* very

much responsible for these further developments in state social policy. As he points out in his article in the *Modern History Review* (September 1990), the difference between the welfare state after the war and social policies before the war is the principle of 'universality': 'the new provisions after 1945 were designed to cover the whole nation, rich and poor, the idea being that if you have services which are only for the poor, which was basically the situation before 1939, they will be second rate services, a debate which faces us again at the present time'.

- *The Butler Education Act (1944).* The work of R. A. Butler, the Conservative President of the Board of Education in the coalition government, this Act made secondary education available to all, free of charge and without restriction, and raised the school-leaving age to 15 (to take effect in 1947). A new Ministry of Education was set up to 'direct and control' local authorities, which were now expected to provide secondary schools 'sufficient in number, character and equipment to afford all pupils such variety of instruction and training as may be desirable in view of their different ages, abilities and aptitudes'. Most local authorities took this to mean the system suggested in the 1926 Hadow Report – three different types of secondary school: grammar, technical and modern. This was a disappointment for many educational experts who believed this system did not offer equality of opportunity and who argued in favour of comprehensive schools. However, the new system was a great improvement, and it enabled many working-class children to go on to university. Calder calls the Act 'the most important gesture towards democracy made in the twentieth century, a fitting product of the People's War'.

- Although no more government legislation came before the end of the war, Clement Attlee, who was Labour leader and Churchill's deputy Prime Minister, kept up pressure in the cabinet so that the Beveridge Report would not be shelved permanently. A Minister for Reconstruction, Lord Woolton, was appointed, and 1944 saw the appearance of three government White Papers (statements of policy which a government hopes to carry out) on a National Health Service, Employment Policy and Social Insurance.

(c) *Political effects*

The main political effect was to cause the election of a Labour government with a huge majority in July 1945. In normal circumstances a general election would have been due in 1940, and looking at the trends during the 1930s, it seems most unlikely that Labour would have won. Even if they had, they would have lacked the programme and the experience to act in the way they did after 1945. The war provided them with both (see Section 29.1 for the reasons for Labour's victory). The trade union movement seemed to be strengthened during the war, with membership rising from 6.05 million in 1938 to almost 7.9 million in 1945.

(d) *A growing sense of complacency*

Many historians have commented on the growing feeling of complacency which was apparent in Britain in the years after the war. Understandably people felt that Britain had done well to survive the supreme test of war and come out on the winning side. They drew the conclusion that the system – both political and economic – must have worked so well that nothing needed changing; except social conditions for a people whose efforts during the war had earned them the right to a better life. Corelli Barnett argues that under the Labour governments of 1945–51, too much was spent on social reform and not enough on economic improvement, and that no serious attempt was made in Britain to modernize industry, roads and railways, which helped to put Britain at a disadvantage in relation to her European competitors (see Section 29.4(c) for a further discussion of this point).

(e) *The war was economically ruinous for Britain*

In 1939, Britain's gold reserves stood at £864 million, but by March 1941 they plunged to only £3 million. At that point the US Congress passed *the Lend-Lease Act* which enabled the British to obtain crucial supplies from the USA, to be paid for later. American help kept Britain going during the war, but it was not given free – by the autumn of 1945 Britain's overseas debts (not all to the USA) stood at well over £3000 million. On the defeat of Japan, Truman, the new American president, abruptly ended Lend-Lease, leaving Britain with much of her foreign investments sold off and her capacity to export sadly reduced. The only solution seemed to be to request another loan from the USA, which was granted, but on unfavourable terms to Britain. Britain was therefore reduced to a close and uncomfortable dependence on the USA.

(f) *Britain's world position changed*

Although Britain's empire had survived intact, British defeats had stirred up nationalist feelings, especially in India and the Far East. Within 20 years most of Britain's empire had become independent, though within the Commonwealth. The war revealed that the USA and the USSR were the world's most powerful states, while Britain, though on the winning side, was now only a second-rate power.

(g) *There was no all-inclusive peace settlement*

There was no big peace conference like the one held at Versailles at the end of the First World War. This was mainly because the suspicion and distrust, which had re-emerged between Russia and the west in the final months of the war, made a comprehensive settlement impossible. The results of a number of separate treaties can be summarized briefly:

● Italy lost her African colonies and renounced her claims to Albania and Abyssinia (Ethiopia).
● Russia took the eastern tip of Czechoslovakia, the Petsamo district and the area round Lake Ladoga from Finland, and held on to Estonia, Latvia, Lithuania and eastern Poland, all of which had been occupied by the Russians in 1939. Russia also took Bessarabia and northern Bukovina from Romania.
● Romania recovered northern Transylvania which the Hungarians had occupied during the war.
● Trieste, claimed by both Italy and Yugoslavia, was declared a free territory protected by the United Nations.
● Later, in San Francisco (1951), Japan agreed to surrender all territory acquired during the previous 90 years, which included a complete withdrawal from China.
● The Russians refused to agree to any settlement over Germany and Austria, except that they should be occupied by Allied troops and that East Prussia should be divided between Russia and Poland.

Questions

1 **Churchill as a war leader**
   Study Sources A to G and then answer the questions which follow.

From the memoirs of Lord Halifax, published in 1957

At the Foreign Office and in the War Cabinet I shared responsibility under the Prime Minister [Churchill] until the end of 1940, through the days which preceded, witnessed and followed the collapse of France and Belgium, and the miracle of Dunkirk. The main burden of all this fell upon Churchill, and inspired him to give leadership to the British people, matchless and unforgettable. . . . I asked him one day if he could ever imagine circumstances in which he might think it right to recommend the King and Government to move to Canada. He thought for a moment, and then he said with great emphasis that he could imagine no such circumstances; every man ought to fight to the death on his own soil, and 'if they come to London, I shall take a rifle and put myself in the pillbox at the bottom of Downing Street, and shoot till I've no more ammunition, and then they can damned well shoot me'.

Source: Lord Halifax, *Fulness of Days*, Collins, 1957.

Source B

Historian Arthur Bryant gives his assessment of Churchill, published in 1959

From first to last, his part in winning the war was greater than any man's – British, American or Russian. He was fertile in resource, inexhaustible in argument, and a spur and stimulus to bold action of any kind. As Prime Minister, Churchill oversaw every department of the country's life and moulded it into an instrument for total war. This gigantic man fired the whole nation with his passionate indignation, pugnacity, impatience and refusal to admit defeat. Even his faults, when tempered by advice, contributed as much to victory as his virtues. Without him there would have been no triumph. . . . When in 1940 Churchill took on the offices of both Prime Minister and Minister of Defence, the three Service Chiefs became responsible to him alone. This close and direct contact between PM and Service Chiefs ensured the correlation of political and military authority and prevented the dangerous division of responsibility, so nearly fatal in the First World War, between politicians ignorant of military matters, and military advisers who had no means of making their advice effective.

Source: A. Bryant, *Triumph in the West 1943–46*, Collins, 1959.

Source C

From the diary of Field Marshal Lord Alanbrooke, Chief of the Imperial General Staff from 1941

October 6th 1943. It is quite clear in my mind that with the commitments we have in Italy we should not undertake serious operations in the Aegean. . . . By 3.25 PM determined to go for Rhodes without looking at the effects on Italy. I had a heated argument with him.
October 7th. Another one-and-a-half hours' battle with PM to hold on to what I think is right. The same arguments brought up again and again.
October 8th. I can now control him no more. He has worked himself into a frenzy of excitement about the Rhodes attack, has magnified its importance so that he can no longer see anything else. He has set his heart on capturing this one island at the expense of the Italian campaign.

January 19th 1944. In all his plans he lives from hand to mouth; he can never grasp a whole plan – selects individual pieces of the vast jigsaw puzzle and concentrates on it at the expense of all others.

March 29th 1945. I feel that I can't stick another moment with him and would give almost anything never to see him again.

July 25th 1945. I shall always look back on the years I worked with him [Churchill] as some of the most difficult and trying of my life. For all that, I thank God that I was given an opportunity of working alongside such a man, and of having my eyes opened to the fact that occasionally such supermen exist on this earth.

Source: quoted in A. Bryant, *Triumph in the West 1943–46*, Collins, 1959.

Source D

The opinion of a military historian, Sir Basil Liddell Hart

Then came the catastrophes of May and June 1940 when France collapsed and Italy entered the war. In that appalling crisis, the first need was to build up the defences of Britain, and the second to provide for the defence of the Mediterranean area. Those two needs were difficult to meet simultaneously. Churchill's boldest and greatest action was seen in the risks he took to strengthen the defences of Egypt before Britain itself was secure against invasion. . . . In March 1941 Churchill declared that the new government of Yugoslavia would receive 'all possible aid and succour from Britain'. Hitler could not tolerate such an insult and at once decided to invade Yugoslavia as well as Greece. Yugoslavia was overrun within a week and Greece in just over three weeks, and the British force was hustled back into its ships. The outcome reflected on Churchill's judgement and on those who had told him military intervention was feasible. . . . The effects of the loss of Singapore and Malaya were disastrous. It is clear that the responsibility for the failure to reinforce Malaya's inadequate defences rests principally with Churchill himself – and was due to his insistence on launching a premature offensive in North Africa.

Source: B. H. Liddell Hart, *History of the Second World War*, Cassell, 1970.

Source E

Letter from Churchill to Sir John Dill, Brooke's predecessor as Chief of the Imperial General Staff, May 1941

I gather you would be prepared to face the loss of Egypt rather than lose Singapore. I do not take that view, nor do I think the alternative is likely to happen. . . . Should Japan enter the war, the US will in all probability come in on our side, and in any case Japan would not be likely to attack Singapore as this would be a dangerous operation for her.

Source: quoted in Liddell Hart, above.

Source F

A British historian, Robert Blake, and an American historian, Wm. Roger Louis, give their joint assessment of Churchill, published in 1993

In May 1940 the failure of the Norwegian campaign brought down Chamberlain and Churchill succeeded him. . . . Seldom has a more crucial decision been made. It meant that Britain had at the head of its affairs the one statesman who, at precisely the moment of the Fall of France, could not only unite all parties by his eloquence but was prepared in the face of all the odds to continue a struggle which objectively seemed hopeless. It was this determination, unflagging energy, and infectious optimism that prevented a dictated peace.... With Britain out of the way Hitler would almost certainly have conquered the Soviet Union, and Japan might not have risked Pearl Harbor. A defeated Russia and a humiliated Britain would have been more vulnerable victims. The United States might not have been drawn into the struggle. Hitler might have ruled a satellite empire from the Urals to the Atlantic. No doubt Churchill's contribution to the outcome, and more specifically to strategy, can be variously assessed. What cannot be disputed is his contribution to morale. As he put it, he gave the roar to the British lion, and in those critical years 1940–1 his eloquence, however dated it may seem today, was of enormous importance.

Source: R. Blake and W. R. Louis (eds), *Churchill: A Major New Assessment of his Life in Peace and War*, Oxford, 1993.

Source G

Extracts from historian John Charmley's reappraisal of Churchill's role as war leader, published in 1993

In the eyes of many sensible folk, [in May 1940] the time had come to think about coming to terms with Herr Hitler ... there was a good deal of support for the idea of at least opening talks to find out what Hitler's peace terms might be. Of Churchill's determination to continue the war there was never any doubt.... But in his determination to see Germany defeated, Churchill neglected to ask himself, until it was too late, what the result of the total destruction of German power would be upon the balance of power.... He had been so fixed upon the German menace to the balance of power that he had signally failed to notice that by destroying German power, he had helped to raise up a new and equally sinister threat; ...

Surveying the situation in July 1945 it was hard to argue that Britain had won in any sense save that of avoiding defeat. He had destroyed the awful tyranny of Hitler, but what had risen in its place? ...

At the end of the war he was, once again, faced with what looked like an attempt by one power [USSR] to dominate the Continent, an odd result for so much expenditure of treasure and manpower ...

Churchill stood for the British Empire, for British independence and for an anti-Socialist vision of Britain. By July 1945 the first of these was on the skids, the second was dependent solely on America and the third had just vanished in a Labour election victory.

Source: J. Charmley, *Churchill: The End of Glory*, Hodder & Stoughton, 1993.

(a) On the basis of the evidence in this collection of sources, suggest why Churchill has been described as 'the Saviour of the Nation'. (16 marks)

(b) From the evidence of Sources C, D and E and the information in Chapter 28, what mistakes did Churchill make and how serious were they? (10 marks)

(c) Compare and contrast Sources F and G in their assessments of Churchill's role as war leader. (12 marks)

(d) Using the evidence of the sources and your own knowledge, explain which of the two interpretations you find most convincing. (12 marks)

(Total 50 marks)

2 Assess the importance of Allied air power in the eventual defeat of the Axis powers.

Labour in power: the Attlee governments 1945–51

Summary of events

As soon as Germany was defeated (7 May 1945), the Labour party was anxious to withdraw from the wartime coalition and fight a general election, since the parliament was ten years old. Churchill would have liked to fight the election as leader of a national government, as Lloyd George had done in 1918, but Labour's attitude made this impossible. Voting day was 5 July, though the results were not declared until three weeks later, to allow the armed forces to vote.

Labour won a massive victory, with 393 seats to the Conservatives' 213; the Liberals could only muster 12, and there were 22 others. This was the first time Labour had enjoyed an overall majority, and it would now be able to achieve its most cherished objectives – a welfare state, nationalization, work for everybody, and an open foreign policy based on genuine co-operation – without too much opposition (except from the House of Lords). Unfortunately the government was hampered by the most appalling economic problems in the aftermath of the war; the USA had immediately stopped Lend-Lease, two-thirds of Britain's export trade had disappeared, much of her merchant fleet had been lost in the war, and without American aid she lacked the capital to bring the economy back to normal peacetime production, so that she could begin to recover overseas markets. There were problems of international relations and the Cold War (see Section 32.1) and there was the dilemma of what to do about India (see Section 32.2) and Palestine (see Section 32.3).

The government was responsible for a remarkable though controversial set of achievements – social reforms, nationalization of key industries, financial measures, economic recovery, and independence for India. Inevitably, aspects of their policies aroused opposition, and in the general election of February 1950, Labour's position weakened as their overall majority fell to only 5. The government struggled on until October 1951 when another election gave the Conservatives a slim overall majority of 17.

29.1 The Labour victory in 1945

(a) Why did Labour win so decisively?

There was general amazement at the election result which gave Labour an overall majority of 146. Most people expected that after Churchill's splendid leadership during the war, the Conservatives would win comfortably. However, Churchill himself had doubts: 'I am worried about this damned election,' he remarked in June; 'I have no message for them now.' The basic reason for their defeat was that though Churchill was still popular, the Conservatives were not. Now that the war was almost over (Japan surrendered on 14 August), many people remembered the depression and held the Conservatives responsible for getting Britain into the war. As Harold Macmillan put it, 'it was not Churchill who lost the 1945 election; it was the ghost of Neville Chamberlain'. The Conservatives seemed to have shown little enthusiasm for the Beveridge Report, and although the government had prepared three White Papers (see Section 28.7(b)) about its proposed social policy, these received relatively little publicity. Labour on the other hand promised to implement the Beveridge Report, offering what people wanted to hear – jobs for everybody, plenty of new houses and a national health service. Churchill struck a false note when he claimed in a radio broadcast that a Labour government would bring with it 'the kind of features that were associated with the Gestapo'; many people thought this excessive, since he had been working closely and successfully for the last five years with Attlee, Morrison and Bevin, who could hardly be described as revolutionaries. The Labour leaders had gained ministerial experience during the wartime coalition, and there could be no doubts about their moderation and competence.

(b) *The new men in power*

The new Prime Minister, Clement Attlee, came from a middle-class background; educated at public school and Oxford, he had intended to become a barrister, but, having a strong social conscience, he became interested in social work in the poverty-stricken East End of London. He was elected MP for Limehouse in 1922 and leader of the Labour party in 1935. In appearance he was mild and inoffensive; he was quietly-spoken and did not waste words, and this led many people to underestimate him. Churchill

Illus. 29.1   The Labour big three: Bevin, Attlee and Morrison, after their victory in 1945

described him as 'a sheep in sheep's clothing', and later as 'a modest little man with plenty to be modest about'. But this was far from the truth; Attlee was shrewd and determined, and like Lord Liverpool, was an excellent manager of the cabinet, which contained several strong-minded and potentially difficult people. According to historian Peter Hennessy, he was good at 'using silence as a weapon, cutting off wafflers, absolutely brutal with the inadequate and the incompetent, far more effective than any Prime Minister since'.

The Foreign Secretary was Ernest Bevin; the son of a Somerset farm labourer, he had started work at the age of 11 as a farm boy. Later he became a drayman and then leader of the Transport and General Workers' Union. After the 1926 General Strike he had turned against industrial action, and was an outstanding success as Churchill's wartime Minister of Labour. Other leading members of the government were Hugh Dalton as Chancellor of the Exchequer (replaced by Sir Stafford Cripps in 1947), Herbert Morrison, leader of the House of Commons, and Aneurin Bevan, Minister of Health. All of them, apart from Bevan, had served in Churchill's coalition, and formed a capable and experienced team.

29.2 Labour and the Welfare State

(a) *Significance of the Beveridge Report*

The phrase 'welfare state' means one in which the government tries to provide the best possible social services for everybody. The Labour governments of 1945–51 are usually given most of the credit for setting up such a system in Britain. *The Beveridge Report of November 1942* (see Section 28.7(b)) had provided plenty of ideas about what a welfare state should aim for – the elimination of want, disease, ignorance, squalor and idleness – though it is now recognized as being far from the revolutionary document that many took it to be at the time. Many of its proposals were just a rationalization and an extension of existing schemes, they were not exactly generous, and they discriminated against working women (see Robert Pearce's article 'Beveridge 1942: Reconstruction or Reform?' in *Modern History Review*, September 1993).

In fact the Labour party already had its own plans for social reform before the Beveridge Report came out. The 1942 party conference committed a future Labour government to a comprehensive social security scheme, family allowances and a National Health Service. In spite of the country's economic difficulties, Attlee was determined to press ahead with this programme; a mass of new legislation reached the statute book, and by July 1948 Britain had a welfare state. It was not perfect, but an attack had been made on all five of Beveridge's 'giants': three of them – want, disease and idleness – had been well and truly tamed, though with the other two – squalor and ignorance – there was still some way to go. Some historians have called this a 'peaceful revolution', though others argue that the changes were merely evolutionary – they occurred naturally as the result of a long process of development. As Derek Fraser puts it: 'the British Welfare State was not born – it had evolved'.

(b) *The National Health Service*

This was the most spectacular of Labour's social reforms. It was the work of the Minister of Health, Aneurin Bevan, a former Welsh miner. Many people thought the task would be beyond him, but Bevan was an outstanding personality: he had educated himself and had read widely, he was a fluent speaker and a formidable debater – one of the few who could successfully stand up to Churchill. Within a very short time he had mastered the intricacies of the health and hospital situation; he had the vision to see exactly what he wanted, and the courage to make sure that he got it, in the face of some strong opposition from the medical profession. Starting on 5 July 1948, the system entitled everybody to free medical care in a range of services from general practitioners, specialists and dentists, to hospital and ophthalmic treatment, from spectacles, false teeth, medicines and drugs, to midwifery, maternity and child welfare services. The scheme was financed mainly from taxation, but some of the revenue came from National Insurance contributions. To make sure that the same standard of health care was provided in all parts of the country, Bevan decided that the hospitals should be nationalized. For health purposes England and Wales were divided into 14 areas, each under a regional hospital board; Scotland had five regional boards. Appointed by the Minister himself, these boards controlled general policy, while the day-to-day running of the hospitals was looked after by local management committees, of which there were 388 in England and Wales and 84 in Scotland.

There was considerable opposition to the scheme from family doctors who disliked the proposal that they should be paid a salary by the government. This, they argued, would deprive them of their professional independence and reduce them to the status of civil servants, which, they seemed to think, was beneath their dignity. It would also in some mysterious way, interfere with the doctor–patient relationship. In February 1948, 90 per cent of the members of the British Medical Association threatened to boycott the whole scheme. Bevan finally overcame their hostility by a clever device: instead of being paid a salary, doctors would receive fees based on the number of patients they had on their lists. This made all the difference, and when the scheme was introduced on 5 July 1948, 90 per cent of all GPs took part.

The service turned out to be more expensive that had been expected, costing more than £400 million in the first year. Prescriptions, which had been running at just under seven million a month under the old system, more or less doubled in September 1948 and had reached 19 million a month by 1951. No fewer than five million pairs of spectacles were given out by opticians in the first year, and the demand for false teeth was double what was expected. This led the government to begin charging adults half the cost of false teeth and spectacles (1951). Bevan resigned from the government, furious that his principle of a free health service had been violated. It was a sad end to his ministerial career but he will always be remembered as the architect of the NHS.

The system worked remarkably smoothly and soon brought a striking improvement in the health of the working class, while deaths from tuberculosis, pneumonia and diphtheria were greatly reduced. According to historians Alan Sked and Chris Cook, the new health service 'constituted an almost revolutionary social innovation since it improved the quality of life of most of the British people; ... it was soon to become the social institution of which the British would feel most proud'.

(c) *The National Insurance Act (1946)*

This extended the original 1911 Act to cover all adults. The scheme was compulsory; in return for a weekly contribution from worker, employer and government, the individual was entitled to sickness and unemployment benefit, old age pensions for women at 60 and men at 65 (26s. a week and 42s. for a married couple), widows' and orphans' pensions, maternity allowances, and death grants to help with funeral expenses. These were all more generous than Beveridge had anticipated, though some Labour left-wingers thought they should have been even higher.

(d) *The National Assistance Act (1948)*

This was designed to fill in any loopholes not covered by the National Insurance Act, which was supposed to apply to the entire population. However, people joining the insurance scheme for the first time were not entitled to full pension benefits for ten years, and there were tens of thousands of old people whose only income was the non-contributory pension (now 10s. a week, but still inadequate) introduced in 1908. Other people not covered were women whose husbands were in jail, unmarried mothers, and the blind, the deaf and the crippled. The Act set up *National Assistance Boards* to which they could apply for further assistance. This was a real innovation, a decisive break with the past, since although applicants had to undergo a 'means test', the money for the extra relief was provided by the government from taxation, and it was a move away from the idea that poverty was a matter for local administration. As well as cash benefits, the Act also provided services for people in need; and here the government did make use of local authorities, placing on them the duty of providing homes and other welfare services for the elderly and handicapped. Together with the National Insurance Act, this measure provided a whole new social security structure. It was generally welcomed, and unusually the Conservatives in opposition chose not to vote against either bill. They had moved a long way since 1900.

(e) *The National Insurance Industrial Injuries Act (1946)*

This was a vast improvement on the old Workmen's Compensation Acts under which it had been difficult and expensive for a workman to prove that an injury or disability had been caused by his job, and since the employer had to foot the bill, it had been even more difficult to win adequate compensation. The new Act made it compulsory for both workers and employers to join the state in making weekly contributions to a fund which would provide compensation to injured workers and pensions for those who were disabled.

(f) *Education*

The government concentrated on carrying out *the Butler Education Act of 1944* (see Section 28.7(b)), making secondary education until the age of 15 free, and providing meals, milk and medical services in schools. An examination (the 11-plus) was introduced to select which children were thought to be suitable for a grammar school education (or for a secondary technical school in the few areas where these existed), and which would go to secondary modern schools. In one sense the new system was an outstanding success: it allowed a whole new generation of talented working-class children to move up the educational ladder, many of them as far as university, which would have been unthinkable before 1939. A successful Youth Employment Service was set up and the government embarked on an expansion of university and technical education. Many Labour supporters and educational experts felt that by merely accepting the Butler Act, the government showed a disappointing lack of imagination. *Two main criticisms soon emerged:*

1 The education provided varied in type and quality from area to area. Some counties, like Lancashire, which could afford to provide technical schools as well as grammar schools, could boast that up to 40 per cent of their secondary places were in grammar and technical schools; but in other counties, like Surrey, the figure was as low as 15 per cent. The 11-plus examination therefore did not indicate which children were suitable for which type of school: it simply selected the required

number of children to fill the places available. In Surrey, children who would have been 'suitable' for a grammar school education had they lived in Lancashire, had to go to a secondary modern school because there were not enough grammar school places.

2   The system was divisive: the view rapidly developed that secondary modern schools were second-class institutions to which the 11-plus failures went; a new type of class distinction was therefore created. Many experts argued that if primary education could work successfully without different types of school, then it ought to be possible for secondary education to be successfully conducted in 'comprehensive' schools to which all children went at the age of 11, without selection. It was felt that Labour had missed a splendid opportunity to introduce a comprehensive system, free from class distinction, before the Butler system became established.

Another disappointment was that the Labour government, faced with heavy defence spending at the time of the Korean War (which began in June 1950), reduced the spending programme on education, so that fewer new schools, nurseries and colleges were built than had been intended.

(g) *Housing was a major problem*

On top of the housing shortage already existing in 1939, a further 700 000 houses had been destroyed in the war. In March 1945 Churchill's government announced that 750 000 new houses would be needed as soon as the war was over. Housing came under the control of Bevan's Ministy of Health, and although he was preoccupied with the Health Service, he still found time and energy to launch a housing drive. Economic conditions were not helpful – raw materials were in short supply and expensive. Nevertheless Bevan had considerable success. Only 55 400 new houses were completed in 1946, but this rose to almost 140 000 in 1947 and to over 284 000 in 1948 (this figure included pre-fabricated houses which Bevan himself privately described as 'rabbit-hutches'). There was a slight decline after that, but in 1949–51 Labour still averaged well over 200 000 houses a year, most of which were council houses.

Bevan had provided far more houses than Churchill had asked for; and what's more, he had insisted that the new council houses were built to higher standards than ever before, including three bedrooms and an indoor bathroom and lavatory. Unfortunately Churchill's figure of 750 000 turned out to be an underestimate; what nobody had foreseen was the increase in marriages and the rapid increase in the birth rate. In spite of Bevan's undoubted achievement, given the difficult economic situation, there was still a serious housing shortage when Labour left office in 1951. One estimate put it as high as 750 000 houses fewer than households. Finally, Bevan protected tenants who lived in houses owned by private landlords, by introducing rent controls.

(h) *Legislation to improve the environment*

1   *The New Towns Act (1946)* – this gave the government power to decide where new towns should be built and to set up development corporations to carry out the projects. The aim was to create towns which were healthy and pleasant to live in, as well as being geared to the needs of the townspeople, unlike the ugly monstrosities which had grown up without any planning during the nineteenth century. The first to be completed was Stevenage, followed by Crawley, Hemel Hempstead and Harlow. Altogether 14 New Towns were operational before the

end of the Labour governments, and these were not just in the south; successful examples elsewhere were East Kilbride, Peterlee and Glenrothes.

2   *The Town and Country Planning Act (1947)* was another Bevan measure designed to make life more pleasant. It gave the job of planning to the county authorities, which were all required to produce land development plans for the next 20 years. The planning authorities were given much wider powers of compulsory purchase and the right to control advertisements and historic buildings. Government grants were available whenever necessary. If there was any increase in land values as a result of profitable development, the government had the power to levy a development charge on the increase.

(i) The Trade Disputes Act (1946)

This repealed Baldwin's 1927 Act of the same title (see Section 24.4(c)). The political levy was now legal again, and it was up to individuals to 'contract out' if they did not wish to make a financial contribution to the Labour party.

29.3 Why and how did Labour attempt to introduce a planned economy?

(a) The ideas and motives behind a planned economy

The idea of a planned economy had been discussed between the wars (see Section 20.5). The Labour government was the first to make a serious attempt to carry out some of the suggestions put forward. Their motives were mixed: the immediate need was to restore trade and prosperity which had been badly affected by the war – it was calculated that about two-thirds of Britain's export trade had disappeared. Declining industries had to be revived so that exports could increase and the massive balance of payments deficit could be eliminated. Over £3000 million was owed, much of it to the USA for goods supplied on credit during the war.

Labour felt that the best way of restructuring and modernizing industry was to nationalize it, that is, to take the most important industries away from their private owners so that they became the property of the state. In this way the government would be able to control 'the means of production, distribution and exchange'. It would permit more efficient planning and more co-operation between industries, and would ensure fair treatment and better conditions for the workers. The coalmining industry was a prime example of inefficiency and poor labour relations which, Labour felt, could be improved only by government control. Above all it was hoped that better planning would eliminate unemployment, the problem which had plagued all the governments between the wars.

(b) Nationalization

This was the most striking of Labour's attempts at planning. Nationalization was a matter of principle for socialists; they believed that it was only right for the country's most important industries to be owned by the state, so that profits would go into the treasury rather than into the pockets of private owners. This would provide much of the extra cash needed to pay for the new welfare state. The programme was carried through under the general direction of Herbert Morrison.

First came the nationalization of the Bank of England (1946) which meant that money would now be available whenever the government needed it for investment. Later the same year air transport was nationalized and reorganized into three companies: British Overseas, British European and British South American Airways. In 1947 it was the turn of coalmining and cable and wireless. In spite of Conservative opposition, some 1500 collieries and about 400 smaller mines were handed over to state ownership, to be controlled by *the National Coal Board*. There was great rejoicing among the miners who felt that at last they were about to get a fair deal. The main Conservative criticism was that the industry, with close on three-quarters of a million workers, was too large to be controlled centrally. The nationalization of cable and wireless meant that the government now controlled all international radio and telegraph services.

Public transport (1948) was to be controlled by *the British Transport Commission* which was divided into six boards: Docks and Inland Waterways, Railways, London Transport, Road Haulage and Road Passenger Transport. The government hoped to create an efficient transport network in which all the different branches were co-ordinated to provide a well-planned system which would serve everybody, including those living in remote areas. The generation and supply of electricity were also nationalized in 1948. The Central Electricity Board with its national grid of pylons and power lines had been owned by the government since 1926. Now the state took over the separate generating companies – about 500 of them – and set up 14 area electricity boards which were able to standardize voltages and prices and provide a more efficient service over the whole country. The same reasoning lay behind the nationalization of the gas industry in 1949. The government was able to organize the hundreds of small companies into an efficient national system.

Iron and steel was the most controversial of Labour's targets for nationalization and showed that the consensus of opinion between Labour and Conservatives on the issue of nationalization had its limits. The iron and steel industry was reasonably prosperous and efficient; Labour was determined that it should be nationalized (though Morrison himself had doubts), since it was clearly one of the 'commanding heights' of the economy. However, the Conservatives believed that nationalization was only justified if an industry was in need of help because it was inefficient or old-fashioned. Profitable industries should be left in the hands of private people who knew how to run them best. They opposed Labour's plans bitterly in parliament and the House of Lords refused to pass the Bill. To overcome this opposition the government passed *the Parliament Act (1949)* which reduced the powers of the House of Lords: instead of being able to delay bills for three sessions of parliament (two years), the delay could now only be two sessions (one year in actual time). At the same time plural voting was abolished and the universities lost their representation in parliament. With all the delays, it was only after the 1950 election that the nationalization of iron and steel took effect; if Labour had lost the election, the bill would have been scrapped. The Conservatives swore that they would denationalize iron and steel as soon as possible, and they did so in 1953.

(c) American aid and the Marshall Plan

In August 1945 an immediate injection of cash was needed to get the economy moving again. Since the Americans had stopped Lend-Lease, Keynes, the famous economist, was sent to Washington to negotiate an interest-free loan of 6000 million dollars. The Americans were unsympathetic and drove a hard bargain – they would lend only 3750 million dollars at 2 per cent interest, and repayments were to start in 1951; in 1947 Britain would be required to make the pound sterling freely convertible (exchangeable) for dollars. The loan was made available in July 1946, but within a year it had almost been used up. Industry was recovering and exports had actually reached 17 per cent above the 1939 level; but this was not enough – the balance of payments deficit stood at £438 million.

However, help was on the way: the American Secretary of State, George Marshall, worried about the poor prospects for American exports and about the possible spread of communism in Europe, launched his *European Recovery Programme*, offering grants to any country in Europe which cared to accept them. In 1948 Britain gratefully took the lead (see Section 32.1(d)), accepting what amounted to a gift of £1263 million (known as Marshall Aid). This enabled the recovery to be completed, and by 1950 British exports stood at 75 per cent above the 1938 level.

(d) *Close control of all aspects of the economy*

This was another feature of Labour's attempts at planning; a new *Economic Planning Council* was set up (July 1947) under Sir Edwin Plowden, together with a whole host of planning committees, such as the Import Programme Committee and the Production Committee. Control was especially marked in 1947–50 after Sir Stafford Cripps had replaced Dalton as Chancellor of the Exchequer. Descended from an aristocratic family, educated at public school, and with a successful career as a barrister behind him, Cripps was 40 when he was converted to socialism. He was a devout Anglican, moral and upright (many thought him sanctimonious), and had a highly developed sense of duty and service to his fellow humans. He was a teetotaller and a vegetarian and believed that *austerity* was the way to conquer Britain's economic problems. Only increased production and exports would provide the necessary resources to make Britain a fairer country. He left people in no doubt about his priorities: 'First are exports, second is capital investment in industry, and last are the needs, comforts and amenities of the family.' The public must 'submerge all thought of personal gain and personal ambition'. No wonder an observer listening to a Cripps speech once remarked: 'you can just see the home-made lemonade boiling in his veins'. *Control measures included:*

- Since there was still a world shortage of food, 'fair shares' wartime rationing was continued. Bread rationing was in operation from 1946 to 1948, and potato rationing was introduced in December 1947; in almost all cases the allowances were lower than the wartime average. As the situation improved, certain commodities were de-rationed, but even in 1951, meat, bacon, butter, tea and sugar were still rationed. However, the government provided subsidies to keep food prices down, and gave help to farmers (price guarantees, subsidies for modernization, and the National Agricultural Advisory Service to provide the expertise).This helped to bring about a 20 per cent increase in agricultural output between 1947 and 1952, and made Britain's farming industry one of the most mechanized and efficient in the world.
- During the disastrously cold winter of 1946–7, demand for coal and electricity was so enormous that all fuels were severely rationed. For several weeks it was illegal to use electricity in the home between 9 a.m. and midday and between 2 p.m. and 4 p.m. Many factories had to close through lack of coal, throwing two million people temporarily out of work (March 1947).
- Building materials were rationed and licences had to be obtained for all new buildings; this was to make sure that resources went into building factories, schools and council houses instead of into less essential projects like dance-halls and cinemas.
- Rents, profits and interest rates were controlled and a tight rein kept on foreign currency, so that holidays abroad were out of the question for most people.
- Imports were controlled in the struggle to achieve a favourable balance of

payments. The government bought supplies of raw materials for industry and allocated them to those industries which would contribute towards the export drive: cars, motorcycles, tractors, ships, engineering products, aircraft and chemicals. Cripps's exhortations to businessmen to export at all costs certainly worked, but it left a chronic shortage of consumer goods for the home market.

● Cripps persuaded the trade unions to accept a policy of wage restraint between 1948 and 1950; at a time of rising prices, this was a considerable achievement.

● In August 1949, in response to a recession in the USA and a drain of Britain's gold reserves, Cripps devalued the pound so that it was worth $2.80 instead of $4.03. Many thought that Cripps had overreacted, but other experts think the pound had been overvalued after the war and that devaluation was a sensible policy, facing up to reality. Although at the time it was seen as a setback for the government, the immediate effects were good: the devaluation made imports more expensive and British exports cheaper, so that for a time exports were boosted.

29.4 How successful were the policies of the Labour governments?

Labour was responsible for a huge body of reform, but inevitably with such controversial policies, historians are divided about their success and their long-term effects. Broadly speaking there are three different interpretations:

● the sympathetic view – Labour was largely successful in carrying out its policies and achieving its main aims, and deserves to be remembered above all as the creator of the welfare state and the party that led Britain to recovery after the Second World War.

● the unsympathetic left-wing view – Labour missed an opportunity to introduce real change and real socialism; their policies were half-hearted and nowhere near radical enough.

● the unsympathetic right-wing view – Labour was so obsessed with its welfare state that it neglected industry and the economy, with disastrous long-term results.

(a) *The sympathetic view*

Historians Kenneth Morgan and Paul Addison are leading exponents of this view. They believe that Labour, boosted by a great vote of confidence in the 1945 election, carried out its mandate for radical change; its social policies were innovative and highly successful, setting the pattern for the next quarter of a century until the appearance of Thatcherism. Labour's attempts at planning the economy surpassed anything previously seen in Britain, and brought considerable success. By 1950 Britain was well on the way to recovery: inflation seemed to be under control, there was full employment, exports were increasing, and there was a healthy balance of payments. Especially impressive was the export of British cars to North America. The 1951 Festival of Britain could be seen as a triumphant symbol of Britain's recovery and revitalization. According to Kenneth Morgan, 1948–50 'was amongst the most thriving periods economically that the country as a whole had experienced since the late Victorian era'. Most Labour supporters were full of praise for the 'mixed economy', that is, partly nationalized and partly privately owned; they hoped that this new 'middle way' (between full capitalism, in which everything was privately owned, and communism, in which everything was owned by the state) would be an example for the rest of the world to follow. Economist Alec Cairncross believes that, given the awesome problems facing the government in 1945, its achievements could hardly have been greater. There were notable achievements in foreign policy too, with Bevin playing an important role in the Marshall Plan and the formation of NATO (see Section 32.1(d and f)) and Attlee handling Indian independence well in difficult circumstances (see Section 32.2).

However, in the final year of its life, the Labour government suffered an economic setback when Britain became involved in the war in Korea (see Section 32.1(g)). The USA, leading the attack on the communists, went in for massive rearmament, forcing up prices of raw materials on the world market, and causing a sharp increase in the price of goods imported into Britain. When Britain also decided to increase her rearmament programme, it led to a period of inflation, shortages and further economies; to save money, Hugh Gaitskell (who had replaced the exhausted and ailing Cripps as Chancellor) introduced charges for spectacles and dental treatment, causing a split in the party. Peter Hennessy sums up the sympathetic view well: in spite of the economic setback of 1951, 'the achievements of the Attlee administration between 1945 and 1951 probably make it the most hyper-achieving peacetime government this century in economic and, especially, social terms. Virtually all the promises in its manifesto were implemented by 1951.'

(b) *The unsympathetic left-wing view*

Historians like John Saville believe that Labour was a great disappointment to real socialists; although the social reforms were quite impressive, the government failed to introduce a genuine socialist system and ended up merely strengthening capitalism:

● The people running Labour's economic policy – Morrison, Dalton, Cripps and Shinwell – were not expert planners and were reluctant to listen to advice. Even a sympathetic historian like Morgan admits that 'Britain's economic planning under Labour was distinctly weak at the centre ... advisers found themselves often frustrated by a government of the left that steadfastly refused to plan'. Their whole approach was piecemeal and indirect, and they tended to deal with specific problems and situations as they arose rather than working out an overall plan to be followed. In spite of all the various planning committees, the government never succeeded in drawing up real targets for investment, production and consumption.
● Nationalization was not carried out in the way many socialists had hoped. Morrison set the newly nationalized industries up as public corporations, like the Central Electricity Board and the BBC which had been introduced by the Conservatives in the 1920s. Each industry was controlled by a small board of experts responsible to a government minister, but there were no workers on the boards, they had no share in decision-making and no share of the profits. This tended to make the structure too bureaucratic and inflexible, and the workers felt excluded, which meant that the mass support for nationalization which in theory there should have been among the working classes, did not exist. It was felt that the previous owners had been compensated excessively: the mine-owners received £164 million and the iron and steel owners £240 million; it was clear that many years' profits would be needed to pay off such large sums. What the government had actually done was to buy out the former owners while keeping the same management.
● Only about 20 per cent of the nation's industries were nationalized, and apart from iron and steel, they were either unprofitable, or in need of investment for development and modernization, or both. Profitable industries remained firmly in the hands of private enterprise. Yet the government felt unable to provide sufficient investment to do the job properly, and consequently the nationalized industries, particularly coal and

transport, continued to provide an inefficient service and ran up large deficits. The hope that profits would help meet the cost of the welfare state proved false. This whole approach convinced the public that nationalization automatically implied inefficiency and waste, and Labour failed to point out that the problems were of long standing and that the payment of compensation to the previous owners was using up most of the profits. There was a strong case for nationalizing other profitable industries, for example those producing consumer goods, to show that state ownership need not be limited to 'commanding heights' industries and failing industries.

However, the Labour leaders were cautious men who had gone as far as they dared. They had no plans to take over any more industries after iron and steel. Instead of being the beginning of a new era of collectivist planning which socialists had been dreaming of, the Attlee government turned out to be the climax of 50 years of economic and social reform. What remained now was not further development, but, as Morrison himself put it, 'consolidation'.

• Labour made the mistake of assuming that Britain must continue to act as if she were a great power, when in fact her economy was incapable of sustaining such action. Holders of this view believe that the government should not have taken the decision to become an atomic power in 1947 and should have kept out of the Korean War.

(c) *The unsympathetic right-wing view*

This view was first put clearly by Corelli Barnett in his book *The Audit of War* which was published in 1986. Barnett would certainly agree with Peter Hennessy that by 1951 Labour had fulfilled virtually all the promises in its manifesto, but he believes that this had disastrous effects. The government was led astray into the 'utopian' schemes of Beveridge, which the economy was incapable of supporting. Labour's obsession with the welfare state used up resources which should have been put into modernizing industry, and then left the country saddled with a long-term burden which hampered the economy and reduced Britain's competitiveness for the next half-century. True, the country needed social reform, but this should have waited until industry had been brought into the highest possible state of efficiency, thus maximizing profits which would have helped towards the cost of the welfare state. Holders of this view believe that the Beveridge Report and Attlee's government between them must bear a heavy responsibility for Britain's post-war decline.

(d) *Conclusion?*

Some more recent writers, including Martin Pugh, Robert Pearce, Nick Tiratsoo and Jim Tomlinson, have swung the argument firmly back in favour of the sympathetic view. They feel that Corelli Barnett overstated his case; there were clearly far more forces at work causing Britain's economic decline for it to be pinned on the Labour government and excessive public spending. Robert Pearce points out that although welfare spending did increase rapidly after 1945, 'this was also the case among Britain's economic rivals and so cannot constitute a distinguishing feature explaining poor economic performance'. Martin Pugh mounts a strong defence of Labour's record, arguing that although huge sums of money *were* spent, especially on the NHS, expenditure did not get out of control. The three Labour Chancellors, Dalton, Cripps and Gaitskell, were all extremely careful to keep expenditure within bounds. Pugh makes the important point that the amount of ill-health which had gone untreated before 1945 was also very damaging to the economy; 'any genuine audit of welfare policy would have to include some assessment of the economic gain from a fit and healthy labour force'.

Nick Tiratsoo and Jim Tomlinson, in their joint study of Labour's economic policy, argue that Labour did not ignore industrial development: on the contrary, important steps were taken:

- the government made sure that building new factories was given priority over hospitals, schools and houses;
- working parties of experts, employers, workers and trade unionists were set up to investigate certain key industries and recommend improvements;
- the *British Institute of Management* was set up (1948) to improve standards in management;
- industrialists and workers went to the USA with government backing, to find out what the latest techniques were;
- there was an official government campaign to encourage joint production committees in factories where employers and workers could come together to sort out differences and improve performance.

If the achievement was less than might have been hoped, this was partly because of a lack of co-operation from employers, who were opposed to all state intervention, fearing that it would lead to nationalization; the idea of actually consulting trade unions was thought to be a sign of weakness, which would also lead to a loss of control by management.

29.5 Why did Labour lose the 1951 general election?

The question has to be faced, if Labour was as successful as these historians suggest, why did the party lose the general election in 1951? Several factors seem to have been at work:

1 The country was tired of rationing and the housing shortage, and there was a feeling that austerity had gone on too long. There was a new round of restrictions and shortages as a result of the government's decision to increase its armaments programme when Britain became involved in the Korean War (1950–3); and above all, the cost of living was rising. The period of compulsory military service (introduced in 1947) was increased from 18 months to two years in 1950, and this was an unpopular move.

2 The government had just had to deal with a crisis in Iran (Persia) when the Iranian government suddenly nationalized the oil refinery at Abadan owned by the Anglo-Iranian Oil Company, in which the British government held a majority of the shares. The Conservatives urged the government to send troops to recapture the refinery, which was the largest single supplier of oil to Britain. The Labour cabinet took no action, and thus laid itself open to the charge of weakness. The Conservatives were able to cash in with the cry that in situations like the Korean War and the Iranian Oil crisis, Churchill was the man needed to lead the country. (A compromise solution was reached in 1954 allowing British Petroleum 40 per cent of the shares.)

3 The Conservatives produced an attractive programme promising to build 300 000 houses a year, to give people 'more red meat', a tempting proposal at a time when meat was still strictly rationed, and to 'set people free' from socialist rules and restrictions. Results suggest that on the whole, working-class voters, especially in the north and west, continued to support Labour; but middle-class voters,

especially in the south east (where Labour lost 20 seats), continued the drift away from Labour which had begun in the 1950 election.

4   Labour campaigned on its achievements in office, which were certainly impressive. However, with the resignation of Bevan and Harold Wilson (President of the Board of Trade) over the introduction of National Health charges, the party seemed to be split, and the government had a general air of exhaustion after its six frantically busy years in office.

5   It is thought that Liberal supporters in constituencies where there was no Liberal candidate (only 109 Liberals stood) tended to vote Conservative. Even so, the Labour defeat was very narrow: Labour actually polled more votes than they had ever done before (13.95 million, compared with 13.26 million in 1950), and *more votes than the Conservatives* (13.7 million, up from 12.5 million in 1950), yet they won only 295 seats to the Conservatives' 311. The main reason for this strange state of affairs was that many Labour MPs in safe seats were elected with huge majorities, whereas, on the whole, Conservative majorities tended to be smaller. The Liberals, who won only 6 seats, saw their vote slip from 2.6 million in 1950 to only 0.7 million.

Questions

1   The Labour government and nationalization
Study Sources A to D and then answer the questions which follow.

___ **Source A** _____

Putting the cart before the horse – a cartoon in Punch *in 1949. The man pulling the cart is Clement Attlee, the Labour Prime Minister*

Figure 29.1

Extracts from a conversation between Attlee and a journalist, Francis Williams

Williams: Had you a complete working pattern of policy in mind when you became Prime Minister?

Attlee: Certainly. I was definitely determined to go ahead with plans of nationalisation. There was no difficulty with the Bank of England, Cable and Wireless, gas and electricity and there wasn't much with the mines. Transport was much more difficult and iron and steel had not been worked out.... There were a lot of problems to clear up but I felt we must push ahead. Nationalisation had to go ahead because it fell in with the essential planning of the country. It wasn't just nationalisation for nationalisation's sake, but the policy in which we believed: that fundamental things – central banking, transport, fuel and power – must be taken over by the nation as an essential part of a planned economy – a basis on which the rest of reorganisation of the country would depend. There was the making of the health service, the co-ordination of all the various social services and the advance in education. All this could not be delayed. And there were practical things – building houses and many new factories ...

Source: quoted in F. Williams, *A Prime Minister Remembers*, Heinemann, 1961.

Extract from a speech by Winston Churchill, the Conservative leader, during the 1951 election campaign

Socialism, with its vast network of regulations and restrictions and its incompetent planning, is proving itself every day to be a dangerous and costly mistake. Every major industry which the socialists have nationalised, has passed from the profitable or self-supporting side of the balance-sheet to the loss-making side.

Source: quoted in A. Sked and C. Cook, *Post-War Britain*, Penguin, 1993 edition.

Historian C. J. Bartlett writes about nationalization

The case for the nationalisation of electricity and gas was strong. Neither, as organized, could undertake ambitious and co-ordinated modernisation programmes. There were over 500 separate electricity undertakings. Gas supply was even more disorganised and inefficient. The case for the nationalisation of the coalmines, the Bank of England, airways and railways was also good and could be justified on grounds other than socialism. All needed lots of capital that was unlikely to be provided by private enterprise. The major debate was over iron and steel. This industry was not obviously inefficient or short of capital, but it was clearly one of the 'commanding heights of the economy'.

Source: C. J. Bartlett, *A History of Postwar Britain*, Longman, 1977.

(a) On the basis of the evidence in Sources B and D, what was the case in favour of nationalization? (7 marks)

(b) From the evidence in Sources A and C, what criticisms were made of Labour's nationalization programme? (5 marks)

(c) Judging by the evidence of the other sources and your own knowledge, how valid were the criticisms made in Sources A and C? (13 marks)

(Total 25 marks)

2 How successfully did the Labour governments of 1945–51 tackle the economic and social problems of post-war Britain? [NEAB]

30 The rise and fall of consensus 1951–79

Summary of events

The Conservatives were in power for 13 years following their narrow election victory in October 1951; they won the next two elections – in 1955 and 1959 – much more convincingly, with majorities of 58 and 100. This period saw four Tory Prime Ministers: Churchill (1951–5), Sir Anthony Eden (1955–7), Harold Macmillan (1957–63) and Sir Alec Douglas-Home, the 14th Earl of Home (1963–4). On the whole it seemed to be a period of prosperity when, as Macmillan put it, people had 'never had it so good'. Eventually, after losing three consecutive elections, Labour succeeded in winning a tiny overall majority of 4 (October 1964). This was soon increased to 96 in the election of 1966, and Labour remained in power, with Harold Wilson as Prime Minister, until 1970.

By this time the economy was far from healthy, and in the election of June 1970 there was a swing from Labour big enough to give the Conservatives an overall majority of 30. Edward Heath was Prime Minister until February 1974, when a confrontation between government and miners led to a narrow Conservative defeat and the return of Wilson as Prime Minister, though without an overall majority. In October 1974 Wilson went to the country again, and although Labour strengthened its position, the results fell well below Wilson's hopes. With 319 seats, Labour had a comfortable lead over the Conservatives (277) and Liberals (13), but there were 26 assorted Nationalist and Northern Ireland MPs, leaving a Labour overall majority of only 3. In spite of this, Labour remained in office until May 1979, though Wilson himself resigned in April 1976. James Callaghan was Prime Minister for the remainder of the Labour government. The election of May 1979 brought a decisive result: the Conservatives won a comfortable overall majority of 43, and Margaret Thatcher became Britain's first woman Prime Minister.

A summary of the different governments, October 1951 to May 1979

Date	Government	Prime Minister
October 1951– May 1955	Conservative	Sir Winston Churchill (October 1951– April 1955) Sir Anthony Eden (from April 1955)

May 1955– October 1959	Conservative	Sir Anthony Eden (until January 1957) Harold Macmillan (from January 1957)
October 1959– October 1964	Conservative	Harold Macmillan (until October 1963) Sir Alec Douglas-Home (October 1963–October 1964)
October 1964– March 1966	Labour	Harold Wilson
March 1966– June 1970	Labour	Harold Wilson
June 1970– March 1974	Conservative	Edward Heath
March– October 1974	Labour	Harold Wilson
October 1974– May 1979	Labour	Harold Wilson (until April 1976) James Callaghan (April 1976–May 1979)

30.1 What is meant by consensus politics?

The period from 1951 until the early 1970s is usually described as *the era of consensus politics*. This means that there seemed to be very little fundamental difference between the policies of the two main parties, though of course there were differences of detail and emphasis. Strictly speaking, consensus began during the Second World War when the Conservatives and Labour worked so well together during the wartime coalition. This continued during Attlee's governments when the only really bitter clash was over iron and steel nationalization, leading to a further reduction in the power of the House of Lords.

When the Conservatives came to power in 1951, there was no dramatic change in policy. In spite of all the party propaganda, the generally Keynesian approach continued: the Welfare State was safeguarded and even extended, and the government accepted Labour's policy of full employment, and the mixed economy; only steel and road haulage (which Labour had been less than enthusiastic about anyway) were denationalized. The term *'Butskellism'* was coined by *The Economist* from the surnames of R. A. Butler (Churchill's Chancellor of the Exchequer) and Hugh Gaitskell (Labour leader from 1955 until his death in 1963), to show how close Conservative and Labour policies were. This consensus lasted through the 13 years of Conservative government (1951–64), and through Harold Wilson's Labour governments (1964–70).

This does not mean that there was *total* agreement about every policy; there were people in both parties who felt impatient with the consensus approach. Some Conservative right-wingers, for example, were appalled at Macmillan's decolonization policies (see Section 32.5–6). Some Labour left-wingers were bitter critics of the official Labour line on defence, which was to go along with the Conservative policy of rearmament and building up nuclear weapons. However, the Conservative leadership kept the right-wingers out of key positions in the government and the consensus was able to continue. With the failure of Edward Heath's government (1970–4) and the election of the right-winger Margaret Thatcher as Conservative leader (1975), the period of consensus came to an end.

30.2 The Conservative governments 1951–64

(a) *Churchill and Eden*

At the age of 77 when he became Prime Minister for the second time, Churchill was no longer the dynamic leader of the early 1940s; he left much of the heavy work to his acknowledged successor, Anthony Eden. When Churchill retired in April 1955, Eden became Prime Minister and immedietely held a general election in which the Conservatives increased their slim lead to an overall majority of 58. Reasons for their victory were the country's growing prosperity and rising living standards, together with the fact that the Labour party was seriously split over defence policy. While the official Labour line was to go along with the government's rearmament programme, Aneurin Bevan and his supporters – Harold Wilson, Richard Crossman, Barbara Castle and others – criticized it bitterly. Bevan was on the verge of being expelled from the party after his attacks on Attlee.

Eden's premiership was a disappointment. Much was expected of him: his reputation as an international statesman stood high, he had a social conscience, and since he was charming and handsome, he even looked the part of the successful Prime Minister. Within a few months, however, he was giving the impression of not being in full control of his cabinet, and even the Conservative press mounted an attack against him, claiming that what was needed was a 'smack of firm government'. His disastrous handling of the Suez Crisis in 1956 (see Section 32.4) and his deteriorating health caused him to resign (January 1957).

(b) *The Macmillan era*

Harold Macmillan was chosen as Conservative leader in preference to R. A. Butler, and was Prime Minister for over six years (1957–63). Macmillan was a member of the famous publishing family, and had aristocratic connections, having married the daughter of the Duke of Devonshire. According to Sked and Cook, he was 'a fascinating personality, a strange mixture of the hard-headed professional politician and the amateurish country gentleman, indulging a somewhat theatrical, Edwardian style of political presentation'. During the 1930s when he was MP for Stockton-on-Tees, he had acquired a reputation as a progressive, forward-looking and radical Conservative with his plans for dealing with unemployment and his book *The Middle Way* published in 1938, in which he set out his radical, but non-socialist solution to the depression.

Macmillan was a 'one nation Tory', believing that the Conservatives should follow Disraeli's example, as Quintin Hogg (another Tory reformer) put it, 'to lead and dominate revolution by superior statesmanship instead of to oppose it, to by-pass the progressives by stepping in front of current controversy instead of engaging in it'. As Housing Minister, Macmillan had recently demonstrated his social awareness by building more houses per year than the previous Labour government. He soon restored party morale, which was in tatters after the Suez debacle, and revealed himself as a natural leader, commanding the respect of his cabinet and establishing a rapport with the public through his television appearances. By the time the next election took place (October 1959) the country seemed to have forgotten Suez, the economy was booming, and the Conservatives coasted to an easy victory under 'Super-Mac's' leadership. It was the third successive election victory for the Tories and a personal triumph for Macmillan.

The Macmillan years were a crucial period in British history; despite the Prime Minister's many gifts, even he was unable to disguise permanently the fact that Britain was no longer a great power. Most of her empire gained independence and Britain got no compensatory influence in Europe. When she missed an opportunity to join the Common Market (1957) and was refused entry in 1963, Macmillan's foreign policy had largely failed (see Section 32.7). In home affairs Britain enjoyed a period of prosperity and rising living standards. But in the early 1960s the economy seemed to be stagnating and by January 1963, almost 900 000 people were out of work. Later that year, Macmillan, approaching 70 and in poor health, decided to resign. Sir Alec Douglas-Home was Prime Minister for a year until the Conservatives lost the 1964 election.

30.3 What did the Conservative governments achieve?

(a) *An improvement in living standards*

This was the most striking feature of the 13 years of Conservative rule.

1   The first sign of improvement was the government's decision to move away from 'austerity' by reducing as many of Labour's controls as possible. During Churchill's government, restrictions of all sorts were swept away: all types of rationing and restrictions on building were ended, income tax was reduced and limits on hire-purchase sales and even on the right to strike were removed.
2   Between 1951 and 1963 wages rose on average by 72 per cent while prices rose by only 45 per cent; this meant that people could afford more consumer goods than ever before. For example, the number of cars rose from under three million to well over seven million, while licensed TV sets rose from 340 000 to almost 13 million. In 1961 the working week was reduced from 48 hours to 42 hours.
3   There was an increase in house building, thanks to the efforts of Macmillan at the new Ministry of Housing. He was determined to outdo the previous Labour government's record – their best year had been 1947 when 284 230 new houses had appeared. Macmillan threw all his energies into the 'national housing crusade', as he later described it. Unlike Labour, he encouraged local authorities to allow private contractors to build more houses and abolished Labour's tax on land development. Churchill told him he must produce 300 000 new houses a year, but Macmillan did even better – 327 000 in 1953, and 354 000 in 1954. The worst of the housing shortage was clearly over.

(b) *Important extensions of the Welfare State*

Benefits were raised, and *the Mental Health Act (1959)* laid down that mental illness was to be regarded no differently from physical illness. However, the introduction of a 2s. prescription charge aroused the Labour opposition to fury. There was also criticism that very few new hospitals were built during the 1950s. In 1962 the government announced that 90 new hospitals would be built over the next 10 years, but the Conservatives were out of office before the programme got under way.

(c) *Help for agriculture*

Help was provided for agriculture in the form of grants and subsidies to encourage farmers to use new fertilizers, new machinery, new techniques and new animal feeds. It was calculated that in the year 1960–1 alone, over £100 million was given to farmers by the state. Farming became increasingly mechanized and highly efficient, and production continued to rise.

(d) *An expansion of education*

About 6000 new schools were built and 11 new universities, while the existing universities were encouraged to expand. Realizing the importance of technological education, the government introduced Colleges of Advanced Technology. The great debate in education during the 1950s was about the relative merits of comprehensive and grammar schools. By the time of the 1959 election, Labour was committed to supporting comprehensive education on the grounds that it would reduce class distinction, and because the 11-plus examination was not thought to be a reliable method of predicting future academic development and achievement. For most of their 13 years the Conservatives supported the grammar schools and prevented county councils from introducing comprehensive systems. By 1963 they were just beginning to recognize the possible advantages of comprehensive education, and their support for the grammar schools was weakening.

Critics of the government pointed out that the list of achievements did not seem particularly impressive compared with what Labour had achieved in a much shorter period. As time went on, more attention began to focus on criticisms of the government.

30.4 On what grounds can Conservative policies be criticized?

(a) *Inconsistent economic policies*

The Conservatives did not find a permanent solution to the interconnected problems of how to stimulate economic growth, while at the same time keeping inflation under control and maintaining a favourable balance of trade. Successive Chancellors of the Exchequer tried different methods, sometimes attempting to limit spending, sometimes allowing more freedom; this approach came to be known as *'stop–go'*.

1   R. A. Butler, Churchill's Chancellor, inherited an unhealthy economic situation from Labour. The Korean War (1950–3) caused a rise in world raw material prices, so that the cost of Britain's imports increased appreciably; Butler found that the balance of payments deficit was approaching £700 million. He decided that he must bring about a reduction in demand; a package of restrictions was introduced, including controls on credit (bank rate was raised from 2 per cent to 4 per cent to discourage people from borrowing money) and strict limits on imports. This was the first of the Conservative 'stop' phases; it seemed to work: by the end of 1952 the deficit had been converted into a surplus of £300 million. It was generally thought that Butler's 'stop' had been responsible for the improvement, but it is now clear to economists that the main reason was that the increase in import prices caused by the Korean War lasted only a short time. During 1952 import prices fell to the old levels, whereas Britain's exports continued to sell at roughly the same

prices. The deficit would probably have righted itself without any interference from Butler, whose measures had the unfortunate effect of reducing investment in industry at a time when industrialists ought to have been aiming for rapid growth. The disturbing fact was that although there was a trade surplus at the end of 1952, British exports were actually falling. The significance of this did not seem to be appreciated at the time: the Tories seem to have drawn the conclusion that whenever an unfavourable balance of payments seemed likely, a quick 'stop' was all that was needed to work the economic miracle. The fact that these stops hindered economic growth was ignored.

2   During 1953 and 1954 Butler operated a 'go' phase, cutting the bank rate, encouraging investment and producing some industrial expansion. There was full employment, exports increased and the economy moved into a period of boom. The situation seemed so promising that shortly before the 1955 election, Butler took sixpence off income tax. Now a different problem developed: full employment brought rising wages, and the demand for goods at home increased, causing rising prices – inflation. The increasing demand was met partly by increasing imports. At the same time exports were adversely affected by large numbers of strikes, and 1955 saw another unfavourable balance of payments. Butler tried to reduce home demand by raising purchase tax and hire purchase deposits. This change of tack so soon after the income tax reduction gave the impression that Butler's judgement was at fault, and he was soon replaced as Chancellor by Macmillan.

3   Macmillan continued Butler's 'stop' policy, raising the bank rate to 5.5 per cent, so that it was more expensive to borrow cash. This was known as a *credit squeeze*: an attempt to reduce spending in order to check inflation and reduce imports, thereby improving the balance of payments. This was successful in that it produced a favourable trade balance for 1956.

4   With the economy apparently going well, the next Chancellor, Peter Thorneycroft (1957–8), decided to relax the squeeze and risk a 'go'. Taxes and credit restrictions were reduced and an export boom followed; but at the same time, more cash was available to spend at home, causing an increase in demand and a consequent rise in prices and imports. Price rises led to wage demands and strikes, so that exports were soon affected and the balance of payments was threatened again. Thorneycroft believed the time had come to get inflation under control by holding down expenditure for 1958–9. There was some opposition to this in the cabinet, since it might mean less cash for social policies; Macmillan, with one eye on the possibility of a 1959 election, also opposed Thorneycroft, who resigned (January 1958).

5   Macmillan pressurized his next Chancellor, Derick Heathcoat Amory, to produce a budget which would be popular with voters. The Chancellor obliged with his 1959 tax-cutting budget, and also relaxed credit controls and allowed wage increases. This certainly helped to woo the voters, but once again, it contributed to a consumer boom, which brought a new flood of imports and an unhealthy trade balance. The Chancellor tried to hold down wage increases and began a further credit squeeze in 1960. This was not enough, and his successor, Selwyn Lloyd, took tougher measures: he raised interest rates, put 10 per cent on purchase tax and raised import duties. He also tried a new idea – a pay pause which succeeded in holding wages of government employees down for almost a year, but was repeatedly breached after that. This was the first attempt at a definite pay policy, and it had failed. By the early 1960s the repeated 'stops' were holding back industrial expansion and Britain was lagging behind her European competitors.

6   The Conservatives realized that a new approach was needed: first in 1961, they

applied for membership of the European Economic Community (EEC), but the application was turned down by France. Later the same year they set up *the National Economic Development Council (Neddy)* followed by a *National Incomes Commission (1962)*. The idea was to bring together representatives of government, business and trade unions to discuss production targets and wages, and generally to encourage more central planning.

(b) *Failure to join the EEC*

The Conservatives can be criticized for failing to join the European Economic Community at the outset in 1957, which had unfortunate consequences for British production and exports (see Section 32.7).

(c) *Not enough investment in industry*

Not enough cash was directed into important industries; this was partly because the 'stops' discouraged industrialists from risking long-term investment and because too much of the available money was invested abroad. Many argued that the government was spending far too much on defence, manufacturing the hydrogen bomb in a vain attempt to keep up with the USA and the USSR. Thus certain industries declined, particularly textiles (hampered by competition from Portugal, Japan and India), and shipbuilding (competition from Japan); although other industries were expanding (aircraft, cars and chemicals), production costs were high, which often made British goods expensive. In the face of some strong foreign competition, exports did not boom as much as they might have done; consequently there was a constant struggle to keep costs down. Unemployment became more of a problem in the early 1960s, especially in the North of England and in Scotland; early in 1963 there were almost 900 000 out of work. A combination of failure to enter the EEC, economic stagnation and a final 'go' period which caused a sudden surge in imports, resulted in a record balance of payments deficit of £748 million for 1964.

(d) *Scandals and cover-ups*

In addition to its economic problems, the government's reputation was tarnished by scandal. First in October 1962, William Vassell, a clerk at the Admiralty, was found guilty of spying for the Russians; he had been blackmailed because he was a homosexual, and it was suspected that two government ministers had attempted a cover-up. Though the two ministers, T. Galbraith and Lord Carrington, were cleared by an enquiry, the affair left an uncomfortable atmosphere. The next scandal was much more damaging to the government since it directly involved the Minister for War, John Profumo. In June 1963 it emerged that he had been having an affair with a call-girl, Christine Keeler, who at the same time happened to be associating with a Russian naval attaché. There was the obvious security risk, plus the fact that Profumo had lied to the House of Commons, denying that there was anything improper in his relationship with Miss Keeler. Macmillan had accepted his statement and was made to look foolish when the truth came out. Profumo was forced to resign, and the new Labour leader, Harold Wilson, seized the opportunity to make a scathing attack on Macmillan for not treating the matter seriously enough at the outset.

Finally, after Macmillan's retirement, there was a rather unseemly squabble to choose his successor. There were three main candidates: Lord Hailsham (Quintin Hogg), who resigned his peerage so that he could become a member of the Commons, R. A. Butler (who seemed the most likely choice), and Reginald Maudling. However, after 'consultations' and 'soundings', Lord Home (Foreign Secretary since 1960) emerged as the new leader. He also had to resign his peerage and became Prime Minister as Sir Alec Douglas-Home. Although he was amiable, honest and popular within the party, and was much more shrewd than the opposition gave him credit for, there was some resentment among Conservatives about the way he had been chosen, which compared unfavourably with Wilson's straightforward election as Labour leader. There was no established method of choosing a Conservative leader; much depended on the preference of the retiring leader, and Macmillan, unimpressed by the three candidates, pushed his own favourite for the post – his Foreign Secretary. Labour was able to claim that Home's aristocratic background, his lack of experience in the Commons and his remoteness from ordinary people made him totally unsuitable for the leadership of the country.

All these Conservative failures and tribulations contributed to the Labour victory in October 1964. Another important factor was that Wilson had revitalized the Labour Party, presenting an attractive programme of improved welfare services, modernization and planning of the economy. Wilson also stressed the need for the government to sponsor scientific and technological development so that Britain could catch up with the USA and Japan in these areas. Even so, the Labour victory was a narrow one – 317 seats against 304 Conservatives and 9 Liberals – but it was enough to bring to an end the 13 years of Conservative rule.

Assessments of these 13 years vary widely. Some historians, pointing to the increasing prosperity and *the affluent society*, as economists called it, claimed that they were largely successful years. The Conservatives themselves emphasized this as their main achievement; their slogans for the 1959 election proclaimed: 'Life is better with the Conservatives'; 'Don't let Labour ruin it'. However, critics of the government suggested that the 'affluent society' developed from the improvement in world trade, which had very little to do with the government's policies. Some economists go further and argue that the government's 'stop–go' policies hindered the country's economic development: Britain's prosperity under the Conservatives should have been even more marked than it was. They see the period as one full of missed opportunities – and the biggest was the failure to enter the EEC at the beginning in 1957. Some historians believe that Macmillan himself ruined Britain's chances of getting into the EEC in 1962–3 by concentrating too much on Britain's 'special relationship' with the USA (see Section 32.7).

30.5 The Wilson governments 1964–70

With a tiny overall majority of 4 when it took office in October 1964, Wilson's new government was precarious. After an encouraging by-election victory at Hull North in January 1966, Wilson decided to risk a general election the following March, in the hope of increasing Labour's majority. He had already been Prime Minister long enough to make a good impression on the electorate; his superb television technique, together with his familiar pipe and Gannex raincoat, combined to project the image of the capable and reliable father-figure who had the country's fortunes well under control. At the same time the Conservatives had a new and untried leader in Edward Heath (elected by ballot in July 1965), and a majority of the voters saw no reason to desert Labour so soon. Wilson won the mandate he had asked for, securing 363 seats against 253 Conservatives, 12 Liberals and 2 others. In spite of their large majority, Labour's path was far from smooth: Wilson and his cabinet seemed to spend most of their time wrestling with insoluble economic problems and strikes; matters were further complicated by the situation in Rhodesia and by violence in Ireland.

(a) *The economy and the balance of payments deficit*

The most pressing problem was the £800 million balance of payments deficit inherited from the Conservatives:

- The Chancellor of the Exchequer, James Callaghan, borrowed heavily from the International Monetary Fund to replenish Britain's rapidly dwindling gold reserves which were being used up to cover the deficit. Many economists have pointed out that there was an excellent case for a devaluation of the pound at this point, since all the evidence suggested that the pound was overvalued against the dollar and especially against the German mark. A quick devaluation would make British exports cheaper and lead to an export boom. However, Wilson decided against this, feeling that, having already devalued once in 1949, Labour's prestige would be ruined if they went in for a second devaluation. Callaghan was therefore forced to fall back on yet another squeeze, holding wages down and raising import duties.

The government's efforts were ruined by a dockers' strike (May 1966) which brought trade almost to a standstill and caused a drastic fall in exports. Some foreign bankers feared that the unions were getting out of control, and the pound was adversely affected on the foreign exchanges. Even after the strike was settled the value of the pound continued to fall, and some members of the cabinet suggested devaluation. Callaghan, who still saw devaluation as a political humiliation, would not hear of it: 'devaluation is not the way out of Britain's difficulties', he declared in July 1967. Soon another dock strike affecting London and Liverpool reduced exports again, and it was clear that there would be a massive trade deficit by the end of the year. With the drain on gold reserves increasing, the government decided that the only alternative was to devalue the pound from $2.80 to £2.40 (November 1967). It was hoped that, apart from stabilizing the financial situation, devaluation would cause a surge in exports. However, the immediate effect was to bring about Callaghan's resignation; after his declaration against devaluation only a few months earlier, it was felt that he could hardly remain at the Treasury. He was replaced by Roy Jenkins.

Unfortunately the main results of the first three years of Labour economic policy turned out to be little different from the previous Conservative 'stop–go' years – economic stagnation. The devaluation did not help Wilson's reputation either; he went on television and told the nation: 'devaluation does not mean that the pound in the pocket is worth 14 per cent less to us now than it was'. The problem, as Ben Pimlott, Wilson's biographer, points out, was that 'the Prime Minister had persistently argued that devaluation did matter to ordinary people. Now that it had happened, he appeared to be standing on his head, cleverly arguing that it did not ... this did the premier's already slippery image limitless harm in the subsequent, inflationary years.'

- During 1968 the new Chancellor cut government spending by £750 million and raised taxes on cigarettes, alcohol and petrol. This aroused bitter criticism from the left wing of the party, but Jenkins was determined to stick by his policies, and eventually they began to show results – a balance of payments surplus of £387 million for 1969. Unfortunately the ending of the pay restraint policy in 1970 led to steep wage increases which in turn brought rising prices; the government had failed to escape from the 'stop–go' economy.

(b) *The failure to reform the trade unions*

The economy was damaged by large numbers of strikes, particularly among dockers and in the motor-car industry. The number of working days lost through strikes increased from 1.75 million in 1963 to 2.9 million in 1965 and to 4.69 million in 1968. One disturbing point was the rapidly growing number of unofficial or 'wildcat' strikes, when shop-stewards led walk-outs instead of going through official union procedures. Although a survey in 1969 showed that 57 per cent of people still thought trade unions were a 'good thing' (the figure had been 70 per cent in 1964), there was a growing feeling among the general public that unions must be more disciplined and unofficial strikes curbed. In 1968 *the Donovan Commission on Industrial Relations* recommended improved voluntary agreements rather than new laws to deal with trade unions.

Wilson, however, decided that public opinion would support some moderate reform, and Barbara Castle, the Employment and Productivity Secretary, brought out a White Paper called *In Place of Strife*, outlining the government's plans (January 1969). There was to be a ballot of all members before a union could call a strike, followed by a 28-day period for further discussions before the strike went ahead; there would be fines for those who broke the rules. There were howls of protest from the TUC and from all sections of the Labour party, and there were real doubts as to whether a bill based on these proposals would have enough support to get it through the Commons. Even the Home Secretary, Callaghan, opposed it, reportedly telling Wilson: 'you won't get it through. You'd better head it off.... If it's [trade union reform] so inevitable, let the Tories pass it.' There were plots to replace Wilson with Callaghan if he tried to push the bill through, and eventually he was forced to accept defeat and drop the proposals. It was a humiliating climb-down: the government had admitted that reform was needed, and had then shown itself incapable of carrying any reform through.

(c) *The problem of Rhodesia*

The situation in Rhodesia was handled sensitively and skilfully by Wilson (see Section 32.6(c–d)). Economic sanctions were placed on the Smith regime, though they were ineffective. Wilson twice met Smith, aboard HMS *Tiger* (1966) and HMS *Fearless* (1968), but no solution was reached.

(d) *Violence in Northern Ireland*

Northern Ireland had been comparatively calm since Lloyd George's 1922 settlement (see Section 26.2(e)). However, the IRA would never rest until the north was reunited with Eire, while the Protestant-dominated Northern Ireland parliament would never agree to this. Violence between Catholics and Protestants escalated, and in August 1969 Wilson sent troops to Belfast and Londonderry to restrain the two factions and particularly to protect Catholic areas from attacks by Protestants (see Section 31.1(d–e) for full details).

(e) *Labour's achievements*

There were constant crises and many of Labour's plans had to be abandoned because of the economic situation. For example, prescription charges were abolished from February 1965 but were reintroduced early in 1968 as part of the emergency measures. But there were some constructive achievements:

- The introduction of rent rebates and votes at 18;

- the abolition of the death penalty and the creation of the Ombudsman, to investigate complaints against inefficient administrators;
- *the Race Relations Act (1968)* made it illegal to discriminate against people on racial grounds in employment, housing, insurance, education and other areas. This had some success and meant that West Indians, Pakistanis and Indians were able to work as lawyers, teachers and doctors and to join the police.
- Many would see Labour's most lasting achievement to be in the field of education. There was a determined move towards comprehensive secondary education, and the Open University was created, using radio and television to enable people to receive a university education at home.
- In general, living standards continued to improve, with a larger proportion of households than ever before having refrigerators, washing-machines and TV sets.

All this was not enough to dispel the impression that Labour, apart perhaps from its last year in office, had made many of the same mistakes as the Conservatives and had not 'got the economy right'. Several key industries – coalmining, shipbuilding, textiles and railways – continued to contract, and this caused unemployment to rise from around 400 000 to just over 600 000 in 1970. Although Wilson could have waited until the following year, some favourable by-election results and opinion polls convinced him that an election victory was possible in June 1970. Unfortunately for Labour, many of their traditional supporters felt that the government had failed to live up to its promises; Jenkins stuck to his severe policies and failed to provide a give-away budget before the election, and this may well have lost the party crucial support. The Labour vote fell by almost a million while the Conservative vote went up by 1.7 million, enough to give them an overall majority of 30.

30.6 The Heath government 1970–4

Edward Heath was a 'one nation' Tory, in the tradition of Disraeli and Macmillan, and was keen to maintain the welfare state. He also believed in planning, and in January 1970 had held the Selsdon Park conference to work out policies to be followed when the party was next in office. Much time was spent discussing trade union reform and the reduction of state intervention in the economy; this has been seen by some historians as the beginning of the end of consensus politics; Wilson strengthened this impression when he talked about the emergence of a new right-wing type of Tory called 'Selsdon Man'. In reality, when the Heath government was in office, many elements of consensus continued.

Heath believed it was possible to escape from the 'stop–go' trap by reducing controls to a minimum and taking Britain into the EEC, which, it was hoped, would stimulate British industry. Unfortunately the government almost immediately suffered a tragic blow with the death of Iain Macleod, the Chancellor of the Exchequer, after only a month in office. He was a politician of enormous ability and expertise who had been working on plans for tax reform. His successor, Anthony Barber, lacked Macleod's experience and authority. After this, very little went right for the government.

(a) *Continuing economic problems*

Barber introduced decisive measures, cutting taxes and reducing restrictions on hire purchase and credit; Britain's entry into the EEC was secured at last in 1972 (to take effect in January 1973), Heath's greatest achievement (see Section 32.7(g)). However, the hoped-for investment in industry failed to materialize and inflation became serious again. This caused Heath to do a sharp U-turn to a policy of holding wages down and reimposing controls; but there was no rapid improvement: 1973 showed a balance of payments deficit of close on £1 billion (a new record), unemployment hovering at over 850 000 and inflation still rising.

(b) *Help for poor families*

Heath strengthened his 'one nation' credentials by introducing the Family Income Supplement, together with rates and fuel rebates to help poor families; but these were criticized by many right-wing Conservatives as being too much like socialism.

(c) *Help for ailing industries*

When Rolls-Royce, Britain's biggest manufacturer of aircraft engines (as well as luxury cars), seemed to be on the verge of bankruptcy, the government rescued it by stepping in and nationalizing it (1971). Later, Upper Clyde Shipbuilders was saved from collapse by a government subsidy of £35 million, preserving thousands of jobs in the Glasgow area.

(d) *The Industrial Relations Act (1971)*

This was an attempt to introduce the sort of moderate trade union reform which had eluded Wilson. Designed to cut down strikes and curb escalating pay demands, the Act set up a National Industrial Relations Court with the power to enforce ballots for strikes, and a 60-day 'cooling-off' period before a strike began. Although in many quarters this was seen as a mild and sensible measure, the unions opposed it bitterly. There was a loophole in the Act which enabled the TUC to defy it successfully: unions were required to register under the Act, and the court would be unable to deal with any union which refused to do so. The TUC instructed all unions not to register, and threatened to expel any union which did. In 1972 there was a wave of strikes in protest at the new legislation, and a record 23.9 million working days were lost.

The most serious was the miners' strike (January–February 1972). The background to the dispute was the steady decline in the coal industry which had reduced numbers of miners from over 700 000 in 1957 to less than 300 000, plus the fact that miners' wages had lagged behind those of other industrial workers. The National Union of Miners (NUM) put in a large pay demand and when this was refused by the National Coal Board, a national miners' strike began. Arthur Scargill, leader of the Yorkshire Miners, masterminded a campaign of mass picketing, using 'flying pickets' who would converge on coal depots and prevent the movement of coal stocks. Soon power stations had to close down, the government declared a state of emergency and a million and a half people were thrown out of work. Heath eventually gave way and conceded all the miners' demands. Meanwhile the Industrial Relations Court stood largely idle.

(e) *Continuing disturbances in Ireland*

The British army found itself in the impossible situation of trying to prevent Catholics and Protestants slaughtering each other, while at the same time having to endure attacks from the IRA and another group calling itself the Provisional IRA (for the Heath government's reaction, see 31.1(f–g)).

(f) *The Local Government Act of 1972*

This was the most important local government reform since 1888, when county councils were introduced. It was intended to improve administrative efficiency and remove anomalies; it combined some small counties, creating new units such as Humberside and Cleveland, while tiny counties like Rutland and the Isle of Ely ceased to exist. However, this was not popular in places where centuries-old county loyalties were outraged by the new boundaries.

(g) *The Arab–Israeli War and the oil crisis*

The problem began in the autumn of 1973, following the short Arab–Israeli War of October 1973. The Arab oil-producing states decided to show their displeasure towards certain countries which, they felt, had been too friendly towards Israel. Britain found that her oil imports were cut by 15 per cent, while the Arabs imposed a series of price increases which more than trebled the cost of Britain's oil imports. Not only did this cause a petrol shortage, it also ruined any faint chance that there would be a favourable balance of payments for 1973. Worse was to follow ...

(h) *Renewed confrontation with the miners*

Heath's U-turn in favour of wage restraint soon produced another confrontation with the miners. They had just put in a demand for a large wage increase (September 1973) when the oil crisis seemed to strengthen their position. After the failure of talks, the NUM introduced an overtime ban (November), to which Heath responded by declaring a state of emergency and appointing the moderate William Whitelaw as Employment Secretary. A similar ban by electricity workers and railway drivers soon followed, adding to the general fuel shortage. Although the miners' leader, Joe Gormley, was also a moderate, they were unable to find a compromise. Heath was determined not to allow his wages strategy to be breached and would make no increased offer to the miners. Instead, a series of drastic emergency measures was introduced to save power: from January 1974 industry was allowed to work only a three-day week, there was to be a 50 mph speed limit and, the most unpopular move of all in the eyes of many – TV was to close down at 10.30 pm. As a strike began to look more likely, the TUC offered Heath guarantees that if he would treat the miners as a special case, other unions would not seek to breach his pay policy. When Heath rejected this offer, the miners held a ballot in which 81 per cent voted in favour of a strike (4 February 1974). Heath decided on a general election, hoping to win public support for his stand against the miners.

(i) *The general election of February 1974*

The election was a bitter and dramatic affair. Heath campaigned on the need for strong government. 'Who governs Britain,' asked the Conservatives, 'parliament or the unions?' Labour seemed to have very little new to offer. However, the miners presented their case well, while a few days before the election two sets of statistics were published which may well have swayed voters: the first showed that food prices had risen by 20 per cent during 1973; the second showed that the trade deficit had just reached another all-time high. Enoch Powell, a leading if rather eccentric Conservative, urged people who were against Britain's membership of the EEC to vote Labour.

The election result was a strange one: there was no great surge of support for Heath's anti-union stand, and the Conservative vote fell by over a million. It was clearly a vote of no confidence in the Conservatives, but it was hardly a positive vote for Labour either, since they polled around half a million fewer votes than in 1970. The Liberals, who had won several sensational by-election results over the Tories, saw their total shoot up to over 6 million (from only 2.1 million in 1970), as they took votes from both major parties. However, the strange British electoral system meant that they still only won 14 seats – the vast majority of Liberal votes were wasted in constituencies where Liberal candidates came second. The final figures were: Labour 301 seats, Conservatives 297, Liberals 14, Nationalists and others 23. Heath did not resign immediately but had talks with Jeremy Thorpe, the Liberal leader, about a possible coalition. He justified this on the grounds that the Conservatives had polled more votes (11.87 million) than Labour (11.64 million) and that there was agreement between the two parties on Europe and on an incomes policy. In the end, the idea of a coalition proved unacceptable to the Liberals, Heath resigned, and Wilson formed a minority Labour government.

30.7 Labour in power again 1974–9

(a) *Wilson's brisk beginning*

Wilson faced an unenviable task in trying to 'get the economy right', as he put it. In spite of the government's small majority, he began briskly. He made a left-winger, Michael Foot, Secretary of State for Employment, which pleased the unions. He settled the miners' strike, though only by allowing their full wage claim, and ended the three-day week. The government's *Trade Union and Labour Relations Act* repealed most of Heath's Industrial Relations Act, and later the National Industrial Relations Court was abolished (July 1974). This was followed by a rash of other wage increases which helped to push up prices and fuel inflation; industrial wages went up by 19 per cent in 1974 and by 23 per cent in 1975. Wilson now introduced a new strategy known as the 'Social Contract'; this was an attempt to improve industrial relations by government and TUC working out agreement on wage levels.

Wilson decided that the situation had stabilized sufficiently for him to hold an election in October 1974, hoping for a repeat of the big Labour victory of October 1966. However, there was only a slight improvement in Labour's position as they emerged with an overall majority of three. By the end of 1974 there was still no sign that the government would be able to remedy the basic weakness of the economy, though in 1975 the Social Contract began to show some results. The TUC agreed to a £6 a week limit on wage rises; and the Chancellor of the Exchequer, Denis Healey, introduced a tough budget, reducing defence spending, raising income tax to 35p in the pound and raising VAT (which he had introduced in 1974 at 8 per cent) to 25 per cent on certain luxury items

(b) *What was wrong with the British economy?*

The simple fact was that British industry was not producing enough goods for export at the right prices; foreign competitors could produce more cheaply and secured a larger share of the market. The statistics of Gross Domestic Product (GDP) for 1977 are very revealing; GDP is the cash value of a country's total output from all types of production. To find out how efficient a country is, economists divide the GDP by the population of the country, which shows how much is being produced per head of the population. Figure 30.1 shows that economically Britain was one of the least efficient

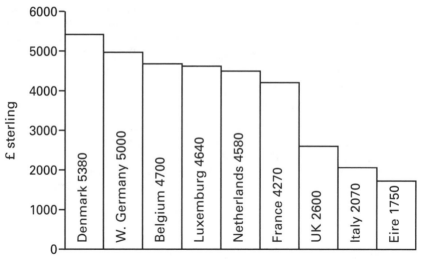

Figure 30.1   GDP per head of the population in 1977, shown in £ sterling

Source: based on statistics in Jack B. Watson. *Success in World History Since 1945*
(John Murray, 1989), p.150.

nations in the European Community, while Denmark and West Germany were top of
the league.

Nor did the situation improve during the Thatcher era: in 1993 Britain's performance was still below the EEC average (see Table 33.2). The reasons for this inefficiency are a matter of controversy; management blamed unions for excessive wage
demands and opposition to new techniques and processes; certainly the power of the
unions had increased over the previous decade, and both Wilson and Heath had failed
to control them; *The Financial Times* went so far as to call them 'the robber barons of
the system'. On the other hand, unions blamed unimaginative management. Some
economists also criticized management on the grounds that they were so greedy for
profit that too little was ploughed back for research and development. It was also suggested that governments should have spent more on grants to develop industry and less
on social services. There can be no doubt that the 'stop–go' policies, which neither
party had been able to escape from, slowed down industrial expansion; average annual
economic growth rates were consistently lower than those of Britain's main competitors.

(c) *The EEC referendum (June 1975)*

As well as all the economic problems, Wilson was also faced by difficulties within the
Labour Party. The left wing of the party, whose leading personalities were Michael
Foot, Barbara Castle and Tony Benn, was becoming stronger. Many constituency party
organizations began to be taken over by left-wing activists, who bitterly opposed any
sort of wage restraint and felt that Wilson was not delivering real socialism; some of
them were members of the Trotskyite Militant Tendency. This alarmed right-wingers
like Callaghan and Jenkins, but Wilson succeeded in holding the party together by
including both Foot and Benn in the cabinet and by appeasing the trade unions.
Another potential split in the party was over membership of the EEC: right-wingers
like Roy Jenkins and Shirley Williams supported Britain's continued membership, but
Benn and the left wanted to withdraw. When Benn suggested a referendum on the

issue, expecting a vote in favour of withdrawing, Wilson agreed. The result appeared to be decisive: 67.2 per cent of those who voted favoured continued membership (but see Section 32.7(g)). The left was defeated for the time being, Benn was demoted to the Department of Energy (from Trade and Industry), and Wilson had maintained party unity again.

(d) *Wilson resigns (April 1976)*

Although there had been rumours, Wilson's sudden resignation came as a complete surprise to the country; but it was something he had been planning for a long time, and he had told several people, including the Queen, of his decision as early as the previous December. He gave as his reasons that he had had enough of the strains of top-level politics, and, though he was only 60, he did not want to lead the party into another general election, having already gone through four. He therefore felt it only right that his successor should be given a chance to establish himself before the next election. Wilson's unkindest critics claimed that his real motive was the desire to escape the humiliation of failure, since he knew that he was incapable of solving the country's economic problems. However, Ben Pimlott sees no reason to disbelieve what Wilson himself said; as he explains, 'he was not ill, but he was ageing. The years of buffeting had left their mark. . . . He had lost none of his acuteness, but he no longer had the same energy, the same aggression or the same ambition. . . . He felt he owed it to Mary [his wife] not to go on too long.'

(e) *Callaghan in charge*

Aged 64, James Callaghan was older than Wilson. He was on the right of the party and had vast experience, having been Home Secretary, Foreign Secretary and Chancellor of the Exchequer. He was a fatherly figure who seemed to inspire confidence, and his style was relaxed and reassuring; he was particularly successful at dealing with the new Conservative leader, Margaret Thatcher, in the House of Commons.

He certainly needed all his coolness, since the government was soon hit by a financial crisis caused by a combination of the huge balance of payments deficit following the oil crisis, inflation running at 16 per cent and rising unemployment which had topped the million mark for the first time since 1939. Confidence in sterling was badly shaken and the pound fell to $1.57. Healey was forced to ask the International Monetary Fund (IMF) for a loan; this was granted, but only on condition that the government made massive spending cuts. Callaghan told the party conference in September: 'you cannot now, if you ever could, spend your way out of a recession'. In December 1976 Healey announced cuts of over £2.5 billion over the next two years, and price increases on alcohol and tobacco. Some experts see this crisis period in 1976 as the point when Keynsian policies were abandoned. These were unpopular moves and Labour soon lost four by-elections, depriving them of their Commons majority.

The government's stringent policies, together with the fact that Britain was beginning to enjoy the advantage of her own North Sea oil, soon brought an improvement in the situation. In 1974 Britain imported over 100 million tons of oil and exported less than one million; by 1980 imports and exports of oil almost balanced. By the end of 1977 Britain was able to repay much of the loan to the IMF, and the balance of payments had moved into surplus. The annual inflation rate, which had touched 24 per cent in 1975, had fallen below 10 per cent. Two other important developments were:

● *The Devolution Act (December 1978)* provided for the establishment of regional assemblies in Scotland and Wales, on condition that 40 per cent of the electorate showed themselves to be in favour. However, in a referendum held the following March, only 12 per cent of the Welsh electorate approved, while in Scotland the figure was 33 per cent. Consequently, devolution was quietly shelved for the time being (see Section 31.2(d) and 31.3(c)).

● *The Lib–Lab Pact.* By January 1977 Labour's overall majority was down to one. To ensure that his government survived, Callaghan made a pact with the new Liberal leader, David Steel. The Liberals would vote with Labour in parliament and in return they would be allowed to see Labour's proposed bills before they were introduced into the Commons. They would then signify whether or not they were prepared to support Labour's proposals, so that in effect they could veto future legislation. Steel was angling for a possible deal on a reform of the electoral system – the introduction of some form of proportional representation, which would give the Liberals a fairer representation in the Commons. Nothing came of Steel's hopes, but from Labour's point of view the pact was a success, lasting until the autumn of 1978 and helping to prolong Callaghan's government.

(f) *The winter of discontent (1978–9) and the election of May 1979*

Most informed observers expected that Callaghan would hold an election in the autumn of 1978, to take full advantage of the improving economic situation. However, he decided to hang on until 1979, and this turned out to be a fatal delay. Callaghan proposed to extend the Social Contract for a further period by limiting wage increases to 5 per cent. Given the fact that inflation was still running at 10 per cent and living standards were falling steadily, this was always going to be difficult to enforce. The TUC rejected it, and even more seriously, so did the Labour Party Conference (October 1978). Neither side would compromise, and after the Ford car workers had won a big wage increase by going on strike, there was a surge of strikes, especially among public sector workers whose wages had been tightly controlled for the previous three years. This was extremely embarrassing for the government, especially when NHS workers, dustmen and even Liverpool grave-diggers went on strike. Strike action dragged on through the winter, 'the winter of discontent' as it became known, and ruined Labour's claim that they could control the unions. In addition there were almost 1.4 million people out of work, and the government seemed to have run out of ideas and reforming zeal.

The election was forced on Callaghan by the government's defeat in a vote of confidence. Disappointed by the failure of the devolution referendum, the Scottish Nationalists voted against the government, which lost by one vote. Callaghan was forced to face an election on 3 May 1979 with the opinion polls running strongly against Labour. By contrast the Conservatives were full of new purpose; the unfortunate Heath had been dropped after suffering two election defeats in 1974, and their new leader, Margaret Thatcher, was aggressive and self-confident, making the most of Labour's failure to cope with the winter of discontent. The results were: Conservatives 339, Labour 269, Liberals 11, others 16, giving a Conservative overall majority of 43. Labour was to be in opposition for the next 18 years.

30.8 Immigration and race relations

(a) *Immigration from former British colonies*

Before the Second World War very few non-white people lived permanently in Britain. After 1945 more of the populations of the British territories in Africa and Asia decided to come and settle in Britain. During the 1950s, on average, about 30 000 immigrants a year entered Britain. During the 1960s the numbers increased, averaging about 60 000 a year. The peak years were 1961 with 115 000 and 1962 with 108 000. During the 1970s immigration was much lower because of government restrictions. In 1971 there were about two million non-whites living in Britain; roughly two-thirds of them had come from Commonwealth countries, mainly from the West Indies, India, Pakistan and Hong Kong. The other third had been born in Britain. Non-whites were only a tiny proportion of the population, at most only 4 per cent.

They came to Britain for a variety of reasons. As members of the British empire and Commonwealth, they had been brought up to admire the British way of life, and they hoped to improve their standard of living by coming to work in Britain. During the 20 years after 1945 Britain was prosperous and there were plenty of jobs available for immigrants. Many came to work in the new National Health Service as doctors and nurses. Many businesses and firms encouraged people to come to Britain by advertising in Commonwealth countries for workers. The sharp increase in immigration in the 1960s was caused by rumours that the British government was planning to restrict further immigration.

(b) *The British government restricts immigration*

There were fears that if the surge of immigration in 1961 and 1962 continued, it could cause serious economic and social problems. There might not be enough jobs to go round, and if there was unemployment among immigrants, that would place an extra burden on the social services. Government restrictions gradually reduced immigration to a trickle:

1 Harold Macmillan's *Commonwealth Immigrants Act (1962)* limited immigration to people who could show that they had a job to come to, and to people who already had close relatives in Britain. This was criticized by the Labour and Liberal Parties because it did not apply to people from non-Commonwealth countries who could still come in without restriction. This seemed deliberately racist, designed specifically to keep out non-whites.
2 Harold Wilson's Labour government (1964–70) tightened restrictions further, in spite of Labour having criticized the Conservatives for starting the policy. But public opinion seemed to be firmly against unlimited immigration, especially among people who were afraid that their jobs would be threatened. From 1965, only 8500 Commonwealth immigrants were allowed into Britain each year, and the quota was later reduced to 1500 a year. This was to keep out thousands of Asians who were leaving Kenya to escape hostile treatment by the Kenyan government. Although they all held British passports, most of them were obliged to go elsewhere – mainly to Canada, Australia, New Zealand and India.
3 Edward Heath's government introduced a period of probation for new immigrants as well as stiff penalties for illegal entry (1971). In 1981 Margaret Thatcher made it more difficult for relatives of non-white immigrants to gain entry to Britain.

(c) *Race relations*

On the whole in Britain there was nothing like the bitterness and violence seen in the USA and South Africa, and all immigrants had full civil rights. But racialism was there; many white people refused to accept non-whites as equals and showed their prejudice in a variety of ways – like refusing to serve non-whites in pubs and restaurants, and making it difficult for them to get jobs and houses. When jobs and houses became fewer, whites felt more threatened, and their hostility to West Indians and Asians increased. Non-whites felt that the police were prejudiced against them, and relations with the police were often tense.

British politicians and governments were, on the whole, more sympathetic to non-white peoples than the general public were, and did their best to encourage racial harmony. There were two important exceptions:

1   Enoch Powell, a leading Conservative MP, believed that continued immigration of non-white people would lead to great social tension and violence between the different races. In 1968, in what became known as 'the rivers of blood' speech, he said: 'We must be mad, literally mad as a nation, to be permitting the annual inflow of 50 000 dependents. It's like watching a nation busily heaping up its own funeral pyre. As I look ahead I am filled with foreboding; like the Roman, I seem to see the River Tiber foaming with much blood.' He suggested that all non-whites should be sent back to the countries of their birth. However, most of the leading Conservatives were much more liberal on the issue, and Heath sacked him from the Shadow Cabinet.

2   The National Front (NF) and its offshoot, the British National Party (BNP) were political parties which campaigned for a 'white' Britain. They failed to win any seats in parliament, though in 1993 a BNP councillor was elected to Tower Hamlets in London. Most politicians were dismayed by the election of a BNP member, because both the NF and the BNP were extremist parties which stirred up racial hatred and violence.

(d) *Government attempts to encourage racial harmony*

The Labour Party hoped to improve race relations. There had been serious racial clashes in Nottingham and Notting Hill (London) in 1958, and the increase in immigration in the early 1960s seemed likely to increase tensions. Wilson realized that Acts of Parliament could not force people of different races to love and respect each other, but he believed it was the duty of the government to show people what sort of behaviour was and was not acceptable in a civilized society. *Labour governments introduced three Race Relations Acts:*

1   1965: this set up *the Race Relations Board* to work towards fair treatment for non-whites. People could be taken to court for inciting racial disorder and for refusing to serve people in pubs and restaurants.

2   1968: this set up *the Community Relations Commission*; its job was to keep an eye on what was happening in areas of mixed race, and to encourage the formation of *Community Relations Councils* in local areas. People could now be prosecuted for discriminating against non-whites in housing and jobs.

3   1976: this set up *the Commission for Racial Equality* which was designed to actively encourage better relations and understanding between peoples of different races. People could be prosecuted for trying to incite racial hatred by using language which was 'threatening, abusive or insulting'.

How successful were these Acts?

The new Commissions did excellent work, but progress was slow. During the 1980s there were some disturbing developments:

●   As unemployment increased to three million, it became more difficult for non-whites to find jobs; unemployment was twice as high among Asians and West Indians as among whites. Many young black and coloured people, resentful of their unfair treatment, joined protest demonstrations which often ended in violence. There were riots in Brixton and Liverpool in 1981 and again in London and Birmingham in 1985.

● Non-whites, especially Asians, began to suffer harassment: houses were covered with insulting graffiti, windows smashed, property vandalized, and people beaten up and stabbed.

● In 1993, Bernie Grant, a black Labour MP, said that many black people were disgusted and disillusioned by the way they were treated in Britain, and felt that there was no future for them there. He suggested that they might be better off going to live in their country of origin.

Clearly it was going to take generations for attitudes to change sufficiently for there to be perfect racial harmony.

Questions

1 Read the following extract from *Harold Macmillan*, by Nigel Fisher, a Conservative MP during Macmillan's premiership, and then answer the questions which follow:

> It must be remembered that the period of his Premiership was one of prosperity, during which inflation and unemployment were low and the standard of living high for a large majority of the British people. History will assess whether it was a time of real achievement or of missed opportunities, diguised by *Macmillan's own inimitable style*. The conclusion may be that it was a combination of the two: that genuine gains were made but that the chance to modernise the industrial structure of Britain was not fully taken.

Source: N. Fisher, *Harold Macmillan*, Weidenfeld & Nicolson, 1982.

(a) Explain what you think the writer means by the phrase in the extract, 'Macmillan's own inimitable style'. (5 marks)

(b) In what ways can Macmillan's premiership be seen as 'a time of real achievement'? (10 marks)

(c) Do you think Macmillan's premiership was 'a time of missed opportunities', and if so, what opportunities were missed? (20 marks)

(Total 35 marks)

2 Why was the Conservative Party more successful electorally in the 1950s than in the 1960s?

3 Explain who was the more successful Prime Minister in domestic politics, Harold Macmillan or Harold Wilson. [AEB]

4 'Twenty-eight wasted years'. Assess the validity of this view of the domestic record of Conservative and Labour governments in the period 1951–79. [AEB]

31) Britain and its parts: England, Ireland, Scotland and Wales

Summary of events

Britain, or the United Kingdom (UK), in 1900 consisted of four parts – England, Ireland, Scotland and Wales, but there was only one parliament which met in London. Scotland was a separate country until 1707 when *the Act of Union* joined Scotland and England into one. The Scots ceased to have their own parliament which had met in Edinburgh, and instead sent their MPs to the London parliament. Ireland had its own parliament until 1800 when it was abolished by the British government; like the Scots, the Irish MPs had to travel to London to sit in the British parliament. The Welsh had never had a parliament of their own and Welsh MPs always sat at Westminster.

The UK was dominated by England which had by far the largest population. The 1901 census showed that out of a total UK population of 41.5 million, 30.5 million (around 73.5 per cent) lived in England. 4.5 million (about 10.8 per cent) lived in Scotland, 4.5 million in Ireland and 2 million (about 4.8 per cent) in Wales. London, the capital of England, was capital of the UK as well, and the fact that the parliament of the UK happened to meet in England only underlined this domination. Many English people saw nothing wrong in this; they thought that to be English was the same thing as being British and vice versa, and they seemed to assume that as time went on, the Irish, Scots and Welsh would become more like the English. However, *in Ireland, Scotland and Wales there were people who were far from happy with this relationship*:

- They believed that they did not receive a fair deal from the English-dominated parliament in London, and blamed all their problems on the English. This feeling was especially strong in Ireland.
- They had no wish to become 'English' and were determined to preserve their separate identity and culture. In Wales, for example, they were keen to preserve the Welsh language.
- There were demands for self-government or *devolution* as it was later called. These feelings were most strong in Ireland where the Irish Nationalist party, and later Sinn Fein, had massive support (see Sections 7.4, 16.1 and 8(b), 21.5). Southern Ireland was allowed to become independent as *the Irish Free State* in 1922, but most of Ulster in the north-east remained part of the UK (see Section 26.2).

Nationalist feelings were never so strong in Scotland and Wales, though both of them had nationalist political parties; the Welsh Nationalist Party was founded in 1925 and the Scottish Nationalists in 1928. Their campaigns for separate parliaments came nearest to success in 1979 when the British government allowed a referendum in Wales and Scotland to find out whether the majority of people really were in favour of devolution. *The Welsh voted four to one against devolution.* Although a majority of Scots who voted were in favour of it (51.6 per cent to 48.4 per cent), this was not a large enough majority and so *devolution for Scotland could not go ahead.* Meanwhile Northern Ireland had its own parliament at Stormont, but when serious violence broke out between Roman Catholics and Protestants, the British government felt obliged to suspend the Stormont parliament and bring Northern Ireland under direct rule from London (1972). All attempts to restore power to Stormont came to nothing. When the Labour Party, which had committed itself to allowing parliaments in both Scotland and Wales, won the 1997 general election, prospects for some kind of devolution seemed brighter.

31.1 Northern Ireland since 1922

From 1921 until 1972 Northern Ireland was governed by its own parliament created by the 1920 Government of Ireland Act, which had begun to operate even before the 1921 Anglo-Irish Treaty set up the Irish Free State. The Northern Ireland parliament was usually known as Stormont, after the place where the new parliament building was situated. It consisted of two houses, a lower house called the House of Commons and a second chamber known as the Senate. The Commons had 52 members each representing one constituency; the Senate had 24 members elected by the House of Commons. There was a Prime Minister and cabinet, and the parliament had very wide powers; only a few matters such as foreign affairs, defence and income tax were still controlled by the British parliament.

Once the excitement at the partition of Ireland had passed and the civil war in the Free State had ended in 1923, most people in the rest of Britain forgot about Ireland and assumed that life in Northern Ireland was going on in much the same way as it was in the rest of Britain. But this was not so – from the beginning Northern Ireland suffered a number of problems which British governments tended to ignore:

(a) *Problems in Northern Ireland*

● The new province had a long frontier with the Free State, and this frontier had a distinctly artificial look about it. It included many areas, such as parts of Tyrone and Fermanagh, south Armagh and south Down, which contained a large number of Catholics who were strongly nationalist and who wanted their areas to be in the Free State. They were bitterly disappointed by the failure of the Boundary Commission to change the frontier (see Section 26.3(a)). This meant that just over one-third of Northern Ireland's population were Roman Catholics, many of whom felt that the whole of the province, not just the Catholic areas, should be part of the Free State. Only the most sympathetic treatment by the Protestant majority could have reconciled these Catholics to remaining citizens of Northern Ireland.
● During the depression of the late 1920s and 1930s, Northern Ireland suffered massive unemployment. In 1929 over 15 per cent of insured workers were without jobs, and this soon shot up to over 30 per cent by 1931. Even in 1937 when the rest of Britain had recovered to some extent, nearly a quarter of insured workers were still jobless, the highest unemployment rate in Britain. There was a shortage of cash for housing, roads, schools and health care, and so all these facilities in Northern Ireland were of a lower standard than anywhere else in Britain.

- Political life in Northern Ireland did not run along normal party lines as it did in the rest of the UK. There were no Conservative, Liberal or Labour parties; political groupings reflected the sectarian divisions in society: Protestants were represented by the Unionist Party, Catholics by various nationalist groups. The Protestant/Unionist-dominated Stormont government deliberately did its best for the Protestants, while Catholics were discriminated against in housing, jobs, education, apprenticeships and public appointments. Constituency boundaries were fixed to give maximum advantage to Unionist candidates in elections (this is known as 'gerrymandering'). The Royal Ulster Constabulary was armed and was supported by a second armed force known as the 'B Specials', whose main function seemed to be to keep the Catholics under control.
- The Catholic population felt frustrated and helpless since the Stormont government was always Unionist. There was no way they could ever win a majority at Stormont and no chance of changing the government as there was in a normal liberal-democracy. Nor did the British government intervene on behalf of the Catholics. Sometimes sectarian violence broke out between Catholics and Protestants (a dictionary definition of a 'sectarian' is 'a bigoted supporter of a particular sect or religion'). The worst case occurred in 1935 when several people were killed in sectarian riots in Belfast.

(b) *Northern Ireland during the Second World War (1939–45)*

The province took on a new importance and enjoyed unexpected prosperity during the war years. Londonderry played a vital role as a naval base, and industry flourished, as it did in the rest of Britain, producing material for the war effort. The famous Harland and Wolff's shipyard in Belfast was kept busy replacing ships sunk by German submarines, and it also manufactured aircraft.

(c) *The situation after 1945*

Despite its comparative prosperity and deceptive calm, the problems of Northern Ireland were still there at the end of the war. In the 20 years after 1945 one of the most striking things about the province was *the continued unfair treatment of the Catholic population*. The unemployment rate among Catholics was three times higher than among Protestants. Well over 90 per cent of the workers at Harland and Wolff's were Protestant and so were 94 per cent of senior civil servants and 90 per cent of the RUC. Eamonn McCann, a Catholic leader of the civil rights movement recalled: 'The Education Act of 1944 gave Catholic working-class children the chance to go to grammar school and university, but we couldn't even get a job as a lavatory cleaner at Derry Guildhall. That made us angry.'

Protestants were more likely than Catholics to get council houses, and there were property qualifications for voting in local elections which excluded many more Catholics than Protestants. According to historian C. J. Bartlett, 'nowhere else in the western world were Catholics so much excluded from positions of influence. The great majority of Catholics were convinced that they were victims of deliberate discrimination.' Protestants defended their behaviour on the grounds that Catholics were enemies of Northern Ireland and were working for unification with the republic. In 1956 the IRA began a terrorist campaign against what they described as 'British rule in occupied Ireland', but this only made the Protestants more determined to defend their position.

(d) *O'Neill, reform and the civil rights campaign 1963–8*

In 1963 a new Unionist Prime Minister, Terence O'Neill, came to power. He had more progressive ideas than the old Unionists and felt it was time to treat Catholics more fairly, so that they would become reconciled to living in Northern Ireland. He believed that greater economic prosperity and closer relations with the republic would help. A programme of gradual reform was started to increase Catholic rights and a plan was drawn up for industrial expansion, including new towns at Antrim, Ballymena and Craigavon. In 1965 O'Neill met the Prime Minister of the republic and a friendly relationship seemed to have been established. Encouraged by this, the Roman Catholic community, after years of helpless inaction, began to organize themselves and in 1967 they founded *the Northern Ireland Civil Rights Association*. This was a non-violent group which had some support from moderate Protestants. Until then things had been peaceful, but tensions began to creep in which soon turned to violence:

- Harold Wilson's Labour government urged O'Neill to speed up his reform campaign, but this alarmed the extreme Protestants who were already suspicious of his meeting with the Irish Prime Minister. They were afraid that further reforms would threaten their supremacy, and leaders like the Reverend Ian Paisley, who had founded an extreme Protestant sect of his own, inflamed the situation by making violently anti-Catholic speeches. (In 1971 he formed a breakaway group from the official Unionist Party known as *the Democratic Unionist Party*.)

Illus. 31.1   Londonderry, 1 January 1968 – civil rights marchers break up after they are headed off by their opponents, on the city outskirts

- The Civil Rights Association planned a large protest march to take place in Londonderry, a mainly Catholic city, but it was banned by Home Affairs Minister William Craig.
- In spite of this the march went ahead (5 October 1968), but violence erupted when it was broken up by the RUC using water cannon and baton charges.

(e) *British troops sent to Northern Ireland (August 1969)*

During 1969 violence escalated as more and more protest marches were held. In January the Civil Rights Association attempted to march from Belfast to Londonderry, but the march was again broken up by the RUC. After more marches, the Protestant Loyalist Associations such as *the Orange Order* and *the Apprentice Boys* began to hold counter-demonstrations. The Unionist Party was now split, and the extremists, blaming O'Neill for the deteriorating situation, forced him to resign (April 1969). Violence reached a new peak in August 1969 when the Protestant Apprentice Boys held a march. When Catholic crowds tried to hold a counter-march, they were attacked by the RUC and the Protestants and driven back into the Bogside, the Catholic area of the city. Feeling themselves under siege, the Catholics barricaded themselves into the Bogside and declared 'Free Derry'. Riots followed in other cities; in the Falls Road area of Belfast, Protestant gangs throwing petrol bombs destroyed over a hundred Catholic homes. The Northern Ireland government had lost control and was forced to ask the British government for help. James Callaghan, the Home Secretary, decided to send British troops to restore order, though he made it clear that they were there not to maintain Protestant supremacy, but to safeguard the rights of all Northern Ireland citizens. Troops moved into the Bogside and the Falls Road, and the RUC and the 'B Specials' withdrew. Catholics welcomed the troops, feeling that they would now be protected from further Protestant attacks.

(f) *Direct rule imposed (March 1972)*

For a time it seemed as though the presence of British troops and the actions of the British government might stabilize the situation. The Westminster government tried to show its impartiality by holding an enquiry (under the chairmanship of Sir John Hunt) into the activities of the RUC and the 'B Specials'. When this condemned their policing methods, Callaghan did not hesitate to act: he reorganized and disarmed the RUC and abolished the 'B Specials' who were hated by the Catholics. Callaghan also began an impressive programme of local government reform – a fairer system of electoral districts, a fairer system of allocating council houses, and a new body to which people could appeal if they felt they were being unfairly treated. All these measures, it was hoped, would show the Catholics that the British government cared about them and would therefore calm the situation. By the time Labour was defeated in the election of June 1970, *the position of Catholics in Northern Ireland had been transformed for the better*. Unfortunately, instead of stabilizing, the situation continued to deteriorate until Edward Heath's government felt it had no alternative but to bring the province under direct rule from Westminster:

- The concessions to Catholics provoked riots from Protestants, especially in October 1969 when the 'B Specials', whom many Protestants saw as their guardians, were disbanded. A number of Protestant para-military groups was formed, it was claimed, in self-defence. In January 1970 the Reverend Ian Paisley was elected to the British parliament in London.

- The IRA began to play an important role. In December 1969 they split into the Officials, who were more moderate, and the Provisionals, who were committed to military action. Their ultimate aim was to drive the British out of Northern Ireland. There were some non-violent Catholic organizations such as *the Social Democratic and Labour Party (SDLP)* led by Gerry Fitt and John Hume, who were both elected to Stormont. But they were always in danger of being overshadowed by the Provisional IRA whose tactics were to turn the Catholic population against the British troops. In this they succeeded: they launched a campaign of terrorism, and the troops found themselves having to search Catholic households for weapons and IRA suspects. Some unpleasant incidents occurred; the first major clash between Catholics and troops took place in April 1970 and the first British soldier was killed in February 1971; in July troops killed two young Derry men.

- Brian Faulkner, the new Northern Ireland Prime Minister, with the full support of the British government, responded by introducing *internment* – arresting and imprisoning people indefinitely without trial (August 1971). Over 300 people were held in an attempt to stamp out the IRA. However, this only served to infuriate the Catholics, and the riots continued. So did Protestant attacks on Catholics, and many Catholics began to seek refuge over the border in the republic.

- A new peak of violence was reached on *'Bloody Sunday'*, 30 January 1972, in the Bogside, Londonderry. A Catholic civil rights march clashed with troops who overreacted, shooting dead 13 unarmed civilians and wounding many more. There was world-wide condemnation of British policy in Northern Ireland. The situation was chaotic: even with 20 000 troops there, it seemed impossible to govern the province. The Catholic side was split between the IRA/Sinn Fein and moderates like the SDLP, and the Unionists were split into at least three groups: the official Unionists (led by Faulkner) who, on the whole, were prepared to go along with what the British government wanted, the Democratic Unionists (led by Paisley) who wanted complete integration with Britain, and a group who seemed prepared to consider an independent Ulster (see Figure 31.1).

It was in this impossible situation that Edward Heath decided to suspend Stormont and bring Northern Ireland under direct rule from London. William Whitelaw as Secretary of State for Northern Ireland had the unenviable job of trying to prevent civil war.

(g) *The failure of the new executive (May 1974)*

Whitelaw tried to please the Catholics by beginning a phase-out of internment. But this further angered the Protestants who were already annoyed by the suspension of Stormont. There was bitter and violent opposition from Protestant groups such as *the Ulster Defence Association*, and the IRA continued its bombing campaign, extending it to England, where six people were killed at the Aldershot army base. In spite of this, the British government made a brave attempt to set up a new and fairer government in Northern Ireland:

- Plans were announced (March 1973) for a new Assembly of 80 members elected on the single transferable vote system, and a new Executive (the group whose job it is to make sure that laws are carried out), in which power would be shared between Protestants and Catholics.
- Elections for the new Assembly were held in June 1973, but were disappointing for the British government. Faulkner's Official Unionists (who supported the plans) won only 23 seats, while the 'Loyalist' Unionists, who opposed the plans because they were against sharing power in the Executive with Catholics, won 27 seats.
- The New Executive was set up in November 1973 consisting of six Faulkner

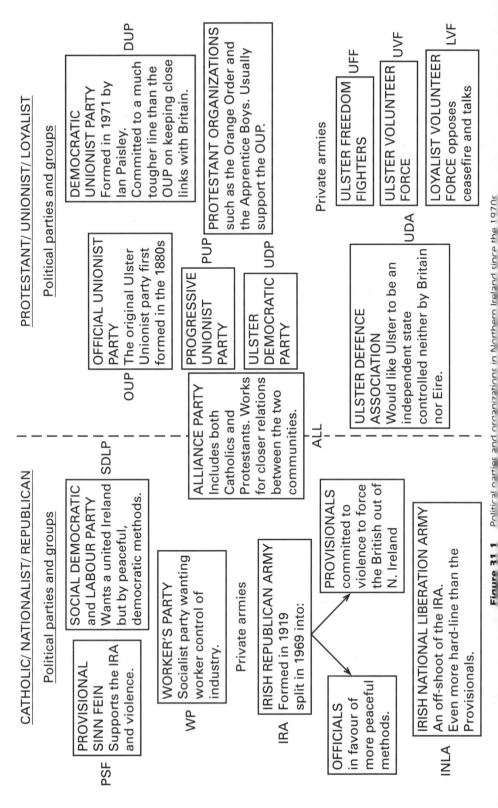

Figure 31.1 Political parties and organizations in Northern Ireland since the 1970s

Unionists, four members of the Catholic SDLP, and one member of the Alliance Party (which included both Catholics and Protestants who wanted to be non-sectarian). There was bitter opposition to this from Loyalist Unionists.

• *The Sunningdale Agreement* seemed to be an encouraging development. This was negotiated in December 1973 by Whitelaw with representatives of the Eire government and of the new Northern Ireland Assembly. It supported the idea of the power-sharing Executive to be led by Brian Faulkner, with Gerry Fitt of the SDLP as his deputy. To calm Protestant fears, it was agreed that no change would take place in the status of Northern Ireland without the approval of a majority of Northern Ireland voters. Also suggested was a Council of Ireland to include MPs from both parts of Ireland, which would gradually move towards joint control of certain matters.

• The new Assembly and Executive formally came into operation on 1 January 1974, but they had to face the most extreme opposition from so-called 'Loyalist' Unionists. In the British general election of February 1974, Protestant opponents of the new system, calling themselves *the United Ulster Unionist Council*, won 11 out of the 12 Northern Ireland seats at Westminster. In May *the Protestant Ulster Workers' Council* organized a massive general strike in protest against power-sharing. Soon the province was at a standstill with no power and no food supplies. Faulkner had little choice but to resign (28 May 1974); the Executive collapsed, and the attempt at power-sharing had failed because of opposition from extreme Protestants.

(h) *IRA violence continues*

Since 1974 all attempts to provide Northern Ireland with a viable government allowing Catholics some say in the running of the province have failed, mainly because of the unwillingness of so many Unionist politicians, especially Paisley, to consider any compromise. On the other hand it has to be said that the continued IRA campaign of violence both in Northern Ireland and England did not help progress towards a solution. For a time they targeted and killed well-known individuals – Ross McWhirter, a right-wing critic of the IRA (1975), Conservative Northern Ireland spokesman Airey Neave (1979) and Lord Mountbatten (1979). Most outrageous of all was the attempt to blow up Mrs Thatcher and her cabinet at the Grand Hotel, Brighton, where they were staying for the 1984 Conservative Party Conference. Though five people were killed, the top politicians escaped.

(i) *The Anglo-Irish Agreement (November 1985)*

Margaret Thatcher was determined to do all she could to bring peace to Northern Ireland. She had already had a summit meeting with Irish Prime Minister Dr Garrett Fitzgerald in November 1981; they met again in November 1985 and signed *the Hillsborough Agreement* (also known as *the Anglo-Irish Agreement*). This acknowledged that any change in the status of Northern Ireland could only come about with the consent of a majority of the people of the province. Britain and Eire would confer regularly about the situation in the north and about security along the border. This was seen by many people as a statesmanlike initiative by the two leaders, especially in the wake of the Brighton bombing. The difficulties facing both governments, no matter how willing they were to talk, were illustrated by the reactions to the agreement. Amid massive demonstrations, the two main Protestant Unionist groups, who appeared to have learnt nothing since 1922, denounced it as a sell-out, while on the other side Charles Haughey, leader of the Eire Fianna Fail party, called it 'a very severe blow to the concept of Irish unity'.

In spite of all the setbacks, it was clear that some progress had been made:

- Blatant discrimination against Catholics in Northern Ireland was a thing of the past.
- Successive British governments since 1963 had poured many millions of pounds into Northern Ireland to improve facilities for *all* citizens.

On the other hand, the province suffered badly from the recessions of the 1980s and early 1990s; it had the highest unemployment rate in Britain, especially in Catholic working-class areas such as Newry and Londonderry, where it was sometimes as high as 40 per cent. The gulf between Catholics and Protestants seemed as wide as ever, and British troops were still there vainly trying to prevent them from killing each other. People in the rest of Britain, where Catholics and Protestants for the most part lived amicably side by side, grew impatient with the problems of Northern Ireland and could not understand why the people continually failed to move away from sectarian bitterness and forgive and forget the past.

(j) *The IRA ceasefire (August 1994–February 1996) and the failure to find peace*

The IRA, financed by Irish Americans, still persisted with its pointless campaign of bombings and assassinations: there was the Remembrance Day bombing which killed 11 people at Enniskillen (November 1987) and the murder of Conservative MP Ian Gow in 1990. Later they changed to placing bombs in business premises and even in shopping areas. When two small boys were killed by a bomb in Warrington (April 1993) there was widespread condemnation of IRA tactics throughout Britain and the republic. Meanwhile the Protestant paramilitary groups continued to retaliate in Northern Ireland by shooting and blowing up Catholics. Pressure was beginning to mount on the IRA to call off the campaign of violence, which was getting nowhere. Secret talks had been going on between representatives of the British government and the IRA, and John Hume, the SDLP leader, worked tirelessly to persuade Sinn Fein to use its influence to bring an end to the violence. President Clinton of the USA threw his weight behind the search for peace; apparently the British government promised that if a ceasefire held for three months, Sinn Fein would be allowed to join peace talks.

John Major took the initiative and had several meetings with the Irish Prime Minister, Albert Reynolds. The two leaders produced a joint statement (known as *the Downing Street Declaration*) setting out requirements for peace talks to begin. It was emphasized again for the benefit of the Unionists that no changes would take place in the status of Northern Ireland without the approval of a majority in the province. Any party could join in negotiations if it renounced violence (August 1994). After some hesitation, the IRA declared 'a complete cessation of violence' and this was followed by a similar declaration from Loyalist paramilitary groups. There was immense relief and rejoicing in Northern Ireland, where over 3100 people had been killed since the violence began in 1969.

Progress was very slow. In February 1995 the government published a framework plan which peace negotiations might follow and there was a proposal for a joint Ulster–Ireland legislative body which could have limited powers. Although this was only a proposal, Unionists were outraged: Paisley called it 'totally and absolutely repugnant' and 'a declaration of war on the union and the unionist people'. In March 1995 the British government demanded that the IRA should begin handing over its weapons before all-party talks could begin, but this was rejected, and stalemate seemed to have been reached. Only at the end of November did things move forward when the British and Irish governments set up a three-member international panel headed by

Senator George J. Mitchell of the USA, to try and find a compromise on the decommissioning of weapons. Immediately afterwards President Clinton visited Northern Ireland where he received an enthusiastic welcome from both Catholics and Protestants (30 November 1995).

Senator Mitchell announced his recommendations on 24 January 1996: he dismissed the demand for weapons to be handed over *before* talks began as unrealistic, since paramilitary groups on both sides had rejected it. He proposed that the parties should commit themselves to a phased disarmament, in parallel with talks, and should undertake to abide by six principles:

1 No guns to be relinquished ahead of talks.
2 Decommissioning would be considered once negotiations started.
3 All paramilitary groups would eventually disarm totally.
4 Destruction of all weapons would be monitored by an independent international commission.
5 All punishment attacks should end.
6 All groups should renounce violence and commit themselves to peaceful and democratic means.

This was widely seen as a sensible and realistic document which provided a basis for all-party talks to get under way. The Irish government, the SDLP, the IRA and the other paramilitary groups accepted it. However, John Major, under pressure from the Unionists and needing their votes to maintain his dwindling Commons majority, tried to sidestep the main thrust of the report and proposed instead, elections to a constitutional convention, an idea already pushed by the Unionists. An exasperated John Hume accused him of buying Unionist votes in the Commons. Whether the IRA was genuine in its acceptance of the Mitchell proposals was never put to the test, and the opportunity was lost. In February 1996 the IRA broke the ceasefire on the mainland by exploding a huge bomb in London's docklands, killing two people. Later, another massive bomb destroyed much of the city centre of Manchester, and it was only by a miracle that nobody was killed.

John Major pressed ahead with his elections in Northern Ireland for delegates to a negotiating forum, drawn from all parties committed to renouncing violence (June 1996). Sinn Fein took part and won 17 out of the 110 seats; however, because of the continuing IRA violence, they were not admitted to the forum. In October 1996 the IRA broke the ceasefire in Northern Ireland and the whole dreary tale seemed set to repeat itself. In the British general election of May 1997 Sinn Fein won two seats and took 16 per cent of the Northern Ireland vote, its best performance for 40 years, in spite of the continued violence. The newly elected Labour government made determined efforts to resurrect the 'peace process', and in July 1997, after the Orange Order had made concessions by calling off some of their provocative marches, the IRA responded by announcing another ceasefire. Negotiations chaired by Mr Mitchell began in September 1997, though prospects for a successful outcome did not seem bright.

31.2 Relations between Britain and Scotland

(a) *Scotland in 1900*

Most Scots were well aware that their country had been a separate kingdom with its own parliament until 1707. Like Ireland, Scotland had had its traumatic times: the most notorious were *the Highland Clearances* of 1782–1820 and 1840–54, when the clan chieftains of the Highlands and Islands had evicted thousands of their tenants to make way for sheep farms. Although there were problems in Scotland – for example, there was considerable economic hardship with the decline of sheepfarming in the 1880s – there was no great desire at this time for Home Rule as there was in Ireland. Most Scots agreed that their country had done reasonably well out of the union with England and felt that it should continue.

Although there was no Scottish parliament, the Scots did have some control over their own affairs. They continued their own system of law and law-courts, their own churches and their own education system which had existed before 1707 and which were quite different from those in the rest of Britain. The Scots believed, with some justification, that their education system was superior to England's. The literacy rate was higher than in England or Wales, and Scottish children from poor backgrounds had a better chance of making it to the top. Scotland had four universities, and this meant that a higher proportion of young people could go on to university than anywhere else in the UK. Since 1872 Scotland had had its own Education Department. In 1884 Gladstone's government set up *the Scottish Office* and created a new official known as *the Secretary of State for Scotland*, whose department looked after matters such as the Poor Law, health, roads, bridges and fisheries. Politically, Scotland was strongly Liberal: if there had been a Scottish parliament it would have had a permanent Liberal majority.

(b) *The Home Rule for Scotland movement up to 1914*

When the campaign for Irish Home Rule gained momentum, it encouraged some Scots to think along the same lines. At the time of the First Irish Home Bill in 1886, a Scottish Home Rule Association was formed in Edinburgh, and the Scottish Liberal Party had some sympathy with the idea of separate parliaments for Scotland, Wales, Ireland and England, within some sort of federal system. In 1908 a Bill to give Home Rule to Scotland was introduced into the Commons and passed with a majority of over 100. Of the Scottish MPs, 41 voted in favour and 12 against. The Conservatives opposed it strongly, as they did Home Rule for Ireland. Not surprisingly the Bill was defeated in the Lords. This happened four times before 1914; when the First World War broke out in 1914, the matter was quietly dropped for the time being.

(c) *The campaign for Scottish devolution*

During the 1920s Scottish nationalism revived, in a rather different form. The Liberal party was in rapid decline by this time and so the National Party of Scotland was formed in 1928; another groups calling itself the Scottish Party was formed in 1930. They amalgamated in 1934 to form *the Scottish National Party (SNP)*, and talked about 'the urgent need and necessity of self-government for Scotland'. Their motives were both economic and cultural:

- *Economic motives:* Like the rest of Britain, Scotland suffered from the inflation at the end of the First World War (see Section 23.1(b) 2). There was rioting in Glasgow, and the government, convinced that it was the beginning of revolution, brought in troops and tanks to restore order. Scotland also suffered badly from the depression of the early 1930s. In 1932 almost 30 per cent of insured workers in Scotland were out of work, higher than any other region in Britain except Wales. In Motherwell in 1934, over 37 per cent of insured workers were without jobs; in Glasgow alone, 90 000 people were out of work in 1936, when the worst of the depression was over in England. Many Scots felt that Scotland was paying more into the Treasury and receiving less than was fair, but the English argued that Scotland was not paying her fair share and was receiving more than she deserved.

- *Cultural motives:* People like Hugh MacDiarmid wanted to preserve what they saw as a genuine Scottish culture against English and American influences, and some Scottish nationalists believed in reviving the old Celtic alliance of Scots, Welsh, Irish and Cornish against the English. They hoped to revive the Gaelic language which was hardly spoken outside the Highlands and Islands.

Although the movement generated a lot of interest, it made no impact on parliament, and no more Scottish Home Rule Bills were introduced. Instead, the English-dominated Westminster parliament gave the Scots slightly more control of their own affairs within the existing system. The SNP succeeded in winning one by-election in Motherwell in April 1945 but lost the seat to Labour in the general election of July 1945. Interest was maintained, however, and in January 1949 John MacCormick founded *the Scottish Covenant*, which collected two million signatures of people who wanted a separate Scottish parliament.

(d) *The SNP begins to take off*

During the late 1960s the SNP began to take off. Again it was economic forces that seemed to be important. The economic performance of Britain as a whole was not impressive towards the end of the 1960s, and many Scots were convinced that Scotland could do better on its own, especially after the discovery of North Sea oil, which was piped ashore to Scotland. The SNP regarded this as Scotland's oil and they could imagine an independent Scotland enjoying new wealth from oil revenues. At the same time many Scots resented the rising unemployment which was again worse than it was in England. Also unpopular was the arrival of American Polaris nuclear submarines based at Holy Loch.

- In 1967 the SNP candidate, Winifred Ewing, won Hamilton in a sensational by-election; it had been held by Labour with a 16 000 majority. The SNP also won sweeping victories in local government elections, taking control of local councils in Glasgow, Dundee, Cumbernauld and East Kilbride.
- Membership of the SNP grew rapidly; by the end of 1968 it had more members than any other party in Scotland and was drawing support from a wide range of people – workers, owners of small businesses, housewives and members of the professional middle classes. Other parties, especially Labour, were losing support to the SNP, which was shown most dramatically by Winifred Ewing's by-election victory.
- The other parties therefore found themselves pushed towards the idea of devolution to win back support from the SNP. In 1968 Edward Heath, the Conservative leader, revealed to the Scottish Conservatives that he was in favour of a Scottish Assembly, and a committee was set up to investigate how this could best be introduced.
- The 1964–70 Labour government appointed *the Kilbrandon Commission (1968)* to draw up plans for both Scottish and Welsh devolution. These were eventually published in 1973 and involved setting up elected parliaments for Scotland and Wales. However, there had been some problems during the discussions, partly because some of the members felt it was unfair not to give England devolution as well.
- The general election of October 1974 was a great success for the SNP: they won 11 seats and took 30 per cent of the votes in Scotland.
- The Labour government which won the election decided to go ahead with devolution; one reason for this was no doubt because it had an overall majority of only

six, and needed the support of the eleven SNP and three Plaid Cymru (Welsh Nationalist) MPs.

However, as the prospect of devolution became brighter, problems and disagreements arose which held things up, and in the end, caused the idea to be dropped altogether:

- There was disagreement about how much power the Scottish parliament should have. The SNP wanted it to have full powers over taxation, and over industrial and economic policy. The London government was not prepared to allow this and insisted on the Secretary of State for Scotland having the power to veto laws passed by the Scottish parliament. Another problem was whether there should be a reduction in the number of Scottish and Welsh MPs sitting at Westminster.
- The discussions again raised the question of a separate parliament for England. Many people in the north of England felt that their area had problems which were just as serious as those of Scotland and Wales and they resented the fact that these areas seemed about to be given special treatment.
- The government eventually produced a Bill for Scottish devolution: there would be a Scottish parliament in Edinburgh, but it would have no powers of taxation and no real control over industry and agriculture; the Secretary of State for Scotland would have the final say over most matters. This was a very weak affair and satisified nobody.
- The government decided to hold a referendum to find out whether a majority of the Scottish and Welsh people themselves were in favour of devolution. A condition attached was that 40 per cent of the total electorate must vote in favour, not just 40 per cent of those who voted, in order for the Devolution Bill to be passed. When the referendum was held (March 1979), a majority of those who voted (51.6 per cent to 48.4 per cent) were in favour of devolution. But over 36 per cent of the electorate did not bother to vote at all, and this meant that only about 33 per cent of the total electorate had shown that they wanted a separate Scottish parliament. Devolution was dropped and Nationalist support declined sharply; the SNP won only two seats in the general election of 1979, two in 1983, and three in 1987 when their total vote was less than half what it had been at its peak in October 1974.

The most striking thing about Scotland, judging by the general election of 1987, was the strength of the people's support for Labour: out of the 72 seats in Scotland, the Conservatives could muster only 10 against Labour's 50. Both Margaret Thatcher and John Major were adamant against devolution which, they claimed, would lead to the breakup of the United Kingdom. Meanwhile the Labour Party became more enthusiastic, and under Tony Blair's leadership, pledged itself to a Scottish parliament with the power to raise taxes and able to control all matters except foreign affairs, defence, immigration, social security and macro-economics. The massive Labour victory in the 1997 election made Scottish devolution much more likely. For Scottish Conservatives the election was a catastrophe: the swing away from them was completed and they lost all 10 of their seats; six of them went to Labour, which emerged with a record 56 seats in Scotland; the Scottish Nationalists doubled their seats to six, and the Liberal Democrats won ten.

During the summer of 1997 the new Labour government, together with the Scottish Nationalists and the Liberal Democrats, campaigned vigorously in favour of devolution. In the referendum held in September 1997, 60 per cent of the Scottish electorate voted; 74.3 per cent of those who voted wanted a Scottish parliament, and 63.5 per cent wanted it to have tax-raising powers. Devolution for Scotland could now go ahead. The first elections for the new 129-seat parliament in Edinburgh were due to take place in May 1999 so that it would be ready for business in 2000.

31.3 Relations between Britain and Wales

(a) *Wales up to 1914*

Although Wales had been officially united with England since 1536, the Welsh people had kept a strong feeling of national identity, preserving their own culture, religions and language. Unlike the Irish and Scots, the Welsh tended not to emigrate to the USA and Canada, though one famous group settled in Patagonia (South America) in 1865. Instead, as industry developed, they moved to the coalmining valleys of South Wales which were one of the most prosperous parts of Britain in 1900. Well over half the population of two million spoke Welsh, and probably 30 per cent of these did not speak English at all. The British government was quite sympathetic towards Welsh cultural interests, and in 1880 it was agreed that the education system in Wales should help to preserve the Welsh language and cultural heritage. There was a university college at Aberystwyth, and two more were founded, at Bangor and Cardiff; in 1893 the colleges were organized into the University of Wales. Issues at stake before 1914 included:

1   *The row over the 1902 Education Act.* Balfour's Education Act (see Section 12.7(e)) caused a major controversy in Wales. Although this was in many ways an excellent reform, it was bitterly disappointing to religious Nonconformists who were strong in Wales, because it gave money out of the rates to support Anglican schools. The Nonconformists had been hoping that Balfour would abolish Anglican and Catholic schools which were mostly on the verge of bankruptcy, but now they were to be rescued by money from local rates, to which Nonconformists had to contribute. In Wales most of the schools were Anglican, whereas about three-quarters of churchgoers were Nonconformists. There was much ill-feeling that so many children of Nonconformist parents would have to continue attending Anglican schools. There was a great outburst of opposition in both Wales and England, but it was in Wales that the desire to safeguard Nonconformist education was most extensive.

   A campaign of passive resistance was mounted which usually involved refusal to pay rates. David Lloyd George, the Welsh-speaking Liberal MP for Caernarvon Boroughs, himself from a Baptist family background, led the attack on the Act in parliament. In the general election of January 1906, the Conservatives failed to win a single seat in Wales, so strong was Welsh feeling against the Balfour Act. However, when the victorious Liberals tried to introduce an Education Bill more acceptable to the Nonconformists, it was thrown out by the Conservative majority in the Lords. The row over Nonconformist education was mixed up with another issue:

2   *The Campaign against the Anglican Church.* The Anglican Church (the Church of England) was the established church (that is, the official state church) in both England and Wales (as it had been in Ireland until it was 'disestablished' in 1869 – see Section 13.3(c) 1). Welsh Nonconformists objected to having the 'English' church forced on them, and they expected the Liberal government to do something about it. *The Welsh Disestablishment Bill*, by which the Anglican Church would cease to be the state church in Wales, was introduced in 1912. Although it had passed the Commons three times by 1914, it was held up by the Conservatives in the Lords. Many Conservatives were staunch Anglicans; in fact the Anglican Church used to be referred to as 'the Conservative Party at prayer'; they opposed the Bill with what now seems rather un-Christian bitterness. F. E. Smith, a leading Conservative MP, even went so far as to say that the Bill 'shocked the conscience of every Christian community in Europe'. In spite of the Lords' disapproval, the

Bill became law in 1914, though its operation was postponed until the end of the First World War.

3 *Home Rule for Wales.* The campaign got under way in 1887 with the founding of an organization called *Cymru Fydd (Coming Wales)*, whose aim was a separate Welsh parliament. Its president was Tom Ellis, who called himself a Welsh Nationalist, although he was Liberal MP for Merionethshire. After Ellis's death in 1899, Lloyd George took over the leadership, and in 1911 the Welsh Liberal party announced its support. However, there was no great interest in Home Rule; a Welsh Home Rule Bill was introduced into the Commons in 1914, but it was dropped when the war broke out.

(b) *Wales between the wars*

The most striking thing about Wales between the wars was its economic decline. Heavily dependent on coalmining, Wales was badly hit by both structural and cyclical unemployment in the 1920s and 1930s (see Sections 20.5 and 25.4), and for much of the time it had the highest unemployment in Britain, even worse than in Northern Ireland. In 1932, 36.5 per cent of all insured workers were without jobs, and the figure was still over 22 per cent in 1937, when the worst of the depression was officially over. In some towns the situation was disastrous: in 1934, for example, 74 per cent of all male workers were without jobs in Brynmawr, 73 per cent in Dowlais and 66 per cent in Merthyr. Unemployment was worst among coalminers, especially in the Merthyr and Rhondda valleys: in 1935 about half the miners in these areas were out of work.

In 1934 Wales was named as a 'Special Area', along with Scotland, Cumberland and Tyneside. This seemed to do very little good, though a trading estate was set up at Treforest and a new steelworks was built at Ebbw Vale. These economic difficulties did not cause any marked outburst of Welsh nationalist feeling. *Plaid Cymru (Welsh Nationalist Party)* was founded in 1925 with a programme of self-government for Wales, but it won no seats in parliament and only had about 2000 members by 1939. In South Wales people seemed to be more interested in supporting the Labour party, which wanted to maintain the union of England and Wales and which hoped to introduce socialist reforms which would benefit both English and Welsh.

(c) *Plaid Cymru and Welsh Nationalism since 1945*

For the first 15 years after the Second World War, Plaid Cymru continued its campaign but won very little support. The 1945–51 Labour governments were unsympathetic, but the new Conservative government appointed *a Minister for Welsh Affairs*, acknowledging that Welsh interests deserved to be given special attention. It was also hoped that the announcement in 1956 that Wales was for the first time to have its own capital city – Cardiff – would please nationalist opinion. There was much investment in Welsh industry during these years, and this brought a marked improvement in the economy. Most people seemed happy for Wales to continue as part of the UK, and Plaid Cymru could make no headway in elections. In the 1959 general election the party ran only nine candidates, and every single one lost his deposit. Only about 5 per cent of the Welsh electorate voted Plaid Cymru. However, during the 1960s there was a surge of support which led to some successes:

● In 1962 the veteran nationalist leader, Saunders Lewis, dismayed at the decline in Welsh speaking, made an impassioned radio broadcast calling for a campaign to protect the Welsh language and culture which, he said, were being ignored by the English-dominated London government. This led to the formation of *the Welsh*

Language Society, and also to an enthusiastic campaign of civil disobedience, in which Welsh-language supporters defaced road signs written in English and damaged TV masts which transmitted English-language instead of Welsh-language programmes. Later some of the extremists became more violent, attacking post offices and holiday homes in Wales owned by English people.

● Plaid Cymru began to attract more votes and in 1966 Gwynfor Evans, the party's president, won a by-election at Carmarthen, their first ever seat in parliament. It was said that many people had voted Plaid Cymru as a protest at the recent closing of the Carmarthen to Aberystwyth railway line. In 1967 and 1968 they came close to winning the safe Labour seats of Rhondda West and Caerphilly; these were coalmining areas where pit closures and rising unemployment were causing criticism of the Labour government (1964–70).

● Labour made some concessions to Welsh opinion. *The Welsh Language Act (1967)* gave the Welsh language equal legal status with English; Welsh began to be used more in government business, and there were more TV programmes in Welsh and more Welsh-speaking primary schools. Even the Royal Family became involved in the campaign to please the Welsh: Prince Charles was invested by the Queen as Prince of Wales at Caernarvon Castle (1969) and he also spent a term at Aberystwyth University College to learn Welsh. In 1968 a Royal Commission was appointed (later known as *the Kilbrandon Commission)* to look into devolution for both Wales and Scotland.

● Plaid Cymru election successes continued when in the general election of October 1974 the party won three seats.

● A separate Welsh parliament now seemed to be a distinct possibility. The Labour government had only a tiny overall majority, and in order to make sure of support from the Welsh and Scottish Nationalist MPs, seemed prepared to go ahead with devolution. In 1978 a Bill agreeing in principle to a Welsh assembly passed the Commons, though the actual proposal was for an even weaker body than that proposed for Scotland – little more than a glorified county council.

Plaid Cymru was in for an even bigger disappointment. In March 1979 when a referendum was held in Wales to find out exactly how strong support for devolution was, the vote went overwhelmingly against it: 243 048 in favour and 956 330 against. There was even a majority against in the Welsh-speaking area of Gwynedd which had two Plaid Cymru MPs. It seemed that this decisive vote against a separate Welsh assembly was because the Labour Party, which had massive support in industrial areas, campaigned against devolution, believing that Wales would be worse off separated from the English economic and social structures. This was a debatable question though; ten years later the Welsh economy was far from healthy. The coalmining industry which had once been such a vital element in Britain's prosperity, had declined beyond recognition. In 1912 over 250 000 men worked in the Welsh coalmines; in 1990 the figure was less than 5000 and still falling.

As the 1997 general election approached, although a section of New Labour still opposed devolution for Wales, official party policy under Tony Blair had swung round to favour some sort of Welsh assembly. In the election the Conservatives lost all six of their seats in Wales, five to Labour and one to the Liberal Democrats. Plaid Cymru held on to the four seats won in 1992. With Labour now holding 34 out of the 40 seats in Wales, the party was hopeful of a 'yes' vote in the referendum due to be held in September 1997. However, the result was extremely close: 559 419 (50.3 per cent of those who voted) wanted a Welsh parliament, while 552 698 (49.7 per cent) voted against it. The turnout was only just over 50 per cent, which meant that the plan had been backed by only 25 per cent of the population. Nevertheless the government was determined to press ahead with legislation to set up a 60-member assembly to begin business in Cardiff in the summer of 1999. Unlike the Scottish parliament, however, the Welsh assembly would not have the power to make laws and raise taxes.

Questions

1 Crisis in Northern Ireland

Study this extract from a journalist's eye-witness account of 'Bloody Sunday' in Londonderry, 30 January 1972, and then answer the questions which follow.

The trouble began when a big civil rights procession organized by *the Civil Rights Association*, defying the Northern Ireland government's ban on marches, approached a barbed-wire barricade in William Street. The procession, estimated at 7000 to 10 000 strong, had intended to march to the Guildhall to hold a protest meeting against the continuation of *internment*. Some of the younger members, despite appeals from stewards, began to throw bottles, stones and bricks at the British troops. As the missiles became heavier, a water cannon filled with purple dye was sprayed on the demonstrators . . . they continued pelting the troops who replied with rubber bullets; the demonstrators lobbed canisters of CS gas among the troops. A few minutes later men of the Parachute Regiment leapt over the barricades and chased the demonstrators. As stated, 13 civilians were killed and 16 wounded. The army insisted that fire had been opened on snipers only after the troops themselves had first been fired on. Demonstrators and relatives of those killed strongly denied this, declaring that those taking part in the march had been completely unarmed.

Source: *Keesing's Contemporary Archives*, January 1972.

(a) Explain what the writer means in the extract by the phrases:
  (i) 'the Civil Rights Association';   (5 marks)
  (ii) 'the continuation of internment'.   (5 marks)
(b) Using the information in Chapter 31, explain why British troops had been sent to Northern Ireland in 1969.   (8 marks)
(c) Using the evidence in the extract and the information in Chapter 31, explain why the British troops reacted so violently on 30 January 1972.   (7 marks)
(d) In what ways does this extract demonstrate the difficulties facing historians when they try to write about the situation in Northern Ireland?   (5 marks)
(e) As a result of 'Bloody Sunday' the British government suspended the Northern Ireland parliament and imposed direct rule on the province (March 1972). However, the government wanted to restore the Northern Ireland parliament as soon as possible.
  Explain why it had been impossible to do this by 1997.   (20 marks)
                                                                 (Total 50 marks)
2 In what ways did the nationalist movements in Northern Ireland, Scotland and Wales differ from each other?
  Why were there still no separate parliaments for these areas in 1992?

32 Britain and her place in the world after 1945

Summary of events

The twenty years after the end of the war saw Britain declining from her pre-war position as one of the world's leading powers, to become a second- or perhaps third-rate power, in comparison with the two superpowers – the USA and the USSR. However, British governments, both Labour and Conservative, seemed unwilling to accept what was happening, and displaying what some historians have called 'delusions of grandeur', tried to act as though Britain was still on an equal footing with the USA and the USSR. In 1946 her empire was still intact, and she had troops in Germany, Greece, Iran, India, Egypt, Palestine, Malaya and Singapore. This was extremely expensive to maintain for a country whose resources had been strained to the limit by the war effort. There were some disagreements in the Labour cabinet about how long Britain could go on maintaining her world-wide military presence; Hugh Dalton, the Chancellor of the Exchequer, was anxious to economize, and felt that at least British troops could be withdrawn from Germany. However, Ernest Bevin, the Foreign Secretary, was a dominating figure who enjoyed the full support of Attlee, the Prime Minister. They were both determined that Britain should play a world role for as long as possible, even to the extent of producing her own nuclear weapons.

The problems which were soon to unfold before Bevin were complex: the need for a settlement of Germany, the Indian demands for independence and the Jewish/Arab violence in Palestine, Britain's role in the Cold War, and the war in Korea. Bevin negotiated these problems with great skill, though he failed to resolve the Arab/Israeli situation which in desperation he handed over to the UN.

After the Conservatives came to power in 1951, foreign affairs were dominated by Anthony Eden, first as Foreign Secretary (1951–5) and then as Prime Minister (1955–7). He seemed to be handling affairs well until the 1956 Suez War ended in humiliation for Britain and caused his downfall. To many people this seemed conclusive proof that Britain, incapable of conducting an independent foreign policy without American approval, was no longer a world power. However, while Harold Macmillan was Conservative Prime Minister (1957–63) he somehow succeeded in keeping up the illusion for a little longer by seeking to renew and develop Britain's 'special relationship' with the USA.

It was under Macmillan's premiership that Britain gave up most of her empire, though the vast majority of the newly independent states chose to remain within the Commonwealth. India (1947) and Ceylon and Burma (1948) had already been granted their independence under Labour. They were soon followed by Malaysia and Gold Coast (1957), Nigeria and Cyprus (1960), Tanganyika and Zanzibar (together forming

Tanzania, 1961), Uganda (1962) and Kenya (1963). Soon after Macmillan's retirement (1963), other territories became independent: Nyasaland, Northern Rhodesia, Guiana and Malta (1964), Bechuanaland (1966) and Aden (1967), and finally, after some delay, Rhodesia became independent in 1980.

At the same time as she was withdrawing from her empire, Britain missed an opportunity to join the other states of western Europe, when she decided not to become a member of the European Economic Community (EEC) on its formation in 1957. When Macmillan eventually decided that it would be advantageous for Britain to join after all, her entry was blocked by the French (January 1963). Britain was thus left largely isolated from the rest of Europe and at the same time had offended the Commonwealth by applying to join the EEC. Britain seemed to be floundering, and it was to be another ten years before Europe opened its ranks to admit her. Dean Acheson, a former American Secretary of State (who was reasonably pro-British) made the much-quoted remark (in December 1962) that Britain 'has lost an Empire but has not yet found a role'.

32.1 Britain and the Cold War

(a) *What was the Cold War?*

Towards the end of the war, the harmony which had existed between the USA, the USSR and the British empire began to evaporate, and all the old suspicions came to the fore again. Relations between Soviet Russia and the west became so difficult that although no actual armed conflict took place directly between the two opposing camps, the decade after 1945 saw the first phase of what became known as *the Cold War*. This continued, in spite of several 'thaws', until the collapse of communism in eastern Europe in 1989–91. What happened was that, perhaps deterred by the fear of a nuclear war, instead of allowing their mutual hostility to express itself in open fighting, the rival powers confined themselves to attacking each other with propaganda and economic measures, and with a general policy of non-co-operation.

Both superpowers gathered allies around them: between 1945 and 1948 the USSR drew into its orbit most of the states of eastern Europe. A communist government was established in North Korea (1948) and the communist bloc seemed to be further strengthened in 1949 when Mao Zedong was at last victorious in the long civil war in China. On the other hand the USA hastened the recovery of Japan and fostered her as an ally, and worked closely with Britain and 14 other European countries as well as with Turkey, providing them with vast amounts of economic aid in order to build up an anti-communist bloc. Whatever one bloc suggested or did was viewed by the other as having ulterior and aggressive motives. There was a long wrangle, for example, over where the frontier between Poland and Germany should be, and no permanent settlement for Germany and Austria could be agreed on.

In the mid-1950s, after the death of Stalin (1953), the new Russian leaders began to talk about 'peaceful co-existence', and the icy atmosphere between the two blocs began to thaw. It was agreed to remove all occupying troops from Austria (1955); however relations did not warm sufficiently to allow agreement on Germany, which remained divided until 1990.

(b) *What were the causes of the Cold War?*

The basic cause lay in the differences of principle between the communist states and the capitalist or liberal-democratic states. Ever since the world's first communist state was set up in Russia in 1917, the governments of most capitalist states viewed it with distrust and were afraid of communism spreading to their countries. Only the need for self-preservation had caused both sides to ignore their differences; as soon as it became clear that the defeat of Germany was only a matter of time, both sides, and Stalin in particular, began to plan for the post-war period. He aimed to take advantage of the military situation to strengthen Russian influence in Europe; this involved occupying as much of Germany as possible as the Nazi armies collapsed, and acquiring as much territory as he could get away with from other states such as Finland, Poland and Romania. When Stalin extended Russian control over most of eastern Europe, the West became more and more alarmed at what seemed to be Russian aggression; they believed that he was committed to spreading communism over as much of the globe as possible.

In the final phase of the war President Roosevelt had been inclined to trust Stalin, but Churchill thought differently. He wanted British and American troops to make a dash for Berlin before the Russians took it, but he was overruled by the Americans. However, after Roosevelt died in April 1945, his successor, Harry S. Truman, was much more suspicious of the Russians, and his misgivings were confirmed at the Potsdam Conference in July 1945, when Stalin refused to come to any agreement about Germany's future. Some historians believe that Truman's main motive for dropping the atomic bombs on Japan was to show Stalin what might happen to Russia if he dared to go too far. Even so, it was not until early in 1947 that Truman completely abandoned his belief in Stalin's good faith.

Ernest Bevin's attitude in this situation was similar to Churchill's. He had no love for communists and thought that Britain must stand up to the Russians in order to maintain a balance of power in Europe. The best way to achieve this was by co-operation with the Americans, and he hoped for a concerted Anglo-American effort to prevent the expansion of Russian power and communism in eastern Europe. But the Americans, even Truman, were reluctant to interfere in the affairs of eastern Europe, believing that, even if Poland and Hungary fell under Russian influence, Stalin would allow them to have democratic governments if they wished. The Americans soon received an unpleasant shock: by the end of 1947, communist governments had been established, under Russian influence, in Poland, Hungary, Romania, Bulgaria and Albania. In addition Stalin treated the Russian zone of Germany as if it belonged to Russia, banning all political parties except the communists, and draining it of vital resources.

(c) *Which side was to blame for the Cold War?*

During the 1950s most western historians blamed Stalin, arguing that his motives were sinister and that he intended to spread communism as widely as possible through Europe and Asia. The formation of NATO and the American entry into the Korean War in 1950 were the West's self-defence against communist aggression.

On the other hand, Soviet historians, and during the 1960s and early 1970s some American historians, argued that the Cold War ought not to be blamed on the Russians. Their theory was that the USSR had been so weakened by the war that Stalin's motives were purely defensive and that there was never any real threat to the west from Russia. Some Americans claim that the USA should have been more understanding and should not have challenged the idea of a soviet 'sphere of influence' in eastern Europe. The actions of American politicians, especially Truman, provoked Russian hostility unnecessarily. This is known among historians as the 'revisionist' view.

Later a third view – known as the 'post revisionist' interpretation – became popular among American historians during the 1980s. They had the benefit of being able to look at lots of new documents and visit archives which had not been open to earlier historians. The new evidence led them to take a middle view, arguing that both sides should share the blame for the Cold War. They believe that American economic policies such as Marshall Aid (see below) were deliberately designed to increase US political influence in Europe. However, they also believe that although Stalin had no long-term plans to spread communism, he was an opportunist who would take advantage of any weakness in the west to expand Soviet influence. With their entrenched positions and deep suspicions of each other, the USA and the USSR created an atmosphere in which every international act could be interpreted in two ways. What was claimed as necessary for self-defence by one side was taken by the other side as evidence of aggressive intent. Sections (d–h) show how this happened.

(d) *The Truman Doctrine and the Marshall Plan*

The situation in Greece led to a closer American involvement in European affairs.

● British troops had helped liberate Greece from the Germans in 1944 and had restored the monarchy. They were now feeling the strain of supporting the king against communist guerrillas who were receiving help from Albania, Bulgaria and Yugoslavia. If Greece fell to the communists, there was every chance that Turkey and Iran would follow. In Bevin's view, only Britain stood between Russian control of the eastern Mediterranean, the Dardanelles and the Middle East.

● Churchill responded to what was happening with a speech at Fulton, Missouri (USA), in which he tried to stir the Americans into action (March 1946). He repeated a phrase he had used earlier: 'From Stettin in the Baltic to Trieste in the Adriatic, *an iron curtain has descended across the continent.*' Claiming that the Russians were intent on 'indefinite expansion of their power and doctrines', he called for *a western alliance* which would stand firm against the communist threat, 'since our difficulties and dangers will not be removed by merely waiting to see what happens'. The speech helped to widen the rift between east and west; Stalin was able to denounce Churchill as a 'warmonger', while over a hundred British Labour MPs signed a motion criticizing Churchill.

● An added difficulty was that Anglo-American relations were strained by the abrupt ending of Lend-Lease and by the unfavourable terms insisted on for the American loan in 1945 (see Section 29.3(c)). Many Americans were hostile to Britain's empire and continued to view Britain as a serious trade rival. This was one reason for the lack of enthusiasm for Britain's anti-communist stand in Greece.

● In February 1947 Bevin told the Americans clearly that Britain's economic position made it impossible for her to continue the struggle in Greece. If they wanted Greece and Turkey saving from communism, they would have to do it themselves. Truman responded with what became known as *the Truman Doctrine*: the USA would 'support free peoples who are resisting subjugation by armed minorities or by outside pressures'. Greece immediately received massive amounts of arms and other supplies and by 1949 the communists were defeated. Turkey, which also seemed under threat, received aid worth about $60 million.

● *The Marshall Plan* (announced June 1947) was an economic extension of the Truman Doctrine. American Secretary of State George Marshall produced his European Recovery Programme (ERP) which offered economic and financial help wherever it was needed. 'Our policy,' he declared, 'is directed not against any country or doctrine but against hunger, poverty, desperation and chaos.' Its aim was to promote the economic recovery of Europe, thus ensuring markets for American exports. In addition, communism was less likely to gain control of a prosperous western Europe.

The only proviso was that the European nations themselves must co-operate with each other to produce a plan for the best use of American aid.

Bevin eagerly took the lead, and together with the French Foreign Minister, called an international conference in Paris. By September 16 nations (Britain, France, Italy, Belgium, Luxembourg, Netherlands, Portugal, Austria, Switzerland, Greece, Turkey, Iceland, Norway, Sweden, Denmark and the three western zones of Germany) had drawn up a joint plan for using American aid. During the next four years over $13 000 million of Marshall Aid flowed into western Europe, fostering the recovery of agriculture and industry which in many countries were in chaos as a result of war devastation. The Russians were invited to the conference but declined to attend. They were well aware that there was more to Marshall Aid than pure benevolence. Although in theory aid was available to eastern Europe, Molotov, the Russian Foreign Minister, denounced the whole idea as 'dollar imperialism'. The Russians saw it as a blatant American device for gaining control of western Europe, and worse still, for interfering in eastern Europe, which Stalin considered to be in the soviet 'sphere of influence'. Russia rejected the offer, and neither her satellite states nor Czechoslovakia, which was showing interest, were allowed to take advantage of it. By now the 'iron curtain' seemed a reality and the Cold War was well under way.

(e) *The Berlin blockade and airlift (June 1948–May 1949)*

This brought the Cold War to its first big crisis, which arose out of disagreements over the treatment of Germany:

1   At the end of the war, as agreed at Yalta and Potsdam, Germany and Berlin were each divided into four zones. While the three western powers did their best to organize the economic and political recovery of their zones, Stalin, determined to make Germany pay for the damage inflicted on Russia, continued to treat his zone as a satellite, draining away its resources.
2   Early in 1948 the three western zones were merged to form a single economic unit whose prosperity, thanks to Marshall Aid, was in marked contrast to the poverty of the Russian zone. At the same time, outraged at the Russian-backed coup in Czechoslovakia (February 1948), the western powers began to prepare a constitution for a self-governing West Germany, since the Russians had no intention of allowing complete German reunification. However, the Russians were alarmed at the prospect of a strong, independent West Germany which would be part of the American bloc.
3   When in June 1948 the west introduced a new currency and ended price controls and rationing in their zone and in West Berlin, the Russians decided that the situation in Berlin had become impossible. Already irritated by this island of capitalism deep in the communist zone, they felt it was out of the question to have two different currencies in the same city, and they were embarrassed by the contrast between the prosperity of West Berlin and the poverty of the surrounding areas.

The Russian response was immediate: all road, rail and canal links between West Berlin and West Germany were closed. Their aim was to force the west to withdraw from West Berlin by reducing it to starvation point. The western powers, convinced that a retreat would be the prelude to a Russian attack on West Germany, were determined to hold on; they decided to fly supplies in, rightly judging that the Russians would not risk shooting down the transport planes. Truman had thoughtfully sent a fleet of B 29 bombers to be positioned on British airfields. Over the next 10 months the Americans and British airlifted 2 million tons of supplies to the blockaded city in a remarkable operation which kept the 2.5 million West Berliners fed and warm right through the winter. In May 1949 the Russians admitted defeat by lifting the blockade.

The affair had important results: the outcome gave a great psychological boost to the western powers, though it brought relations with Russia to their worst ever. It caused the western powers to co-ordinate their defences by the formation of NATO. It meant also that since no compromise seemed possible, Germany was doomed to remain divided for the foreseeable future. The German Federal Republic (West Germany) came into existence in August 1949; the Russians set up their zone as the German Democratic Republic (East Germany) in October 1949.

(f) The formation of NATO (North Atlantic Treaty Organization) – April 1949

The Berlin blockade demonstrated the west's military unreadiness and frightened them into making definite preparations. Already Bevin had made the first moves to bring about closer co-operation in western Europe: in March 1948 Britain, France, Belgium, Holland and Luxembourg had signed *the Brussels Defence Treaty* promising military collaboration in case of war. Now they were joined by the USA, Canada, Denmark, Portugal, Italy and Norway. All signed *the North Atlantic Treaty*, agreeing to regard an attack on any one of them as an attack on them all, and placing their defence forces under a joint NATO Command Organization which would co-ordinate the defence of the west. This was a highly significant development: the Americans had abandoned their traditional policy of 'no entangling alliances' and for the first time had pledged themselves in advance to military action. Stalin took it as a challenge and tension remained high.

Bevin was justifiably exultant, seeing NATO as the crowning achievement of his career: he had contributed to the formation of the Truman Doctrine, taken the lead in planning for Marshall Aid, played an important part in preparations for the Brussels Treaty, and supported Truman in the Berlin airlift. The climax of the process was NATO.

(g) The war in Korea (1950–3)

The origins of the war lay in the fact that the country had been divided into two zones in 1945 at the end of the Second World War. It was divided at the 38th parallel by agreement between the USA and the USSR for purely military reasons – so that they could organize the surrender of the occupying Japanese forces; it was not intended to be a permanent political division. However, the unification of communist North Korea with the non-communist South soon became part of the Cold War rivalry, and no agreement could be reached. In 1949 Russian and American troops were withdrawn, leaving a potentially dangerous situation: most Koreans bitterly resented the artificial division forced on their country by outsiders. Without warning, North Korean troops invaded South Korea in June 1950.

The communists had just gained control of China under the leadership of Mao Zedong. Truman was convinced that the attack on South Korea, coming so soon after Cold War events in Europe, was part of a vast Russian plan to advance communism wherever possible in the world; he believed it was essential for the west to take a stand by supporting South Korea. American troops in Japan were ordered to South Korea *before* the UN had decided what action to take. The UN Security Council called on North Korea to withdraw her troops, and when this was ignored, asked member states to send assistance to South Korea. This decision was reached in the absence of the Russian delegation who were boycotting meetings in protest against the UN's refusal to allow Mao's new Chinese regime to be represented, and who would certainly have vetoed such a decision. In the event, the USA and 14 other countries (including Britain, Australia, Canada and New Zealand) sent troops, though the vast majority were Americans. All forces were under the command of the US General MacArthur.

Their arrival was just in time to prevent the whole of South Korea from being overrun by the communists. By September 1950 communist forces had captured the whole country except the south-east, around the port of Pusan. UN reinforcements poured into Pusan, and there was soon a complete turnaround – communist forces were chased out of the South and by the end of October UN troops had occupied two-thirds of North Korea, and reached the Yalu River, the frontier between North Korea and China.

The Chinese government was seriously alarmed: in November they launched a massive counter-offensive with over 300 000 troops described as 'volunteers'. By mid-January 1951 they had driven the UN troops out of North Korea and crossed the 38th parallel; Seoul, the capital of South Korea was captured again. MacArthur was shocked at the strength of the Chinese forces; he argued that the best way to beat them and stop the spread of communism was to attack Manchuria, with atomic bombs if necessary.

At this point Clement Attlee, still British Prime Minister, paid a surprise visit to Washington to urge Truman not to use atomic bombs on China. Possibly influenced by Attlee, Truman decided that this would be too risky and might cause a large-scale war which the USA did not want. He decided to settle for merely 'containing' communism; MacArthur was removed from his command. In June UN troops cleared the communists out of South Korea again and fortified the frontier. Peace talks at Panmunjom lasted for two years, ending in July 1953 with an agreement that the frontier should be roughly along the 38th parellel.

Although Britain sent the second largest contingent of troops, suffering over 4000 casualties (almost 700 killed), this was small compared with the American commitment (they lost over 33 000 killed). The main importance of the war for Britain was the way in which it set back her economic recovery (see Section 29.4(a)) and caused a split in the Labour Party (over how to meet the expense) which contributed to its defeat in the election of 1951 (see Section 29.5).

(h) *Britain and her defences*

Attlee and Bevin had authorized the manufacture of an atomic bomb, though this was not given much publicity. The bomb was successfully tested in 1952, and it was thought that this put Britain back on a level with the USA and the USSR. However, development of atomic weapons moved fast; before long Britain had to decide whether to produce a hydrogen bomb. In 1954 Churchill announced that Britain would go ahead with its manufacture, and by 1957 the first British H-bomb had been successfully exploded.

However, the nuclear arms race soon became far too fast and too expensive for Britain. The next development (by the Russians) was the intercontinental ballistic missile (ICBM) – a nuclear warhead carried by a rocket so powerful that it could reach the USA even when fired from inside the USSR. When Britain tried to develop her own rocket system – *Blue Streak* – it proved impossibly expensive and was abandoned in 1960.

At about the same time, *the Campaign for Nuclear Disarmament (CND)* was started. Its supporters argued, on moral grounds, that Britain should withdraw from the nuclear arms race and disarm unilaterally; it was hoped that the USA and the USSR would follow Britain's lead and scrap their nuclear weapons too. Their case was strengthened when evidence began to build up showing that nuclear tests carried out in the atmosphere caused a highly dangerous radioactive fall-out. CND held mass demonstrations and rallies, and every year at Easter held a protest march from London to Aldermaston (where there was an atomic research base) and back. No British government dared risk unilateral disarmament, which, they believed, would leave Britain vulnerable to a nuclear attack from the USSR; they would only consider abandoning their nuclear weapons as part of a general agreement by all the major powers (multilateral nuclear disarmament).

Harold Macmillan quickly built up an impressive reputation as an international statesman. He was convinced that Britain's future was inextricably bound up with the USA and was anxious to renew the 'special relationship' between the two states which had been seriously damaged by the Suez war (see Section 32.4). He saw this as the best way of maintaining Britain's 'great power' status. He formed good relationships with Presidents Eisenhower and Kennedy; he was a great believer in the value of summit conferences between world leaders and worked hard to organize one. He visited Moscow (February 1959) and established good relations with Nikita Khrushchev, the Russian leader. Macmillan could claim to be at least partly responsible for Khrushchev's decision not to press for a western withdrawal from Berlin. Soon afterwards Macmillan went to Paris, Bonn and Washington, and as the Cold War tensions eased, he was able to persuade the western leaders that a summit with the Russians might be fruitful. Unfortunately when the conference eventually met in May 1960, it was unsuccessful. An American U-2 spy plane had just been shot down over a thousand miles inside Russia. The Russians demanded an apology, and when Eisenhower refused, Khrushchev walked out.

Illus. 32.1   President Kennedy of the USA and Harold Macmillan, working at 'the special relationship'

By 1963 it was clear that Britain had ceased to be a world power. She had been humiliated at Suez in 1956; she simply lacked the economic strength and the resources to remain on a level with the two superpowers, and had been forced to abandon the idea of manufacturing her own nuclear weapons. The best Macmillan could manage was to persuade John F. Kennedy (at a meeting in Nassau in December 1962) to supply Britain with American nuclear Polaris missiles which could be fired from British nuclear submarines. During the Cuban missile crisis (October 1962) Britain was unable to play any useful role. The crisis occurred when Kennedy demanded the removal of Russian missiles from Cuba, less than 100 miles from the American coast. The two powers seemed to be on the verge of nuclear war, but common sense prevailed and Khrushchev agreed to remove the missiles. Soon afterwards Britain was refused entry to the EEC (see Section 32.7(f)), and at the same time had lost most of her empire.

Macmillan had one final achievement before his retirement: he played an important role in the signing of *the Nuclear Test Ban Treaty (August 1963)* by the USA, the USSR and Britain. It was agreed that in order to avoid polluting the atmosphere, nuclear tests would only be carried out underground. The Americans had not been enthusiastic about the treaty, and it was Macmillan's persistence that eventually brought success. Kennedy paid Macmillan a handsome tribute, acknowledging that the British premier's role in limiting nuclear testing had been indispensable.

32.2 Why and how did the British leave India in 1947?

(a) *Why did the British leave India in 1947?*

By 1945 and the end of the Second World War it seemed clear that Indian independence could not be delayed much longer. The nationalist campaign had been gathering strength for many years (see Section 26.4), and in 1942 Sir Stafford Cripps, acting on behalf of the war cabinet, had offered India dominion status once the war was over; the Labour government, wanting to show that it disapproved of 'exploiting' the Indians, was anxious to go ahead. Bevin had earlier toyed with the idea that independence might be delayed for a few years to enable the British government to finance a development programme for India. This idea was abandoned partly because the Indians would be intensely suspicious of any delay, and partly because Britain could not afford the expense, given her own economic difficulties. India became independent and was divided into two states – India and Pakistan – in August 1947.

The reasons why the British eventually decided to leave India have been the subject of some lively debate during recent years. In the period immediately after independence, the withdrawal seemed a perfectly straightforward affair: it was presented by official sources as the culmination of a process going back to the 1919 Government of India Act by which British politicians carefully moved India towards independence. It had been intended all along and was a triumph of British planning and statesmanship. It was not just British historians who held this view: V. P. Menon, Indian constitutional adviser to the Governor-General for the last five years before independence, believed that Britain's decision to quit India was 'her finest hour ... it not only touched the hearts and stirred the emotions of India, ... it earned for Britain universal respect and goodwill'.

This view was later challenged by a number of Indian historians, including Sumit Sarkar and Anita Inder Singh. They argue that Indian independence never was a long-term British goal, and that the 1919 and 1935 Government of India Acts were designed not to prepare for independence but to postpone it. The credit for Indian independence belongs entirely to Congress. As Anita Inder Singh puts it:

> drawing on popular anti-imperialist sentiment, the Congress became one of the biggest mass movements in history; it engaged the Raj in a protracted trial of strength, and through an adroit mixture of negotiation and civil disobedience, it led India to independence. Generally, Indians do not perceive independence as a gift from the British or as an easy success. To them independence was the hard won fruit of struggle and sacrifice made by millions of Indians against an oppressive Raj, symbolized by the imprisonment of Gandhi and Nehru for eleven and nine years respectively.

True the Labour government offered independence in March 1946, but that was only because the pressures from below – agrarian troubles, demands for the overthrow of the Raj, mutinies in the Royal Indian Air Force and Navy – had become intolerable and the government knew that Britain was too weak to keep control if widespread revolution broke out.

Some other historians take a middle view: while accepting that inter-war Conservative-dominated governments did everything in their power to thwart progress towards Indian independence, they believe that great credit is due to the Labour government for its positive role in 1945–7. Howard Brasted, for example, presents a fair and balanced view: he disputes the claim that the government made its India policy up as it went along and ended up running away from the problem. He points out that the Labour Party had already, *before* the Second World War, produced a clear policy on British withdrawal from India; this was embodied in *the Attlee Report on India (1934)*, which was later discussed by Attlee, Cripps and Nehru in 1938, when they worked out a framework of British withdrawal by a future Labour government, to be preceded by democratic elections. Nehru and Gandhi knew that with the massive Labour victory of July 1945, Indian independence could not be far away. On 20 February 1947 Attlee announced the timetable for unconditional independence, during which the Indians would work out their own constitution through a representative Constituent Assembly. If the plan was not carried through in the way Attlee envisaged, this was partly because, as Brasted points out, the Viceroy, Lord Wavell, was not in sympathy with Labour's plans: 'proclaiming, despite constant briefings, that he did not know what Labour's itinerary was, the Viceroy persistently departed from the route Labour had long proposed to take; hence his dismissal'. The other problem was the difficulty of preserving the unity of India, and it was this problem which proved impossible to solve.

(b) *Why was the partition of India necessary?*

1   The problem sprang from the religious hostilities between Hindus, who made up about two-thirds of the population, and the rest, who were mostly Muslims. After their victories in the elections of 1937, the Hindu Congress Party unwisely called on the Muslim League to merge with Congress. This alarmed the League who were now convinced that an independent India would be dominated by Hindus. M. A. Jinnah, the Muslim leader, demanded a separate Muslim state of Pakistan.

2   Attempts to draw up a compromise constitution acceptable to Hindu leaders (Nehru and Gandhi) and to Jinnah, failed. The British proposed a federal scheme in which the central government would have only limited powers, while those of the provincial governments would be extensive. Provinces with a Muslim majority would be able to control their own affairs, and there would be no need of a separate state. Both sides accepted the principle but could not agree on details.

Illus. 32.2 Lord and Lady Mountbatten with Gandhi in 1947

3   Violence broke out in August 1946 when the Governor-General, Lord Wavell, invited Nehru to form an interim government, still hoping that details could be worked out later. Nehru formed a cabinet which included two Muslims, but Jinnah, convinced that the Hindus could not be trusted, called for 'direct action' to achieve Pakistan. Fierce rioting followed in Calcutta, where 5000 people were killed; it spread to Bengal where Muslims set about slaughtering Hindus. As Hindus retaliated, the country seemed on the verge of civil war.

4   To try and force the Indians into a more responsible attitude, Attlee announced in February 1947 that the British would leave no later than June 1948. The new Viceroy, Lord Mountbatten, turned out to be an inspired choice by Attlee. He quickly decided that partition was the only way to avoid civil war. He realized that there would probably be bloodshed anyway, but felt that partition would produce less than if Britain tried to insist on the Muslims remaining inside India. Within six weeks of arriving, in spite of all the complexities, Mountbatten had produced a plan by which the country could be divided and power transferred from the British. This was accepted by Nehru and Jinnah (though not by Gandhi). Afraid that delay might cause more violence, Mountbatten advanced the date for British withdrawal to August 1947.

(c) *How was the partition carried out?*

The Indian Independence Act was rushed through the British parliament (August 1947) separating the Muslim majority areas (the north-west and north-east of India) from the rest of India as the independent state of Pakistan, which was in two sections, over a thousand miles apart (see Map 11.1 on p. 144). But it was not easy to carry out the terms of Act:

- It had been necessary to split the provinces of the Punjab and Bengal which had mixed Hindu/Muslim populations, and inevitably millions of people found themselves on the wrong side of the new frontiers.
- Fearing persecution, millions headed for the frontier, Muslims trying to get into Pakistan and Hindus into India. Clashes occurred which developed into near-hysterical mob violence, especially in the Punjab, where about 250 000 people were murdered. Violence was not quite so widespread in Bengal where Gandhi, still preaching non-violence and toleration, managed to calm the situation.
- Violence began to die down before the end of 1947, but in January 1948 Gandhi was shot dead by a Hindu fanatic who detested his tolerance towards Muslims. It was a tragic end to a disastrous set of circumstances, but the shock seemed to bring people to their senses, so that India and Pakistan could begin to think about their other problems.

Attlee insisted, probably rightly, that Britain could not be blamed for the violence which followed independence; this was due, he said, with his inimitable knack of under-statement, 'to the failure of the Indians to agree among themselves'. Howard Brasted believes that a less sensitive handling of the situation by the British government could have produced an even more catastrophic bloodbath. 'The fact that a constitutional set-tlement was achieved which transferred power to chosen successors, legally, legisla-tively and amicably rather than through bitter armed struggle, should not be taken for granted.'

32.3 Britain withdraws from Palestine

In 1945 Britain was still heavily committed in the Middle East; Palestine had been a British mandate since 1919, British troops were still stationed in the Suez Canal zone of Egypt, and Britain owned a controlling interest in the Anglo-Iranian Oil Company. Serious problems arose in all three areas, but it was in Palestine that the first crisis occurred.

(a) *What caused the crisis in Palestine?*

1   The problem originated soon after the First World War when large numbers of Jews began to settle in Palestine, hoping to set up a Jewish 'national home' (see Section 26.5(c)). The Arabs in Palestine were implacably hostile to the idea of a separate Jewish state in what they considered to be their homeland. In order to retain Arab friendship and their own oil supplies, the British limited Jewish immigration to 10 000 a year (1939).

2   The Second World War intensified the problem, with hundreds of thousands of refugees from Hitler's Europe looking for somewhere to go. In 1945 the USA pressed Britain to admit 100 000 of them into Palestine; this demand was echoed by David Ben Gurion, one of the Jewish leaders, but the British refused, not wanting to offend the Arabs. The British were particularly exasperated by Truman's attitude: he criticized the British government for not admitting the refugees, yet would give no help and refused to allow any more Jews into the USA.

3   The Jews, after all that their race had suffered at the hands of the Nazis, were determined to fight for their 'national home'. They began a terrorist campaign against both Arabs and British; the most spectacular incident was the blowing-up of the King David Hotel, the British Headquarters in Jerusalem, with the loss of 91

lives (1946). The British responded by arresting Jewish leaders and by turning back ships such as the *Exodus* crammed with intending immigrants.

4 Bevin hoped to be able to find some sort of compromise to satisfy both Jews and Arabs, and one which would preserve British influence. He met the leaders of both sides, but no compromise was possible: the Jews wanted their own state, the Arabs refused all concessions, and neither side would budge. By February 1947 therefore Bevin invited the United Nations to deal with the problem, and in November the UN voted to partition Palestine, setting aside roughly half of it to form an independent state of Israel for the Jews. The UN also suggested that Britain should put the plan into operation. Bevin was against partition, even though the UN announced that the existing Arab population would be able to continue living in Israel. His argument was: why should the Palestinian Arabs be forced to become a minority in a Jewish state when the Jews were refusing to become a minority in an Arab state? Consequently the British refused to carry out the partition, and in May 1948 they withdrew altogether from Palestine, thus ending the mandate.

(b) *Why did the British decide to withdraw?*

There were several motives. British public opinion had gradually turned against the Jews because of their terrorist outrages; the peace-keeping operation had already proved expensive, and the prospect of enforcing the partition (which they did not approve of and which would be even more costly, at a time when Britain was in economic difficulties) to the advantage of the Jews, appalled Bevin. Nor did Bevin see why the British should have the sole obligation of acting as international policemen in the Middle East; there was a strong feeling that since the Americans had taken up a pro-Jewish stance, then they ought to be allowed to get on with carrying out the partition. Finally there was the possibility that British troops might be needed in Europe, given the growing tension over Berlin.

Map 32.1 The Middle East

When the British withdrew, fighting had already broken out between Jews and Palestinians, who bitterly resented the loss of half of their homeland. Ben Gurion declared the new state of Israel independent and it was immediately attacked by Egypt, Syria, Jordan, Iraq and Lebanon. Amid general surprise, the Israelis defeated their enemies and their new state soon became established. They have defended it successfully ever since.

The most tragic result of the war was the plight of the Palestinian Arabs who found themselves inside the new state of Israel. After Jewish terrorists had slaughtered the entire population of an Arab village, nearly a million Palestinians fled into Egypt, Lebanon, Jordan and Syria where they lived in miserable refugee camps.

(c) *Who was to blame for the tragedy?*

● Most of the rest of the world, and the Conservatives, blamed Britain's Labour government for its handling of the situation. It was said that British troops should have stayed on to ensure that the partition of Palestine was carried out smoothly. The Arabs accused the British of being pro-Jewish for letting far too many Jews into Palestine in the first place and for causing them to lose half their homeland. The Jews accused the British of being pro-Arab for trying to limit Jewish immigration.

● Bevin defended his actions and blamed the USA for the chaos; there is some evidence to support his case. It was US President Truman who pressurized Britain to allow 100 000 extra Jews into Palestine in April 1946. Although this was bound to upset the Arabs even more, Truman refused to provide any American troops to help keep order in Palestine, and refused to allow any more Jews to enter the USA. It was Truman who rejected the British *Morrison Plan of July 1946*, which would have set up separate Arab and Jewish provinces under British supervision. It was the Americans who pushed the plan for partition through the UN, even though all the Arab nations voted against it; this was bound to cause more violence in Palestine.

● Some historians have defended the British, pointing out that they were trying to be fair to both sides, and that in the end, it was impossible to persuade both Arabs and Jews to accept a peaceful solution. The British withdrawal was understandable: it would force the Americans and the UN to take more responsibility for the situation they had helped create. It would save the British a lot of expense: since 1945 they had already spent over £100 million trying to keep the peace, and they could not afford to continue.

32.4 Britain and the Suez crisis 1956

(a) *The causes of the crisis were complex*

It was partly a continuation of the Arab–Israeli conflict; it was partly a struggle between Arab nationalism (in the person of the Egyptian leader, Colonel Nasser) and the British (and French), who wanted to prolong British influence in the Middle East; and it was an episode in the Cold War between the USA and the USSR.

1 Colonel Gamal Abdel Nasser, the new ruler of Egypt (who came to power in 1954 soon after the overthrow of the unpopular King Farouk), was aggressively in favour of Arab unity and independence, including the liberation of Palestine from the Jews. Almost everything he did irritated the British, the French or the Americans. He organized guerrilla bands (*fedayeen* – self-sacrificers) to sabotage

and murder inside Israel and blockaded the Gulf of Aqaba leading to the Israeli port of Eilat.

2   He insisted that Britain evacuate her military base at Suez (the agreement signed in 1936 allowing her to keep the base expired in 1956), sent aid to the Algerian Arabs in their struggle against France, prodded the other Arab states into opposing the British-sponsored Baghdad Pact, and forced King Hussein of Jordan to dismiss his British army chief of staff.

3   In September 1955 Nasser signed an arms deal with Czechoslovakia for Russian fighters, bombers and tanks, and Soviet experts went to train the Egyptian army. The Americans saw this as a Russian attempt to 'move into' the Middle East, and tried to placate Nasser by offering to finance the building of a dam at Aswan. However, Nasser upset the west further by officially recognizing communist China, and the Americans cancelled the promised grant of $46 million (July 1956).

4   Nasser immediately retaliated by nationalizing the Suez Canal, intending to use its revenues to finance the dam. Share-owners, a majority of whom were British and French, were promised compensation.

5   Anthony Eden, Britain's Conservative Prime Minister, convinced that Nasser must be got rid of, took the lead at this point. He believed that Nasser was on the way to forming a united Arabia under Egyptian control and communist influence. Two-thirds of all Britain's oil supplies came via the Suez Canal, and these could now be cut off at Nasser's whim. Eden viewed him as another Hitler or Mussolini, and according to historian Hugh Thomas, 'saw Egypt through a forest of Flanders poppies and gleaming jackboots'. He was also influenced by the fact that the Conservatives had criticized the Labour government which took no action in a similar situation in 1951 when Iran nationalized the Anglo-Iranian Oil Company, and he was infuriated by the taunts of the Tory press that he was indecisive. Eden had plenty of support for some sort of action against Nasser; Churchill remarked: 'we can't have this malicious swine sitting across our communications', and the new Labour leader, Hugh Gaitskell, agreed that Nasser must not be appeased in the way that Hitler and Mussolini had been appeased in the 1930s. Most people in Britain seemed to ignore the fact that Nasser had offered compensation to the shareholders and had promised that the ships of all nations (except Israel) would be able to use the canal.

(b) *Anglo-French-Israeli plans*

Secret talks took place between the British, French and Israelis, and a plan was hatched: Israeli troops would invade Egypt across the Sinai peninsula, whereupon Britain and France would issue an ultimatum to both sides to withdraw. The Egyptians would not be able to agree to this, so British and French troops would attack Egypt and occupy the Canal zone on the pretext that they were protecting it from damage in the fighting. Anglo-French control of the canal would be restored, and the defeat, it was hoped, would topple Nasser from power.

Recent research has shown that the war could easily have been avoided and that Eden was more in favour of getting rid of Nasser by peaceful means. The Americans had made it clear that they had no desire to get involved in military action in the Middle East; President Eisenhower was facing an election in November, and did not want to appear too aggressive. In fact there was a secret Anglo-American plan (*Omega*) to overthrow Nasser using political and economic pressures. In mid-October 1956 Eden was still willing to continue talks with Egypt; he had called off the military operation, and there seemed a good chance of compromise being reached over control of the canal. However, Eden was under pressure from several directions to use force.

MI6 (the British intelligence service) and some members of the cabinet, including Macmillan (the Chancellor of the Exchequer) and Selwyn Lloyd (the Foreign Secretary) were in favour of military action. Macmillan assured Eden that the USA would not oppose a British use of force; 'I know Ike', he told Eden. 'He'll lie doggo!' In the end it was probably pressure from the French government which caused Eden to opt for the joint military operation with France and Israel.

(c) *The war against Egypt*

The plans were duly put into operation and militarily were a brilliant success. The war began with the planned Israeli invasion of Egypt (29 October), which within a week had captured the entire Sinai peninsula. Britain and France delivered their ultimatum and proceeded to bomb Egyptian airfields and land troops at Port Said, at the northern end of the Suez Canal. The attacks caused an outcry from the rest of the world: the Americans, who were afraid of upsetting all the Arabs and forcing them into closer ties with the USSR, refused to support Britain. In fact at the UN both the Americans and Russians, for once in agreement, categorically condemned the British and French action and the UN accused them of aggression. The UN went on to demand an immediate ceasefire, threatened oil sanctions and prepared to send a peace-keeping force of its own. With the pressure of world opinion against them, Britain, France and Israel agreed to a ceasefire (6 November) and began to withdraw, while UN troops moved in to police the frontier between Egypt and Israel.

(d) *The outcome of the war*

The war was a diplomatic disaster for Britain and France; as Peter Clarke puts it: 'once the cover story was blown, the British appeared doubly guilty – not only of aggression against Egypt but guilty too of calculated deceit of their great ally'. None of their aims was achieved. They had failed to overthrow Nasser, and his prestige as leader of Arab nationalism against European interference was greatly enhanced. He simply replaced the American and western aid he had lost with aid from the USSR. The Egyptians blocked the canal and the Arabs reduced oil supplies to western Europe, where petrol rationing was introduced for a time. To back up its condemnation in the UN, the USA withdrew its support for the pound, which caused a disastrous fall in Britain's gold reserves – a quarter of her entire gold and dollar reserves were lost in November alone. The British action soon lost them a valuable Middle East ally in Iraq where the pro-British King Feisal and his premier, Nuri-es-Said, came under increasing attack from other Arab governments; both were murdered in 1958. Even more serious, the Anglo-American alliance was weakened at a time when it needed to present a strong front against the Russians who were in the process of crushing the Hungarian uprising. Britain was seen to be weak and incapable of conducting a foreign policy independently of the USA. It has been suggested that Britain's humiliation helped to speed up decolonization by encouraging independence movements in Africa.

On the other hand some historians have sought to play down the ill effects of Suez. David Carlton points out that although Nasser was still in power, Egypt had in fact suffered a devastating defeat at the hands of Israel, losing at least a third of her army and its equipment. British influence in the Middle East was not completely finished since pro-British regimes survived in Jordan and Kuwait. The breach with the USA was soon healed when Macmillan became Prime Minister.

(e) *The war a personal disaster for Eden*

In some quarters Eden was criticized for having sent troops into Egypt in the first place, without any real moral case (the fact that Nasser had offered compensation was consistently ignored). Others thought that having gone in, Britain should have ignored the UN and captured the whole canal zone, which would have been possible within a few days. What would have happened then is not certain; it seems that Eden had not thought the consequences through clearly enough, and Britain's actual war aims were vague. Always highly strung, he was exhausted by the crisis, and on his doctor's orders, he resigned in January 1957. His political career was finished. The irony was that though Eden is remembered as the scapegoat for Suez, he was succeeded as Prime Minister by Macmillan, who was arguably just as responsible for the disaster as Eden. Macmillan had urged Eden to opt for military action, and after talking to Eisenhower, he misled Eden into thinking that the Americans would not oppose it. Yet as Chancellor of the Exchequer responsible for Britain's dwindling reserves, Macmillan was the one who changed his tune and urged a ceasefire, realizing that this was the only way to get back American support for sterling.

32.5 Britain, Malaya and Cyprus

(a) *Problems involved in the British withdrawal from Malaya*

Malaya was liberated from Japanese occupation in 1945, but there were two main problems to be faced before the British could think of withdrawing:

● How could such a complex area be organized? It consisted of nine states, each ruled by a Sultan, two British settlements, Malacca and Penang, and Singapore, a small island less than a mile from the mainland. The population was multi-racial: mostly Malays and Chinese, but with Indians and Europeans as well. It was decided to group the states and the settlements into *the Federation of Malaya* (1948) while Singapore remained a separate colony. Each state had its own legislature for local affairs; the Sultans retained some power, but the central government had firm overall control. Since everybody had the vote, the Malays, the largest group, usually dominated affairs.
● Chinese communist guerrillas, who had led the resistance to the Japanese, now began to stir up strikes and violence against the British, and the situation was serious enough for a state of emergency to be declared in 1948. The British dealt with the problem successfully, though it took time: all Chinese suspected of helping the guerrillas were resettled into specially guarded villages; it was made clear that independence would follow as soon as the country was ready for it; this ensured that the Malays remained firmly pro-British and gave little help to the communists who were mainly Chinese. Even so the emergency remained in force until 1960.

The move towards independence was accelerated when the Malay party under their capable leader, Tunku Abdul Rahman, joined forces with the main Chinese and Indian groups to form *the Alliance Party*, which won 51 out of the 52 seats in the 1955 elections. This seemed to suggest stability, and the British were persuaded to grant full independence in 1957 when Malaya was admitted to the Commonwealth.

(b) *The Federation of Malaysia founded (1963)*

Malaya soon settled down under the leadership of Tunku Abdul Rahman, and its economy, based on exports of rubber and tin, was the most prosperous in South East Asia.

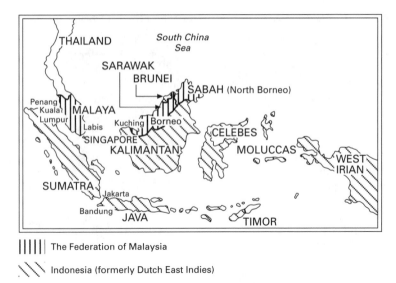

IIIIII The Federation of Malaysia

\\\\\ Indonesia (formerly Dutch East Indies)

Map 32.2 *Malaysia and Indonesia*

Thus in 1961 when Abdul Rahman proposed that Singapore and the three British colonies of North Borneo (Sabah), Brunei and Sarawak should join Malaya to form the Federation of Malaysia, Britain agreed. The Tunku had an ulterior motive: the island of Singapore with its prosperous port would be a valuable acquisition, but since three-quarters of its population were Chinese, the Malays would be outnumbered if union took place just between Malaya and Singapore; if the other three colonies with their predominantly Malay population also joined the federation, the Malay majority would be preserved. Singapore, Sarawak and Sabah were in favour of joining, but *objections came from two quarters*:

- In Brunei, groups of people opposed to joining the federation started a revolt (December 1962). Although this was quickly suppressed by British troops flown in from Singapore, the Sultan of Brunei decided not to join. This was a disappointment for Abdul Rahman, since Brunei had rich oil resources.
- President Sukarno of Indonesia protested because he hoped that Sabah and Sarawak would become part of Indonesia once the British left.

After a United Nations investigation team reported that a large majority of the populations concerned was in favour of the union, the Federation of Malaysia was officially proclaimed (September 1963). Malaysia survived an attempt by neighbouring Indonesia to bring about its disintegration (1963–6). Britain, Australia and New Zealand provided vital military assistance so that the Malaysians could control the situation. However, in 1965, Singapore, under the leadership of Lee Kuan Yew, chose to leave the Federation, becoming an independent republic. Brunei ceased to be a British colony and became an independent state within the Commonwealth in 1984.

(c) *Complications in Cyprus*

The Labour government (1945–51) considered giving Cyprus independence, but progress was delayed by complications, the most serious of which was the mixed population – about 80 per cent were Greek-speaking Christians of the Orthodox Church, while the rest were Muslims of Turkish origin. The Greek Cypriots wanted the island to unite with Greece (*enosis*), but the Turks were strongly opposed to this. Churchill's government (1951–5) inflamed the situation in 1954 when their plans for self-government allowed the Cypriots far less power than Labour had envisaged. There were hostile demonstrations which were dispersed by British troops.

Eden, Churchill's successor, decided to drop the idea of independence for Cyprus, believing that Britain needed the island as a military base to protect her interests in the Middle East. He announced that Cyprus must remain permanently British, though the Greek government promised that Britain could retain her military bases even if *enosis* took place.

The Greek Cypriots, led by Archbishop Makarios, pressed their demands, while a guerrilla organization called *Eoka*, led by General Grivas, waged a terrorist campaign against the British who declared a state of emergency (1955) and deployed about 35 000 troops to try and keep order. British policy also involved deporting Makarios and executing terrorists. The activities of Colonel Nasser in Egypt only served to strengthen Eden's resolve that Britain must keep her foothold in the Middle East.

(d) *Macmillan favours compromise*

The situation became even more difficult in 1958 when the Turks set up a rival organization which favoured dividing the island. Eventually, to avoid civil war between the two groups, Macmillan (who became Prime Minister in 1957 when Eden resigned following Britain's humiliation at Suez) decided to compromise. He appointed the sympathetic and tactful Hugh Foot as governor, and he soon negotiated a deal with Makarios: the Archbishop dropped *enosis* and in return Cyprus was granted full independence; Turkish interests were safeguarded, Britain retained two military bases, and, along with Greece and Turkey, guaranteed the independence of Cyprus. In 1960 Makarios became the first president, with a Turkish Cypriot, Fazal Kutchuk, as vice-president. It seemed a masterly solution, but unfortunately it only lasted until 1963, when civil war broke out between Greeks and Turks. In 1974 Turkey sent troops to help establish a separate Turkish state in the north, and the island has remained divided ever since. The Turks occupy the north (roughly one-third of the island's area), and the Greeks the south, with UN troops keeping the peace between the two.

32.6 The end of the British empire in Africa

Why did the British decide to leave Africa?

During the 1990s, as more and more government documents dealing with decolonization became available, historians have had a great time investigating the motives behind the withdrawal of all the European powers, not just Britain, from their empires, and the different ways in which these withdrawals were conducted. The main debate which has developed (as we saw in the case of India in Section 32.2) is about the extent to which decolonization was caused by the local nationalist movements and how far it was brought about by outside political and economic considerations. Robert Holland, a leading exponent of what has become known as the *'metropolitan thesis'*, believes that outside forces – metropolitan factors – were more important. 'The great colonial powers,' he writes, 'divested themselves of their subordinate possessions, not because internal pressures within their colonies left them with no other choice, but in the wake of a revisionist process whereby imperial roles came to be seen as incongruent with more "modern" goals in the fields of foreign and economic policy.'

Other historians feel that more credit must be given to the strength of local nationalist movements and they acknowledge that in some cases the imperial power was quite simply expelled by sheer force. The sorts of questions that historians have to try and answer are, for example: would the British have left East Africa and Central Africa for purely 'metropolitan' reasons *if there had been no nationalist movements in those areas*? However, each case was different, and more research will be needed before clearer conclusions can be reached.

What can be said with certainty is that African nationalism spread rapidly after 1945; this was because more and more Africans were being educated in Britain and the USA, where they were made aware of racial discrimination. Colonialism was seen as the humiliation and exploitation of blacks by whites, and working-class Africans in the new towns were particularly receptive to nationalist ideas. The British, especially the Labour governments of 1945–51, were prepared to allow independence, and were confident that they would still be able to exercise influence through trade links, which they hoped to preserve by including the new states as members of the Commonwealth. This practice of exercising influence over former colonies after independence by economic means is known as *neo-colonialism*, and it became widespread in most of the new states of the Third World. Even so, the British intended to move their colonies towards independence very gradually, and the African nationalists had to campaign vigorously and often violently to make them act more quickly.

There were plenty of 'metropolitan factors' at work too. The USA, the USSR and the UN were all against imperialism. Britain had been seriously weakened economically by the Second World War and the sheer cost of maintaining her empire, while at the same time developing her own nuclear weapons, was spiralling out of control. It was Macmillan who accelerated Britain's decolonization, apparently because he thought it foolish for a country which was so economically weak to attempt to maintain an imperial role. According to Martin Pugh, it was more than just a loss of nerve after Suez; already as Chancellor of the Exchequer, Macmillan 'had drawn up a profit and loss account for every colony in order to determine where the balance of advantage lay'. His conclusion was: withdraw with as much dignity as possible, while presenting it as a generous and noble response to rising African nationalism. As Iain Macleod, Macmillan's Colonial Secretary, later put it: 'we could not possibly have held by force our territories in Africa; the march of men towards freedom cannot be halted; it can only be guided'.

The British colonies in Africa fell into three distinct groups which had important differences in character, and these affected progress towards independence.

West Africa: Gold Coast, Nigeria, Sierra Leone and the Gambia

Here there were relatively few Europeans, and they tended to be administrators rather than permanent settlers with profitable estates to defend. This made the move to independence comparatively straightforward.

East Africa: Kenya, Uganda and Tanganyika

Here, especially in Kenya, things were complicated by the 'settler-factor' – the presence of European and Asian settlers who feared for their future under black governments.

(a) West Africa

1 The Gold Coast

The Gold Coast was the first black African state south of the Sahara to win independence after the Second World War, taking the name *Ghana* (1957). It was achieved fairly smoothly, though not without some incident. The nationalist leader, Kwame Nkrumah, educated in London and the USA and since 1949 leader of *the Convention People's Party (CPP)*, organized the campaign for independence. There were boycotts of European goods, violent demonstrations and a general strike (1950), and Nkruma was twice imprisoned. However, the British, realizing that he had mass support, agreed to allow a new constitution which included the vote for all adults, an elected assembly and an eleven-person Executive Council of which eight members were chosen by the assembly. In the 1951 elections, the first under the new constitution, the CCP won 34 seats out of 38. Nkrumah was invited to form a government and became Prime Minister in 1952. This was self-government but not yet full independence. The Gold Coast had a small but well-educated group of politicians and other professionals who, for the next five years, gained experience of government under British supervision. In 1957 Ghana received full independence.

2 Nigeria

Nigeria was easily the largest of Britain's African colonies, with a population of over 60 million. It was a more difficult proposition than Ghana because of its great size and because of its regional differences between the vast Muslim north, dominated by the Hausa and Fulani tribes, the western region (Yorubas) and the eastern region (Ibos). The leading nationalist was Nnamdi Azikiwe, popularly known to his supporters as 'Zik'. He had been educated in the USA, and after his return to Nigeria in 1937 he soon gained enormous prestige. In 1945 he showed that he meant business by organizing an impressive general strike, which was enough to prompt the British to begin preparing Nigeria for independence. It was decided that a federal system would be most suitable; in 1954 a new constitution introduced local assemblies for the three regions with a central (federal) government in Lagos, the capital. The regions assumed self-government first and the country as a whole became independent in 1960. Sadly, in spite of the careful preparations for independence, tribal differences caused civil war to break out in 1967, when the Ibos declared the eastern region independent, calling it Biafra. Only after long and bloody fighting was Biafra defeated (1970) and Nigerian unity preserved.

3 Sierra Leone and the Gambia

These two remaining British colonies in West Africa achieved independence without serious incident – Sierra Leone in 1961 and the Gambia in 1965.

The Central African Federation 1953–63
Northern Rhodesia (Zambia), Southern Rhodesia (Zimbabwe) and
Nyasaland (Malawi)

R Ruanda 1962
B Burundi 1962

Map 32.3   Africa becomes independent

(b) *East Africa*

Originally the British thought that independence for the colonies of East Africa was not so necessary as for West Africa, and that when independence did come, it would be in the form of multi-racial governments, in which the European and Asian settlers would play a significant part. But Macmillan (Prime Minister 1957–63) was responsible for the important change in British policy towards the remaining African colonies. He had come to realize the strength of black African feeling and the strain it would place on Britain if she attempted to crush it. In a famous speech in Cape Town in 1960 he talked of 'the wind of change blowing through the continent. Whether we like it or not, this growth of national consciousness is a political fact, and our national policies must take account of it.'

1 Tanganyika

In Tanganyika the nationalist campaign was conducted by *the Tanganyika African National Union (TANU)* led by Dr Julius Nyerere, who had been educated at

Edinburgh University. He insisted that the government must be African, but he also made it clear that whites had nothing to fear from black rule. Macmillan's government, impressed by Nyerere's ability and sincerity, conceded independence with black majority rule (1961). The island of Zanzibar was later united with Tanganyika and the country took the name *Tanzania* (1964). Nyerere was president until his retirement in 1985.

2 Uganda

In Uganda independence was delayed for a time by tribal squabbles; the ruler (known as the Kabaka) of the Buganda area objected to the introduction of democracy. Eventually a solution was found in a federal constitution which allowed the Kabaka to retain some powers in Buganda. Uganda itself became independent in 1962 with Dr Milton Obote as Prime Minister.

3 Kenya

Kenya was the most difficult area to deal with because there were some 66 000 white settlers who were violently opposed to black majority rule. They refused to negotiate with the African nationalist leader, Jomo Kenyatta and his *Kenya African Unity Party (KAU)* and were determined to prolong white settler rule. They provoked a confrontation, hoping that violence would destroy the African party. The British government was under pressure from both sides, and the white settlers were supported by certain big business interests in Britain; even so, it did not handle the situation with much imagination. KAU was able to make little progress, the only British concession being to allow six Africans to join the Legislative Council of 54 members.

African impatience burst out in a campaign of terrorist attacks on European-owned farms and on black workers. It was organized by the *Mau Mau* secret society, whose members were mainly from the Kikuyu tribe, who had been deprived of much of their best land by the white settlers. A state of emergency was declared (1952) and Kenyatta and other nationalist leaders were arrested. Kenyatta was kept in jail for six years (1953–9) although he had publicly condemned terrorism. The British committed 100 000 troops to flush out the terrorists, and over the next eight years some 10 000 people, mostly Africans, were killed, and about 90 000 Kikuyu imprisoned in what can only be described as concentration camp conditions. There was a scandal in 1959 with revelations of brutal treatment of prisoners and mysterious deaths in captivity.

The terrorists had been defeated by 1960, but by then, ironically, the British, encouraged by the 'wind of change', had performed their policy U-turn. They realized that Kenyatta was, after all, a moderate, and allowed him to become Prime Minister when Kenya became independent in 1963. In spite of his treatment by the British, Kenyatta favoured reconciliation; whites who decided to stay on after independence were fairly treated provided they took Kenyan citizenship.

c) *Central Africa*

This was the most difficult area for Britain to deal with because this was where the settlers were most numerous and most deeply entrenched, particularly in Southern Rhodesia. Another problem was that numbers of well-educated Africans were much smaller than in West Africa, because the settlers had made sure that very little money was spent on further and higher education for black Africans. Alarmed at the spread of nationalism, the whites decided that their best policy was to combine resources. They persuaded Churchill's government to allow them to set up a union of the three colonies – Nyasaland and the two Rhodesias – to be known as *the Central African Federation* (1953). Their aim was to preserve the supremacy of the white minority – about 300 000

Europeans out of a total population of around 8.5 million. The federal parliament in Salisbury (the capital of Southern Rhodesia) was heavily weighted to favour the whites, who hoped that the federation would soon gain full independence from Britain, with dominion status.

The Africans watched with growing distrust, and their leaders, Dr Hastings Banda (Nyasaland), Kenneth Kaunda (Northern Rhodesia) and Joshua Nkomo (Southern Rhodesia) began to campaign for black majority rule. As violence spread, a state of emergency was declared in Nyasaland and Southern Rhodesia, with mass arrests of Africans (1959). However, there was much support for the Africans in Britain, especially in the Labour party and among moderate Conservatives. The Conservative Colonial Secretary, Iain Macleod, was sympathetic and the government appointed *the Monckton Commission* to investigate the situation. In 1960 this recommended votes for Africans, an end to racial discrimination and the right of territories to leave the federation.

1 Nyasaland and Northern Rhodesia

The British government introduced new constitutions in Nyasaland and Northern Rhodesia, which in effect allowed the Africans their own parliaments (1961–2). Both wanted to leave the federation, which was therefore terminated in December 1963, signalling defeat for the settlers. The following year Nyasaland and Northern Rhodesia became fully independent, taking the names *Malawi* and *Zambia*. There was bitter opposition from some Conservative right-wingers, led by Lord Salisbury, who were strongly pro-settler; but most Conservatives were reconciled to decolonization by this time, and the government was able to ignore their protests.

2 Southern Rhodesia

Rhodesia, as it was now known, took much longer to deal with, and it was 1980 before the colony achieved independence with black majority rule. It was here that the white settlers fought most fiercely to preserve their privileged position. There were just over 200 000 whites, about 20 000 Asians, and four million black Africans; *the Rhodesia Front*, a right-wing racist party, was determined never to surrender control of the country to black African rule. The black African parties were banned.

When Zambia and Malawi were given independence, the whites assumed that Rhodesia would get the same treatment and requested independence. The Conservative government refused, making it clear that independence would be granted *only if the constitution was changed to allow black Africans at least a third of the seats in parliament*. Ian Smith (who became Prime Minister of Rhodesia in 1964) rejected this idea, arguing that continued white rule was essential in view of the problems being faced by the new black governments in other African states, and because the Zimbabwe nationalists seemed bitterly divided. When the Labour government (1964–70) refused to compromise, Smith declared Rhodesia independent, against the wishes of Britain, in November 1965 (this was known as UDI – unilateral declaration of independence).

There were mixed reactions to UDI. Harold Wilson soon decided it was out of the question to use force against the illegal Smith regime, and hoped to bring the country to its knees by economic sanctions. The UN condemned UDI and called on member states to place a complete trade embargo on Rhodesia. The Commonwealth was divided – Ghana and Nigeria urged Britain to use force, while Zambia and Tanzania hoped economic sanctions would suffice. However, South Africa, also ruled by a white minority government, and Portugal, which owned neighbouring Mozambique, were sympathetic to Smith, and Rhodesia was able to continue trading through these coun tries. Many Commonwealth countries felt that Britain was soft-pedalling sanctions, especially as Zambia was suffering more from them than Rhodesia. When Wilson twice met Smith (aboard HMS *Tiger* in 1966 and HMS *Fearless* in 1988) to put new ideas forward, there were howls of protest in case he betrayed the black Rhodesians. Perhaps fortunately for the future of the Commonwealth, Smith rejected both sets of proposals.

In 1970 Rhodesia declared itself a republic, and the rights of black citizens were gradually whittled away until they were suffering similar treatment to that being experienced by blacks living under *apartheid* in South Africa (see (d) below). In 1976 the first signs began to appear that the whites would have to compromise, and they were eventually forced to give way:

● Mozambique's independence from Portugal (June 1975) was a serious blow to the Smith regime. The new president, Samora Machel, applied economic sanctions and allowed Zimbabwean guerrillas to operate from Mozambique. Thousands of black guerrillas were soon active in Rhodesia, straining the white security forces to their limits.
● The South Africans became less inclined to support Smith, fearing that the USSR and Cuba (who were involved in Angola) might start interfering in Rhodesia unless some compromise could be found. Both Americans and South Africans urged Smith to make concessions to the blacks before it was too late.
● By 1978 nationalist guerrillas controlled large areas of Rhodesia and the whites were on the verge of defeat.

Smith still tried everything he knew to delay black majority rule as long as possible. He was able to present the divisions between the nationalist leaders as his excuse for the lack of progress, and this was a genuine problem:

● *ZAPU* (Zimbabwe African People's Union) was the party of the veteran nationalist *Joshua Nkomo*.
● *ZANU* (Zimbabwe African National Union) was the party of *the Reverend Ndabaningi Sithole*.
These two parties, representing different tribes, seemed to be bitter enemies.

● *UANC* (United African National Council) was the party of *Bishop Abel Muzorewa*.
● *Robert Mugabe*, leader of the guerrilla wing of ZANU, was another powerful figure.

Smith tried to compromise by introducing his own scheme, a joint government of whites and UANC, the most moderate of the nationalist parties, with Bishop Muzorewa as Prime Minister (April 1979). However, it was ZANU and ZAPU which had mass support and they continued the guerrilla war. Smith had to admit defeat and the new Thatcher government called *the Lancaster House Conference* in London (September–December 1979). All parties were represented and after some skilful manoeuvring by Lord Carrington, the Foreign Secretary, the conference reached agreement:

● There was to be a new constitution which would allow the black majority to rule.
● In the new republic of Zimbabwe, there would be a 100-seat parliament in which 80 seats were reserved for black Africans.
● Muzorewa would step down as Prime Minister and the guerrilla war would end.

In the elections which followed, Mugabe's ZANU won a sweeping victory, taking 57 of the 80 black African seats. This gave him a comfortable overall majority, enabling him to become Prime Minister when Zimbabwe officially became independent in April

1980. The transference to black majority rule was welcomed by all African and Commonwealth leaders as a triumph for common sense and moderation. However, some Conservatives accused the government of betraying Muzorewa and allowing Zimbabwe to fall to Marxism. Civil war between ZANU and ZAPU, which many had feared, did not materialize; the two parties merged in 1987, when Mugabe became the country's first president. He was re-elected for a further term in March 1996.

(d) *South Africa*

The situation in the Union of South Africa was different from that in the other British parts of Africa. South Africa had enjoyed dominion status since 1909 (see Section 21.2) and therefore had more say over its own affairs than the other areas, which were colonies. The majority of the white population was of Dutch Boer origin and therefore did not have the same close affiliations with Britain as the whites in the British colonies. While the colonies gained independence under black majority rule and stayed within the Commonwealth, South Africa preserved white minority rule and left the Commonwealth in 1961.

The whites formed less than 20 per cent of the population. In 1974 there were almost 18 million black Africans, known as Bantus, 2.3 million coloureds, 700 000 Asians and 4.2 million whites. Roughly two-thirds of the whites were of Dutch origin (known as Afrikaners) and the rest were of British origin. With the granting of independence to India and Pakistan in 1947, white South Africans became alarmed at the growing racial equality within the Commonwealth and were determined to preserve their supremacy. Most of the whites were against racial equality, but the most extreme were the Afrikaner Nationalists, led by Dr Malan, who claimed that the whites were a master race and that non-whites were inferior beings. The Dutch Reformed Church (the official state church) supported this view, though the Christian Church in general believes in racial equality. The Nationalists won the 1948 elections with promises to rescue the whites from the 'black menace'. Malan's policy was *apartheid*.

What was apartheid?

It was a policy which involved separating or segregating the different races, in order to preserve the racial purity of the whites, and thus their supremacy. There had been some segregation before 1948; for example, Africans were forbidden to buy land outside special reserve areas. But Malan's apartheid was much more systematic: Africans had to live in special reserves and townships, with separate and inferior facilities. If an existing black township was thought to be too close to a 'white' area, the whole community was uprooted and 'regrouped' somewhere else to make separation as complete as possible. There were separate buses, trains, coaches, cafes, toilets, park benches, hospitals, beaches, picnic areas, sports and even churches. Black children went to separate schools and were given a much inferior education. Every person was given a racial classification and an identity card, and marriage and sexual relations between whites and non-whites were forbidden. Black Africans had no political rights and were not represented in parliament.

There was mounting criticism of apartheid from all over the world. Most of the Commonwealth members were strongly opposed to it, and early in 1960 Macmillan had the courage to speak out against it in the South African parliament in Cape Town, during his famous 'wind of change' speech. His warnings were ignored, and shortly afterwards the world was horrified by the Sharpeville massacre when 67 Africans were killed in clashes with the police.

At the 1961 Commonwealth Conference, criticism of South Africa was intense, and many thought she should be expelled. In the end the Prime Minister, Verwoerd, withdrew South Africa's application for continued membership (in 1960 she had decided to become a republic instead of a dominion, thereby severing the connection with the British crown; because of this she had to apply for readmission to the Commonwealth), and she ceased to be a member of the Commonwealth.

The end of apartheid and white supremacy

Apartheid continued without any concessions to black people until 1980. But pressure for drastic change was building up. It was a serious blow to the white South African regime when in 1975 the white-ruled Portuguese colonies of Mozambique and Angola achieved independence. The African takeover of Zimbabwe in 1980 removed the last of the white-ruled states which had been sympathetic to South Africa and apartheid. Now she was surrounded by hostile black-ruled states, and many Africans in these new states had sworn never to rest until their fellow-Africans in South Africa had been liberated. Moderate Afrikaner leaders realized that they had to make concessions or risk losing everything. In the early 1980s much of the apartheid system was dropped: in 1990 the African National Congress (ANC) was legalized and Nelson Mandela was released after 27 years in jail.

President F. W. de Klerk (elected 1989) had privately decided that black majority rule would have to come eventually; he wanted to move the country towards it in a controlled way rather than have it imposed by violence. He deserves great credit for the courage and determination he showed in the face of bitter opposition from right-wing Afrikaner groups. Nelson Mandela, now leader of the ANC, responded well, condemning violence and calling for reconciliation between blacks and whites. After long and difficult negotiations, a new constitution was worked out (1993), and a general election was held in which the ANC won almost two-thirds of the votes (May 1994). Mandela became the first black president of South Africa. It was a remarkable achievement, shared by both Mandela and de Klerk, that South Africa was able to move from apartheid to black majority rule without civil war.

32.7 Britain, European unity and the European Community

(a) *Reasons for wanting more unity*

In every country in western Europe there were people from all parts of the political spectrum who wanted more unity. They had different ideas about exactly what sort of unity would be best; some simply wanted the nations to co-operate more closely; others (known as *federalists*) thought in terms of a politically united Europe with a federal system of government like the one in the USA. Their reasoning was simple: only by a co-operative effort and a pooling of resources could Europe recover from the ravages of the war; the countries were too small to be economically and militarily viable separately in a world dominated by the superpowers, the USA and the USSR. The more the countries of western Europe worked together, the less chance there would be of war breaking out between them again, and it seemed the best way for a speedy reconciliation between France and Germany. Finally it was thought that the threat to western Europe from Russia and communism could best be met by joint action. West Germany was especially keen on the idea because it would gain her early acceptance as a responsible nation again.

Winston Churchill was one of the strongest advocates of European unity; in March

1943 he spoke of the need for a Council of Europe, and in a speech in Zurich in 1946 he suggested that France and Germany should take the lead in setting up 'a kind of United States of Europe'.

(b) *First steps in co-operation*

The first steps in economic, military and political co-operation were soon taken, but the federalists were bitterly disappointed that a United States of Europe had not materialized by 1950.

● *The Organization for European Economic Co-operation (OEEC)* was the first move towards unity; it was created in 1948 as a response to the American offer of Marshall Aid, when Ernest Bevin took the lead in organizing 16 European nations to draw up a plan for the best use of American aid (see Section 32.1(d)). The 16-nation committee became the permanent OEEC, and it was extremely successful in apportioning American aid and encouraging trade among its members by reducing restrictions.
● *NATO was another example of European co-operation*, set up in 1949 as a mutual defence in case of an attack on one of the member states (see Section 32.1(f)). However, France withdrew in 1966.
● *The Council of Europe (1949)* was the first attempt at some sort of political unity. Its founder-members were Britain, Belgium, Netherlands, Luxembourg, Denmark, France, Eire, Italy, Norway and Sweden. By 1971 all the states of western Europe (except Spain and Portugal) had joined, and so had Turkey, Malta and Cyprus, making 18 members in all. Based at Strasbourg, it consisted of the Foreign Ministers of the member states, and an assembly of representatives chosen by the parliaments of the states. It had no powers, however, since several states, including Britain, refused to join any organization which threatened their own sovereignty. It could debate pressing issues and make recommendations, and it achieved useful work sponsoring human rights agreements; but it was a grave disappointment to the federalists.

(c) *The European Economic Community (EEC) set up (1957)*

Known in Britain in its early years as *the Common Market*, the EEC was set up by *the Treaty of Rome (1957)* and came into operation on 1 January 1958. There were six founder-members – France, West Germany, Italy, Belgium, Netherlands and Luxembourg. Britain refused to join. *The stages in the evolution of the Community were:*

1   *Benelux.* In 1944 the exiled governments of Belgium, Netherlands and Luxembourg formed *the Benelux Customs Union*, a customs and trading association which came into operation in 1947.
2   *The Treaty of Brussels (1948).* By this treaty, Britain and France joined the three Benelux countries in pledging 'military, economic, social and cultural collaboration'. The military collaboration eventually resulted in NATO; the next step in economic co-operation was the ECSC.
3   *The European Coal and Steel Community (ECSC) set up in 1951.* This was the brainchild of Robert Schuman, the French Foreign Minister, who hoped that involving West Germany would improve relations between France and Germany and at the same time make European industry more efficient. Six countries joined – France, West Germany, Italy, Belgium, Netherlands and Luxembourg. All duties and restrictions on trade in coal, iron and steel between the Six were removed, and

a High Authority was created to administer the community and organize a joint programme of expansion. However, the British refused to join because it would mean handing over control of their industries to an outside, supra-national authority. The ECSC was an outstanding success; steel production rose by almost 50 per cent during the first five years, and the Six decided to extend it to include all production.

The British decision not to join is usually seen as a serious mistake; but it is easy to be wise with the benefit of hindsight. In defence of the government it has to be pointed out that they were in the throes of nationalizing iron and steel, and coal had just been nationalized; these would be pointless exercises if the industries were immediately to be handed over to the High Authority. Nor were there any guarantees that the ECSC would be a success; at that point the six states which joined were much weaker economically than Britain. As historian Stephen George points out, 'by joining in, Britain might have been tying itself to a sinking ship which could pull down the British economy with it'. Attlee therefore announced that although Britain sympathized with any activities which improved Franco-German relations, she could not undertake to join the scheme immediately.

4   *The Treaty of Rome (1957)* setting up the EEC specified that the Six would gradually remove all customs duties and quotas so that there would be free competition and a common market. Tariffs would be kept against non-members, though even these were reduced. The treaty also mentioned improving living and working conditions, expanding industry, encouraging the development of the world's backward areas, safeguarding peace and liberty, and working for a closer union of European peoples; obviously something much wider than just a common market was in the minds of the statesmen of the Six. Jean Monnet, for example, the French chairman of the ECSC High Authority, set up an action committee to work for a United States of Europe. The EEC was soon off to a flying start; within five years it was the world's biggest exporter and biggest buyer of raw materials, and was second only to the USA in steel production. Once again, however, Britain had refused the invitation to join.

By 1967 the machinery to run the EEC had been refined to include the following:

●   *The European Commission* based in Brussels was the body which ran the day-to-day work of the Community. It was staffed by civil servants and expert economists who took important policy decisions. It had strong powers so that it would be able to stand up to criticism and opposition from the governments of the Six, though in theory its decisions had to be approved by the Council of Ministers.

●   *The Council of Ministers* consisted of government representatives from each of the member states. Their job was to exchange information about their governments' economic policies and to try and co-ordinate them and keep them running on similar lines. There was some friction between the Council and the Commission: the Commission often seemed reluctant to listen to the advice of the Council, and kept on pouring out masses of new regulations.

●   *The European Parliament* met at Strasbourg and consisted of 198 representatives chosen by the parliaments of the member states. They could discuss issues and make recommendations, but had no control over the Commission or the Council. From 1979 the representatives (Euro MPs) were directly elected by the people of the Community.

●   *The European Court of Justice* was set up to deal with any problems which might arise out of the interpretation and operation of the Treaty of Rome. It soon came to be regarded as the body to which people could appeal if their government was thought to be infringing the rules of the Community.

- Also associated with the EEC was *EURATOM*, an organization in which the Six pooled their efforts towards the development of atomic energy.

In 1967 the EEC, the ECSC and EURATOM formally merged and became known simply as *the European Community (EC)*.

(d) *Why did Britain refuse membership of the EEC?*

It was ironic that though Churchill had been one of the strongest supporters of the idea of a unified Europe, when he became Prime Minister again in 1951 he seemed to have lost any enthusiasm he might have felt for Britain's membership of it. Attlee had drawn back from entering the ECSC and both Churchill and Eden were doubtful about any deeper co-operation. Both Eden and Macmillan were very cool towards the negotiations which preceded the signing of the treaty of Rome.

Their main objection was that Britain would no longer be in control of her own economy, which would be at the mercy of the European Commission in Brussels. Although the governments of the other six states did not seem unduly worried by this prospect and were prepared to make the sacrifice in the interests of greater overall efficiency, the British government was not.

There was also the fear that Britain's relationship with the Commonwealth might be ruined if she were no longer able to give preference to Commonwealth goods such as New Zealand lamb and butter. Around 40 per cent of all Britain's exports went to the empire (or what would soon become the Commonwealth). The Commonwealth, with a population of around 800 million, seemed a more promising market than the EEC which had less than 200 million.

Britain's 'special relationship' with the USA had to be taken into consideration; this was not shared by the other states of Europe, and if the British became too deeply involved in economic integration in Europe, it could damage their special relationship with the Americans. Underlying all this was the fact that most British politicians were deeply suspicious that economic unity would lead to the political unity of Europe, and that was even less appealing to the British, who were determined that British sovereignty (that is, supreme control of their own internal affairs) must be preserved.

On the other hand Britain and some of the other European states outside the EEC were worried about being excluded from selling their goods to EEC members because of the high duties on imports from outside the Community. Consequently in 1959 Britain took the lead in organizing a rival group, *the European Free Trade Association (EFTA)*. Britain, Denmark, Norway, Sweden, Switzerland, Austria and Portugal agreed gradually to abolish tariffs amongst themselves. Britain was prepared to join an organization like EFTA because there was no question of common economic policies and no Commission to interfere with the internal affairs of states. By 1961, however, the British had had a complete change of mind, and Macmillan announced that they wished to join the EEC.

(e) *Why did the British change their minds and apply to join the EEC?*

In the first place it was clear by 1961 that the EEC was an outstanding success – without Britain. Since 1953 French production had risen by 75 per cent, while German production had increased by almost 90 per cent. Britain's economy was much less successful – over the same period British production had risen by only about 30 per cent. Britain's economy seemed to be stagnating in comparison with those of the Six, and in 1960 there was a balance of payments deficit of some £270 million. Although EFTA had succeeded in increasing trade among its members, it was nothing like as successful as the EEC. The Commonwealth, in spite of its huge population, had nothing like the same purchasing power as the EEC; with so many colonies now gaining independence, there was no guarantee that trade with them would continue at the same level, whether they were in the Commonwealth or not. Macmillan now thought that there need not be a clash of interest between Britain's membership of the EEC and trade with the Commonwealth, especially as dominions like New Zealand and Australia were showing more interest in trading in their own regions. There were signs that the EEC was prepared to make special arrangements to allow Commonwealth countries and some former European colonies to become associate members.

Another argument put forward was that once Britain joined, competition from other EEC members would stimulate British industry to greater effort and efficiency. Macmillan also made the point that Britain could not afford to be left out if the EEC developed into a political union. He seems to have had some idea that Britain could take over the leadership and build the Community up into a strong defensive unit against the USSR, and in partnership with the USA. This may well have been Macmillan's primary motive, though he could hardly give it much publicity. Meanwhile the Labour Party opposed British entry; Wilson said it would mean 'selling our friends and kinsmen down the river ... for a marginal advantage in selling washing-machines in Dusseldorf'.

Macmillan gave the job of negotiating Britain's entry to Edward Heath, who had been an enthusiastic supporter of European unity since he first entered parliament in 1950. Talks opened in October 1961, and although there were some difficulties, it came as a shock when the French president, de Gaulle, broke off negotiations and vetoed Britain's entry (1963).

(f) *Why did the French oppose British entry to the EEC?*

The Dutch and Belgians welcomed Britain's application to join, seeing British membership as a counter-balance to the danger of Franco-German domination; the West Germans too saw Britain as a promising market. However, de Gaulle claimed that Britain had too many economic problems and would only weaken the EEC. He objected to any concessions being made for the Commonwealth, arguing that this would be a drain on Europe's resources. Yet the EEC had just agreed to provide economic and technical aid to France's former colonies in Africa. The British believed that de Gaulle's real motive was his desire to continue dominating the Community. If Britain came in, she would be a serious rival. Nor was de Gaulle happy about Britain's 'American connection'; he thought that because of her close ties with the USA, Britain's membership would allow the USA to have a major and unwelcome influence in European affairs. 'England is insular and maritime', he complained. 'The entry of Britain would completely change the Common Market which would become a colossal Atlantic grouping under American dependence and control.' He was probably annoyed that Britain, without consulting France, had just agreed to receive Polaris missiles from the USA. He was certainly furious with President Kennedy for not having made the same offer to France. He was determined to prove that France was a great power and had no need of American help. It was this friction between France and the USA which eventually led de Gaulle to withdraw France from NATO in 1966.

In fact some of de Gaulle's suspicions may well have been close to the mark. According to historians Alan Sked and Chris Cook, 'Macmillan had no intention of making Britain a European power. The real reason behind the British application was the need for Britain to find somewhere to act a leading role and improve her international reputation. Once inside the Common Market, Macmillan planned to organize it in co-operation with America, as part of an extended Atlantic partnership.'

Finally there was the problem of French agriculture: the EEC protected its farmers with high tariffs (import duties) so that prices were kept much higher than in Britain. Britain's agriculture was highly efficient and subsidized to keep prices relatively low. If this continued after Britain's entry, French farmers with their smaller and less-efficient farms, would be exposed to competition from Britain and perhaps from the Commonwealth.

Meanwhile the EEC success story continued. The Community's exports grew steadily, and the value of its exports was consistently higher than that of its imports. Britain on the other hand usually had a balance of trade deficit, and Harold Wilson's Labour government (1964–70) was forced to begin its term in office by borrowing heavily from the IMF to replenish its dwindling gold reserves (see Section 30.5(a)). This convinced Wilson that the only solution was for Britain to join the EEC, though until then Labour had opposed it. However, in 1967 de Gaulle once again vetoed the British application.

(g) *Britain enters the Community at last (1973)*

Britain's application remained on the table and eventually, on 1 January 1973, along with Eire and Denmark, she was admitted to the Community. The Six became the Nine. Britain's entry was made possible mainly by the resignation of de Gaulle in 1969, and the fact that his successor, Georges Pompidou, was more friendly towards Britain. The French were beginning to feel somewhat perturbed by the increasing economic power of West Germany, and hoped this might be offset by Britain's membership. Conservative Prime Minister Edward Heath (1970–4) was in a good position to press Britain's claims strongly. He negotiated with great skill and tenacity, and it was fitting that, having been a committed European for so long, he was the Prime Minister who finally took Britain into Europe.

Public opinion in Britain was divided over whether it was a wise move to join the Community, and many people were worried about how far British sovereignty would be affected. The Labour Party was split on the issue, and after coming to power in 1974, Wilson held a referendum (see Section 30.7(c)). The people were asked to vote (1975) about whether or not they wanted Britain to stay in the EC. Sixty-seven per cent of those who voted expressed approval of Britain's membership. But this was not as decisive as it might seem, since only two-thirds of the electorate voted. This meant that less than half the voters were convinced that membership was a good thing; the rest either did not want to stay in the Community or did not care enough either way to bother to vote.

32.8 Britain and the Community since 1973

The main developments and problems since Britain became a member of the Community in 1973 were:

(a) *The Lomé Convention (1975)*

Responding to criticism that it was too inward-looking and self-centred, EC representatives, meeting in Lomé, the capital of Togo in West Africa, agreed that goods produced in over 40 countries in Africa and the Caribbean, mostly former European colonies, could be brought into the Community free of duties. The agreement also promised economic aid, and other poor Third World countries were added to the list later.

(b) *Direct elections to the European Parliament (1979)*

Although it had been in existence for over 20 years by this time, the EC was still remote from ordinary people. One reason for introducing elections was to try to arouse more interest and bring 'the people in the street' into closer contact with the affairs of the Community.

The first elections took place in June 1979, when 410 Euro-MPs were chosen. Britain, France, Italy and West Germany were allowed 81 each, the Netherlands 25, Belgium 24, Denmark 16, Eire 15 and Luxembourg 6. For Britain the elections came immediately after Margaret Thatcher's victory in the UK general election of May 1979 (see Section 30.7(f)), so it was no surprise when the Conservatives swept the board in the Euro elections as well: they won 60 out of the 81 seats, while Labour could manage only 17. The turnout was disappointing – less than a third of the British electorate was interested enough to bother voting. Overall in the new European parliament, the right-wing and centre parties had a comfortable majority over the left.

Elections were to be held every five years; by the time the next elections came along in 1984, Greece had joined the Community, and was allowed 24 seats, bringing the total to 434. This time in Britain the Conservatives lost ground to Labour, winning 45 seats to Labour's 32; overall the centre and right kept a small majority. For the results of later elections see Table 32.1. In July 1997 the new Labour government announced that a proportional representation system of voting would be introduced for the 1999 elections, replacing the 'first past the post' system. This would bring Britain into line with the rest of the Community. The new system would be based on large multi-member constituencies in which electors would vote for lists of candidates drawn up by the parties.

Table 32.1 British seats in the European Parliament

	1979	1984	1989	1994
Labour	17	32	45	62
Conservatives	60	45	32	18
SNP	1	1	1	2
Official Unionist	1	1	1	1
Democratic Unionist	1	1	1	1
SDLP	1	1	1	1

Source: D. Childs, *Britain Since 1939: Progress and Decline* (Macmillan, 1995) p. 248.

(c) *The introduction of the Exchange Rate Mechanism (ERM)(1979)*

This was introduced to link the currencies of the member states in order to limit the extent to which individual currencies (Italian lira, French, Luxembourg and Belgian franc and German mark) could change in value against the currencies of other members. A country's currency could change in value depending on how well its domestic economy was performing: a strong economy usually meant a strong currency. It was hoped that linking the currencies would help to control inflation and lead eventually to a single currency for the whole of the Community. Britain decided not to take the £ sterling into the ERM; though Chancellor Nigel Lawson wanted Britain to join in 1985–6 when the economy was booming, Mrs Thatcher refused (see Section 33.4(b) 2). When Britain did eventually join the ERM in October 1990, the economy was weaker and the exchange rate relatively high. This meant that the pound was overvalued and difficult to defend; within less than two years (September 1992) Britain had been forced to withdraw sterling from the ERM, and John Major's government suffered a humiliating blow (see Section 33.6(c) 2).

(d) *Community membership grows*

Greece joined the Community in 1981, followed by Spain and Portugal in 1986, bringing the total membership to twelve and the Community population to over 320 million. Spain and Portugal had not been allowed to join earlier because their political systems were undemocratic. Their arrival caused new problems: they were amongst the poorest countries of Europe and their presence increased the influence within the Community of the less industrialized nations. From now on there would be increasing pressure from these countries to help the less developed states, and so improve the economic balance between rich and poor nations. Membership increased again in 1995 when Austria, Finland and Sweden, three relatively wealthy states, joined.

(e) *Britain and the EC budget*

During the early years of their membership, many British people were disappointed that Britain did not seem to be gaining any obvious benefit from the EC. Eire, which joined at the same time, immediately enjoyed a surge of prosperity as her exports, mainly agricultural produce, found ready new markets in the Community. Britain on the other hand seemed to be stagnating in the 1970s, and although her exports to the Community did increase, her imports from the Community increased far more. Britain was not producing enough goods for export at the right prices; the statistics of GDP for 1977 show that Britain was one of the least efficient nations in the EC, while Denmark and West Germany were at the top of the league (see Section 30.7(b) for more details and explanations; and 33.6(c)).

A major crisis erupted in 1980 when Britain disovered that her budget contribution for that year was to be £1209 million, whereas West Germany's was £699 million and France only had to pay £13 million. Britain protested that her contribution was ridiculously high, given the general state of her economy. The difference was so great because of the way the budget contribution was worked out: this took into consideration the amount of import duties received by each government from goods coming into that country from outside the EC; a proportion of those duties received had to be handed over as part of the annual budget contribution. Unfortunately for the British, they imported far more goods from the outside world than any of the other members, and this was why their payment was so high. Margaret Thatcher was determined to get it reduced; after some ruthless bargaining, a compromise was reached: Britain's contribution was reduced to a total of £1346 million over the next three years. Similar wrangling took place during the summer of 1983 and again in 1984 before a compromise agreeable to Britain could be arrived at. By that time, Mrs Thatcher had offended most of the other European leaders and was being referred to as 'Lady de Gaulle'. However, her efforts saved the British taxpayer billions of pounds over the next 13 years.

(f) *The 1986 changes*

Encouraging developments occurred in 1986 when all twelve members, working closely together, negotiated some important changes which, it was hoped, would improve the EC. They included a move, by 1992, to a completely free and common market with no restrictions of any kind on internal trade and movement of goods. There was to be more Community control over health, safety, protection of the environment, and protection for consumers; there would be more encouragement for scientific research and technology and more help for backward regions. The most controversial changes were those affecting the Council of Ministers and the parliament: there was to be majority voting on many issues in the Council of Ministers; this would prevent a measure from being vetoed by just one state which felt that its national interests might be threatened by that measure. The European parliament was to have more power so that measures could be passed with less delay. This meant that the domestic parliaments of the member states were gradually losing some control over their own internal affairs.

Those people who favoured a federal United States of Europe were pleased by these developments, but in some countries, especially Britain and Denmark, they stirred up the old controversy about national sovereignty. Mrs Thatcher upset some of the other European leaders again when she spoke out against any movement towards a politically united Europe: 'a centralized federal government in Europe would be a nightmare; co-operation with the other European countries must not be at the expense of individuality, the national customs and traditions which made Europe great in the past' (for Mrs Thatcher's later policies towards Europe see Section 33.4(c)).

(g) *The Common Agricultural Policy (CAP)*

One of the most controversial aspects of the EC was its Common Agricultural Policy. In order to help farmers and encourage them to stay in business, so that the Community could continue to produce much of its own food, it was decided to pay them subsidies (extra cash to top up their profits). This would ensure them worthwhile profits and at the same time would keep prices at reasonable levels for the consumers. This was such a good deal for farmers that they were encouraged to produce far more than could be sold. Yet the policy was continued, until by 1980 about three-quarters of the entire EC budget was being paid out each year in subsidies to farmers. Britain, West Germany and the Netherlands pressed for a limit to be placed on subsidies, but the French government was reluctant to agree to this because it did not want to lose the votes of French farmers, who were doing very well out of the systen.

In 1984 maximum production quotas were introduced for the first time, but this did not solve the problem. By 1987 the stockpiling of produce had reached ridiculous proportions. There was a vast wine 'lake' and a butter 'mountain' of one and a half million tonnes – enough to supply the entire EC for a year. There was enough milk powder to last five years, and storage fees alone were costing a million pounds a day. Efforts to get rid of the surplus included selling it off cheaply to the USSR, India, Pakistan and Bangladesh, distributing butter free of charge to the poor within the Community, and using it to make animal feed.

All this helped to cause a massive budget crisis in 1987: the Community was £3 billion in the red and had debts of £10 billion. In a determined effort to solve the problem, the EC introduced a harsh programme of production curbs and a price freeze to put a general squeeze on Europe's farmers. This gradually brought down the surpluses and improved the situation, but ten years later, in 1997, CAP was still absorbing almost half of the Community's budget – about £27 billion a year. Among other reforms introduced in 1992 were changes designed to protect the environment and promote more ecologically friendly farming methods. It was calculated that by 1997 these had reduced the use of fertilizers and pesticides by up to 30 per cent.

Further reforms proposed for 1998 included reducing subsidies paid to farmers and introducing a more open market for agricultural products. Experts predicted that although this would mean British farmers losing some £450 million in annual subsidies, this would be more than offset by the freedom to sell on the world market.

(h) *Greater integration – the Maastricht Treaty (1991)*

A summit meeting of all the heads of the member states was held in Maastricht (Netherlands) starting in December 1991, and an agreement was drawn up (February 1992) for 'a new stage in the process of creating an even closer union among the peoples of Europe'. Some of the points agreed were:

- more powers for the European parliament;
- greater economic and monetary union – this was intended to culminate in the adoption of a common currency (the euro) shared by all the member states, around the end of the century;
- a common foreign and security policy;
- a detailed timetable of the stages by which all this was to be achieved;
- the Community was to be known as *the European Union (EU)*.

Britain objected very strongly to the ideas of a federal Europe and monetary union; the treaty therefore did not mention the phrase 'federal state', and it was agreed that Britain and Denmark could opt out of a single currency of they decided to do so. In fact most British businessmen seemed to favour a common currency, believing that it would eliminate the uncertainties of fluctuating exchange rates between currencies.

Britain also objected to a whole section of the treaty known as *the Social Chapter*, which was a list of regulations designed to protect people from exploitation at work. There were rules about safe and healthy working conditions, equality at work between men and women, consultation with workers so that they were kept informed about what was going on, and protection of workers made redundant. Britain argued that these would increase production costs and therefore cause unemployment. The other members seemed to think that proper treatment of workers was more important. In the end, because of British objections, the Social Chapter was removed from the treaty and it was left to individual governments to decide whether to carry it out. This caused protests among European businessmen who claimed it would give British business an unfair advantage, since British firms did not have to keep to the same rules on working terms and conditions as the rest of the European Union. These opt-outs and omissions were seen as a personal achievement by John Major (see Section 33.6(a)). The rest of the Maastricht Treaty had be to ratified by the national parliaments of the twelve members, and this had been achieved by October 1993.

The French, Dutch and Belgian governments supported the treaty strongly because they thought it was the best way to make sure that the power of the reunified Germany was contained and controlled within the Community. The ordinary people of the Community were not as enthusiastic about the treaty as their leaders. The people of Denmark at first voted against it, and it took determined campaigning by the government before it was approved by a narrow majority in a second referendum (May 1993). The Swiss people voted not to join the EU (December 1992), and so did the Norwegians; even in the French referendum, the majority in favour of Maastricht was tiny. In Britain, where the government would not allow a referendum, the Conservatives were split over Europe, and the treaty was approved only by the narrowest of majorities in parliament. Major was harrassed by the Conservative anti-Europeans (Eurosceptics) for the rest of his premiership (see Section 33.6(c) 6).

The Labour victory in the 1997 election heralded a different British approach to Europe. Although the Labour Party was doubtful about a federal Europe, their general approach under Tony Blair's leadership, in striking contrast to that of the Conservatives, was 'Euro-friendly', and the new Prime Minister said that he wanted Britain's attitude to the EU to be positive and constructive. At a summit meeting in

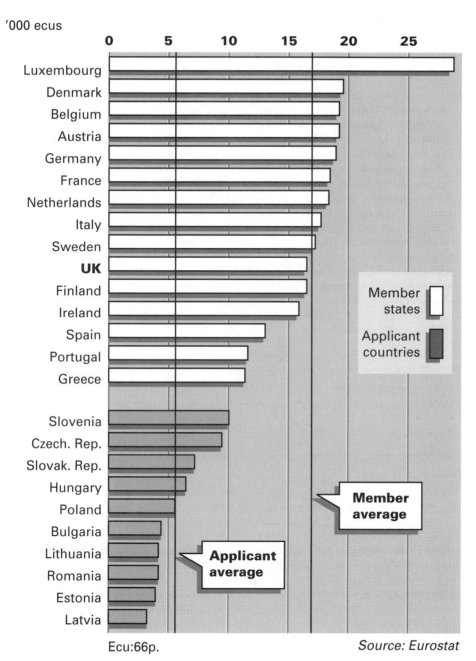

'000 ecus

Figure 32.1 GDP per head of the population of EU members and applicants, 1995

Source: The Guardian, 17 July 1997, p. 12.

Amsterdam (June 1997) it was agreed that the Social Chapter would be put back into the Maastricht Treaty, after Britain had indicated that she was now willing to accept it.

As the European Union approached the millenium, there were some vital issues to be faced:

- How much further could political integration go? The Amsterdam summit was unable to come up with any acceptable reforms of the EU institutions and voting procedures, and this suggested that the momentum towards closer political union was flagging. Nor was any progress made towards a common defence policy.
- The goal of European monetary union (EMU) and a single currency by 1999 was causing problems for all the member states. The requirement for joining the single currency was that a country's budget deficit must be less than 3 per cent of its GDP. By the end of 1996 governments were reducing spending and cutting welfare benefits in the struggle to keep their deficits low, and this provoked criticism and ill-feeling. In France the unpopular right-wing Juppé government was defeated and a socialist government came to power (May 1997). The British government said it was keeping its options open: although it was unlikely that Britain would join EMU in 1999, she might well do so later, at a time which would be most beneficial to British interests.
- The EU was already making preparations to admit Cyprus and some eastern European countries around the year 2002: the most likely ones from the list of applicants were Poland, Hungary, the Czech republic, Slovenia and Estonia. Negotiations were expected to begin in 1998, the year in which Britain would hold the presidency of the Union. The problem was that these countries were among the poorest in Europe, so the contributions of the wealthier members could be expected to rise to meet the extra expense and increased economic aid. This could mean that Britain and Eire, which were two of the poorer members in 1997 (see Table 33.2 on p. 586), could lose economic aid.

Questions

1 The Suez War 1956
   Study Sources A to D and then answer the questions which follow.

Source A

Sir Anthony Eden's speech to the cabinet, 27 July 1956

The nationalisation [of the Suez Canal] is not just a legal matter, it is one of the widest international importance. . . . Colonel Nasser's action has presented us with an opportunity to find a lasting settlement of this problem, and we should not hesitate to take advantage of it. . . . Our essential interests in this area must, if necessary, be safeguarded by military action and the necessary preparations to this end must be made. Even if we have to act alone, we cannot stop short of using force to protect our position, if all other means of protecting it prove unsuccessful. . . . Any failure on the part of the Western Powers to take the necessary steps to regain control over the Canal would have disastrous consequences for the economic life of the Western Powers and for their influence in the Middle East.

Source: quoted in R. Lamb, *The Failure of the Eden Government*, Sidgwick & Jackson, 1987.

Source B

Information from Anthony Nutting, Minister of State at the Foreign Office, who resigned on 6 November in protest at Eden's policy

Challe [Deputy Chief of Staff for the French Air Force] outlined a possible plan of action for Britain and France to gain control of the Suez Canal. Israel would be invited to attack Egypt, and then France and Britain, having given Israeli forces

---

time to get through Sinai close to the Canal, should order 'both sides' to withdraw their forces from the Suez Canal and permit an Anglo-French force to intervene and occupy the Canal with the excuse that they were saving it from damage by fighting.... This would restore the running of the Canal to Anglo-French management and enable us to supervise all shipping movements through the Canal and so break the blockade of Israel.

I knew that no matter what contrary advice he might receive over the next 48 hours, Eden had already made up his mind to go along with the French plan ... designed to topple Nasser and sieze the Suez Canal. Relations would be poisoned between Britain and Egypt and the Arab world for generations to come. To make matters worse, Britain had obviously acted in collusion with Israel; proof of this was plain in the ultimatum which demanded that both sides withdraw to a distance of 10 miles from the Canal at a moment when the Egyptian army was still trying to halt the Israelis 125 miles to the east of the Canal. This meant that Britain and France, who were pretending to put a stop to the fighting, were ordering the victim of aggression to withdraw 134 miles, while the aggressor was being allowed to advance up to 115 miles!

Source: A. Nutting, *No End of a Lesson*, Constable, 1967.

___ **Source C** _____

Speech by Selwyn Lloyd, the Foreign Secretary, in the the House of Commons, 31 October 1956

The Right Hon. Gentleman asked whether there had been collusion with regard to this matter.... It is quite wrong to state that Israel was incited to this action by Her Majesty's government. There was no prior agreement between us about it. It is of course true that the Israeli mobilisation gave some advance warning, and we urged restraint upon the Israeli government and in particular drew attention to the serious consequences of any attack on Jordan.

Source: *Hansard*, October 1956.

___ **Source D** _____

Historian Richard Lamb writes about Suez in a book published in 1987

The cabinet agreed that they were on weak ground over the question of the illegality [of Nasser's nationalisation of the Canal], since Nasser was offering to pay compensation to shareholders in the Suez Canal Company.... Eden intended to keep the collusion plan secret indefinitely. Without doubt he destroyed all English copies of the document. They are not in the Public Record Office.... It was an amazing error of judgement for a statesman with Eden's experience to imagine this would be possible. It is hard to avoid the conclusion that his health and the remedies prescribed by his doctors had affected his judgement... it was bound to be leaked by the French and Israelis. The plan was not even disclosed to the cabinet, which was downright dishonesty ...

On 30 October the ultimatum was delivered. On the night of 31 October the British dropped bombs on thirteen targets ... on 5 November British seaborne landings were made at Port Said which surrendered.... *On the 30 November the decision was taken to withdraw British troops....* Clearance of the Canal was now

[4 December] in the hands of the UN. Nasser was triumphant. His propaganda was that his army had defeated the British, French and Israelis, so that they had been obliged to withdraw ignominiously. His popularity in Egypt and the Arab world soared.

Source: R. Lamb, *The Failure of the Eden Government*, Sidgwick & Jackson, 1987

(a) On the basis of the evidence in these sources, explain the motives behind the British military action in Egypt. (12 marks)

(b) What criticisms of the British plan of action can be made, according to the evidence of the Sources? (10 marks)

(c) According to Source D, 'on the 30 November the decision was taken to withdraw British troops'. Using your own knowledge, explain why British troops were withdrawn after an apparently successful beginning to their action. (8 marks)

(d) From your own knowledge, how serious a setback was Suez for Britain and for Sir Anthony Eden? (10 marks)

(Total 40 marks)

2 How useful to Britain in the period 1945 to 1973 was the 'special relationship' with the USA? [AEB]

3 To what extent were the aims and course of Britain's foreign policy after 1945 determined by her 'special relationship' with the USA?

4 Why did Britain join NATO in 1949, refuse to join the EEC in 1957, and apply for membership in 1961?

5 What were the motives behind Britain's move to decolonization after 1945, and how smoothly was the process carried out in the period 1945 to 1964?

33 Thatcherism and the New Right 1979–97

Summary of events

With a comfortable overall majority of 43 after the election of May 1979, Mrs Thatcher, Britain's first woman Prime Minister, prepared to grapple with the country's problems, following Callaghan's 'winter of discontent'. She called the strikes 'a reversion to barbarism', and made it clear that she would stand no more nonsense from the unions. She offered a new policy – monetarism – to cure the country's economic ills and revitalize capitalism. She was firmly on the right of the party, having none of the traditional Conservative paternalism of Disraeli, Macmillan or William Whitelaw, who had been her chief rival for the leadership. By the early 1980s her beliefs and policies were being referred to as 'Thatcherism' and her supporters were described as the New Right.

During *her first government (1979–83)* Mrs Thatcher and her team applied monetarism, with mixed success. The most disturbing result was the rise in unemployment to over 3 million. The Conservatives' popularity waned rapidly and they began to lose by-elections to the Liberals and to the newly formed Social Democrat party (which had just split from the Labour party in March 1981). However, Conservative fortunes revived after Mrs Thatcher's decisive handling of the Falklands crisis and Britain's victory in the war with Argentina (April–June 1982). In the election of June 1983, with the Labour party in complete disarray, the Conservatives won a landslide victory, giving them an overall majority of 144.

The second Thatcher government (1983–7) is regarded as the heyday or 'high noon' of Thatcherism, during which New Right policies such as privatization, 'rolling back the state' and controlling government spending were vigorously pursued. Mrs Thatcher again decided to go to the country early, after local election results seemed favourable. In June 1987 the Conservatives were once again victorious; though losing some seats to Labour, they still emerged with an overall majority of just over 100.

But storm clouds were soon gathering over *the third Thatcher government (1987–90)*. Mrs Thatcher insisted on pushing ahead with a new and extremely unpopular policy, the poll tax, though most of her cabinet was against it. There were disagreements within the party over Europe, and criticism of Mrs Thatcher increased. By the autumn of 1990 many Conservatives saw her as a liability, and to the amazement of most of the nation, who knew nothing about the back-stage manoeuvrings, she was forced to resign (November 1990). John Major was elected leader of the party and he became Prime Minister.

John Major began well, dropping the disastrous poll tax, but unemployment was soon rising again, and the Conservatives had to fight the next election (April 1992) in the middle of a recession. Against all expectations, Major won a small overall majority of 21.

But things soon began to go wrong for the new government; later the same year, Britain was forced to leave the ERM (see Section 32.8(c) for an explanation of the ERM), and the Conservatives' traditional reputation of being good managers of the economy was left in tatters. Differences in the party over Europe became ever more serious.

Meanwhile the Labour Party under its new leader, Tony Blair, had been busy modernizing itself and projecting its non-socialist image of New Labour. It was no surprise when the Conservatives lost the election of May 1997. What *was* surprising was the magnitude of the Conservative defeat: Labour emerged with 418 seats and an overall majority of 179, and the Conservatives were reduced to only 165 – their lowest total since 1906.

33.1 What is meant by 'Thatcherism'?

Margaret Thatcher was the daughter of a Grantham grocer, Alfred Roberts, who was a local Conservative councillor and alderman. After reading Chemistry at Oxford, she married Denis Thatcher, a rich industrialist. She stood for parliament, unsuccessfully, in 1950, at the age of 23, and was eventually elected MP for Finchley in 1959. Before her election as leader in 1975, her experience of high office had been unusually limited – her only major post was Secretary of State for Education under Heath. She was influenced by the ideas of Enoch Powell and Sir Keith Joseph, two right-wing Conservative MPs, who believed that during the years of consensus politics under Macmillan and Heath, the Conservatives had strayed too close to socialism and the mixed economy; it was time to return to 'economic liberalism'. This involved reducing state intervention to the absolute minimum and allowing what they called 'market forces' to rule the economy. Powell and Joseph had themselves been influenced by an Austrian, F. A. Hayek, who had set out the New Right ideas in his book *The Road to Serfdom*, first published in 1944. *Thatcherism, as it developed from these ideas, was basically an attack on socialism and collectivism, and involved a number of principles:*

(a) *The role of the state in society must be reduced*

There was too much planning and too many restrictions; people should be given more freedom to show their initiative in business. This sounded very much like the old nineteenth-century *laissez-faire* ideas, and in fact Mrs Thatcher talked about a return to Victorian values. The economy must be left free to develop according to the demands of the markets (market forces). Hard work and enterprise would be rewarded, and the power of the trade unions, which Mrs Thatcher saw as 'wreckers', must be curbed. Direct taxes must be reduced so that people could spend their money largely as they wished. It was acknowledged that there would be inequalities of wealth in such a system, but this was to be welcomed in an 'enterprise culture' where the prospect of wealth must be the great driving motive behind people's desire to advance themselves. Eventually (though not much was said about this in the 1979 manifesto) the state would be 'rolled back' even further by privatizing all the nationalized industries. The belief was that privately owned concerns were always more likely to produce positive results – greater efficiency and greater profits – than those owned by the state.

(b) *Monetarism was the best way to make Britain prosperous again*

Another influence on the New Right was the American economist, Milton Friedman, who believed that governments and businesses ought to spend less; this was the opposite of Keynes's theory that governments should spend their way out of depressions. Previous governments in their 'stop' phases had controlled the money supply temporarily by raising the bank rate. Mrs Thatcher aimed to pursue this policy wholeheartedly and without any relaxation. The theory was that a tight hold must be kept on the money supply via the Bank of England by maintaining high rates of interest, so that firms and individuals were forced to reduce borrowing. Management must therefore keep costs down by laying off workers and streamlining operations for greater efficiency. There would be no government grants to prop up inefficient firms, so that only those which made themselves competitive would survive. Such a policy meant a high unemployment level, but its supporters claimed that it was like a major surgical operation – drastic, but effective in the long term: British industry, though much contracted, would be more efficient and competitive overseas.

With purchasing power reduced as unemployment rose, inflation would be controlled and wage demands moderated accordingly. One advantage of monetarism was that the control it exercised was more impersonal than Heath's wage restraint, and therefore there was less chance of a direct confrontation between government and unions. A further advantage, particularly attractive to the Conservatives, was that trade unions would be less powerful: workers, thankful to be in a job during a time of high unemployment, would be less willing to strike. It was expected that in due course, joblosses would be offset by the creation of large numbers of new jobs in the service industries (like leisure, tourism, advertising, banking, insurance and information technology); many of these would be less well-paid, less secure, and less trade union dominated than before. Monetarism would keep inflation low – always one of the government's main aims – and this would encourage people to save more.

(c) Self-help and individualism

Mrs Thatcher rejected the idea that it was the job of the state to care for people from 'cradle to grave'. Individuals must make their own provision for sickness and old age and not expect the welfare state to do it for them. Only those who were incapable of looking after themselves would be helped by the state. This would enable the government to save vast amounts of money and seemed to herald less commitment to the welfare state – the health service, education and social services – than under any government since 1945. One popular item in the 1979 Conservative manifesto was the sale of council houses to sitting tenants at well below market prices.

(d) A strong element of British nationalism

Many right-wing Conservatives had not come to terms with the loss of Britain's empire in the 1950s and 1960s (see Chapter 32) and her general decline as a great power. Nor had they approved of Heath's enthusiasm for joining the EEC. Mrs Thatcher was prepared to do all she could to safeguard Britain's sovereignty and stand up for Britain's rights in Europe, and she would not be pushed around by foreigners. Later she enjoyed being portrayed in *Sun* cartoons 'handbagging the Frogs', and she revelled in it when the Russians dubbed her the 'Iron Lady'. She preferred to foster Britain's special relationship with the USA, especially with President Ronald Reagan, another committed monetarist and market forces enthusiast. Other objects of Mrs Thatcher's disapproval were Scottish and Welsh Nationalists who, she believed, wanted to break up the UK.

(e) Thatcherism was radical and anti-establishment

Mrs Thatcher felt herself to be an outsider in terms of the traditional Tory leadership:

she was from a lower-middle-class background and she was a woman; her beliefs marked her off as different from most of the Tory 'grandees' like Lord Carrington, William Whitelaw and Sir Ian Gilmour who, she felt, had taken the party perilously close to socialism. She was impatient with civil servants who had spent their careers making consensus politics work. In particular she resented the Foreign Office diplomats whom she saw as overcautious, patronizing and far too liberal. She disapproved of the Rhodesia settlement reached in December 1979 (see Section 32.6(c)), blaming Carrington and the Foreign Office because it gave power to a socialist government. This experience made her determined to follow her instincts against their advice if necessary (as in her refusal to support sanctions against South Africa and her insistence on launching the campaign to recapture the Falklands). Eventually she fell out with most sections of the British establishment, including the universities, the BBC and the Church of England. When a group of Anglican bishops expressed disquiet at the plight of the poor in Liverpool, Mrs Thatcher was displeased, feeling that the Church of England had become tainted with socialism; she had apparently missed the point that it was Christianity which was motivating the bishops. Her suspicion of the 'establishment' mentality was the reason why Mrs Thatcher always took care to ask the question, when making appointments both in government and administration, 'is he one of us?' and why she surrounded herself with reliable New Right advisers.

In practice many of these Thatcherite principles had to be modified. As Peter Clarke points out, Mrs Thatcher 'was a political opportunist in the best sense, always quick to seize the opportunities which came her way and exploit them. . . . She made up policies as she went along and used off-the-cuff public utterances to bounce her colleagues into accepting initiatives that had not been previously agreed.' Monetarism eventually had to be abandoned as unworkable, though the government never admitted it. Although Mrs Thatcher opposed too much state interference and wanted people to have more freedom in economic affairs, more restrictions than ever were introduced on civil liberties, and the government took on more powers in areas like education and local government. However, all this was in the future; in April 1979 Mrs Thatcher seemed exactly the sort of decisive, forceful, strong-willed and self-assured leader which Britain needed. 'The mission of this government,' she announced soon after her election victory, 'is much more than economic progress. It is to renew the spirit and the solidarity of the nation. At the heart of a new mood in the nation must be a recovery of our self-confidence and our self-respect.'

33.2 The first Thatcher government 1979–83

(a) *Monetarism in practice*

Mrs Thatcher had to proceed cautiously at first since only three other members of her cabinet (Sir Geoffrey Howe, Sir Keith Joseph and John Biffen) shared her ideas; all the rest she regarded, in varying degrees, as 'Wets'. Nevertheless, with Howe as Chancellor of the Exchequer, she was able to make the first moves towards monetarism. Howe's budget of June 1979 was designed to control inflation which was running at 10 per cent when the government took office. The basic rate of income tax was reduced from 33 per cent to 30 per cent, VAT was raised from 8 per cent to 15 per cent (to offset the losses from income tax), cash limits were introduced on public spending, which affected housing, education and transport, and there was a cripplingly high minimum lending rate which had gone up to 17 per cent early in 1980. At first the problems seemed to get worse: the annual rate of inflation soared to 22 per cent by May 1980, but this was

Illus. 33.1   Margaret Thatcher and Sir Geoffrey Howe

partly because the government had honoured pay rises agreed under Labour. Thatcher and Howe confidently predicted that the inflation rate would be down to 10 per cent by the end of 1981. Their predictions were not far wrong; in fact by 1983 the rate had fallen to 4.5 per cent, and the government had therefore achieved its primary aim.

Unfortunately there were some drastic side-effects:

● The British economy suffered the worst depression for 50 years, partly because the pound was strong, and this made exports more expensive and encouraged imports. There was also a deepening world recession which would have affected Britain anyway.
● Hundreds of firms went bankrupt, as the high interest rates and tightly controlled money supply prevented people from borrowing, and there was no help forthcoming from the government. In 1981 alone the economy shrank by 2 per cent and by the end of 1982 something like 25 per cent of British manufacturing capacity had been destroyed. The de-industrialization of Britain was well under way.
● Unemployment shot up to 2.8 million in the autumn of 1981, almost double the figure when the Conservatives came to power. A year later it had reached 3.3 million. Most of the jobs lost were in the manufacturing industry, and the worst hit areas were the north of England, Wales and Scotland. In the summer of 1981 there were riots in Brixton (London), Liverpool and Manchester.

Opinion polls showed that the government was extremely unpopular, but Mrs Thatcher stuck doggedly to her policies. She had already told the party conference in October 1980, 'You turn if you want to. The lady's not for turning.' When some cabinet 'Wets' ventured to criticize her economic strategy, they were unceremoniously removed and replaced by Thatcherites (1981). Two of these were self-made men – Cecil Parkinson (who became Party Chairman) was a successful industrialist and son of a railwayman from Carnforth (Lancashire), and Norman Tebbit (who became Secretary for Employment), a tough politician known in some party circles as 'the Chingford skin-head', was a former pilot and son of a shop manager. Nigel Lawson, an economic jour-nalist and a 'true-believer', was brought in to head the Department of Energy.

Whatever her private thoughts were, Mrs Thatcher seemed obsessed with self-help and apparently showed little sympathy for the plight of the 3 million unemployed. The government lost a number of by-elections, the most spectacular defeat being at Crosby where a Conservative majority of over 19 000 was converted into a 5000 majority for Shirley Williams, the candidate of the newly-formed Social Democrat party (November 1981).

(b) *The formation of the Social Democrat Party (SDP)*

If the Conservatives had their internal squabbles, the Labour party was in a much worse state. The right wing of the party was becoming more and more impatient with the left because of its support for militant trade unionism, unilateral disarmament, withdrawal from the EEC and further nationalization. The election of the veteran left-winger, Michael Foot, as party leader (1980) convinced some of the right that they had no future in the Labour Party. Four of them, Roy Jenkins, Dr David Owen, Shirley Williams and William Rodgers – soon to be known as *the Gang of Four* – left the party and in a blaze of publicity launched the new SDP (March 1981). Jenkins narrowly failed to win a by-election at Warrington, but after the SDP formed an alliance with the Liberals, successes followed. A Liberal, William Pitt, won Croydon, Shirley Williams won Crosby, and in March 1982 Jenkins captured Glasgow Hillhead. All three seats were taken from the Conservatives. Suddenly, soon after the Hillhead by-election, the political scene was transformed by the Falklands War.

(c) *The Falklands War (April–June 1982)*

1 The Argentinian claim to the British-owned Falkland Islands in the South Atlantic had been discussed on and off by the two governments for the previous 20 years. The Argentinians may well have got the impression that the British would not be averse to an eventual transfer of power; but the stumbling-block was that the 1800 Falklanders were adamant that they wished to remain under British sovereignty. Two decisions taken by the Thatcher government, on the advice of the Foreign Office, were probably interpreted by the Argentinians as signals of Britain's declining interest: the ice-breaker ship *Endurance* was removed from the Falklands, and an elderly aircraft carrier was to be scrapped, which would make it more difficult to defend the islands.

2 Argentinian forces invaded the islands (2 April) as well as their dependency, South Georgia. The UN Security Council and the EEC condemned their action and urged the Argentinians to withdraw, but to no avail. Mrs Thatcher acted decisively and astonished the world by the speed of her response. Against the advice of the Foreign Office, a British task force was swiftly assembled and sent off to recapture the Falklands. It consisted of some 79 ships including the aircraft carriers *Invincible* and *Hermes* and about 6000 troops.

3 During the three weeks it took the task force to sail the 7000 miles via Ascension Island to the South Atlantic, frantic attempts were made, notably by Alexander Haig, the American Secretary of State, to reach a negotiated solution. However, the British, refuting South American charges of colonialism, pointed out that the

islanders wished to remain associated with Britain; they refused to negotiate unless Argentinian troops were withdrawn. The Argentinians, safely in possession of the islands, refused to budge, and Haig's efforts came to nothing. Meanwhile Lord Carrington, the Foreign Secretary, had resigned, accepting responsibility for 'the humiliating affront to this country'. He was replaced by Francis Pym. Mrs Thatcher showed considerable determination and nerve, since the operation was risky in the extreme: weather conditions were highly unpredictable and there was insufficient air cover. But she viewed all attempts at negotiation as appeasement, and fortunately the opposition leaders supported her.

4   The task force arrived in Falklands waters during the final week of April and soon enjoyed complete success. South Georgia was recaptured (25 April) and the *General Belgrano*, an elderly Argentinian cruiser carrying troops and deadly Exocet missiles, was sunk by a British nuclear submarine with the loss of 368 lives (2 May). This prompted the *Sun* to come out with the triumphant front page headline 'GOTCHA'. The sinking caused much controversy, since the vessel was outside the total exclusion zone which the British had declared around the islands. HMS *Sheffield* was badly damaged by an Exocet missile (4 May), but this did not prevent successful landings at Port San Carlos (21 May) and later at Bluff Cove and Fitzroy near Port Stanley (early June); two British frigates were sunk during the landings. British troops won engagements at Darwin and Goose Green and finally captured Port Stanley. On 14 June the Argentinian troops surrendered and the recapture of the Falklands was complete. The British had lost 254 men killed, the Argentinians 750. The expedition cost Britain around £1600 million.

5   The effects of the war on the home front were little short of sensational. There was an outburst of patriotism such as had not been seen since the Second World War, and approval of the government's decisive action caused their sagging popularity to revive with a vengeance. This was reflected in the local election results in May 1982 and in two by-elections which the SDP could have been expected to win, judging from their earlier performances, and which the Conservatives won comfortably. In the euphoria of the Falklands victory the government was able to ignore questions such as: What had it all been for? What good did it do? To Mrs Thatcher the answers were obvious: a military dictator had been taught a sharp lesson, and Britain's prestige in the world had been restored. Critics were given short shrift and told to 'rejoice'! On the other hand, the cost of defending the islands since then has been enormous.

(d) *The election of June 1983*

With over 3 million still out of work, Labour ought to have had a fighting chance of victory, but several factors worked in the Conservatives' favour:

●   They had succeeded in bringing the annual inflation rate down to around 4 per cent which they had claimed all along to be one of their main aims.

●   Critics of the trade unions were pleased with the government's actions to curb trade union powers. Already *the 1980 Employment Act* had restricted picketing to the pickets' own place of work. *The Employment Act of October 1982* went further and restricted the operation of closed shops – a closed shop could only exist when a ballot showed 85 per cent support. Trade unions were made more accountable for their actions and could be fined for unlawful strikes; compensation was to be paid to workers who had been sacked from their jobs for non-membership of a union. The election manifesto promised more legislation to force trade unions to hold ballots before calling a strike and ballots about whether or not to continue the political levy.

- The Labour party did itself no good with a left-wing manifesto which included restoration of full trade union rights, withdrawal from the EEC and from NATO's defence policy, and unilateral nuclear disarmament. One disgruntled right-wing Labour MP called it 'the longest suicide note in history'.
- Above all, there was the continuing effect of the 'Falklands factor'.

The Liberal/SDP Alliance conducted an impressive campaign projecting itself as the only viable alternative government to the Conservatives. Though it failed to make a breakthrough in terms of seats, it took crucial votes away from Labour. The results showed an overwhelming Conservative victory with 397 seats, against only 209 for Labour, 23 for the Alliance and 21 others. It was a disaster for the Labour party which polled its lowest vote since 1935.

The Conservatives and most of the press enthused about their landslide victory. But in fact the voting figures revealed something rather different. The Conservative vote had actually fallen from the 1979 figure (from 13.69 million to 13.01 million) suggesting not that there was a great surge of enthusiasm for Mrs Thatcher, but rather that the electors decidedly did not want a Labour government (Labour's vote fell from 11.53 million to 8.45 million). Many Labour voters and some disillusioned Tory supporters switched to the Alliance, whose 7.8 million votes were one of the most striking features of the election. This revealed more clearly than ever the unfairness of the British electoral system. Labour's 27.6 per cent of total votes cast entitled them to 209 seats, but the Alliance, not all that far behind with 25.4 per cent, secured only 23 seats. It was the old story of the single vote, single member constituency system working to the disadvantage of a party which came second in a large number of constituencies. The demand for proportional representation revived, but there was little prospect of its being introduced in the near future, since the Conservative government, not unnaturally, was happy with the existing system.

33.3 Mrs Thatcher's heyday 1983–7

Fortified by her huge Commons majority, Mrs Thatcher reshuffled her cabinet, bringing in more Thatcherites, and pushed ahead with her programme against a background of continuing monetarism. The government's record contained some major achievements, though all were highly controversial:

(a) *Privatization*

This was strongly advocated on the grounds that it would increase efficiency, encourage more concern for the customer, and enable the general public and employees to become shareholders. Also attractive to the government were the proceeds – £2500 million in 1985–6 and about £4700 million in each of the next three years. By January 1987 no fewer than 14 major companies (including British Aerospace, British Petroleum, British Telecom, Britoil, the Trustee Savings Bank and British Gas) had been sold off into private ownership. This was bitterly attacked by the Labour party with its belief in nationalization, and even some Conservatives felt that things were going too far; Lord Stockton (formerly Harold Macmillan) called it 'selling off the family silver'.

(b) *A tough line with the trade unions*

The government continued to take a tough line with the unions, quickly introducing the new regulations about compulsory ballots. Union membership was banned at Government Communications Headquarters (GCHQ). The biggest confrontation came with the miners. When the National Coal Board announced the closure of 21 uneconomic pits, with the expected loss of 20 000 jobs, the executive of the National Union of Miners, led by Arthur Scargill, voted for a national strike. They had defeated the Heath government, why not Thatcher too? There was an excellent response from the miners, except in Nottinghamshire and Derbyshire, where they were at least risk. The strike dragged on for a year (March 1984–March 1985), but it was soon clear that Scargill had miscalculated badly – the government, anticipating a strike, had made sure that large coal stocks were built up, plenty of cheap imports were available, and demand was decreasing as summer approached. The new regulations made it more difficult for pickets to stop the movement of coal, and Scargill had made the fatal mistake of failing to hold a national ballot on whether to strike. There were some ugly scenes between police and strikers; miners and their families suffered great hardship, but the government refused to compromise, and the miners were gradually forced to return to work. The strike fizzled out, ending officially in March 1985, but it had been a bitter struggle and it seemed to exacerbate the divisions in society. The government's victory was seen by many observers as Mrs Thatcher's revenge against the miners for bringing Heath's government down in 1974.

A second major dispute occurred in 1986 when Rupert Murdoch, owner of Times Newspapers, sacked 5500 workers, members of the print union, following a strike. He transferred printing to a newly built and specially fortified plant at Wapping, where he successfully resisted union attempts to prevent new work practices being introduced. The unions had to accept defeat, after being heavily fined under the new legislation. By this time the trade union movement had lost all heart for action, though in a final show of defiance, all 37 surviving unions voted to continue their payments to the Labour party.

(c) *Strict maintenance of law and order and public security*

The army and police were used several times to remove peace campaigners from Greenham Common and Molesworth RAF bases; they were protesting against American Cruise missiles being deployed there. The BBC was continually attacked for allegedly being biased against the government; the BBC offices in Glasgow were raided and films said to threaten Britain's security were seized (February 1987). Among them was a programme about Zircon, a new spy satellite for eavesdropping on the Russians.

(d) *Close control of government and local authority spending*

Top-spending local authorities, many of them Labour controlled, had a maximum rate placed on them (rate-capping) to force them to economize (February 1986). The Greater London Council (GLC), also Labour controlled, and the six other English Metropolitan County Councils were abolished on the grounds that they were a costly and unnecessary layer of government. Norman Tebbit made no secret of the fact that the real reason for the abolition of the GLC was because it was 'Labour-dominated, high-spending and at odds with the government's view of the world'.

(e) *The Anglo-Irish Agreement (November 1985)*

This was a new attempt to secure peace and stability in Northern Ireland (see Section 31.1(i)).

(f) *A tough stance against international terrorism*

Britain broke off diplomatic relations with Libya after a policewoman was killed by shots fired from the Libyan People's Bureau in London (April 1984). In April 1986 Mrs Thatcher supported the USA's punitive action against Libya, allowing American F-111 bombers to fly from bases in Britain to take part in air strikes on Tripoli and Benghazi which killed over a hundred people. The US claimed that they were aiming for 'terrorist-related targets', but the raids aroused world-wide condemnation for causing the deaths of so many innocent civilians. Britain also broke off relations with Syria (October 1986) whose government was allegedly involved in an attempt to blow up a jumbo jet at Heathrow Airport.

(g) *The agreement with China (1984)*

Britain promised to hand Hong Kong over to China in 1997, and in return the Chinese offered safeguards, including maintaining the existing economic and social structure for at least 50 years. The handover was in accordance with the 1842 Treaty of Nanking by which Britain leased Hong Kong until 1997.

Meanwhile the government came under increasing fire from its critics. Unemployment stubbornly refused to come down below 3 million and it seemed that Britain was rapidly becoming 'two nations'. The government's own statistics revealed (1987) that 94 per cent of job losses since the Conservatives took office were in the North, while the South was largely thriving and prosperous. Since 1979 there had been a 28 per cent drop in manufacturing and construction jobs, which compared badly with an 8 per cent drop in Germany, a 2 per cent drop in the USA and a 5 per cent increase in Japan. Inner cities were neglected and there was a rundown in public services, especially the Health Service, where in 1986–7 a chronic shortage of beds caused many people to be turned away and lengthened waiting-lists for operations. When challenged before the 1983 election, the government had assured the public that the Health Service was safe, but now there seemed a real danger of creating a two-tier Health Service: for those who could afford it, a private sector which was flourishing and efficient, for those who couldn't, a public sector which was short of cash, under-staffed and generally second-rate.

In addition the government suffered a number of embarrassments and scandals. There was a public conflict of attitude between two cabinet ministers (Heseltine and Brittan) over the future of the ailing Westland Helicopter Company, the only remaining British helicopter manufacturer. No help was forthcoming from the government, though it would surely have been in Britain's defence interests to own at least one plant which could produce military helicopters. Brittan, a free-marketeer and definitely 'one of us', wanted the company to be taken over by the American firm of Sikorsky, but Heseltine wanted it to become part of a European consortium. Mrs Thatcher supported Brittan, but she handled the affair badly and it ended with both ministers resigning (January 1986). Early in 1987 there was a scandal on the Stock Exchange when it emerged that some directors of the Guinness Company had illegally bolstered the price of their own shares during their battle to take over the Distillers' Company.

A measure of their unpopularity was the fact that the Conservatives lost four by-elections (three to the Alliance and one to Labour) between June 1984 and May 1986. However, as another election approached, the Chancellor, Nigel Lawson, suddenly announced extra spending of £7.5 billion for 1987 on education, health and social services. This seemed to be a U-turn away from monetarism, though the government did not admit it. With the inflation rate well under control at only 3 per cent and the promise of good times ahead, the opinion polls showed a revival in the Conservatives' popularity.

(h) *The election of June 1987*

Although the Labour party fought a lively campaign under its new leader, Neil Kinnock, the Conservatives won a third successive victory. They took 380 seats against 229 for Labour and 22 for the Alliance, giving them an overall majority of 102. *Reasons for the Conservative success were:*

- The relatively prosperous South and Midlands were apparently well satisfied with Tory rule and were confident that the economic recovery would continue.
- Some historians believe that privatization and the increase in home ownership were an important ingredient in winning working-class support, since this was part of the move towards a 'property-owning democracy'. Above all, the sale of council houses may have been a vital factor. First introduced in 1980, the sales meant that by the time of the election in 1987, over a million council houses had passed into private ownership. As historian Peter Clarke puts it: 'on council estates, a freshly painted door and a copy of the *Sun* in the letter box were a signal of Thatcher's achievement at remaking the Conservative Party'.
- Labour's defence and economic policies continued to put people off.

It was clearly a remarkable achievement by Mrs Thatcher to lead her party to three successive election victories, and in January 1988 she broke Asquith's record as the longest-serving British Prime Minister this century. There were two other striking points about the 1987 election: the Conservatives did badly in Scotland, winning only 10 out of the 72 seats, and further entrenching the North–South divide. Over the country as a whole, *almost three people in five voted against the Conservatives*. The Conservatives took 42.2 per cent of the votes, Labour 30.8 per cent and the Alliance 22.6 per cent. Under the existing electoral system, with Labour and Alliance candidates splitting the anti-Tory vote, it was difficult to see how the Conservatives could ever lose an election.

Important developments soon took place in the Liberal/SDP Alliance camp. Bitterly disappointed by their poor election performance, at least in terms of seats, the two parties began talks to try and bring about a merger. The negotiations went well, and in January 1988 the new party – the Social and Liberal Democrats – was born. After 12 gruelling years as Liberal leader, David Steel decided to stand down, and Paddy Ashdown was elected leader of the new party. It remained to be seen whether the Lib Dems (as they soon became known) would be able to make any real contribution towards ending the period of Tory domination.

33.4 Triumph, decline and downfall 1987–90

(a) *The triumph of Thatcherism*

After her success in the 1987 election it seemed that Mrs Thatcher could be Prime Minister for life if she wished. Although she was now 62, she told interviewers that she had no thoughts of retirement and was looking forward to a fourth election victory. For about a year after the election everything seemed to go well: the economy had moved into a boom period and unemployment was falling. After reaching a peak of 3.4 million in January 1986, it fell steadily to 1.6 million in June 1990. Economic growth averaged 3.7 per cent in the years 1984–8.

Mrs Thatcher was keen to show that her government was not losing its drive; Thatcherite changes came thick and fast, though again, they were all highly controversial:

- *Privatization continued* with the government selling off its remaining holdings in BP and going on to sell electricity and water. By 1992 only coal and railways of the main industries and utilities remained in state ownership.
- *The Education Reform Act (1988)* was designed to improve what Conservatives saw as Britain's failing education system. They blamed this on poor quality teacher training, informal teaching methods, insufficient attention to the 'three R's', lack of testing and streaming, and a breakdown in discipline. The Act introduced a national curriculum which all pupils had to follow, and pupils were to be tested at 7, 11, 14 and 16. Parents were given the right to choose which school they wanted their children to go to in a particular area, and control of school budgets was taken out of the hands of local authorities and given to individual head teachers. If a majority of parents wished, a school could opt out of local authority control to become 'grant-maintained'; it would then be financed directly by the government, side-stepping the local authority, and would be run by its governors.

Critics of the Act argued that most of these changes were unnecessary and poorly thought through; the main problem with education was that it was a two-tier system. The public and private schools, to which most of the wealthy sent their children, were well financed and had excellent facilities, whereas the state system was underfunded, and suffered from insufficient teachers, oversized classes, and in many cases inadequate facilities and crumbling buildings.

- *The government introduced market forces into the Health Service* to make it more efficient. For example, hospitals were encouraged to opt out of the system and handle their own finances. But this had unfortunate results as some managers went to extreme lengths in the drive for greater efficiency, running hospitals as though they were businesses instead of services. While efficiency was a laudable aim, it could hardly be called efficient that hundreds of hospital wards were closed, that thousands of nurses left the profession because of low pay, and that hospital waiting lists were getting longer; in some areas, people were having to wait over two years for operations.
- *There were further reductions in income tax.* In his budget of March 1988, seen by many as the high point of Mrs Thatcher's third government, Nigel Lawson reduced the basic rate of income tax from 27 per cent to 25 per cent and the top rate from 60 per cent to 40 per cent. Income tax reductions had been one of the Conservatives' election promises, and Lawson could claim at this point that all his goals had been achieved: inflation, interest rates and unemployment had all been brought down, while economic growth was going up.

(b) *The government begins to lose its way*

Things began to go wrong soon after Lawson's budget:

1   The tax cuts caused a big increase in consumer demand; this in turn fuelled inflation which rose from 4 per cent to over 10 per cent by September 1990. To try and counteract this, interest rates were raised from 7.5 per cent at the time of the

budget to 15 per cent in October 1989, which was highly unpopular with mortgage holders.

A rift gradually opened up between Mrs Thatcher and Nigel Lawson over the question of Britain joining the Exhange Rate Mechanism (ERM) (see Section 32.8(c)). Lawson had wanted Britain to enter the ERM in 1985 when the economy was in good shape. His argument was that it would make the pound more steady by locking it into the other major European currencies, since this would bring a more stable exchange rate and keep inflation low. 1985–6 would have been a good time to join, when the economy was booming and the exchange rate reasonably low. But Mrs Thatcher was against the idea, fearing that it would lead to a loss of government control over its own economic policy. Lawson resigned in October 1989 after Mrs Thatcher refused to sack her economic adviser, Alan Walters, who disagreed with Lawson. Mrs Thatcher was eventually persuaded to join the ERM – by John Major – in October 1990. However, by that time the exchange rate was relatively high and the economy weaker than it had been in 1985–6; this meant that the pound was overvalued and was therefore more difficult to defend.

The introduction of the community charge (or poll tax, as it became known), first in Scotland (1989) and then in England and Wales (1990), was the government's biggest mistake. This was a new system of financing local government, which the Conservatives had promised to reform. The old payment of rates by household was abolished and replaced by a flat-rate charge to be paid by every adult, irrespective of the size of his or her house. It was an attempt to make every taxpayer pay an equal contribution to costs under high-spending Labour councils, rather than forcing wealthy property-owners to pay well over the average.

Mrs Thatcher and Nicholas Ridley, the minister handling the introduction of the poll tax, pressed on enthusiastically with the new scheme, which was described by Mrs Thatcher as the 'flagship' of her government, though Lawson and most of the cabinet were against it. 'Every time I hear people squeal,' said Ridley, 'I am more than ever certain that we are right.' But it didn't seem fair that 'the rich man in his castle' should pay the same as an ordinary worker living in a small terraced house. The new tax caused uproar: there were protest demonstrations and riots, and a concerted campaign to persuade people not to pay. In Liverpool in 1990, 51 per cent of adults evaded payment and the tax became more and more difficult to collect. The government's standing in the opinion polls plummeted, and in a by-election in October 1990 the Conservatives lost the safe seat of Eastbourne to the Liberal Democrats.

c) *The downfall of Mrs Thatcher*

Although things were clearly not going well for the government, Mrs Thatcher's down-fall still came as a surprise to most people. The crisis began when Sir Geoffrey Howe unexpectedly resigned from the cabinet, and on 13 November 1990 delivered a devas-tating speech in the Commons, criticizing Mrs Thatcher's attitude towards Europe. By 7 November she had resigned and her successor had been chosen. Yet as Conservative leader she had won three consecutive elections with large majorities, and had never lost an election. *Why did the Conservative Party drop Mrs Thatcher?*

Dissatisfaction had been increasing for some time in the cabinet with Mrs Thatcher's style of government. Full cabinet discussion of policies became increasingly rare, and decisions were taken by Mrs Thatcher after consultation with small groups of cabinet members or with her personal advisers. This was one of the reasons given by Heseltine for his resignation in January 1986: 'the prime minister's methods,' he said, 'are not a proper way to carry on government and ultimately not an approach for which I can share responsibility'. An important issue like membership of the ERM was never discussed in full cabinet. Her style became increasingly dictatorial and she took to undermining ministers who criticized or displeased her by allowing press leaks from No 10 Downing Street. She developed an irritating habit of referring to herself in the royal plural; on one famous occasion she told a group of TV reporters outside No 10: 'we have become a grandmother'!

- She gradually lost touch with her original power base in the parliamentary party. This was made worse by the retirement, after the 1987 election, of William Whitelaw, an expert parliamentarian on whom she relied heavily for advice. Although he was never a Thatcherite, Whitelaw remained loyal to his leader, and according to Nicholas Ridley, 'was possessed of almost supernatural political antennae and knew when to warn Mrs Thatcher that a situation had reached breaking point'. The departure of Norman Tebbit and Lord Young, two reliable Thatcherites, left her increasingly dependent on Lawson and Howe, who, as time went on, became more impatient with her methods. Her loss of touch was never illustrated better than in her refusal to abandon her 'flagship', the poll tax.
- By the autumn of 1990 it was clear that Thatcherite policies had not delivered an 'economic miracle', and were seen to be a failure on all fronts (see next Section).
- Disagreements over the government's policy towards Europe became more serious. Mrs Thatcher had never been enthusiastic about Britain's membership of the EEC, and was convinced that the sovereignty of the British government was being threatened. Her attitude to Europe had been aggressive right from the beginning. She was alarmed at the moves towards further political and economic union, especially in July 1988 when Jacques Delors, a French socialist who was President of the European Commission, made a speech in which he said that in six years there would be 'an embryo European government'. Within ten years '80 per cent of the laws affecting the economy and social policy would be passed at a European and not a national level'. Mrs Thatcher declared that Delors had 'gone over the top', and many Conservative MPs agreed with her. However, there were many pro-European Conservatives who, together with the Foreign Office, felt that Britain should play a positive role in Europe instead of the negative approach adopted by Mrs Thatcher.

The following September she responded with a speech in Bruges (Belgium) in which she attacked the whole idea of further European unity and control from Brussels. 'We have not successfully rolled back the frontiers of the state in Britain,' she said, 'only to see them reimposed at a European level.' According to Hugo Young, Mrs Thatcher's biographer, this speech 'was viewed with amazement across Europe, dismay in the Foreign Office and with especial weary horror by the Foreign Secretary, Sir Geoffrey Howe'.

However, it wasn't long before Howe and Lawson seemed to make some progress: they had been wanting to take Britain into the ERM, but Mrs Thatcher would not hear of it. At a summit meeting in Madrid (June 1989), they pressurized her, by threatening to resign, into accepting in principle the idea of joining the ERM and a common monetary policy, when the conditions were right. Mrs Thatcher was furious at having been outmanoeuvred, and in July she sacked Howe as Foreign Secretary and replaced him with John Major. Howe became Leader of the House of Commons and Deputy Prime Minister, but he was angry at the way he had been treated. Clearly the three senior figures in the government were on bad terms, and it wasn't long before Lawson resigned after further disagreement over the ERM (October 1989). At a summit meeting in Rome in October 1990, Mrs Thatcher condemned the idea of European economic and monetary union, even though at Madrid she had committed her government to it. This upset the pro-European Tories, especially when she began the usual leaks and rumours to discredit Howe, in preparation for removing him from the cabinet.

Sir Geoffrey pre-empted these sordid goings-on by getting his resignation in first and making his sensational Commons speech. Dennis Healey once remarked that having an argument with Sir Geoffrey, a mild-mannered and quietly spoken man, was like being savaged by a dead sheep. But this speech must rank as one of the most devastating ever delivered in the House of Commons; in reality it was a signal to the party that he thought it was time for Mrs Thatcher to go.

● Michael Heseltine, who had waited in the wings for a moment like this since his resignation in 1986, now challenged Mrs Thatcher for the leadership of the Conservative Party. Although Mrs Thatcher won by 204 votes to 152, she was three short of the number needed to avoid a second ballot, and there were 16 abstentions. Roughly 40 per cent of Conservative MPs were not prepared to support Mrs Thatcher. In fact, even in her heyday, there was never a majority of Conservative MPs who could be described as Thatcherites. As historian Martin Pugh puts it:

> They had accepted her as long as she delivered victory at the elections; but by 1990 they judged that public disenchantment over the poll tax and the economy was so deep that she would lead the party to defeat next time. This feeling spread rapidly once the Prime Minister had failed to win on the first ballot.

Most of her cabinet colleagues felt the same and advised her to step down. She was clearly now seen as an electoral liability; she therefore decided not to go forward into the second ballot. John Major and Douglas Hurd now came into the contest; in a determined effort to prevent Heseltine, who had dared to challenge her, from becoming leader, Mrs Thatcher let it be known that she supported Major. The ballot was won by John Major, who immediately became Prime Minister as well as party leader. Major had 185 votes to Heseltine's 131 and Hurd's 56.

33.5 Assessment of Mrs Thatcher's governments

(a) Mrs Thatcher's achievements

There can be no doubt that it was a brilliant personal achievement by Margaret Thatcher to win three successive elections and spend eleven and a half consecutive years as Prime Minister. Only Lord Liverpool (1812–27) had spent a longer continuous period in office. She was a figure of international standing, highly respected both in the USA and in Russia, and, more grudgingly, in Europe too. *What did her policies achieve?*

The most striking change in direction which was maintained right through the Thatcher years was privatization. The curbing of trade union powers was an important and necessary step, and resulted in fewer strikes than at any time since the 1930s. Another notable feature was the sale of council houses, which brought house owner-ship in Britain up from 44 per cent to about 66 per cent of the population, the highest in western Europe. During Mrs Thatcher's first few years in power, the 'enterprise cul-ture' showed many successes, with a record number of small businesses being set up. Many firms, which had slimmed down during the first burst of monetarism, became extremely efficient and increased their productivity and competitiveness, so that they could rival the best in Europe. In fact during the 1980s productivity (the amount pro-duced per worker) grew by over 4 per cent a year. Income tax was reduced steadily over the 11 years, and living standards improved for most people.

One of Mrs Thatcher's greatest achievements was to renegotiate Britain's contribution to the EEC budget (see Section 32.8(e)) and Britain became more fully integrated in Europe in spite of Eurosceptic doubts. Her policy towards Russia was a success: she formed a good relationship with Gorbachev on his first visit to Britain (December 1984). 'I like Mr Gorbachev,' she told TV viewers; 'we can do business together.' During her later visit to Russia (March 1987) they had long talks, and she could claim that she had helped to pave the way for the end of the Cold War.

Thatcherism also had an effect on the Labour Party: by moving the Conservative Party firmly to the right, Mrs Thatcher forced Labour, under Neil Kinnock, John Smith and Tony Blair, to adapt to changing circumstances, modernize its image and drop most of its socialist ideals, such as nationalization and the restoration of full trade union powers. Thus Mrs Thatcher could claim, with some justification, to have set a new political agenda, changed the course of British politics and played a vital role in the disappearance of socialism from Britain.

(b) *Thatcherite policy failures*

On the other hand some of her aims had clearly not been achieved. Monetarism was quietly abandoned as unworkable and inflation had not been controlled – when she left office it had risen again to 10.6 per cent, higher than when she came to power. Pressure of public opinion prevented her from dismantling the Health Service or from interfering too much with free education and other social services. In fact spending in all these areas increased between 1979 and 1990, much of the extra cash being spent on unemployment benefit. In spite of her reservations about Europe, Britain had been drawn more deeply into the EEC, even joining the ERM in 1990.

Overall, Mrs Thatcher's policies had unfortunate effects:

● During the first bout of monetarism (1980–1) Britain lost between 20 and 25 per cent of her manufacturing industry – sometimes referred to as a 'de-industrialization' process. Although there was a recovery during the years 1984–8, this soon deteriorated into another recession, as the 'economic miracle' failed to materialize. The government, now bereft of ideas, fell back on raising interest rates, but this made the situation worse. Investment fell, borrowing was too expensive, and about 29 000 businesses went bankrupt in 1990 alone. The most recent statistics show that between 1979 and 1991, the average annual rate of economic growth was only 1.75 per cent, below that of most other developed nations. This was worse than the 2.4 per cent average for the previous ten years, which had been considered poor and which the Conservatives had vowed to improve on. According to Martin Pugh, who takes a bleak view of the situation, by 1982 Britain 'had ceased to produce a wide range of sophisticated items of the sort that had once been the basis of her wealth: typewriters, computers, washing machines, television sets, sewing machines and motor cycles. Her companies had been driven out of motor cars and shipbuilding except for small remnants; and aerospace, railways and coal were fast going the same way. Whereas in the late 1950s 8 million people had worked in British manufacturing industry, by 1991 fewer than 5 million still did so.' Not surprisingly, Britain's share of total world trade continued to decline (see Table 33.1) while Japan's increased.

● The loss of so much of Britain's manufacturing industries meant that more goods had to be imported. This led to a balance of payments deficit of £13.6 billion in 1989, which had risen to £16 billion in 1990. There was not enough investment in industry, so that in the early 1990s, British capital stock – machinery, buildings and techniques – was older and smaller than that of many of its main competitors. Faced with competition from cheap imports, many British manufacturers of goods like textiles,

Table 33.1 Percentage shares of world trade in manufactures (1950–90)

	France	W. Germany	UK	Japan	USA
1950	9.9	7.3	25.5	3.4	27.3
1958	8.6	18.5	18.1	6.0	23.3
1970	8.7	19.8	10.8	11.7	18.5
1979	10.8	20.7	9.8	13.6	15.9
1989	9.0	20.4	8.2	17.6	15.8

Source: D. Childs, *Britain Since 1939: Progress and Decline* (Macmillan, 1995), p. 253.

shoes, and consumer electronics either stopped producing or set up factories in Asia where labour was cheaper. Total output in Britain declined in 1991 and 1992.

● Unemployment had fallen from a peak of 3.4 million in 1986 to 1.6 million in June 1990; but the recession had sent it up again to almost 2 million when Mrs Thatcher resigned, and it continued to rise, reaching 2.6 million by the end of 1991. However, the real unemployment figure was much higher than that, because the government's methods of counting always underestimated numbers out of work. In addition, about half a million people had been placed on official training schemes which kept them off the official registers. The real total of unemployed at the end of 1992 was at least 3.5 million. Payment of unemployment benefit and social security was a constant drain on the budget; so many households on low incomes meant a massive loss of purchasing power, which did nothing to help the economy recover.

● The gap between rich and poor widened. Successive income tax reductions, particularly in 1988, benefited the rich more than the poor: over the eleven and a half years of Mrs Thatcher's governments, the richest 20 per cent gained by almost a third, whereas the poorest 20 per cent gained only 1 per cent in income. Higher direct taxes such as VAT meant that people on low incomes had to pay the same VAT increases as those on the highest incomes, for example on commodities like petrol, and they were therefore relatively worse off. Although the wages of most people in work rose, salaries of top people rose by much more than those of unskilled workers. By 1993 the gap between the highest and lowest wages was the widest since records began. According to the Rowntree Trust, between 1979 and 1991, the incomes of the top 10 per cent rose by more than 50 per cent, while the real incomes of the bottom sixth actually fell. Another distressing development was the deliberate casualization of the workforce: in order to maximize profits and dividends paid to shareholders, managers began to employ a higher proportion of part-time workers, who could be paid lower rates and could be hired and fired at short notice whenever necessary. At the same time tighter regulations made it more difficult for young people to get social security benefits, and it was no surprise when beggars began to appear on the streets again. With unemployment running permanently at around 3 million, it seemed that Thatcherite policies had created, or at least had failed to prevent, the emergence of a permanent 'underclass' for whom there was no longer any role in society. As unemployment and poverty increased, so did the crime rate.

● Thatcherite financial policies led to freedom from regulation for the City of London and the banking system. This too had unfortunate side-effects. Many foreign banks seized the opportunity to set up in London, so that by 1991 around half the banking houses in London were foreign-owned. According to economic journalist Will Hutton, writing in 1995 (in *The State We're In*, Vintage, 1996), 'the City of London has become a byword for speculation, inefficiency and cheating. Given the power to regulate their own affairs, City financial markets and institutions have conspicuously failed to meet any reasonable standard of honest dealing with the public or their own kind.' There was the Guinness case already referred to, and this was quickly followed by many examples of 'sleaze' and fraudulent dealings. It became commonplace for insiders with privileged information to manipulate share prices on the Stock Exchange for personal profit. Fraud and theft led to the collapse of the Barlow-Clowes financial empire. In 1991 the Bank of Credit and Commerce International (BCCI) was forced to close after fraud on a huge scale was revealed; an enquiry blamed the Bank of England for not acting early enough to prevent the collapse. In the two and a half years after 1990, no fewer than 100 000 jobs were lost in the City, and it seemed likely that the Frankfurt money market might soon become more important than London.

Another failure of the City was that it tended to reward companies which concentrated on 'short-termism'; this includes, among other practices, paying high dividends to shareholders, and taking over other companies, rather than spending sufficient cash on research and development (R & D). On the other hand, companies which *did* invest more of their profits in R & D were undervalued on the Stock Market. Shareholders were doing well, but enterprise and expansion were being discouraged, since investment was much lower than it should have been. Will Hutton provides some revealing statistics: in 1994 only 13 British companies, four of them drug companies, appeared in the world's top 200 spenders on R & D. In British industry during the 1980s, investment rose by only 2 per cent per annum, profits rose by 6 per cent per annum, while dividends jumped by 12 per cent per annum. The world's top 200 companies spent three times more on R & D than on dividends; however, in Britain, even the top research companies spent only two-thirds of the amount they paid out in dividends.

A further unhealthy trend was that the country came to rely on foreign investment to develop new industries and training. By 1995 no less that 25 per cent of British manufacturing capacity was owned by foreigners, who employed 16 per cent of all British workers. It seemed strange that a government which was so touchy about losing *political* control to foreigners in the European Community should show so little concern that the country was fast losing *economic* control of its own vital industrial base.

33.6 John Major's governments 1990–7

(a) Major's first term

John Major was virtually unknown to the wider public until he was unexpectedly made Foreign Secretary in 1989, soon afterwards replacing Nigel Lawson as Chancellor. He was chosen as leader because he had received Mrs Thatcher's blessing; she thought he was 'one of us' – the best man to carry on her policies. He had the added attraction of being one of the 'new generation' of Tories – he had never been to university and had even been on the dole for a time before finding a job in a bank. He gave the impression of being a genuinely likeable man who understood the needs of ordinary people. His task now, as historian John Charmley puts it, 'was to move the Thatcherite agenda on to the next phase and to unite the Party in order to retain power'.

In the Gulf War (1990–1) he soon found himself carrying out a policy initiated by Mrs Thatcher. When Saddam Hussein, the ruler of Iraq, sent his forces into the neighbouring state of Kuwait (August 1990), President Bush of the USA took the lead in pressing for action to remove the Iraqis; Saddam was ordered to withdraw his troops by 15 January 1991. Mrs Thatcher, who happened to be in the USA with Bush when the news of the invasion was announced, fully supported Bush's stand: Saddam controlled too much of the oil which the industrial west needed for him to be allowed to keep Kuwait. 'Remember, George, this is no time to go wobbly, George', she told the President. When the 15 January deadline passed, Major was Prime Minister, and he went ahead with Britain's contribution – sending some 45 000 British military personnel to join operation *Desert Storm*, which soon chased Saddam's troops out of Kuwait.

However, Major soon showed that he had no intention of simply continuing Thatcherite policies. In the run-up to the next election (April 1992) he took a number of actions which disappointed the right wing of the party: he

- announced that he wanted a classless society;
- appointed Chris Patten, who was on the left of the party, as Party Chairman;
- dropped the disastrous poll tax and replaced it with a new council tax based on property values;
- made it clear that he believed more money would have to be spent on health and education;
- signed *the Maastricht Treaty (December 1991)* which committed Britain to greater integration in Europe (see Section 32.8(h)). Major negotiated a special agreement which allowed Britain to opt out of the social chapter and some aspects of the common economic policy. This was seen in many circles as a considerable achievement by the Prime Minister; however, it was not enough for the Thatcherites, who felt that he was too pro-Europe. They demanded a referendum on whether or not Britain should accept the treaty, but the Prime Minister refused. This disagreement over Europe was to split the Conservatives right through Major's period in office, and was to play an important part in the massive Conservative defeat in 1997.

The government faced other problems: the economic depression grew worse, and in 1991 alone, 48 000 businesses went bankrupt. Unemployment continued to rise, and there were record numbers of house repossessions as people fell behind with their mortgage repayments.

(b) *The election of April 1992*

With the country in the middle of a depression, the opinion polls predicted either a narrow Labour victory or a hung parliament in which the Liberal Democrats would hold the balance. The Labour Party had been revitalized under the leadership of Neil Kinnock: he had got rid of the militant extremists, or 'loony left' as the Conservatives called them, played down the socialist element in the manifesto and united the party. At a big election rally a few days before voting, he was introduced as 'the next Prime Minister'. Against all expectations, the Conservatives won a narrow victory; the figures were: Conservatives 336, Labour 271, Liberal Democrats 20, and various others 24, giving an overall Conservative majority of 21.

Reasons for John Major's victory:
- Mr Major was a popular leader who came over as honest, caring and reliable – a sort of Stanley Baldwin figure. Although the country was suffering a severe recession, voters seemed to blame Mrs Thatcher for that, and were prepared to give the new Prime Minister a chance to prove himself. The victory was seen as a genuine personal success for Mr Major.
- Labour had not quite succeeded in throwing off its old image as a party of high spending and high taxation. John Smith, the Shadow Chancellor, was honest enough to admit that taxes would have to go up to enable more to be spent on health, education and social services.
- Some statistics suggest that as many as one million voters, who would most likely

have voted Labour or Liberal Democrat (if they had voted at all), had dropped off the lists because of their refusal to pay the poll tax.

● Seven out of the eleven main daily newspapers, which accounted for two-thirds of all sales, supported the Conservatives and ran campaigns to ridicule and discredit Neil Kinnock.

(c) *A catalogue of disasters*

Mr Major had very little time to enjoy his victory before things began to go wrong. It soon became clear that a majority of the new Conservative MPs were supporters of Thatcherite ideas; this increasingly hampered Mr Major, who was quietly trying to move the party away from Thatcherism. But the party in parliament was probably now more Thatcherite than when Mrs Thatcher herself had been Prime Minister. *The main problems were:*

1   *The recession continued*, thousands more jobs were lost and unemployment rose. The housing market remained depressed, and many housebuyers found that their homes were worth less than they had borrowed to buy them (this was known as 'negative equity'). The Chancellor, Norman Lamont, talked about 'the green shoots of recovery', but these were difficult to detect. In 1993 Britain's economy compared badly with those of other leading European Union states: in the league table of Gross Domestic Product, Britain came in eighth place out of twelve and performed below the average (see Table 33.2).

Table 33.2   Average Gross Domestic Product per head (GDP) in 1993 in European Union states, according to purchasing power (Average = 100)

Greece	48
Portugal	58
Eire	72
Spain	77
Britain	96
EU average	100
Germany	102
Netherlands	103
Italy	104
Belgium	106
Denmark	108
France	112
Luxembourg	130

Source: D. Childs, *Britain Since 1939: Progress and Decline* (Macmillan, 1995) p. 267.

2   *Britain was forced to take sterling out of the ERM (September 1992)*. During the election campaign, Major had emphasized that Britain's membership of the ERM was his central strategy for defeating inflation and making Britain fully competitive. But it now emerged that when (as Chancellor of the Exchequer) he had taken Britain into the ERM (October 1990) the pound had been overvalued (at 2.95 German marks). Unfortunately, because of the weak economy, the pound lost value within the ERM, and it became more and more difficult to maintain the exchange rate. The government tried to defend the pound by raising interest rates, but by September 1992 dealers were selling the currency so fast that the value continued to fall. Lamont put interest rates up briefly to 15 per cent and spent £60 billion in an attempt to save the pound. All his attempts failed: on 'Black

Wednesday' (23 September 1992), sterling had to be withdrawn from the ERM and allowed to find its own level. In practice this meant that the pound had been devalued by about 15 per cent.

This was a devastating blow for the government. Its main economic strategy had failed and the economic competence of Major and his Chancellor was now open to serious doubts. Ironically the weaker pound made British goods cheaper abroad and exports gradually increased; but this was no thanks to the government.

3 *There was uproar when the government announced (October 1992) that in preparation for the privatization of coal, 31 of the remaining 50 pits were to be closed, throwing about 30 000 miners out of work.* This was in spite of the fact that the coal industry had become much more efficient since the miners' strike. Public opinion, on the whole, supported the miners and wanted the pits to remain open. Critics of government policy pointed out that it would be ludicrous if the country found itself at some later date having to import expensive foreign coal when it could have continued to produce British coal at lower prices. There was also the argument that all the energy industries (electricity, gas, coal, oil and nuclear power) ought to be under state control, otherwise it would be virtually impossible to have a carefully thought out, long-term, co-ordinated energy policy. Michael Heseltine, the minister responsible, agreed to reconsider the plan; but although it was postponed for a time, by June 1993 all the pits had been closed and the number of miners in the country had roughly halved. The government had apparently committed itself to buying gas and nuclear power, though the latter was uneconomic and was having to be subsidized by the government. This was certainly not Thatcherite economics.

4 *Another unpopular step was the extension of VAT to domestic fuel (May 1993).* So great was the outcry that Lamont was forced to resign and was replaced by Kenneth Clarke. The government was losing by-elections, both to the Liberal Democrats and Labour, and eventually its majority was reduced to one.

5 *In an attempt to rally the party, Major launched a new campaign – 'back to basics',* which seemed to be an updated version of Mrs Thatcher's Victorian values: a return to a stricter morality and a strengthening of family life. This was introduced with the best of intentions, but the party soon let Mr Major down. Within a few months the campaign backfired when eight Conservative MPs had made the headlines, amid accusations of adultery or corruption. One area where 'back to basics' might have been effective was in cleaning up and improving standards in television. However, the government's deregulation policies made this impossible. For example, BSkyB, the satellite TV company owned by Rupert Murdoch, was freed from the regulatory standards applying to terrestrial broadcasters, partly, according to some commentators, as a political favour to Murdoch.

6 *Meanwhile the dispute in the party over Europe rumbled on as a permanent theme;* the Eurosceptics made life difficult for Mr Major every time there was a Commons vote on anything to do with Europe. As the Conservative majority dwindled, the Prime Minister had to resort to threats of resignation and later an agreement with the Ulster Unionist MPs to make sure that the legislation got through. Once, he deprived a group of nine Eurosceptic MPs of the party whip, but he took them back again later, even though their attitude had not changed; this did nothing to strengthen his authority.

When rumours of a challenge to his leadership began to circulate, Mr Major boldly seized the initiative by announcing that he was offering himself for re-election in the summer of 1995 instead of waiting until the autumn. He told his critics to 'put up or shut up'. The Welsh Secretary, John Redwood, a Thatcherite and Eurosceptic, resigned from government and challenged Mr Major. The election resulted in a comfortable victory for Major with 218 votes (out of 329) against 89 for Redwood. Michael Heseltine, who had earlier suffered a heart-attack, decided not to stand, and his supporters voted for Major. Heseltine was rewarded with the post of Deputy Prime Minister.

7   The situation in Ireland took a turn for the better in August 1994 when the IRA called a ceasefire (see Section 31.1(j)). But although the ceasefire lasted for 18 months, very little progress was made in the peace process. The government was in a difficult situation: the slightest sign of any concessions to the nationalists infuriated the Unionists, and with such a slender majority Mr Major could not afford to alienate the Ulster Unionist MPs. The IRA called off the ceasefire in February 1996.

8   *The government mishandled the crisis over BSE and the safety of British beef.* After outbreaks of a cattle disease known as bovine spongiform encephalitis (BSE) (commonly known as 'mad cow disease), some scientists claimed that eating beef from diseased cattle caused Kreuzfeldt Jacob's disease, a deadly disease in humans which always proved fatal. Although government scientists denied that there could be any connection, many people in Britain stopped eating beef. It emerged that BSE was caused by contaminated cattle food which contained animal protein made from sheep which had been suffering from a disease called 'scrapie'. There was outrage in some quarters where it was felt that making cattle eat animal protein was something akin to cannibalism. However, it seemed that this had been going on for some time without any ill-effects, until Mrs Thatcher's government relaxed controls, so that animal feed could be processed at lower temperatures, which was cheaper. These lower temperatures failed to destroy the BSE organisms, hence more outbreaks of the disease.

The Major government, to its credit, banned the use of cattle feed containing animal protein and introduced new hygiene regulations in abattoirs.

Unfortunately the government then made two mistakes: it failed to ensure that the new regulations were enforced rigorously enough; some farmers continued to use up stocks of contaminated feed and many abattoirs ignored the new rules. Secondly, not wanting to antagonize farmers, the government failed to introduce a sufficiently rigorous policy of slaughtering diseased animals early enough. It should have been possible, with prompt action, to eliminate all diseased herds. The result was further outbreaks of BSE. There was great public concern also when more cases of Kreuzfeldt Jacob's disease were reported in humans, and there were fears of an epidemic developing.

In the end, the government got the worst of both worlds. By 1996 there was worldwide concern about the safety of British beef and the European Union banned further imports. The government was therefore forced to introduce a large-scale slaughtering policy anyway. The whole thing was a tragedy for the farmers; by the time of the next general election (May 1997) the ban on British beef exports to Europe had still not been lifted.

As the 1997 election drew nearer, the situation in the country seemed to improve and Mr Major could point to some positive achievements. Britain began to move out of the recession at last; the economy began to grow again and became the healthiest in Europe (or so the government told the public). Unemployment was falling and inflation was low and well under control. 'Britain is booming! Don't Let Labour Spoil It', urged the election posters. Another achievement was the setting up of the National Lottery, an idea rejected by Mrs Thatcher. This raised lots of money for charity, sports, the arts and the national heritage, though Michael White (writing in the *Guardian*, 3 May 1997) called it 'an example of degenerate Majorite radicalism'. None of this was enough to restore the Conservatives' popularity, and the opinion polls consistently predicted a comfortable Labour victory.

(d) *The Conservative defeat – 1 May 1997*

Most people seemed to expect a Labour overall majority of 40 to 50 seats and were unprepared for the huge Labour landslide victory which gave them an overall majority of 179. Labour emerged with 418 seats, their highest total ever, beating even their famous landslide victory of 1945 (393 seats). The Conservatives had 165 seats, their lowest total since 1906 when they were reduced to 157. The Liberal Democrats won 46 seats. Seven members of the cabinet and many former ministers lost their seats. The Conservatives were left with no seats in Scotland and Wales, suggesting that the Scots and Welsh did not like the Conservatives' opposition to devolution; and they had very few seats in the large English cities. It was a devastating rejection of a particular brand of Conservatism which had moved too far to the right. At the age of 43, Tony Blair became the youngest Prime Minister since Lord Liverpool in 1812.

There were some other remarkable points about this election. More women MPs were elected than ever before; the number just about doubled to 119, of whom 109 were Labour. The voting system as usual played some strange tricks. The Liberal Democrats doubled their seats, although their share of the vote fell by 1 per cent. Although the Conservatives won 31 per cent of the votes, this only brought them 25 per cent of the total seats in the UK. The Conservatives polled more votes in Scotland than the Liberal Democrats, yet won no seats, whereas the Liberal Democrats won ten. The discrepancy was even more pronounced in Wales where the Conservatives polled twice as many votes as Plaid Cymru, who won four seats, while the Conservatives had nothing to show. In the past the system had always benefited the Conservatives; in 1997 for the first time, in Scotland and Wales, the Conservatives had to cope with the problem which usually faced the Liberal Democrats – it is difficult for minority parties, whose support is widely spread out, to win seats under the first-past-the-post system. *Why did the Conservatives lose so heavily?*

● Some experts feel that the Conservatives had never recovered from 'Black Wednesday' when the pound was forced out of the ERM. A financial disaster of this magnitude, resulting in a 15 per cent devaluation of the pound, had never happened before under a Conservative government. Previous financial crises – 1931, 1949, 1967 and 1976 – had all occurred under Labour. The Conservatives' reputation for economic competence had gone and they never succeeded in regaining it.

● Although the government kept on saying that Britain was booming, many voters were clearly not feeling the benefit of it. Exit polls suggested that there was a big swing to Labour in middle-class seats among people in junior managerial and clerical jobs – the sort of people who had suffered most from negative equity when the housing market collapsed. In an age of permanent casualization and down-sizing, more and more people felt insecure in their jobs – and this included people in the South and the London area, which were now feeling the pinch like the Midlands and North.

Critics of the government claimed that the sole reason the British economy seemed to be performing better than the European economies, was because Britain had an unfair advantage: its refusal to accept the social contract of the Maastricht Treaty had left Britain with one of the cheapest labour markets in the Community. British workers now had very little legal protection of any kind. There was no limit on working time, no minimum wage, and no legal right to representation at the workplace. This was a return to Victorian times with a vengeance: employers were now under no legal obligation to pay their workers fairly, or to treat them as anything other than disposable commodities. Unemployment benefit (now called 'job-seekers' allowance') was limited to six months, and it was more difficult to get sickness benefit.

● Many people felt that privatization had gone far enough. Although the privatized industries which had to face real competition were now competitive and sure-footed in the global marketplace (after years of hardship and job losses both before and after privatization), it is debatable whether privatization was necessary for this to happen. The privatized utilities (such as gas, electricity and water) attracted criticism because they exploited their monopoly positions in the UK market, and their directors awarded themselves huge salary increases and share options which made them millionaires several times over. However, their increases in profit were not achieved by any particular business skill or genuine entrepreneurship, but simply by cutting staff and raising prices. Yet the government, even with its tiny majority, still pushed ahead with plans for privatizing the railways and nuclear fuels. Rail privatization aroused criticism in the South and South-East; again there were immediate staff lay-offs, and these led to poor services and left commuters struggling.

● The split in the party over Europe lost the Conservatives support. In 1906 the party had been split over tariff reform, but the result was the same; a divided party never does well in general elections. The Eurosceptics claimed that they spoke for a majority of the country, but the voting showed no obvious swing to Eurosceptic candidates. The general feeling was more that Mr Major, struggling to find an acceptable middle course for Britain's membership of the European Union, had been let down by the Eurosceptics.

● Sleaze was an important issue in the election and dominated the first two weeks of the campaign. Having been in power for so long, many Conservatives, though certainly not Mr Major himself, seemed to get careless, feeling that they could get away with all sorts of corrupt practices: asking questions in the Commons to further the interests of certain companies, and accepting cash from individuals to ask questions, were two of the activities now seen as acceptable. Two of the most notorious cases were those of junior ministers Tim Smith and Neil Hamilton, who were accused of accepting £2000 each and other rewards from an Egyptian financier, Mohammed al Fayed, to ask questions in the House. They eventually resigned from the government, as did Jonathan Aitken, who was alleged to have breached the government's own embargo on arms exports to Iraq, in his capacity as a director of a defence contracting firm. Mr Major appointed the Nolan Committee to consider how to improve standards in public life. This suggested that MPs should disclose all payments received for consultancy work; however, most Conservatives rejected this and insisted that parliament should be left to regulate itself. Voters did not like sleaze. Neil Hamilton, though protesting his innocence, lost his seat to an independent 'anti-sleaze' candidate, Martin Bell, a well-known BBC TV reporter, who turned Hamilton's 20 000 majority into an 11 000 majority for himself. Jonathan Aitken also lost his seat.

● The Labour party had been transformed almost out of recognition since 1992. The process of reform had been started by Neil Kinnock, but he resigned after Labour's defeat in 1992, and was replaced as leader by John Smith, a Scottish barrister. In 1993 he manoeuvred the party conference into accepting reforms which would reduce direct trade union influence on party policy. When John Smith died suddenly in May 1994 he was replaced by Tony Blair, an Oxford-educated barrister. According to Professor Anthony King (writing in *The Daily Telegraph* on 3 May 1997), 'Mr Blair was the kind of leader for the 1990s that might have been produced by computer-aided design; young, classless, squeaky-clean, with no close connections to the unions. Mr Blair knew that radical change was needed if Labour was to become electable.'

And radical change was what Mr Blair provided: the famous clause 4 of the 1918 party constitution, which committed Labour to nationalization, was dropped, and it was made clear that a Labour government would not repeal the Conservative trade union reforms. Mr Blair promised that there would be no big tax and spending increases – *New Labour was to be a party of social democracy, not socialism.* Another new departure was the way Mr Blair wooed business leaders, explaining his plans for a partnership between New Labour and business to take Britain into the twenty-first century. He even had a meeting with Rupert Murdoch, owner of *The Times*, *The Sunday Times*, the *Sun* and BSkyB. In the end, the *Sun* and the *Evening Standard* switched support from the Conservatives to Labour, while *The Times* told people to vote for Eurosceptics of whichever party.

● Finally, tactical voting probably made an important contribution to the sheer size of Labour's majority. Blair made this possible by making a deliberate effort to improve relations with the Liberal Democrats, promising a referendum on proportional representation. In return Paddy Ashdown said he would support a Labour government. Given the amount of common ground between the two, this made it easy for voters of either party to vote for the other in marginal constituencies, rather than splitting the anti-Conservative vote evenly. Michael Portillo, the Defence Secretary, was defeated by his Labour challenger at Enfield-Southgate, where the Liberal Democrat vote fell by 4 per cent from 1992, just enough to unseat Mr Portillo.

The defeat of Mr Portillo was a particularly serious blow for the Conservatives, since he was widely viewed as the most likely successor to Mr Major, who announced his resignation as Conservative leader the day after the election. The party was left stunned, confused, demoralized and leaderless, and the immediate need was to find a leader who could unite the various factions. In June, after a lively campaign, the Conservative MPs elected William Hague as the new party leader. At 36, the youngest Tory leader since William Pitt in 1783, Mr Hague was on the right of the party. In *The Guardian* the following day (20 June 1997), Hugo Young wrote: Hague's election is the delayed revenge of the Thatcherites for what happened in 1990. The party is unequivocally back in their hands, led from the right, where the noisiest heart of modern Conservatism beats'.

Sources: the statistics in this chapter are taken from the following sources:
J. Charmley, *A History of Conservative Politics 1900–1996* (Macmillan, 1996, pp. 225–51)
D. Childs, *Britain Since 1939: Progress and Decline* (Macmillan, 1995, pp. 196–267)
W. Hutton, *The State We're In* (Vintage, 1996 edition, pp. 7–8, 172, 330)
M. Pugh, *State and Society: British Social and Political History 1870–1992* (Arnold, 1994, pp. 302–34)

Questions

1 **Thatcherism and its legacy**
   Study Sources A to D and then answer the questions which follow.

--- **Source A** ---

John Charmley, a Conservative historian, gives his view

If Mrs Thatcher came from the traditional bastion of British Conservatism, she was able to fashion an appeal to the aspirational working classes through the attempt to create a genuinely popular capitalism . . .; she knew that the claim that government was a cure for all society's ills was essentially fraudulent. . . . This helps to explain the passion she brought to her task – it was an expression of the deepest parts of a forceful personality – and the areas which she felt most strongly about. The sale of council houses to their tenants, the curbing of union power by getting rid of the 'closed shop' and making ballots for strike action compulsory, the sale of shares in the privatized industries – all these expressed her vision in which individuals were the basic unit. In the areas mentioned she did genuinely touch a popular nerve.... It is too soon to reach anything like a considered verdict on her long period in office.... On a personal level it was a towering achievement. Economically the record was cloudier.

Source: J. Charmley, *A History of Conservative Politics 1900–1996*, Macmillan, 1996.

Source B

Extracts from a biography of Mrs Thatcher by Hugo Young

Was she truly a visionary? Did she possess a strategic idea, or ideas, commensurate with the length of time she served and the powerful personal influence she exercised? Some close members of her staff, when asked this question, would reply with raised eyebrows. They regarded her as a politician who never thought far ahead. She had neither the patience nor the strategic cunning necessary for a political visionary.... All the same it would be a mistake to say she had no large picture of what she wanted to achieve. She certainly did. She may have lacked strategic vision in the sense of an all-embracing plan. But her politics were informed more than any other post-war Prime Minister's by guiding beliefs to which she referred in almost all situations. She saw a smaller state, a more market-oriented economy ... weaker unions and stronger businessmen, an enfeeblement of collective provision and greater opportunities for individual self-help. All of these she succeeded in filling with powerful moral purpose, which proved that she was, in some absolute sense, right, and socialists were with equal certainty wrong.... She was determined to erase socialism from the British agenda.

Source: H. Young, *One of Us*, Macmillan, 1991 edition.

Source C

The view of Professor Martin Pugh, another historian

Thus by the end of 1992 the accelerating decline of the British economy had cast the whole experiment of the 1980s into perspective. Although Mrs Thatcher had appeared to be an immensely powerful Prime Minister, she had wholly failed to prevent Britain being drawn inexorably into Europe; indeed the country had, by 1990, lost many of the attributes traditionally associated with a sovereign state. Her economic strategy had been a doomed attempt to recapture a half-remembered, half-imagined era in which the state had played a minimal role in economic and social affairs. By the early 1990s a reaction in favour of Keynesianism had set in. Thatcherism in this context seemed increasingly a Quixotic attempt to tilt at such windmills as Europe and socialism; *essentially an aberration in the course of British history.*

Source: M. Pugh, *State and Society: British Political and Social History 1870–1992*, Arnold, 1994.

Source D

Journalist Charles Leadbeater writing in The Observer, *4 May 1997*

More of this state is now in the hands of quangos and executive agencies. Power has been centralized, local government neutered. The Tories' mixed record of achievement makes it all the more remarkable that their ideological triumphs have been so sweeping. The market is dominant; privatisation is irreversible, union reform unchallenged, socialism vanquished; a culture of individualism is more deeply rooted than the current vogue for community suggests. The Tories may have departed but they – and Thatcher in particular – have mapped out the path down which we walk. It will be hard for us entirely to escape Tory ideas and values, because they have had such a powerful influence on us. They preached an ethic of responsibility but relieved most of the middle class of guilt or obligation to the less fortunate. That legitimized a low-level, everyday culture of greed; taking responsibility for yourself has increasingly come to mean grabbing what you can in a society where winners take a disproportionate share of the rewards. The enterprise culture of risk and reward, the Victorian values of work and thrift, have given way to the lottery culture of random selection and the Cedric Brown culture of rampant greed . . . and the explosion of inequality which will be their most lasting and damning legacy.

Source: C. Leadbeater, 'The Tory Years', in *The Observer*, 4 May 1997, p. 28.

(a) From the evidence of these four sources, how far do you think there was ever a genuine Thatcherite vision of the future?   (5 marks)

(b) What evidence is there in these sources to explain why Mrs Thatcher won three general elections between 1979 and 1987?   (5 marks)

(c) Professor Martin Pugh in Source C writes that Thatcherism was 'essentially an aberration in the course of British history'. Using these sources and the evidence from Chapter 33, explain to what extent you would agree with this statement.   (15 marks)

(Total 25 marks)

2 Explain why John Major and the Conservatives won the general election of 1992 against most expectations, but lost the election of 1997 so disastrously.

Further reading

General

Highly recommended, especially for 'A' level students, is the *Modern History Review*, published four times during the academic year, by Philip Allan, Market Place, Deddington, Oxfordshire. Some of the most useful articles are mentioned under the separate chapter headings.

Blake, R., *The Conservative Party from Peel to Thatcher* (Fontana, 1985)

Chamberlain, M. E., *Pax Britannica? British Foreign Policy 1789–1914* (Longman, 1988)

Charmley, J., *A History of Conservative Politics 1900–1996* (Macmillan, 1996)

Childs, D., *Britain Since 1939 – Progress and Decline* (Macmillan, 1995)

Clarke, P. F., *Hope and Glory – Britain 1900–1990* (Allen Lane/Penguin, 1996)

Marwick, A., *British Society Since 1945* (Penguin, 2nd edn 1990)

McCord, N., *British History 1815–1906* (Oxford, 1992)

Morgan, K. O., *The People's Peace: British History 1945–1990* (Oxford, 1992)

Peden, G. C., *British Economic and Social Policy: Lloyd George to Margaret Thatcher* (Philip Allan, 1985)

Pugh, M., *State and Society: British Political and Social History 1870–1992* (Arnold, 1994)

Royle, E., *Modern Britain: A Social History 1750–1985* (Longman, 1988)

Sked, A. and Cook, C., *Post-War Britain: A Political History* (Penguin, 1993 edition)

Stevenson, J., *British Society 1914–45* (Penguin, 1984)

Taylor, A. J. P., *English History 1914–45* (Oxford, 1965)

Thompson, F. M. L. (ed.), *The Cambridge Social History of Britain 1750–1950, Vols 1–111* (Cambridge, 1993)

Chapter 2   Britain under the Tories 1815–30

Beales, Derek, *From Castlereagh to Gladstone, 1815–55* (Nelson, 1969)

Belchem, J., *'Orator' Hunt: Henry Hunt and English Working Class Radicalism* (Oxford University Press, 1985)

Brasher, N. H., *Arguments in History – Britain in the Nineteenth Century* (Macmillan, 1968)

Cookson, J. E., *Lord Liverpool's Administration, 1815–22* (Scottish Academic Press, 1975).

Dinwiddy, J. R., *From Luddism to the First Reform Bill* (Blackwell, 1986)

Evans, E. J., *Britain before the Reform Act: Politics and Society 1815–1832* (Longman, 1989)

Evans, E. J., 'The Premiership of Lord Liverpool', in *Modern History Review*, April 1990

Gash, N., *Lord Liverpool* (Weidenfeld & Nicolson, 1984)

Goodlad, G., ' "Liberal" and "High" Tories in the Age of Liverpool', in *Modern History Review*, November 1995

Hargreaves, J. A., 'Luddism', in *Modern History Review*, September 1995

Hilton, Boyd, *Corn, Cash and Commerce – The Economic Policies of the Tory Governments, 1815–30* (Oxford University Press, 1977)

Hinde, W., *George Canning* (Collins, 1973)

Hinde, W., *Catholic Emancipation: A Shake to Men's Minds* (Blackwell, 1992)

Longford, E., *Wellington, Pillar of State* (Weidenfeld & Nicolson, 1972)

Reid, R., *The Peterloo Massacre* (Heinemann, 1989)
Revill, P., *The Age of Lord Liverpool* (Blackie, 1979)
Thompson, E. P., *The Making of the English Working Class* (Gollancz, 1963; Penguin, 1980)
White, R. J., *From Waterloo to Peterloo* (Mercury, 1963)

Chapter 3   Foreign affairs 1815–30

Chamberlain, M. E., *Pax Britannica? British Foreign Policy, 1789–1914* (Longman, 1988)
Chapman, T., 'A Just Equilibrium? The Congress of Vienna', in *Modern History Review*, September 1996
Derry, J. W., *Castlereagh* (Allen Lane, 1976)
Dixon, P., *Canning: Politician and Statesman* (Weidenfeld & Nicolson, 1976)
Ward, D. R., *Foreign Affairs, 1815–1865* (Collins, 1972)

Chapter 4   Parliament and the Great Reform Act of 1832

Brock, M. G., *The Great Reform Act* (Hutchinson, 1973)
Derry, J. W., *Charles, Earl Grey* (Blackwell, 1992)
Hamburger, J., *James Mill and the Art of Revolution* (Yale University Press, 1963)
Hobsbawm, E. J. and Rudé, G., *Captain Swing* (Lawrence & Wishart, 1969)
Phillips, J. A., *The Great Reform Bill in the Boroughs* (Clarendon Press, 1992)
Smith, E. A., *Lord Grey* (Oxford University Press, 1990)
Thompson, E. P., *The Making of the English Working Class* (Gollancz, 1963; Penguin, 1980)
Wright, D. G., *Democracy and Reform* (Longman, 1970)

Chapter 5   Whig reforms and failures 1833–41

Brundage, A., *The Making of the New Poor Law, 1832–39* (Hutchinson, 1978)
Cecil, D., *Melbourne* (Constable, 1954)
Finlayson, G. B. A. M., *England in the 1830s* (Arnold, 1969)
Jenkins, T. A., *The Liberal Ascendancy 1830–1886* (Macmillan, 1994)
Longmate, N., *The Workhouse* (Temple Smith, 1974)
Mandler, P., 'The New Poor Law', in *Modern History Review*, November 1993
Rose, M. E., *The Relief of Poverty, 1834–1914* (Macmillan, 1972)
Watson, R., *Edwin Chadwick, Poor Law and Public Health* (Longman, 1969)

Chapter 6   Chartism

Behagg, C., 'Taking Chartism Seriously', in *Modern History Review*, April 1996
Briggs, A. (ed.), *Chartist Studies* (Macmillan, 1969)
Cole, G. D. H., *Chartist Portraits* (Macmillan, 1965)
Cunningham, H., 'The Nature of Chartism', in *Modern History Review*, April 1990
Jones, D., *Chartism and the Chartists* (Allen Lane, 1975)
Read, D. and Glasgow, E. L., *Feargus O'Connor* (Arnold, 1961)
Royle, E., *Chartism* (Longman, 1980)
Thompson, D., *The Chartists* (Temple Smith, 1984)
Ward, J. T., *Chartism* (Batsford, 1973)

Chapter 7   Sir Robert Peel, the Conservatives and the Corn Laws 1830–46

Adelman, P., *Peel and the Conservative Party 1830–50* (Longman, 1989)
Blake, R., *The Conservative Party from Peel to Thatcher* (Fontana, 1985 edn)
Clark, G. Kitson, *Peel* (Duckworth, 1936)
Evans, E., *Sir Robert Peel* (Routledge, 1991)
Foster, R., 'Peel and his Party', in *Modern History Review*, September 1993
Gash, N., *Sir Robert Peel* (Longman, 1976)
Gash, N., 'Sir Robert Peel and the Conservative Party', in *Modern History Review*, February 1990
Grinter, R., *Disraeli and Conservatism* (Arnold, 1968)
Hinde, W., *Richard Cobden* (Yale University Press, 1987)
McCord, N., *The Anti-Corn Law League* (Allen & Unwin, 1958)
Randell, K. H., *Politics and the People 1835–1850* (Collins, 1972)
Read, D., *Cobden and Bright* (Arnold, 1967)

Chapter 8   Domestic Affairs 1846–67: Russell, Gladstone, Disraeli and the Reform Act of 1867

Blake, R., *Disraeli* (Eyre & Spottiswoode, 1966; Methuen, 1969)
Briggs, A., *Victorian People* (Penguin, 1965)
Cowling, M., *Disraeli, Gladstone and Revolution* (Cambridge, 1967)
Gash, N., 'The Peelites after Peel', in *Modern History Review*, February 1994
Kinealy, C., 'The Famine 1845–52: How England Failed Ireland', in *Modern History Review*, September 1995
Kinealy, C., *This Great Calamity: The Irish Famine 1845–52* (Gill & Macmillan, 1994)
Magnus, P., *Gladstone* (John Murray, 1963)
Smith, F. B., *The Making of the Second Reform Bill* (Cambridge, 1966)
Vincent, J., *Disraeli* (Oxford University Press, 1990)
Walton, J. K., *The Second Reform Act* (Methuen, 1987)

Chapter 9   Lord Palmerston and foreign affairs 1830–65

Chamberlain, M. E., *Pax Britannica? British Foreign Policy 1789–1914* (Longman, 1988)
Chamberlain, M. E., *Lord Palmerston* (University of Wales Press, 1987)
Goodlad, G., 'With Generous Sympathies and Hearty English Pluck', in *Modern History Review*, September 1996
Jenkins, T. A., *The Liberal Ascendancy 1830–1886* (Macmillan, 1994)
Ridley, J., *Lord Palmerston* (Constable, 1970)
Southgate, D. G., *The Most English Minister: Policies and Politics of Palmerston* (Macmillan, 1966)
Steele, E. D., *Palmerston and Liberalism 1855–65* (Cambridge, 1991)
Taylor, A. J. P., *The Struggle for Mastery in Europe* (Oxford, 1954; paperback 1971)
Ward, D. R., *Foreign Affairs, 1815–1865* (Collins, 1972)

Chapter 10   The Crimean War (1854–6)

Anderson, M. S., *The Eastern Question* (Macmillan, 1966)
Hibbert, C., *The Destruction of Lord Raglan* (Penguin, 1963)
Lambert, A., *The Crimean War: British Grand Strategy Against Russia, 1853–56* (Manchester University Press, 1990)
Lambert, A., 'The Crimean War: An Historical Illusion?', in *Modern History Review*, November 1991
Taylor, A. J. P., *The Struggle for Mastery in Europe* (Oxford, 1971) chapters 3, 4 and 5
Thomas, D., *Charge! Hurrah! Hurrah! A Life of Cardigan of Balaclava* (Routledge, 1974; Futura, 1976
Woodham-Smith, C., *The Reason Why* (Constable, 1953)

Chapter 11   Britain, India and the Mutiny of 1857

Edwardes, M., *British India* (Sidgwick & Jackson, 1967)
Farwell, B., *Queen Victoria's Little Wars* (Allen Lane, 1973)
Harris, J., *The Indian Mutiny* (Hart Davis MacGibbon, 1973)
Porter, B., *The Lion's Share: A Short History of British Imperialism 1850–1970* (Longman, 1975)
Spear, P., *A History of India* (Penguin, 1965)
Woodruff, P., *The Men Who Ruled India* (Cape, 1953)

Chapter 12   Social Reform: factories, mines, public health and education

Battiscombe, G., *Shaftesbury* (Constable, 1974)
Briggs, A., *Victorian Cities* (Penguin, 1963)
Chesney, K., *The Victorian Underworld* (Temple Smith, 1970)
Finer, S. E., *The Life and Times of Sir Edwin Chadwick* (Methuen, 1952)
Fraser, D., *The Evolution of the British Welfare State* (Macmillan, 1973)
Longmate, N., *King Cholera* (Hamish Hamilton, 1966)
Musgrave, P. W., *Society and Education since 1800* (Methuen, 1968)
Royle, E., *Modern Britain: A Social History 1750–1985* (Arnold, 1988)
Thompson, E. P., *The Making of the English Working Class* (Gollancz, 1963; Penguin, 1980)
Thompson, F. M. L. (ed.), *The Cambridge Social History History of Britain 1750–1950, Vols I–III* (Cambridge University Press, 1993)
Waller, P. J., *Town, City and Nation. England 1850–1914* (Oxford, 1983)

Walvin, J., *English Urban Life, 1776–1851* (Hutchinson, 1984)
Wardle, D., *English Popular Education 1780–1970* (Cambridge, 1970)
Watson, R., *Edwin Chadwick, Poor Law and Public Health* (Longman, 1969)

Chapter 13   Gladstone's first ministry 1868–74

Abbott, B. H., *Gladstone and Disraeli* (Collins, 1972)
Adelman, P., 'Gladstone and Liberalism', in *Modern History Review*, February 1991
Biagini, E. F., *Liberty, Retrenchment and Reform: Popular Liberalism in the Age of Gladstone, 1860–1880* (Cambridge, 1992)
Chamberlain, M. E., *Pax Britannica? British Foreign Policy 1789–1914* (Longman, 1988)
Cooke, A. B. and Vincent, J., *The Governing Passion: Cabinet Government and Party Politics in Britain, 1885–86* (Harvester Press, 1974)
Feuchtwanger, E. J., *Gladstone* (Allen Lane, 2nd edn, 1989)
Feuchtwanger, E. J., 'Gladstone's Irish Policy: Expediency or High Principle?', in *Modern History Review*, November 1991
Foot, M. R. D. (ed.) *The Gladstone Diaries* (Oxford, 1968)
Jenkins, T. A., *Gladstone, Whiggery and the Liberal Party, 1874–1886* (Oxford, 1988)
Jenkins, T. A., *The Liberal Ascendancy, 1830–1886* (Macmillan, 1994)
Jenkins, T. A., 'The Nonconformist Anglican', in *Modern History Review*, November 1996
Lyons, F. S. L., *Ireland Since the Famine* (Fontana, 1974)
Magnus, P., *Gladstone* (John Murray, 1963 edn)
Mathew, H. C. G., *Gladstone, 1809–1874* (Oxford, 1986)
Parry, J., *The Rise and Fall of Liberal Government in Victorian Britain* (Yale University Press, 1993)
Winstanley, M., *Gladstone and the Liberal Party* (Routledge, 1990)

Chapter 14   Disraeli and the Conservatives in power 1874–80

Abbott, B. H., *Gladstone and Disraeli* (Collins, 1972)
Adelman, P., *Gladstone, Disraeli and Later Victorian Politics* (Longman, 1970)
Beloff, M., 'The British Empire', in *History Today*, February 1996
Blake, R., *The Conservative Party from Peel to Thatcher* (Fontana, 1985 edn)
Blake, R., *Disraeli* (Eyre & Spottiswoode, 1966; Methuen, 1969)
Blake, R., 'Disraeli – Political Outsider', in *Modern History Review*, November 1989
Farwell, B., *Queen Victoria's Little Wars* (Allen Lane, 1973)
Grinter, R., *Disraeli and Conservatism* (Arnold, 1968)
Hobsbawm, E., *The Age of Empire 1875–1914* (Weidenfeld & Nicolson, 1987)
Jenkins, T. A., *Disraeli and Victorian Conservatism* (Macmillan, 1996)
Jenkins, T. A., 'Disraeli and the Art of Opposition', in *Modern History Review*, February 1997
Porter, B., *The Lion's Share: A Short History of British Imperialism 1850–1970* (Longman, 1975)
Shannon, R., *Gladstone and the Bulgarian Agitation, 1876* (Nelson, 1963)
Shannon, R., *The Age of Disraeli, 1868–1881* (Longman, 1992)
Smith, P., *Disraelian Conservatism* (Routledge & Kegan Paul, 1967)
Taylor, A. J. P., *The Struggle for Mastery in Europe* (Oxford, 1971 edn)
Vincent, J., *Disraeli* (Oxford, 1990)

Chapter 15   Victorian prosperity and depression

Aldcroft, D. H., *The Development of British Industry and Foreign Competition 1875–1914* (Allen & Unwin, 1968)
Aldcroft, D. H. and Richardson, H. W., *The British Economy 1870–1939* (Macmillan, 1969)
Barker, T., 'Workshop of the World', in *History Today*, June 1994
Daunton, M., *The Political Economy of Britain 1850–1939* (Oxford, 1996)
Evans, E., *The Forging of the Modern State: Early Industrial Britain 1783–1870* (Longman, 1983)
Hobsbawm, E., *Industry and Empire* (Penguin, 1969)
Kennedy, W. P., *Industrial Structure, Capital Markets and the Origins of British Economic Decline* (Cambridge, 1987)
Mathias, P., *The First Industrial Nation* (Methuen, 1969)
Saul, S. B., *The Myth of the Great Depression* (Macmillan, 1969)

Thompson, F. M. L., 'The Golden Age of Farming?', in *Purnell's History of the English Speaking Peoples* (BPC Publishing, 1971) pp. 3400–5.

Wiener, M. J., *English Culture and the Decline of the Industrial Spirit, 1850–1980* (Cambridge, 1981)

Chapter 16   Gladstone and Salisbury 1880–95

Adelman, P., 'Gladstone and Liberalism', in *Modern History Review*, February 1991

Chamberlain, M. E., *The Scramble for Africa* (Longman, 1974)

Coleman, B., *Conservatism and the Conservative Party in Nineteenth Century Britain* (Arnold, 1988)

Farwell, B., *Queen Victoria's Little Wars* (Allen Lane, 1973)

Foster, R. F., *Lord Randolph Churchill: A Political Life* (Oxford, 1981)

James, R. R., *Lord Randolph Churchill* (Weidenfeld & Nicolson, 1969)

James, R. R., *Rosebery* (Weidenfeld & Nicolson, 1963)

Magnus, P., *Gladstone* (John Murray, 1963 edn)

Marlowe, J., *Mission to Khartoum: General Gordon* (Gollancz, 1969)

Moorehead, A., *The White Nile* (Hamish Hamilton, 1960)

Morton, G., *Home Rule and the Irish Question* (Longman, 1980)

Pakenham, T., *The Scramble for Africa* (Weidenfeld & Nicolson, 1991)

Parry, J., *The Rise and Fall of Liberal Government in Victorian Britain* (Yale, 1993)

Porter, B., *The Lion's Share: A Short History of British Imperialism 1850–1970* (Longman, 1975)

Shannon, R. T., *Gladstone* (Methuen, 1984)

Taylor, R., *Lord Salisbury* (Allen Lane, 1975)

Winstanley, M.J., *Ireland and the Land Question 1800–1922* (Methuen, 1984)

Chapter 17   Ten years of Conservative rule 1895–1905

Chamberlain, M. E., *The Scramble for Africa* (Longman, 1974)

Chamberlain, M. E., *Pax Britannica? British Foreign Policy 1789–1914* (Longman, 1988)

Churchill, W. S., *Frontiers and Wars* (Penguin, 1972)

Coleman, B., *Conservativism and the Conservative Party in Nineteenth Century Britain* (Arnold, 1988)

Farwell, B., *Queen Victoria's Little Wars* (Allen Lane, 1973)

Fraser, P., *Joseph Chamberlain* (Cassell, 1966)

Goodlad, G. D., 'Lord Salisbury and Late Victorian Conservatism', in *Modern History Review*, February 1996

Jay, R., *Joseph Chamberlain: A Political Study* (Oxford, 1981)

Longford, E., *Jameson's Raid* (Weidenfeld & Nicolson, 1982 edn)

Magnus, P., *Kitchener: Portrait of an Imperialist* (John Murray, 1958)

Marlowe, J., *Cecil Rhodes* (Elek, 1972)

Pakenham, T., *The Boer War* (Weidenfeld & Nicolson, 1979)

Pakenham, T., *The Scramble for Africa* (Weidenfeld & Nicolson, 1991)

Taylor, R., *Lord Salisbury* (Allen Lane, 1975)

Thomas, A., *Rhodes: The Race for Africa* (BBC, 1996)

Watts, D., *Joseph Chamberlain and the Challenge of Radicalism* (Hodder & Stoughton, 1993)

Young, K., *Balfour* (Bell, 1963)

Chapter 18   The Dominions: Canada, Australia and New Zealand before 1914

Bloomfield, P., *Edward Gibbon Wakefield* (Longman, 1961)

Clark, C. M. H., *A History of Australia* (Macmillan, 1982)

Metge, J., *The Maoris of New Zealand* (Routledge, 1976 edn)

Morton, W. L., *The Critical Years: The Union of British North America* (Toronto, 1964)

New, C. W., *Lord Durham* (Dawson, 1969)

Chapter 19   The growth of the trade unions and the Labour Party to 1914

Adelman, P., *The Rise of the Labour Party, 1880–1945* (Longman, 2nd edn 1986)

Benn, C., *Keir Hardie* (Hutchinson, 1992)

Cole, G. D. H., *The Life of Robert Owen* (Cass, 1965)

Howell, D., *British Workers and the Independent Labour Party 1888–1906* (Manchester University Press, 1983)

Howson, J., 'The Dock Strike of 1889', in *Modern History Review*, February 1996
McKibbin, R., *The Evolution of the Labour Party 1910–24* (Oxford, 1974)
Morgan, K. O., *Keir Hardie: Radical and Socialist* (Weidenfeld & Nicolson, 1984)
Musson, A. E., *British Trade Unions, 1800–1875* (Macmillan, 1972)
Pelling, H., *A History of British Trade Unionism* (Penguin, 1968)
Pelling, H., *The Origins of the Labour Party, 1880–1900* (Oxford, 1965)
Pugh, M., *State and Society: British Political and Social History 1870–1992* (Arnold, 1994)
Tanner, D., 'Keir Hardie and the ILP, 1900–15', in *Modern History Review*, April 1994
Tanner, D., 'The Rise of the Labour Party', in *Modern History Review*, November 1989
Tanner, D., *Political Change and the Labour Party 1900–18* (Cambridge, 1990)

Chapter 20   The State and the People from the 1880s to 1939

Birch, R. C., *The Shaping of the Welfare State* (Longman, 1974)
Chinn, C., *Poverty Amidst Prosperity: The Urban Poor in England 1834–1914* (Manchester University Press, 1995)
Constantine, S., *Unemployment in Britain between the Wars* (Longman, 1980)
Crowther, A., *British Social Policy 1914–39* (Macmillan, 1988)
Fraser, D., *The Evolution of the Welfare State* (Macmillan, 2nd edn 1984)
Harris, J., *Private Lives, Public Spirit: A Social History of Britain 1870–1914* (Oxford, 1993)
Lowe, R., 'The Origins of the Welfare State in Britain', in *Modern History Review*, September 1989
Peden, G. C., *British Economic and Social Policy: Lloyd George to Margaret Thatcher* (Philip Allan, 1985)
Stevenson, J., *British Society 1914–45* (Penguin, 1984)
Read, D., *Edwardian England* (Harrap, 1972)
Roberts, R., *The Classic Slum* (Penguin, 1973)
Thane, P., *The Foundations of the Welfare State* (Longman, 1982)
Thane, P., 'The Impact of the Welfare State on British Society, 1906–51', in *Modern History Review*, September 1989
Thompson, F. M. L. (ed.), *The Cambridge Social History of Britain 1750–1950, Vols I–III* (Cambridge, 1993)

Chapter 21   The Liberals in power 1905–14

Adelman, P., *The Decline of the Liberal Party 1910–31* (Longman, 1981)
Blewitt, N., *The Peers, the Parties and the People. The General Elections of 1910* (Macmillan, 1972)
Clarke, P. F., *Lancashire and the New Liberalism* (Cambridge, 1971)
Dangerfield, G., *The Strange Death of Liberal England 1910–14* (1936; Fontana edn 1982)
Green, E., 'Neutering Mr Balfour's Poodle', in *Modern History Review*, April 1996
Henig, R. (ed.), *The Origins of the First World War* (Routledge, 1993)
Jefferies, H. A., 'Germany and the First World War', in *Modern History Review*, September 1995
Jenkins, R., *Asquith* (Collins, 1964)
Joll, J., *The Origins of the First World War* (Longman, 1984)
Lemieux, S., 'The Liberal Party 1910–14. Still a Going Concern?', in *Modern History Review*, September 1995
Liddington, J. and Norris, J., *One Hand Tied Behind Us: The Rise of the Women's Suffrage Movement* (Virago, 1979)
Lloyd, T. O., *Empire to Welfare State* (Oxford, 1970)
Murray, B. K., *The People's Budget 1909–10* (Oxford, 1980)
Pugh, M., *The Making of Modern British Politics 1867–1939* (2nd edn Blackwell, 1993)
Pugh, M., *Lloyd George* (Longman, 1988)
Pugh, M., 'Votes for Women', in *Modern History Review*, September 1990
Read, D., *Edwardian England* (Harrap, 1972)
Searle, G. R., *The Liberal Party: Triumph and Disintegration 1886–1939* (Macmillan, 1992)
Steiner, Z., *Britain and the Origins of the First World War* (Macmillan, 1977)
Tanner, D., 'New Liberalism 1906–14', in *Modern History Review*, November 1990
Wilson, K., 'The Multiple Wars of 1914', in *Modern History Review*, September 1995

Chapter 22   Britain, the First World War and its aftermath

Bourne, J. M., *Britain and the Great War 1914–1918* (Arnold, 1989)
James, R. R., *Gallipoli* (Batsford, 1965)
Liddell-Hart, B., *History of the First World War* (Pan, 1972)
Macdonald, L., *They Called it Passchendaele* (Michael Joseph, 1978)
Marwick, A., *The Deluge: British Society and the First World War* (Macmillan, 1973; 2nd edn 1991)
Morgan, K. O., *Lloyd George* (Weidenfeld & Nicolson, 1974)
Pugh., M., *Lloyd George* (Longman, 1988)
Sharp, A., *The Versailles Settlement: Peacemaking in Paris, 1919* (Macmillan, 1991)
Taylor, A. J. P., *An Illustrated History of the First World War* (Penguin, 1963)

Chapter 23   Politics in confusion 1918–24

Adelman, P., *The Decline of the Liberal Party 1910–1931* (Longman, 1981)
Adelman, P., *The Rise of the Labour Party 1880–1945* (Longman, 2nd edn 1986)
Clarke, P. F., *Lancashire and the New Liberalism* (Cambridge, 1971)
Cook, C., *The Age of Alignment 1922–29* (Macmillan, 1975)
Kinnear, M., *The Fall of Lloyd George* (Macmillan, 1973)
Marquand, D., *Ramsay MacDonald* (Cape, 1977)
McKibbin, R., *The Evolution of the Labour Party 1910–24* (Oxford, 1974)
Morgan, K. O., *Lloyd George* (Weidenfeld & Nicolson, 1974)
Phillips, G., *The Rise of the Labour Party, 1893–1931* (Routledge, 1992)
Pugh, M., *The Making of Modern British Politics, 1867–1939* (Blackwell, 1982)
Searle, G., *The Liberal Party: Triumph and Disintegration, 1886–1929* (Macmillan, 1992)
Tanner, D., *Political Change and the Labour Party, 1900–18* (Cambridge, 1990)
Taylor, A. J. P., *English History 1914–45* (Penguin, 1970)
Wilson, T., *The Downfall of the Liberal Party 1914–1935* (Collins, 1966; Fontana, 1968)

Chapter 24   Baldwin, the Conservatives and the General Strike

Ball, S., 'The Conservative Dominance 1918–40', in *Modern History Review*, November 1991
Howson, J., 'The General Strike: A Bluff Which Was Called?', in *Modern History Review*, September 1996
Hyde, H. M., *Baldwin – the Unexpected Prime Minister* (Hart-Davis, 1973)
Macleod, I., *Neville Chamberlain* (Muller, 1961)
Morris, M., *The General Strike* (Penguin, 1976)
Morris, M., 'The General Strike', in *Modern History Review*, February 1991

Chapter 25   The second Labour government (1929–31), the world economic crisis and the National governments

Adelman, P., *The Rise of the Labour Party, 1880–1945* (Longman, 1986)
Aldcroft, D. H., *The British Economy Between the Wars* (Philip Allan, 1983)
Aldcroft, D. H., 'The Locust Years? Britain's Inter-War Economy', in *Modern History Review*, November 1993
Ball, S., *Baldwin and the Conservative Party: The Crisis of 1929–31* (Yale University Press, 1988)
Bassett, R., *Nineteen Thirty One: Political Crisis* (Macmillan, 1958)
Constantine, S., *Unemployment in Britain between the Wars* (Longman, 1980)
Cross, C., *Philip Snowden* (Barrie & Rockcliff, 1967)
Donaldson, F., *Edward VIII* (Weidenfeld & Nicolson, 1978)
Garside, W. R., *British Unemployment 1919–39* (Cambridge University Press, 1990)
Marquand, D., *Ramsay MacDonald* (Cape, 1977)
Skidelsky, R., *Politicians and the Slump: The Labour Government of 1929–31* (Penguin, 1970)
Thorpe, A., *Britain in the 1930s: The Deceptive Decade* (Blackwell/Historical Association, 1992)
Thorpe, A., 'The 1931 Crisis', in *Modern History Review*, November 1993
Williamson, P., *National Crisis and National Government: British Politics, the Economy and Empire 1929–32* (Cambridge University Press, 1992)
Williamson, P., 'The King, Politicians and the 1931 Crisis', in *Modern History Review*, November 1993

Chapter 26 Britain and the problems of Empire between the wars

Brown, J. M., *Gandhi: Prisoner of Hope* (Yale, 1989)
De Paor, L., *Divided Ulster* (Penguin, 1971)
Foster, R. F., *Modern Ireland 1600–1972* (Penguin, 1989)
Gopal, S., 'Churchill and India', in Blake, R. and Louis, W. R. (eds), *Churchill* (Oxford, 1993)
Gopal, S., *Jawaharlal Nehru: A Biography* (Oxford, 1990)
Lee, J. J., *Ireland 1912–1985* (Cambridge, 1989)
Lyons, F. S. L., *Ireland Since the Famine* (Fontana, 2nd edn. 1985)
Moore, R. J., *The Crisis of Indian Unity 1917–1940* (Oxford, 1974)
Pandey, B. N., *The Break-up of British India* (Macmillan, 1969)
Porter, B., *The Lion's Share: A Short History of British Imperialism 1850–1970* (Longman, 1975)
Watson, J. B., *Empire to Commonwealth, 1919–1970* (Dent, 1971)

Chapter 27 Appeasement and the outbreak of the Second World War: foreign affairs 1931–9

Bullock, A., *Hitler: A Study in Tyranny* (Penguin, 1969)
Charmley, J., *Chamberlain and the Lost Peace* (Hodder & Stoughton, 1989)
Cockett, R., 'Appeasement: Britain's Prime Minister in the Dock', in *Modern History Review*, February 1990
Fest, J., *Hitler* (Penguin, 1982)
Gilbert, M. and Gott, R., *The Appeasers* (Weidenfeld & Nicolson, 1967)
Martel, G. (ed.), *'The Origins of the Second World War' Reconsidered: The A. J. P. Taylor Debate after Twenty-Five Years* (Unwin Hyman, 1990 edn)
McDonough, F., 'Why Appeasement?', in *Modern History Review*, April 1994
Neville, P., *Neville Chamberlain: A Study in Failure?* (Hodder & Stoughton, 1993)
Overy, R. and Wheatcroft, A., *The Road to War* (Macmillan, 1989)
Rock, W. R., *British Appeasement in the 1930s* (Arnold, 1977)
Taylor, A. J. P., *Origins of the Second World War* (Penguin edn., 1974)
Taylor, P. M., 'Appeasement: Guilty Men or Guilty Conscience?', in *Modern History Review*, November 1989
Watt, D. C., *How War Came: The Immediate Origins of the Second World War, 1938–39* (Heinemann, 1989)

Chapter 28 Britain and the Second World War 1939–45

Addison, P., *The Road to 1945* (Pimlico, 1994 edn)
Barnett, C., *The Audit of War* (Macmillan, 1986)
Blake, R. and Louis, W. M. (eds), *Churchill: A Major New Assessment of His Life in Peace and War* (Oxford, 1993)
Brivati, B. and Jones, H. (eds), *What Difference did the War Make?* (Leicester University Press, 1993)
Calder, A., *The People's War: Britain 1939–45* (Cape, 1969)
Calvocoressi, P. and Wint, G., *Total War* (Penguin, 1974)
Charmley, J., *Churchill: The End of Glory* (Hodder & Stoughton, 1993)
Gilbert, M., *Second World War* (Phoenix, 1996)
Liddell-Hart, B., *History of the Second World War* (Cassell, 1970)
Lucas, S., 'Hiroshima and History', in *Modern History Review*, April 1996
Marwick, A., 'Two World Wars: Their Impact on Britain', in *Modern History Review*, September 1990
Neville, P., 'Dunkirk and the Myths of 1940', in *Modern History Review*, September 1991
Pelling, H., *Britain and the Second World War* (Collins Fontana, 1970)
Ponting, C., *1940: Myth and Reality* (Sinclair-Stevenson, 1990)
Roberts, A., *Eminent Churchillians* (Phoenix, 1993)
Roberts, A., *The Holy Fox: A Biography of Lord Halifax* (Weidenfeld & Nicolson, 1991)
Robbins, K., *Churchill* (Longman, 1993)
Smith, H. L. (ed.), *War and Social Change* (Manchester University Press, 1986)
Taylor, A. J. P., *The Second World War* (Hamish Hamilton, 1975)
Thoms, D. W., 'Blitz, Work and Women', in *Modern History Review*, November 1996

Chapter 29   Labour in power: the Attlee governments 1945–51

Addison, P., *The Road to 1945* (Pimlico, 1994 edn)
Barnett, C., *The Audit of War* (Macmillan, 1986)
Cairncross, A., *Years of Recovery: British Economic Policy 1945–51* (Methuen, 1985)
Calvocoressi, P., *The British Experience, 1945–75* (Penguin, 1979)
Foot, M., *Aneurin Bevan* (Paladin paperback edition, 1975)
Fraser, D., *The Evolution of the British Welfare State* (Macmillan, 1973)
Harris, K., *Attlee* (Weidenfeld & Nicolson, 1984)
Hennessy, P., *Never Again: Britain 1945–51* (Jonathan Cape, 1992)
Jefferys, K., *The Attlee Governments 1945–51* (Longman, 1992)
Morgan, K. O., *Labour in Power 1945–51* (Oxford, 1984)
Pearce, R., *Attlee's Labour Governments, 1945–51* (Routledge, 1993)
Pearce, R., 'Beveridge 1942: Reconstruction or Reform?', in *Modern History Review*, September 1993
Pelling, H., *The Labour Governments 1945–51* (Macmillan, 1984)
Pimlott, B., *Hugh Dalton* (Macmillan, 1986)
Saville, J., *The Labour Movement in Britain* (Faber, 1988)
Tiratsoo, N. and Tomlinson, J., *Industrial Efficiency and State Intervention: Labour 1939–51* (Routledge, 1993)
Tiratsoo, N. (ed.), *The Attlee Years* (Pinter, 1991)
Tiratsoo, N., 'The Attlee Years Revisited', in *Modern History Review*, February 1994

Chapter 30   The rise and fall of consensus 1951–79

Calvocoressi, P., *The British Experience 1945–75* (Penguin, 1979)
Campbell, J., *Edward Heath* (Weidenfeld & Nicolson, 1993)
Fisher, N., *Harold Macmillan* (Weidenfeld & Nicolson, 1982)
Goodlad, G., 'The Premiership of Harold Macmillan', in *Modern History Review*, February 1997
Healey, D., *The Time of My Life* (Michael Joseph, 1989)
Hennessy, P. and Seldon, A. (eds), *Ruling Performance: British Governments from Attlee to Thatcher* (Blackwell, 1987)
Holmes, M., *The Labour Government 1974–79* (Macmillan, 1985)
Horne, A., *Macmillan, Vols 1 and 2* (Macmillan, 1988 and 1989)
Lamb, R., *The Failure of the Eden Government* (Sidgwick & Jackson, 1987)
Lamb, R., *The Macmillan Years 1957–63: The Emerging Truth* (John Murray, 1995)
Lapping, B., *The Labour Government 1964–70* (Penguin, 1971)
Pimlott, B., *Harold Wilson* (Harper Collins, 1993)
Ponting, C., *Breach of Promise: Labour in Power 1964–70* (Hamish Hamilton, 1987)
Ramsden, J., *The Age of Churchill and Eden, 1940–1957* (Longman, 1995)
Ramsden, J., *The Winds of Change: Macmillan to Heath* (Longman, 1996)
Turner, J., *Macmillan* (Longman, 1994)
Wilson, H., *The Labour Government 1964–70: A Personal Record* (Penguin, 1974)

Chapter 31   Britain and its parts: England, Ireland, Scotland and Wales

Arthur, P. and Jeffery, K., *Northern Ireland Since 1968* (Blackwell, 1988)
Buckland, P., *A History of Northern Ireland* (Holmes and Meier, 1981)
Clutterbuck, R., *Britain in Agony: The Growth of Political Violence* (Penguin, 1978)
Cook, C. and Ramsden, J., *Trends in British Politics* (Macmillan, 1978)
Lee, J. J., *Ireland 1912–1985* (Cambridge, 1985)
Philip, A. B., *The Welsh Question* (University of Wales Press, 1975)
Rees, M., *Northern Irleland: A Personal Perspective* (Methuen, 1985)
Wichert, S., *Northern Ireland since 1945* (Longman, 1991)

Chapter 32   Britain and her place in the world after 1945

Aldous, R. and Lee, S. (eds), *Harold Macmillan and Britain's World Role* (Macmillan, 1996)
Brasted, H., 'Decolonisation in India: Britain's Positive Role', in *Modern History Review*, November 1990
Carlton, D., *Britain and the Suez Crisis* (Blackwell, 1988)
Carlton, D., 'Suez 1956: The Consequences', in *Modern History Review*, February 1990

Darwin, J., *Britain and Decolonisation* (Macmillan, 1988)

George, S., *Britain and European Integration since 1945* (ICBH/ Blackwell, 1991), and in *Modern History Review*, April 1992

Goodlad, G. D., 'The Premiership of Harold Macmillan', in *Modern History Review*, February 1997

Hargreaves, J. D., *Decolonisation in Africa* (Longman, 1988)

Holland, R. F., *European Decolonisation 1918–81:An Introductory Survey* (Macmillan, 1985)

Holland, R. F., 'Imperial Decline: A New Historiography', in *Modern History Review*, February 1992

Horne, A., *Macmillan,* 2 vols (Macmillan, 1988–9)

Kyle, K., *Suez* (Weidenfeld & Nicolson, 1991)

Lamb, R., *The Failure of the Eden Government* (Sidgwick & Jackson, 1987)

Lamb, R., *The Macmillan Years, 1957–63: The Emerging Truth* (John Murray, 1995)

Nutting, A., *No End of a Lesson* (Constable, 1967)

Ramsden, J., *The Winds of Change: Macmillan to Heath* (Longman, 1996)

Singh, A. I., *The Origins of the Partition of India 1936–1947* (Oxford, 1990)

Turner, J., *Macmillan* (Longman, 1994)

Young, J., *Britain and European Unity 1945–1992* (Macmillan, 1993)

Chapter 33　Thatcherism and the New Right 1979–97

Childs, D., *Britain Since 1939: Progress and Decline* (Macmillan, 1995)

Clark, A., *Diaries* (Weidenfeld & Nicolson,1993)

Crick, M., *Scargill and the Miners* (Penguin, 1985)

Howe, G., *Conflict of Loyalty* (Pan, 1994)

Hutton, W., *The State We're In* (Vintage edn, 1996)

Lawson, N., *The View From No 11* (Bantam, 1992; Corgi, 1993)

Riddell, P., *The Thatcher Era and its Legacy* (Blackwell, 1991)

Thatcher, M., *The Downing Street Years* (HarperCollins, 1993)

Young, H., *One of Us* (Macmillan, 1991 edn)

Index